Prais

The Greatest Band

"*The Greatest Band That Never Was* is a moving, often heart-warming story that brought me to tears a handful of times. The sense of community and goodwill and a group of people working together is very striking. The book is a rollercoaster of compulsive energy that makes for one feel-good experience. Addictive reading." – *David Schloss, Professor of Creative Writing, Miami University (Ohio)*

"I proofread one to two books a week, and this is easily one of the absolutely best books I've read in the past few years. I laughed, I cried, and I had all the feelings. This would make a FANTASTIC limited series. Thank you for writing it and sharing it with the world." – *BE Allatt*

"An unassuming paralegal embarks on a quest to reunite past and present by locating the members of a band that broke up almost four decades before. In the process she rescues an ailing family business, reunites a community, and reignites the unique creative spark that turns a group of forgotten musicians into living legends. *The Greatest Band That Never Was* deftly weaves multiple narrative strands to tell a story of self-discovery, unconquerable resilience, and the power of music to bring people together and transform lives. Meshel has written something magical — and epic." – *Ian Boyle, author of* What the Dormouse Said

"*The Greatest Band That Never Was* is a warm and wise reflection on how the Woodstock era changed the American way of life. It is a humorous and thoughtful story of a small-town band who is reincarnated years after its demise to become the focus of another social movement, spreading pride, hope and American values." – *Mike Berlin*

"If you combined a seasoned playwright, a deep music expert, a meticulous culture archivist, a practical psychologist and a jazz improviser, you'd get the author of *The Greatest Band That Never Was*. Meshel has composed a riveting tale, hilarious and heart-warming and wise." – *Yuri Gittik*

"Shelly's need to find something exciting to do with her life and the escape from her smothering dad are meticulously crafted. Her hunt for the band members was a real page-turner. Her quest and romantic arc held my interest, first page to last. The drama, humor, and dialogue! An amazing accomplishment." – *John Kehe*

"My Book Club's been looking for this one! These unforgettable, self-empowered women doing their thing create a vibe that easily passes the Bechdel test. Couldn't put it down! Highly recommended." – *Shari Giddens*

"Jeff Meshel's love song of a novel has the big-hearted feel of "It's a Wonderful Life" and the reality check of "Almost Famous." You'll wish this celebration of life wasn't over when you get to the last page—with a smile on your face." — *Sally Schloss, author of the novel* Helping Howard

Praise for Song of The Week

(https://jmeshel.com/sotw/)

"Your blog is in my RSS reader. When a new post comes out, I drop everything and come here and read and listen and think and sometimes shed a few tears. Thank you for this. It's magical. Worth the extraordinary effort you put into it." —*Seth Godin, author of* This is Marketing, (SoTW 163, Joni Mitchell, 'For Free')

"Jeff, this is such brilliant writing. It deserves a huge audience. I just love your sense of humor and we really need one now." – *Judy Labensohn, author of* Our Names Do Not Appear (SoTW 247, Perry Como, 'Kol Nidre')

"Jeff, you are a life-blood of music. Those who love music love you, me included."—*John Radoszewski* (SoTW 301, Erik Bosio/ Jeff Meshel, 'Galia')

"Great writing, great insight, great song. Like "In My Life" itself, your observations took me down memory lane and Life in the Time of Covid at the same time."—Alan Tigay, *World Listening Post* (SoTW 053, The Beatles, 'In My Life')

"Thank you for your insight, Jeff!" – *Laurie Verchomin, Bill Evans' widow* (SoTW 124, Bill Evans, 'Nardis')

"Thank you so very much for your wonderfully eloquent and engaging posts. They not only bring back so many memories of the music of my misspent youth, but deepen my understanding and appreciation of the universal interconnections that music creates. It's always a joy to read – so thank you for writing with such love."—*Linda Seru* (SoTW 292, My 10 Life-Changing Albums)

"In many ways your essays are a work of art. This was wonderful, almost sublime."— *Dr. Aryeh Levenson* (SoTW 193, The Band, "Rocking Chair')

"Beautiful, witty, sly, and profound, Jeff. Like you."— *John Kehe* (SoTW 248, 'You Ain't Going Nowhere')

"You sound like someone who has an unhealthy relationship with both women and himself." — *Stephen Linhart* (SoTW 272, Vilray/Rachael Price, 'Do Friends Fall in Love')

"Your curiosity and passion are an inspiration to me. You've pushed me to become an accomplished listener. Thank you for your tenacious search for music that lies off the beaten path."— *Maggie Evans* (SoTW 069, Cat Russell, 'New Speedway Boogie')

"Thanks again for your enlightening article. I'm a superficial music 'lover' that never gets below the surface of the song. You provide the 3rd dimension. I really appreciate your first-hand experiences and the ties between the songs, artists, other happenings that explain how it all fits together."—*Ellis Koch* (SoTW 070, Buddy Holly, 'That'll Be the Day')

"You not only write with an open mind, but with an open heart as well."—Jackson Ahern (SoTW 012, Arvo Pärt, 'De Profundis')

"Eloquent, sublime. Bach 'attempts to impose an artificial order upon an inherently chaotic world.' Great working image. Thank you for a really nice essay this week." – Howard Jacobson (SoTW 077, J.S. Bach, 'Art of the Fugue')

THE
GREATEST
BAND
THAT NEVER WAS

JEFF MESHEL

atmosphere press

To Yonit, for making the best of me.

Characters

Aaron Woodwright	1947	Bandleader
Sam Miller	1948	Singer-songwriter
Kathleen Brinker	1950	Singer
Gavin Grover	1944	Drummer
Vaneshi	1949	Multi-instrumentalist
Bev Hunt	1948	Band Coordinator
Shelly Griffin	1963	Paralegal
Col. Charles Griffin	1931	Judge Advocate, US Army (Ret.)
Allie Bauer	1937	Owner, Bauer's Brewery
Brandi	1983	Receptionist, WFOR
Johnny Walker	1944	Disk Jockey, WFOR
Gerald Bridges	1946	Billionaire
Matt Hinton	1980	Handyman, Shortstop
Robbie Pettiford	1989	Bev's son
Diane Hobgood	1956	Florida State Senator
Justine Brinker	1990	Diane's Niece
Winston	1961	Cook
Dog	?	Mutt
Gruenhaus	1903-1904	Farmhouse

Part 1

Something in the Water

1

Pedro's Cantina

– April 1970 –

Years later, hundreds of people would swear they'd been at Pedro's Cantina the night Sam Miller and Aaron Woodwright first met. But the truth is that the taco-and-beer hangout could hold no more than a few dozen sweaty Steuben College students at a time, even on an Open Mic Wednesday.

"Hi, Aaron," fluttered the three fresh-faced, eager coeds sitting right in front of the little stage, regulars: a chubby blonde, a plain brunette, and a freckled redhead with braces.

Aaron had his circle of devotees. They told each other they loved his voice and his piano, and told their dates that Pedro's had the best tacos in Steubenville. But it was Aaron they were coming to see, his well-tended shock of jet-black hair, his long eyelashes, and his only-for-you smile. He knew it, he cultivated it, and he used it.

"What's going on, ladies?" he asked, smiling at each one of them, even the chubby blonde.

"Oh, not much at all," drawled the plain brunette, wiping a line of beer foam from her upper lip with her little finger. One night during a break, he had squeezed her in the storeroom—Janet? Janice?—but felt she wasn't quite ripe for picking.

Tonight, he was entranced by the new waitress, surveilling her hips as she navigated the tables in her very tight jeans and

3

a light blue blouse with a scooped neck that said hello with a big smile when she bent down to serve a trayful of pitchers and mugs and greasy Mexican food. She had strong shoulders, a jet-black pageboy, large gray eyes, and a crinkled smile—a fine-looking waitress, and Aaron Woodwright was an avid fan of fine-looking waitresses in low-cut peasant blouses.

As he played, he followed her gliding and squeezing between tables, carrying mugs and pitchers, and seating the mix of date couples, the frat and sorority crowd, and recently a smattering of longhairs, a new sight around Steuben College. He tried to catch her eye, but she seemed focused on her work. The more she didn't notice him, the more he aimed his singing at her.

"*If you see me walking down the street,*" he crooned at her. He was almost certain that a small smile snuck out once or twice, but she continued to not look at him.

"We're going to take a short break now, and then we'll be back with our open mic set," Aaron grinned, but the crowd was already talking among themselves. "And don't forget tonight's special," he added dutifully, "Pedro's tasty tamales and a pitcher of Creston Gold for only $2.50."

Pedro was running back and forth behind the counter, serving up the tamales and beer, enchiladas and beer, tacos and beer, and just plain beer. "Ten minutos," he warned Aaron, splashing down a mug on the bar in front of him and adjusting his sombrero.

For some misguided reason, Youngstown-born-and-bred Pedro believed that donning the cheesy garb and bogus accent of a B-movie-stock Mexican brought a bit of exotic glamor to Rust Belt Steubenville. But he was a fair boss, even though he lived devoutly by his motto, "A peso is a peso."

"Excuse me," said the new waitress, pushing past Aaron.

"Excuse you?" he said as she squeezed between him and the bar, with her finally looking directly into his face up close. "You're my inspiration. My muse. I'm indebted to you from the bottom of my heart."

"Gimme a break." She rolled her eyes, pushing past him to put two pitchers under their taps, but he thought he caught a bit of a smile.

"Can I ask you a question?"

"You have till these pitchers fill."

"I'm Aaron Woodwright."

"That's not a question," she responded, her back to him, but he sensed her smiling.

"Okay, New Waitress, what's your name?"

"Don't give my name to strangers," she said.

"We're work colleagues," said Aaron, smiling right into her eyes.

"Kathleen," said New Waitress.

"You're a student at Steuben?"

"Maybe," she answered, wiping and bustling.

"Do you sing? You look like a singer."

"Hup," she said, lifting the two pitchers in one hand and what looked like a dozen mugs in the other. "Gotta go!"

"Just tell me that!"

"I can carry a tu—" and she disappeared between the tables.

"You talk to the senorita affer work, si?" said Pedro in his flat, Midwestern, ersatz South-of-the-Border accent.

"Know anything about her, Pedro?"

"She work good, look good." He clapped Aaron on the shoulder and nudged him towards the stage. Aaron pushed back through the crowd, which had thickened with a couple of open mic guitar slingers and a few more gawkers. Pedro lowered the lights in the room and flicked the single spotlight on the tiny stage.

"Hey everyone, welcome to Pedro's Open Mic Night. It's really great to see you all here," he said to a smattering of applause led by his three little groupies in the front row. "I'm sure you're all as excited as I am to see what kind of surprises we're going to have tonight."

New Waitress was busy bouncing from table to table, bringing orders, clearing, wiping tables, and seating students as they came in.

"But first, we have a tradition here, the guest appearance by a member of—the staff! I've already done my set, and trust me, you really don't want to hear Pedro do his Speedy Gonzales routine. So, please help me give a warm welcome to: 'New Waitress—Kathleen!' "

As the half-drunk, horny college kids cheered and howled on cue, she turned to stare at him with a mixture of consternation and pique, which melted into an "Oh, yeah?" grin. It seemed you didn't fool around with New Waitress Kathleen.

She untied her half-apron, tossed it over her shoulder, and sauntered up to the matchbox stage. She sat down on the stool next to the piano and covered the mic with her hand. "You know you're making a fool out of both of us, don't you? I've never sung in public before." But she made no move to escape.

"I can't imagine anyone making a fool out of you," he said with his sparkling smile. "Call it."

No one even noticed the stranger standing by the door.

"Um—'Different Drum'?"

Aaron played a couple of chords, and she sang a couple of notes. "Can you lower it a little?"

Aaron nodded, counted himself in under his breath, and began a cloppy, reeling intro.

"*You and I ...*"

The first verse went smoothly, him grinning at her, her taking it cautiously, sticking closely to the melody. By the beginning of the second verse, Aaron was focusing on his playing. This was too good to mess up. She laid back on the beat and punched out "*Oh, you cry-y*" in a syncopated funk that made Aaron smile at the keyboard. Then, she looped a giant slur down on "*... and a-a-all you can say,*" and the few students who were still busy with their beer or chatting sat up and started to listen. By the chorus, Aaron had forgotten about her peasant blouse for the moment and was thinking only of following the husky alto kneading and probing the words, an edgy declaration of female independence.

Kathleen ended with a flourish and enthusiastic applause from the crowded little room. She took a deep, exaggerated bow, clearly pleased with herself. Pedro was waving a beer pitcher at Aaron from behind the bar, pointing at it.

From the back of the cantina, the stranger was clapping and shrieking whistles with his fingers in his mouth so loudly that people were covering their ears and turning to stare. He didn't look like a student—scruffy, in a WWII field jacket, with a mess of sandy brown hair and a tattered guitar case. No one had ever seen him before at Pedro's. He kept on shouting, "Yo, New Waitress!" and shrieking those whistles.

"We're going to take a short break, give you all a chance to top up," said Aaron. "And don't forget tonight's special, Pedro's tasty tamales and a pitcher of Creston Gold for only $2.50."

"Hey," Aaron grinned at her as she was filling pitchers.

"I never did anything like that before!" she said, gleaming. "It was *fun!*" Her forehead and her chest were damp with sweat.

"You're fabulous!" he said, letting himself get pushed up against her accidentally.

"Down, tiger," she said, a hand on his chest. But her cheeks were shining, and there was a glow in her eyes.

"You sing as good as you look," he said.

"I got work to do," she said, smiling to herself, pushing off into the mass of beer-guzzling students.

2

One-Lane
Road to Nowhere

– May 9, 2006 –

"God *damn* it!" Shelly seethed, as she drove straight past the Antique Mall, missing her turnoff to I-76.

Monday morning, she was driving down to Creston to meet a new client about closing down an old family brewery. The road was familiar, but all she could see in her mind's eye was Derek looking up at her from underneath his ex-wife Marcia, riding naked on top of him.

"Shelly, wait!" he had called after her. "It's not what it looks like!"

It's not what it looks like? Gee, Derek, lose your car keys in there? That's what she should have said!

"Fuck!" she blurted, whacking her fist against the steering wheel, pulling into a Wendy's to make a U-turn.

She stomped on the brake, jolting to a stop, rerunning in her mind his oh-so-pitiful attempt to look innocent while buck naked, the both of them.

"Fuck!" she shouted again, banging her fist for emphasis. "Fuck! Fuck! FU-UCK!"

She gasped, looking at the heel of her hand, tears beginning to well. It really hurt. She sniffled and turned back towards the turnoff. Ouch! God *damn* him. Her BlackBerry rang. She pulled a tissue out of her purse quickly, blew her nose, put on a smile, and answered.

"Hi, Dad."

"Hi, Shel. Good morning. Everything okay?"

"Sure. How're you?"

"You took all the client agreement forms?"

"Yes," she snapped.

"And the list of documents you need to get from her?"

"Dad, I've done this a dozen times." Shelly ran her father's law firm, an office of six lawyers and five assistants, and handled the most complicated paperwork herself, but her father was her father and a colonel in the Army Reserve.

"Just get all the stuff you need and get back."

"What's that supposed to mean?"

"You know, don't waste more time down there than—"

"Dad, I've got to go. There's an accident up ahead,"

The Colonel thought she wasted far too much time talking to their clients. He also thought that spit-shining one's shoes every Friday kept chaos at bay.

She passed Neumann's Funeral Home and took the I-76 West turnoff. She looked at her watch. She was going to be half an hour late, at least. Damn, her hand really hurt.

It wasn't simply him cheating on her that hurt so much. They didn't have an expressed "exclusivity" agreement or anything, even though they'd been dating for seven months. But the deceit! The endless hours lying in his bed, listening to him whine about Marcia, about how she never listened to him, how she didn't really understand him, and how all she cared about was her damned volleyball team. What on earth made that asshole think that she was interested in hearing—endlessly—about Marcia and her fucking volleyball team? While she was naked in his bed? All she could think of was the look on their faces when she walked into his apartment bedroom, both with their eyes closed, moaning—

The phone again.

"Shelly, we got cut off. Is everything okay?"

"Everything's fine," she said, trying to sniffle quietly.

"Are you sure?"

"Yes, I said it is."

"You got all the papers?"

"You already asked me that."

"Call me on your way back."

"Okay, but it will probably take the whole day."

"Make sure you get back while it's still light out. The forecast says rain this evening."

"All right, Dad."

She waited, knowing it was still coming.

"I thought you were staying over at Derek's."

"Yeah, well, I decided not to."

"Is everything okay?"

"Daddy, I'm almost there. I have to go." And she hung up.

And then the tears just burst out.

Goddamn him.

Derek coached the Youngstown Bulldogs, a local celebrity of sorts in an area sorely devoid of stardust. He had played cornerback for the Browns for six seasons until a tight end from the Green Bay Packers hit him with a low block, ruining his left knee for life. Any high school football coach was a minor deity in rural Northeast Ohio, let alone one who had played for the Browns. And everyone agreed that Derek was one good-looking football coach. A lot hunkier than anyone else she had ever dated. *Of course, that had its price*, she thought, remembering how he'd check himself whenever he passed a mirror. And he missed a lot of her jokes.

She dug the last tissue out of her purse and blew her nose. She kept meaning to get herself a new bag, one with a pouch for her cell phone on the outside, but the stores in Warren had so little to offer, and she was always too busy at the office to take a day off to go into Cleveland for shopping.

But the local newspapers sought every opportunity to feature a large picture of Coach Derek Turnbull, and the guys in the office were always asking, "How's it going with Derek?" with a big grin and a hint of a wink. The girls were constantly harping on what a catch he was and fishing for details from the bedroom. Well, he was certainly better than nothing, and she certainly didn't mind the stardust overflow.

But she had to admit that she wasn't totally surprised. He had canceled the last two Sunday night dates in a row because he said he had his kids for the weekend. "I'll see you this Sunday?" she had asked him. "Yeah, probably," he had answered. The schmuck.

So, she drove to Youngstown, all primped and primed. She'd even stopped at the market on 422 that carried his favorite beer, Creston Gold. When she had gotten to Derek's, six-pack in hand, she was ready for a fun evening. Instead, she had been treated to Marcia's bare ass. The dick!

She pulled the donut that she'd grabbed on her way out of the house from her purse. She'd stayed up till almost two, killing half a bottle of wine to dull the fury and the humiliation, oversleeping and rushing to put herself together for the drive to Creston. She tried to extricate the donut from the bag carefully, but the powdered sugar, of course, managed to sprinkle itself all over her dark blue top. She tried to brush it off, managing only to smear it. She threw the donut out the window.

"Let the birds choke on it," she growled aloud.

For months, she had kept telling herself that Derek was basically a good guy, that she had to give him some time to settle into a new relationship after a rough divorce, always hoping that he'd invite her to a family picnic or a work banquet. He did, sometimes. And sometimes not. When she was with him, he was always eager enough to get her into the bedroom. But she spent a lot of time waiting for him to call.

She passed the turn-off to Ravenna and fished through the pocket on the door till she found a crumpled napkin and blew her nose. She really should take the car in for a wash and vacuum.

But he usually didn't call. Because he was apparently more interested in screwing his ex-wife and listening to her ramble on about her volleyball team.

Leaving Shelly without a glimmer of hope of finding someone to spend those long nights with. Interesting and available men over forty were about as common in Warren, Ohio, as Emperor Penguins. Derek was the first guy she'd seen semi-regularly since—well, since forever. She didn't count Tim, the paunchy pharmacist she'd known since high school, her emergency fallback option. He would call her to go see a new "art" film, their one common interest, or she would call him to accompany her to some unavoidable social obligation, usually a wedding or funeral. She supposed Tim wanted to have sex with her, but she had casually avoided his occasional fumbling attempts at touching her arm or sitting hip-to-hip, and he seemed easily enough dissuaded.

She looked at her watch—ten to ten, and she was still more than half an hour away. *"It's not what it looks like."* The asshole. She blew her nose again and tried to rub off the powdered sugar, to no avail. She pulled the bottle of water from her purse and poured a little on her knit cotton top, trying to rub out the white streaks, leaving only a blotch.

Nor did she count Brian, the lawyer from St Louis whom she'd met in Cleveland about the purchase of a tooling company that was closing down. They were both stuck in the city overnight. They'd had a couple of drinks in the hotel bar, and spent the night together. He was sweet and appreciative, and his ginger hair and warm voice really appealed to her. Months later, he called to tell her that he was coming to Cleveland for a few days, and they spent a very passionate weekend together in his room. After that, he wrote her some pretty gooey emails that she answered curtly or not at all. She knew there was no future in seeing a married man.

Ordinarily, she wouldn't have allowed herself to succumb, but life in Warren was so suffocatingly dull she sometimes thought she would explode from boredom. In its prime it was nowhere, and now it was decaying from industrial depression, unemployment and Stage IV drabness. The few friends she tolerated from high school had long ago escaped, except for Denise, who got knocked up during her senior year, but she was always busy with some family emergency.

So she worked. And worked. And worked, running her father's law office. And here she was, dependable, humiliated and livid, with splotches on her top, driving on a Monday morning to yet another small-to-medium business falling victim to the ravages of post-industrial middle America, this time an old family-owned brewery. Going to pore over the books of one more failing business her father made his living from, accompanying them to a legally tidy and efficient demise. Some people called them sharks. "Those Griffins, they smell blood." As if the economy was any more her father's fault than an undertaker was responsible for the deaths of his clients. What did they think, that you just locked the door of a lost cause and walked away?

"It's not what it looks like." Grrr!

She passed the interchange to Deerfield Road, the road she used to take down to Athens. She and Randall had lived together during her senior year and the year after, when she stayed on as shift manager in the campus bookstore while he finished his master's degree. She'd thought of moving on, but there weren't a lot of job options open to her with a BA in English Lit, and campus life was fun. There was always something going on, and in between the weekend parties and world music festivals, there was a lot of great sex, she had to give that to Randall. She'd even thought of registering for an MA herself but didn't see the point in knocking herself out for another useless degree, and at the end of the year, Randall informed her that he was flying back home to Oregon. Sixteen years later, she could hardly remember his face.

She stayed on in the apartment for a while, not having anywhere else to go, hanging out with a mix of grad students and locals, partying relentlessly and recklessly. Those months were hazy, and she didn't care much to try to dispel the haze. She wasn't particularly proud of some of the things she did remember. A few desperate, cheap thrills, and no clue what to do with herself.

But her mother had solved that for her by getting sick. Home she came, the good girl that she was, back to the bleakness that was Warren, shuttling her mother to doctors and clinics and physical therapy, and then supervising renovations in the house, including a chair lift to the second floor, while her father struggled to keep his law office afloat and pay the crippling medical bills. Two years she slaved, and then her mother died.

She exited at Route 3 and turned left towards Seville. Two miles to Creston. Her top was still blotched. Shelly sighed and checked herself in the mirror. Her eyes were still a little puffy and red. Why did people think that being blonde and pale was a gift?

Her father had convinced her to come into his little firm, to help out "for a while" while she figured out what she wanted to do. And then Shawn walked into the office, in his Hawaii shirt and his cocky grin, knowing exactly what he wanted— the inheritance of his recently deceased aunt. He'd smiled at her, and she'd smiled back.

"Is there a restaurant around here where a guy could take a pretty girl to impress her?" he'd asked her.

"Langton's, out on Route 62," she'd answered, blushing.

Over fine steaks and an excellent local beer, he told her about the prime location he'd discovered right on the beach in Miami. He had dreams and dimples, and spun enchanting stories of a tropical paradise.

Afterwards, in his room that night, in his soft, confident

voice, he told her how he was going to use the eight thousand dollars he was inheriting from his aunt—Widow Dougherty out on the old Garretsville Road—to sign a long-term lease at a bargain price and open a chic coffee shop right across the street from the beach. On the second night, he said casually that she should come down to visit him. On the third night, they began to discuss it in earnest. On the fourth, his last in Warren, they made plans that she would fly down the next week "to hang out for a while".

She made the left at Wooster Pike, past the Abundant Life Choices church, and took the second right, onto Stuckey Road.

She packed for a week's stay, but found that between beach and bed she didn't need many clothes at all, and the week quickly turned into a month, and then two. She helped him move his few possessions into the tiny apartment above the café. Then she helped him buy a few second-hand furnishings, and added some curtains and decorations. They spent the days sanding and polishing and painting, the afternoons on the beach, the evenings in bed. By the time the tourist season rolled around, the sun and the sea and the sand and the sex had melted away the memory of the hospitals and the bed pans and Warren like a patch of snow on I-76 in the Florida sun.

But as the seasons passed, so did Shawn's enthusiasm for the café. The meager profits seemed to disappear—up Shawn's nostrils, she suspected. And then he was gone. She struggled valiantly to keep the café afloat, but found herself at thirty-one penniless, homeless, directionless.

So twelve years and seven pounds ago she moved into her father's basement apartment and began working for him as a paralegal, her tail between her legs, her spirits as flat as the landscape and as gray as the horizon here in Creston, Ohio, on a dreary mid-Monday morning. How had she gotten stuck in this rut? Where had her car turned off the interstate and onto a one-lane country road going from nowhere to nowhere?

3

The Stranger
– April 1970 –

"Hi-i, Aaron," smiled the very short Open Mic regular in wire glasses and an unfortunate halter top.

"Hey there," Aaron grimaced, trying to sound encouraging. "You up next?"

"Yeah. I'm going to play a couple of my old favorites."

"Great." He hesitated. "Remind me?"

"Beverly. Bev. Hunt. Remember, you introduced me three weeks ago?" She chattered like an insecure chipmunk.

"Right. Of course." He turned into the mic with all his emcee charm. "Ladies and gentlemen, friends and lovers, our first guest is someone you've all heard and enjoyed before. Please welcome— Bev Hunt!" trying unsuccessfully to elicit some acknowledgment from the clinking and guffawing audience.

Little Bev shuffled on stage, squinting and trying to ignore the swelling noise in the room. She perched herself on the stool. *At least she's wearing pants*, thought Aaron, recalling the slippage disaster from her last appearance.

She began with a tedious Welsh ballad about a mining disaster. "*There's blood on the coal ...*"

In the middle of the room was a table with two frat couples. Both males were wearing Steuben College Wrestling Team sweatshirts. One was short with close-cropped hair, protruding ears and muscles all over, the other tall and wide with simian features. Their dates were pink and indistinguishable. As the beer entered their bloodstream and the desperation of the miners grew, so did the raucousness of the frat boys.

"When the ground gets restless, miners die ..."

It was one with the big ears who started it, in a low voice at first, then growing, backed by the extra-large partner and, hesitantly, the girls.

"Bea-ver hunt. Bea-ver hunt! Bea-ver hunt!" It was the chant that had accompanied her humiliation some weeks earlier, when her wraparound skirt unwrapped in the middle of the fourth verse, just as the widows and mothers were receiving news of the mine's collapse.

But she continued singing the woeful tale, choking back the humiliation.

Now boisterous and unrestrained, they were shouting and clapping, "Bea-ver hunt! Bea-ver hunt"

Aaron vaguely registered a figure moving through the tables of Pedro's Cantina towards the frat boys when a crash stopped the music. The entire room turned to stare at the stranger in the army jacket, whose guitar case had just knocked a full pitcher of beer into the laps of the hecklers, drenching the girls' fancy date outfits. The two wrestlers stood up, affronted and dripping, their dates aghast.

"What the hell?" whined the large one, looking down hopelessly at his shirt and crotch.

"Accident," said the stranger, turning to walk away.

But the one with the muscles and the silly big ears grabbed him by his shoulder and turned him.

"You did that on purpose, you jerk." His date's cheeks were as pink as her sweater.

"Fuck you," said the surly stranger, his nostrils flaring, his shoulders rising and falling, packed nose to nose opposite the frat boys.

"Hippie faggot," said the big, drenched one. His fists hung

almost to his knees, clenching and unclenching.

"Asshole," said Protruding Ears, giving the stranger's shoulder as much of a shove as the cramped tables and chairs allowed. The stranger dropped his guitar, turned and shoved the big wet one sprawling into the lap of a girl at the table behind him, knocking over their table, mugs and pitchers splashing and flying and crashing in a groping, stumbling mass of bodies and shouts and confusion. The stranger tried to grab the short one, but suddenly Kathleen was in the middle of the fray, sorting out bodies, placing herself between the brawlers. She was pushing chairs aside with her hips, wiping the foam from the blouse of the girl underneath the guitar guy, untangling the knot of limbs and suds.

Over the shouting and crashing, Aaron began to pound out some funky Motown chords. "*Calling out around the world—* C'mon, you lazy drunks! Move those be-hinds!" No one noticed Bev Hunt packing her guitar, and slinking off to sit by herself.

Most of the audience was on their feet, straining to see the action, and Aaron smoothly channeled the energy into a dance party. Pedro was smoothing feathers and picking up tables.

The shaggy stranger wanted to get back into the fracas, but Kathleen firmly pushed him back and eased him into a chair next to the stage. "You okay?" she said into his ear, her hands on his shoulders. He was still panting, and his eyes were careening about the room like a crazed bird trapped in a smoky college bar.

"Are you all right?" She shook his shoulders. "Hey!"

His eyes settled on hers for a hush of a moment, and he smiled. "Sure," he said.

"Hey, piano man, let's hear what the tough guy's got," the waitress called to Aaron and shoved the stranger up onto the little stage, hoping he couldn't get into too much trouble while performing.

The room was reeking of noise, smoke, beer, and hormones. The frat boys and their pink dates were getting drunk, raucous, and overcharged. *What the heck*, thought Aaron. *Let's see how the hotshot handles this.*

"Hey, man, how you doing? Aaron Woodwright," said Aaron, holding out his hand.

"Miller," he said to the floor. "Sam."

Aaron handed him a cable for his guitar, a beat-up acoustic with an electric pickup.

"Okay, folks, please give a warm welcome to Sam Miller!" he said and stepped off the stage to watch what would happen.

Sam stood staring at the floor for a full ten seconds, oblivious to the mix of polite clapping, drunken disregard, and catcalls from the frat boys.

Then, he ripped into a driving, muscular "*If you knew Peggy Sue*," rough and riveting. "*Mah-hah Peggy Sue-ha-hu*," he growled, rhythmic and deep. The entire room could see her, that Peggy Sue, and feel the passion driving the rumpled stranger to utter consternation. His baritone was raspy, insistent, and probing. In the verses, his voice was controlled and commanding, but by the refrain, it was outright raunchy. Aaron's three little groupies were staring up at this Sam Miller, their mouths half open. The frat boys' dates were transfixed, their tight cashmere sweaters rising. The frat boys were wondering if what that asshole was generating would still be warm when they got back to the car.

Kathleen stopped serving beer to stare. *Not a college kid*, she thought. *Street-wise. Scrappy. Scary. But, oh my, how that boy sings.*

"He's good!" said Aaron into her ear, his mouth brushing her very fragrant black hair.

"He's great," she answered, staring at the singer.

Aaron looked at her looking at him.

Finally, she tore her eyes away and went back to sloshing pitchers and mugs.

"Hell," Aaron said to himself and went up to the piano. He

comped some simple fill chords, catching the sense of Sam's quirky syncopations, but Sam was so deep inside the song that he didn't even seem to notice that Aaron had joined in.

Sam's guitar grew more and more percussive, thick chords pummeling more rhythmic excitement than Pedro's Cantina had ever witnessed. Aaron's left-hand chords kept the beat, while Sam ventured further and further out into crazy, stretched rhythms, howling like a banshee in heat, "*My Peggy Sue-hu-hu-a-hu-u-ue,*" Aaron miraculously there to catch him on the beat as he came down.

At the beginning of the instrumental break, Sam went back to playing a straight rhythm. Aaron was taken aback for a moment but then jumped in to take the lead with his right hand, florid pianistic lines rolling and rocking all over the keyboard, an improvised jazz infusion Buddy Holly would never have dreamed of. Together, they ran through another instrumental verse, Sam providing the rhythm, Aaron creating a melodic line that wound and twisted through the chord changes, probing and questioning, and trying to entwine that oh-so-elusive Peggy Sue.

The room was rising and swaying with the music, the frat boys and the hippies and the pocket protectors moving and perspiring in the smoke and the sweat on the beer-sticky floor. Aaron glanced up and saw Pedro next to the stage, waving his sombrero exuberantly, guiding Kathleen through the steps of what was supposed to be a Mexican hat dance but actually resembled more a Pennsylvania polka.

And bam, back in the final verse, Sam at the mic, his eyes closed, his shaggy hair matted, transporting every person in the room with the beat and the hunger, Aaron keeping him on track. It ended with a crash and the crowd on its feet, clapping and cheering, Sam's old buddies, the frat boys, the loudest of all.

"Where are you from, Miller?" asked Aaron, a little patter for the crowd.

"'Round."

"Sorry, where?"

"Around. You know."

"O-kay ... Well, welcome. Steubenville could sure use some new blood." Cheers from the crowd. "So, you're a Buddy Holly fan?"

Miller peered at Aaron. After a pause, "Yeah, Buddy Holly."

"I guess he's also new to the English language," Aaron mugged in an aside to the audience.

Miller fiddled with his guitar

"What else you got for us, Miller?"

He stood motionless, his eyes closed. The room went silent.

"*Just—you—know—*" he began, his raspy voice alone, his lips touching the microphone, then stopped, frozen in mid-air, and finally, "*why,*" and his guitar came in with a sweet, swaying slow-dance swing. He crooned the love song, dripping desire.

"What do you think?" Bev dared to ask the glamorous waitress who was staring at the stranger.

"A girl could get pregnant just listening to that," she answered and headed back into the kitchen with her tray of empty mugs.

On the break, Aaron supplied a lilting arpeggio while Sam punctuated it with wordless scatting. He finished slowly, word by word, just his voice, until the final "*ways*" just hung in the air, suspended.

And the college crowd went wild, hooting and stomping and jumping and calling for more.

Sam smiled at an imaginary spot on the floor. Aaron was grinning despite himself, clapping along with the audience.

Then, Sam Miller began strumming a series of impassioned, church-tinged chords. "You can sing along here, if you want to," he mumbled too far from the microphone to be heard. "*If you ever change your mind,*" he sang, his guitar pounding a forceful, insistent beat. His eyes were closed to the smoky cantina, sweat dripping down his gaunt cheeks. His voice was fierce, gravelly, fervent. "*Oh, oh, bring it on home to me.*"

On the refrain, he called out to the crowd, his eyes closed, his face glowing, and they responded in unison, a choir of young believers. "*Yeah! (yeah!), yeah! (yeah!), yeah! (yeah!).*"

The three groupies gaped, gripping each other's hands.

When Sam began the second verse, Aaron joined above him in a joyous harmony, which Sam seemed to have been expecting.

The brunette dug her fingernails into the blonde's hand so hard that the girl yanked it away, but neither moved her eyes from Sam, his eyes still closed but smiling, his lips touching the microphone, his voice moving the crowd with gospel fervor.

"*Bring it on home to me,* yeah!" and the whole smoky cantina responded with a delirious "*Yeah!*"

"*Yeah?*" Sam challenged them.

"*Yeah,*" they responded, the frat boys loudest of all.

"*Yeah?*"

"*Yeah!*" And the crowd was on its feet, shouting and clamoring and clapping for more. Aaron came forward and put his arm around the guest singer. "SamMiller! SamMiller!" the room chanted. Sam smiled at the floor. The walls of Pedro's Cantina seemed to heave from the shouting and shrieking and stomping, everyone on their feet, jumping and cheering. Through the commotion, Aaron saw Pedro gesticulating furiously at him from behind the bar.

"Well, well!" said Aaron into the mic through the shouting and applause. "We're going to take a very short break. Remember tonight's spe—"

The waitress was squeezing between tables with tray after tray of pitchers and mugs, the pocket protectors and the long hairs and the frat boys with their pink dates all guzzling and chattering in the afterbuzz.

Pedro turned off the spotlight, and Aaron looked for Sam, but he had disappeared into the crowd. He asked Kathleen if she saw where he'd gone, but she was busy with the customers.

"Hey, Aaron," said little Beaver. "How about that?"

"Yeah. Did you see where he went?"

"I think maybe he left. Wow. He's, like, incredible."

Despite himself, Aaron felt a tinge of jealousy. *I should care about* Beaver? he thought.

No one had the courage to try the open mic afterward, so Aaron played one more set. The crowd was already thinning out. Even the three groupies had gone. He sat by the door to the kitchen, nursing a beer, as he watched Kathleen bobbing and weaving through the tables, serving the last couple of mugs, and clearing the vacated tables. There was still a lot of mess on the floor from Sam's little mayhem.

"Can we talk?" he asked as she approached, a tray piled high with an aftermath of dishes and pitchers.

"I'm working," she answered as she hurried past him into the kitchen.

"What time do you finish?" he tried.

"When I finish," she said on her way back out of the kitchen, barely glancing at him.

"I'll wait," he called after her as she headed into the wreckage of the room. "I'll wait till you finish," he repeated as she brought another load into the kitchen.

"It'll be too late," she said.

He wasn't sure, but he thought she might be playing him. And he was flustered because he could usually read these signals clearly.

"Of course, you could help," she said without turning, unloading the dishes into the sink.

"Me?"

She isn't even listening, he thought. *Or is she?*

"Hey, I'm the entertainment."

She turned to face him, standing close. "You trying to start up with me?" she asked, looking him right in the eye.

He nodded.

She handed him a broom and dustpan, wiped her hands on a towel, and headed back out to the carnage of the room, rag and mop in hand.

The downtown streets of little Steubenville were deserted when they finally finished cleaning up.

"So, how was your first night at Pedro's?"

"Pretty neat, I guess," she said.

He stopped in his tracks. "You *guess?*"

"That Sam guy," she said.

"Yeah, that Sam guy. Strange dude."

"Oh, yeah! But, wow, he's a fucking force of nature."

"You've got a great voice yourself," said Aaron, deftly changing the subject.

"It was cool," she said, looking at Aaron, remembering the thrill she'd felt singing on stage. "I've never sung for an audience before."

"Really? You seemed so confident."

"I mean, I know I can carry a tune. I was just hoping I'd remember all the words."

"No, you have a real stage presence. No jitters."

She looked at him sideways, knowing he was flattering her and enjoying it. Maybe it was that thick black hair. Aaron was indeed a very nice-looking pianist. Or maybe it was the two beers on top of an empty stomach on top of an adrenaline high. She felt a woozy glow throughout her body.

"I'm used to shutting out crowds," she said.

"How's that?" He moved a little closer to her as they walked so that their shoulders would brush accidentally.

"I used to swim. Competitively."

"No shit. A jockette?"

"Surprise, surprise."

"All full of surprises."

She stopped. He stopped with her. She turned to him, so he turned to her. She took the front of his shirt in her hand and pulled him down to her for a deep, long, tongued kiss.

"Want to come up to see my etchings?" he managed to say.

"They any good?"

4

Allie Bauer's Brewery
– May 9, 2006 –

At the Bauer mailbox, Shelly turned and drove up the long, crunchy driveway to a sprawling, green farmhouse with a stately porch in front and a single car tucked at the side. A short, sturdy woman with cropped white hair in her late sixties came down from the porch on the side of the house and walked towards her.

"Hi, Allie Bauer," she said, extending her hand.

"Hi, I'm Shelly Griff—aah," she yowled at the woman's firm handshake and burst out in a flood of tears, clutching her hand in pain.

"Come into the house, honey," said Allie, leading her into the kitchen. "Here, hold it under the cold water while I make you up an ice pack."

"I'm so sorry," choked Shelly, struggling to control the tears, feeling the mucus dripping down from her nose.

"Here," said Allie, handing her a box of tissues, guiding her to a seat at the kitchen table, and wrapping a towel neatly around ice from the old refrigerator. She brought Shelly a glass of water and sat next to her, her hand on Shelly's arm, while the distraught young lady collected herself.

"I'm—I'm so sorry, I have never—" Shelly choked.

"Shh," said Allie. "Take your time."

Shelly sipped her water and tried to focus on breathing regularly.

"I'm so sorry," she managed after a few moments. "This has never happened to me before."

"We all have our days, Mrs. Griffin," said Allie gently.

"Oh, I'm not Mrs. Griffin," she sniffled. "That was my mother."

"Oh, I'm sorry, I assumed Mr. Griffin—"

"He's my father. I work with him in the office."

"I see."

"I'm Ms Griffin. Miss Griffin."

"Allie Bauer, pleased to meet you," she said, giving Shelly's left hand a gentle squeeze.

"I'm okay now, thank you so much. I had a little accident—"

"You don't need to explain."

"Thanks. Anyway, I apologize."

"And you certainly don't need to apologize."

"I appreciate that. I'm fine now, really."

"Why don't I make us some coffee, and we can sit in the office."

"You live—here?" Shelly asked, looking around the large old country kitchen.

"We call this the annex. Back in the old days it used to be the offices of the brewery. But when my husband Paul died, I moved in here and closed up Gruenhaus. That's what the house was always called."

"You live here alone?"

"Yes, I do. Yes, ma'am. Since my husband Paul died, back in 1993. Lived here all my life. I was born in this house."

"Wow. Well, actually, me, too. I live in the house I was born in. My father and I."

"Nothing like staying close to your roots."

"I guess."

"Here we go," she said, holding a tray with a coffee pitcher, a plate of muffins, and a box of tissues. "We can sit in the office if you like. The books are all in there."

Allie led her through the small dining room, where two large photographs were hung prominently, one of a man in his fifties, the other of a young man in an Army dress uniform.

Shelly followed her into a tightly packed room, tidy except for the desk. Three of the walls were filled with black and gray ledgers. Above the desk hung a dozen plaques and faded framed certificates—"Bauer's Brewery, for Excellence in Quality, 1957," "For Outstanding Achievement in Business: Bauer's Brewery, 1952" from the Ohio Brewer's Association, "The Wayne County Chamber of Commerce 1948 Merchant's Award: Bauer's Brewery."

Shelly wasn't surprised to see there was no computer. Many of her father's clients had no interest in joining the twenty-first century. Much of her work consisted of digitizing books that had been kept for decades by hand.

"We can sit at my desk. I've prepared all the papers your father asked for as best I could."

"I'd like to get some background first," said Shelly, indicating the worn plush couch, "if that's okay with you."

"I surely don't mind." Allie smiled. "I don't get many nice young visitors out here. But your father said something about you being in a big hurry."

Shelly waved her left hand dismissively. "Colonel Griffin."

"I'm sorry?"

"That's what I call him when he acts like my commanding officer."

"He was in the military?"

"Thirty years. Retired early when my mom got sick, went into private practice."

"He was a judge advocate?"

"Yes, he was," she said, repressing the desire to roll her eyes.

"Very impressive."

"Well, the Army certainly molds men," said Shelly.

"In what way?"

"Conscientious," she said, choosing her words carefully. Allie was a lovely woman, but a client, nonetheless. "Ver-ry conscientious. About my time."

"He sounded quite to the point over the phone," she said, "very efficient."

"Oh, efficiency is his middle name."

"Don't be so hard on him." Allie smiled. "He sounds like a very nice man."

He would like this lady, thought Shelly. "It's just that he can be a little, ah, overly focused on the paperwork."

"What do you mean?"

"In my experience, it's good to hear the story from the beginning so that we can weigh all the options."

"Well, that's fine with me, whatever you need."

They settled into the couch, Allie placing the tray between them. Shelly dried her eyes and blew her nose for what she hoped was the last time.

"I understand you've done this a lot?" Allie asked.

"What?"

"Closing up businesses. Selling out."

Shelly shifted uncomfortably. She set down her coffee cup and saucer on the tray.

"Look," she said, looking Allie directly in the eye. "I know what people say about us. 'The sharks,' smelling blood, making money off of the misfortunes of others."

"Well, yes," Allie said, looking down at her coffee, "but they also say you're the best at it in this whole part of the state."

"Allie, nobody's trying to sell you a bill of goods here. The economy is really, really tough. A lot of businesses are going under. It's very sad. But behind each business is a person, or people, or a family. Somebody has to help them through this. That's our job. We're experienced because we're good at it. We're honest and we're fair. That's why people come to us."

Allie looked at her, weighing her words.

"Trust me," Shelly said, "I promise we'll check out all the options and try to help you through whatever is best for you."

"Okay," said Allie, with a small smile of resignation. "Do you like cornbread muffins? They're fresh."

"They smell delicious," Shelly said.

"My mother's recipe from way back when," said Allie with a smile. "I've been baking them for, oh, sixty years now."

"Mmm," said Shelly, chewing. "They *are* delicious."

"Why, thank you, honey."

"So, tell me the story. Tell me about Bauer's Brewery and why you want to sell out."

"About a month ago—"

"Start at the beginning. How long has Bauer's Brewery been around?" asked Shelly, chewing hungrily, looking at the faded placards on the wall.

"Oh, forever, more or less. It was established in 1872 by my great-grandfather, Gunther Bauer, and the family has been making beer ever since. Except for the Prohibition, of course. That's when my grandfather bought this farm. My uncle Fred worked it, then his son, my cousin Jimmy, till he went away to the war."

"Wow. That's some history!"

"One of the oldest businesses in Northeast Ohio still run by the original family."

"So, what happened?"

"After the war, the big breweries started growing, taking over everything. The smaller breweries started dropping like flies all over the county."

"Why?"

"Bottling costs, for one. People started to take bottles home from the store rather than hang out in a tavern and drink draft. So, we had to expand from one production line to three. And then came distribution costs. You needed a whole fleet of trucks to distribute the bottled beer, and only the major breweries could afford that. By the time my father retired, in '71 or

'72, and Paul and I started running the business, we were the only local brewery left in these parts."

"You were living here?"

"Yes, in Gruenhaus. My mom had passed long ago, so it was Dad and Paul and I. And Jimmy, our son. Named after his uncle. Oh, and Dad's old-maid aunt, Georgina. She lived with us, too. Lived to be a hundred and two!"

"You kept your maiden name?"

"Yes, well, the brewery was always run by a Bauer. Father to son. But I'm an only daughter. So, when I married Paul, I decided to keep my maiden name. Let me tell you, it raised quite a few eyebrows."

"A woman ahead of her time," Shelly said and smiled.

"Well, there wasn't much choice. Paul was a good man, but people around here put stock in the Bauer name. At least they used to."

"What do you mean?"

"Well, it's all changed, hasn't it? I remember when I was a little girl, back in the late forties, early fifties, when my grandfather was still running the company, we were something special in these parts. This whole part of the state, out to Columbus, Cleveland, Youngstown, Mansfield, Canton, Zanesville—everybody knew the Bauers.

"Our beer was a symbol of local pride. People swore by it. You know, there was never really much to brag about in this part of the state. There were the factories, and the steel foundries, and the rubber plants and all. Those were prosperous times. Good times. People worked and raised families and went to church and to their local high school's football games and drank Creston Gold."

"That's your beer?" asked Shelly, surprised. "I had no idea. I just bought a six-pack last night."

"You're a Creston Gold drinker?"

"Not me. My boyfriend—my ex-boyfriend—this guy that I was seeing—he drinks it. Creston Gold. He lives in Youngstown, and he can't find it there. So, when I drive down from Warren, I pick him up a six-pack from this convenience store that carries it."

"Sure, Schnee's. On 422."

"You know every single place that sells your beer?"

"Well, there aren't that many of them anymore. But, yes, we have a long history here."

"Wow. So. Creston Gold."

"Yes, that's our beer. Back in the '40s and '50s, we tried a couple of other brews, but that was the one people kept coming back to. The water for it comes from Lake Traumsee, just down past the southern pasture here. You can see it from the other side of Gruenhaus. People used to say there's something special in the water," said Allie with faded pride.

"Then what happened?"

"Well, it was a real struggle. As I said, we were the only local brewery left. We tried our best to keep it going, Paul ran the plant, down past Wooster, I kept the books here." Allie paused. "And then, ah—" She stopped talking. Her eyes teared up, and she took a tissue from the box to dab her nostrils and the corners of her eyes. "And then one night in 1993, a few days after Christmas, he was coming home late from the brewery, and it was snowing, and—"

Shelly waited patiently.

"And a truck swerved, and—" She made a gesture with her hand. She unrolled the tissue in her hand and blew her nose.

"Your son?"

"Jimmy was a senior in high school. I wanted him to go to college, but he insisted on enlisting. 'That's what Bauer's do,' he said. He promised me he'd be all right." She blew her nose and sat with her hands in her lap, her head bowed. "He didn't keep his promise."

Shelly leaned forward and gently squeezed her hands.

"Why didn't you sell out then?"

"Gruenhaus was my home. Bauer's Brewery was all I had

31

ever known. My name and the brewery—that was all I had left. So, I kept going on my own. And have been for over ten years now. But it's a losing battle. A quality beer with limited distribution. Costs keep going up, and sales keep dropping. We're down to one production line and three trucks when they're all working. About twenty-five employees." She paused. "There's a man who runs the daily operations, been with us for about fifteen years, but he's about to retire."

"You've tried to sell it?"

"I put it on the market a year ago. Not a nibble. Our machinery is too old to be worth investing in. Distribution, they have sewn up anyway. And it seems goodwill and a reputation aren't worth anything in the open market."

They sat in silence for a long moment.

"I'm sorry," said Shelly.

"I gave Bauer's Brewery my life, Shelly. I'm almost seventy, and I just don't have any strength left. I'm giving up." Allie lifted her head. "That's why I called your father. I just want to get out from under this already," she sighed.

Shelly sighed as well. "That must be a very hard decision for you."

"Well, I won't lie. Yes, it hurts. It hurts that I'm closing my family's business. It hurts that the family name won't—" Allie stopped to blow her nose. "Now *I'm* crying? Someone would think we're a couple of over-emotional women here."

No, thought Shelly, *they'd think we're a couple of women who got screwed.* But she said nothing, waiting patiently for this dignified, heroic lady to regain her composure.

"But you know what hurts the most?" Allie asked, looking up at Shelly. "That this whole part of the country is dying. A slow, painful death. Just closing down, like Bauer's Brewery. And there's nothing anyone can do about it."

They both sat in silence. Shelly had no intention of mouthing any empty words of comfort. It sucked.

"So, I guess we should get to work on the books," said Allie finally.

"I guess we should," Shelly agreed, trying to maintain a professional veneer of cheer.

"Maybe we'll have a bite to eat first?" Allie suggested, smiling through the gloom. "I want to hear about this ex-boyfriend who drinks Creston Gold."

"As far as I'm concerned, he should choke on it," said Shelly, and they both laughed as they walked back into the kitchen.

5

The Aaron Woodwright Smile

– April 1970 –

Two days after Open Mic Night, Aaron was eating a ham and cheese sandwich in the Student Union cafeteria when Beaver came up to him.

"Hey, Aaron."

"Hey, how are you?" he forced out. He glanced around, hoping no one was watching.

"That Sam Miller! Wow!" she chirped.

"Yeah," he answered with no smile at all.

"Aaron, listen, I was talking to my cousin Marty ..." Two girls walked by. He smiled at them. "He goes to Ohio State. He's driving through here on Wednesday, and he's going to stay over." They smiled back. "So, I thought I'd take him to Pedro's."

What did I do to deserve this? Aaron asked himself.

"He's a really cool guy, Marty. He's involved in the protest movement there."

"Oh, yeah?"

"He's organizing a big anti-war demonstration there. At Ohio State."

"Right," he squirmed, "Listen, I have to—"

"He's looking for people to perform."

"I'm not really into politics," he said, rising.

"The last one had about two thousand people," she said, looking up at him. "He said he's expecting twice that many next time."

"Really?" Aaron sat back down.

"So, I thought I'd bring him to Pedro's."

Aaron's heart rose. "Wednesday's not the best time. It's Open Mic."

"I thought maybe Sam Miller will show up again."

Aaron's heart plummeted.

"And maybe you could work something up with him?"

"What, m-me and that Miller?" Aaron stuttered.

"I mean, you're both so good."

"He's weird," said Aaron.

"But the two of you together?" she said, awed by the thought.

"But—I mean—I don't even know the guy. That was just a one-time thing."

"He said they're expecting a crowd twice that size next time."

Aaron looked at her. "Four thousand people?"

"Uh-huh," she said, her heart pounding.

"Wow. But I wouldn't even know how to contact—"

She handed him a small piece of paper. Sam Miller, 251 McMillan Street.

"Oh. Ah. Thanks, ah—"

She showed him the other side of the note. Bev Hunt. 421-3305.

"Bev," he said.

"See you Wednesday?"

"I guess. Yeah. Sure. Four thousand people?" he repeated.

Bev nodded rapidly.

"Thanks. Uh, Bev. Yeah, great. Thanks." And Aaron bestowed upon little Bev a full-fledged Aaron Woodwright smile.

She gazed at him as he walked away.

6

Creston Gold

– May 9, 2006 –

"Why didn't you answer your phone?" snapped the Colonel.

"Because I was working!" Shelly snapped back.

"Until now?"

"Yes, until now!" Shelly looked at her watch. Four-thirty, but the sky was already dark and ominous.

"Why did it take so long?"

"It took! Dad, will you get off my back?"

"All right, all right," he said, retreating without apologizing. "How was it?"

How was it? Shelly had no idea how to answer that in curt military syntax.

"It was fine. Standard stuff. I don't know how she kept the brewery going this long. It should have been put down twenty years ago. The books are a mess. She's been doing them by herself, doesn't own a computer. Nothing surprising."

"Did you get—"

"Yes, I got everything, and I'm on my way back, and I'll talk to you later," she said, hanging up. Thick, heavy drops began to splatter the windshield. But Shelly's mind was on that warm, brave woman fighting a futile battle by herself, every twist of fate just looking for a new way to screw her, and facing it with a spirit and courage that made Shelly want to curl up under her quilt until the world decided to change.

Of course, she couldn't say that to her father. He would lecture her, as he had done so many times before, that this was their job, to crunch the numbers, advise the client, and facilitate what needed to be done. And hand on her heart, from what Shelly had seen, there was no question—keeping Bauer's Brewery alive would be like resuscitating a dead horse.

But even that wasn't what was on Shelly's mind. It was what Allie had said to her as she was about to leave. Allie had handed her a bag of the very delicious cornbread muffins.

"Oh, that's so sweet," Shelly had said, patting her hips, "but I don't need them."

"Oh, don't be silly," she'd said. "Share them with that nice father of yours."

"Oh. Well, I'm sure he'll appreciate them."

"And—" Allie hesitated. "Can I speak frankly with you, honey?"

"Of course," said Shelly.

"Don't let yourself get stuck."

"I'm sorry?" she said, turning bright red. Her entire life, she'd had to deal with a complexion that advertised her embarrassment.

"You're too good to let yourself waste away working for your father and closing down businesses in this God-forsaken corner of nowhere, waiting for a Prince Charming who doesn't exist. Don't get stuck here. Like I did."

Alone in the car on I-76 East, driving back to Warren, Ohio, Shelly felt herself flush again.

The rain was coming down steadily. Shelly turned up the windshield wipers and turned on the radio, hoping to distract herself. It was the one radio show she followed, Johnny Walker, "Johnny at Six" from WFOR in Cleveland. He had a warm bass and always struck her as a really nice guy. Her father had once had some dealings with him about a real estate case but, ever the tight-lipped Colonel, had nothing to say other than he seemed like a decent enough person.

Listening to Johnny Walker's show was always a pleasant surprise. Unlike other programs, he seemed to have no set format, which she found appealing. Sometimes he would just play popular music, sometimes he'd go off on some musical tangent, sometimes he'd do interviews around a certain subject. But it was always done in a human voice that spoke to her strongly.

This evening, he was talking about the recently deceased Linn Sheldon, host of the local children's TV show *Barnaby*, which she had grown up on. Johnny was talking in a homey, intimate tone to people who had worked on the show, family and friends, and people like herself for whom *Barnaby* had been a significant part of their childhood landscape for thirty-two years. Shelly thought there could be no more fitting tribute.

Then, the theme song from *Barnaby* came on, a satiny impressionistic melody full of strings and flutes. The puppets and the cartoons on the show, the hot chocolate her mother had made for her as a treat on Saturday mornings, the smell of her mother sitting next to her, all these drifted across Shelly's mind as she sped through the darkening mid-May evening, wondering just where it was that she was going.

Late that night, Shelly dialed into the internet. She waited impatiently through the wee-oo-ee till the connection finally succeeded, annoyed once more at her father's refusal to pay for a broadband connection at home. She finally connected and tried "Bauer's Brewery" and "Creston Gold" on Yahoo! but came up empty-handed. Then, she tried Google. Again, nothing. She searched for information about the local brewing industry, but it gave her nothing of interest. On Wikipedia, she found an article on the history of breweries in the US and one on the rapid growth of craft and microbreweries in recent years. They only drove in how much of an anachronism Bauer's was in 2006.

Discouraged, she looked for *Barnaby* and for Johnny Walker on the WFOR site but again found nothing of interest. On the Plain Dealer site, she found their obituary for *Barnaby* but nothing more. It was past midnight, and she was tired from the day, but she still felt unsettled and poured herself another half glass of wine. She went on YouTube and found an old clip of the *Barnaby* show, which she enjoyed greatly, but it increased her feeling of loss. She tried "Bauer's Brewery," hoping against hope. Nothing. She yawned and was about to close down the computer. *Last try,* she thought. In the YouTube search bar, she typed in "Creston Gold" and hit Enter.

She waited for the query to go through and yawned aloud again, long and disheartened.

A match appeared.

"Creston Gold - Decapede" was there, with a picture of five young people grinning in front of a rundown storefront. She sat up straight, clicked, and after an endless half-minute, a wistful, lulling song began to play.

Storm clouds are gathering way out there
Soon it's gonna rain—but I don't really care
Lying with you on the ground
Grass and sunlight all around
Nothing's gonna bring me down
Pass me another Creston Gold.

Fully awake now, she looked at the file details: "Creston Gold" - Decapede, uploaded by WhoDeMan, 4 views, February 15, 2006. Four months ago. That was all. She clicked on WhoDeMan, but there was no more information. She clicked on Show More—nothing.

She listened again. And again. It was a beautiful song, soft and summery, floating on the wings of young, optimistic love.

Lake Hope lapping at the shore
This must be the place I've been searching for
Holds me close and takes me in
To a place I've never been
Never gonna leave again
Have another Creston Gold.

She stared at the picture—a tall, very handsome guy with aviator shades and a shock of hair to die for; an elegant tawny man, impeccably dressed; a barefoot monk attired in a white robe, with endless black hair and beard; and a fetching girl with a black pageboy, hoop earrings, and a peasant blouse was holding back a rough, haggard guy trying to walk away.

What the hell? Who were these people? Decapede, what was that? Was this crazy salad actually the band that made this beautiful record?

But fatigue overtook her, and Shelly fell into a deep sleep, dreaming of the lawyer from St. Louis eating a powdered donut, Casper the Friendly Ghost floating over a pastoral meadow, and a white-faced young man in dress blues inside a picture frame, soundlessly mouthing an unheard song.

7

Chez Sam

– April 1970 –

251 McMillan was above Steubie's Subway Sandwiches. As Aaron climbed the stairs, the door on the second floor opened a crack. A very old woman with a blue-gray bouffant and thickly caked makeup peered out. She looked like she'd been mummified.

"Hi there," he said, smiling his Aaron smile.

She looked at the guitar case he was holding, snorted, and slammed the door.

He climbed to the top floor. "Gnossos Pappadopoulis" was written neatly on the door to the right. The other door had no name, only a large crack at eye level. All he could see through it was an empty pizza box and an empty beer bottle. Aaron knocked. He heard some sort of rustle. He waited. And knocked again, harder.

The door opened. Sam was standing there, mostly asleep, buck naked. "Angf?" he said, yawning with his mouth wide open and stretching. Clothesless. Bare. His thing just hanging there in the open air.

"Hey. Aaron. From Pedro's," Aaron said cheerily to no visible response.

Sam turned, and his bare backside walked away. Aaron stepped in, hesitantly closing the door behind him. It was a

41

large kitchen covered with what had once been food containers and other random refuse. He heard a harsh stream in the toilet and wandered into the other room, picking his way cautiously among the clutter on the floor. A double bed, a post-apocalyptic mess. A bay window looking down at the corner and a small table with an ashtray overflowing with butts of hand-rolled cigarettes. A guitar case. A hookah held together with duct tape. A beat-up old stereo and pile of records, on top, someone named Sandy Bull. A poster with red-white-and-blue stars-and-stripes lettering, reading "Fuck America." Above the stereo, another poster, one of Frank Zappa sitting on a toilet. Next to it, one of Fred Astaire and Ginger Rogers in mid-swirl.

Sam came out, drying his face on a towel so grimy Aaron shuddered at the thought of it touching human skin. Sam tossed the towel in the direction of a kitchen chair, but it missed and fell to the floor.

Aaron's eyes locked on Sam's face. Not even underpants. "Listen, you really rocked the room at Pedro's."

"Oh, yeah."

"I wanted to talk to you."

"Shoot," said Sam distractedly, attempting to bite off a piece of ossified pizza crust, spitting it back into the box, and closing the lid over it. He took a swig of tap water, swished it around his mouth, and spit it into the sink.

"Some guy heard about us singing at Pedro's, you know, you and me—"

Sam walked past him, au naturel, to the bay window and began foraging through the ashtray.

"He's organizing a big demonstration at Ohio State."

Finally, Sam came up with a roach long enough to extract another toke or two.

"Five thousand people."

"Do you have a light?"

"Could you maybe hold off with that?" asked Aaron. Sam

looked at him with disdain but tossed the roach back into the ashtray. "Could you please listen to me?"

"What? I'm listening!"

"And could you maybe—?"

"What? Oh, that?" He snickered at Aaron's discomfort but grabbed a pair of jeans from the floor, sitting on the bed to slip them on underwearless. Aaron looked unsuccessfully for a chair, and perched himself gingerly on a corner of the bed.

"So, listen," Aaron began, "There's someone who heard about the two of us singing at Pedro's, you know, me and you. He's organizing a big anti-war demonstration at Ohio State in a couple of weeks. Five thousand people. And they need performers. So he's coming here on Wednesday to check us out."

"Us?"

Aaron nodded. He was trying not to think about the sheet he was sitting on, what unspeakable acts had occurred on it, what residues and stains had been secreted there. "I thought we worked pretty damned well up there, the two of us."

Sam was rummaging through a pile of discarded clothing on the floor.

"So what do you say?"

"About what?" Sam asked, smelling the armpits of a St Mary's of the Assumption Nursing School sweatshirt.

"Wednesday. The guy coming to hear us. Would you concentrate?" said Aaron, standing up.

"Jesus, I just woke up!" grumbled Sam.

"So do you want to do it?"

"Do what?"

Was this guy serious?

Aaron raised his voice and tried to sound organized and stern: "A guy's coming to Pedro's next week to check us out, you and me, for a big gig in Columbus. You want to work up some songs with me, yes or no?"

" 'You and me'?"

"Yeah, you know, some protest songs or something."

"Not interested," said Sam.

"Chance to play for thousands of people?"

"Ain't interested."

"I assume you're against the war."

"You can assume whatever you want," he growled as he pulled the sweatshirt over his head. "I don't like crowds and I don't like protest songs."

"Could we at least just try some stuff together?" said Aaron. "I brought my guitar."

"What, that Muzak shit you were playing?"

"The audience seems to like it," said Aaron, prickling.

"Blood, man. It ain't got no blood."

"What do you mean, 'blood'?"

Sam picked up his guitar, dumped the entire pile of dross from a dilapidated bridge chair onto the floor—clothing, books, a three-ring binder, a leather aviator's hat with fur flaps, and a crumbled travel poster advertising Ibiza—sat down, played two strong chords, and a string snapped.

"Ah, fuck!" muttered Sam. "You got a spare A string?" For a full five minutes Sam searched the two-room apartment, Aaron warming up and trying to show off with some fancy runs, but Sam was furrowing deep under the bed, where he extracted a mud-crusted poncho, a large broken peacock feather, a paperback with no cover, an almost empty box of cheese crackers, and finally, a packet of strings. Sam stuffed the last cracker into his mouth while he changed the string and tuned, and without warning jumped into "Bye Bye, Love."

They ran through it easily, a fun three-chord warm-up, Sam singing a muscular lead, Aaron providing a fluid, precise harmony. On the last verse, they both did a surprisingly accurate imitation of The Everlys' nasal twang.

"Nice," said Aaron, when they finished, although it was much better than just "nice". "Can I show you something?"

Sam looked at Aaron's right hand.

"You see how he slaps it?"

Sam tried to copy him. "How did you—"

"You hit all the strings at once, and then you muffle it with the back of your hand."

"Ah," he said, shifting his chair to face Aaron, practicing the riff over and over. They began to run through some basic Chuck Berry and Elvis, feeling each other out. As often as not, Sam would switch songs in mid-verse with no warning, and Aaron would scramble to catch up.

"I love those oldies," said Aaron, and he began the bouncy bass intro to "Pretty Woman."

"Do it slower," said Sam. "Slower," he repeated. "I said slower."

"Jeez," Aaron complained, but he slowed to an amble.

"Now, dirty it up," said Sam. "More." And when he was ready, Sam began flicking a sassy, high-heeled pulse on his guitar and then growling a sultry, *Pretty woman walking down the street,*" Aaron following in skintight harmony, steel against gravel, sparks flying. They finished together in a triumphant "*Oh- oh, pret-ty wo-man.*"

"Whoo!" said Aaron.

"I'm hungry," said Sam, tossing his guitar on the bed and pulling on a shoe.

"Where are you going?" asked Aaron.

"Steubie Subways downstairs."

"But we just got started."

"I don't know who this 'we' is you keep talking about, man," said Sam, rubbing his hand over his empty stomach underneath the droopy sweatshirt, "but I got to eat. See my other shoe?"

Aaron jumped up. "If I go get you a sandwich, will you, like, hang out and play for a while?"

Sam weighed that for a moment. "Yeah," he said. "Why not?"

Aaron looked at him.

"Well?" Sam looked at him. "Go! Italian Deluxe."

Aaron opened the door.

"And a root beer," Sam added.

Aaron closed the door behind him.

Sam opened the door. "With extra baloney," he called.

Aaron bounced jauntily down the steps.

"And onions."

As he passed the second floor, the mummified old lady was holding open the door a crack, the chain on, staring out at him. "Clementine Wilson," read the sign. He smiled at her. She scowled.

Do I really want to hook up with a weirdo like that? Aaron reflected as he waited in line for the sandwich. *And the way he never looks at you? God only knows what's going on inside that head. I get it, I can't transform a song like he can. But if it weren't for me, he'd get so far into a song that he'd drown. It's me who keeps the rhythm going, I remember what verse we're singing. He couldn't carry off that act of his without me.*

And as he climbed back up the stairs, the mummy was still peering out, waiting for him to place a bomb or turn into a vampire. "Hi, Clem!" he said with a chipper wave. She stared for a moment, then slammed the door shut.

Sam ingested the entire submarine sandwich more quickly than Aaron thought possible, extra baloney and onions included.

After a resounding root beer belch, they went through some workhorses from the radio, Beatles and Byrds and Springfield, nothing too gritty for Aaron, nothing too smooth for Sam, who would flick skittishly from song to song after a verse or two. On the songs Aaron knew, he would add a harmony and some musical counterpoint, garnishes and decorations and spices. On those he didn't know, he did a respectable job of filling in behind Sam, enabling him to experiment vocally and rhythmically. At one point, Aaron began to play the introduction to "In-A-Gadda-Da-Vida," but Sam gave him such a withering glare that he hurried to change the tune.

For hours, they played blues and country rock, Oldies but

Goodies and Rhythm and Blues and Motown, jousting with each other higher and harder. Sam would make some fast ones slow and some slow ones fast, and his voice made every song fresh. Aaron's guitar and his harmony vocals made every song shine.

Aaron was used to leading, but he understood that if he wanted to make music with Sam, he'd have to do it on Sam's terms. And Aaron knew he wanted very badly to make music with him.

"You like Mexican food?"

"Hell yes," said Sam.

"I'll tell you what. You come play at Pedro's, I'll buy you dinner."

"I dunno, I got a lot to do—"

"All you can eat," said Aaron.

"Yeah?" Sam peered at him sideways.

"Nine-thirty, we go on."

Sam picked at his guitar. "I gotta check with my secretary," he said.

"Ah, come on. This was fun."

Sam continued picking and thinking.

"All the enchiladas and tacos and frijoles you can eat."

"They got chili con carne?"

8

C. Griffin, Attorney at Law

– May 10, 2006 –

"Hey, Shel," the Colonel called to her as she tried to slip past his office door. She stopped and stood in his doorway, holding the coffee mug to her nose, inhaling the caffeine. "Where's the original of the 2003 tax return for Bauer's Brewery? I only see a copy."

"Good morning to you, too."

"What? Oh, good morning."

"Mrs. Bauer couldn't find it. It's okay, they accept certified copies except for the previous year."

"Are you sure?"

"Yes, Dad."

"Mmm," he said, perusing the pile of files. "It looks like it's all here," he said without looking up.

"You're welcome," she said and turned to leave.

"Hey, Shel," he called after her, "is everything okay?"

"Yeah, fine. I took a look at the numbers. Pretty dismal. It's a sinking ship."

"You'll start filling out the corporation dissolution forms?"

"If you'll let me get to my desk."

"Hey, what's the matter?"

"Nothing," she said and paused. "It's sad."

"What is?"

"It's an old family brewery. The pride of the whole region."

"I used to drink Creston Gold myself."

"Allie Bauer's been keeping it afloat for years, by herself, against all odds."

"And?" That was civilian for "Dismissed."

"And nothing. It's sad."

"Okay. Let me know when the forms are ready, I'll go over them," he said, reading.

"Did you find the muffins I left in the kitchen?"

"Yes, very tasty."

"You're welcome."

He peered up over his reading glasses.

"Thank you."

"They're from her. From Allie."

"So please tell her thank you for me when you speak to her."

"Tell her yourself. She sent them to you."

"To me? What for?"

"To be nice. I'll explain that concept to you someday."

"Don't be sarcastic."

"She's a very nice lady. A widow. Her son died in the service."

The Colonel looked up.

"She seemed to think you sounded nice over the phone."

"Me?" he responded.

"Go figure. She's very warm. And good-looking for her age. I think you'd like her."

He looked at Shelly for a moment. "Could be," he said and returned to the papers on his desk.

Shelly sat at her computer, taking advantage of the office's broadband connection, listening to the song over and over with earphones till it was running through her brain unassisted. The dissolution forms sat in a pile on the corner of her desk while she searched the web again for Decapede, for Creston Gold, for Bauer's Brewery. Nothing.

She picked up the phone and called Allie, who said how much she'd enjoyed the visit despite the dispiriting circumstances. Shelly responded in kind and told her how much her father had appreciated the muffins. Allie had never heard of the song and had only a vague notion of what YouTube was. They both hoped they would meet again sometime soon.

Shelly thought about Allie, her heart-wrenching life of toil and loss. *Damn it, people loved that beer. Why should such a business fail?* The song, with all its sweet, innocent optimism, kept running through her mind. *"Lying with you on the ground / Grass and sunlight all around / Nothing's gonna bring me down / Pass me another Creston Gold."*

It just wasn't fair.

In the afternoon, she called the office's tech guy and asked him if there was a way to trace who posted a clip on YouTube. He told her there wasn't.

So, Shelly worked. She filled out the dissolution forms, tallied the figures for Bauer's Brewery, organized the files, and submitted the applications to the Bureau of Business Registration.

On her way home after work, Johnny Walker was bewailing budget cuts for inner city playgrounds, waxing passionate that for many kids growing up in a gray concrete world, these parks were the only glimmer of light in their lives. He played some old songs Shelly loved—"The Circle Game," "Where Do The Children Play?" and "Sugar Mountain."

On impulse, she pulled into the parking lot of the Carpet King Factory Outlet and called information for the telephone number for WFOR. The line was busy. She tried again, to no avail. She tried again when she got home but got a recording that the switchboard had closed for the evening.

After a desultory dinner alone, she tried to find something to occupy her mind on television, but it all seemed stale and irrelevant. She dialed into YouTube. Staring at the picture of this mysterious Decapede on the screen, she quietly sang along with the song. *Storm clouds are gathering way out there / Soon it's gonna rain—but I don't really care.*

The picture was black and white, the clothes a mix of late collegiate and early hippie. Late 1960s? Outwardly, the five appeared unconnected. But they must be the band. *Pass me another Creston Gold.* And it had to be local. Decapede. What kind of name is that?

Shelly showered and went to sleep early.

The next morning from work, she tried the radio station again. After twenty minutes, she managed to get a girl on the line.

"Could I please speak to Mr. Johnny Walker?" Shelly asked, coloring.

"Who is this?" the girl asked curtly, and Shelly hung up, flushed with embarrassment. The phone rang, and Shelly jumped.

"Shelly, hi. It's me," said Derek. "You haven't answered any of my—"

"Oh, go fuck yourself!" she barked and threw down the receiver.

She sat there fuming, angry and embarrassed and frustrated. Her pulse was racing, and her mind was in turmoil— Derek looking up at her wide-eyed from underneath his ex-wife, *Nothing's gonna bring me down,* five young people in black and white outside time and place, the busy signal at the radio station. "Don't let yourself get stuck," Allie had said.

A feeling welled up in Shelly that she had reached a dead end, and something had to change. She didn't know what it was, but she knew that it was up to her.

9

Woodwright and Miller

– April 1970 –

Steubenville was well off the beaten path, snuggled into the rolling hills of Eastern Ohio and content with that. Locals liked to tell how the town weathered the Great Depression. "The zipper factory. Even in hard times, people need zippers." Folks supported President Nixon and minded their own business. Except when the hippies were disrespectful to the flag.

Aaron usually played his eight o'clock set for the waitresses, Pedro, and the cook, but when he arrived on Wednesday, the room was half full. Several of the tables were occupied by longhairs, an uncommon sight in backwater Steubenville.

Bev was waiting for him breathlessly.

"Hiya," she bubbled.

"Hi, Bev. Is your cousin here?"

"He's on his way. Where's Sam?"

"We go on at ten."

"Oh, Aaron, it's going to be so cool."

From the corner of his eye, he saw Kathleen in the kitchen and abruptly detached himself.

"Hey there," he said and smiled.

"Oh, hi." She gave him a quick smile, then continued to

dry and stack plates.

"I'm sorry I didn't call," he offered in embarrassment.

"What did you say?" she responded, her back to him, shelving the plates.

"I'm sorry I didn't call you."

"Oh, that's okay."

"I've been really busy with that weirdo, Miller. It's not that I wasn't thinking about you," he said with his warm and winning smile.

"Don't worry about it," she said, tossing the knives and forks and soup spoons into separate bins with a grating clang.

"I mean, you shouldn't think—" he said, touching her waist.

"Aaron," she said coolly, pulling away, "I wasn't expecting flowers. Don't you need to go play?"

He looked at her. With a shrug, he went to the piano to limber up his fingers and warm up his voice.

"Hey, ladies," he said to the three little groupies in the front row, giving each of them her own personal Aaron Woodwright smile. "You're back," he said.

"Are you kidding?" said the brunette.

"Thanks," he said. *She's actually not so bad.*

"I mean, you were really good, too," said the redhead.

"He is coming, isn't he? That Sam guy?" asked the blonde, and the three of them looked at each other and giggled.

By nine o'clock, all the tables were full. By nine-thirty, people were standing in the back and on the sides. By ten o'clock, Aaron had somehow managed to get through his second set, although it seemed no one was listening. The room was vibrating and buzzing. Bev was sitting by the counter with her cousin Marty, a grad student with a solid tie over a checkered shirt.

Sam Miller was nowhere to be seen.

"Hey, everyone," said Aaron into the mic, "we're going to take one more short break to let you order another round—

don't forget tonight's special, tacos with frijoles and a pitcher of Creston Gold for only $2.50—and then we'll be back, yours truly and—" He made a dramatic pause to which no one was really listening. "Our mystery guest, Sam Miller!" The room murmured audibly.

Aaron made his way through the throng to the counter.

"Hoo hoo," said Pedro, moving plates from the kitchen window to the counter and trays of emptied plates back for washing and refilling. The waitresses were moving pitchers and mugs as fast as the taps could fill them.

"Mucho business, ah?" Aaron asked him.

"Where's your amigo?"

"Good question."

"Why you standing here?" asked the man under the sombrero. "You go play."

"*Well, I think I'm going out of my head,*" crooned Aaron, but even the three girls in the front row were chattering among themselves.

At twenty after ten, Aaron spied Sam outside on the sidewalk.

"Be right back, folks," said Aaron and shoved his way through the crowd.

Sam was standing there, guitar in hand, wearing his Army jacket and a Marble Oaks Lacrosse team T-shirt. Two girls with bellbottoms and headbands were jabbering at him. He looked like he wanted to escape.

"Goddamit, where have you been?" Aaron hissed.

"Whoa, relax, man," said Sam.

The girls backed away.

"You were supposed to be here an hour ago."

"You better take a step back, real fast."

People inside were pointing and whispering.

"I told you we go on at ten," Aaron seethed. "The audience is waiting, the guy from Columbus is waiting—"

"I don't give a flying fuck, and if you don't get your nose

out of my face—" said Sam, dropping his guitar case heavily.

But then Kathleen was standing between them. "Hey, you guys, people in there are getting restless."

Aaron glowered at Sam. Sam's eyes were darting and diving like bats in the night.

She slipped her hand under Sam's right arm and pressed it firmly to her. "Hey, I hear you guys are great together. Come on, let's hear some music."

Sam looked at her, and his panting slowed. She motioned to Aaron to go inside. He stalked off, angry and exasperated.

She stood next to Sam while his breathing relaxed. He looked through the window but didn't move. Inside, a glass shattered.

"Come on, my butt's catching a cold out here," she said finally, picking up the guitar case, prying open his clenched fingers and wrapping them around the handle.

He muttered something.

"Talk up," she said.

"I said there's an awful lot of people in there."

"Yeah, and they all came to hear you."

They stood in silence.

"I don't like crowds," he said.

"I know," said Kathleen, still holding his arm. "That's why you close your eyes when you sing."

He looked at her for a moment, then back down at the sidewalk.

"You guys sound good together?" she asked.

Sam shrugged. "He's okay," he said, still looking down, but she could see him smile.

"Come on," she said, tugging him inside. He followed close behind in her wake as she forged a path through the sea of revelers.

Aaron tapped on the mic. "Hey, you all. Thanks for coming out tonight. Wow, what a trip, huh?" Shouts of expectation.

Putting on his best "remember who's paying the bills"

smile, he interjected, "And don't forget tonight's special, tacos with frijoles and a pitcher of Creston Gold for only $2.50." On the last words, Aaron heard a number of members of the audience jokingly join in with him. He paused for drama, checking that Marty was listening.

"Ladies and gentlemen, cowboys and Indians, friends and lovers: I'm Aaron Woodwright"—he figured he'd better get it in while he could—"together with *Sam Miller!*" The crowd was stomping and shouting.

"Start with Peggy Sue!" the waitress called to Sam as he shuffled towards the little stage.

He didn't indicate that he'd heard her, but as soon as he began with the percussive, full strumming and "*If-a you knew, a-Peggy Sue ...*" the throng began to clap in time and shout encouragement. Some of the younger coeds and some under-age high-school girls began to yelp and shriek, but the older students hushed them.

Sam sang with his eyes closed, his lips touching the mic, Aaron making magical music behind him. He crooned "True Love Ways," dripping sweat and oozing grit, punctuated with girls sighing and squealing. Kathleen wondered who he was thinking about while he was singing.

He roused the crowd with "Bring It On Home" till they were on their feet, bopping and bouncing with all the fervor of a tent revival. Then, when everyone thought Sam and Aaron couldn't go any higher, Aaron looked at the audience with a big grin and began pounding the "bm-bm bm-bm-bmmm!" intro, gritty, slow, and seductive, and the audience was on their feet and shouting and cheering and singing at the top of their college voices with them, "*Pretty woman walking down the street ...*"

It was after midnight, and Pedro had just locked up. Aaron and Sam were sitting with Bev and her cousin while the waitresses cleaned up the considerable mess.

"Well, that was some show," said Marty.

"Thanks," grinned Aaron.

Holding a well-laden tray in one hand, Kathleen wiped the table with the other. She laid down mugs of beer and plates of greasy Mexican delights, starting with a large bowl of chili for Sam. Aaron spied her smiling as she watched him attack his plate.

"This is only the second time they've played together," Bev chirped to Marty. "Right, Sam?"

"Mm-hmm," he mouthed, his fingers wrapped tightly around the spoon.

"It's incredible," basked Aaron. "We met on stage just last week, rehearsed a little, and—well, you saw."

"It was really great," said Marty. "I mean, wow. You guys are something special."

"Thanks," said Aaron, beaming. "Thanks very much." He nudged Sam under the table.

Sam grunted his appreciation into the bowl.

"So," said Aaron, "Columbus?"

Aaron and Bev listened raptly as Marty explained. He was about twenty-six, older than everyone else and with longer hair. He had come to little Steubenville from Ohio State, with its masses of students and worldliness. Sam continued to spoon the chili.

"We've been demonstrating against the war for months now. In the beginning, there were just a few dozen activists. But it's growing by hundreds every day. Washington pretends that the protests are just at Berkeley, Harvard, but it's happening all over the Midwest, too, man. On every campus, students are organizing and protesting. We're closing down classes, occupying buildings. The national leadership wants to show—"

"National leadership of what?" Aaron asked. Sam was mopping up his plate with some sort of cornbread.

"The SDS, Students for a Democratic Society. They're coordinating protests on campuses all over the country. They say we have to show the world that America's heartland won't stand for this war."

"Is it dangerous?" Aaron asked.

"The Columbus Police Department has a rapid response team for protests. They call it the 'D Platoon.' They're a bunch of bloodthirsty fascists. Billy clubs, tear gas. They're looking to beat on the hippies."

Aaron looked at Sam, but he was focused on the bowl.

"So, we've planned this mass demonstration three weeks from now. In the Oval. We're setting up a stage and a sound system and everything. There'll be speeches and music. I'd love for you guys to come play."

Aaron smiled graciously.

"But you know, it's an anti-war demonstration. Do you think you could play some protest songs?"

Aaron looked at Sam, but he was busy spooning chili into his mouth, spoonful after heaping spoonful.

"Sure," said Aaron.

"And, you know, with thousands of people, I have to give them more than two guys singing. I need some *sound*, you know what I mean?"

"You mean we'd need to plug in?" asked Aaron.

"Not just that," answered Marty.

"You all need anything else?" asked Kathleen.

"No, we're good, thanks," said Aaron and Marty.

"You got any more of that chili?" asked Sam, still chewing.

Aaron was trying to stay focused on what Marty was driving at, but he thought he saw her wink at Sam.

"What you need is a band."

"A band?" Aaron asked.

"Yeah. You know. A couple of stoned troubadours just won't cut it in front of thousands of people. You need to give it some oomph."

"In three weeks?" Aaron asked hesitantly.

"May fourth," said Marty. "A Monday."

"To get a band together in that time?" asked Bev, wide-eyed.

"Yeah," said big-city Marty.

Aaron looked at Sam. "What do you say?"

Sam sniffed Kathleen's shoulder as she lay a clean napkin, a clean spoon, and a frosty mug of Creston Gold in front of him.

"Sam," said Aaron, "are you with us?"

"Uh-huh," he said to the steaming bowl of chili.

"Have you ever heard of Vaneshi?" asked Marty.

"No," said Aaron, "what's that?"

"Not what, who," laughed Marty. "He's this guy, lives in a trailer out in the woods down by Lake Hope, walks around barefoot in a white robe, even in winter. Hardly talks. The guy's a guitar legend. You could try to get him."

"You think he'd be interested?"

"No idea. But you could try."

Aaron hesitated.

"Listen," said Marty, "there's a lot of bands around that are dying for the opportunity to—"

"Hey, waitress, c'mere," Sam called through his full mouth without moving his eyes from the chili bowl.

"You talking to me?" she said, still mopping.

"Yeah, I'm talking to you," he answered.

"Well, I got a name."

"Oh, yeah?" he asked.

"Oh, yeah," she answered.

"So, what is your name?"

"Kathleen," she said, leaning her chin on the mop.

"Could you pay attention here?" Aaron scolded Sam, but Sam ignored him.

"C'mere, would ya?"

"Ask me nicely," she said from her mop.

"Hey, Kathleen," he said, turning to her, "would you please get your butt over here?"

She put down the mop and sauntered over to their table. Aaron shot Sam what was intended to be a withering look, but he wasn't looking.

"Yeah, cowboy, what's on your mind?" she said, suppressing a smile.

"Want to join a band?"

"Hey—" said Aaron.

"What did you say?" she laughed.

"I asked if you want to sing in a band. With me and him."

"What he means is—" Aaron attempted.

"I'm not a singer," she said.

"I heard you," said Sam. "You're good enough."

"Listen, guys—" Aaron tried, but Sam held up his hand. Aaron stopped.

Kathleen and Sam looked at each other.

"Are you serious?" she asked.

"Marty here says we need to give it some oomph," said Sam.

" 'Oomph'?" She smiled skeptically.

Sam smiled and nodded. He turned to Aaron. "You want to tell me she isn't 'oomph'?"

Aaron weighed his lack of options. "Yeah, she's 'oomph,' " he admitted.

They looked at Kathleen.

"What the hell?" she said.

And so, they were three.

10

WFOR

– May 16, 2006 –

Shelly sat sweating, her heart thumping, picturing the career-ending act of fraud she was about to commit. She tried to distract herself by deciphering the young receptionist. The right side of her head was shaven almost up to the top, but then a giant shank of dark black hair flipped over to the opposite side, completely hiding her left eye and ending in tips splotched with pink. She had globs of black eyeliner and mascara, a nose ring, a lip ring, and fire-alarm-red lipstick.

"You can go in now," she said. She had a stretch top with horizontal red and black stripes, a wide black patent leather belt, and a blood-red very mini skirt. With black tights. And black platform heels. With silver studs.

"Mrs. Griffin?" said Johnny, slouching towards her with a paunch and a ponytail and an outstretched hand.

"Ms. Miss. Shelly." Her cheeks were on fire.

"Hi Shelly, pleased to meet you. What exactly is this document I need to sign? Leasing that property must have been, what, twenty years ago?"

Shelly swallowed. "Well, Mr. Walker, I have to confess that—"

"Johnny, please," he said warmly.

"Johnny," answered Shelly. She hadn't met many celebrities before. Any, actually. "I'm here under false pretenses."

He looked at her over his reading glasses.

"I do work for the Charles Griffin law firm, but there is no document for you to sign. I used that as a pretext to—"

"Brandi!" he called to the receptionist, his smile fading.

"The firm is dealing with the dissolution of an old family brewery, Bauer's, down in Creston—"

"Brandi, would you please show this woman out?"

"—they make Creston Gold, and it's a really heartbreaking story, and I heard that tribute you did for *Barnaby*, and I—"

He signaled to Brandi to wait.

The patter she had rehearsed now evaporating, she could feel her face quickly approaching tomato, but the words kept flowing out in a tumble.

"I think it's unfair that a family business that's been in Northeast Ohio for over a hundred years, that's a symbol of local pride, with one woman trying to keep it afloat against all kinds of odds and market trends, with a really tragic personal story, that this kind of business, with twenty-five employees, should just tank without anyone even noticing—"

"Creston Gold?"

She nodded as she pulled a tissue from her pocket and dabbed at the corner of her eye. "And I think this lady, and this family brewery, and all the people who work there, and all the people who have been drinking Creston Gold for so many years, they at least deserve to be noticed before they all just disappear."

She stopped to breathe. He was listening.

"And I heard that beautiful tribute you gave *Barnaby*, about how much he meant to all of us who grew up on his TV show. And I think you should talk about this lady and her brewery on the radio. And tell Cleveland, and all of Northeast Ohio, that this local symbol is about to go under. And that we should all at least pause for a minute and be sad."

Remarkably, he was still listening. Brandi cracked her gum.

"Because people listen to you. A lot of people. You have the power to do the right thing, to give this lady a respectful goodbye and thank-you for all the pride her family has given us. She deserves that."

She sniffled.

"And I tried to get through to you by phone and stuff, but I couldn't, so I wrote that fake letter. I apologize. It's very unprofessional."

She sniffled again and dabbed her eyes. She didn't even see Johnny's annoyed scowl turning into a smile of sympathetic amusement.

"That's all."

Johnny gestured to Brandi that she wasn't needed, but she ignored him.

"Come over here, have a seat," he said, leading her to two low chairs in the corner of the room. "Shelly?"

She nodded.

"Creston Gold, you said?"

She nodded again. Her cheeks were no longer on fire, but her heart was still thumping.

"I used to drink Creston Gold in college." He smiled nostalgically. "Everyone did. Oberlin, class of '67. I spent four years doing little other than drinking Creston Gold."

"Same for me. OU, Class of '85. Same for everyone," she said. "And now it's closing down."

"Why is that?"

She recounted for him the economics of the beer industry as she had come to understand it over the previous few days, how the giant national breweries had swallowed up the smaller local ones, and the trendy craft breweries had crippled the few that were left. She told him about the Bauer clan and about Allie's hard life and her courage. She confessed to him that her father's firm made its living from the dubious task of closing down businesses.

"I was born and raised in Warren," she said. "Did you know that in my lifetime, the population there has dropped from sixty thousand to forty thousand? You know what's going on around here economically. It's not pretty."

"No, it's not," he agreed.

"It seems to me," said Shelly, looking Johnny directly in the eye, "that Northeast Ohio doesn't have a very good self-image. There's not much around here that people are proud of. But you, people listen to you. Creston Gold has been a symbol for generations. The brewery shouldn't just go gentle into that good night."

Johnny looked at her steadily, stood up, and gathered her into a wide, warm hug. She had no idea what was happening. His gray ponytail brushed her nose, and his paunch was substantial.

Finally, he broke the embrace and, at arm's length, looked her in the eye. "Shelly, I think that's a wonderful, wonderful idea."

"Oh!" she blurted. "The song!"

"What song?"

"I found a song on YouTube—"

"That's part of the internet, right?" he asked Brandi, who rolled her eyes.

"Well, yes," said Shelly.

"I'm not much of a computer person," he explained.

"That's okay, lots of our clients aren't," she said and smiled. "We have a, ah, *mature* clientele. Can I show you?"

"Use my computer," said Brandi with the raccoon eyes.

"Search for 'Creston Gold,' " Shelly instructed her over one shoulder, Johnny squinting over the other.

"My father used to drink Creston Gold," said Brandi, typing. "I never see it around anymore."

Shelly and Johnny exchanged looks.

On Brandi's screen, the hourglass twirled and twirled. Finally a picture began to emerge, pixel by pixel.

"See?" said Shelly, reading from the screen, "Creston Gold—Decapede, thirty-one views."

"Who is this Decapede?" asked Johnny. Brandi clicked on the picture of the band.

"That's exactly the point!" said Shelly. "No one knows. There's no other mention of them on the internet. Thirty-one views on YouTube, almost all of them are mine."

"What does that mean?" asked Johnny.

"That no one's ever seen this," Brandi answered him with just a hint of condescension.

They waited while the file loaded. Finally the song began to play.

"Turn it up a little," Johnny told Brandi.

"The world out there don't look so kind / But I don't care, 'cause love is blind / You're the one thing on my mind / Pass me another Creston Gold."

"That's a *good* song," said Johnny, staring at the screen.

Shelly felt her heart leap.

Brandi cracked her gum and pressed Replay.

The three of them huddled together, studying the faded black-and-white photo on Brandi's screen—the pretty boy with the black hair smiling right at the camera, the stylish black guy, impish and embarrassed, the barefooted monk gazing off into the sky, the scowling, intense one trying to escape the frame, the womanly girl holding him back.

"That's the band?" asked Johnny.

"Duh," said Brandi.

"So, what I thought was—" said Shelly and then hesitated.

Johnny and Brandi looked at her, waiting.

"What I thought was that maybe you could do some kind of search or competition or something on your show to try to find out where this song came from. Who this band was. Because obviously, they're local, 'Creston Gold.' And if that really is a picture of this Decapede, they're pretty old. To ask if anyone recognizes the name or the song. Somebody might remember. And that would be, like, a way to talk about the brewery and—"

Johnny straightened up and again enwrapped Shelly in his bear hug. Over his shoulder, Shelly saw Brandi rolling her eyes.

In the elevator going down, Shelly looked at the woman in the mirror. "What just happened?" she asked her, but the woman had no idea.

11
Minor in Percussion
– April 1970 –

They drove across town to the graduate dorms in Aaron's old powder-blue Beetle. There had been several hours of real spring sun, but now it was late afternoon, the throes of winter chill.

"Where'd you hear about this guy?" Aaron asked Kathleen.

"A guy at Pedro's said he heard we were looking for a drummer."

"Tijuana Brass?" snickered Sam, looking through the 4-tracks on the back seat where he was scrunched.

"Pedro wants me to learn some Mexican music. Want me to put it on?" asked Aaron.

"Hell no," said Sam.

"Oh, come on, it's not that bad," said Kathleen, turning around to Sam.

He put his finger to his temple and pulled the trigger.

"Know what I was thinking about for our anti-war song?" said Aaron. "*Love is but a song we sing / Fear's the way we die—*"

"Oh, that's a cool song," said Kathleen.

"—with three-part harmony for '*Come on, people, now / Smile on your brother—*' "

"Hippie-dippie shit," said Sam from the back seat.

"Why do you say that?" asked Kathleen, shifting to look at him.

"Holding hands and singing 'Kumbaya' ain't going to end no war."

"So, what is?" asked Kathleen.

Sam shrugged and looked out the window.

"If enough people come to protest—" she attempted.

"Then the fuzz will shut it down. Just like in Chicago."

"But a singer still has to try to talk about things that matter," said Kathleen. "Doesn't he?"

"Bullshit," Sam growled.

"There are great anti-war songs," said Aaron.

"They're all crap."

" 'Blowing in the Wind'?" said Aaron.

"Blowing wind," said Sam.

" 'The Sound of Silence'?" said Kathleen.

"Headache!" answered Sam.

" 'Eve of Destruction'?" said Aaron

Sam groaned in disbelief.

"Oh, sorry, Mr. Blood, what would you suggest?"

"Write your own," said Sam.

"Write your own," snorted Aaron. "Just like that."

"A protest song?" said Sam. "How hard can that be? You just get all indignant and whine the same line over and over with a couple of changes."

"It's not that easy," said Aaron.

"Course it is," said Sam.

"So, you're going to write one?" He mugged at Kathleen. Kathleen looked at Sam.

"Sure," said Sam.

They parked, and Sam squeezed out of the back seat of the Beetle. "Apartment three-twenty-nine," Kathleen read from a note as they climbed the stairs. The sign on the door said Paul Mize / Gavin Grover.

Aaron knocked.

"What kind of name is Gavin?" Sam said.

"Shh!" said Aaron and knocked again.

A young man with sepia skin answered the door, wearing a delicate peach-colored shirt with light beige slacks and Oxford loafers.

"Hello," he said, in a clipped accent that sounded like an art museum, smiling with polite surprise. "Can I help you?"

"Hi, I'm Aaron Woodwright. This is Sam and Kathleen."

"Hi," said Kathleen with a smile.

"We're students at Steuben, and—"

"Want to join a band?" asked Sam.

"*Vraiment?*" uttered Gavin with an amused double-take. "Well, I suppose you should come in. Come, come." He ushered them in and disappeared into the kitchen.

"It's very, um, aesthetic," said Aaron, looking around as they stepped inside.

"Somebody's got an eye for design here," said Kathleen, looking at a large, framed poster of Judy Garland and a Kandinsky reproduction that matched the metallic aqua chair she settled into.

"Too clean," said Sam.

There was one shelf of art albums (Impressionists and Modern), one of books (Truman Capote, Tom Wolfe, Buckminster Fuller, Alvin Toffler), and one of jazz albums (Getz, Mulligan, Monk). Above the fastidious work desk were neatly ordered textbooks on Functional Analysis, Operator Theory, and Operator Algebras. Sam plopped on the floor, his legs stretching out into the middle of the room.

"Doesn't he look a little serious?" Aaron asked Kathleen in a low voice.

"They say he's good," she shrugged.

Gavin came in carrying a large tray with a matching glass tea set, stepping over Sam's ragged boots.

He poured four cups methodically. "There's sugar and cream here. And biscuits. Please, help yourselves."

"Cool pad," said Sam. He scooched over to the tea tray, added two heaping teaspoons of sugar to his cup, grabbed a handful of cookies, and then slouched back against the wall, slurping and chomping.

"*Merci*. We're quite pleased with it."

"Your accent?" Kathleen asked. "It's lovely."

"Oh, thank you! *Quebecois*."

"It's beautiful."

"You're very sweet. Well," he said, turning to Aaron, "I admit that you have my interest here."

"It's pretty simple, really. I play piano at Pedro's Cantina in town."

"I'm afraid I don't know it."

"It's a beer joint for undergrads," Kathleen explained.

"Oh, I see. I don't really go out very much."

"Waddya do for fun?" asked Sam through the cookies and tea.

"Fun? My roommate, Paul, and I are math grad students," he explained, and everyone chuckled.

"Anyway," said Aaron, "Sam dropped in at an open mic night last week, and then we played together, and it went over really well."

"They're really, *really* good," said Kathleen.

"A guy from Ohio State invited us to play at a big anti-war demonstration in a few weeks," said Aaron, "but for that, we need a band,"

Sam took another handful of cookies.

"I play piano, guitar, bass," said Aaron. "Sam plays rhythm guitar. All three of us sing."

"We understand you play drums?" Kathleen asked.

"Oh, I see," said Gavin, gently setting down his teacup. "That's not really the sort of thing I do."

"But you do play drums?" Aaron persisted.

"Well, yes, I minored in percussion at McGill. And I played in some jazz groups around Montreal."

"Well, then—" said Aaron.

"But I assume you fellows play rock music?"

"To tell you the truth," said Aaron, "we're just starting. We're working on developing our style. I was actually thinking about an amalgam of fluid rock with some elements of jazz and a lot of emphasis on vocals—"

"It's a pick-up band," said Sam, spewing crumbs.

"I don't know," said Gavin. "It's not really my kind of music—"

"We're just going to play a few simple songs—" Kathleen reassured him.

"And there's supposed to be five thousand people there—" said Aaron, smiling his most charming smile.

"Five *thousand?*" said Gavin.

"And what about the war?" asked Kathleen.

"What about it?"

"Soldiers are dying over there every day," she said with passion.

"You Americans should get out of there," said Gavin, but he was looking at Aaron, thinking.

"Still, we all have to do whatever we can to stop it," said Kathleen.

Gavin didn't disagree. "I have a seminar paper—"

"It's gonna be a fucking gas, man!" said Sam, sitting up straight. "Spring is coming, you know? There's people out there, and birds and nature and stuff coming to life. Singing and dancing and drinking beer."

"The birds are drinking beer?" asked Gavin.

"The cool ones are," answered Sam.

Gavin sipped his tea.

"It's only for three weeks," said Kathleen.

"We'll have a few rehearsals. Nothing too complicated," said Aaron.

"You have to hear them," Kathleen added. "They're incredible. Everyone's talking about them. You wouldn't believe the crowd that came to Pedro's just for them."

"Really?" weakened Gavin.

"They got chili con carne," said Sam.

"I like chili," Gavin said into his teacup. "Three weeks?"

They nodded.

"Including a couple of warm-up gigs at Pedro's," said Aaron.

Gavin hesitated.

"Gavin," said Kathleen, looking at him with her giant gray eyes, "you seem like a really cool guy, and we'd love it if you'd come give us a chance."

Gavin smiled mischievously. "There's a drum kit in the music room. I have a key."

As they walked down the stairs, Aaron said to Kathleen in a low voice, "Did you notice there's only one bedroom there?"

"Oh, you're quick!" mocked Kathleen, knocking on his head.

"Shotgun!" shouted Sam, running ahead.

And then they were four.

12

Who is Decapede?

– May 24, 2006 –

One week after Shelly lied her way into Johnny Walker's office, he broadcast his tribute to the Bauer saga. She was still floating as she sat with her father to go over the forms for the dissolution of the brewery.

"You look all chipper this morning."

"How sweet of you to notice," she said.

Her phone rang. It was a number she didn't recognize.

"Shelly Griffin," she said.

"Hey, Shelly, this is Brandi from WFOR. How are you?"

"Oh, hello," she said in her most officious voice. "Could you hold on just one moment? Sorry, Dad, I have to take this," she said, rising.

"We're just getting started. There's a ton of stuff to go through here—"

"I'll be right with you, Brandi."

"Who the heck is *Brandi*?" her father asked, but she pretended not to hear him.

"Hi," said Shelly in her normal voice. She could feel her heart thumping. "How are you?"

"Me? How are *you*?" Brandi asked. "Did you hear the show yesterday?"

Johnny had dedicated his entire hour to Bauer's Brewery,

to Allie Bauer, and to Creston Gold. "And our very warm thanks to Shelly Griffin from Warren, Ohio, for bringing to our attention this whole very sad story, so emblematic of the times we live in," he had said.

Shelly had never before heard her name on the radio, let alone spoken by someone like Johnny Walker.

"Wow. I mean, just, wow," said Brandi. "Here, I've got Johnny on the line for you."

"Hi, Shelly?"

"Yes, hi."

"It's Johnny."

"Oh, Mr. Walker!"

"Please, call me Johnny."

"I thought the show was just wonderful. Especially the interview with Allie. I cried through most of it. You have no idea what it meant to her."

"I'm so glad you liked it, Shelly. Allie Bauer really is a very sweet woman. And heroic."

It was so strange for Shelly, and a little thrilling, to be able to visualize the man behind that voice.

"Listen, I have some bad news."

"Oh," she said, her heart plummeting.

"I did everything I could. I played 'Creston Gold'—"

"Three times!"

"And I offered two tickets to the Tim McGraw show for any caller who could provide information?"

"I know—Johnny," she said, waiting for the axe to fall. *Me*, she thought despite her dread, *on a first-name basis with a radio star!*

"And you heard me thank you?"

"I can't tell you how much I appreciated that."

"But no one could tell us anything about Decapede or the song. Nothing. Zip. Empty-handed," he said, his rich bass heavy with disappointment.

"I understand," said Shelly quietly, deflating as quickly as a pin-pricked balloon. "It was a shot in the dark. So many years—"

"Bu-ut—" he said, his voice suddenly upbeat, "we've been getting a crazy number of calls, people saying how much they enjoyed the show, how much they love the beer—"

"Really?"

"—and requesting the song! Deep into the night and from early this morning—people just keep calling, wanting to hear 'Creston Gold.' And asking if we've learned anything at all about Decapede."

"That's wonderful—"

"So-o ..." he dragged it out, making her heart flutter like a fourteen-year-old girl being flirted with by the most popular sixteen-year-old guy in the school. "So-o, tomorrow night, I'm going to do a follow-up show about the response."

"*Omigod*," she thought, and her heart danced a little jig.

"Shelly, it seems like we've struck a really responsive chord here. You were right. Creston Gold is a local symbol. People really care about it. There's a whole groundswell of support out there."

"Well, you did a really wonderful show about it."

"It was your idea."

Shelly felt herself turning red.

After they hung up, she could still hear Johnny Walker saying, "It was your idea." *Damn.*

"Shelly!" her father called from his office.

She groaned, stood up, and went to him.

"Who was that 'Brandi'?" he asked.

Shelly looked her father in the eye. "A friend," she said, with finality.

"Gee, Shel, I just asked. Can't a father ask?"

"Can we just work, please?"

On his six o'clock show, Johnny retold the story. He played 'Creston Gold' three more times, passionately calling for anyone who had ever heard of the band to get in touch with the station and win the tickets. In response to all the requests to see the band's picture, he directed listeners to "the YouTube."

" 'Creston Gold,' folks—it's got to be a local band. Come on, Cleveland, someone out there must recognize them. *Who is Decapede?* Please, call!"

Late that night in her room, Shelly stared at the picture as she listened to the song. *Nothing's gonna bring me down / Pass me another Creston Gold.* She tried to conjure up the band from the one photo, but they were as unfathomable as a pirate ship laden with gold bullion lying on the floor of the Caribbean Sea, exotic fish swimming through the portholes.

They looked like college kids, all eager and optimistic, trying on identities like new costumes. The hot kid with the hair and that killer smile. She could see coeds screaming and pulling their hair over him. She could see their moms doing it as well. The natty black guy. He looked so—*tidy.* What was he doing with these ruffians? The girl, with her headband and ripe figure and those big eyes. Shelly pictured the guys in the audience drooling over her. The monk, who let him out of his ashram? He was barefoot!

But it was the guy moving off to the side who really caught her imagination. She guessed that he was the singer. The shaggy hair, the lean body. That intense, hungry look. What was he looking at outside the frame? He would be the challenging one.

She tried to imagine what they looked like today. They'd be in their fifties, at least.

"Creston Gold—Decapede." That's all the screen said. Before Johnny's show, it had 51 hits. Now there were 438.

13

Radio Roulette
– April 1970 –

To his great chagrin, Aaron had an exam on Friday, so he had no choice but to send Kathleen and Sam to look for the mysterious guitarist. Bev proudly chipped in her car, a snazzy 1968 maroon Mustang convertible.

"Can we put down the top?" asked Sam, running his hand over the smooth black leather of the bucket seat.

"Maybe, if you behave yourself," said Kathleen, and drove off, shining in her tie-dyed top and beaded Navaho headband. He was in mud-caked cut-off jeans, ragged work shoes with one black and one green sock, and a bowling shirt with "Ray" stitched over the pocket.

They talked about Nixon and McNamara and the growing opposition to the war. They talked about their favorite candy bars—Almond Joy for her, Tootsie Rolls ("Yech, are you kidding me?") for him. The sun was radiant after a long, gray winter, and after half an hour, he asked Kathleen again if they could lower the roof.

"The forecast said it might rain," she said.

He looked at the sky and sniffed. "Nah, we'll be okay."

Kathleen studied Sam, slouched in his black leather bucket seat with his beat-up shoes on Bev's dashboard. She made a mental note to brush it off later.

She'd never seen him relaxed before, she realized. Around people, he was so jumpy. Wary, like he needed to always be ready to flee. Or fight. Now, he was grinning into the wind like a long-haired collie.

He was certainly good-looking enough, with his lean body and rugged features and shaggy, thick brown hair that looked like he'd cut it himself. Tough. Strong. That's what a cowboy should look like, she decided.

She thought about the way he attacked those two wrestlers. He's probably been in a barroom brawl or two. Probably started them. She felt a tingle of fear, not unpleasant, like a good horror film.

But on stage, his whole face squinched up when he sang, his eyes closed to the world, singing from inside each song, his lips so close to the mic you could hear his moist breath, his low, gravelly voice. *Mah-hah Peggy Sue-ha-hu ...* Kathleen pressed down on the gas pedal, and all of the Mustang's eight cylinders began to churn as they cruised along the two-lane country road, over gently sloping hills bordered by fields, woods, and the occasional sleepy hamlet, their hair fluttering gloriously in the wind.

"Can we turn on some music?" he asked.

"You know about 'radio roulette,' right?" she asked.

"What's that?" he chuckled.

"First song that comes on? It's going to have some special meaning."

"What kind of meaning?"

"Depends on the song," she said with a smile.

"You believe in that stuff?"

"No," she said, "but it's fun."

"How do you turn this thing on?"

Kathleen pressed the green button.

A wall of sound came blasting from underneath the dashboard, jangling guitars and maracas and castanets and timpani and all the vibrations of a new world coming alive. "*Well, he walked up to me, and he asked me if I wanted to dance—"*

Kathleen began to bop and dance as she drove, hands on the wheel and eyes on the road, singing along at the top of her lungs out into the country air. Sam joined on top in a silly falsetto, and they started laughing so hard Kathleen had to turn off the music.

They debated the perfect road trip song and tested each one together—a sloppy "Ticket to Ride," a sloppier "Daytripper," a campy "If You're Going to San Francisco." Then, Sam began a sweet, heartfelt "Grooving," and Kathleen stopped singing to listen. His voice was moist and raspy and trusting, like a dog's tongue. His eyes were open.

They gossiped about Gavin, agreeing he was a sweetheart (her word), trying unsuccessfully to imitate his accent, laughing wildly at his wide-eyed bewilderment when they piled in on him with their outlandish offer. They speculated together about the mysterious Vaneshi. Kathleen thought he was probably a legend, the Loch Ness monster of Lake Hope. Sam said that he didn't believe in that legend, that the guy was probably an alien. Or a yeti, he wasn't sure which.

"Ooh, ooh," he said, pointing at a sign, McDonalds Zanesville 14 mi.

"Already?" she said, smiling.

They rode in comfortable silence.

"Worst summer job ever?" she asked.

"Worst?" he said, smiling and thinking. "Been a few. I can tell you the weirdest one. Varnishing mannequins in a mannequin factory."

She laughed. "Where was that?"

"Syracuse, New York. Fucking cold up there! Ah, the worst?" he remembered. "Sorting the catch at a fishery in upstate Michigan. I stunk for months afterwards. You always been a waitress?"

"I used to work summers as a lifeguard."

He stole a quick look at her. "No shit?"

"No shit," she laughed. "Feel that." She held up her arm for him to feel her swimmer's biceps, which he did, firmly. She was, indeed, a muscular waitress.

"Do you swim?" she asked.

"No, ah, water and me, uh, I'd rather be the one doing the drinking."

"My relatives have a country club near my home, up near Erie."

"Sounds pretty cushy."

"It was great, except I had to help out waiting table at fancy affairs. And one night, at a bar mitzvah," she began to stutter with laughter, "a guest felt me up—"

"So, you quit?"

"I bloodied his nose, so they fired me," she howled, and Sam howled with her. "I'm starting, I'm starting—" she choked, stuttering and snorting, holding her stomach, "to think I wasn't meant to be a waitress."

"Wh— Wh—" he tried, but he was laughing too hard.

"Last September, I started working at the Student Union dining hall. On the last Friday of the semester," she said, gasping for breath, "they have a fancy sit-down dinner. To celebrate, yeah?"

She slipped into the patter of a standup comedian, rolling with her yarn, Sam happily playing the audience, the laughter bouncing back and forth between them, rising and swelling.

"So, usually, on a Friday, a couple hundred people would show up for dinner. But here, they advertised steak and ice cream and everything, so everyone with a dining card came. Almost four hundred people. We had to open spare tables and everything, except the idiots, they had prepared food for just two hundred. And the guy in charge, this uptight little pipsqueak with a bowtie and a high voice, like with a carrot up his ass? He won't let us start serving till we have portions for everyone."

"Course not," he said, laughing hard already.

"So, we ran down to the freezer, took out piles of steaks, and brought them up to the kitchen. But they were frozen solid, yeah? And it's already after six o'clock, and the hordes are starting to get restless, starting to bang on the tables. And he's barking out orders like a chihuahua, driving everyone crazy. So, we're doing all kinds of crazy stuff, trying to get the goddamn steaks to defrost, yeah? We filled up all the ovens, turned them on high. Stuck them in pans, put them on the fire. A big mess, and then we're trying to get all the plastic wrapping off the frozen steaks so we can fast-heat them, which doesn't work anyway, but we don't know that, yeah?"

Sam was whooping with laughter.

"By now, they've finished off all the bread and vegetables and stuff and are about to start eating the plates and the silverware, and they start throwing things. First, napkins. And then this disgusting corn-and-mayonnaise salad that was left on the table because no one would touch it."

Sam was writhing in his seat, tears running down his cheeks.

"So, the pipsqueak finally gives us the sign to start serving. And guess who's first?"

Sam was doubled over, howling and choking with laughter so hard that he could only point at her and stutter "Y— Y—"

"So, I'm loaded up with like twelve plates of steak on this giant tray, and I come breezing in from the kitchen through these double doors, and everybody's looking at me, shouting and yelling, and I'm almost running. And there's this patch of water or corn salad or something, and my legs just go out from under me, and I land wha-a-ah, BOOM on my butt. The tray and the plates and the steaks go flying all the hell around, and I'm lying on my back with my goddamn skirt up over my face, advertising my privates to these four hundred hunger-crazed Cossacks, and I'm sliding on my behind in the steaks and the plates and the corn salad, trying to figure out where the hell up is, and I finally get on my feet, and everyone is stone silent, and I look around, and I see the mess, and I let out this giant 'F-U-U-U-U-C-K!' and I—"

"Stop," he begged, twisting and convulsing from laughter, "please, stop!"

They took a long moment together to catch their breath.

"And that," she said, struggling to get the words out, "was the end of my career at the Steuben Student Union dining hall."

"Oh!" he held up his hand, begging her to stop talking, bent over and struggling for breath in between the whoops of laughter.

At the McDonald's, she pulled into an empty parking spot next to an Ohio State Highway Patrol cruiser. Two uniformed and armed patrolmen were eating their burgers and fries. They turned to stare at the girl with the headband and her long-haired passenger from behind their aviator sunglasses.

"Sam, is something wrong?" Kathleen asked.

"Move the car, will you?" he croaked, studying the Mustang's black floormats. "They make me nervous."

In line, waiting for their order, three good old boys were watching them from a table.

"Forget to get your hair cut, cutie?" said one.

Sam's eyes began to jump.

"Sam," she said, laying a hand on his arm and turning him to her, "are you listening to me?"

"You got money for a hamburger, but you don't got money for a haircut?" said his friend.

Sam turned to them, his chest rising.

"Please?" she pulled at his sleeve, but he wasn't listening.

"Faggot," said the first one.

"Hippie commie," said the second.

"Yeah, faggot," said the third.

Sam started to move towards them, but she blocked his path, planted her feet, and stuck her finger in his chest.

"Listen to me," she said in a firm, low voice.

He was staring at them over her shoulder, his chest heaving.

"Listen to me!" she demanded. She pulled his face to look at her. "Sam!"

"Ooh, look at the pussy pushing him around."

"Them hippies don't got no balls at all."

She turned Sam to face the counter, her fingers digging deeply into his arm.

"What's a good-looking piece of ass doing with a fairy like that?"

He tried to turn, but she dug in her nails.

"Okay," he grunted. "Ow."

Their order finally came. She paid, put the bags in both his hands, and steered him toward the door.

Then, Kathleen stopped in the middle of the restaurant, leveled her eyes at them, and said in her strong, even voice for the entire McDonald's to hear, "Just so you morons should know—he's got a dick bigger than the three of yours put together," and shoved Sam out the door.

They drove through the rolling hills, eating their Big Macs and fries and drinking their milkshakes, the early spring sun melting the last patches of snow, their own private heaven in a maroon Mustang with black bucket seats and the top down, the wind blowing their hair, their whole lives ahead of them just waiting to be lived, not a care in the world.

14

Like a Virus

– May 25, 2006 –

On Wednesday evening, Johnny dedicated the entire show to interviewing listeners about Creston Gold. Some were pleading passionately that the beer was a matter of local pride and that it would be a tragedy if Bauer's Brewery closed down, some were speculating about the band ("from England, maybe they have a beer with that name over there"), and some were simply exuding love for the innocent, moving song.

Johnny announced that the station had decided to offer a reward of $500 for information leading to the band's identity, with a special phone line dedicated to Creston Gold callers.

At night, alone in her room, Shelly looked at "Creston Gold—Decapede" on YouTube. 1,238 views.

15

Then They Were Five

– April 1970 –

Near the entrance to the park, Kathleen and Sam stopped at Nick's Gas Bait Tackle & Souvenirs, a two-pump gas station that looked like it hadn't seen a customer since the previous summer.

"You wait here," she said.

"You gonna finish your fries?" He watched her walk towards the door. "I sure could go for a beer," he called.

"Excuse me, sir," she said to the young man behind the counter, twenty-three and looking like a young version of American Gothic.

"Yes, ma'am. How can I help you?"

"Beer?"

"Back in the cooler to the left of the fishing tackle. We got a special on Creston Gold three-point-two, six-pack for a buck ninety-eight."

She browsed over a display of tourist paraphernalia, picking up a small 79¢ snow globe with **LAKE HOPE STATE PARK** printed on the base. Inside there was a blue fish standing on its tail with a stupid, toothy grin. She shook it, and snow fluttered all around it.

"Six dollars premium, please, and these," she said, placing the beer and the glass ball on the counter. "And this," she added, picking up a Tootsie Roll from the candy rack.

"Tell me," she asked as she was paying, "do you know a musician who lives around here named 'Vaneshi'?"

"You mean that hippie in the crazy-colored trailer up by the lake?"

"Could be," she said and smiled.

"With the long hair and the white robe?" he asked dubiously.

"I'm guessing that's him." She smiled.

He looked hard at her.

"You ain't one of them hippies, are you?"

"Me? Oh, certainly not, sir. Not at all. I'm a Christian."

He stared, unconvinced. "Well," he shrugged finally, figuring it wasn't none of his business who a nice girl like this was going to visit, " 'Bout a mile and a half up 278, you got your turn-off to Lake Hope State Park? So, you go another couple hunrit yards, you got a little road off to the right. You take that and follow it for half a mile."

"Okay! Thanks."

"Then there's a wooden gate, but it's gonna be locked."

"Okay," she said.

"So, you climb over it and walk up this dirt road about another two hunrit yards."

"Great, got it, thanks."

"Then there's a little path going up through the trees to the right."

She waited.

"You follow that, and up at the top, you'll see it. Crazy-colored trailer, right up on the lake."

"Okay, great, thanks so much."

"Pretty little place."

"Looking forward to seeing it."

Just then, Sam walked in, his sandy mane stragglier and puffier than ever from the wind. Gothic Junior just stared.

"Peace," she said, flashing him a V and pulling Sam outside.

The little trailer sat in a small clearing, surrounded by trees and brush, a hundred feet from the shore of Lake Hope. It was covered with loopy, droopy designs in diaphanous colors, dotted with yins and yangs and disembodied floating eyes. The windows and door were open.

"Yo?" Sam yelled.

"He-lloooooooooo!" she called. But the woods were quiet.

They looked inside the tiny trailer. There was an unmade cot, a sink, and a table with a Bunsen burner and dishes. Exotic instruments were strewn about, most with a wooden body, a neck, and strings strung between them. They were propped against the wall, hanging from the wall, lying on the table, resting on the floor, or just lying askew.

Sam picked one up carefully to examine it.

"What's that?" asked Kathleen.

"An oud. From the Middle East."

"This one?" she asked, pointing at a flat, wooden instrument with a neck as long as an arm.

"Never seen anything like it."

"It's a kantele," said a voice behind them in a strong Brooklyn accent.

They turned to see a beanstalk of a young monk in a once-white linen robe-like garment, his stringy black hair hanging loose past his shoulders, an unkempt black beard down to his navel.

"It's Finnish. Can have anywhere from five to forty strings."

"Cool."

"This one's got nineteen." The bearded young man picked it up to show Sam. He was barefoot, with a ripe bouquet.

"It's related to the harp. You hold it on your lap like this and pluck it with both hands. And you can also operate these stops with your left hand."

"Can I—?" asked Sam.

"Here," said the monk, seating Sam on the one rickety chair, showing him where to strum, where to press. Sam experimented gently.

"Ah," he said. "Thing's got some serious bass tones."

Sam strummed and pressed while the bony young man watched, occasionally guiding him with a word or showing him with his own fingers.

After a few minutes, Sam was making music from it.

"That's very cool."

The young man might have been smiling, but his beard completely hid his mouth.

"I'm Kathleen. This is Sam."

"*Namaste*," he said, bringing his palms together, closing his eyes and bowing slightly. "Vaneshi. Would you like some tea?"

"I'd love some," said Kathleen.

"Can I—?" Sam asked, indicating the instruments.

"Please," said Vaneshi. "An instrument unplayed is like a woman unloved."

"I like this guy," Kathleen said to Sam. "You don't look Indian."

"By choice," he grinned. "I'm from Flatbush."

Sam took an acoustic guitar into his arms and began tuning it.

Vaneshi lit the Bunsen burner, filled a tin can with water from a large plastic jug, and placed it on the fire. Then he took three plain brown paper bags and measured out a handful of dried weeds from each into a bowl. Sam began picking a gentle country blues. Vaneshi took a pestle-shaped rock and began grinding the dried leaves into a powder, smiling, his eyes glazed and floating as he swayed to Sam's guitar.

His pupils are very wide, thought Kathleen. "What exactly is in the—"

"Nettle and alfalfa," said Vaneshi. "With a little horsehair for tang. It all grows right here."

"Far out," she said.

"Could you watch the water?" he asked her. "When it boils, just add the infusion and stir it a bit."

"I can handle that."

Vaneshi took an old, battered acoustic guitar, sat cross-legged on the floor facing Sam, and began to play fills and decorations around his rhythmic picking pattern. Sam played a twelve-bar blues through a couple of times, then comped for Vaneshi to play a melodic lead, a winding, serpentine line weaving and bobbing in and out of Sam's strumming.

Kathleen set a glass of the brew next to each of them and sat on the cot. "Mm, delicious!" she said, trying to sound sincere. Sam slurped his. "How long have you lived here?" she asked.

"All winter," he said.

"Isn't it a little isolated?"

"I needed space," he said softly. "And cold."

"You don't get lonely?"

"We spend too much time reflecting other people." He spoke in a whisper, Kathleen straining to hear. His pupils were still very wide. "You see, when I'm talking to you, I'm also looking at you, perceiving you, reacting to you. What I say, what I think, it isn't 'me.' It's the part of me that I choose to show to you, to share with you. It's as much you as it is me. A person needs solitude to become whole within himself. To become one with his own energies before he interacts with the world."

"How's that going for you?" asked Sam.

"Winter's over. I think I'm ready to move back."

They nodded to each other.

"We're putting together a band," said Sam. "Me and Kathleen here, and this piano bar guy and a drummer."

"We have a gig at a big anti-war demonstration at Ohio State in two weeks," said Kathleen. "Supposed to be five thousand people."

"That's a lot of people."

"You play rock and roll?" Sam asked.

"Every chance I get," said Vaneshi, smiling underneath all the hair.

Sam picked the familiar opening riff, *Bam, ba-ta-ta, Bam! ba-ta-ta.*

Vaneshi somehow rose from the floor by simply unfolding his legs. He rummaged in a cardboard box under his bed, extracted two brightly painted maracas, and handed them to Kathleen. Then, he sat back down on the floor opposite Sam, counted him in, and began the opening riff. Sam doubled him on the intro, then began a hard, rhythmic accompaniment. Kathleen shook her shakers, grinning widely, and broke into joyous song.

"*Well, he walked up to me, and he asked me if I wanted to dance ...*"

And then they were five.

16

Sleepover

– May 26, 2006 –

In the afternoon, Brandi called, pumped with excitement.

"Shelly, it's a madhouse here."

"What is?"

"The phones. Nobody's talking about anything else. Who is Decapede? Where did 'Creston Gold' come from? There's a million calls, but zilch. Wait, Johnny wants you. Line six!" she hollered.

"I got it, you can hang up," Johnny hollered back. "Hi Shel."

"Hey, Johnny," she managed to answer, her heart thumping.

"Listen, this thing is growing out of all proportion. The phones just don't stop. Nobody knows anything, but people keep calling, all day and most of the night, to ask if there's anything new."

"Seriously?"

"Yeah. Listen, Shelly, I need to knock around some ideas with you. And there's a friend of mine who wants to meet you."

"What sort of—"

"I'll explain it all tomorrow. Eight o'clock?"

"Could we make it at nine?" said Shelly. "It's impossible to get into the city at that hour."

"No, sorry, we have an eight o'clock meeting on that, oh, waddaya call it?"

"Skype," said Brandi.

"I told you to hang up," said Johnny.

"You can sleep at my place," said Brandi.

Shelly wondered what sort of den of iniquity she was walking into, but Brandi's apartment was clean and colorful and surprisingly cheerful. Except for the large black and white photo above her bed of a polar bear with a seal in its jaws.

Brandi had brought in tortilla chips, salsa, and a six-pack of Creston Gold. Looking at this young, frankly carnal fashion freak made Shelly acutely aware of the twenty years and twenty leagues of inhibitions that separated them. But after a beer and a little weed ("just one puff" for Shelly), they were giggling and gossiping and getting all pajama party.

"So, who's this videoconference with?" Shelly asked.

"Johnny swore me to secrecy," said Brandi.

Shelly frowned at her.

"Gerald Bridges!" she whispered conspiratorially.

"Come on," said Shelly. "You're serious?"

"Yup," smirked Brandi, inhaling.

"He's like a multi-trillionaire! The guy invented leveraged buyouts. He owns his own island in Hawaii!" said Shelly, giddy from the beer, the puff, and the girlie camaraderie. "What does he want with me?"

"He and Johnny, like, grew up together," squeaked Brandi, holding her breath.

"Okay, so?"

"So, this Gerald Bridges has been in hiding ever since the tape came out," said Brandi, still holding her breath.

"What tape?"

"Seriously?" asked Brandi.

Shelly shrugged.

"Where do you live? He married this tennis player-model, thirty years younger than him and a foot taller." Brandi exhaled. "And so, she's raking him over the coals in their divorce trial. And then this tape came out. People are saying he released it himself to cut down the settlement. Really, you haven't seen it?"

Shelly shook her head.

"It's all over the internet. Her and these two big hairy guys—"

"I get the point," laughed Shelly.

"Time-stamped. Two weeks after the marriage!"

"Ouch," said Shelly. "Poor guy. But how's he connected?"

"Johnny was telling him all about Decapede, to cheer him up, I guess."

"What the heck does he want with me?"

Brandi shrugged. "Johnny caught me listening in. I had to hang up. Beer?"

"Oh, no," said Shelly.

"C'mon, one more."

"I have to watch my weight."

"Oh, bullshit," Brandi protested, opening herself another bottle. "You look amazing."

"I bless Spanx every morning."

"I look the way I want. I don't give a flying fuck what anyone thinks."

"I admire that in you."

"What, you do? This look, you like it?" Brandi asked, her tongue loosened by the beer.

"Not exactly my style," said Shelly, and they both guffawed at that image, "but I admire your courage."

"My courage? I'm a secretary, big fucking deal. I'm in awe of you."

"Of me?" asked Shelly, genuinely surprised.

"The way you lied your way into Johnny's office? That is so ballsy."

Shelly flushed with pleasure. She had never in her life thought of herself as "ballsy."

"The way you convinced him in one minute to go on your wild goose chase? Sister, I idolize you. You are *amazing!*"

"I don't think anyone's ever called me 'amazing' before." She smiled.

Brandi told Shelly how she'd grown up in Canton helping out in her mother's bridal salon, reading fashion magazines slavishly and dreaming of opening her own boutique someday. But money was tight, and she got edgy for a taste of the big city. The radio station liked to present a hip young look, so they hired her as a receptionist, which was a whole lot better than waitressing or working as a salesgirl.

They agreed that despite his age and fame, Johnny could be quite childish. But sweet. Brandi told Shelly how much her friends from the bars and clubs around Cleveland loved "Creston Gold," how they had been flooding all their AOL chat groups with buzz about Decapede, telling their friends to check out the clip and asking if anyone knew anything about the band.

Well past midnight, exhausted from gabbing, they logged into YouTube. 3208 views. They looked at each other and smiled slyly.

Shelly was taken aback when she realized that she'd be sharing Brandi's bed, but it was queen-sized, and they lay tipsy and giggling next to each other under the covers till far too late, gabbing about the Decapede picture.

"Which one would you do first?" asked Brandi.

"Brandi!" protested Shelly.

"Oh, come on," said Brandi, elbowing her under the covers. "In theory."

"I don't know, really. Between the one with the nice hair and the shaggy one," she confessed finally. "How about you?"

"Well, first choice would be both of them together."

"Bran-di!"

"But if I had to pick just one at a time? Start with the pretty one, you know, for a warm-up. But that bad boy? Oh, would I jump that!"

Shelly looked in Brandi's mirror and was pleased with what she saw. She'd brought her most serious work outfit, a tailored navy business skirt suit with a pale blue blouse buttoned up to the mandarin collar. She'd spent twice as long as usual on her makeup, even applying a bit of mascara.

"Well?" she asked with a bright smile.

Brandi, with her implausible hair and dark mien, studied her and frowned.

Shelly lost her bright smile. "What?"

Brandi pulled an unfolding cosmetics case from the closet, hairdressing instruments on one side and make-up equipment on the other.

"Sit," she ordered.

Shelly sat.

Brandi wiped clean the makeup Shelly had so laboriously applied and set to work with the grave focus of a brain surgeon.

"No raccoon eyes, okay?"

"Don't knock it till you've tried it," laughed Brandi. After a few minutes, she stood back to examine her work. "You know you have a complexion to die for. Your skin is like milk. I just added a little blush."

"I can't tell a lie without turning purple."

"You just need more practice," said Brandi and began combing and snipping and reshaping Shelly's fine blonde hair.

Twenty minutes later, Shelly looked at herself in the mirror. Her hair was mostly pinned back behind her ears, with a few well-placed strands spilling down to frame her face. Her eyes looked larger and softer, and her lipstick three shades hotter than she had ever worn before. She smiled at her revamped self, and the comely lady in the mirror smiled back.

"Stand," said Brandi.

Shelly stood.

Brandi reviewed her outfit and frowned.

"What?" said Shelly. "I want to look serious."

"Oh, that'll get you real far in a room full of men. Lose the jacket."

Shelly lost the jacket.

Brandi opened Shelly's collar button, stepped back to survey her, then opened two more.

"Brandi!" protested Shelly, trying to rebutton the third one, but Brandi slapped her hands away. Shelly tugged up the blouse as a gesture to modesty.

"Pull your shoulders back," ordered Brandi.

"You sound like my father," answered Shelly.

Brandi stood behind Shelly, hooked her fingers into the crooks of her collarbone, and jammed her thumbs hard against Shelly's shoulder blades, forcing her to thrust out her chest.

"Ow," said Shelly.

"You got it? Show it!" commanded Brandi. She studied Shelly and smiled proudly.

Shelly looked at her new profile in the mirror. "This skirt doesn't make my butt look fat?"

"You've got a great ass," said Brandi, smacking it smartly. "And if you'd just stand up straight, you'd have knockout boobs."

She pulled her shoulders back. She'd never thought of her boobs as "knockout," but Brandi seemed to be an expert on the subject.

Brandi burrowed in a drawer, came up on Shelly from behind, and hung around her neck a long filigree chain with a polished oval seashell reaching down towards her newly revealed cleavage.

Shelly scrutinized herself in Brandi's mirror. "Yeah?"

"I'm telling you, you are one hot piece of ass!" Brandi smiled. "Damn, girl, you do blush easily."

17
Lake Hope
– April 1970 –

"Do you want me to drive?" Sam offered, clearly hoping she'd refuse.

"No, I got it," said Kathleen. "So, what did you think of him?"

He grinned. "I think maybe we got ourselves a band."

"Who would have believed it?" she smiled. "One day a waitress at Pedro's Cantina, the next a singer in a band."

"You got anything to eat?" Sam asked.

"Look in the bag on the back seat."

Sam stuck his hand in the paper sack and pulled out the snow globe with the grinning fish.

"What's this for?" he asked, shaking the fish and studying the little snow storm.

"It's a gift," she said. "To remember today."

"For me?" he asked.

"Yeah, for you," she answered.

"Oh," he said, studying the flurry.

"You're supposed to say thank you," she said.

He looked at her and then at the globe.

"Thank you," he grunted, and continued to watch the slowly falling snow.

"There's something else in there for you."

He extracted the Tootsie Roll. He looked at her, and she grinned. Sam smiled and peeled away the shiny white and brown wrapper. He bit off a big chunk and chewed at the stiff, unyielding glob. Kathleen watched him, and she smiled, too.

"You want a bite?" he offered.

"No, it's all for you."

"Ah," he said, chewing and thinking. "Thank you."

"You're welcome," she said.

"I'm not used to presents," he said.

"I know," she answered.

They rode in comfortable silence, the two-lane highway curving along the lake.

"I gotta pee," she said.

"There's probably a gas station somewhere up ahead."

"I don't need no gas station, you city slicker you," she said, pulling off the little highway onto a narrow dirt path. It led through a cluster of trees, rose over a small bank, and ended at a small patch of grass on the bank of the lake itself.

Kathleen ran off into the bushes, and Sam stood at the lake's edge skipping stones, eight, even ten hops out over the placid water. The trees and foliage were just beginning to show signs of late April green. A few birds were flying high in the fine, almost-spring sky, and squirrels were chattering in the trees.

"Want to go in?" she asked, looking out at the lake.

"Oh, sure," he scoffed.

"Come on, chickenshit!" she challenged him. When he didn't react, she pulled off her T-shirt. Her bra was white and lacy. Her breasts were full and mesmerizing. His mouth went dry.

"I—I—"

"Oh, don't be a pussy," she said laughing and teasing, reaching out her hand. He moved back. She looked at him. His eyes were skittering.

"What's the matter?" she asked, not joking now.

"You go in. I'll wait," he said, turning from her.

"What's wrong?" she asked quietly, taking his hand. It was cold and clammy.

"Nothing," he mumbled.

She touched his shoulder. He jerked away, but she held on to his hand more tightly.

"What is it?" she asked gently. Again she laid her hand on his shoulder, holding his hand tightly. This time he didn't try to move away, but his chest was rising and falling. His palm was sweating.

She stood next to him, her breasts touching him, her hand barely moving on his shoulder. He looked away.

"I—" he began, and stopped. She waited, her hand gentle on his arm. "I've never—"

"Never?" she asked softly.

"Please," he added in a whisper, "please don't laugh."

"Come on," she coaxed him gently. "Just up to your waist?"

He shook his head, looking at his feet.

"Just up to your knees?"

He shrugged, still avoiding her eyes. And her breasts.

"Just up to your little toesies?"

He shrugged again.

"Come on," she whispered. "You can if you want."

She watched him steal a look at her and stepped back.

"Only if you want to," she smiled slyly, pulling off her shorts, her eyes holding his. Her panties were cream-colored. Her whole body was cream-colored. His breathing slowed gradually.

She turned her back to him, just an arm's reach away, and unhooked her bra. She paused to look at him over her shoulder, then slipped off her panties and went sloshing into the water.

"Ay," she shrieked with delight. "It's so fucking cold!"

She turned to him and spread her arms. "You coming?"

He stared.

"Okay then," she said.

He watched as she waded in till the water reached her bare ass and then dove headfirst and disappeared with a ripple. The water continued to lap the shore. Finally, her head broke through the surface, shaking and squealing, peeling her wet hair back from her face. She stood. The water reached almost to her waist. Her breasts were glistening, the nipples tight from the shock of the cold. As far as the lake was concerned, it was still winter.

"I'm dying," she shouted, laughing, hugging herself.

Sam stared at the ground.

"You're going to lose your singer to hypothermia!"

He looked around frantically.

"Come warm me up, you idiot!"

He looked at her looking at him, her breasts shining, the water dripping down her creamy body.

He pulled off his shirt and threw it on the ground, kicked off his shoes, and pulled off his jeans. He tried to hide John Thomas rising, but lost his balance while pulling off a sock and plopped clumsily onto his butt.

"Ow!"

"Would you please hurry up?"

He tried to walk casually down to the water's edge, but the stones were sharp. He started jumping, but that only made them dig into his feet more deeply.

She walked towards him till the water was halfway to her knees, but Sam was looking at the ground, picking his way around the sharper stones.

"There, that's the worst part," she said.

He stopped and gaped at her.

"Sam, come here."

He looked at her.

"Come on," she repeated gently.

She was standing there, knee-deep in the gently lapping water, naked as the April trees around them, shining and glistening and looking into his eyes.

"You're past the hardest part."

Sam took a deep breath. He was standing naked, the water almost touching his toes. There was no going back.

She moved towards him, only a few feet from him now. The water touched his feet. His head was spinning. Kathleen extended her hand to him. He reached out and grabbed it, and she coaxed him in a small step.

"YAH, FUCK THAT'S COLD!"

"Shhh," she said, taking his hands, drawing him, inch by inch, into the cold, wet, unfathomable depths. "Come. I'm here."

She smiled to calm him, but he was staring at the water around his ankles. She moved back slowly, small step by small step, drawing him in.

"Look at me," she said, but he didn't seem to hear her, staring only at his feet. "Sam! Look at me," she insisted.

He raised his head till he was looking at her face. She smiled. "That's it. Come on." The water was at his calves now. At his knees. He began shaking. "It's only water," she said, holding his hands, leading him deeper and deeper.

"Fucking cold water!" he said, his teeth chattering, his eyes wide with fear, careening furiously, with nowhere to hide.

"That's right," she said softly. "Fucking cold water. You're doing great."

"Ow!" A rock.

"That's it," she said, tugging his hands gently. "Come on."

When the water had reached her breasts and the middle of his torso, she stopped and continued pulling him to her till she enfolded him in her arms. He was shaking hard now. She held him to her tightly, laid her head on his chest, and stroked his back till he caught control of his breathing. Every few breaths, he shuddered, but she held him close, pressing his trembling body against her firm, determined nakedness.

She began to hum in his ear. He didn't recognize the tune, but he didn't care.

"Better?" she whispered.

He nodded into her shoulder. "Can we get out now?"

"Come," she said, leading him by the hand to a patch of grass. He was quivering. "Come, lie down here," she said, laying him on his back, patting him with his shirt, then rubbing him with it till the shirt could absorb no more. His lips were pale, his eyes red and tearing. His breathing was hard but even. She lay down beside him and turned him on his side to cradle him in her arms from behind, stroking his chest with her open hands, cooing into his ear, warming him.

Eventually, he stopped shuddering. His breathing relaxed. She held him, front to back, her hands on his arms, his shoulders, his chest. "Shh," she whispered in his ear. Her hand traveled over his drying skin, strong and gentle and firm. She rubbed his chest, his abdomen. She reached down and wrapped her hand around his penis. It began to awaken.

"You okay?" she whispered.

He nodded slightly, then turned to her and kissed her deeply.

He entered her blindly. She held him with all her strength, opening to take him in, clutching him to her as he pumped himself into her, whimpering and shaking his head, pounding her violently. When he came, he let out a broken cry of anguished release.

Afterward, he lay on top of her, the sun on his back, breathing together. Finally, he rolled off and lay next to her, staring at the cloudless, endless sky. Her fingers moved over his shoulder, lightly, barely touching, fulfilled.

"I was born in Wilmington, Delaware," he said in a low, even voice. "When I was five, my mother left."

She said nothing but continued to stroke his arm.

"I never found out why, nothing. My father never said anything. After a while, this Molly moved in with us. She was pregnant with my father's kid. Neither of them really wanted me around. So, they sent me to live with my grandmother in

Florida. On the couch of a little apartment, nothing but old people around. After a couple of years, I got to be too much for her, so I got sent to my aunt in Syracuse. I was getting into trouble in school and in the neighborhood. She couldn't handle me. I don't blame her. I was pretty rough."

He fell silent. She stopped moving her fingers, resting her hand on his shoulder.

"They sent me to this school for tough kids. It was pretty bad. I was pretty bad. I had this rich friend, Joey. He was getting picked on all the time, and I liked fighting, so I'd protect him. He bought me a guitar. One Thanksgiving, he took me home with him. That was pretty cool. But then he got sick and left school. Never saw him again. On vacations, I'd just stay in the dorm. It was in this little town in Connecticut, Mansfield. I'd just wander around down in the lousy part of town, getting into trouble. Summers were the worst. One I stayed with my father. That was really hell. One I went down to Florida, but my grandmother was getting really old. I dragged that out till I was sixteen."

He fell silent again. She could feel him swallow.

"Since then?"

"Just getting by on my own. Jobs, here and there. Then I met this woman in Indiana, Sara Beth. She had a little girl, Kimmie. I really liked her. I lived with her for about a year. Went to night school for a while, finished high school."

Then he stopped talking. They lay together, her head on his chest, listening to the birds and the squirrels and the waves lapping at the shore. Then they made love again, slowly, with a different kind of need.

18

The Phone Call

– May 27, 2006 –

"What do you call this thing again?" asked Johnny.

"Skype," said Brandi, opening the program for him at her desk.

"Remember, don't mention anything about a videotape," he whispered to Shelly.

Brandi clicked on Connect and seated him. After an endless minute, a pixelated, jerky Gerald Bridges appeared on the screen.

"Hey, Gerry!" shouted Johnny, as pumped as a Cleveland boy at his first Indians game.

"You don't need to shout," whispered Brandi.

"Hiya, Johnny," answered Gerald Bridges.

"How's the weather in Hawaii?"

"Paradise," answered the 5'1" tycoon, the world's most famous cuckold.

"Remember Flash Gordon's video camera?" shouted Johnny.

"Exactly!" said Gerald, sitting forward. "So, did you get any leads yet?" He was bald as a cue ball on top, with a ring of long hair covering his ears and neck and a piercing voice.

"No leads. But calls are still lighting up the switchboard, as they used to say."

"Say that to a kid today, he won't know what you're talking about."

"You wouldn't believe how this Decapede thing has caught on," shouted Johnny. "I've done shows three straight nights. The phone just keeps ringing here at the station. Everyone, old hippies, soccer moms. The kid from the coffee truck outside was pumping me for information about the band. A kid! And 'Creston Gold'! How do you like that song?"

"That song!" Gerald gushed.

"Right? I told you!" said fourteen-year-old Johnny.

"Amazing," said eleven-year-old Gerry. "So, is, ah, Shelly there?"

Shelly took a deep breath.

"Wait, I'll put her on," said Johnny, and gave Shelly the chair.

"Hello, sir," said Shelly.

"Hi, Shelly, very pleased to meet you," said the sixth-richest man in the world.

"Likewise," she said, blushing.

"I don't know if you know this, but Johnny and I go way back. He's always been a little bit older and a whole lot cooler than me. He's been telling me all about this mystery band of yours, trying to cheer me up. I've been going through a rough patch recently, and I just wanted to tell you, Shelly, that song has kept me going for the last few days. *Nothing's gonna bring me down / Have another Creston Gold*," he sang. "I used to drink Creston Gold when I was young."

"Well, I'm very glad to hear that," was the best she could come up with.

"Johnny told me that it was your idea, tying a tribute to the brewery with the song and a treasure hunt for the band."

"Well, yes, sir, I guess you could say that I'm the guilty party."

"Outstanding," he said.

"Thank you, sir."

"And he told me how you lied your way into his office," Gerald cackled.

"Oh, that—" Shelly colored.

"Very ballsy. I like you," said Gerald Bridges, staring at Shelly, unblinking.

"Thank you, sir," she said. *Are all tycoons this weird?* she wondered.

"You work in your father's law office?"

"Yes, sir, I'm a paralegal. And I run the office. Jill of all trades."

"I'm surprised that hippie vibe speaks to someone as young as you," said Gerald Bridges.

"I suppose," Shelly agreed, "but there's something so pure, so innocent, so hopeful about that song. Something so lacking in the world today. It's like—it's what people need today."

"Hmm," he said. "How old are you?"

"Excuse me?" stammered Shelly.

"I'm rich enough to get away with asking that." His laugh was sharp and shrill, but his eyes continued to stare. "How old are you?" he repeated.

"I'm forty-three."

"Doesn't it surprise you that people of all ages are calling?"

"To tell you the truth, sir, no, it doesn't. You mention Creston Gold to anyone around here, they all have the same response. 'Oh, Creston Gold,' and they say it with a sort of sad sigh. But I am surprised by the numbers."

"What numbers?" he asked.

"Well, I've been following the number of hits on YouTube."

"Tell me," said Gerald, cocking an eyebrow.

"When I crashed Johnny's office, there were twenty views. That was four days ago. Last night, there were about four thousand."

"In four days?" said Gerald, scratching some numbers on a legal pad. "That's impressive."

"That's because the YouTube is the only place people can

hear the song," said Johnny, proudly showing off his techno-logical acumen. "Other than WFOR."

"Wrong," said Brandi with a pop of her gum off-camera.

"Who said that?" asked Gerald.

Brandi stuck her piercings and lopsided hairdo into the frame.

"People I know are downloading it like crazy. eDonkey, Kazaa. Hi, I'm Brandi."

"Hi, Brandi," said Gerald. "Very interesting."

"And they listen to it on their iPods," added Shelly.

Johnny looked at them as if they were speaking Greek.

"Hmm," said Gerald, tapping the pen on his bald pate. "Has anybody else picked up on this outside of WFOR?"

"I don't think so," said Johnny.

"Hmm," said Gerald, thinking.

The phone on Brandi's desk rang.

"Hello," she said.

"Can't you take that elsewhere?" said Johnny, annoyed.

"Well, Shelly," said Gerald, "it was certainly a pleasure meeting you. I just wanted to tell you that I really appreciate your gumption."

"Oh, thank you, sir."

"And your initiative. And your vision."

"Thank you."

"And, who knows? Maybe someday—"

Just then, Brandi came clomping back into the room excitedly on her patent leather goth platform boots. "There's a call!" she said, cracking her gum like a string of firecrackers.

Johnny and Gerald and Shelly stared at her, dumbfounded. Brandi looked at Johnny and at Gerald Bridges on the screen and handed the phone to Shelly.

"What am I supposed to do?" mouthed Shelly in a panic, covering the mouthpiece.

"Answer it!" cried Johnny.

"Answer it!" commanded Gerald Bridges.

"Answer it!" urged Brandi.

"This is Shelly Griffin speaking," she said, switching the phone to speaker.

"Hello. I'm calling about that song you're playing on the radio."

"Yes! What's your name please?"

"Eddie. Eddie Basinski."

"Could you spell that, please?" said Shelly.

He spelled it, and Brandi scribbled.

"And your phone number, in case we get cut off?" Brandi wrote. "Where are you calling from, Eddie?"

"I'm from over in Wakefield."

Gerald's eyes grew even wider, and he leaned forward.

"And you have some information?" Shelly asked.

"Yeah, well, my nephew showed me the picture of that band on the interweb, singing that song about Creston Gold."

"Yes?" she said, her voice rising in anticipation.

"There's really a five-hundred-dollar prize for someone who knows something about it?"

Shelly glanced at Johnny, who nodded vigorously. "Yes, that is correct. Do you know something about Decapede?"

"Nah, I never heard of no Decapede," he said, and they all sighed. "And I never heard that song. Sure is pretty, though." Their shoulders all sagged. "But I know that band. They used to play down at Steuben College."

They all jerked upright.

"Steuben College? In Steubenville?"

"Yeah. I was down there on a wrestling scholarship."

"When was that?"

"Oh, it must have been around '69. Or '70. Or '71. They used to play at a place called Pedro's, on State Street. Fine tamales, that Pedro had. They played there. Then at some hall in town." And then, as an afterthought, he added, "Fine beer, Creston Gold. Ain't seen it around for a while. Is it true they're closing down that brewery? That'd be a damn shame."

Johnny and Brandi and Gerald Bridges stared at Shelly.

"Do you remember any of their names?"

"Am I gonna get them five hundrit bucks?"

Shelly looked at Johnny, who nodded furiously.

"Oh, absolutely."

"Now?" she mimed to Johnny.

He nodded.

"A check?" she mouthed.

"Yes!" he answered, shouting soundlessly.

"Eddie, if it's convenient for you, I'd like to come down to Wakefield right now and bring you a check and ask you some questions."

"You know that McDonalds on West 65th near Loraine?"

"In an hour?"

"See you there, lady. I'll be the guy with the big grin and his hand out."

As soon as she hung up, Johnny and Brandi and Gerald Bridges began to speak loudly, but she didn't hear anything they were saying.

Johnny shuffled around the table to where Shelly was sitting, the receiver in her hand. He took her hands, pulled her up, and gathered her into a big hug. She looked at Brandi over his shoulder and patted him on the back like she was trying to burp him.

"Shelly! Shelly!" called a shrill voice from the little speaker on Brandi's desk. "You have to call me as soon as you talk to him!"

But no one was paying attention.

19

The First Rehearsal
– April 1970 –

Aaron arrived at four thirty to set up the gear in the music room. Gavin and Vaneshi arrived at five, one after the other. Aaron introduced them to each other and thanked them for coming.

"*Namaste*," said Vaneshi from within his thick black beard, bowing. He shuffled barefoot to an amp, plugged in his guitar, sat cross-legged on the floor in his threadbare white pajama, and began picking scales.

Gavin set up the refreshments he had brought—a bottle of tropical fruit juice, a thermos of herbal tea, and home-baked banana bread.

At twenty after, Aaron finally went outside to look for Kathleen and Sam. He saw them half a block away, chattering with their heads together, her arm in his. When Kathleen spotted him, she stood up straight, removed her arm, and greeted Aaron with a wave and a smile.

"Hey, Aaron, what's up?" said Kathleen.

Aaron shook his head, exasperated.

"I'm sorry we're late," she said. "We were supposed to—"

"The new guys have been waiting."

"Yeah, so let's get started," Sam growled.

"Do you not give a shit about anyone?" Aaron hissed.

"Hey, man," said Sam, "you want to cool down, it's all—"

"Don't you get that we have a gig tomorrow night?"

"We do," said Kathleen, insinuating herself between them, laying her hand on Aaron's arm, "I'm really sorry we're late. There was a mix-up—"

"And we haven't had one single minute of rehearsal?" said Aaron, shaking her hand off, making no attempt to veil his vexation.

"Hey," said Sam, coloring and edging forward, "she said we're sorry."

"*You*," he said, his finger pointing at Sam's chest, "have no right to even open your mouth about—"

"Don't you *ever*—" said Sam, knocking away Aaron's finger.

Kathleen turned Sam and gently moved him away, holding his shoulders and whispering in his ear for a long moment while his eyes shot knives in Aaron's direction over her shoulder.

"Okay?" she asked him.

But he just glowered at Aaron.

"*Okay?*" she demanded.

Sam looked at her and nodded. He glared back at Aaron but allowed her to push him towards the door to the music room.

"Listen," she said, turning to Aaron, "I wanted to tell you—"

"So, you're with him?" he cut her off.

"I—We sort of—" she squirmed.

"Just say it."

"Yes," she snapped. "I'm with him. Okay?"

"Great."

"Look, Aaron," she said as soothingly as she could. "We had a little thing, it was nice, but—"

"And now you're coming late, too?"

"—don't make it into more than it was."

Aaron said nothing, seething.

"Okay?" She tried touching his arm, but he shook her off. "Okay?"

"I hate to see you getting dragged down into his shit."

"Look, Aaron, I'm not his mother."

"So, I see."

"And I know he can be a handful."

Aaron snorted.

"But I promise you, I'll do everything I can to make sure he does his job. All right?"

Aaron studied the sidewalk.

"Your chances are better dealing with him through me than on your own, no?"

The sidewalk hadn't changed much.

"Aaron?"

"Okay," he said petulantly.

"And listen—would you look at me, please?"

Aaron raised his head to face her.

"This thing, Sam and me—it's new. I don't know exactly what it is or where it's going. But it's not nothing. It's not just, you know, for kicks. It—means something. I don't know what, but something."

"Congratulations," he said, bruised.

"So, I'm asking you—I'm pleading with you—don't tell him about us." She paused, looking at him with her big gray eyes. "It won't do anybody any good."

"Come on, let's go in."

"Please?" she implored him.

"Okay, listen up," Aaron said, clearing his throat. "It's great having you all here. I can't wait for us to get to know each other musically and personally. We only have two and a half weeks till the demonstration, and we need a whole set for Pedro's."

"When's our first show?" Gavin asked.

Aaron took a deep breath. "Tomorrow night," he said and paused. "And every Wednesday and Friday night."

"Are you serious?" said Kathleen, wide-eyed.

"Oh, that's impossible," said Gavin.

Vaneshi crooked an eyebrow.

Sam stuffed a whole slice of banana bread into his mouth.

"We'll work through the songs that Sam and I have tried out—"

"Ankafln," interjected Sam through the banana bread.

"And Kathleen," said Aaron. "It's nothing fancy, you guys'll catch on in seconds. So, I made a list here."

Sam clambered up from the floor and wiped his mouth with the back of his hand while he was still chewing. Everyone watched as he strapped on his guitar, plugged it in, and blasted the ear-shattering *Bam!Bam!Bam! Bambam!* of "Louie, Louie." Vaneshi, who was cradling his guitar cross-legged on the floor, flicked it on and ramped it up. Gavin jumped up and grabbed his sticks, leaving Aaron no choice but to strap on his bass. Sam was screaming a hilarious garble of lyrics so hoarsely and coarsely that they were all afraid he'd shred his voice. But they all followed, glued together by Gavin's very insistent beat.

"I don't know the words," shouted Kathleen, laughing.

"No one does," Sam shouted back.

Vaneshi played a frenetic, searing solo that had them all gaping in amazement. At one point, the tip of his beard got snarled between the bottom strings, but he kept on playing high notes valiantly while Kathleen ran over and untangled him. They finished together in a crash of Gavin's cymbals, everyone grinning and high-fiving each other. Even Sam looked pleased.

"Mr. Vaneshi!" grinned Aaron, and the skinny monk put his hands together and bowed slightly.

"I thought you said you didn't play 'that kind of music,' " laughed Aaron to the drummer.

"I don't think I've ever whacked the drums so hard in my life," smiled Gavin shyly.

"Nice, man," said Sam.

Kathleen walked over to Gavin and planted a big, wet kiss on top of his shaven head. He beamed like a child with a big, dripping ice cream cone.

"Twelve-bar blues?" suggested Aaron, and they all agreed.

"Here, I got one," said Sam, and he played a raunchy riff.

Aaron fiddled with a bass line for a moment. "In A, okay? Gavin, count us in?"

"*Oh, sweet Mama / Why'd you leave me all alone?*" Sam sang in his grittiest baritone, "*Oh, sweet Mama / Why'd you leave me all alone? / I tried to do you right / But everything just came out wrong.*"

"Woo, get the white boy!" whooped Kathleen.

"What you got, honky?" Sam challenged Aaron.

"*I got a wooooooooman in Jersey,*" sang Aaron, wagging his head like a mop top, and Kathleen jumped up to dance in front of him. "*Makes me sing all night and day / I got a woman in Jersey / Makes me sing all night and day / My fingers got such bad blisters / I just had to run away.*"

Vaneshi played a high-voltage solo, and then Sam took the mic.

"*I got a girl in Vegas,*" howled Sam in a voice grungy enough to peel the paint from the walls of the music room. Kathleen bopped towards him, undulating and rippling with the music. "*Makes my eyes turn green / I got a girl in Vegas / Makes my eyes turn green / She got curly hair / The sun ain't never seen.*"

Kathleen clapped for him, with everyone grinning and grooving, then grabbed the mic and shouldered Sam out of her way.

"*I got a man in Memphis / Makes my eyes turn blue,*" she wailed in her deep, muscular alto, "*I got a man in Memphis / Makes my eyes turn blue / Turns my innards to molasses / When he do the things he do.*"

By this time, all five of them were laughing so hard that the song fell apart.

"Gavin, are you blushing?" asked Kathleen through her laughter.

"Oh, my," he said, turning a very rosy shade of sepia but clearly enjoying himself.

"But, seriously, guys," said Aaron, unstrapping his bass

and walking towards the piano, "I made a list of actual songs that we can perform tomorrow."

"Can't we just play, man?" said Sam.

"I want to start off with some easy ones," said Aaron, ignoring him.

Sam began to play a loud riff, and Aaron flicked off Sam's speaker.

"Hey, what the fuck?"

"I'd rather try to polish up a few we've done alrea—"

"Don't you ever—"

"We're going to need a whole bunch of songs for tomorrow," said Kathleen. "How about let's start with Aaron's list?"

Sam looked at her. Then, he grumbled something and let Aaron do his job.

"Okay, let's warm up with a Chuck Berry," Aaron suggested, and everyone seemed to like the idea.

"Ah, like 'Memphis, Tennessee'?" suggested Gavin.

"Something with backing vocals," said Aaron.

" 'Almost Grown'?" offered Kathleen.

"Oh, I know that one," smiled Gavin.

"Can you play that?" Aaron asked Vaneshi.

Vaneshi nodded beatifically, his beard tickling his ankles. "In D?" he asked and ripped into it. Sam took the lead on the first verse, with Aaron and Kathleen providing the *A-Ah-Hah! Wo! Yeah!s*. Kathleen did the second verse solidly, and Aaron took the third. But it was Vaneshi's showpiece, his smile serene and his fingers like razors. Gavin had no problem rising to the occasion in volume and grit, knocking everyone for a loop with his muscular, driving drumming.

"I guess we can mark that one down," said Aaron, smiling as broadly as everyone else in the room.

Aaron explained "Shout" to them, with each of the members taking a turn at singing lead (even Gavin was convinced to do the "*A little bit softer now*" section), and they played it through quickly. Even though Sam kept mixing up the order of the parts, they felt confident they could hoof it on stage and preferred to leave time and energy to work on their showpieces.

Then they ran Sam's "Peggy Sue." Gavin kept Sam's rhythmic quirks in check with the original drumroll backing, and Vaneshi provided a raucous lead. At the last, rousing chord, Sam pointed his finger at Gavin, shouting, "Yes! Yes!" which made the drummer glow.

"It's a shame you don't play bass," Aaron said to Kathleen as he moved to the piano. He was trying to maintain his bruised façade but was having too much fun.

"Maybe someday I'll learn it," she answered with a wink.

For "True Love Ways" Gavin used his brushes, Vaneshi supplied a twinkling lead, and Kathleen sat in the corner sipping Gavin's tea, staring at Sam. *Just you know—why,* he lilted the delicate melody in his naked, sandpaper voice, and the tea went down her wrong pipe, sending Kathleen into a coughing fit.

Then they ran "Bring It On Home to Me," Sam singing his soulful lead. Aaron strained to reach the high harmony, but Kathleen hit it easily, and everyone joined in zealously, shouting out the congregation's *Yeah? Yeah! Yeah? Yeah* call and response.

Gavin grew more secure in his role as timekeeper and less and less apprehensive of these very loud, very messy undergrads.

Vaneshi was light years ahead of the rest musically. He rarely spoke but, when addressed, would smile angelically and agree with whatever was said.

Sam sang them "Pretty Woman," stealing glances at Kathleen, slowing it down into a deliberate, lustful grind, with Aaron backing him on vocals. Vaneshi and Gavin knew the song well and figured out their parts quickly.

"The crowd's going to love that," said Kathleen.

"I hope so," said Aaron, checking his list.

"*You and I travel to the beat of a different drum,*" Kathleen sang. They ran it once, then a second time, Kathleen delivering the story each time with more confidence and control.

"Great," said Aaron, "now let's do my 'Walk—'"

"I got another one for you," said Sam to Kathleen.

"Maybe later—" she attempted, but Sam began the irresistible *Bam, ba-ta-ta, Bam!, ba-ta-ta.* Vaneshi joined in, doubling him. Gavin smiled in recognition and began a rat-a-tat line of rim shots. Kathleen smiled self-consciously but picked up a tambourine and approached the mic. Aaron, left with no choice, joined in, comping heavy chords on the piano.

"*Well, he walked up to me*"—she grinned at the two of them, and then back at Gavin and Vaneshi—"*and he asked me if I wanted to dance,*" she sang, with a saucy little shimmy with the mic stand.

She smiled at Aaron and then at Sam. They looked at each other and began to "*ooh-ooh*" behind her, higher and higher.

Half an hour later, the song was theirs, and everyone was pleased as punch, even Aaron, although he was becoming visibly impatient for his turn.

"Do you think maybe we could do my 'Walk On By' now?" he asked.

"Muzak," muttered Sam loudly enough for Aaron to hear.

"Maybe I'll add a verse about blood," he sneered at Sam.

"Might help," answered Sam.

"Or do you just need to sing whatever comes into your head?" jabbed Aaron.

"Seems to me it was you who was—" Sam stopped mid-sentence and sniffed the air.

"What?" asked Kathleen.

Sam stared at the door.

"I didn't hear anything," said Aaron.

There was a low thumping. Kathleen ran to open it, and there was little Bev, hidden by a heavy brown paper bag in one hand and two six-packs of Creston Gold in the other, struggling to knock with her foot. Kathleen grabbed the bag.

"Pedro thought you guys might be hungry."

Sam leaped to grab the beer and shoved a pile of jackets and bags from the one table onto the floor.

Bev stood by the door.

"Uh, I guess we'll take a break," said Aaron.

Sam was already unwrapping Pedro's savory goodies. "Slow down, soldier," said Kathleen, shooing him away from the table and tidying up while Gavin pulled chairs around for everyone. Sam tried to stick a hand into one of the bags, but Kathleen smacked him on the wrist.

He stood back grouchily until she had laid places for the band.

"This is lovely," said Gavin to Bev. "Thank you so much."

"How's it going?" Bev asked Aaron.

"Pretty good," he answered, annoyed at the interruption but distracted by the waft.

"Poor guys have been playing their fingers to the bone," said Kathleen, popping beers for the pack of musicians feeding on Pedro's steaming fare.

"Well, enjoy," said Bev, edging towards the door.

"Sit," said Sam through his mouthful, pushing back a chair for Bev with his foot.

She hesitated.

"Come, join us," said Kathleen.

"Oh, yes, please, do," Gavin added quickly.

"Yeah, sure," said Aaron politely.

Hesitantly, Bev took her place at the table.

Sam pushed a plate of tacos in her direction while he chewed.

Bev stared at Sam.

I will never forget this moment as long as I live, she thought to herself, her heart afloat.

As they were slowing down, sated, Aaron turned to Sam. "Hey, Miller, didn't you say you're going to write a protest song?"

"I dunno, did I?" asked Sam, mopping up the remainder of

his enchilada with a tortilla.

"Sounded to me like you promised us one," taunted Aaron.

"I did, huh?" Sam peered at Aaron and took a last bite and a slug of beer. He wiped his hands on the greasy waxed paper and then again on his pants for good measure, picked up his guitar, and sat on an amp, staring at the floor as he began to strum an ominous minor chord. Everyone's chewing slowed.

Cuyahoga rising, river gonna overflow
Cuyahoga rising, river gonna overflow
You looking for a place to hide
But you ain't got no place to go.

Run to the levee, levee bout to give
Run to the levee, levee bout to give
Too late for prayin',
You judged by how you live

Cuyahoga rising, river gonna overflow ...

As he repeated the chorus, Gavin and Vaneshi looked at each other.

Fly to the moon, but you just can't run away
Fly like Appollo 11, but still you got to pay
You gotta come back down to earth
Meet your judgment day.

Cuyahoga rising, river gonna overflow ...

Kathleen looked at Aaron, but he was watching Sam's fingering.

In the morning, drop the napalm, go to sleep at night.
In the morning, drop the napalm, try to sleep at night.
Your dreams, they won't forgive you.
Cuyahoga make it right.

Bev remembered to swallow the bite of burrito she'd been holding in her mouth.

Cuyahoga rising, there's a price you have to pay
Cuyahoga rising, there's a price you have to pay
Ain't no place to hide
Cuyahoga wash your sins away.

Aaron clapped his hands slowly, one clap at a time, in undisguised esteem.

Vaneshi stared at some molecule in the air, nodding slightly.

Gavin put both hands over his heart.

Bev shifted in her chair and cleared her throat.

Kathleen hugged Sam from behind, resting her cheek on his back.

Sam smiled to himself.

"Again?" said Aaron, playing the chords while Bev scribbled down the words.

Aaron sat at the piano, playing snatches and scratching notes as he worked. Bev was writing out copies of the words in her girlish hand with the i's heart-dotted. Kathleen was hugging Sam's arm as he picked through the remnants of Pedro's bag of goodies. After ten minutes, Bev handed out the lyrics to the band.

"Looks okay to you?" Aaron asked Sam.

Sam grunted without looking.

"Can I show you an idea I had for a couple of different chords, give it a really spooky feeling?" asked Aaron.

"Where?" asked Vaneshi, watching as Aaron demonstrated. "Nice," he said, fingering the progression. Sam ran it as well.

"I'm just going to play tambourine on this," said Gavin. "At least in the beginning. If that's all right."

They all reassured him that that was fine.

Sam began the eerie song in his grainy voice. Aaron gradually insinuated the piano backing, never stealing focus, following Sam, providing a rhythmic counterpoint to the percussive guitar. Vaneshi danced around the melody in ghostly, serpentine lines. At the appointed place, Aaron added a light harmony above the vocal, a haunting, holy echo.

Aaron took the lead on the second verse, his agile tenor lighter, brighter than Sam's rasping baritone. *"Fly to the moon, but still you got to pay."*

Kathleen sang lead on the third verse, reading the dense lyrics for the first time. But her rich, husky alto was a clarion warning. *"Your dreams, they won't forgive you / Cuyahoga make it right."*

But what stuck in everyone's ears and minds was the refrain, *Cuyahoga rising, there's a price you have to pay / Cuyahoga rising, there's a price you have to pay / Ain't no place to hide / Cuyahoga wash your sins away,* and how Aaron stacked the voices on each repetition, the harmony growing and swelling with the river.

At the end, there was a long moment of silence.

"Yeah," said Aaron quietly.

Bev just stared at them.

"I don't know if that was all right," said Gavin. "In the last two verses, I added some bass drum with brushes on the high-hat—"

They all shushed him, and all six of them sat for a moment without talking.

Finally, Aaron got to sing his "Walk On By," and Sam was grinning as he sang the *"Don't! Stop!"* backing vocals on the same mic with Kathleen.

It was getting late, so Aaron had them run through all the songs one last time. By midnight, they were confident that each person knew his role in each song and they could get through them without snags.

"What do you think?" Gavin asked Aaron as they were packing up. "Are we ready?"

"You bet your booties we're ready," he said confidently. Confidence was one of Aaron's more attractive qualities. When it came out as cockiness, it was less appealing. "They're going to love us."

"Oh, you guys are going to be just great," fluttered Bev.

They all chattered excitedly, except for Vaneshi, who was fingering scales in the air.

"What should we wear?" Gavin asked. Everyone shrugged.

"You can wear whatever you like," Aaron said to the band. Turning to Sam, "No American flag T-shirt, okay?"

"It's at the dry cleaner," answered Sam.

"Hah. There's just one more thing before we go home," said Aaron, pausing dramatically. "We need a name." They all began talking excitedly to each other, shouting suggestions and laughing and horsing around till he rapped on the table. "I think everyone should make a suggestion, and we'll discuss them. Then we'll vote." Everyone looked at him, then continued chattering.

"Head Cleaner," said Sam.

"What?" Gavin asked.

"That's kind of trippy," Aaron said. "Sounds like a name for a psychedelic band. We play more, like, hard-core rock."

"How about something local?" Kathleen asked. "The Steubens." Everyone stared at her. "Okay, bad idea."

"Something connected to Pedro?" Bev offered.

"The Flying Burrito Brothers," said Aaron.

"Frijoles and Beer," said Kathleen.

"I'm hungry," said Sam.

"That's a name for the band?" asked Aaron.

"Works for me," answered Sam.

"Which?" asked Gavin, "Frijoles and Beer or I'm Hungry?"

"Something that makes you think of hard rock," said Aaron. "Something like 'The Mothers of Invention.'"

"The Fruits of Labor," suggested Gavin.

"The Fruits of the Loom," said Aaron.

"The Fruits," said Sam.

They all sat, thinking.

"My Foot."

"The Wet Rags."

"The Living Daylights."

"Monkey's Uncle."

"My Uncle's Monkey."

"Hell's Bells."

"Heck's Wrecks."

"Sudden Death Playoff."

"Dickie and the Carburetors."

"Who's Dickie?"

"The Hypnic Jerks," said Gavin, with a wide smile. Everyone stared. The smile faded.

"Planned Obsolescence."

"The New Deal."

"TVA."

"San Andreas's Fault."

Vaneshi stopped playing his scales. Everyone turned to look at him.

"Visuddhimagga," he said.

Everyone looked at each other. Vaneshi returned to his scales.

"Victory in our Time."

"The Wooden Nickels."

"Aunt Martha's Compote."

"The Polar Opposite."

"Listen," said Gavin, rising, "I hate to be a party pooper, but it's getting quite late—"

"Sit!" said everyone in unison. Gavin sat.

"Look," said Kathleen after a frustrating group silence, "it's late, and we need to get some sleep. It's just a name. Let's just pick something safe."

"Like what?" Gavin asked.

"How about an insect name?" offered Aaron. "The Beatles.

The Crickets. It gives a sense of belonging to The Tradition."
Everyone concurred.
"The Monarchs," said Gavin. Everyone groaned.
"Lacewing," said Kathleen. Nobody reacted.
"Brown Recluse?" offered Vaneshi. Everyone frowned.
They all sat thinking.
"Aaron and the Ants?" said Sam. Everyone snickered.
"Gavin and the WASPs," said Aaron. Everyone laughed.
"It really is getting la—" Gavin tried.
"Decapede?" offered Bev.

20

Protruding Ears
– May 27, 2006 –

"Do you remember any of their names?" Shelly repeated.

"Just Sam," said Eddie Basinski, staring at her open button as he slurped his strawberry McDonald's milkshake. He was muscular for a man nearing sixty, but short and bald with comically protruding ears.

"Which one is Sam?" she asked, placing the picture in front of him.

"That one," said Eddie, pointing at the scruffy one. "He might of wrote the song."

"Sam what?" Her pulse was racing.

"I don't know. Sam—just Sam," he concluded.

"You're sure it's him?"

"Hell, yes, we were buddies. I remember the very first night he came into Pedro's. He tripped over me, going up on the stage, almost fell over."

"And this one?" she asked, indicating the tan, well-dressed one.

"He played drums, I think. I don't know his name. Oh, and I remember that guy," he said, pointing at the tall one in the white robe. "Played these long, crazy guitar solos. Oh, man, was he good!"

"And this one?"

"Ah, he played piano really good and did all the talking. It was like his band, I guess. He was kind of a pain in the ass."

"Do you remember what he was called?"

"Some Jew name. Abraham. Moses. Something like that."

"And her?"

"They just called her Waitress. She had these big gray eyes. I don't remember her name. But I sure remember those knockers, if you'll pardon my French. Didn't wear no bra-ssiere, either. That was pretty cool."

Eddie continued to stare at her décolletage. Shelly didn't move for fear of derailing his slow-moving train of thought.

"Were they students at the college?"

Eddie shrugged his shoulders. The check was in his shirt pocket.

"Can you try to remember what year it was exactly?"

Eddie thought hard, gnawing on a French fry. "Nah, sorry," he said finally.

"How long were they around for?"

Eddie rolled that around his mind slowly. "Not long at all," he said finally. "It musta been—"

She stared at his Dumbo ears while he thought.

"I know!" he said, sitting up straight and inhaling the milkshake down the wrong pipe. He began coughing harshly till Shelly finally got up from her seat and went around to smack him hard on his very thick back. Then, she brought him a cup of water. Finally, he caught his breath. Shelly had a sneaking suspicion that Eddie was dragging it out, relishing his moment of glory.

"I remember now. It was right before the shooting over at Kent State. They were going to play at some pep rally or something. I don't know what happened afterwards 'cause they closed down the school. I missed going to the division wrestling championship. I was ranked second in the conference in the hundred-fifty-two-pound weight class."

"They were playing right before the shooting? So it would

have been, what, April? May 1970?"

"I guess. I don't remember exactly."

"Is there anything else you can remember, anything at all that might help me track them down?"

Eddie ruminated on that for a while, picked up his mobile phone, and dialed.

"Yo, Dinks, how you hanging, bro? How's life out in Cal-i-for-ni-yay? Listen, crazy thing here. You remember that band used to play at Pedro's, the one where the waitress with the big boobs sang?" He made a gesture of apology to Shelly. "You won't believe this, man—they got a song that's all over the interweb. A picture of them, too. I don't know, somewhere on the interweb." Shelly wrote "YouTube" on a napkin. "It's on YouTube, man. They called themselves—" She wrote Decapede on the napkin. "The Decapedes. Yeah, I never heard that name, neither. That's right. Yeah. Listen, you remember any of their names or anything? Yeah, just that Sam guy. Me, too. What? Oh, yeah? Yeah, that's cool, man. I'll catch you. Take care."

"That was Dinks."

"So I gathered."

"He don't remember the same stuff as me."

Shelly smiled at him, but he was busy studying her bust.

"But—" he drawled.

"What?" she asked.

"He did say that there was some newspaper article about the band back then."

"In what paper?"

"The Steubenville paper. He remembered 'cause it was on the back of a story about the wrestling team. He saved it in his crap book." Eddie laughed. "We used to call it a 'crap book.' Get it? Scrapbook/crap book?" He waited for Shelly to respond, but she was interested only in the article. "But he don't got that no more. Lost it when his trailer burnt down."

"Oh, boy," said Shelly, "that could be a gigantic help."

Shelly left him her number in case he dredged some additional image from his very sludgy memory and hurried to the car to call the station.

"Did you get it all down?" asked Johnny, hungry for every scrap of new grist for his show.

"I recorded it and signed him on a release form," said Shelly proudly.

"Yes!" said Brandi.

"Outstanding," said Gerald Bridges from his private Hawaiian island.

"Thanks," said Shelly, "but it's not much to go on."

"So, what are you going to do?" asked Gerald Bridges.

"Tomorrow's Saturday," Shelly answered. "I think I'll take a drive down to Steubenville."

"Hey, Johnny, where'd you find this girl?" said Gerald Bridges.

21

The First Gig

– April 1970 –

Aaron recognized only a few Steuben students among the dozens of people milling restlessly on the sidewalk outside Pedro's. Most of them were clearly not locals—hair, beards, bellbottoms, beads, embroidered vests, paisleys, tie-dyes, flowers, and that waft of a fragrance he was beginning to recognize as grass.

"What's going on here?" he asked a group of strangers.

"They're not letting any more people in."

"It's full."

"This guy—"

"—who sang here last week—"

"—Sam something—"

"—really fantastic—"

"—sing again tonight—"

"What, by himself?" Aaron heard himself asking.

"I don't know," said one scrawny guy with straggly hair down to his American flag T-shirt.

"Someone said there's another guy with him," said one of the girls.

"No, there's going to be a whole band."

"All these people—?" Aaron asked.

"From Wheeling, from Cambridge, from Canton even."

"Isn't it *cool*?"

Aaron looked around him. The crowd, it seemed, was growing.

"Word gets around, man."

"Even around here."

"There's a whole generation—" said one.

"—with a new explanation," the others chimed in.

"Everybody's been talking about him, this Sam guy."

"They're all saying he's going to play at the big demonstration at Ohio State."

"Really?" said Aaron.

"That's so ex-*ci*-ting!"

"Somebody from around here playing at the demonstration, that is so cool!"

The door opened a crack, and Pedro slipped out in full regalia, sombrero and poncho and droopy mustache.

"What the hell?" Aaron said to him quietly.

"Everybody come in, no problemo!" Pedro shouted to the growing swarm.

The jumble of people murmured confusedly.

Aaron looked at him askance and whispered, "There's no room inside for all these people."

Pedro shrugged with an innocent smile. "Good abbertise, mucho hombres make wait."

Aaron looked at his watch. A quarter to ten.

Gavin came out to see the hubbub on the sidewalk. "Excuse me?" he said politely. "I'm set up."

"Great. We'll start soon," said Aaron. "Vaneshi's okay?"

"Yes, he's warming up. This—this—" He indicated the crowded sidewalk. "Is this normal?"

"No, Gavin," Aaron answered, scouring the crowd desperately for Sam. "There is nothing normal about this."

"They're all here to hear us?"

"Yeah," he said. *Sam Miller and his backing band.*

At ten of ten, Sam and Kathleen appeared. She was shining in a puffy white blouse pulled down to reveal her bare shoulders. Her face was glowing, framed by her black pageboy, punctuated by gold hoop earrings. Sam was decked out in battered jeans, a Harvey's Mufflers T-shirt, work boots, and a Davy Crockett cap complete with raccoon tail.

Aaron was about to explode at him when he noticed people in the crowd pointing and whispering.

"Hey, Sam!" called one guy, waving. "Kill 'em in there."

"Thanks, man," Sam waved back.

"You're late," said Aaron to the two of them. "For a change."

Sam surveyed the clamor with a sly smile. He looked at Aaron with a grin and a twinkle in his eye, grabbed his head in his hands, and gave him a big, sloppy kiss on the cheek. Kathleen tried to keep a straight face as Aaron wiped off the slobber.

"C'mon already," said Aaron. "Vaneshi and Gavin are inside. We're ready to start." But the doorway to Pedro's Cantina was clogged, so he led them around to the narrow alley in back with a green door opening into Pedro's kitchen. Aaron's groupies from the front row were lying in wait.

"Hi," said the chubby blonde.

"We came back to see you," said the freckled redhead.

"Hi there," said Aaron with his Aaron smile.

"Hey, Sam," said the brunette, sidling up to Sam and smiling widely, showing off her gleaming orthodontic rails. Sam mumbled something and began examining the garbage cans. She took his hand, put a magic marker in it, and pulled down the neck of her already plunging T-shirt to present her noteworthy writing pads.

"Would you sign me?" she smiled enticingly, trying to catch his eye. Aaron's smile faded quickly, and Kathleen stifled a laugh. Sam tugged on her sleeve, and she led him into the kitchen.

"Any chance I can get some—" Sam attempted, pointing at the pots, but Kathleen pulled him on through the steaming kitchen and out into the smoke-filled, beer-sloshed, hormone-choked horde calling for loud music.

Pedro was furiously directing the waitresses, but when he saw Sam, he stopped and came over to give him a big Mexican hug and pushed them into the roiling waves. The crowd was on its feet, clapping and shouting and stamping their feet as the band squeezed their way to the tiny stage.

The matchbox platform at Pedro's Cantina couldn't hold the five of them. Sam was sandwiched between Aaron's upright piano and Gavin's pared-down drum kit. Vaneshi was perched placidly cross-legged inside a recessed windowsill behind the piano. Kathleen teetered on the far corner of the platform.

Aaron, Kathleen, Vaneshi, and Gavin exchanged looks of bewilderment as the crowd kept cheering, but Sam stood at the mic, fiddling with his guitar. Finally, he raised both hands, and the crowd went quiet.

What's he going to do now? Aaron wondered. *Preach a fucking sermon?*

Sam Miller waited, eyes shut, his upraised hands commanding complete, deafening silence, and when the room finally went still, he let loose with, *"Weh-heh-eh-eh-eh-eh-e-hell——- You know you make me want to SHOUT!"*

The band —for they were now, in fact, a band—played better than they had dreamed of. The edges were ragged, and the singers had difficulty hearing each other when the instruments were playing loudly, but somehow Gavin managed to keep them in time together, and Aaron made sure they didn't try anything too fancy. They were actually making joyous music together, these five strangers.

And the people loved them, standing throughout the set, dancing as much as they could without being able to move their feet. The band was theirs, the music was theirs, and this new world was theirs.

There was a spirit in the air, bigger than its parts—five musicians discovering each other and themselves, shaking and rocking the room crammed with unfettered hair, carefree hearts, and expanding minds, the Spirit of 1970 blossoming in this sweaty, murky little beer bar in Steubenville, Ohio.

Late that night after the show, the five of them sat together, exhausted. Aaron had just finished obtaining the phone number of a tall girl with a boyish haircut and a womanly body. He seemed to be relaxed for the first time in days. Sam was wolfing down a large plate of tamales and huarache. Kathleen brushed back his sweat-matted hair, smiling as she watched him feed. Gavin was nursing a beer, his eyes glazed. Someone in the audience had given Vaneshi a kaleidoscope, and he was looking into it, turning it slowly, transfixed.

Pedro came over with Bev and a young man.

"You guys, you were *fabulous*," squealed a beaming Bev.

They all nodded thanks, even Aaron.

"This is my friend Larry," said Bev. "He writes for the *Ohio Valley Press*."

Larry wore the uniform of a conservative Steuben student, a pressed Oxford button-down shirt, chinos, Weejuns, and an incongruous Peace pendant. Every night the people of Northeast Ohio watched the body count on the news. And every day a few more people began to question Nixon's Vietnam policy.

"Hi," said Larry, shaking hands first with Aaron, who stood and offered him a chair; then with Sam, who transferred the fork to his left hand while continuing to chew; then Kathleen, who gave him her hand and a warm smile; and then Gavin, who stood to greet him properly. "Pleased, I'm sure." Vaneshi was still lost deep inside the kaleidoscope. There were broad smiles all around.

"I just wanted to tell you all how much I enjoyed your show. Wow. Decapede!"

"Oh, thanks," said Aaron. "We really didn't expect anything like this."

"This was really Decapede's first-ever appearance?" Larry asked.

"Absolutely," said Aaron. "Brand new. First gig."

Sam scooped up another tamale with his hand, the sauce running down his wrist as he chomped into it. Kathleen handed him a napkin.

"Incredible. I'd love to do a story about the band. Is there any chance I could do an interview with you tomorrow?" Larry asked the group. "Talk about how you met, the story about this demonstration at Ohio State."

"Sure!" answered Aaron. "What time?"

"One o'clock, at the newspaper office?"

"No problem."

"Great. Meet you at 141 Fourth Street."

"Tell them about kibahnes," Pedro said to the young reporter.

Aaron had long ago given up on trying to understand Pedro's ersatz pidgin Mexican gibberish.

"Right," Larry smiled. "Pedro was asking me if I know of a bigger place around here he could rent for you guys. I told him I have connections down at the Kiwanis lodge."

"They have a hall?" asked Gavin.

"With a nice stage. You could fit a couple of hundred chairs."

"Standing?" Aaron asked.

"Oh, probably three hundred, three fifty."

"Tree hunrit peoples!" Pedro snatched a napkin and began writing numbers. Aaron and Kathleen and Gavin watched him. Sam was still absorbed in his plate, Vaneshi in his kaleidoscope.

"Sam?" Aaron asked.

"What?" He looked up.

"What do you say to us playing in a hall?"

"Need more amps," said Sam.

Pedro finished his calculations. "Tree hunrit peoples?" he asked Larry again.

"At least."

Pedro nodded. "Pedro bring you ebryting what you need."

Steubenville was a poster town for Middle America. People flew the flag and kept their hair cropped short. But the winds of change had begun to blow even in this backwater. The scattered longhairs from neighboring counties heard there was a new band, a local band, playing *their* music, and word spread like a brush fire.

Pedro knew which side of a tortilla was buttered with pesos, so he quickly booked the Kiwanis hall for all the Wednesday and Friday nights leading up to the demonstration.

He had his waitresses draw a big poster for the front window of the café, "Pedro's Famous House Band / DECAPEDE / Tickets $1 Advance, $1.50 at Gate / 3 Tickets for $2.50 when you purchase the Daily Special."

The tickets were selling faster than hot tamales, so he had flyers printed as well.

Bev bought herself a clipboard and assumed the role of coordinator, making sure everyone knew where to be and when and what instruments and cables to bring, making runs to the printers, to the hall, to Pedro's. No one questioned her being there, and she blossomed, allowed to hang out with Steubenville's overnight stars. As a joke, Kathleen brought her a whistle on a lanyard, but Bev wore it proudly everywhere she went. She even let her hair get a little frizzy.

The legendary Decapede shows, the ones that would be described and discussed and dissected so extensively and apocryphally in the media and at breakfast tables and water coolers, the ones that many hundreds, if not thousands, of Eastern Ohioans would claim to have been present at, were the handful of shows at the Kiwanis that spring.

Legally, the hall held two hundred and fifty people standing. But the fire chief was from Southern Texas, raised on Mexican cuisine, so that ordinance was conveniently ignored, though no one in Steubenville was happy to see so many hippies all in one place. They were even less happy that so many of their own high school kids were rubbing shoulders with them.

Many of the attendees came in twos and threes from small neighboring towns, long-haired and flowered and anti-war anti-draft lovers of this new music, young shop workers and students and waitresses and dentists' receptionists and electricians, and even one apprentice bookkeeper. In their hometowns, they were sneered at for their anti-patriotic sentiments and hedonistic lifestyles, greatly exaggerated in the minds of their working-class white-boxer-shorts fathers and dinner-on-the-table mothers.

But for the freaks and peaceniks, the dropped-out, turned-on pot-smoking misfits, the ones who suffered daily the slings and arrows of derisive looks and snide comments from teachers and parents' friends and pretty sorority girls, it was a tribal gathering, a validation of a new generation, with values fundamentally different from their union-dues paying parents. And it wasn't on the cover of Time or an item on the Walter Cronkite Show, it was *right here*, at the Kiwanis Club hall in Steubenville.

So when Sam sang, *"Cuyahoga rising, river gonna overflow / You looking for a place to hide / But you ain't got no place to go,"* the audience felt he was talking to them about themselves.

The first show was full. The second, at least a hundred people were left clamoring outside. The box office showed almost four hundred tickets sold. By the last week, Pedro was running two sets a night, with concessions from the taco stand bringing in even more than the ticket sales. Pedro was a very happy faux Mexican.

Inside the hall was a whirlwind of excitement, a crush of

bodies, a pandemonium of energy engendered by the sweaty, gritty, horny rock music fueling this new generation's transcendent sense of discovering itself.

Many of the people in the audience were returnees, even buying tickets for both sets on the same evening, so they quickly learned Decapede's small repertoire. "Shout" was the showstopper, raising the tumult to the pitch of a call-and-response Southern Baptist revival, the audience whooping "Shout!" on cue and echoing "Hey-ey-ey" to the exhortations of Preacher Sam.

They would follow that with the hymnal "Cuyahoga Rising." When the entire room joined in on the refrain of "Cuyahoga rising, river gonna overflow," even the fire chief had to admit that there was "something happening here." In Thomas L. Ewing's book Decapede: Culture & Community (Toreador Press, 2011), numerous locals are quoted saying that it was that performance that made them re-examine their views about the war.

The favorite of the hard-core Decapede hippie devotees—Decaheads, they called themselves—was the endless instrumental jam they dubbed "Bug Juice." It began with an eerie, psychedelic chord progression for a couple of verses, then evolved into Vaneshi's guitar solo, meandering and snaking and weaving a mesmerizing journey through a spaced-out soundscape beyond time and place.

The members of the band hadn't expected any payment, but they heard the cash register ringing at an energetic clip, so the question was in the air. Aaron offered to speak to Pedro, and everyone readily agreed. When he asked Bev if she'd like to come along, she nodded YES!

The sign on the front door of Pedro's Cantina said Closed, but the green alley door was unlocked. Aaron and Bev followed a voice from the office.

"Guido? It's Lonny Hinton. How you doing? Yeah, a month

of Sundays. How've you been?"

Aaron peeked in. It was indeed Pedro, speaking in fluent American English.

"Me too. Listen, you remember that fifty bucks you owe me? No, I know. Will ya listen to me? Just listen. I got a deal for you, help you out, too. I need a recording studio in Columbus a week from Sunday. May third. I don't know, from noon. A rock and roll band. What do I care what kind of studio?" He paused, listening. "You're joking, right? I'm talking about a Sunday, off the books!" Another pause. "That's your problem, Guido. Do whatever you need to do. Either the fifty bucks cash or a studio." A pause. "Okay, we'll talk again tomorrow," said Pedro/Lonny, sounding very satisfied.

Aaron and Bev tiptoed outside, closing the door quietly behind them. They looked at each other in astonishment, hugged and jumped up and down, and ran to tell the band.

The next two weeks were a blur for everyone, with rehearsals every evening except for show nights.

A photo of Aaron's most sparkling smile appeared on the back page of the *Ohio Valley Press*, and he was squeezing the most out of his celebrity, spending as much time as he could drinking coffee in the Student Union, holding court for a gaggle of adulating coeds.

Bev was darting with a fury from place to place with her clipboard and whistle and lists, chattering and harried but beaming all the while.

Gavin, who was accustomed to being at the gym promptly at seven and at his library desk at eight, was sleeping in most mornings. No one had ever seen him smile so much.

Vaneshi was happily ensconced back in the attic of a garage in Zanesville, playing at night and, during the day, building a twenty-three-stringed kantele with an electric pickup and exploring his inner universe. After a winter of deprivation of the flesh, each afternoon, he walked barefoot down to Dairy Queen for a super-sized banana split.

Sam and Kathleen were never apart. When she attended classes, he would wait for her outside. On campus and in town, people began pointing at them walking arm in arm. They called them "The Golden Couple."

Some of the Decaheads were starting to turn up outside the music room to watch their rehearsals, but Bev maintained a firm No Outsiders policy. So it was only the band who knew what was really happening in the music room—the six of them, for Bev was now a permanent sixth wheel, as indispensable as she was annoying.

Every rehearsal, Sam would show up just late enough to provoke Aaron. If Aaron called a song, Sam would start to play something else. If Sam said he wanted a break, Aaron would insist they play the song through again, at which point Sam would put down his guitar and go outside for yet another "breath of fresh air." When he returned, he was more relaxed but distant, engrossed in his own private world.

Gavin asked Kathleen if she couldn't control him, but the more she cajoled Sam, the more contrary he became. She found that the most effective way to keep him calm was to touch his arm or lay a hand on his shoulder.

Aaron couldn't hide his irritation at her constant rubbing up against Sam and became more and more overbearing. Bev saw this and tried to distract him, but she lacked the power to deflect his attention. Sam saw it as well, and took the opportunity to drape his arm over Kathleen territorially. Once or twice, the tension grew so strong that Sam gave Kathleen a deep, long kiss in the middle of the room, embarrassing her, making everyone else uncomfortable, and incensing Aaron.

Still, the music was coming together despite all the tension in the room, or perhaps fueled by it. Aaron and Sam tried to avoid each other as much as possible or were steered apart by the others, but within the music, they were becoming the most intimate of partners, a couple despite themselves. Their tight vocals were as close as gravel and steel melded together. Sam provided the core for most of the songs, rhythm guitar and lead vocals. Aaron supported him on piano or bass, embellished him, shaping Vaneshi and Gavin and Kathleen to fill Sam's sketch into an explosion of color full of indelible phrases and unforgettable hooks.

On stage, each show forged Decapede into a more and more cohesive unit, learning each other's habits, adapting to each other's quirks, compensating and complementing and building each other's confidence in themselves individually and as a band, till they began to feel they had their own sound, their own voice.

As the band's frontman, Aaron managed the flow of the shows, calling the songs, reminding each member of what they had worked on in rehearsal, and pattering with the audience to growing response. More and more frequently, the local high school girls would squeal in excitement. The hippies who gravitated in from neighboring counties were older and regarded the teeny-boppers with snobbish disdain, but by the end of the show, they, too, were shouting with them for yet another encore.

Try as Aaron might to lead the band, the spotlight always fell on Sam. Aaron composed the sound that made it all listenable and accessible and fun. But everyone knew it was Sam's raunchy magnetism that made the guys gape and the girls gasp. He sang with his eyes closed, his mouth almost touching the mic so that the words seemed to be coming directly from his gut with raw passion, sweat streaming down his face, his tawny hair matted. Every word he sang was true, whether a love paean to Peggy Sue or a nightmare spiritual. He believed, and the audience believed with him.

22

Dickenson's Hardware
– May 28, 2006 –

Shelly took Carlton Salt Springs Road south out of Warren, skirting Youngstown. Derek flitted through her mind. *Derek who?* She smiled to herself. The fine, late May sun was shining as she drove through field after lush field, corn, barley, wheat. *Grass and sunlight all around / Nothing's gonna bring me down / Pass me another Creston Gold.*

But then her phone rang, dispelling the reverie.

"Hi, Da–"

"Shel, where the heck are you?" he asked.

"I'm fine, Dad, how are you?"

"Me? I haven't been AWOL for three days."

"Three days?"

"I haven't seen you since Thursday."

"Thursday night. That's less than two days."

"Thursday, Friday, Saturday. That's three days in my book."

"Thursday evening till Saturday afternoon is less than forty-eight hours. That's two days in my book."

"What got you into such an argumentative mood?"

"Sorry, I have another call. Catch you later," she said, thanking the telephone god. "Allie, hi!"

"Oh, Shelly, honey, it's so nice to hear your voice."

"Yes, I've been thinking about you a lot. Have you been

141

listening to the radio show?"

"Of course. It's—well, I hardly know what to say. It's really quite amazing, what you've done."

"They're going crazy at the station. It seems like all Northeast Ohio is talking about Decapede."

"Well, that's the thing, Shelly—that's why I'm calling. Ever since that Johnny Walker started playing 'Creston Gold' on the radio, things have been going a little crazy at the brewery, too."

"What do you mean?"

"Our orders just picked up like nobody's business. We can't hardly keep up with it. The workers down at the brewery are doing overtime, first time in I don't know how many years. I even asked a retired driver to come in and help out."

"Oh, Allie, I'm so happy to hear that."

"It's all thanks to you, sweetie. You know, the foreman was asking about hiring some new workers. I told him I have no idea how long this is going to last."

"Good question. But you know what?" Shelly paused. "Why don't we wait a little bit with those dissolution forms," she said. "There's no rush, right?"

"That sounds to me like a very good idea," said Allie.

Shelly drove through Canfield, Columbiana, Calcutta, East Liverpool, and Wellsville, finally pulling into the parking lot of the Steubenville Public Library.

"Excuse me," she said to the librarian, who looked as though she'd been pickled sometime during the Eisenhower era. "I'm doing some historical research on Steubenville."

"Yes, how can I help you?" Her voice was uninflected, her eyes expressionless.

"I'm looking for an article that appeared in a local newspaper in about 1970."

"The only newspaper around here was the *Ohio Valley Press*, and that closed down in 1986." She paused. "1987," she corrected herself. "No, 1986," she ruled, leaving no room for appeal.

"Do you perhaps have an archive? Microfiche?"

"I'm sorry, ma'am, we do not."

Shelly pondered that.

"Could you tell me where I might find an archive of the paper?"

"Dickenson's Hardware, down on Fourth Street."

Shelly waited for some elaboration, but as none seemed forthcoming, she thanked the lady and drove downtown to Dickenson's. She parked on what had once been the main drag of Steubenville. It looked exactly like Warren, only more so. She vaguely remembered having seen this street in an episode of Twilight Zone, where the hero steps out of his car into 1957.

The bell above the door of the hardware store rang as she entered. The store was dank and dreary, the only light coming through the front window, empty except for dust and the smell of hardware. She was sure that this was what the 1950s had smelled like. A man came out of the back room. He wore horn-rimmed glasses, a short-sleeved white shirt with a tie that had not been stylish in any decade.

"And how can we help yo-ou this morning?" he asked, his eyes scouring her candidly. She was wearing an airy tunic with large, bright green and blue flowers over jeans.

"Hi, my name is Shelly Griffin," she said.

"Marvin George," he said, extending his hand. It was clammy and creepy, and she extracted hers with a tug.

"I'm doing some research for WFOR radio in Cleveland. I was told that you might know something about the *Ohio Valley Press*?"

Marvin cleared his throat. "Oh, I know just about everything there is to know about the *Ohio Valley Press*. I was the owner and publisher of that fine journal till it closed."

"Really?" she asked, her pulse beginning to thump.

"Yup. Bought the paper in 1974. Ran it till it died."

"And tell me," she asked, her heart pumping, "I'm looking for an article from 1970. Is there an archive of the paper that I could see?"

"I don't know if you'd call it an archive, but there's piles of the paper down in the basement going back to World War II."

"Do you think I could take a look?"

"Well, I don't know," he drawled, staring at her. "I wouldn't want to leave the store unattended. We're pretty busy here."

Shelly looked around. Apparently he was saving money on electricity. "If you could just show me? I promise to be as little bother as possible," she said, turning on her biggest smile.

He leered back with his yellow-toothed smirk and led her through a small door in the back, down a creaky staircase into the bowels of the store, lit by a single 40-watt bulb.

"Let's see," he said, perusing the towering, teetering stacks of papers. "Over here's the late 80s. And here's the early 80s. The late 70s. 1974. 1973, 1972. 1971. Here we go," he said, patting a stack that reached above Shelly's head. "What month are we talking about?"

"April or May, I think," she said.

He pulled down the top pile, a foot-high bundle tied with brown twine. A flurry of dust swirled around them in the meager yellow light. "October," he said. "They're not in exact order," he smiled at her chest.

"Let's see," he said, pulling down bundle after bundle. "August. February. Here we go, April 1970." He plopped it down on a small table in a thick cloud of dust, picked up a very long pair of scissors and cut the cord. "All yours," he said. But he continued standing right next to the pile of papers. "It came out twice a week, Tuesdays and Fridays."

She moved forward gingerly. He was standing so that she would need to bump up against him to look at them. She reached forward awkwardly, lifting the top paper. "Friday, April third, 1970," she said. She flipped through the paper quickly in the dim light, sixteen pages, mostly advertisements. The basement was silent except for Marvin George's breathing.

"If you tell me what you're looking for, perhaps I could help you," he said, inching closer.

"I'm not completely sure, but I'll know it when I see it," she said, trying to focus on the brittle, yellowing newspapers. She laid April 3 to the side and picked up April 6. He was almost touching her. There was more room on the other side of him, but it was in a corner. She sidled past him, straining to brush against him as little as possible.

She finished skimming April 6, folded it neatly, and laid it to the side.

"You know, I usually don't let people nose around down here," he said in a low, pulsating voice, angling himself closer to her.

"I appreciate that," she said, picking up April 10 and leafing through it quickly, struggling to focus on the article.

"You should," he said, his knee bumping hers.

Her mouth went dry.

"You should show me—"

And they both heard the bell above the front door ring. They stood staring at each other, his knee touching hers.

"I—I wouldn't want you to miss any business on my account," she croaked.

"Shh," he said, his body touching up against hers.

Shelly looked him directly in the eye, only inches away, took a deep breath, and shouted as loud as she could, "We'll be right u-up!"

Marvin George leaned in against her, inhaled, and pushed himself off her.

"I'll be right back," he said.

As soon as he began climbing the stairs, Shelly grabbed the April and May bundles and chugged up the stairs, through Dickenson's Hardware—ignoring his shout of "Hey, wait a minute!"—and out onto Fourth Street. She opened the passenger door, threw the papers in, jumped into the driver's seat and sped off, coughing from the dust.

She stopped at a traffic light two blocks away and checked that she wasn't being followed. Then she looked at herself in the rearview. Then she looked down at the pile of yellowing *Ohio Valley Press* newspapers on the seat next to her. Then she looked at herself again in the rearview mirror and saw her face shining.

The light changed. Shelly found a Starbucks and sat in their parking lot with a large latte for over half an hour, leafing through edition after edition. She finished April, draining her coffee with a growing sense of dread.

And then there it was, May 1, 1970, on the back page. "Steubenville Band Draws Crowds" and under that, "To Play at Mass OSU Demonstration, Says Group Leader" with the byline "By Larry Dickenson."

There was one picture. It was the guy with the hair and the smile. Shelly's heart did a backflip with a perfect landing.

" 'Rising Star in Steubenville, by Lawrence Dickenson,' " she read into her phone. " 'It was a fine April afternoon when your *Ohio Valley Press* reporter sat down to interview a local musician who is making a lot of noise (hah hah!) in and around Steubenville. Aaron Woodwright, a senior at Steuben College—' "

"Wait," said Johnny, "I want to get Brandi on the li—"

"How do you spell Woodwright?" asked Brandi.

"I told you not to—"

"W-r-i-g-h-t," said Shelly and paused. "Can I go ahead?"

"Yes," shouted Johnny and Brandi simultaneously.

" 'Aaron Woodwright, a senior at Steuben College, has been tinkling the ivories and serenading the audience at Pedro's Cantina for two years now. His musical prowess, charming demeanor, and, last but not least, good looks have made Aaron a local celebrity, drawing crowds of students, Steubenvillians, and music (and tamale) lovers from the surrounding area.' "

"Unbelievable," said Johnny.

"Then there's a picture with the caption 'Aaron Woodwright, rising Steubenville musical star.' " She took a very deep breath. " 'But recently a new figure emerged on the scene at Pedro's, one Sam Miller, a soulful dynamo of a singer-guitarist. He seemingly appeared out of nowhere to take the stage at the regular Wednesday night Open Mic and rocked the audience onto their feet with his earthy performance. Aaron invited Sam to back him for a couple of songs, together with Kathleen Brinker, a sophomore at Steuben College.' " Shelly spelled the name. "Got that?"

"Yeah, yeah," said Brandi. "Go!"

"Unbelievable," said Johnny.

" 'Kathleen just began her career as a waitress at Pedro's Cantina, only to discover that she's now also a songbird. In the short time since Sam and Kathleen appeared, Aaron's band has been attracting Standing Room Only crowds to Pedro's, mostly of the long-haired type. Their reputation has grown quickly, and the number of fans showing up to hear them has been increasing from show to show. According to information received at OVP's desk, Aaron's band may soon be appearing at the Kiwanis club in Steubenville, which has a much larger capacity than Pedro's Cantina, in order to accommodate the growing numbers of new fans.' "

"Unbelievable," said Johnny.

" 'However,' " Shelly continued reading, " 'that is just the warm-up! Aaron has been invited, together with the entire band—himself, Sam, Kathleen, drummer Gavin Grover, and guitar wizard Vaneshi—to appear at a mass anti-Vietnam war protest demonstration at Ohio State University in Columbus on May 4.' "

"Wait," said Brandi, scribbling.

"Unbelievable," said Johnny.

"Okay, go," said Brandi.

" 'Stay tuned for updates about this exciting new group of local performers!' " Shelly concluded with a flourish.

They waited while Brandi finished writing.

"Shelly?" said Johnny.

"Yes?" she answered.

"You're a magician."

"Oh, cut it out," she smiled, her head spinning.

"You should call Gerald, read it to him."

"Oh, come on," she said. "I'll fax it to him when I get to the station."

"He'll want to hear it right now," said Johnny.

"Are you kidding?" asked Shelly.

"I haven't seen him this excited in years. He's Decapede's biggest fan."

"Fucking Wonder Woman!" said Brandi.

23

Sheek Records

– May 3, 1970 –

Bev set the departure for eight sharp Sunday morning in front of Pedro's. The streets of downtown Steubenville were empty. Even Sam showed up on time, overnight bag in hand, dragged by Kathleen, his eyes mostly closed. They all greeted each other with claps on the back and hugs, palpably excited despite the hour. Sam and Aaron managed a perfunctory hug.

Gavin was beaming, in dark brown slacks and an avocado shirt. Vaneshi was smiling to himself in his own private world, humming a cheery Indian scale up and down. He had even donned sandals for the occasion. Kathleen was radiant in bell-bottom jeans and a paisley blouse under a fringed leather vest, a red bandana over her hair, her gray eyes shining. Aaron was wearing new opaque sunglasses and trying to look cool. Sam looked like a somnambulant derelict.

"Okay, listen up," said Aaron. "We meet at the Pancake House in Zanesville at eleven o'clock. It's right on Route 40, at the corner of Graham Street. Sam, what?"

"Do we get to order whatever we want?"

Everyone booed and jeered him, as charged as school kids setting out on a spring day's excursion. Bev tooted her whistle.

"Come on, can you be serious for a minute?" Aaron said. "We meet the recording engineer at one o'clock. We only have

149

four hours in the studio, and we're going to try to cut nine songs, so we need to be really focused. We have them down pat, so we shouldn't need more than one take for each, two at the most," he said confidently. "Then we go to our motel. The demonstration is scheduled to start around noon, so we need to leave by ten. Okay?" Everyone nodded in assent except Sam, who was already shuffling towards Bev's Mustang. "Just one more thing," Aaron called.

Sam kept walking.

"Miller!" snapped Kathleen.

Sam turned wearily.

"Ta-dah!" said Bev dramatically, pulling a small camera out of her purse. "Decapede! For posterity!"

Kathleen pulled Sam to stand next to her. Bev arranged them all in front of Pedro's, with the sign above them.

"Cheese!" said Bev with her camp counselor's chipperness. One click, and Sam was shuffling back to the car. "One more!" Aaron called after him, but Sam climbed into the back seat of Bev's Mustang and stuck his tattered work boots out the window.

Bev looked at Kathleen. "I guess you're with me," she said.

"Gavin, Vaneshi, you're with me," said Aaron. "So, ah, good luck to everyone. Big day. Let's kill 'em."

"Big day, big day," they all agreed and set out to meet their destiny.

Vaneshi looked at Gavin, hiked up his Indian pajamas and folded his skinny 6'2" frame into the back seat of Aaron's Beetle.

As Kathleen was getting into the passenger seat of Bev's Mustang, she stepped on something hard. Inside the paper bag was the glass snow globe with the grinning fish. She slipped it into her big beaded bag.

And so they drove, chatting girl talk over the background of an 8-track of Blood, Sweat and Tears. Bev was in awe of Kathleen, her warmth, her earthiness, her figure, her way of drawing guys like Aaron and Sam to her. And she was nice!

As she drove, Bev checked out Sam in the rearview, dead to the world in the back seat, the length and breadth of his taut, fierce body in repose. For a fleeting moment, she pictured Kathleen and him in the act itself, that glowing, earthy Her enveloping that needy, unbridled Him. She took a deep breath, gulped guiltily, and shook her head.

Look at you, she said to herself in the mirror, *on your way to a recording studio with the coolest bunch of people you've ever met, leading them through the rolling hills of provincial Ohio, a modern Pocahontas, chatting like an equal with gorgeous Kathleen, within touching distance of that Sam Miller—I could die right now.*

In his Beetle, Aaron was recounting piano-bar stories from Pedro's for the first half hour. Then Gavin was modestly awing Aaron and Vaneshi with stories of the jazz scene in Montreal. Then Vaneshi and Gavin got into a long, technical discussion about Indian percussive instruments, from the naal and the tabla to the kanjira and the thavil and the ghungroo. Aaron turned on the radio, but the only station with decent reception was broadcasting a Baptist church service.

At the Zanesville Pancake House, two local couples were sitting at the next table, each with a baby, all with ample rolls of padding, evidence of many heaping orders of Today's Special at the Pancake House. The band couldn't hear what they were saying, but they could pick up the two men discussing Sam's and Vaneshi's long hair in a clearly uncomplimentary tone. The fatter of the two fat women looked at Gavin and said in a stage whisper, "... coming into a place like this with that ..." and she mouthed the word "Negro."

"How're your pancakes?" Kathleen asked Sam.

"Mmm," he said, nodding and chewing.

Bev hustled them outside without a second cup of coffee and paid the bill from the money Pedro had given them for expenses.

In Columbus, they pulled up in front of Smokey Joe's Bar

& Grill. The few people they had seen on the street were black, one of whom was sleeping on the stoop next door. It was not a neighborhood they would have felt comfortable walking around in at midnight. Or, in fact, even at noon on a sleepy Sunday. The door to the bar looked like the gate to Hell.

"Are you sure this is the place?" Aaron asked Bev.

She looked at Pedro's directions and nodded.

"Who's going in?" asked Kathleen.

"Gavin?" suggested Aaron.

"Me?" he responded, aghast. "Why me?"

"Well," said Aaron. "It's a Negro neighborhood. You're—you know, Negro."

"It looks rather unsavory," said Gavin.

Everyone stood looking at each other.

"What's the guy's name?" asked Sam.

"Marvin," said Bev. "He's the bartender."

He climbed out of the back seat of the Mustang and walked towards the door.

"Sam?" called Kathleen, but he just waved over his shoulder.

Everyone looked at each other for a long moment.

"He won't know what to say," said Bev. No one disputed that.

Bev hesitated for a long moment, then went chugging after him. Aaron looked at the rest of the band, who were watching him to see what he would do.

"Bev, wait," he called unenthusiastically, and followed her through the metal-barred door into the dark.

They stood just inside the door, Bev holding onto Aaron's arm. The lights were low and the air was true to the bar's name. *Mih-hih-hih-stakes, I know I've made a few* lilted from the juke box. When their eyes adjusted, they saw Sam in animated conversation with Marvin, who was pointing and gesturing, apparently giving Sam directions. They were laughing about something Aaron and Bev couldn't hear. The only other customers were a couple of men staring at them from a dark corner. Finally, the bartender handed Sam a hefty brown paper bag and two six-packs of Creston Gold. Sam stood up and gave Marvin an elaborate handshake like Aaron had seen on television between athletes. Sam grabbed the bag in one hand and the beer in the other and motioned with his head for Aaron and Bev to follow him.

They drove several blocks off the main street, deeper into a neighborhood which rarely saw white faces, and parked in front of a run-down row of shops. One bore a sign, "Sheek Records." The windows and door were boarded and covered with wire mesh. Sam banged on the door while everyone else watched from inside the two cars. He banged again. Then he found a doorbell and pressed it long and hard. Finally, a window opened on the second floor and a young man with a massive Afro orb leaned out.

"What the fuck you want, boy?"

Sam looked up. "Hey, man. Marvin sent me. Brought you something," he said, holding up the bag.

The young man smiled. "Yeah, I be down."

He led them in through a small waiting room with a single office desk. On the walls were album covers. "Something Sweet for the Lady" showed an unclothed Black woman (with an exposed nipple) licking the whipped cream off the top of a chocolate ice cream sundae. Next to that was Moms Mabley's "I Like 'Em Young."

They filed through the tiny control room into a small soundproofed studio full of chairs, microphone stands, a drum kit, an upright piano that looked like it had been through more than one bitter war, a pile of worn-out girlie magazines, and assorted refuse. Sam sniffed the room and smiled.

"Awright, y'all, I'm Junior," he said. He was wearing a shiny maroon paisley shirt with a wide, open collar and a jaunty beret. "Bathroom's by the office. Mi casa su casa. You got till five sharp."

They looked at each other.

"Hi," said Aaron, stepping forward, extending his hand.

"I'm Aaron. How are we going to work this?"

"First time in a recording studio?" asked Junior.

"No," answered Aaron. "Not—well, kind of."

"Ain't no thang," said Junior. "I press Record, you play your music."

"What about balance?"

"Yeah, thass a good thing," he said. "Okay, you, Mr. Drummer Man—"

"Gavin," said Gavin, smiling and incongruous in his pressed avocado shirt.

"Yeah," Junior smirked. "You be sure not to whop them cymbals too close to this mic. Got that?"

"What if—"

"You," Junior said, indicating Vaneshi, "you good right there. You need to turn up your volume more'n one notch, you tell me, I do it from the board. You hear?"

"Namaste," said Vaneshi.

"Yeah, right," said Junior, and turned to Kathleen. "Lady, you just sing into this here mic. Hope you sing as pretty as you look."

"Why, tha-ank you, Mr. Junior," she said and smiled.

Junior laughed, lapping it up.

"What about me?" asked Aaron.

Junior turned and looked at him. "Play yo' piano, sing into yo' mic. You think you can handle that?"

Aaron forced himself to smile.

"Sam, where dat bag of delights you brung?"

Sam pointed at Bev as he focused on peeling the crunched-up wrapper off a wad of Tootsie Roll. Junior turned and looked down at her. The big greasy brown paper bag she clutched was pushing her breasts up and out into the public domain.

"Why, thank you, li'l girl," he leered down at her.

Bev looked up at him, with his mushroom cloud Afro and his shiny dark skin. She smiled nervously. He just kept smiling down at her.

"I have a set list here," she said finally, flustered, fumbling with the paper bag.

"Now why don't you just come on in here," he said, relieving Bev of the bag and steering her towards his booth. "Wha' you all call yoselves?"

"Decapede," said Bev, as he pulled her a chair next to his, facing the band through the soundproof window.

"How you spell dat?" he asked, closing the door behind them.

Through the window, the band could see Junior unwrap something that looked like it had until recently been part of an animal with four short legs. He teased Bev, offering her a greasy glob of something. She squealed in mock horror, and they both laughed. Bev gawked while Junior chewed slowly, staring her right in the eyes, his mouth open and grinning.

They began unpacking their instruments and arranging the chairs and the mics. Gavin cleared away some of the strewn trash and unidentifiable waste matter, then folded up extra chairs. From inside a bongo drum he extracted a ball of nylon, which he unrolled to reveal a pair of fishnet pantyhose. He jammed them into the overflowing trash pail.

Through the monitor, Junior addressed them. "Awright, y'all play sumpin."

"Ready?" Aaron asked, and they all nodded at each other. Gavin called out: "One, two, one two three—" and they played Aaron's "Walk On By" all the way through, flawlessly, charged with energy, and grateful to finally be making music.

"How was that?" Aaron asked Junior.

"Thas about the whitest music ever get made in this room," said Junior over the squeaky little speaker.

Through the soundproof window, they saw Bev lean up against him and say something in his ear. He laughed and smiled broadly.

"Okay, I think we're ready to record it," said Aaron.

"You just done that," said Junior.

"I'd like to try it again, please," Aaron flashed his smile at Junior through the soundproof glass. "I thought the tempo was dragging a little in the second verse—"

But Aaron was speaking to a soundproof window.

"Next," said Junior over the studio speaker, scooching a little closer to Bev.

The session went more smoothly than anyone had expected. They ran through "Peggy Sue" and "True Love Ways" in a single take ("That boy got *mojo*," said Junior to Bev) and "Bring It On Home to Me" in three because Sam kept mixing up the verses ("Thass some shit-ass jive, man" he whispered right into Bev's ear, and she nodded rapidly in agreement).

"Cuyahoga Rising" took longer. Aaron had them repeat it several times to get the vocal balance just right. Sam sang the first verse, ominous and ghostly, goading Aaron to an uncommonly passionate performance on his verse. Kathleen in turn moved them all on the third verse, singing from the very depths of the earth. On the chorus, their three-part harmony vibrated. When they listened to the playback, they all got chills.

"Wass next?" Junior asked Bev, laying his arm on the back of her chair.

"Kathleen's songs," said Bev, looking at the play list on her knees. She could feel his hot, moist breath on her shoulder.

"Can you give me a little more piano in my headphones?" asked Aaron.

"Ah give you piano up the wazoo, man," answered Junior through the speaker. He looked at the song list. "My, my, what pretty handwriting you have," he said, reaching deep into Bev's lap to take the sheet.

Bev touched the back of his hand.

"Awright, Kathleen," Junior said through the studio speaker, "you want to stand right up next to dat microphone. Closer."

Bev's eyes widened.

"A little closer."

Bev's eyes widened a little more.

"Right there."

Bev gasped.

"And take the headphone thing offa one ear, you hear yo' band better like dat."

"Okay, thanks," said Kathleen, all business. "Can I try just a little bit to hear how it sounds before we record?"

"Iss mah pleasure," he grinned widely at Bev.

Kathleen sang a verse, getting used to hearing herself in one ear and the band in the other, and hoping the microphone wouldn't pick up the sound of her heart pounding. She took a few deep breaths and told them she was ready. Aaron began the clip-clop intro, and Kathleen lit into the take-no-shit-from-a-guy declaration of independence.

She laid back on the beat with panache and punched out, "*Oh, you cry-y,*" in a syncopated funk that made everyone smile. Then she looped a giant slur down over "*... and a-a-all you can say is it'll work out,*" and she lit up the dingy Sheek studio. As the final, jangling chord was fading, Kathleen let out a joyful titter which the mic picked up. She was afraid she'd spoiled the entire take, but everyone else thought it was charming, so they left it in.

"Whas next on that list of yo's?" asked Junior right into Bev's ear.

"'And Then—'" she gulped. "'And Then—'"

Vaneshi hit the first indelible *Bam, ba-ta-ta, Bam!, ba-ta-ta.* Aaron doubled the second one with his left hand, and Kathleen stepped up to the mic with her maracas like she'd been doing it all her life. "*Well he walked up to me, and he asked me if I wanted to dance ...*" At the end, she froze, grinning wildly, signaling everyone to wait until the final jangling chord had completely faded.

"Well, ladies and gennelmen," drawled Junior, standing up, pointing at his watch and stretching, "iss been a pleasure—"

Aaron stood up reluctantly. Vaneshi and Gavin began to unplug their gear and pack up. Kathleen returned her maracas to her bag. Sam was sitting in the corner, strumming a sweet chord progression as the others were rolling up cables.

"Sam, you want to help us?" said Aaron, but Sam continued strumming, and then humming over it a sweet, lilting melody.

"What is that?" asked Gavin.

"Oh, I like it," said Kathleen.

Sam looked at Kathleen and nodded slightly.

"A new song?" asked Aaron.

"Yeah, I been working on it for a couple of days," said Sam as he strummed. "Not sure if it's finished."

"Can we hear it?" asked Gavin.

They looked up at the booth.

"Sorry, man, I got to—" said Junior over the squeaky speaker.

Through the glass, they saw Bev tug Junior's hand off the Speak button. She pulled his ear down to her mouth to whisper, even though no one could hear. Junior's eyes opened wide, he paused, then broke into a wide grin.

"Change in schedule. Y'all can keep on doing your thang for a while," Junior's voice squeaked through the speaker. Gavin and Aaron and Vaneshi and Kathleen stared as Bev and Junior left the booth and closed the office door behind them.

Sam reached into the front pocket of his jeans and spread out the contents on a folding chair—some coins, a Zippo lighter, a pack of cigarette papers, and the last chunk of a Tootsie Roll. From his other front pocket he extracted a small tin container, which he stuck back in his pocket. Then he patted his back pocket and withdrew a crumpled copy of the Kiwanis flyer with something scrawled on the back. He flattened it out and slipped the strap of his acoustic guitar over his head. He played a few chords, made some minor tuning adjustments, and hummed a snatch of a melody. He paused to look at Kathleen. Then he began to strum a soft, wistful introduction, full of minor sixths and major sevenths.

Storm clouds are gathering way out there
Soon it's gonna rain—but I don't really care
Lying with you on the ground
Grass and sunlight all around
Nothing's gonna bring me down
Have another Creston Gold.

Lake Hope lapping at the shore
This must be the place I've been searching for
She holds me close and takes me in
To a place I've never been
Never want to leave again
Have another Creston Gold
Have another Creston Gold.

And when she holds my hand
I know she understands
Understands ...

Sometime tomorrow, we'll be far away
All we have for sure is what we have today
The world out there don't look so kind
But I don't care, 'cause love is blind
You're the one thing on my mind
Have another Creston Gold.
Have another Creston Gold.
Have another Creston Gold.

No one spoke as the final chord faded into silence. After a long moment, Kathleen went over to Sam and hugged him from behind, resting her cheek on his back.

Gavin began to clap, slowly and quietly, in hushed appreciation. Vaneshi, and then Aaron, joined in.

"Not bad, man," said Aaron in earnest admiration, "not bad at all." Despite everything, he knew a good song when he heard it.

"AABA?" spoke Vaneshi, to everyone's surprise.

"I guess," said Sam.

"It'll be too short," said Aaron, taking his bass. "Let's try AAB, Vaneshi, you solo on A, then BA. Yeah?"

"There's a pair of bongos here," suggested Gavin meekly. "I thought I'd—"

Everyone assured him that was fine.

Sam showed Aaron and Vaneshi the chord changes. They worked through it, Sam and Vaneshi sitting face to face, both of them playing acoustic guitars, giving the song a sweet, lilting color. Vaneshi played a beautiful harmonic line beginning in the second half of the verse. Aaron surprised them all by suggesting that Kathleen sing it as a counterpoint while he joined them on bass. They ran through the song a few times, respectful and subdued, till they felt they had given it a suitable shape. They ran it twice, three times.

Bev and Junior reappeared in the recording booth.

"Y'all ready?" asked Junior amicably through the speaker.

Bev smiled demurely, though her face was puffy and her cheeks were flushed.

They nailed the song in a single take, and they all felt quite buoyed.

"Closing time, gennelmens an' ladies," said a very compliant Junior.

"Well!" said Gavin.

"Well, well, well," said Aaron.

Sam acknowledged the compliment with a small nod of his head.

"But it'll be too soft for the demonstration," added Aaron.

24

Driving Upriver

– May 28, 2006 –

Shelly began the drive north back to Cleveland with Aaron's picture looking at her from the *Ohio Valley Press* on the passenger seat. On her right, the Ohio River was wide and serene, but Shelly's mind was churning. She knew Gerald Bridges was waiting for her call, but she wanted time to process the new information. She turned on the radio, tuned to WFOR, and after the song, a promo came on: "*Who Is Decapede? For a daily report on all the latest updates, tune into The Johnny Walker Show, weekdays at six o'clock,*" with "Creston Gold" of course providing the background music.

" 'Who is Decapede?' " asked a young female DJ with a breathy voice. Then she whispered conspiratorially, "And I can tell you that I just heard in the hallway here at WFOR that Johnny will have some very exciting *new information* on Decapede this evening. But don't tell anyone!"

Shelly flicked off the radio. She needed to think.

When the Ohio bent eastwards, she stopped for gas and to stretch her legs. She walked across the road to the bank of the river and stood, watching the river flow. *Aaron Woodwright,* she replayed in her mind, *leader, vocals, piano and smiles.* "Pain in the ass," *Protruding Ears had said. Well, not your most reliable witness. Kathleen Brinker, vocals and charm.* "Big gray eyes and knockers." *Gavin*

Grover, drums and class. Vaneshi, guitar and beard. Sam Miller, "soulful dynamo." "Oh, would I jump that!" Brandi had said. Pedro's Cantina. Kiwanis. May 4, 1970. I was just figuring out how to tie my shoes.

She went into the station to pay for the gas, and picked up a pocket-sized green notepad.

"Say, do you carry Creston Gold?" she asked the skinny, pimpled kid at the register.

"No, sorry," he smiled, showing off his braces. "You're the third person to ask today."

"Really?"

"Don't you listen to the radio?" he asked.

"No, why?"

"They got this mystery band on the radio that made a really cool song about Creston Gold. You haven't heard it?"

"Don't think so."

" 'Storm clouds are gathering way out there / Soon it's gonna rain— but I don't really care,' " he sang. "No?"

"Sounds nice," she said.

"That's all everyone's talking about around here. Nobody knows who they are, this band, The Decapedes. You should listen."

"Okay, I will," said Shelly pleasantly.

"That'll be $32.47 altogether."

Shelly turned north on East Liverpool Rd, thinking and thinking.

Aaron Woodwright. Kathleen Brinker. She peeked at the paper. *Gavin Grover. Sam Miller. Vaneshi.*

Aaron Woodwright.

W-o-o-d-w-r-i-g-h-t.

She watched the trees go by as she drove through the gentle hills, and thought some more. She plugged the earpiece into her BlackBerry and dialed 0.

"Information, Leslie speaking, how may I help you?" said a woman's nasal voice.

"Hi, Leslie," said Shelly, with all the personality she

could summon, "I have a name, but I have no idea where the person lives."

"What is the party's name, please?"

Shelly spelled it out for her.

"I think he—" she attempted, but realized she was talking to elevator music.

A moment later, the nasal voice returned.

"I'm sorry, we have no such listing," she said with finality.

"Wait, please don't hang up."

"Yes ma'am, how may I help you?" she said.

"You just looked in the 220 area code?"

"Yes, ma'am," she said.

"Could you possibly check some other area codes for me?"

"No ma'am, one query per call," she said.

"Tell me, Leslie, do you have access to other area codes?"

"Yes, ma'am, but you need to make a new call."

"Well, you see, Leslie, I have a name, but no idea what area code the person lives in. Is there any kind of larger data base or whatever?"

"I'm sorry, you need to make a new call for each request. Those are the regulations," she said mechanically.

"Leslie, have you heard about the band Decapede on the radio?"

There was a pause.

"Leslie?"

"Yes, ma'am. Yes, I have heard of them."

"My name is Shelly. Shelly Griffin. I'm with WFOR."

"Oh."

"I'm the one looking for this band."

There was another pause.

"Leslie?"

"Yes, ma'am. I understand." She still sounded like a machine with a nasal voice.

"And I just got the name of the band leader. Just now. Less than an hour ago. Do you know what his name is, Leslie?"

"No, ma'am."

"Aaron Woodwright. And as you can imagine, I'm very, very interested in contacting him."

Another pause.

"And I think there are a lot of other people out there who would really like me to find him."

"Just one moment, please."

Shelly listened to the elevator music for several minutes. She was about to give up hope when nasal Leslie returned.

"I do have an Aaron Woodwright in Chicago."

Shelly swerved sharply onto the shoulder of the road and stopped the car. She pulled the little green notepad from her purse.

"Okay, I'm writing it down."

"708-331-4785."

"Thank you so, so much, Leslie," said Shelly, her heart still thumping.

"You're welcome," said Leslie, her voice still nasal but now a little more human. "I hope you find him."

Shelly sat in her car on the side of the country road, her mind doing somersaults. She looked at the number again, and at the phone. She dialed, her finger jittering.

The phone rang once. Twice. Shelly hung up.

She got out of the car, walked along the side of the road, sat down and dialed again. One ring. Two. Three. With each ring, she thought her heart would explode. Four. Five. Six. Seven. Eight. A recording answered: "Please leave your name and number after the beep."

Beep.

"Hello," she said, trying to control her voice. "My name is Shelly Griffin. I'm looking for Mr. Aaron Woodwright. If this is he, I'd appreciate it if you would call me back as soon as possible. It's quite important."

Beep.

Oh, my God, she thought to herself.

The road curved gently left. Then it went straight for a while. Then it went past some stores or something. Then it curved right. Then the phone rang, with an 808 area code Shelly didn't recognize.

"Shelly?" asked a man's shrill voice.

Hawaii. Jeez. "Oh, Mr. Bridges," said Shelly. "Hi."

"I just talked to Johnny! How the hell did you find that article?"

"Well, it took some digging. It's a long story."

"Tell me, tell me!" said the sixth-richest man in the world.

"Well, sir, I have something even more interesting to share with you," she teased. "Something even Johnny doesn't know yet. Something that's actually happening right now."

"What? What? What? You're killing me!"

"I just got the telephone number for the bandleader, Aaron!" she exulted.

"Seriously?!"

"And," she said, recovering her serious voice, "I hope I didn't overstep my authority here, but—I called him."

"*And?*"

"I left a message."

"Oh my God!" His voice dropped into a somber business register. "Did you say what it's about?"

"No," she answered cautiously, "I want to make sure it's actually him. And if it is"she took a deep breath—"I don't want to spill the beans over the phone."

"Outstanding," said Mr. Gerald Bridges. "Where is he?"

"The number is in Chicago. Was I right to call him? Maybe I should have waited for Johnny to—"

"Shelly," Gerald Bridges cut her off. "Don't you wait for anyone. Do you hear me?" he asked pointedly. Shelly could picture that disconcerting stare of his.

"Yes, sir," said Shelly.

"This is your baby. You do whatever—"

Shelly's BlackBerry vibrated in her hand, and she heard

the beep of an incoming call. Area code 708.

"I think it's him!" she shouted into the phone.

"Omigod. Call m—" he shouted before she cut him off.

"Shelly Griffin speaking," she said in the most controlled voice she could muster.

"Hello," said the man's voice, with a cheerful, businesslike lilt.

"Hi," said Shelly. "Am I speaking to Aaron Woodwright?"

"Yes, you are. Hello?"

"Yes, hi. Um ... Thank you so much for calling me back." She took a deep breath. "Are you by any chance the Aaron Woodwright who was living in Steubenville, Ohio, around 1970?"

He chuckled. "Yes, I was. I mean, I am. What is this about?"

Shelly pulled over sharply and yanked hard on the hand brake.

"My name is Shelly Griffin, I'm with WFOR radio in Cleveland."

"Okay."

He sounds interested. How could he not be? "There's something I'd like to discuss with you. About those days."

"Please don't tell me that I'm the biological father you've never met," he said, laughing cautiously.

"No, no, it's nothing bad. Nothing bad at all. But it is rather complicated. I'd like to meet you to discuss it in person."

"Cleveland, you said?"

"That's right. WFOR."

"I'm in Chicago," he said.

"Yes, I know," she answered. She paused to think if her credit card would cover the ticket. "I'll come to you."

He thought for a moment. "Sure, why not? I'm pretty busy this week, but maybe sometime next week—"

"Oh, I was hoping we could do it much sooner than that."

"What were you thinking?"

"Like tomorrow?"

"It's that urgent?"

"Well, yes, in a way. It's pretty pressing."

"You've got my curiosity now, Shelly Griffin."

"I'll explain everything. So, when do you think—"

"Tomorrow's Sunday."

"Right. Whenever is convenient for you."

"You must be very anxious to talk to me." He sounded amused and intrigued, flowing with the game. Shelly thought about that smile in the photo and decided she liked him.

"I guess I must be," she said, with just a bit of flirtation.

"A hint?" he asked playfully.

"Not even a hint of a hint," she bantered back. "But I promise you, no paternity suit."

"All right, well, I'm playing golf at seven. After that, I'm free all day."

"If I can catch a morning flight, how about lunch?"

"Fine by me," said Aaron.

"I'll check flight schedules as soon as I get to a computer. I'll text you to confirm."

"Great. I'll text you the name of a restaurant."

"Wonderful," said Shelly.

"Any preferences?"

"How about Mexican?" she said.

"Fine," he said. "I know a nice place downtown, Alejandro's. There won't be much traffic on a Sunday."

They hung up. Shelly sat breathing. The BlackBerry rang again. 808.

"What? What? What did he say? Is it him?" fired Gerald.

"Y-yes!" said Shelly, laughing.

"YES!" he shouted right into Shelly's ear. "And?"

"I'm having lunch with him tomorrow. In Chicago.

The line went silent. Shelly waited.

"If I can get a flight," she said finally.

"There are flights every two hours, starting at six a.m.," said Gerald Bridges, then nothing.

"Mr. Bridges?" she asked finally.

"What are you going to say?" he asked.

"Well, I don't know! I need to meet him, to see what kind of a person he is. What if he's a Unabomber or something?"

"Outstanding, Shelly. Good thinking," said Gerald Bridges. "How did he sound?"

She shrugged. "Feet on the ground. Charming."

"But what are you aiming for? What would be your ideal scenario?"

Shelly pondered that for a moment and smiled. "Sorry, sir, if you tell a wish, it won't come true," she chuckled.

He chuckled, too, and Shelly guessed they were thinking the same thing.

"And you can cut the 'sir' stuff already. 'Gerald.' "

"If you say so," she smiled.

"Listen, when you get to the station, I'm going to have a credit card waiting for you. For any expenses you might have. Anything. And you go out and get yourself something snazzy for the trip."

"Well—" she hesitated, embarrassed.

"Shelly, I'm indecently rich. Please spend a few bucks. It's my way of saying thank you. Do you know how long it's been since I've looked forward to getting out of bed in the morning?"

"Well, thank you."

"Shelly?"

"Yes, Gerald?"

"Go get 'em, girl."

"I'll try, sir."

25

The Big Show

– May 4, 1970 –

Bev had intended to assign rooms—herself and Kathleen in one, the guys in two others, with Sam and Aaron kept apart. But Sam simply grabbed one key, grunted goodnight, took Kathleen's arm, and dragged her off. She waved back at them as she was being pulled away, smiling apologetically, and told them she'd see them in the morning.

"What am I supposed to do now?" said Bev.

"If you don't mind," Gavin said to Bev, "you and I can share a room."

Bev looked at him.

"I promise to behave honorably," he said.

The band was exhausted, physically, mentally, emotionally, and tomorrow was The Big Day, so they retired early. Only Vaneshi availed himself of the motel pool, swimming laps like a seal on diet pills.

Aaron lay on the motel bed, eyes open, with Vaneshi breathing regularly next to him. He could hear muffled voices on the other side of the motel wall. A woman. Laughing. And a man. The woman was singing. He tiptoed outside, barefoot in the chilly night air, and listened at the window. The man said something several sentences long. Aaron could pick out some words. "Second time." "Tried to." "Pathetic." And then a long, throaty laugh that he recognized as Kathleen's. He stood there trying to make out what they were saying, balancing first on one foot on the cold concrete, then on the other, but the voices had stopped. He gave up and went back to his room.

Vaneshi was still breathing regularly and Aaron's eyes were still open when it began. A small, regular thump on the wall by his head. At first he thought it might be some sort of a water pump. Or a door banging somewhere. Regular and low, pausing on occasion. And then picking up speed, what seemed like half an hour of taps in rapid succession. Right by his head. He thought he heard the woman's voice emit a high sigh, drifting downward like a floating feather. He looked at the clock. Two-thirty.

He turned on his side, staring at the black television screen, trying not to think about the performance tomorrow. The noise stopped, finally. He nestled his head into the pillow, thinking that he had done a pretty good job of leading the recording session—his first!—despite all the obstacles. *The next time*, he thought to himself, *I'll prepare a*—and then there was a loud thud on the wall, inches from his ear. Then another. Then another. Then a male's groan, the roar of a tawny-maned lion who'd just bitten through an antelope's neck. Then it stopped. He listened. Nothing but Vaneshi's breathing.

And then he heard it clearly, a woman's low moan. And again. Whack. Whack. Whack whack. Whack whack whack whack—

He got up to pee, even though he wasn't sure he needed to. He stood there waiting, listening to the buzz of the neon light till he finally had a little something to flush. He opened the bathroom door carefully. Nothing. He slipped back under the covers. Three-oh-five. Only Vanashi's breathing.

Finally, he thought to himself, and concentrated on breathing regularly. As the light slowly grew dimmer in his mind, his thoughts gathered around Kathleen. Her peasant blouse. Her shoulders. Her bare shoulders and her tipsy smile—

Thwack! His eyes opened wide. He looked at the wall next to his head. Thwack! Thwack! Thwack thwack thwack thwack—

Aaron climbed out of bed, livid. He looked at the clock. Three fifteen. He gathered up the blanket and pillow and went out to the pool, where he straightened out a plastic lounge chair to its flattest position and lay down, adjusting the blanket and pillow angrily. He found the least bumpy position and closed his eyes. The pool was well-lit, even at night. He covered his head with the blanket.

At six fifteen he slapped the mosquito in his ear with a vengeance, jarring himself awake. He dragged his blanket and pillow back to the room in the dawn's early light and slept solidly till eight o'clock, when Bev's insistent rapping on the door woke him.

They stood behind the impromptu stage in front of Hagerty Hall, nervously awaiting their turn.

Marty himself was addressing the sea of protestors milling over the entire Oval, thousands of freaks and hippies, thousands of clean-cut student types, even faculty members in ties and jackets. There were signs saying "End The War," signs saying "D Platoon Go Home," signs with the peace symbol, and even one saying "Fuck The Pigs." For the first time on the Ohio State campus, marijuana was openly wafting through the air. The atmosphere was charged, a revolutionary carnival. Someone was playing bagpipes.

"Look at them!" Marty shouted indignantly into the mic, pointing at the hundreds of uniformed soldiers gathered on a grassy knoll at the edge of the crowd, a line of trucks and troops armed with rifles and fixed bayonets. "The National Guard? On our campus! Armed forces, called in by Governor Rhodes to gag us, to silence our protest against this senseless, futile war. Armed forces sent by a government waging an illegal, unpatriotic war to quash our right to free speech, our legitimate ..."

"How many people do you think are here?" Gavin asked Bev.

"Marty said it's bigger than they expected."

They stood together, waiting their turn, Gavin and Bev and Vaneshi and Aaron and Kathleen. Gavin was holding his sticks, Vaneshi wearing his guitar.

"The First Amendment to the Constitution of the United States of America ..." A cheer spread through the crowd. " 'Congress shall make no law respecting the right of the people peaceably to assemble and to petition the Government for a redress of grievances.' So I say to you—we *all* say to you, Chief of Police Dwight W. Joseph, Governor James Rhodes, President Richard Milhous Nixon—we all say to you, GET THE FUCK OFF OUR CAMPUS!" The crowd cheered. "Get the fuck out of Vietnam!" The crowd cheered louder. "And listen to what we're saying to you," he said as he raised his fist in the air in defiance: "Hell no! We won't go!" And the chant rose, louder and louder. *Hell no! We won't go! Hell no! We won't go!*

Marty left the stage and walked over to the band, grinning.

"Wow," Bev said to him, wide-eyed.

"I told you guys there'd be a crowd."

"You were great," said Kathleen.

"This whole thing is great," said Aaron. "We're proud to be here."

"You ready? You're on after this guy."

"Oh, we're ready!" said Aaron.

A tall, bearded young man with a mop of curly hair, an Army jacket, and an American flag tie took the mic. "*I saw the best minds of my generation destroyed by madness ...*"

"Where's your boyfriend?" Aaron asked Kathleen, glaring at her bare shoulders and hoop earrings. She was even wearing lipstick for the occasion.

"Would you cut it out already?" she asked, annoyed. "I'm trying to concentrate."

"What's the matter, you didn't get enough sleep last night?"

"You can be a real asshole sometimes, you know?" she said, moving away from him.

Aaron saw Sam's back behind the stage area. He went up to him.

"Are you ready? We go on next, if it's not too much trouble for you."

Sam turned, smiling, and blew a stream of smoke right into Aaron's face. Aaron saw a hand-rolled joint in his hand.

"Are you completely crazy?" he hissed, and slapped it out of Sam's hand. "You're going to go on high?"

"If you ever touch me again," said Sam, poking his finger hard into Aaron's chest, "I will beat the living shit out of you, you pompous little prick." He picked up the joint, took another toke, and went over to join the band.

"And now," said Marty into the mic, "it's my pleasure to introduce to you a great new band, all the way from Steubenville, *Decapede!*"

To scattered applause, the band took the stage. Gavin adjusted his drum kit. Aaron played a couple of chords on the piano and spoke, "Testing, one two," into his mic. Kathleen lowered her mic stand to her height. Vaneshi ran through a quick scale. Sam plugged in his guitar, and moved his mic stand to the right.

"You're standing in front of me," said Aaron.

Sam ignored him, raising the mic stand.

"I said you're blocking me. Move over."

But Sam just kept playing with the mic stand, his back to Aaron.

Aaron got up from behind the piano and grabbed Sam's stand to move it, but Sam held it in place.

"You pathetic little shit," said Sam, "it's all about Kathleen, isn't it?"

"You're such an asshole, you don't even—"

"She sees right through you."

"Oh, fuck you."

"You just can't handle it that she wants me, not you."

Thousands of people were watching the stage, waiting for the music to begin.

Aaron's hands were trembling. He wondered if he'd be able to control them enough to play the piano.

"Oh yeah?" he hissed. "So how is it that I fucked her first?"

Sam froze. "Wha—What?"

"Oh, you don't like the idea of sloppy sec—"

Sam reared back, his right hand clenched in a fist of rage, and slammed Aaron with a hook to the side of the face that knocked him unconscious for a full two minutes.

When he woke up, Sam was gone.

Part 2

Like a Virus

26

World-Famous in Steubenville

– May 29, 2006 –

Shelly stared down at the clouds over Ohio or Indiana, trying to picture Aaron today. In the Decapede photo he was wearing dark glasses, standing tall and straight, self-confident. In the photo from the *Ohio Valley Press*, he was smiling right at the camera, the charm turned on full-blast. And that hair.

She looked out the window at the plane's wing and the clouds beyond. *"I've looked at clouds from both sides now,"* she sang to herself. *"From la-la-la to la-la-la, I really don't know clouds at all."* Boy, that's true, she thought.

She kicked off her new shoes and flexed her toes. The shoes still pinched, but Shelly had to admit that they were very pretty. And *very* expensive.

The minute Brandi had heard about Gerald's credit card, she hurried Shelly out to do some strategic shopping before the stores closed.

"Where are you taking me?"

"On corporate plastic? No-brainer. Tower City Center."

"Out of my league," Shelly had panted as they walked quickly from the station's office.

"Mine, too, but I go gawking there on my lunch hour. A

girl can dream, can't she?"

They only had two hours to completely deck her out, from toothbrush to the elegant peach suit Brandi convinced her to wear for the meeting with *Aaron Woodwright*. Shelly usually went for restrained, somber colors, but Brandi raved about how well the peach complemented her blonde hair and light complexion. So despite the color, the deeply scooped neck and the price tag, she allowed herself to be convinced. They giggled as they accoutered her with undergarments at Victoria's Secret, which was indeed quite different from J.C. Penney!

"What was the word he used?" laughed Brandi.

" 'Snazzy,' " Shelly said, and they had giggled together as they headed down towards Le Parfumerie.

Shelly protested at the $130 bottle of Chanel No. 5, but Brandi was insistent.

"I feel like you're pimping me out!" Shelly laughed, and Brandi had winked.

Shelly had to get up early for her ten o'clock flight, so she made sure to get to bed on time. But as she lay next to Brandi in the dark, her adrenaline was pumping, and she found herself recounting to Brandi the story of Marvin George and his Basement of Horrors. Shelly tittered as she told the story in graphic detail. But when she came to him rubbing up against her in the dim light of that bare bulb, she began to shiver. Brandi put her arm around her and told her that she was a true hero. They swapped stories of humiliating encounters, and Brandi admitted that catching Derek underneath Marcia took top honors. Brandi speculated, laughing softly in the dark, about Aaron's "charming demeanor and (last but not least) good looks."

"But he'd be middle-aged by now," Shelly said.

"Don't knock it till you've tried it," Brandi laughed and poked her under the covers.

Leaning against the airplane window, Shelly chortled aloud at the memory, and the prunish old lady in the seat next to her gave her a scowl. Shelly looked back out at the clouds, cuddled up with her thoughts, and tried to process the maelstrom raging in her brain.

She was early, so she asked the taxi driver, a young Asian guy with muscles and a tattoo of a barcode on his neck, to take a detour along the shore of Lake Michigan, which she had never seen before. *Looks pretty much like Lake Erie*, she mused, but the skyline of downtown Chicago reminded her that she was playing in a different league. In the back seat of the taxi, she checked her makeup and the deep neckline.

"You look fine, lady," he said, grinning at her in the rearview mirror.

"Why, thank you!" she said, beaming.

"Fancy restaurant," he said. "Big date?"

"Oh, just business," she answered, smiling nervously.

She stepped out onto the sidewalk with her new leather overnight case on wheels. She took two slow, deep breaths and pulled open the heavy wooden door. She walked into the lush, hushed restaurant and saw him there in the corner, rising as she approached.

"Hi," he said, extending his hand, "Aaron." As hard as she had tried, she was unprepared for his dazzling smile, his thick black hair handsomely specked with gray, and his strong jaw line.

"Hi," she said, shaking his hand firmly, "Shelly Griffin."

From outside her body, she saw herself standing there holding his hand, with no idea what to do next. Then she heard "I gotta pee" in the air, in her own voice, and understood that the words had somehow popped out of her mouth without bothering to go through her brain.

She smiled in embarrassment and pointed herself in the direction of what she hoped was, indeed, the restrooms. She opened the fancy water faucet just to hear the steady flow in the sink, and checked herself in the mirror. She was flushed to a rich shade of flamingo. There was nothing to do but to look herself in the eye and breathe deeply again, twice. Her makeup was fine. She tugged her scooped neckline up a tad. Then tugged it back down. Then breathed once more, turned off the water, and walked back to the table with all the confidence she could summon.

"Well!" she said.

"Well!" he responded in kind. "You came straight from the airport?"

"Yes, straight here."

"It must be very important. I admit you've piqued my curiosity."

"I can imagine." Her breathing seemed to be functioning. "So. Just to make sure: Your name is Aaron Woodwright, and you were living in Steubenville in 1970?"

"That's right. It was my last year at Steuben College."

"And you play piano?"

"Well," he said, smiling quizzically, "yes, a bit."

Shelly nodded, drew a photocopy of the newspaper article from her bag, and laid it on the table in front of him.

He put on his reading glasses.

" 'Pedro's Cantina,' " he murmured, shaking his head in wonder. " 'Musical prowess, charming demeanor, and, last but not least, good looks,' " he read aloud, chuckling ironically at the compliments. "It was worth coming here just for that."

" 'Sam Miller, soulful dynamo,' " he read, in a tone Shelly couldn't quite put her finger on. "Kathleen Brinker," he mouthed slowly, with warmth. "Gavin Grover! Oh, boy. Vaneshi? My gosh, Shelly, where in hell did this come from?"

"That's you?"

"Oh yes, that's me, all right. From a different life, but—yes."

"Well, well," she smiled coyly, buoyed by his tickled consternation as he read the article again more carefully.

"I mean, we had a pretty enthusiastic little following at

the Kiwanis club there for a while, but I didn't expect a fan club to come crawling out of the wall almost forty years later!" He shook his head, staring at the article. "Can I keep this?"

"Of course. So you have no idea why I'm here?"

"No idea whatsoever. Please."

"I can't believe I'm actually sitting here talking to you."

He made a gesture of amused bewilderment.

"I—I have no idea how to tell this in an organized way. So I'm just going to start at the beginning, if that's okay with you."

"You have my full attention."

"Would you like to order?" asked the waitress.

"Yes?" Aaron asked Shelly.

"Sure," she said, studying the menu.

"Ah," he said after a moment, wagging his finger at her. "Mexican! Cute, cute."

She smiled, and they placed their orders.

"So. From the beginning," he said.

"I work for a law firm in a small town an hour from Cleveland."

"I thought you said you're from a radio station."

"Well, I am. Aaron," she said forthrightly, "this is just such a ridiculously absurd story that you're just going to have to suspend your disbelief for a few minutes."

"Okay," he said, enjoying the mystery.

"But I promise you, it's all true."

And Shelly began to recount the saga. The dissolution of Bauer's Brewery. Allie Bauer's long struggle. Discovering 'Creston Gold' on YouTube.

"Oh, jeez, I haven't thought of that song in—in, well, almost forty years! '*Nothing's gonna bring me down / Pass me another Creston Gold,*'" he sang softly. "What's the matter?"

She motioned to him that everything was fine, and sipped her water.

"Do I sing that badly?" he asked.

"Wait till you hear the rest of the story, you'll understand."

"But how did the song get on YouTube?"

"I have no idea! We're still working on that." She slowly drew another sheet of paper from her bag and laid it in front of him. The photo of Decapede.

"Oh, my God," he said quietly. "I've never seen this before."

"It's Decapede?"

"Sure," he said, studying it closely. "Me. Kathleen. Gavin. Vaneshi. Miller."

Shelly shivered, and began to tell him about her first meeting with Johnny Walker—leaving out the part about the extra-legal pretense—and about his tribute to the brewery, about the song on his show, about the response at the station, and about the 'Who Is Decapede?' mania sweeping Northwest Ohio.

"When was this?" he asked.

"If I tell you, you won't believe me," she smiled.

"That's okay, I don't believe anything you've told me up till now," he smiled back.

"Johnny's original Creston Gold tribute show was"—she paused for dramatic effect—"exactly one week ago."

"All week he's been playing the song?"

She nodded, grinning. "And people keep calling, asking for more."

"Un-fucking-believable," he said, shaking his head and staring at the picture.

I could die right now, Shelly thought to herself. *It's never going to get any better than this.*

"Who ordered the carne asada?" asked the waitress.

"You're right, I don't believe you. That's for the young lady." He gave his head a shake, as if dazed. "Could we see the wine menu, please?"

"So, Mr. Woodwright—'Who Is Decapede?' "

"Where the heck do I start?"

"I've got a million and a half questions."

"I'm afraid the facts aren't quite so glamorous. We were a

few college students who happened to cross paths. We played some pretty good music together, and some locals got excited. But we were never even really a band. We only played together for a short while. We hardly even knew each other."

"But you made a recording and everything—"

"Gosh, I forgot that. Yes, that's right, we were in a studio. In Columbus." Aaron was speaking slowly, exhuming long-buried memories. "We were on our way to play at the demonstration at Ohio State, but something happened." He shook his head. "Kent State. It was the day of Kent State."

"The newspaper article makes you guys sound like Ohio Valley's Beatles."

"Oh, we were quite a local hit. World-famous in Steubenville."

"So, 'Who Is Decapede?' "

"That's it, see, the name, Decapede? No one even knew the name back then. I hardly remember it. It was just 'Aaron's band,' with Kathleen and Miller and a couple of other guys. I don't even remember where the name came from. But we didn't think of ourselves as 'Decapede.' We didn't even really think of ourselves as a band."

"But you were. You played gigs, you made a recording. You must have had other songs that you played."

"Oh, yeah. We were actually pretty good, all things considered. But the whole life of the band didn't last any longer than your story. A few months, maybe."

" 'Creston Gold,' how did that happen?"

"Oh, that was Miller's song. I don't know, he just came in with it one day. I might have done the arrangement. Geez, it's been so long. Who can remember?"

The waitress poured their wine.

"Well, to Decapede," said Aaron, raising his glass.

"To Decapede," said Shelly, and their glasses made a delicate *ping*.

As they ate, Aaron began to recount the history of the legendary Decapede, with Shelly recording him on the fancy little voice recorder Brandi had insisted she buy. He told her how he'd played at Pedro's for pocket money, and how he'd convinced the pretty waitress to sing.

"I didn't even know her name," he recalled, smiling at the memory. "I used to call her New Waitress."

"You had never heard her sing?"

He shook his head. "She just looked like a singer," he said, looking tenderly at the picture. Aaron looked at Shelly playfully. "And I guess I was trying to make an impression. I just had a gut feeling, called her up on stage."

"I get the picture," she winked knowingly.

"She was a very pretty girl, Kathleen," he said fondly.

"Were you two a couple?"

"Oh, for a little while. But you know, the '60s," he said, smiling to himself. She could see him conjuring up images of the womanly girl with the pageboy.

"Go ahead."

"So Kathleen was helping me out, singing harmonies and all. And then, one night this stranger walked in, Miller. Wow, Sam fucking Miller."

"What?"

"He was a real case. I mean, he was talented as hell, I'll give him that. As a singer, as a songwriter. But he was crazy. You couldn't really communicate with him. You'd say something, and his eyes would just be jumping all around, and then he'd laugh this rough laugh of his, and you never knew what he heard, what he was thinking. Now that I think back on him, I guess he was, you know, on the spectrum."

"So how did it work, the two of you together in a band?"

"All we did was argue, the two of us. It would be me taking responsibility for everything and him screwing around and doing whatever came into that head of his. So, yeah, I was always shouting at him. I mean, someone had to, if you're going to have a band."

"So why did you put up with it?" she asked, sipping her wine.

Aaron paused for a moment, unpacking dusty memories, and took a sip of his wine.

"He was just so damn good," said Aaron. "When I could get him to focus—it was like a gift to be playing with him."

"Were he and Kathleen together at any time?"

"Gee, I don't remember. They might have been, for a little while. It's been a long time. How's your food?"

"Mmm, fabulous," she said. "We don't have restaurants like this in Warren."

"That's just south of Cleveland, right?"

"About an hour. Anyway, go ahead. Tell me about how the band got together."

"Well, I had been playing at Pedro's for a while, and I'd built up a following. And then I got Kathleen to sing with me. And then Sam came along and added his stuff. And people really liked us. We played some at Pedro's—" He stopped and picked up the photo of Decapede. "That's Pedro's," he pointed. "The picture was taken in front of Pedro's Cantina. See, that's the front window of the café."

"What was the occasion?"

He paused, dredging through his memories. "Sorry, I can't remember. Maybe it will come to me."

"That's okay. Anyway, the rest of the band?"

"At some point we were getting popular, and I decided to ramp it up. We were singing acoustic stuff, three-part harmony, Kathleen and Sam and I. But I guess I wanted to give it a kick. So I added a guitarist, Vaneshi."

"Tell me about him."

"Ta-all, skinny guy. A regular stringbean. With a long, long beard. Wore this white robe all the time, nothing else. Not even underwear," he smiled. "Au natural. And barefoot. And he didn't shower too often. Hardly talked, but when he did, it was very softly, like a monk. Except with a Brooklyn accent. He'd just sit in a corner, playing scales all the time. I mean, he was a magician on the guitar. Another glass?"

"Whoa, are you trying to get me drunk here?"

"If this isn't cause for celebration, what is?"

"You have a point there, Mr. Aaron Woodwright," she said, allowing him to fill her glass. "I can't believe I actually found you."

"I can't believe someone was bothering to look for me."

"Tell me about Gavin."

"Ah, Gavin was a sweetheart. Gentle, innocent. Everyone loved Gavin. Great drummer. Great drummer."

Shelly watched him walking through his memories of Steubenville, 1970. He was awfully handsome in a mature, masculine way. She guessed that there wouldn't have been many coeds who could resist him back then.

"So the five of you were playing at Pedro's—"

"And the place would be full every time we played," he said, speaking slowly, reconstructing the memories piece by piece. "The place was packed. My regulars, plus some of the crowd that Miller attracted. So Pedro moved us—"

"Pedro?"

"The guy who owned the beer joint. I guess you'd call him our patron."

"Mexican?"

"Nah, it was all a put-on."

"Do you remember his real name?"

"It's been a lot of years," he said, shaking his head.

"So he moved you—?"

"Right, to this hall at the Kiwanis, selling tickets and everything. And more and more people kept coming to see us. There were some crazy nights there." He took another bite and chewed, ruminating on the Kiwanis club. "I guess we really were kind of a local phenomenon."

"And that's when this article was written?"

"Right." He stopped to think. "I went with Beaver down to the newspaper office on 4th Street—"

"Who's Beaver?"

186

"Oh. What was her name? Ah—Bev! She was this girl who hung around with us. Kind of like a groupie, I guess. A bit of a pest, actually. Always chattering. But then when we started getting really popular, and playing more, she sort of attached herself to us."

"Bev what?"

"Oh, jeez, Shelly. It's been so many years. She was really short." He chuckled to himself. "God, I haven't thought of her in—in almost forty years."

"So, you had this gig in Columbus—" she said, drawing him back to his narrative.

"Right. We were playing at the Kiwanis, and people were getting pretty excited about the band, so we got invited to play at this big anti-war demonstration. In Columbus. That's where we made the recordings."

"Tell me about that," she said, sipping her wine. *The annals of Decapede*, she thought, *as told by Aaron Woodwright himself. My gosh. Johnny's going to go crazy. And Gerald?*

He chewed, trying to reconstruct the events.

"Pedro got us into a studio. Just for a few hours. This crazy place in Columbus, really sleazy."

"That's when you recorded 'Creston Gold'?"

"Right. And a few other songs."

"There are more recordings?" she asked, choking on her food. "You okay?"

She nodded, coughing, taking a drink of wine. Her eyes were teared. She took another sip.

"Yeah, about half a dozen. 'Walk On By,' that was my big song. 'Peggy Sue.' That was Sam's. Gee, what else was there? 'Different Drum,' that was Kathleen's feature. Ah, and 'Cuyahoga Rising.' That one was really good."

"I don't know that song."

"I think Miller pinched it from somewhere, I'm not really sure."

"Where are they, these recordings?" she asked, her pulse

pumping. "Do you have them?"

"No idea. I never even heard them."

"So how did 'Creston Gold' get onto YouTube?" she said, puzzled.

He shook his head. "No idea. After Kent State, I don't think we ever met up again."

"What do you mean?"

"You've heard of the Kent State shootings?"

"Of course."

"You can imagine, it was a big deal, the National Guard shooting students. Anyway, they closed down all the schools right away. Even Steuben College. Everybody went home. It was my last year there, so I left and never went back."

"Are you still in contact with any of them?" she asked, hoping against hope.

"Nah," he said. "We just all went our own ways, I guess. I don't remember."

They ate in silence as he ruminated over the dross of his memories.

"Help me kill the bottle?" he asked.

"Just a drop," she said.

She saw him turning something over in his mind.

"What?" she asked him.

He motioned to her to let him think. After a few moments, he spoke.

"I got a Christmas card," he said, carefully unwrapping the memory.

"From whom?" she asked quietly, urging him without interfering with his reverie.

"From Gavin. Oh, gosh, it must be—ten, fifteen years ago. At least."

She saw the wheels turning and waited patiently. She checked the voice recorder to make sure that history was being documented.

"He was living somewhere weird. Wait a minute."

Shelly felt like she should be holding her breath. After an agonizing long moment, he looked up and opened his eyes wide.

"Ah—ah—"

"What?"

"Wait. Wait, I got it," he said, furrowing his brow. And then he began to sing to himself, "*Bye-bye, Miss American Pie ...*"

"Aaron?"

"Mason City."

"What?"

"Mason City, Iowa," he pronounced as if he had decrypted the Rosetta Stone.

"Mason City, Iowa?"

"That's where he was living."

"How exactly is that connected to 'American Pie'?" she asked.

"Buddy Holly."

"I'm sorry?"

"Buddy Holly, the singer?"

"Yes?"

" 'American Pie'?"

She shrugged, wondering if it was the wine talking.

"Mason City, Iowa. That's where Buddy Holly crashed. Where he was killed."

"I'm sorry?"

"Bye-bye, Miss American Pie. The day the music died."

"In Mason City, Iowa?"

"Right. That's where Gavin was living."

"And you remember that because?"

"Buddy Holly! Who doesn't remember where Buddy Holly was taken from us?" he smiled, proud of his archaeological skills.

"Mason City, Iowa?" she repeated so loudly that the people at the next table turned to look.

Aaron pulled back in mock fright.

Shelly pulled her cell phone from her back and dialed 114. "Hi. I'd like a number for Mason City, Iowa," she said slowly and clearly. "Gavin Grover." She pulled her green notebook and a pen from her bag and wrote down a ten-digit number.

"Seems he still lives in there," she said, glowing with pride and excitement.

They looked at each other without speaking and smiled. Shelly dialed and handed him the phone.

"Hi, Gavin? I'm guessing you don't recognize my voice. It's Aaron Woodwright. Yeah, yeah, I'm fine, how're you? I don't know, somehow I remembered. Right, Buddy Holly. Listen. Umm ... I need to talk to you. No, everything's fine. It's just a story that's not exactly for the phone. I was wondering if we could meet. Chicago." He listened. "Ah," he said, deflating. "Okay, just one second," he said, covering the mouthpiece and speaking disappointedly. "He's going to Colorado tomorrow on a skiing trip for three weeks."

Shelly thought for a moment. "What time is he leaving?" she said as if it were the most natural question in the world.

"What time are you leaving? One in the afternoon."

He looked at Shelly. Shelly looked at him and nodded, and they both laughed.

"Are you free for brunch? Okay. No, no, nothing bad. It's just—I can't explain it over the phone. Let me see if it's doable. I'll call you back, okay? Yes, it would be great. Talk to you real soon."

Shelly and Aaron looked at each other.

"It's almost two o'clock," said Shelly.

"Could I have the check, please?" Aaron asked the waitress.

"I'll take care of it," said Shelly.

"No," said Aaron, "it's my pleasure."

"No," said Shelly firmly, pulling Gerald Bridges' credit card from her wallet, "it's my business."

27

White Terry-Cloth Robes

– May 29, 2006 –

As they drove to the airport in Aaron's car, he dialed a number.

"Hi, Julie, sorry to bother you on the weekend. I was called out of town. Can you please cancel all my appointments for tomorrow? Thanks. I'll be back on Tuesday. Call me if there's anything urgent." He hung up.

"Just like that?" Shelly asked.

"Just like that. The business pretty much runs itself already."

"I'm impressed. Family?"

"Never been my thing. You?"

"Free as a bird," Shelly smiled, pushing out of her mind all the unanswered calls from her father.

The man at the counter told them it was a two-hour flight to the nearest airport, in Rochester, Minnesota, but there weren't any flights till the next day. And Mason City was a six-hour drive.

"How much would it cost to charter a plane?" she asked the man nonchalantly.

"Just like that?" Aaron asked.

"Don't ask," answered Shelly. "You wouldn't believe me."

#

At five o'clock, Shelly and Aaron boarded the little Cessna. She held his hand very tightly during take-off but relaxed once they were airborne. As the tiny plane flew over the endless cornfields of Illinois and Iowa, they gazed silently out at the light fading over the flat landscape, each from his own window, each content to process all that had transpired.

Derek was pounding on her office door, but she was shouting at him, refusing to let him in, when the entire building jolted as the plane jarred against the runway. She looked at Aaron and saw the wet spot of drool she had left on his jacket shoulder.

"Oh, shit, I'm sorry!" she said over the din of the engine, trying futilely to wipe away the splotch with her fingers.

"That's okay," he smiled. "I enjoyed it."

Shelly looked at herself. The neckline of her dress had crept down way too far. She adjusted herself demurely and tried to push aside the cobwebs from the edges of her mind.

"Was I asleep long?"

"For about three hundred miles. You looked bushed. You've earned it."

"Mmmm," she said, stretching and smiling.

They landed at the tiny Mason City airport—a landing strip with an office—caught a cab, and asked the driver to stop at a Walmart so Aaron could pick up a toothbrush and a few other necessities.

They checked into a Hampton Inn on the corporate credit card—two rooms, after a moment's awkwardness, and agreed to meet up in an hour. After showering, Shelly lay down on her bed in her white terry-cloth robe to call Brandi.

"Where are you?" shouted Brandi.

"You won't believe me," said Shelly.

"Spill it!"

"Mason City, Iowa." She paused. "I flew here in a teeny

private plane." Pause. "With Aaron Woodwright, who is in the room next door."

"NO FUCKING WAY!"

Shelly laughed and dictated the story to her in brief, punctuated only by Brandi's shrieks of excitement.

"What's he like?"

"Who, Aaron?"

" 'Who, Aaron?' " echoed Brandi, mocking her. "What's he like?"

"Oh, he's very nice. He seems as befuddled by this whole thing as I am."

"Cut the crap. What does he look like?"

Shelly giggled. "Think Robert Redford, just with dark hair. Tall, confident."

"You going to bang him?"

"Brandi!"

"Brandi what?"

"I gotta go. I'll call you when I get a chance."

"Do it for WFOR!" urged Brandi.

Shelly glanced at the emails on her laptop, but there was nothing more urgent than several reminders from Gerald Bridges to keep him up-to-date. Missed Calls. Allie Bauer. Shelly looked at her watch. Too late to call her back. Derek. "Revenge," she smirked to herself, "is a dish best served cold." Delete Contact! Dad, four missed calls. "Kidnapped by aliens," she thumbed, then deleted and wrote, "All fine, will be in touch." Gerald Bridges, seven missed calls. Shelly sighed and dialed the 808 number.

He answered in the middle of the first ring. "Where are you? What's been going on? Johnny got a message that you were flying to Iowa? Did you meet him? Is he—"

"Gerald!" said Shelly sternly. "I have a lot to tell and not much time."

Gerald stopped talking.

Shelly told him the story in brief, rebuffing his repeated

requests for detail, patiently promising to tell him "the *whole* story." "And tomorrow we're meeting Gavin for brunch."

There was silence on the line.

"At his house." No response. "Gerald?"

"I was just bowing down to you."

"Stop it, sir," she said, blushing.

"That article, Shelly? You should have heard Johnny. He read it on the air, word for word, slowly. And the way he told your story? I swear, Shelly, it was like Homer reciting the Odyssey. Live!"

This bed, she noted, *is very comfortable. And so is this robe.*

"Johnny's right. Do you know what he calls you? A sorceress."

"I'm a very lucky country hick, sir."

"Shelly?"

"Yes, sir? Gerald?"

"What the hell is going on here?"

"I don't know, sir. I'm about as clueless as you are. I'm just going through the motions."

"Oh, give me a break."

"Let's see what Gavin's like."

"All right," he said, "but tomorrow, I want to talk to you and Johnny as soon as you get back to Cleveland. Call me from the station."

"Sir, there is one thing I need to talk to you about," said Shelly, lifting herself up off the bed and padding over to an armchair by the window. "I'm in Mason City, Iowa, and when I don't show up for work tomorrow morning, I'm going to be declared AWOL."

"Of course," said Gerald Bridges, "dumb me, not thinking of that. Can you send me your father's phone number on ICQ?"

"If you don't mind me asking—what are you going to do?"

"I'll lease you."

"The Colonel's not going to like that. He's very dependent on me."

"I'll make it worth his while."

"He's *very* dependent on me."

"I'll make him an offer he can't refuse," cackled Gerald.

"Can I make a suggestion, sir?"

"Only if you stop calling me 'sir.' "

"Yes, sir," she chuckled. "How about if I bring him to the meeting?"

"Shelly, this is your show. Whatever you say."

Did I just hear that? Shelly asked herself.

"Shelly, I do have one favor to ask of you," he asked breathlessly, an octave higher. "Do you think it would be possible for me to talk to Aaron?" There was a knock at the door. "There's so many things I want—"

Shelly jumped up and shuffled quickly to open, her finger on her lips.

"I'm so sorry, Gerald," she said in utter earnest. "I'm sure he'd love to talk to you, but he was just so bushed from the trip that he went right to bed. Which is where I—"

"I get it, I get it," said Gerald. "You keep in touch now, okay?"

"I promise," she sang sweetly as she closed the door softly behind Aaron. "I'll call you as soon as there's anything to tell. Nighty-night now."

"Who was that?" Aaron asked.

She looked at him and sighed.

"Dr. Pettiford speaking," said Bev.

"It's me," Bev's sister Arlene shouted over the screams of a hysterical six-year-old. "We have an emergency. Ashley jammed her little finger really badly at soccer. I'm afraid it might be broken."

Bev held the phone away from her ear. "Can she move it?"

"Can you wiggle it for me, honey?" she asked her daughter. "Yes, but she says it really hurts."

"Put it under cold water," said Bev. "It's nothing."

"Okay, thanks," said Arlene. "So, did you talk to the asshole?"

"I tried, but you know how that goes."

"He knew about it?"

"He figured it out two weeks ago. He told me that Robbie promised him he'd never do it again. Can you believe that? He *promised*."

"What did you say?"

"You should have heard me. I was vicious," Bev said lividly, the sisters laughing. " 'He *promised*,' Lenny says to me. Can you believe that? The schmuck. So I said to him, 'And what exactly was the punishment? The sanction? The consequence? Did you understand perhaps one of those words? Our son is selling drugs in school, and he *promised* to *stop*? How sweet. Really, that just brings tears to my eyes.' He asked if I'd be willing to meet with him somewhere to discuss it calmly. I told him when his nuts turn to rhinestones. Arghh!"

"Bev, Robbie's a special kid."

"He's a drug pusher!" she said, laughing through her misery.

"He gave his friends some pills."

"Sold them."

"Do you know that?"

"Not for sure," she admitted.

"Look, I'm not making light of it. But keep it in perspective. He did something wrong, but he's a good kid, Bev. You know that. And he's so talented, with that electronic stuff he does—"

"Arlene, right now I don't give a fuck about his music and his computers," she said, her fury turning to frustration, almost to tears. "I'm afraid he's going to get into serious trouble. He's not far from it."

"So what happened with the principal? Did they expel him?"

"No. His asshole father turned on the charm and got it

lowered to a week's suspension. God, I *hate* that school."

"Bev, it's one of the best schools in Los Angeles County."

"That's where he turned into this, this, *thing* with a hoodie over his headphones and slumped over and not coming out of his room for days at a time."

"You're not overreacting?"

"My son is peddling Percocet at school, and you say I'm overreacting?"

A child screamed in the background.

"Bev, I'm sorry, I gotta go, Ashley's driving me crazy here."

"Okay, have a good night."

"Oh, wait, hey, listen. I saw something on Yahoo! What was the name of that band you ran around with in college?"

"Wow. Where did *that* come from?"

"What were they called?"

"Decapede," said Bev, smiling at the memory. "Why?"

"Look them up on YouTube. Okay, Ashley, I'm coming, you're not going to die from a sprained finger!"

Dr. Beverly Pettiford typed in the band's name and stared at the picture she had taken thirty-six years earlier. Then she heard the voice of Sam Miller, singing *"Storm clouds are gathering way out there / Soon it's gonna rain—but I don't really care,"* with Kathleen singing harmony.

6583 hits. She walked to the foot of the stairs.

"Robbie! Get! *Down! Here!*"

"You just hung up on Gerald Bridges?" asked Aaron.

"He can get a little tiresome at times," Shelly sighed. "Overenthusiastic."

They were sitting in the two armchairs in her room, drinking mini-bar wine from bathroom glasses.

"Gerald Bridges sits around waiting for your phone call."

"He wanted to talk to you. You should thank me. He would have kept you for hours."

Aaron just shook his head in disbelief.

"What do you know about him?" Shelly asked.

"Other than the sex tape? Just what I read in *Business Week* and *Forbes*," said Aaron. "That he made his money in LBOs. You know what they are?"

"I may be blonde, but I work in a law office," she said.

"That he's one cutthroat sonofabitch. People call him the Barracuda of Buyouts." He sipped his wine. "And here he is, eating out of your hand like a tame lion."

"I don't know. One minute he's this serious, sharp businessman, the next he's a whiney little fangirl with Decapede's picture inside a pink heart." She sipped her wine. "He's very insecure. But he sure loves him some Decapede."

Aaron stared at the floor, shaking his head. "Gerald fucking Bridges."

Shelly could feel the wine warming the outer perimeter of her brain. "So, Mr. Woodwright, what do you do when you're not busy being a musical legend?"

"Ha," he scoffed, "the most obscure legend in the history of legends."

"You know, that's already not true. A lot of people are waiting to hear this story. All over Northeast Ohio."

"I don't know, it's not even a story, is it?"

"It sure is. You can't imagine what kind of commotion is going on around 'Who Is Decapede?' The station is getting dozens and dozens of calls every day. When they hear about you—well, I think that might just generate a whole shitload of interest."

"Seriously?"

"You should hear the way Johnny describes the band. He's so good with words. I heard him say on one of his shows that Decapede 'strikes a resonant chord on the acoustic strings of our hearts.' "

"Jeez."

"And no one really believed I would actually find someone from the band."

"Two someones."

"Two someones. Do you know what he called me, Gerald Bridges?" she confided. "A *sorceress*."

Aaron reached across the little table that separated them and squeezed her hand.

"Do you think there's any chance that Gavin is in contact with any of the others?" she asked.

"Hard for me to believe. We hardly knew each other," said Aaron. "But who knows? You're the sorceress here."

"Why, how sweet of you, Mr. Woodwright," she said, "I don't think anyone has ever called me a sorceress before."

He smiled a very broad and very handsome smile and refilled the bathroom glasses.

"Seriously, what do you do in real life?" she asked.

"I own a wholesale hardware company. Woodwright Tools and Supplies. Very romantic."

"Big business?"

"I employ about thirty people. Distribute over most of the Midwest."

"So you're doing pretty well."

"I can't complain. I'm comfortable."

"You said no family? Never been married?"

"Twice, both short-lived. Last one ended eight years ago."

"You can just take off like this?"

"The only ones who will miss me are my golf partners," said the debonair bachelor.

"So you're a pretty independent guy," she said, sipping her wine.

"You could say that. I've worked hard. Made some money. That's it."

"Do you still play?"

"For a bunch of years I used to play and sing at a cocktail lounge on Wednesday nights."

"Why'd you stop?"

"I can't stay up that late anymore," he chuckled. His headful of rich, peppered hair was still wet from his shower. In his white terry-cloth robe, he did look very comfortable. "What about you?"

"Not much to tell. I work in my father's law firm. In exotic Warren, Ohio."

"What's that like?"

"Think Mason City, a thousand miles to the east."

"No significant other?"

Shelly thought of Derek for a nanosecond and looked at this ridiculously handsome guy with that smile and that hair still damp from the shower, next to a lush double bed, both of them in robes with little or nothing underneath, sipping wine and stone-drunk on adrenaline.

"Not even an insignificant other. Work."

"So how did all this happen?"

"Damned if I know," she said, shaking her head and smiling.

"Quite a trip."

"Quite a trip. Beyond my wildest imagination."

"So tell me, Ms Griffin—"

"Yes, Mr. Woodwright?"

"What's going on here?"

"What do you mean?"

"Where is this all going?"

"No one knows. There's all this interest at the station. And now I actually found you. And Gavin. No one knows where it's going."

"And if the interest keeps growing? Who makes the decisions?"

She pondered the question.

"I guess I do."

"You know, I've had a pretty successful career in the world of nuts and bolts, but I feel like I'm watching you pull a sword from a stone."

Shelly flushed. "Oh, cut it out."

"Shelly, you do realize that you're talking about potentially a very big operation here? With a lot of money involved, potentially. A *lot* of money. Fame. And God knows what else."

She nodded.

"Are you up to this?" he asked, dazed.

"I don't know!" she said jokingly, but seriously.

They sat in silence for a long moment.

"Shelly?"

"Yeah?"

"This is a good thing."

She nodded.

"Shelly?"

"Yeah?"

"What's your dream?"

"What do you mean?"

"Your dream for Decapede. Your ultimate, ultimate dream. The whole world is chasing you, throwing money at you, private planes, like your finger is a magic wand. Ms Griffin, it seems you can do anything that you want in the whole wide world. What do you want?"

She looked at the carpet, thinking. Finally, she raised her eyes.

"I don't know. No one's ever asked me that before in my whole life."

Aaron Woodwright looked at her long and deeply.

Well, we wouldn't want to disappoint Brandi, would we?

"Mmm," she said, stretching and smiling.

"Mmm, yourself," said Aaron, cuddling up against her under the covers.

"What time is it?"

"Eight twenty," he said, his mouth muffled against the crook of her neck.

"We should get up," she said.

"We have time," he said, pulling her to him.

Afterward, they lay on their backs, staring at the crinkles

in the plaster of the white ceiling.

"I know," she said.

"What?" he asked.

"I want to reunite the band."

28

Shelly's Baby

– May 30, 2006 –

"Gavin!"

"Aaron!"

Shelly watched them shake right hands, clap shoulders with the left hand, hesitate awkwardly, then give each other a should-we-shouldn't-we hug. *Man-dance*, she thought. A small suitcase was standing next to the door.

"Gavin, this is Shelly Griffin."

"Hi, Shelly," he greeted her warmly. "Please, come in."

Gavin led them through the lovely living room, all restrained beige garnished with dark greens. Shelly saw a large framed Andy Warhol poster of Judy Garland as they passed through to the veranda, where a tastefully set table was waiting for them with an offering of cheeses, crackers, and sliced fruit.

"I really appreciate your agreeing to see us," said Shelly.

"I'm so sorry I don't have more time. I'm being picked up in an hour."

"I understand. Really, I appreciate it."

"You didn't give me much time to prepare," he said apologetically. "The lemonade is fresh, from my own tree there. Be careful," he said naughtily, "it's got a little ginger-flavored vodka in it. I hope it's not too early."

"Oh, we're living on the wild side here, Gavin," said Aaron.

"So what the heck brings you to Mason City, Iowa, of all the places in the world?"

"My partner, Dale, got a job here. As a food engineer for Jell-O. And I followed. I've been teaching math at a junior college nearby."

"Sounds riveting," Aaron said.

"It was supposed to be for just a year or two," said Gavin with thinly veiled discontent. "But somehow it's turned into forever. But what in heaven's name brings you two here?"

Aaron and Shelly exchanged looks and laughed.

"What?" asked Gavin.

"I'm going to record this, okay?" Shelly asked.

Gavin's eyes shifted from Shelly to Aaron and back. They were both smiling giddily.

Shelly laid the article from the *Ohio Valley Press* on the table. Gavin read it carefully.

"Okay," he said guardedly.

Then Shelly laid the picture in front of him.

"Oh my gosh," he said, agape. "I've never seen this before."

Shelly and Aaron exchanged knowing smiles.

"Bev took this," said Gavin.

"*What?*" Shelly exclaimed, clapping her hands and rising an inch off the white wicker chair. "Do you remember her last name?"

Gavin shrugged. "Sorry, just 'Bev.' She was the band's, ah—" He looked to Aaron for help. " 'Coordinator,' would you call her?"

"Pest."

"Oh, Aaron, she was a nice girl."

"Yeah," he admitted. "Coordinator. Drill sergeant. Camp counselor," he offered.

"Do you remember when the picture was taken?" Shelly asked, her heart thumping.

"Yes, it was the day we traveled to Columbus, to the recording studio. And the demonstration. Bev took it just before we set out."

"Okay," said Aaron, trying to reconstruct that morning in his mind.

"Oh, my!" Gavin said, gazing at the picture. "Whew," he said with a low whistle, "Sam Miller." Then he brightened. "Kathleen. What a sweetie."

Shelly and Aaron smiled.

"Aaron Woodwright! Gosh, you were handsome!" said Gavin, punching him gently on the shoulder.

"What do you mean 'were'?" grinned Aaron.

"Vaneshi," he said, pleased to recall the name. "That's so strange. I ran into him once."

"What?" they exclaimed simultaneously.

"In New York City. Dale and I took a trip to celebrate my forty-fifth birthday and to see some shows. That would have been 1993. Thirteen years ago." He spoke slowly, blowing dust off the events. "Dale wanted to buy a camera. So we went to this store people told us about. On 9th Avenue. Midtown. Big store."

"*And?*" Shelly asked, realizing she'd been holding her breath.

"He recognized me. He had, ah—changed. I didn't recognize him at all."

"Changed how?"

"Oh, boy. His clothes, everything. His name, even."

"What did he change it to?" she asked anxiously.

Gavin shook his head. "Sorry."

"Do you have any contact information?"

"No. It was nice to run into each other, but he was busy, working there in the store. He was a salesman. B&H! That's the name of the store. Great store, if you're in the market for any electronics or whatever, you should go there. If you're ever in New York."

"Do you remember anything else? Some way to locate him?"

"No," he said finally. "It was very brief. Just a few hellos, how've you beens, that sort of thing."

"Nothing else?" Shelly asked.

"No, I'm sorry. But, what exactly—what the heck is going on here?" Gavin asked finally, losing his politesse.

"Can I show you something on your computer?"

Gavin brought his laptop.

"Go to YouTube," Shelly said. "Type in 'Decapede.' "

They watched as Gavin typed, the page came up, and "Creston Gold" began to play. He gazed, speechless.

"That's me, playing the bongos," he said finally, his eyes moist.

Aaron shook his head in disbelief.

Gavin sat staring at the picture, mesmerized by the song. Finally, he spoke. "Would anyone like some more lemonade?"

So Shelly recounted the whole fantabulous story. Each time "Creston Gold" ended, Aaron pressed Replay, providing a soundtrack for her implausible, true fairy tale.

"You mean this thing might just be getting started?" asked Gavin.

"Well," said Shelly, measuring her words, "it could also all just die out tomorrow."

"Or it could continue to grow," countered Aaron.

"It sure could," she admitted. She looked at the two of them, the leader-pianist and the drummer of Decapede. "But if—and I really mean 'if,' nothing whatsoever is certain here— if I tried to do something—to organize some sort of get-to-gether. Let's say for a weekend. Would you guys be up for it?"

Shelly and Aaron looked at Gavin.

"Oh, gee," said Gavin, "you'll have to give me some time to think about it. Okay, I'm done thinking. Yes. I'm mildly interested."

"Aaron?" said Shelly.

"I'm right behind you," said Aaron.

They sat in silence, thinking about the past and about the future, with "Creston Gold" playing on Gavin's wood-planked veranda in Mason City, Iowa.

The song ended.

"That really is a lovely song," said Gavin.

"Yes, it is," said Aaron.

They exchanged looks, three innocents setting out together into uncharted territory.

Aaron's phone rang. He looked at the number.

"It's the office, sorry," he said and walked off into the living room.

Gavin looked at his watch and turned to Shelly in a hushed voice.

"We don't have time," said Gavin, scootching closer to Shelly, "so I'm going to cut to the chase."

"Okay," she said, sitting up straight.

"This article? It's a little, let's say, slanted."

"In what way?"

"Don't get me wrong. I give Aaron lots of credit. He led the band, he organized everything. Without him, nothing would have happened. And basically, he's a really good guy. As far as I know him. Which isn't very much. And from a very long time ago."

She waited tensely for the "but."

"But it was Sam that people were coming to see. He was The One."

"Tell me," Shelly urged him.

"Sam was a difficult person, there's no denying that. But he was a—a force. He had this, intensity, this—danger. I guess that's what made him so appealing to the girls."

"Really?" asked Shelly.

"Oh, Shelly, he would sing with his eyes closed, his lips right up against the mic," said Gavin, savoring the image. "It was—carnal. Raunchy. They just melted. I've never seen anything like it. But he was in his own world. I don't think he was even aware of the effect he was having."

Shelly nodded, taking it in. "What was he like as a person?"

"Sam? Where do I start?"

"Aaron said he did a lot of drugs?"

"I don't really know about that. I was quite innocent, to tell the truth. But I wouldn't be surprised."

"Was he difficult to get along with?"

"He was always very nice to me. But for the most part, he didn't really relate well to people. There was something very angry about him all the time. He and Aaron were always at odds."

"Over what?"

"Over everything. The music. Running rehearsals. Everything. Kathleen."

"What about Kathleen?"

"Kathleen was the only person who could get through to Sam."

"They were together? A couple?"

"Oh, my, yes. I didn't know them all that well personally, but it seemed to me like a pretty strange relationship. Almost like she was his, I don't know, his *trainer*. He used to have these—meltdowns. He'd start panting, and his eyes would get all wide and jumpy. And Kathleen—she would sort of pet him. You know, hold him, stroke him. To calm him down. Physically. It was pretty bizarre."

"The performance in Columbus," said Shelly. "You never performed. Why was that?"

"There was that fight," said Gavin. "Between Sam and Aaron."

"Aaron never mentioned that," Shelly said to him.

"Well, you know," he said, clearing dishes.

"So what happened?" she asked Gavin.

"I'm not really sure exactly. I was setting up my drum kit. But at one point they came to blows. As we were getting ready to give our big show. Right there on stage."

Gavin was washing the dishes when Aaron returned.

"Shelly was just asking me about Sam," he explained to Aaron.

"Of course she was," said Aaron.

"I was telling her about the performance in Columbus," said Gavin uncomfortably.

"What happened after that?" she asked.

"I really don't remember," said Aaron.

"I guess the news came in about the shootings at Kent State," said Gavin. "After that, everything's just kind of a blur." He looked at Aaron. "You and I drove back to Steubenville together, I think. With Bev and Vaneshi."

"Could be. I really don't remember."

"What about Kathleen and Sam?" Shelly asked.

"I don't know," said Gavin. "I never saw them again. Never heard from them. Aaron?"

"Nope. And I didn't want to," he said bitterly. "He fucked up everything he touched."

"What about the tapes from the recording session?"

Aaron and Gavin shook their heads and shrugged.

"Look, Shelly," said Aaron, "he was very talented, I'm not denying that. More talented than me. But he was an asshole." Aaron looked to Gavin for confirmation. Gavin shrugged, not contradicting him. "A very talented asshole."

Gavin wiped his hands without speaking, embarrassed.

"I never said we were a band of angels," said Aaron. "When you look back at it, Decapede was a creepy, ten-footed bug."

Shelly slept all the way back to Chicago, leaning against the window of the tiny plane.

"Look, Shelly—" Aaron said as they were saying goodbye at the Transfers gate.

"Aaron, it's okay."

"I don't want you to think—"

"I don't think anything," she said, amiable but proper.

"Don't worry about it."

"You're sure?"

"I'm sure," she said, patting him on the arm. "I've got a lot on my mind."

"I should say so," he said and paused. "Listen, Shelly, can I give you some advice? As a friend?"

"Sure," she said, smiling at the irony.

"From everything you've told me, the people at the station, Johnny and this Gerald Bridges, they don't know what they want any more than we do. Than you do. But I can tell you this—either you steer the train, or the train will steer you."

"Okay."

"What I mean is that this thing is potentially so big, so overwhelming, that no one has any idea where it's going."

"I get that," she said, listening.

"What I think you don't get is what a great job you've been doing."

"Okay. Thanks," she said, flushing.

"No, you're not hearing me. You've been working miracles. Johnny Walker knows that, and Gerald fucking Bridges knows that. You've discovered something outrageously exciting." He paused. "No, not discovered. You've created it. 'Who Is Decapede?', that's down to you. That's Shelly's baby."

She nodded.

"And where it goes, that's up to you. Gavin's with you, I'm with you. Whatever you decide. I can't believe that you'll find any of the others, but up till now, you've done the impossible. So I'm telling you— I'm *advising* you: set the agenda. Don't ask them what they want. Tell them. You're a bright, persuasive young woman. This is all yours. They'll listen."

"Okay," she said, nodding seriously. "Thank you. I appreciate that."

They parted with a kiss on the cheek and a warm, friendly hug.

Never in her life had Shelly imagined herself running up to a counter in an airport and breathlessly panting, "Can you get me on the next flight to Cleveland?" without even asking how much the exorbitant last-minute one-way short-term ticket would cost. *Is this the way businessmen really live?* she asked herself.

She had half an hour till boarding, so she called Brandi as she stood in line at a coffee bar.

"Hi, you're still at the office?"

"What's going on? Everyone's dying to hear!"

"Oh, I have a lot to tell."

"Omigod!" squealed Brandi.

"Listen, can I ask you to do a couple of things for me?"

"I'm writing."

Shelly reached the front of the line. "A latte and a tuna salad sandwich, please. Excuse me, do you have wi-fi here?

"No, ma'am, sorry, but there's an internet kiosk over there," said the barista.

"Sorry, Brandi. Set up a meeting for tomorrow in Johnny's office with Mr. Bridges. Invite my father also."

"What time?"

"Two o'clock. If the Colonel complains about it being last minute, involve Mr. Bridges."

"Okay."

"If anyone asks, tell them it's important."

"What's going on?"

"I got Gavin."

"No!"

"And Aaron."

"Seriously?"

"I got him to commit to 'the project,' whatever it is. They're both interested in being involved."

"Shelly, they're not going to believe this."

"Update Johnny, too, okay?"

"Got it. Anything else?"

Shelly pulled the little green notepad out of her bag and read. "Yes! First thing in the morning, call Steuben College, find out if they have contact information for former students."

"Okay. Anything else?" asked Brandi.

"$8.29, please," said the barista.

"Call me if you get any leads," said Shelly. "If my phone's turned off, write an email."

"Okay. Anything else?"

She looked through the scribbles in her notebook. "Damn, there was something else. I don't even have time to write myself notes. No, that's it for now."

"I've got one thing. A woman called from California about half an hour ago. A Dr. Beverly Pettiford. She insisted on talking to the person in charge of Decapede. Johnny's on the air, so the switchboard gave her to me."

"Okay, and?"

"She said that she has important information about Decapede. So I gave her your email."

"That's all she said?" said Shelly, chewing the rubber tuna salad sandwich.

"Yeah. Did I do right?"

"Great, perfect. Brandi, I have to run. Call me in the morning if you have any information from the college."

```
Subject: Decapede
Sender: Dr. B. Pettiford


Dear Ms Griffin,
    I was referred to you by WFOR regarding
'Who Is Decapede?'
    My name is Beverly Pettiford, nee Hunt.
In 1970, I was a student at Steuben College
and was involved with the band Decapede.
```

It appears that my son found some old
materials about them in my closet and, without my knowledge, uploaded the picture of
the band and the song "Creston Gold" to
YouTube.

I would be happy to discuss this surprising chain of events with you at your
convenience. I can be contacted at …

"Dr. Pettiford?"

"Speaking."

"Hi. This is Shelly Griffin. From WFOR in Cleveland. Regarding Decapede."

"Oh. Oh! Hello."

"Yes, hello. If I understand correctly—you're the Bev Hunt who was the 'coordinator' or whatever of Decapede? Who drove them to the demonstration in Columbus?"

"Coordinator? I guess you could call it that. Wow. How do you know about me?"

Shelly took a deep breath. "Dr. Pettiford, are you sitting down? I've just come from meeting Aaron Woodwright and Gavin Grover. Dr. Pettiford? Are you there?"

"Yes, yes. I'm just a little, ah, stunned."

"Join the club. I've been having surprises like this about three times an hour."

"How in the world—"

"Dr. Pettiford, I have to run to catch a flight in just a min-ute. But I really need to talk to you. As soon as possible," said Shelly. "There's something happening here."

"Please, call me whenever you—"

"No, no, in person. You're in LA?"

"Y-yes."

"Today's Monday. I could fly out there on Wednesday, if that would be okay with you."

"Oh. My. What, from Ohio?"

"Dr. Pettiford, this thing seems to be catching on."

"Bev, please. About Decapede?"

"Decapede is—I don't know how else to put this—becoming famous around here. In Cleveland. Overnight."

"So, what exactly is happening there?"

Shelly paused for a moment and decided it was time to say it out loud. "I'm trying to get the band back together."

There was a long silence. "American Airlines Flight 3682 now boarding at Gate 22. American ..."

"Dr. Pettiford? I really have to run."

"I'll come to you."

"What? Really?"

"I need to get away for a few days," she said. "I'll let you know the details as soon as I can get a flight."

There was a pile-up on the expressway, and Shelly was running late. Just as she reached her exit, her phone rang.

"Shelly Griffin speaking."

"Hi, Shelly, it's Allie Bauer."

"Oh, Allie, I'm so glad you called. I have so much to tell you, but I'm really in an incredible rush right now to get to a really important meeting."

"That's all right," said Allie. "We'll talk some other time."

"Wait," said Shelly, "what is it? Is something wrong?"

"I don't want to keep you."

"No, what? What is it?" Allie didn't sound good.

"Shelly, it's just that things are starting to get out of hand at the brewery. I'm really quite ..." Her voice trailed off. "Shelly, it's too much for me."

"Allie, we need to talk about this. I have to go into this meeting now, but I promise I'll be in touch absolutely as soon as I can."

#

Brandi was waiting for her in the station parking lot. Shelly gave her a quick, warm hug.

"All here. Meeting starts in ten minutes," said Brandi.

"Okay," said Shelly as they walked quickly into the station. "Who would expect heavy traffic from Warren in the middle of the day on a Tuesday? Shoot. Did you get through to the college?"

"I talked to the woman in charge of alumni relations," said Brandi, reading from her list.

"And?"

"They have addresses for graduates."

"Email or regular?"

"Whatever they have. But she warned me it's not kept up-to-date. And it's only for graduates."

"Did you by any chance—"

"Give her the names? Of course I did. Kathleen Brinker, Sam Miller, Vaneshi."

Shelly stopped suddenly, grabbed Brandi by the shoulders, and gave her a big kiss on the cheek. Then she turned and they continued bustling towards the building.

"And?"

"They had one Sam Miller, but he graduated in 1937. No listing for a Vaneshi."

"Fuck!" said Shelly, without breaking her pace, her heels clicking on the pavement.

"She said they have an old address for a Kathleen Brinker," said Brandi, trying to keep up with Shelly as she read, "but she wouldn't send it to me. She said the only way they'll do it is to send her a letter informing her that such-and-such is trying to contact her—"

"So you put in a request?"

"Yeah, of course. But it will take weeks. If the letter reaches her at all."

Shelly stopped. "We don't have weeks." Then she looked Brandi in the eye and smiled. "Thanks."

"And that suit looks *great* on you," Brandi whispered as they walked into the revolving glass door where her father was lying in ambush.

"Well, hello, stranger," scowled Colonel Griffin.

"Hi Dad!" she said, all chipper and panicked, and gave him a peck on the cheek without breaking her pace, clicking quickly across the lobby, with Brandi clomping on her platform shoes in her wake.

"Dad, meet Brandi," said Shelly as the elevator door closed.

"Oh, so this is Brandi," he said, looking at her censoriously.

"My pleasure," she said, cracking a gumshot.

"Shelly, what in heaven's name have you been up to?" he asked in a low voice.

"Good to see you, too, Pop. What's up?" she asked breezily, enjoying his consternation.

"What on earth is going on with you and this radio station and Gerald *Bridges*?" he asked, struggling to maintain his military demeanor.

"Oh, he called you?" she asked casually.

"Yes, he called me!" he hissed in her ear.

"What did he say?" she twinkled at him.

"We came to an agreement that you can take a short furlough." The left corner of his mouth flickered.

"And you agreed?" she said in mock shock.

"He put the firm on a very generous consultancy retainer," said the Colonel, tight-lipped. "He was *very* persuasive."

"That's great news!" said Shelly.

"Shelly," he said, breaking into open awe, "he talks about you like you're—I don't know—Superlady."

"I don't think there is such a character."

"Don't be a smart aleck. What's going on?" he asked, touching her shoulder.

"I'll explain it inside," she said as she walked out of the elevator and into the outstretched arms of Johnny, who engulfed her in a bear hug. She hugged him back until she patted his shoulder to signal she needed to breathe.

"Shelly, you're amazing," fawned Johnny. "You're a sorceress."

Brandi snapped her gum happily.

"Charles Griffin, Johnny Walker," she introduced them. "I believe you've met."

They shook hands manfully, the hawkeyed Colonel and the ponytailed teddy bear.

"Sir!" said the Colonel in acknowledgment.

"Colonel," said Johnny. "Your Shelly is—" and he broke into a little jig, singing "Colonel Griffin, you've got a lovely do-tah" in his best Mancunian accent.

Colonel Griffin looked at him and forced a smile.

Brandi had crowded three chairs in front of the webcam so they could all Skype with Gerald Bridges at the same time. There was an awkward moment, but Johnny insisted that Shelly sit in the middle.

Shelly clicked Connect, and Gerald Bridges appeared on the screen. He was lying in a hammock with his private Hawaiian ocean in the background.

"Gerald!" said Shelly.

"Hey, Shelly!" he shouted as he thrashed about in the hammock, trying to sit up. "Shelly?" he said.

'First name basis?' Shelly could hear her father thinking.

"Yes, sir?"

"I'm ready. Go ahead."

"What, me?"

"It's your meeting," he smiled, still struggling to gain his balance in the hammock. "You called it."

"Oh. Okay. Right. Well, introductions. This is my father, Colonel Charles Griffin, attorney at law. This is Johnny Walker, raconteur extraordinaire. This is Gerald Bridges, president of the Hawaiian branch of the Decapede fan club," she smiled.

"Hi, I'm Brandi," said Brandi, stooping down into the frame from behind.

"Come on already, Shelly," said Gerald, "I'm dying here!"

So Shelly recounted the saga of the past few days while her father and Johnny and Brandi and Gerald all listened, wide-eyed as children at story hour, enrapt by the wild and wondrous events Shelly had traversed.

"... and took the Cessna back to Chicago. That's it," she said with finality. "Finito."

They sat in stunned silence.

"Oh, and one more thing," she started with a little jump. "Dr. Beverly—"

"Pettiford," said Brandi.

"Pettiford. Nee Bev Hunt, the secretary/gofer/agent/roadie/groupie/integral member of Decapede?" Shelly looked at her watch. "She should be landing right about now. From Los Angeles."

Nobody spoke.

"So what's been going on here?" she asked nonchalantly.

"Shelly, you wouldn't believe the response," said Johnny. "I've been retelling the same stories over and over, and people just can't get enough," Johnny chuckled. "Ratings are off the charts. It's like all of Northeast Ohio is following this. When they hear about Aaron and Gavin—"

"And Bev," added Shelly.

"People keep asking where they can get the record," said Brandi. "Other than downloading it on Napster."

Everyone looked at her, and she popped her gum.

"Hmm," said Gerald Bridges. "Has anyone else picked up on Decapede yet? Any other media outlets?"

"Channel Nine news was looking for me," said Johnny. "But I wanted to hear from Shelly before I talked to them."

"Hmm," said Gerald. "Outstanding."

"What are they like, Aaron and Gavin?" asked Johnny. "Are they into this whole—whatever?"

"They're both cool guys in their late fifties, bored out of their minds, dying for a little excitement."

"And Bev?" asked Johnny.

"I'll know more after I meet her. But if she's flying out here at the drop of a hat, my guess is that she would want to be involved."

Shelly paused. Everyone waited for her to continue.

"So I suppose the question is, what's the next step?" Shelly waited for an answer, but they all just continued to look at her.

Shelly cleared her throat. "I suggest we start thinking about a—a get-together. A reunion. For a few days. They'd catch up, swap stories, Johnny could interview the three of them."

"WFOR's 'Decapede Weekend,'" said Johnny, running with the idea. "Have them meet for the first time live on the air."

"Reality radio," said Brandi.

"Hmm," said Gerald Bridges.

"Old friends patching together memories," Johnny imagined. "Audience can call in with questions. It could be really nice."

"When were you thinking?" asked Mr. Bridges.

"As soon as possible," said Shelly, and paused. "But not yet."

"Why not?" asked Brandi.

"I want to see how things play out."

"Shelly?" asked Gerald. He had finally balanced himself in the hammock. "Do you really think—" he asked, tiptoeing around the question no one wanted to say out loud.

"I have a couple of very, very flimsy leads. Even back then, they hardly knew each other."

"But you'll try?" he asked.

"I'm going to try," Shelly reassured him.

"Well, you're the sorceress," said Johnny.

"Just one last thing," said Shelly, looking at her green notebook. "We need to do something about Mrs. Bauer down at the brewery."

"Why?" asked Mr. Gerald Bridges and Colonel Charles Griffin together.

"The whole Decapede thing started when I discovered 'Creston Gold.' And now, with all this publicity, she's flooded with customers shouting for shipments."

"Good for her," said Mr. Bridges.

"So what's the problem?" asked the Colonel.

"If you remember," she said, looking at her father, "we got involved with this because she wanted to close the brewery. Because it was dying and it was too much work for her. Then this happened, and now she's overwhelmed."

"Why is that our problem?" asked the Colonel.

"Because it's the right thing to do," answered Shelly.

Johnny turned to look at Shelly. "Beautiful," he said and hugged her shoulder.

"How do you see that happening?" asked Gerald Bridges.

"I'd like to see Colonel Griffin get involved down there, hands-on," said Shelly.

"I don't know anything about brew—" the Colonel began.

"Outstanding," Gerald Bridges cut him off, "great idea, Shelly. I'll leave you to work out the details."

As the meeting was breaking up, Shelly pulled her father to the side.

"Well?" she asked, thinking he perhaps had something nice to say to her. He didn't. "Listen," she said, "I need to go down to Steubenville tomorrow. I'd like to swing by Creston, stop in to check up on Allie."

"Okay," he said.

"I'd like you to come with me."

"I can't. I have a day full of meetings with clients at the office. I need to put things in order there so that I can—"

"No, I'd like you to come with me."

Colonel Griffin crooked his eyebrow at his daughter. She crooked right back.

"Okay," he said finally. "We can take my car."

"I'll drive," she said.

"Excuse me, Ms Griffin?" called the young receptionist.

"Shelly."

"Sorry."

"You don't need to apologize. What's your name?"

"Brittany."

"Nice to meet you, Brittany. What can I do for you?"

"A Dr. Pettiford called for you. I can dial her for you if you like."

"Thanks, Brittany."

"Shelly?" Brittany looked to the sides conspiratorially as she dialed and spoke in a hushed voice. "Is Aaron that hot in person?"

The best-kept secret in Cleveland, Shelly thought to herself.

"Hello, Shelly?"

"Bev!" Shelly answered, "THE Bev!"

"Hi, we just landed. We're still waiting for our bags."

"Welcome to Cleveland! I'm sorry—'we'?"

"I thought I'd told you. My son, Robbie, is with me. He's seventeen."

"Okay. Great." Her mind was running at double time. "Are you up for a field trip tomorrow?"

"Oh, boy. We're pretty bushed."

"To Steubenville. I have to go there tomorrow. Bev?"

"Wow. I just had this time-tunnel flash. It's been thirty-six years. Yeah, sure."

29

Dr. Bev

– June 1, 2006 –

They set out on their field trip early, the fields and the forests all awakening with a smile to the fine early summer sunshine. Despite the exhausting pace of the previous days, Bev was high on adrenaline. As they cruised down I-71, she and Shelly were exchanging great quantities of information at a breakneck speed in private, low voices. The men in the back seat were both under earphones, Robbie deep asleep, the Colonel reading *The Wall Street Journal* and listening to his military history podcasts.

First, Shelly summarized for Bev the previous day's meeting, and was surprised by her corporate acumen.

"You have quite a business head for a radiologist."

"I own a chain of six clinics around LA. I haven't practiced for years," said Bev.

"Wow," said Shelly.

"As Shakespeare said, 'Money can't buy you love,' " Bev answered cynically. "But wow to you! Decapede! That's *really* impressive."

"You're sweet."

"And the coolest thing I've heard of in the last thirty-six years."

"So, if I can ask, Bev—" Shelly asked hesitantly, "What are you *doing* here?"

Bev had invented a cover story about a crisis at work to justify her sudden jaunt to Ohio, but quickly found herself pouring her heart out to Shelly—her messy divorce, her husband's tacit acceptance—or worse—of Robbie's recreational drug use, Robbie's increasing withdrawal into his own private netherworld, her own mid-life malaise from years spent chasing something that now seemed meaningless.

"I think Aaron feels the same way," said Shelly. "About money. And Gavin, too. He's on his way to dying of boredom."

" '*We are stardust, we are golden,*' " sang Bev. "Life can't live up to that."

"I guess not," said Shelly. She mulled that over for a long moment. "How long are you here for?"

Bev turned to make sure Robbie was asleep. "I don't know. Robbie was suspended for a week. When I heard that he was selling his father's pills to his 'friends' at school, I said to myself, 'Bev, that's it. The clinics don't matter, the money doesn't matter. You have a son that you've been neglecting, and he's sinking down a deep, dark hole. You have to do something drastic.' "

"You can just get up and leave like that? What about the clinics?"

"I'm in partnership with my ex. The lazy dickhead will just have to manage. Are you married?"

"Nope. Single lady."

"Smart lady. If you're ever tempted, call me. I don't know who invented the stupid institution. Never again!"

Shelly laughed. She liked Bev. Tough, successful businesswomen were rare in Warren, Ohio. "You said Robbie's into electronics and stuff?"

"That's all he does. Headphones and computer and electric piano. That's his whole life. He has his own little studio in his room. He lives there. He doesn't eat anything but candy bars. Not a drop of color. I'm afraid he's going to lose his eyesight, like those cave fish."

Shelly laughed again.

"This is so freaky," said Bev, gazing out the window at flat, green Ohio. "Thirty-six years. A whole lifetime." They rode in silence. "I still remember driving to Columbus with Sam and Kathleen in my car. I thought they were the coolest people I ever met." She stared out the window, deep in her memories. "Still do."

Shelly told Bev about her previous trip to Creston, incomprehensibly a mere two weeks earlier, to begin proceedings to dissolve Bauer's Brewery. Bev told Shelly how she'd hung out at Pedro's just for the opportunity to gape at Aaron and about how the very first time Sam walked into Pedro's, he had punched a guy who was heckling her.

Shelly told Bev how she'd lied her way into Johnny's office and about the basement of Dickenson's Hardware. Bev choked on laughter, stifling it so as not to disturb the men. She told Shelly about how she had taken Aaron down to the very same store for the interview. Shelly turned on her voice recorder and begged for more, so Bev told her about how Aaron had dragged Kathleen on stage the first time, about how they were invited to Columbus, and about how Sam had played "Creston Gold" for the first time right there in the studio.

"For the one and only time, no?" asked Shelly.

"That's true," Bev nodded somberly.

"Tell me about Aaron and Sam," said Shelly.

Bev sighed. "Aaron liked being the leader, and Sam didn't like being led. He had this 'Fuck it' attitude towards everything and everyone. Angry. Impulsive. Unpredictable. God, he could drive a stone crazy." Bev browsed through her memories. "But Shelly, the way he sang when he got going? He'd close his eyes and snuggle all close up to the mic and sing from his fucking gonads. I want to tell you, Shelly, he starred in a lot of girls' dreams back in those days."

"And Aaron?"

"Aaron was a real flirt, that hair, that smile," Bev smiled. "He was a charmer, on stage and off. And he scored a lot. I mean, a *lot*. But Sam, he was this raw *essence*. Girls creamed over him, if you'll pardon the expression."

Shelly looked at Bev.

"Me? Oh, no, I was nowhere near Aaron's league. And Sam, he was very shy around girls. Except, of course, Kathleen."

"Why 'of course'?"

"Kathleen was so much *there*. Present. Warm, and gentle, and funny, and *so* beautiful, with those giant gray eyes. And she was always right between them, keeping them apart."

"What was going on 'romantically'?"

"Oh, gosh. Sam and Kathleen. Yin and yang, inseparable. She always had her hands on him, to keep him calm. Sam was this mad *force*. And she was this, this—Earth Mother. Nineteen years old, with the soul of an old medicine woman." Bev chuckled. "They were so damn glamorous, Shelly. There must have been some mean sex going on there."

"Was Aaron jealous of them?"

Bev shrugged. "You have to understand, I wasn't really their friend. They just let me hang around. But it was Sam that people were coming to see. Aaron knew it, and I know he was jealous of that."

"The fight?"

Bev fell silent. "I really don't know. They were in each other's face all day, Sam and Aaron. I guess everyone was nervous. They were on stage, setting up. They had some words, and boom! Sam just hauled off and decked Aaron."

"Right on stage?"

"Right on stage, in front of five thousand people," she said. "And then he stalked off, and we never saw him again."

"Jeez."

"End of story," said Bev. "Or so we thought."

Shelly looked in the mirror at Robbie and her father sleeping. *What have I wrought?* she asked herself.

"Yeah," said Bev to herself.

"What?" asked Shelly.

"I might not have been in the inner circle. But at least I got to watch." They drove past a green sign reading WINDFALL, 3 MI. "Those were the best few weeks of my life. No contest."

"So how did 'Creston Gold' get on YouTube?" Shelly asked.

"My genius son was snooping through my closet. Probably looking for a stash of pills I was hiding from his father. He found a box of some of my old stuff from college. With a reel-to-reel tape and some photos and whatnot. He took it from there."

"Wait, you have the original tape of Decapede?"

"Yeah, sure."

Shelly gulped. "Where is it?"

"In the hotel. I brought the whole box."

The horizon did a backflip and landed on its feet.

"You're a genius," said Shelly.

"I think it's pretty clear who the genius is in this car, and it ain't me," said Bev.

"What else is there?"

"The pictures."

"The one of the band on YouTube?"

"Yeah, but there are a bunch more. Some are even in color." The car swerved. "Wait, I might have stuck them in my purse." She rummaged. "Here you go. Here's the band rehearsing. Here they are playing at the Kiwanis. Oh, wow, here's one from Pedro's. I think there are some more from the recording studio."

This must be how Neil Armstrong felt, Shelly thought to herself. "And you brought them?"

"I brought everything. I thought you might find it useful."

" 'Useful'? My gosh. You have no idea. Wait till Johnny sees this!"

Allie Bauer was waiting for them in a yellow dress as they pulled into the driveway. Shelly was surprised how tightly

Allie hugged her, and she hugged her back warmly.

"And this is Dr. Beverly Pettiford."

"Bev, please. I've heard so much about you."

"I'm very pleased to meet you."

"And this is my father, Colonel Charles Griffin."

"Hello, Allie Bauer," she said, extending her hand. "It's a pleasure to finally meet you, Colonel."

"Yes, hello," he said, shaking her hand firmly and almost smiling. "Please, call me Charles."

Shelly had never heard him say that to a stranger in her life.

"And that's my son, Robbie," said Bev, indicating the hoodie in the back seat of the car.

"Hi Robbie. Welcome to Creston," Allie said warmly, but the hoodie didn't react.

"Sorry, these kids and their earphones," said Bev, embarrassed.

Mr. Griffin turned to Robbie. "Son?"

But Robbie was under his hood, inside his earphones, within his iPod, and took no notice.

"Son?" the Colonel repeated quite loudly. Robbie acted as though he hadn't heard him. The Colonel reached in through the window and yanked the earphones off Robbie's head, the iPod falling to the floor of the car.

"Dad!" said Shelly in alarm.

"Hey!" said Robbie indignantly. "What the fuck?"

"This lady was addressing you."

"So what, that doesn't give you the right to—"

"Son!" said Colonel Griffin, leaning his head in through the window, nose to nose. Robbie glowered at him. "I don't know how it's done where you come from, but around here, when a lady welcomes you into her home, you say 'thank you.' "

All eyes were on the man and the boy. No one spoke, including Bev, who seemed to have no intention of interfering.

Robbie stooped down to pick up the iPod and stuck it in

the pocket of his hoodie, still scowling insolently. Colonel Griffin leaned over him, motionless, glaring icily.

"Thank you!" said Robbie snidely, and slouched deeper into the back seat. But without the earphones.

Shelly thought she heard a snicker, and when she turned, she caught Bev winking at Allie.

"I hope you're all hungry," said Allie.

The adults exchanged pleasantries over the prodigious meal Allie had prepared—fried chicken, mashed potatoes, yams, a mix of stewed vegetables, and fresh biscuits. She also served, to the delight of all, cold bottles of Creston Gold.

"This is *sooo* delicious," said Shelly. "You really didn't need to go to all this trouble."

"Cooking's my therapy," said Allie. "Do you drink beer?" she asked Robbie.

"I'm too young," he said, looking at his mother.

"You're seventeen, right?"

He nodded.

"If it's okay with your mother, we Bauers always let the youngsters drink a little beer. You get them used to it at an early age, it's not such a big deal when they get older."

Bev nodded deferentially.

"That's sound reasoning," said Colonel Griffin.

"If it's all right, I'd like to make a toast," said Shelly, rising with her beer bottle in hand. "To Allie Bauer, the most courageous woman I've ever met—"

"Oh, go on, now," said Allie, embarrassed.

"—who was the inspiration for this whole crazy roller coaster ride. And to Bev Hunt, for shepherding five college kids into a band that has come back to haunt us a lifetime later." Everyone laughed and clinked bottles, even Robbie.

"And to Shelly Griffin," said Colonel Griffin, rising. "I had no idea I was raising a sorceress," he said, smiled, and turned to Allie. "That's what Johnny Walker calls her," he said proudly.

Everyone voiced approval.

"Okay, Daddy, cut it out," she said quietly, touched.

As they were eating, the phone in the office rang, but Allie ignored it. The second time, Colonel Griffin asked if she wasn't going to answer it.

"It'll just have to wait," she answered, her face tightening.

They all noticed with amusement the quantities of food Robbie was devouring, helping after helping.

"Robbie," said Allie after the homemade apple pie a la mode, "I understand you're interested in old musical devices? You might want to take a look in the music room."

"Where is that?" he asked.

"In Gruenhaus," Allie answered. "That's what we call the main house."

"Isn't this the house?" he asked.

"We call this the annex. It used to be the servants' quarters way back when. The house got too big for me a long time ago. The music room's on the main floor, off the living room. You'll find it. The door from here is stuck, you'll have to go around through the front porch."

"Do I need a key or anything?"

"Oh, we don't lock doors around here."

Robbie looked at his mother. For all his sullen bravado, he was still a kid in unfamiliar territory.

"Go ahead," said Allie, "I think you might find it interesting."

"Okay," he said, as if he were doing them all a favor, and shuffled away from the table.

"Well, that was quite a meal," said Bev. "I don't think I've seen my son eat that much—ever."

"Growing boy," said Allie.

"Delicious," said the Colonel, squelching a belch. "Oh, sorry."

"We Bauers are Old World enough to consider that a compliment," she smiled.

"So," said Shelly, turning the conversation to business, "tell us what's been going on here."

"I'll tell you," Allie began, drawing a deep breath. "Ever since the story broke on the radio, all my old customers have been pleading for me to double shipments, triple them. One market in Akron that usually gets fifteen cases a month asked me for a hundred. Old customers have been coming out of the woodwork."

"What has your production been up till now?" asked the Colonel.

"About half a million barrels a year," said Allie. "A little less in the past few years."

"And now?" he asked. "What do you think you could ship today if production could handle it?"

"I have no idea," she said haplessly.

"No idea at all?" he asked.

"Maybe double," she said glumly. "Maybe more. I don't know."

"Isn't that a good thing?" asked Bev.

Allie raised her eyes. She looked as though she were going to cry.

"Allie," said Shelly, "what's the matter?"

"I—I—" She lowered her gaze to her plate.

"What?" said Shelly, scooting her chair closer to Allie and covering her hand with her own.

"I just can't take it anymore," she said in a small voice. "I can't even keep track of the phone calls. I'm running back and forth to the brewery, trying to squeeze out as much production as I can, trying to keep track of the orders, the billing." She shook her head. "I'm just feeling rather overwhelmed."

"Aw, Allie, I'm so sorry," said Shelly.

The Colonel watched, tight-lipped.

"These are people that have been ordering from us for generations. Struggling through hard times, just like us. And now, when something good is finally happening—I don't want to let them down. But I just can't handle it on my own like this." She looked at Shelly, struggling to maintain her composure. "I've been working ten, twelve hours a day. I just can't keep up with it all. I'm afraid I'm about ready to break."

They all sat in silence.

"So how did you have time to make this delicious meal?" asked Bev, trying to lighten the atmosphere.

"I just closed the door to the office. Let the gol-darned phone ring," she said bitterly. She looked around at the three of them. "To tell you the truth, I feel like just getting into the car and driving away."

"I'm so sorry, Allie," said Shelly. "I had no idea."

No one knew what to say.

"Dad, don't you need the powder room?"

"No, why?"

"Well, I do."

"Okay," he said, clueless.

"Dad, would you please come with me to the bathroom?"

He looked at her quizzically. "Oh. Oh! Yes, sure. Where is it?"

"Come, I'll show you," she said, leading him from the kitchen into the small sitting room. She stood him in front of the picture of Allie's son.

"Fine-looking boy," he said. "82nd Armored Battalion."

"Do you see why I wanted you to get down here?"

"I get it, Shel!" He stared at the picture.

"Dad, you saw what's going on back at the station. Nobody knows how big this is going to get. A lot of people are rooting for us. But in the meantime, it's breaking this poor woman's back!"

He pondered her words. "That's not right," he said.

"No, Dad, it's not. And it's you who needs to step in."

"Shelly, I have a law office to run. I'm not like you, I can't just take off—"

"There's nothing so urgent in the office that the other people can't handle."

"Shelly, with you being gone, I can barely keep up there myself."

"Dad, they call us sharks. Do you want to go to your grave known as an undertaker for failed businesses? Or do you want to bring Creston Gold back to life?"

"Humph," he said, with a flicker of a smile breaking the stern lines of his military demeanor.

"You've got to get down to the Brewery to see how things are running, start hiring. God knows there are enough people around here looking for work."

"Don't tell me my job," he said, secretly enjoying her command of the details.

"Daddy, think about this: Decapede is a fad. In half a year, everyone may have forgotten about them, I don't know. No one knows. But Creston Gold will still be on the shelf, and people will still be buying it. A lot of it, if we can help her get it out there."

"When did you get so smart?"

"While you weren't looking."

"So where is the bathroom?"

Shelly walked back into the kitchen, nodding to Allie and Bev. "He's got a good heart. It's just his head that's a little rigid sometimes."

"Fathers," said Bev, and the three of them laughed.

"Why don't you let Bev and me clean up?" offered Shelly.

"Oh, no, this is my kitchen," said Allie.

Robbie came in, bubbling with excitement.

"What?" asked Bev.

"That house? It's a mansion!"

"Yes," laughed Allie, "it's quite large."

"How many rooms does it have?" asked Robbie.

"I have no idea, never counted. Back in the old days, this was the Bauer homestead. You could find three or four families living here, brothers and sisters and parents and kids. Running the brewery, working the farm." She looked at the Colonel as he returned. "We have about six hundred acres here. Potatoes, cabbage, oats, squash."

"Really?" he said, impressed.

"It's all leased out now. When I was a little girl, we used to have these wonderful Sunday picnics down by the lake. Thirty, forty adults. And whole passels of kids."

"You have a lake?" Robbie asked.

"Yes, Lake Traumsee, down the hill on the far side of the house. That's where we take the water for the brewery." She smiled proudly. "People say there's something special in the water there. It's very nice, you should go take a look. Do you swim?" Allie asked the boy.

"Hey, I'm from California." He was smiling.

"I can find you some trunks if you'd like to go in. There's a nice diving board, too."

"Thanks. Maybe later. What I'd *really* like to do is take a look inside that old stereo set in the music room. If I'm allowed."

"Robbie," said Allie, "you can do whatever you like in there. Nobody even goes in there anymore."

His eyes widened.

"But you should still check with Allie first," said his mother.

"Mom!"

"Okay," said Bev, "okay."

"What kind of a set is it?" asked the Colonel.

"You know vintage hi-fi equipment?" snarked Robbie.

"It wasn't called 'vintage' when I worked on it."

"You worked with vacuum tube components?"

"I used to build audio kits back in the Fifties," said the Colonel, "when I was about your age."

"Yeah?" said Robbie, skeptical.

"I used to build receivers. Scott, Fisher, American-made. Best vacuum tube components ever manufactured."

"Do you know what I found in there? A Marantz Model 2 amp."

"I built one of those from scratch."

"Are you serious?"

"I'm always serious, son," said the Colonel seriously.

"Maybe you could take a look at it together?" suggested Shelly.

"Sure," said the Colonel, "after he finishes washing the dishes."

As they were preparing to leave, Shelly pulled Allie to the side.

"What do you think of Robbie?"

"Oh, Shelly, he's a breath of fresh air."

"He was getting into some trouble in California."

"Well, California's full of trouble, isn't it?"

"He's not a bother?"

"Don't be silly. It's such a relief to have something to think about other than the brewery."

"And my father?" she asked, nudging her.

"Cut it out," said Allie, embarrassed. "I think he did a very fine job of raising you. And it's nice having a man to cook for."

"Okay, listen. I have to get down to Steubenville with Bev."

"All right."

"So I'm going to leave the men here with you if that's okay."

"Of course."

"You can introduce Dad to the books."

"And it looks like Robbie will have enough to keep himself busy," said Allie.

"Right. So, I was thinking—and please, if there's a problem with this, just say so—"

"What?"

"I might have some car trouble later."

"Oh, do you want to borrow my car? That's no prob—"

"No, my car's fine. But I was thinking that it might develop some problems later on."

Allie looked at her uncomprehending.

"I might get stuck somewhere. I might not make it back to pick them up."

The Greatest Band that Never Was

"Oh. Oh! *Oh!*" Allie smiled. "Well, those things are out of our control, aren't they?"

Shelly smiled.

"And heaven knows, I have plenty of room."

"Great. Allie, thanks."

"Don't you go thanking me." They hugged and began to walk back to the car. "Shelly, honey?"

"Yes?"

"Did you plan this?"

"Me?" she said innocently. "Who could plan such a thing?"

30

Steubenville Redux

– June 1, 2006 –

Shelly drove south on State Route 3 through Wooster. "Oh!" she said.

"What?" asked Bev.

"Could you make a note for me to call a piano tuner?"

Bev dialed a number on her phone.

"Hi, could I have the number for a piano tuner in Youngstown? Thanks, can you connect me? Hi, I need a piano tuned at the Bauer residence at—" She held the phone to Shelly's mouth.

"2147 Seville Rd," said Shelly.

"Creston. Great, what time?" asked Bev. "Thanks very much." She hung up the phone. "Two o'clock tomorrow."

"We need to let Allie know."

Bev began to dial.

"No, wait, let's not disturb them right now. They're probably working."

They drove in silence for a couple of minutes.

"So, tell me about finding Aaron and Gavin?" Bev said, now that they were finally alone. Shelly related the whole story, tickled to have the most appreciative pair of ears in the world to share it with. She told her how she'd found Aaron's phone number and flown to Chicago to meet him.

"He must have been knocked for a loop," Bev said, imagining the scene.

"No, I'd say he took it with admirable aplomb."

"Always the charmer."

"Oh, he's charming, all right. He's a businessman. Pretty successful, I think. Bored out of his mind. Divorced a couple of times, no family."

"Still thinks he's God's gift?"

Shelly mulled that over. "Yeah," she said finally.

"But he kind of is, right?" Bev asked slyly, girl to girl. "At least he was back then. Jeez, he must have scored with half of the girls in the county."

"I guess," said Shelly, beginning to color. "What about Sam?"

"Oh, God, no. I mean, maybe in my dirtiest dreams, but in real life? No way. I'd be terrified. Way too much for me to handle."

"What was he like towards you?"

"Sam?" She reflected on those distant days, piecing together fragments of memories. "That's the thing. He was so angry. I was terrified of him at first. But he was always really good to me. He always kind of looked out for me. He—he was really smart in some ways. Like, he always saw through a lot of bullshit. But boy, he was one piece of work. Anyway, we were talking about you and Aaron. So?"

"He called Gavin on the spot," Shelly said, "and Gavin said he was going on vacation for a couple of weeks the next day. I didn't want to miss him, but there was no way to get there. So I used Mr. Bridge's credit card and hired a private plane. On the spot."

"Who's Mr. Bridges?"

"Oh, no one's told you?" said Shelly, bracing herself. "Gerald Bridges."

"Gerald Bridges?" exclaimed Bev. "*The* Gerald Bridges?"

"Yup," said Shelly.

"The asshole bazillionaire with the wife and the tape with the two—"

"Yes, him," said Shelly. "There's a lot to fill you in on."

"Tell me about Gavin."

"Oh, he's *so* sweet!"

"Isn't he, though? Gay, yes?"

"I suppose. I didn't think to ask him."

"I didn't know Ohio was so liberated."

"We have internet, you know."

"God, I'd barely recognize it," said Bev as they climbed the stairs of the staid, Colonial-styled McNally Hall. "It's like a dream. Everything's the way it should be. Kind of. But not exactly."

They found Sue Stevenson sitting at her desk in room 113, playing solitaire on her computer with intense concentration.

"Excuse me," said Shelly.

"Just a minute," said Sue officiously, finishing the game. "Yes, please?"

"Hi," said Bev, "I graduated from Steuben in 1970. I was hoping you could help me. I'm looking for contact information for a friend of mine."

"Fill out this form and sign it. We mail your request to the person to inform him or her that such and such a person is inquiring after them, and if they're interested, they make contact."

"That would take weeks."

Sue shrugged. Her eyes drifted back to her screen.

"Well, I'm in quite a hurry. I was hoping perhaps you could give me, you know, some *extra* help."

"Sorry, those are the rules." She returned to her computer.

"Excuse me," said Shelly, "have you heard of Decapede!?"

"Who hasn't?" she answered snottily. "Just for your information, that band started right here at Steuben College!"

"Right, well, you see, my name is Shelly Griffin."

"So?"

"And I'm looking for Kathleen Brinker. The singer for Decapede."

"Everybody's looking for her. Turn on your radio."

"I'm the one who's actually looking for her. For WFOR. I'm in charge of Decapede."

"Johnny Walker is in charge of Decapede."

"I'm Johnny Walker's boss."

"Yeah, sure."

"Yes. And I really need to find Kathleen."

"Show me some ID."

"What?"

"Show me something that says that you're really from the radio."

Shelly looked at her bag. "We're just printing up business cards now."

"Sorry," said Sue and clicked Deal.

Bev tapped Shelly on the shoulder and handed her the photos of Decapede.

"Here," said Shelly, "look at these."

"What's that?"

"Photos of Decapede."

"There aren't any pictures of them. Just the one on YouTube. Johnny Walker said so."

"We've just discovered some new ones. Johnny doesn't know about them yet."

"Yeah, sure."

"Look. Here's the one from the Creston Gold clip on YouTube. Recognize it?"

Sue Stevenson looked at the picture and looked up at Shelly.

"How do I know you didn't just copy it off the internet?"

Shelly handed her the pile of a dozen small black-and-white glossy photos with a datestamp of 11-70.

Sue looked at them, one by one, lifting her eyes to try to figure out if Shelly could really be from the radio.

"So, can you help me?"

"If you give me this picture." She held up one of Aaron flashing his flashiest smile.

"I really need them all, actually."

"Sorry, those are the regulations." She returned to her game.

Bev drew herself up to her full 4'11" and put her fists on the counter. She spoke in a voice that implied she had a loaded machine gun in her purse. "Okay, this can go one of two ways. One, you can give us the information you have for Kathleen Brinker, and on his show tonight, Johnny Walker will personally thank you for your invaluable contribution to finding Decapede," Bev said as she smiled as sweetly as a cobra, "or two, we march upstairs to the president's office and say to him, 'Hello, we're from WFOR, and we need the *urgent* assistance of Steuben College in helping to locate your most famous alumna, but there's this twit of a secretary named Sue Stevenson downstairs who's too busy playing card games on her computer during work hours to help us.' "

The secretary handed her a slip of paper: Kathleen Brinker, 12290 State Route 99, Edinboro, PA 16412.

They stood between the portico columns of McNally Hall. Bev asked, "Where to now, boss?"

"Damn," said Shelly.

"What?"

"I thought we could swing by Pedro's."

"Great! What's the problem?"

"I forgot to bring a camera."

"You can't think of everything all by yourself," said Bev, smiling proudly and pulling a fancy little digital camera from her purse. "C'mon. Let's see if I remember the way."

The front window of Dee's Hair & Beauty Supplies sign was boarded up, a desolate store on an empty street in a depressed little town.

"What do you think?" asked Bev.

"How old was Pedro back then?" Shelly asked.

"I don't know, he was a grown-up. Grown-ups were all kind of the same age. Maybe fifty?"

"So he's probably frying frijoles in that Great Cantina in the Sky?"

"Yeah, I guess."

"Well, we're here," Shelly said. "Let's try anyway."

They banged on the front door, but there was no answer. They peered through the dirty show window and saw no one, but they could hear a faint banging.

"There's a back entrance," smiled Bev, dredging up the memory.

In the narrow alleyway, they could hear banging from inside. Shelly knocked, but there was no answer, so she opened the green door.

"Oh my God," said Bev, looking around at the bare walls, "I feel like I'm walking into a time tunnel."

A young man was deftly hammering a plank into the wall, one precise blow after another. A black wire ran from his earphones down his strapping, bare, sweaty back to the iPod tucked into the back pocket of his snug work jeans. "*Woke up in the Hotel California*," he croaked as he hammered. His highly evolved muscles rippled with every thwack.

"Excuse me?" called Shelly. "Hello!"

He turned, pulling off the earphones, a sandy-haired young man with well-sculpted chest muscles, wearing a backward baseball cap and a wide-open smile. "Hi," he said brightly. He had dimples, too, and placid blue eyes. "Can I help you?"

"It's a crazy story," said Shelly, "but we're interested in a restaurant, Pedro's. It used to be in this location, back in the Sixties."

"That was way before my time," the young man explained to them.

"Do you know where we could find the owner?" asked Bev.

"Oh, that's me, actually. Matt Hinton," he smiled, pulled off his work glove, and extended his broad, moist hand. His bare chest was still sweating from his thwacking.

The ladies introduced themselves.

"Really?" said Shelly. "Who owned it before you, if I may ask?"

"I inherited it from my great-uncle Lonny."

"Lonny what?" blurted Bev.

"Hinton."

Bev squeezed Shelly's wrist so hard her nails dug in.

"He didn't have any kids, so he left everything to me. Not that there was much to leave. A rusty eighteen-foot outboard, twelve hundred bucks in the bank, this store, and a couple more like it. Not worth nothing, just eats up money with taxes. Been empty for as long as I can remember. I'd get rid of it if I could, but nobody wants it. I'm just fixing it up for something to do."

"What do you mean?" asked Shelly.

"I do construction in the off-season, ma'am, but there isn't much work around here. End of June, the league starts up, me and my buddies, we play for the Rapids, over in Cuyahoga Falls. Ohio Valley League. Double-A."

"Baseball," Shelly explained to Bev.

"How come you're interested in Uncle Lonny?"

"Matt, have you heard of Decapede?" Shelly asked.

"Sure. 'Have another Creston Gold,'" he croaked. "That mystery band." He smiled. He had very nice teeth. "Me and my buddies listen to that radio show all the time."

Bev cleared her throat. "This is where Decapede was born," she said.

Matt continued to look at her with the same smile.

Shelly explained the story to Matt patiently, slowing down the tricky parts. Matt just kept smiling, so Shelly wasn't sure how fully he had grasped the basics. Shelly took his number and gave him hers, just in case.

"Who knows?" said Shelly.

"Who knows?" answered back Matt, still bare-chested, still wearing the same smile.

Back in the car, Shelly turned to Bev. "Do you think I should get Johnny to interview him on his show?" she asked, and they broke into laughter at the same time, giggling like teenagers.

"We're going back to Allie's to pick up the guys?" asked Bev as they pulled out of Steubenville.

"We need to talk," said Shelly.

"So serious! About what?"

"Your plans."

"My plans," said Bev, growing serious herself. "Yeah."

"Do you know what your plans are?"

"I know that today was the most fun I've had since—I don't know, since the last time I was in Steubenville. Of all places."

"I'm glad," said Shelly, smiling. "We all need a little of that Decapede magic once in a while."

"And I know that I'm in no rush to get back to LA."

"Well, Bev, would you like a suggestion?"

"Yes, Shelly, I would greatly appreciate a suggestion."

"I'm going to take you back to your hotel now. And tomorrow you're going into the office of WFOR with your box of Decapede stuff. Have Brandi find you a desk. Go through the box with Johnny and Brandi and organize whatever's usable. Get that reel-to-reel tape digitized. Get all the pictures digitized."

"Wait, I'm writing." She pulled a notepad from her bag. "Digitize tape and pictures."

"Call Mr. Bridges and update him."

Bev looked at her. "You expect me to call Mr. Gerald Bridges and tell him about Sue Stevenson?"

"Exactly," Shelly nodded. "Every detail."

"You're joking."

"Bev, he's the biggest fan of Decapede in the world."

"Gerald Bridges? The guy who owns an island in Hawaii, with the trophy wife with the sex tape?"

"He and Johnny grew up together. He's all depressed about that tape, so I guess being involved with Decapede is some sort of distraction, I don't know. Oh, and be sure to tell him my father said we need some sort of legal entity. Maybe an LLC with WFOR as an affiliate? He should ask his lawyers."

Bev shook her head in disbelief as she wrote.

"Where will you be?"

Shelly shrugged and smiled. "Chasing wild geese."

"What about the guys?"

"What guys?"

"Your father and my son?"

"What about them?"

"Don't we need to go get them?"

"What for?"

"Oh." Bev pondered that for a long moment. "Allie?"

"It's fine with her."

"You're sure?"

"I asked her."

"When?"

"This morning."

"Shelly, did you plan this?"

"Really, Bev, who could plan such a thing?" said Shelly, without blushing.

31

Goose Chase

– June 2, 2006 –

The mailbox at 12290 State Route 99 said Lauterman, but Shelly knocked anyway. She saw a curtain move, but no one answered. She listened closely. The only sound was the man next door sharply clipping his hedges. She knocked again and thought she heard a sound. From the corner of her eye, she saw the neighbor staring at her as he sliced the branches of his hedge. She knocked a third time, insistently.

The door opened a crack. A frumpy woman in a half-buttoned, once-white robe peeked out.

"Hi, my name's Shelly Griffin. I'm sorry to bother you, but I'm looking for the Brinker family who used to live here."

"Ain't no Brinker here," she said and slammed the door.

Shelly's heart sank. As she turned to go back to the car, the hedge clipper furtively averted his eyes. She walked toward the car, turned, and caught him staring at her again. She walked over to him.

"Hi," she said brightly.

"Hello," he mumbled and kept clipping, staring at the hedge. Branch after branch fell victim to the metallic slicing clicks. He was pushing fifty, and Shelly assumed that he lived in the house with his decrepit mother. *Yeah, I'd cast him as a serial slasher,* she thought to herself.

"Excuse me, but have you lived here for long?"

He grunted something and kept his eyes fixed on the hedge, as if he were afraid of what he might do if he looked at her.

"You wouldn't happen to remember a Brinker family that lived here, would you?"

"Mebbe," he said.

"Would you know where I could find them?"

"Dunno," he said, slicing the hedge, avoiding eye contact.

"Okay, thanks," she said and started to walk away.

"Try Stancliff Country Club," he said to her back.

"Stancliff?" she asked.

But the man just kept slashing branch after branch with the cold metal blades.

Shelly drove out of town to the country club. She was surprised at how different the terrain was over here in Pennsylvania, sloped and hilly, a mere hour from billiard-table Ohio. A well-kept older receptionist in the clubhouse asked how she could help.

"I'm looking for someone from the Brinker family?" she said.

"They're probably out on the course."

"Who is?" asked Shelly, her heart lifting.

"Hugh, DeWitt, and Louis."

"And they are?"

The woman looked at Shelly as if she were speaking a foreign language. "The Brinker brothers."

"Ah."

"But you might find one of them in the Pro Shop."

"Okay, thanks," she said.

"Excuse me," she said to the man behind the counter in the Pro Shop, "I'm looking for one of the Brinkers."

"They're all out on the course."

"Right. When do you think they might be back?"

He looked at her as if she were cognitively challenged.

"After they finish," he explained, even though it was clear he didn't think she'd understand.

"I'll just wait here, if that's okay."

He looked at her, shook his head, and walked away.

After twenty minutes of looking at clubs, cleats, and ugly clothes, Shelly saw an older man carry his big golf bag into an office. Shelly followed him.

"Excuse me, Mr. Brinker?"

"Yes?"

"Hi, my name is Shelly Griffin. I was wondering if you could help me. I'm looking for a woman named Kathleen Brinker. She'd be about fifty-five years old, used to live out on State Route 99."

"Kathleen Brinker? Nope, sorry, doesn't ring a bell."

Shelly's heart sank.

"But you should ask my sister. She knows more about the family than I do."

Her heart lifted. "Where would I find her?"

"She runs the pool office. Paula. Paula Morningstar."

Shelly hiked from the clubhouse over to the swimming pool. The day was warming. In the office of the pool Shelly found an older woman poring over some papers.

"Excuse me, my name is Shelly Griffin."

The woman looked up, keeping her finger on the page.

"I just spoke to your brother, he said perhaps you'd be able to help me. I'm looking for a Kathleen Brinker. I believe she lived in Edinboro some thirty or forty years ago."

"Kathleen?" the woman repeated. Shelly's heart hung in mid-air. "Not sure, sorry." Her heart sank. "There was a Diane Brinker, Aunt Lucy's girl. She moved to Florida a long time ago." Shelly's heart lifted.

"Would you have any contact information for her?"

The woman shook her head. "Haven't heard from her in years and years." She returned to her work.

Shelly sighed deeply.

"Maybe you've heard of Decapede?"

"What, that band from Steubenville that's all over the radio?" said Paula.

"Exactly," said Shelly, buoyed. "I'm from the radio station. This woman I'm looking for, she was a member of that band."

"Really?" she said, peering over her glasses. "A girl from Edinboro?"

"That's right. Kathleen Brinker."

"Son of a gun. Let me see." She flipped a Rolodex but couldn't find what she was looking for. Then she went to her purse, withdrew a ratty little address book held together by a rubber band, and thumbed the little pages.

"Hey, Corrinne, it's Paula Morningstar. Aunt Bert's daughter. Yeah, okay, how're you? Oh, she's doing fine, chugging along. Ninety-three in July. Yes, all of us. Tell me, do you remember a Diane Brinker, Aunt Lucy's girl? The one who moved to Florida. Yes, that's right. Didn't she have a sister? Would it be Kathleen? No, I wasn't sure either. Anyway, would you by any chance have an address or a phone number for that Diane?" She waited. And waited. Finally, Corrinne returned and dictated an address to Paula. "And give my love to everyone, okay?"

"Here you go," she said, turning to Shelly. 4270 Blue Beech Ct, Tamarac, Florida, said the note. "But she doesn't know her married name."

"Thanks very much," said Shelly, her spirits cautiously rising.

"I guess we'll hear about it on the radio if you find her."

"Oh, for sure. Say, would you like to hear your name on the radio?"

"My name? I've never been on the radio before."

"Well, you listen to Johnny's show today at six o'clock, on WFOR. Do you get WFOR here?"

"We sure do. That Johnny Walker is just the sweetest man in the world!"

"Well, I'll tell him you said that. And I'm going to have

him thank you for this by name."

"Really? You can do that?"

"Yes," said Shelly, "I can do that."

As she drove, Shelly called Bev to pass on to Johnny the regards to Paula Morningstar. Bev told her that since that morning, she'd rented office space on the floor above WFOR, ordered phones and internet, made appointments with two human resources companies, and sent the master tape to a local studio.

"They're working over the weekend to digitize it and clean it up and everything, and they promised me a demo CD by Monday morning."

"Great."

"Just one thing I thought you ought to be aware of."

"What's that?"

"The box the tape was in, it had written on it 'For Lonny Hinton,' " said Bev. "You know, Pedro."

"I get it. Matt's uncle. Ownership rights—"

"I didn't know whether to say anything—"

"No, you're absolutely right." Shelly thought. "Okay, this is what I want you to do. Call the Colonel, explain the situation to him. Ask him to get in touch with Matt and set up a meeting for me with him when I get back."

"Which is when?"

"You'll know when I know. But have the Colonel get in touch with Matt now. I have a feeling he could be helpful."

32

Mendel

– June 3, 2006 –

It was a short walk from the Port Authority building down 9th Ave. As she craned her neck to look up at the skyscrapers, Shelly recalled the jokes about yokels from the Midwest buying the Brooklyn Bridge. She'd only been to New York City once as a child, but it appealed to her more than Chicago, certainly more than Cleveland. She was looking for a photo shop and was taken aback to find that B&H Photo wasn't a shop but a mammoth superstore occupying two floors over an entire city block.

There were dozens of colorful departments, with a hundred salesmen bouncing around in black and white with little black beanies. Some of them were wearing fringed poncho T-shirts with a lot of strings dangling down to their knees, speaking between themselves in a language that sounded something like German, but Shelly couldn't be sure. Some had curly locks growing out from above their ears.

Shelly had once visited Amish country in Eastern Pennsylvania, but they had seemed shy and withdrawn. These men were darting around the giant store, shouting in English and that other language, running and bringing and returning and sending and opening boxes of everything from watches to hair dryers to video games to security cameras to the biggest television screens she had ever seen.

She followed signs directing her to the office on the second floor.

"Excuse me," she said to a heavyset woman at the reception desk who was wearing a lot of jewelry and a wig, "I'm looking for someone who used to work here about ten years ago."

The woman looked at her guardedly. "What's his name?"

"I don't know his name, but—"

"Sorry can't help you," she said and answered the phone. "B&H, Feiga Malka speaking, how can I help you?"

Shelly continued deeper into the hub of offices and found three men in that strange garb talking animatedly to each other in that other language.

"Excuse me," she said, "I'm looking for someone who used to work here about ten years ago."

"What's his name?" asked a portly, smiling older man with a red nose, sitting at a large, mayhem-ravaged desk. Shelly tried to repress the thought of how much he looked like Santa Claus.

"I don't know his name, but he used to play guitar."

"Meidel'e," he said, "seriously?" And returned to his chatter with the younger one.

"Have any of you heard by any chance of Decapede?"

"What is that?" asked Santa.

"A college rock band," said Shelly. "From Ohio. In 1970." They looked at her as if she had green skin and antennae. "Look, this is really important," she pleaded. "I really need to find this guy."

"What do you want from him?" asked Santa guardedly.

"He may have an opportunity to make a lot of money," said the shiksa.

"You're looking for him to make an investment, maybe?" asked the younger man.

"No, no, nothing like that. More like an inheritance. He

251

may have some information that would help a lot of people."

They consulted among themselves in that language.

"Ask the floor manager down on the first floor," said Santa. "He's been here since forever."

"What's his name?"

"Yerachmiel Nisson," replied St. Nick.

"I'm sorry?" said Shelly.

"Yerachmiel Nisson. Just ask for Yerach. Medium size guy, long beard, peyos."

She stared at him.

"What? No good?" he said good-naturedly.

"I'm sorry," said Shelly, coloring. "I don't think—"

"That's okay, you all look the same to us. Come, I'll help you find him."

"Mr. Yera?"

"Yes, how can I help you?"

"I'm looking for a man who worked here ten years ago. It's a long story. He'd be in his mid-fifties now."

"You know how many people we got working here?" he said, gesturing at the giant store.

"He played guitar really well."

"Mendel?"

"I don't know what that means."

"His name. Mendel Shochenstein. Over in the telephone department. I heard him play guitar once at a Simchas Beis Shoyva party. Very good, very good."

"Thank you very much," she said.

"But you'd better make it quick, we're closing soon."

"It's only one o'clock," she said.

"Shabbos," he explained and walked away.

She found Mendel explaining passionately to a customer that on a BlackBerry phone, one could actually write and receive emails. They were quite new on the market, but Shelly had been using one for months, like all the young lawyers in the Colonel's office.

This Mendel was a mountain of black and white—beanstalk height, humpty-dumpty girth, a wild and unkempt gray beard, fringes and strings and tassels and earlocks hanging everywhere, and a booming bass voice.

"Yes, how can I help you?" he asked Shelly. He smelled like the Old Country.

"Excuse me, you are Mendel Shkone—Shocken—?"

"Mendel," he smiled through the black-and-gray jungle. "How can I help you?"

"Hi, my name's Shelly Griffin," she said, extending her hand.

"Sorry, lady, I don't shake hands with women. I know," he said with a twinkle of irony, "it sounds crazy. It's a religious thing. How can I help you?"

Shelly smiled nervously. This jolly mountain of a guy was too sweet to be true. And too photogenic. She was praying against impossible odds for a miracle.

Shelly pulled from her bag the photo of Decapede in front of Pedro's and handed it to the man. He stared long and hard.

"*Gevalt*," he whispered.

"I'm sorry?"

"Where did you get this?"

"Is that you?" Shelly asked.

"It used to be, a very long time ago," said the man, stunned.

Shelly's heart did a backflip.

"What— Where—" he stammered, dumbfounded.

"You haven't seen the clip?"

"What clip?" he asked, staring at the picture, stunned.

"On YouTube."

"I'm sorry, I don't use the internet."

"You're selling all these new technologies, but you don't use the internet?"

"Just when I need to look things up. There's too much

there I prefer not to see. Where did you get this?" he asked, indicating the photo.

"Can I show you something? On the internet?"

"Sure. As long as it has the Good Housekeeping Seal of 'Guaranteed not to offend even the biggest prudes,' " he smiled. She repressed the urge to give this big, cuddly guy a big, teddy bear hug. That was it, she was in love.

Mendel gaped at the picture on the screen and flopped into the chair to listen to "Creston Gold."

"That's me playing guitar," he said, shaking his head in disbelief.

"15,239 hits," she said, pointing at the bottom of the screen.

"15,239 hits," said Mendel, trying to grasp it all.

"In less than two weeks."

"In less than two weeks," he repeated. "My, my."

"Listen, Mendel, we really need to talk."

"I guess we do," he said, smiling under his massive beard.

"Could we get a cup of coffee?"

"No," he said, "it's Friday."

"You don't drink coffee on Fridays?"

"No," he laughed. "It's Shabbos. From sundown. The Sabbath."

"But it's not sundown now."

"No, but a person needs to prepare."

"Oh," she said, seeing that he expected her to understand.

"Come to my home tomorrow?" he said, writing his address on a piece of B&H notepaper. "After shul?"

"After shul," she said. "What time is that exactly?"

Outside was all the glitter and the dazzle of a Friday night in midtown Manhattan, but Shelly was on the phone in her hotel room with her green notebook open. "Everyone's here?" she asked, giddy with excitement.

"Here," said Johnny from the station.

"Here," said Bev from the station.

"Here!" chimed in Gerald Bridges from Hawaii.

"Present," pronounced the Colonel from his office in Allie's annex.

"I'm taking notes," said Brandi, and cracked her gum right in Johnny's ear.

"Hi, everyone," said Shelly. "Sorry to be bothering you on the weekend."

"No, it's fine—have you—we can't wait—what's been—don't worry—how is—" they all clamored at once.

"Whoa!" said Shelly, and they were quiet. "I have some news," she said and paused.

They waited.

"Now listen, this isn't at all for sure, I have no idea if it's going to work out, but—" She paused again for dramatic effect, picturing each wide-eyed face. "Can everyone hear me?"

"Yes!" they all shouted.

"Okay," she laughed. "I'm not sure how it's going to happen, if it's going to happen, bu-ut—"

"Say it already, I'm dying!" pleaded Gerald.

Shelly took a deep breath. "I found Vaneshi," she said, and held the receiver away from her ear.

She waited for the hubbub to subside.

"Okay, okay, come on, listen up." She waited. "There's nothing about him that hasn't changed, including his name. It is now—are you ready for this?—Mendel Shochenstein."

"Spell it," said Brandi, and Shelly did, slowly and carefully.

"He's the sweetest guy in the world, but he lives a very *special* life. I'm not at all sure that he'll want to be a part of anything to do with Decapede. I talked to him for just a couple of minutes, but he invited me to his house tomorrow morning."

"But it's really him?" asked Johnny.

"For sure?" asked Gerald.

"It's really him," said Shelly, dizzy at her own words. Again, she waited for the commotion to die down. "But really, let's not get our hopes up too high. I have no idea if he's on board for—you know, some sort of something." She paused. "Please, guys, I want to hear an update from each of you. Gerald, can you begin, please?"

Gerald told everyone that he'd gone ahead and had his lawyers file incorporation papers, naming Shelly as CEO.

"It takes thirty days in Ohio," said Shelly. "We don't have that kind of time."

"I spoke to the governor," said Gerald. "He'll have it taken care of on Monday. Oh, and the corporation signed an arrangement with the station. An LLC affiliation, like you suggested, Charlie, good call! They'll provide us with whatever services we need, but we're a separate business entity."

"Great," said Shelly. "Johnny, what's going on at the station?"

"It's crazy. I had a two-hour show this afternoon. Bev was telling some hilarious stories about the session when 'Creston Gold' was recorded. Hundreds of people were calling in with questions."

"Do you know who called to ask *me* about *Decapede*?" exuded Bev. "Drew Carey!"

"Yeah, he's a Cleveland boy," said Johnny. "We've knocked back a few Creston Golds together. And listen, Shel, some other stations have started playing the song."

"Local stations?" asked Gerald Bridges.

"Greater Cleveland," Johnny answered.

"And Pittsburgh," added Bev.

"And Toledo," added Brandi.

"Brandi, I want a daily report about the extent of airplay outside Greater Cleveland," Mr. Bridges instructed her.

"Sure," Brandi popped her gum. "*Sir*," she added with an ironic lilt.

"People are calling the station, wanting to know where they can buy the record," said Bev.

"Wait a sec," said Shelly, cradling the receiver with her chin. "*Royalties›Mendel*," she wrote in her green notebook.

"What about the tape?"

"Being done over the weekend," said Bev. "The studio is getting it digitized and mastered and remastered and whatever they do. We'll get an advance copy on Monday."

"How many songs?" asked Shelly.

"About half a dozen," said Bev.

"Omigod," blurted Gerald.

"As far as I can remember," said Bev. "But it's been a very long time."

"I'm going to have a special gala show, big build-up," Johnny gushed. " *'Decapede! The Lost Recordings! Let's listen to them together for the very first time, you and me, Johnny Walker. Right here on WFOR!'* "

"That sounds amazing," said Shelly.

"The pictures," Brandi reminded Johnny.

"Oh, right," said Johnny, "we got back the color prints. They're beautiful! That Bev was some photographer!" Everyone laughed. "The negatives are a little faded, but the lab can enhance them."

"Outstanding," said Mr. Bridges.

In her notebook, Shelly wrote *Photos → Deca.com*. "Just make sure everything's in place legally before you broadcast. Colonel?"

"Yes, Miss Griffin?" he said.

That's him being a jokester, Shelly mused. He must be having a good time. "Did you have a chance to check out the ownership rights of the tape?"

"Not yet. Shelly, I've got my hands full with the brewery."

"That young man Bev and I met down in Steubenville, Pedro's nephew—" Shelly explained to the others.

"Matt Hinton," said Bev.

"Right," said Shelly, "he might well be the legal heir. Dad, we need to talk to him."

"Let me read up first so we know where we stand."

"What's going on at the brewery?"

"Things have been neglected down there, I can tell you that. I got a retired foreman to come back, at least for a while. And I've been looking to hire some production hands."

"Talk to that Matt Hinton."

"I want to read up on ownership statutes first."

"About hiring. He must know people around there." She paused. "Okay?"

"Yes, ma'am," said the Colonel, recognizing that he was outranked.

"You know what?" said Shelly. "He's a handyman. Why don't you ask him to come up to Gruenhaus, fix that door between the annex and the house? It sticks."

"I don't think—" said the Colonel.

"I'm sure Allie has some odd jobs for him to do. I have a feeling he might be helpful," said Shelly.

"Copy that," groused the Colonel.

"How's Allie holding up?" asked Shelly casually.

"Fine," said the Colonel, and not a word more.

Shelly pictured herself choking him. "How's Robbie?" she asked.

"Capable kid. He organized that wide internet in the office," said the Colonel, "so I've been able to work here."

"Broadband," said Shelly.

"Be that as it may," said her father.

"Robbie's having the time of his life," said Bev. "He can't stop raving about the music room."

"You should go down and visit him," said Shelly.

"I think that's exactly what I shouldn't do," Bev answered, and everyone laughed. "I'm staying out of his hair. Anyway, I'm way too busy."

"Brandi?"

"Shelly! I miss you!"

"I miss you, too. You got anything for me?"

"It's really fun here, with all people coming and going and phone calls and noise about Decapede, but it's starting to get hard on the station."

"Got it," Shelly said. "*Office*," she wrote in her notebook. "Give me just one second here."

Shelly jotted a few words in the notebook, drawing circles around two words with arrows leading to an exclamation point.

"Okay," she said. "This is what I need. We need a website. Buy the decapede.com domain before someone else does, top-top priority."

"I'll send in a media team from my office in California," said Gerald Bridges.

"No," Shelly answered, and everyone went quiet. People didn't say "no" to Mr. Gerald Bridges.

"I want to hire locally," she continued, "for everything connected to Decapede."

No one spoke.

"Shelly," said Johnny finally, "that's beautiful."

"Yes, it is," Gerald followed suit. "I'll find a local outfit as soon as we finish here. Good catch about the domain name."

Shelly looked at her notebook. She drew a sharp circle around *Royalties›Mendel*. "Okay, anything else?"

"What about you?" asked Johnny. "Is the sorceress planning to share her plans with us?"

"Plans?" said Shelly. "I don't think I know that word. I'm just letting the wind carry me. As soon as I finish here in New York, I'm flying down to Miami."

"Miami?" asked her father.

"I'm chasing a lead on Kathleen."

"Anything solid?" asked Johnny.

"Couldn't be flimsier."

"What about Sam?" asked Gerald.

"Not even a hint of a hint."

"Well, they were a couple, him and Kathleen," said the president of the Hawaii branch of the Decapede fan club. "So maybe, if you find her?"

"Gerald, sir, it's all a very, very long shot. Don't get your hopes up."

"I understand that, Shelly. You're amazing."

"Cut it out, sir."

"What's your gut feeling about Vaneshi?"

"Gerald, I have no idea whatsoever."

"But you'll try, won't you?" he said. Shelly pictured that stare.

"Yes, sir," said Shelly Griffin, CEO of Decapede, Inc. "I'm going to do my best."

"And you'll let me know?" asked Bev.

"The minute I know," said Shelly.

"And me as well," said Gerald.

"I wish I could call each of you about everything, but it's going to happen through Bev now, okay? Bev, could you please be in touch with everyone and write an email update every—well, whenever." She paused and sighed. "But, Gerald, I promise I'll text you about Mendel as soon as I hear."

"Oh, no need," he said, but Shelly knew he didn't mean it.

"So, Shelly," said Johnny, "how are you going to celebrate your big Friday night in Manhattan?"

"You should be careful out there," said the Colonel.

"You should go out and have some fun," said Bev.

"You should go spend some of my money," said Gerald.

"You should do something you'll regret in the morning," said Brandi.

"I'm going to sleep," said Shelly. "I have a big day tomorrow."

Shelly sat in the hotel room chair, sipping on a glass of wine from the mini-bar. The hotel-fresh terrycloth was pleasantly rough on her freshly showered skin. Just like in Mason City, she smiled. Six days ago. Six. Days. Ago.

She opened the curtain and stared down at the little people and cars scurrying around down on 7th Avenue. She closed the curtain and stared at the wall.

Her eyes began to stumble their way through the angular maze in the aqua wallpaper, bumping against culs-de-sac, retreating, changing direction again and again, accelerating, shifting sharply, faster and faster, bouncing from wall to wall till she found herself floating, weightless, soaring, then suddenly a bob and a swoop and—

Shelly sat up and looked at her watch. She picked up the phone and dialed.

"Hi, Allie, how are you?" she asked. "Aww, I'm so glad to hear that. Really? I'm not surprised. Nothing makes him happier than taking charge. And you're getting along okay? How's Robbie? Does Bev know? And they're not being a bother? Oh, Allie, that's just wonderful! Great, great, chasing all over the country. Allie, listen, I want to throw an idea at you. And you have to be perfectly honest with me ..."

33

After Shul

– June 4, 2006 –

Mendel lived in a row of tired brick homes in the Borough Park neighborhood of Brooklyn. The sidewalks were full of multi-childrened families strolling lazily on a Saturday morning. The men were regal, with shiny black coats down below their knees, extravagant round fur hats, and those long curls hanging down over the ears. The women wore hats and wigs and jewelry, and most were very pregnant. The little boys all seemed to be in perpetual motion, their caps and strings and curls and shoelaces and limbs flying out in all directions. The girls, even the very little ones, were matronly and demure, with long sleeves and braids, thick stockings and glasses. Each family seemed to have about seven children packed into a three-year span. *Maybe they practice different rules of gestation,* Shelly wondered.

Mendel and Fruma Reizele welcomed her warmly, seating her on a well-worn sofa. There was little in the room other than a tattered easy chair and a dining table with twelve chairs. The walls were lined with tall, heavy, very old-looking black books. On one bookshelf was a dusty radio/cassette/CD player. She saw no television, no computer.

Mendel listened intently to her long, fantastical story of the previous two weeks, about 'Creston Gold' on its way to becoming a hit record, about the crazy interest in Decapede, about Aaron and Gavin and Bev. Mendel just kept shaking his head and, with it, the jungle of a beard. As they talked, various family members of a wide variety of ages came and went. Fruma Reizele tried to follow Shelly's story but kept popping up to deal with the needs of a tribe of tykes. For the life of her, Shelly couldn't tell which were children and which grandchildren. But they were all adorable, with all their fringes and earlocks and pink cheeks. Each one gave her heart a tweak.

"So, Mr. Mendel," said Shelly finally, "imagine running into you here." Mendel laughed. "What have you been doing with yourself all these years?"

"Being fruitful and multiplying," he said, indicating the gaggle of giggling children running through the little living room.

"How many children do you have?"

"It's bad luck to count. The evil eye."

"Oh, I'm sorry," she said, retreating.

Mendel winked. "It's just a superstition. Eight, *Baruch Hashem*. And thirteen grandchildren. With two on the way. Excuse me, three."

"Wow."

"Yes, wow. *Keneine hora*."

"You've come a long way since Vaneshi, Decapede."

"Thank God. I've been very fortunate. So, Ms Shelly Griffin, what can I do for you?"

"I don't know!"

He laughed, a deep, booming, heartfelt laugh.

"What?" she asked.

"You come in here like a fairytale, pulling these impossible recordings and pictures and articles out of the air, and you say you don't know what you want?"

"I don't!" she said, laughing with him.

"*Vey iz mir*," he chortled, "the girl's got *neshoma*."

"What's 'neshoma'?" she asked.

"It's like 'soul,' only a different color."

She sipped her cup of sweet, tepid tea. Despite the alien black-and-white surroundings, his warm teasing made her feel comfortable and welcome. "So how does it feel to have a hit record?" she asked.

" 'Creston Gold,' " he said, pulling the memory out of the attic of his mind, blowing off the dust. "I had forgotten that song completely. If I remember correctly, Sam came up with it at the very end of the recording session. Out of nowhere. It almost didn't get recorded. What a beautiful song! I've been hearing it in my head over and over all Shabbos."

"Oh, wait till Johnny hears that one!" said Shelly, feeling a little shiver herself. "Do you still play?"

"After college, I moved to New York, played in wedding bands. To make a living. Hassidim make big weddings, and a lot of them. That's how I encountered this world," he said. "And then I got drawn in. I had my own band. For twenty years. We were doing very well, actually. But then, with a family, I had to get a day job."

He laughed and slurped loudly from his glass tea cup. "So, Shelly, you avoided the question. What do you want?"

Shelly looked him in the eye and said it aloud. "I want to get you guys together."

"Explain?"

"Come to Cleveland for a weekend. Together with Aaron and Gavin and Bev."

"To do what?"

"A get-together at the radio. Swap stories on the air. Do some interviews. You'll love Johnny, I promise."

"That's it? To talk?"

Go on Shelly, she said to herself. *Say it.*

"Do you think the three of you, you and Aaron and Gavin—do you think you could actually play together?"

"To play? Yeah, sure. They're great musicians. We played great together back then—if I remember correctly," he guffawed. "But if you mean to play 'Creston Gold'—you'd need Sam for that."

"Okay, okay." *One step at a time.* "Would you be willing to come out to Cleveland for a weekend?"

"What weekend?"

"Oh, like next weekend."

Mendel laughed aloud. "Look, Shelly, this sounds very nice. And I really do think you're some kind of magician to have found me. But I don't think this is for me."

A small girl came running into the living room with a scraped elbow, screaming like it was the End of Days. Chasing after her came a very young mother or a much older sister, Shelly couldn't figure out which.

"I have a very *full* life," he said, laughing over the child's screams.

"I understand that. Of course, you'd be fairly compensated for participating."

"I'm sorry, Shelly, I don't talk business on Shabbos."

"Can I talk, you listen?"

"Eyes you can close. Mouths you can close. Noses you can even close. Ears you can't close. Right?" His eyes crinkled when he smiled.

"We'd be offering you an honorarium of $10,000 to come out to Cleveland for the weekend. And of course, take care of all your expenses. And needs."

Mendel stroked his beard. "And you realize that from sundown Friday to sundown Saturday, no radio interviews, no making music, nothing?"

Shelly gulped. *That's half the weekend.* "I understand that," she said. "No problem." Shelly wished she had a beard to stroke. It looked so soothing. And wise.

"You have no idea how complicated my lifestyle can be. Where exactly would this be?"

"How about if we did this little reunion—at a farm house, out in the country?"

Mendel shook his head. "I don't know, Shelly," he said reluctantly. "I'll need to think about it."

"Mendel, we don't have time!" said Shelly. He was so sweet, so warm, that the unadorned truth just came tumbling out of her mouth, straight from her heart. "I have no idea what I'm doing here. I don't have a plan. We don't even have a band yet. Just Aaron and Gavin. And Bev. And hopefully, you. I have a maybe-maybe lead on Kathleen. And maybe maybe maybe she knows something about Sam. And I'm going to do whatever I can to track them down.

"But this thing is growing, Mendel. The song. The band. A whole feeling of—something *right* in a world that has way too much *wrong*. My gut is telling me that it's going to catch on beyond Cleveland. And if it does—and I'm not promising anything, yeah? But if it does—we're talking about the Big Time. Including financially. But for anything at all to happen, I need to work fast, and that means I need to know that I can count on you."

It was hard to judge his reaction, his face covered with hair. Finally, he spoke. "Even with all my crazy religious restrictions?"

"Even. We'll do everything you need to make it work for you. I promise."

He sank back into thought. As the house began to fill with children and grandchildren of all ages, they agreed to talk on the phone "after Shabbos" for him to give a final answer.

"Would you like to join us for lunch?"

"Oh, that's so sweet! No, thanks, I need to get down to Florida."

Mendel walked her out.

"That Kathleen, she was a very lovely girl. Very caring. I hope you find her."

"And Sam?"

"Sam, he's—how shall I put it? Sam was high maintenance. Brilliant. Talented. But not easy."

"That's what everyone says."

"Personally, I never had any problems with him. But remember, I was the last person to join. I was only in the band for a few weeks."

"Tell me, do you know why he and Aaron fought?"

"I don't know the details. But they were always at each other's throats. Two young bulls, you know? It was always Kathleen who was keeping the peace between them."

"Right."

"Boy, I remember when I first met them."

Shelly took the voice recorder out of her bag.

"Please, not on Shabbos."

"Oh, sorry. But go ahead."

"You're interested?"

"Are you kidding? I'm dying to hear."

"They're the ones who came to see me, Sam and Kathleen. To 'interview' me for the band. I was living in this psychedelic trailer in the woods by a lake. Down south of Zanesville. And all of a sudden, they drove up. In Bev's car. A fancy Mustang."

"Bev didn't even remember that," said Shelly, straining to memorize every word.

He was speaking slowly, retrieving the images one at a time. "I remember it was a particularly beautiful day." He sighed, his eyes distant. "And they were in love. Real *achdus*." He gazed at the picture in his mind, smiling.

"The song, 'Creston Gold'?"

"He wrote it about that day. 'Lake Hope lapping at the shore / This must be the place I've been searching for.' "

"That's where your trailer was, at Lake Hope?" asked Shelly.

He nodded.

A warm tingle ran through her. "Did you by any chance have any contact with Kathleen or with Sam after that day in Columbus?"

"No, never saw them again. We weren't, you know, friends or anything." He stood on the sidewalk in front of the row of brown brick townhouses, thinking. The only noise was the children playing on the sidewalk in front of the house. "Sorry."

"No, Mendel, this has been great. I just love your life here, it's so—full of life," she laughed.

"Someday you'll come spend Shabbos with us."

"Maybe someday. You'll call me?"

"I'll call you, *bli neder*. I need to talk to Fruma Reizele."

"It was very nice meeting you, Mendel. I hope to see you again soon."

"Very nice meeting you, Shelly Griffin. Gut Shabbos."

"Gut Shabbos to you. OH!"

"What?"

"Before I go. A picture." She fished her camera from her bag.

"Sorry Shelly, not on Shabbos."

"But everyone will want to see what you look like, and I for sure won't be able to describe you," she said, laughing.

"Take a picture off the internet. We all look alike." His laugh was so loud and deep that Shelly thought she felt the Borough Park sidewalk shake.

"Hi Bev. What's up?"

"It's not too late?"

"No, I was just going to sleep. I have an early flight to Miami."

"How did it go?"

"God, I hope he's in. He's the sweetest guy I've ever met."

"And?"

"And he'll call me. He's very reluctant to leave his world. But he looks like he could really use the money. So I've got my fingers crossed. Ah, and do you know what he told me?"

"What?"

"That Sam and Kathleen came down to find him where he was living, in a place called—are you ready for this?—Lake Hope!"

"Like in the song?"

"In your car."

"Really?" Bev thought a moment. "Nah, that memory's gone."

"And that he wrote 'Creston Gold' about that day."

"No shit? Wow. Wait till Johnny tells that little tidbit on his show. They're going to go ballistic."

"Oh! And that it almost didn't get recorded, just at the last minute—wait. Damn, I have another call. I'll talk to you tomorrow."

"Have a good flight."

She didn't recognize the number. "Shelly Griffin speaking."

"Hi, Shelly. It's Mendel."

"Oh, hi, how are you? I was just telling Bev about you."

"Oh. Well, I hope I get to meet her soon."

"That means you're—"

"That means I am."

"Oh, I'm so happy."

"Well, I'm happy too. And I'm happy that you're happy."

"I'll be in touch very soon about the details. Or Bev will."

"Wonderful."

"Hope to see you soon."

"*Gut voch.*"

"Sorry?"

"Have a good week."

"You, too, Mendel."

Shelly stared at the ceiling. She thumbed a message to Bev.

```
Mendel in, Allie hosting next weekend at
Gruenhaus.
```

Shelly lay in the dark, her mind careening. She sat up with a start and thumbed a message to Mr. Bridges.

```
Mendel    committed    to    next    weekend    at
Gruenhaus.  $10K.
```

A short moment later, her phone beeped:

```
YEEEEEEEESSSSSSSSSSSSSSSSSSS!!!!!!!!!!!
```

The phone beeped again.

```
Can I come?
```

Shelly turned off her phone and lay back down. *Idiot, why didn't you ask Mendel to pray?* She lay thinking in the dark.
Oh, Kathleen, please be there.

34
Almost Grown
– June 6, 2006 –

The sky was a tropical azure blue when Shelly left the Miami airport, but on the drive to Broward County it turned from ominous gray to sinister black. As she exited I-95, the celestial dam split open, and Lake Heavens emptied itself onto poor little Tamarac, accompanied by a full-scale apocalyptic lightning-and-thunder show. She drove at a crawl through the tasteful neighborhood, peering through the downpour till she found 4270 Blue Beech Court. She parked in the driveway and turned off the motor to listen to the stampede of crazed buffalo on the roof. A sign on the front yard read "Hobgood for Congress," with the picture of a handsome, commanding woman. She decided to wait out the rain but lost patience after a minute and ran to the front door through an innocent-looking puddle that swallowed her left foot all the way up to the ankle.

There was no name on the door. Shelly rang the bell.

The woman from the sign opened the door. She was wearing a beautiful floor-length red-and-gold lounging robe that looked as if it had been purchased on a trip to Ecuador or Morocco.

"Yes?"

"Hi, I'm very sorry to bother you, but—"

"Come in, please, don't stand there."

"Oh, thanks. I'm sorry, I'm dripping—"

"We're used to that, it's okay. Here, please, come in."

"Thanks," said Shelly, wiping the rivulets from her face. "Whew. I'm—I'm looking for a Diane Brinker?"

"Oh, boy."

"I know, it's a long story, I—"

"I'm Diane Brinker-O'Neil-Hobgood, so I guess that's me. You're not a disgruntled taxpayer or anything, are you?"

"No," said Shelly, "just a very wet one. And I pay my taxes in Ohio."

"Wait, let me get you something." She brought Shelly a beach towel, which she used to dry her face and hair.

"You can take off your shoes if you like," said Diane.

Shelly did and dried her feet.

"We don't get rain like this in Ohio."

"Here, come on in."

"I don't mean to impose—"

"I'm not going to send you back out into this rain. Come in, sit down." Diane led her into a large Florida room with bamboo couches in patterns of large green and blue flowers and a glass wall looking out on a well-manicured little lake.

A girl of fifteen or sixteen with arresting gray eyes was sitting on the sofa, holding a guitar. "This is Justine," said Diane, and disappeared.

"Hi, I'm Shelly."

"Hi," said the girl softly. She was wearing sweatpants and an oversized black T-shirt, her dark hair straggly and unkempt.

"I'm sorry to barge in on you like this."

"Oh, it's okay. I was just ..." The girl's voice faded out.

"Here, this will warm you up," said Diane, handing her a cup of steaming tea. "You can sit anywhere. This furniture is used to wet."

Shelly took a sip and coughed. "Whoa, what did you put in here?"

Diane smiled warmly, crossing her legs. "Just a little something to take the chill out on a stormy day."

Shelly took another sip. "I really didn't mean to disturb—"

"It's no problem. Justine was just playing me a new song she's learned."

"Oh, you sing?"

"I guess," said the girl without raising her eyes.

"Could I hear also?" asked Shelly.

The girl half-shrugged. There was something in her vulnerability that touched Shelly, and she sensed Diane wanted her to encourage the girl.

"Please, Justine, go ahead. I'd love to hear your new song," she said. The girl looked up at her. "Really I would."

"Okay," said the girl, and began playing a mournful ballad about a robin crying over her empty nest. The girl spoke in whispers but sang in a warm, confident contralto. She hesitated in the middle of the third verse and stopped playing in mid-sentence.

"That's all I remember," she said.

"Beautiful," said Diane.

"That was just lovely," said Shelly.

"Thank you," she said softly. The telephone rang in the kitchen. Justine leaned her guitar against the sofa and trotted off to answer, relieved to escape the stage.

"She seems like a very sweet girl," said Shelly.

"Yes, she is very sweet," said Diane. "So! How can I help you?"

"Well, it's a very long story, but actually I'm looking for someone who might be a relative of yours, a Kathleen Brinker?"

Justine came back into the room with the phone. "It's Senator Quinlan," she said, holding the phone out to Diane.

"Hello, Senator," said Diane. "No, the vote will be postponed till next week. I'll make sure. No, it's under control. Listen, I can't talk now. I'll see you in Tallahassee first thing tomorrow morning, okay?" And she hung up. "Ah, Justine, would you excuse us?"

"Sure," she said and turned to leave.

"Nice meeting you," called Shelly.

Justine turned with a small smile. "Nice meeting you," she said softly and padded off.

A bolt of lightning lit the room like a strobe, and the thunder that followed rattled the glass wall. Shelly took another sip of her spiked tea.

"I'm a state senator," Diane explained. "And I'm running for Congress."

"Oh, my, how impressive," said Shelly.

"Running's one thing, winning's another. I'm running as an independent, so it's quite an uphill battle."

"Even more impressive," said Shelly.

"Thanks. So. Kathleen! What do you want with Kathleen?"

"You are a relative? You know her?" said Shelly brightening.

"Sister," said Diane.

"Omigod!" said Shelly. "You're Kathleen's sister?"

"Was."

Shelly froze.

"Kathleen died four years ago. She was killed in an accident."

"Oh no," said Shelly, her heart collapsing.

"She was driving home at night," said Diane, "up in Morris County, New Jersey. She swerved to avoid a deer."

"Oh, no. Oh, how terrible."

"How did you know Kathleen?"

"I didn't," said Shelly, deflated and disheartened. "I—" And she began to cry.

Diane moved next to her and lay her hand on Shelly's back, clueless. She had seemed like a pleasant enough young woman. And sane. "Can I get you anything?"

"Yes, please." Shelly held out her cup of tea for a refill, hoping there would be alcohol in it again. She was trying to stifle her tears and her embarrassment.

By the time Diane returned with the spiked tea and a box of tissues, Shelly had managed to compose herself and was drying her eyes on the damp towel.

"Thank you," Shelly said, holding the mug tightly in both hands. "I'm so sorry. This is so embarrassing."

Diane sat on the couch next to her. "That's okay. We all have our days."

Shelly sniffled and blew her nose. She put the dirty tissue in her bag, extracted a Shelly Griffin, CEO, Decapede, Inc., business card, which she handed to Diane, and sniffled again.

"Have you heard of Decapede?" she asked.

"That mystery band from YouTube? Sure."

"Right. That's me. I'm—I'm head of the campaign."

"Oh. Oh, my. What brings you all the way from Cleveland?"

Shelly pulled a copy of the Decapede photo from a manila envelope in her bag. Diane glanced at it. "Yes, I've seen this on YouTube," she said and handed it back.

"Look at the girl," said Shelly.

Diane examined the grainy photo. "Katie?" she whispered, thunderstruck. "Where— How?"

Shelly handed Diane the box of tissues.

And Shelly told her the whole story, about Aaron and Gavin, Bev and Colonel Griffin, Allie and Johnny, WFOR and Mr. Gerald Bridges and Mendel, and the entire Decapede saga.

"That's why I reacted like that," Shelly explained, "when you told me that—"

"It ruins everything for you," said Diane.

"I had this pipe dream of getting the band back together," Shelly sniffled. "I felt like I was getting to know Kathleen. She was very—dear, to me, in my thoughts. In my imagination."

"What about Sam Miller?" asked Diane.

"I don't even have a clue. I was hoping against hope that Kathleen—"

"I understand," said Diane. "I suppose there's a lot of money at stake."

"There is. But that's really not the point. It could have been—I don't know, a legend coming alive. I had dreams of them performing, recording. But, well—" Shelly shrugged. "You know. 'Dreams.'"

They sat in silence, listening to the rain. Finally, Diane spoke.

"I guess we should tell Justine," Diane said softly.

"Why Justine?"

"Oh—" she started. "She's Kathleen's daughter."

They both used the box of tissues for a long minute.

"When Kathleen was killed, Justine came to live with me. There wasn't anyone else."

"Her father?"

Diane shook her head. "IVF. Justine's a test-tube baby."

"Really? No other family?"

Diane shook her head. "Just the two of us. Kathleen was six years older than me. My gorgeous big sister, I idolized her. But we were very different. I wanted to go conquer the world. She was a homebody."

"She never married?" asked Shelly.

"No. After college she moved back to New Jersey to be near our folks. She took over our mother's job as a swimming teacher at a college up there," Diane smiled through her tears. "But then the folks died, and she was turning forty, wanted a child. So she went to a clinic." She paused. "That's all she ever wanted, really, was to nest."

Shelly sipped her tea.

"Justine was her whole world. They were awfully close, just the two of them. And then the accident happened. Justine was twelve. She—" Diane stopped to fight back tears. "It was just the worst age. It was the end of the world for her. She was completely broken."

She blew her nose.

"Anyway, I moved to Florida a long time ago, so Kathleen and I didn't see each other that much. And, growing up—she was so much older than me. So we weren't, like, buddies, you know?"

"I wish I knew. I'm an only child."

"It was more a warm, close feeling," Diane said softly. "I really did love her very much." She wiped her eye, but the heavy crying was past. "So there was no question that I'd take Justine in. But I had just been elected to the State Senate, and I was already spending the work week up in Tallahassee, so it was a really lousy solution. Don't get me wrong, I love Justine with all my heart. And, you know, if she had been like a baby or something, I might have dealt with it differently. But she was almost thirteen. You know, *almost grown.* Anyway, she came to live with me. I've been trying to do the best I can, you know? And Justine's been trying, too. She really is a great kid. But you know, not a kid, not an adult. And I'm not her mom. I'm her, I don't know—her aunt."

"I understand," said Shelly, wiping her nose and sipping the tea.

"I hired this great Jamaican guy, Winston. He's been with us for about half a year now, keeps house for me, cooks, cleans. Basically, he mothers Justine and me. She's finishing eleventh grade in a couple of weeks, but she's never really made any connections here. She hardly ever leaves the house. She's very"—Diane chose the word carefully, with sadness—"*fragile.* She's so sweet. She's just—sad. Just her and her guitar. You should hear her. She just sits in her room, singing all these heartbreaking songs."

The rain seemed to be letting up a little.

"I guess we should talk to her," Diane said

"I guess so," said Shelly.

35

The Girl

– June 6, 2006 –

"Justine, can you come in here a minute?" Diane called.

"Yes?" she said quietly.

"Shelly has something she wants to tell you."

"Okay," said the girl.

"Come, sit with us," said Diane, moving to a chair so Justine could sit next to Shelly. "It's about Mom."

Justine looked at her aunt.

"It's okay," Diane smiled. "It's all good."

The girl sat next to Shelly.

"Justine, I just want to tell you how sorry I am to hear about your mother. Your aunt told me the story."

"Okay. Thanks."

"Did your mother ever tell you about a band she sang with in college?"

Justine shrugged. Shelly waited.

"Just once."

"Can you tell me what all she said? What you remember?"

She shrugged again. "I don't think it was any big deal or anything. They were just some people who met up and played together."

"Do you remember the name of the band?"

She shook her head. "I just know that's where she met this guy."

"What guy?"

She thought for a moment. "I think she didn't know him for very long. But I guess he was pretty special for her."

"Why do you say that?"

Justine stood up and walked out of the room. Shelly and Diane looked at each other. Justine returned holding a heavy little glass ball and handed it to Shelly.

"She kept this on top of her dresser. I asked her about it once. She said it was from a very special day with a guy. She said—" Justine bit her lip. "She said it was the most beautiful day of her life. Except for the day she gave birth to me. And then she started crying, so I never asked her about it again."

Shelly examined the snow globe. A grinning blue fish was standing on its tail in a snowstorm. On the base was printed **LAKE HOPE STATE PARK.** Underneath was a price sticker, **Nick's 79¢.** She handed it back to Justine.

"It's pretty stupid," said Justine, looking down at the glass ball, turning it upside down, righting it, and watching the snowflakes fall around the fish with the silly smile. "But I guess it was important to her, so I kept it."

Shelly touched Justine's shoulder. She jerked a little but didn't withdraw. Her thoughts were deep inside the snow globe.

"Justine, have you heard of Decapede?"

"Sure," she said. "That band from YouTube. It's really cool, like this big mystery," she explained to Diane. "They sing that really pretty song, 'Creston Gold.' "

"Have you ever listened to the words?" asked Shelly.

"Not really." The girl began to sing in a tender alto, "*Storm clouds are gathering way out there, soon it's gonna rain—la la la la la la la, pass me another Creston Gold.* Something like that."

Shelly fished in her manila envelope and handed the girl a copy of the words.

"Storm clouds are gathering way out there, soon it's gonna rain—but I don't really care," declaimed the girl. "Lying with you on the ground, grass and sunlight all around, nothing's gonna bring me down, have another Creston Gold. Lake Hope lapping at the shore ..." Her voice slowed and ground to a stop.

The girl looked at Diane and then at Shelly. Shelly handed the picture of the band to Justine.

"Yeah, I've seen it. It's all over the web."

"Look at the girl in the picture, Jus," said Diane.

Justine studied at the picture, furrowing her brow, then looked up at Diane, then down at the picture again, then up at Shelly.

"It's—" she said and stopped. Diane and Shelly both nodded and waited patiently while the girl processed it all.

"That's Sam," said Shelly, pointing at the boy looking off to the side. "He wrote that song for your mother about their visit to Lake Hope."

She handed Justine the box of tissues and began to tell her the tale of Decapede, about Bauer's Brewery and about Johnny and WFOR, and about Aaron and Gavin and Bev and Mendel, and about the upcoming weekend.

"Can I come?"

Shelly looked at Diane, who nodded.

"Sure," smiled Shelly. "We'd love that."

"Will you take me to see Lake Hope?" said the girl, looking up at Shelly with her big gray eyes.

"Sure," Shelly said, "I can do that."

36

Like a Virus
– June 7, 2006 –

It was not even eight-thirty on Monday morning when Mr. Gerald Bridges walked into the office, but a workman was already attaching a "Decapede" sign to the office door, two burly guys were maneuvering a copying machine on a hand truck down the hallway, and half a dozen cleaners were vacuuming and polishing all the glassed-in cubicles like a colony of very busy bees. At the folding table where the reception desk should have been, a very short woman was sitting on a stool with her back to him, shouting into her phone.

"No, I said I need someone to cater in lunch *and* keep the break room stocked with light food and snacks. Sorry, it's a deal breaker. So hire someone. Yadda, yadda, figure it into your bill. No, I need an answer now." She smiled. "Terrific. Get your guys shaking. I want the kitchen up and running by the end of the work day. You got that?"

Two guys in mover uniforms came through lugging a bulky desk. "The executive chair and table go back in the corner office," she ordered. "All the other office tables, one to a room. Make sure you put them on the wall with the DSL outlet."

"Excuse me," said Gerald.

The woman swiveled around and jumped down from the stool. They stood looking at each other, eye to eye, 5'1" to 4'11".

"Dr. Pettiford, I presume," said the sixth-richest man in the world.

"Bev," said Bev. "I left the doctor back in Los Angeles."

"I'm Gerald Bridges," he grinned.

"I know who you are," she smiled, shaking his hand firmly.

Of course you do, he told himself, *"Gerald Bridges: Cuckold."* Out loud, he said, "And I know who you are," pumping her hand and looking her in the eye.

"You do?" asked Bev.

"Are you kidding? Decapede's manager! I heard Johnny's interview with you," he said, still pumping her hand. "I couldn't wait to meet you."

"It wasn't an official title, but—well, yeah, I guess I was," she said. *Crowned after thirty-six years,* she glowed. *And by Mr. Gerald Bridges, no less.*

"That is *sooo* cool," he prattled on. "I'm jealous."

He must be so embarrassed every time he meets someone new. "I'll tell you all about it sometime," she grinned back at him.

"I can't wait—" he bubbled.

"Sorry," she interrupted and turned to holler at two movers lugging more furniture. "I told your boss that the blue table goes in the break room! Doesn't anyone pass on instructions around here? Put it under the window." She returned to him. "Sorry."

"You're in charge here?"

"Shelly asked me to set up an office. We're just trying to hold down the fort till she gets back."

"Who's we?"

"Well, Brandi and I. She was Johnny's secretary, but Shelly stole her. She's terrific. I rented this place," she said, indicating the beehive behind her, "and started hiring staff. By the afternoon, there will be four receptionists on the phone lines during business hours, one overnight, two girls on the internet, one tech guy—"

"You did this over the weekend?" *She's very capable, this Bev.*

"It's not so complicated. All you need is telephone lines, broadband lines, office supplies, and some employees. And Brandi helped a lot," said Bev. "I'm sorry, sir, but—"

"Gerald, please."

"I'm sorry, Gerald, but what are you doing here exactly?"

"Johnny called to tell me about Decapede. I've known him since I was a kid."

"WATCH WHERE YOU'RE GOING WITH THAT! Sorry," she said, touching his arm.

It's very nice to look a woman in the eye, he thought, remembering how he'd needed to strain his neck to talk to his supermodel ex. "Anyway, that song, 'Creston Gold'?" he said. "It helped me through a rough patch. So, when Johnny told me about all this 'Decamania,' I thought maybe I'd just come to see if I could help out."

"In—in what capacity, Gerald?"

"No 'capacity.' Just to help out. Whatever I can do. No title. God, I love the sound of that!" he exuded.

Bev's phone rang. "Sorry, it's the internet service," she said to him. "No!" she shouted into her BlackBerry, "I said I need the intranet to run on *both* DSL *and* a cable modem, with two different providers. Total redundancy. I didn't ask you how much it's going to cost, I asked if you can do it, yes or no? No, Wednesday is not an option." Bev frowned. "Let me speak to your supervisor, please. When will she be back? Hello? Hello?" Bev slammed the phone down. "The sons of bitches have a three-day waiting list, no matter—"

But Gerald was already dialing his cell phone. He smiled at Bev warmly and put the phone on speaker.

"Sebastian?"

"Yes, Mr. Bridges, sir."

"Have the head of the AOL internet division in Metro Cleveland call me."

"Call you personally, sir?"

"Was I not clear the first time?" he asked, not blinking.

"Yes, sir. No problem."

"It's eight-thirty Eastern Daylight here. I expect my phone to ring by nine."

"Yes, sir, I'm on it, sir."

Gerald snapped his phone shut and puffed out his chest.

"You just did that?" choked Bev, laughing.

Gerald shrugged modestly. "So do you think there'll be a desk for me here?"

"Oh, no, I'm sure Johnny will give you his office downstairs. We don't even have a coffee machine yet."

"Want me to go out and get one?" he offered.

"Sorry. STOP DRAGGING THAT—" Bev charged off after two workmen, shouting down the hallway. Through the glass, she saw that Gerald was watching, and she shouted at them a little louder.

He chuckled, watching her berate the men. *She's very nice,* thought Gerald as she returned. *People are always nice to your face. It's behind your back that they snicker.*

"Sorry, it's a madhouse."

"Don't apologize, please. It's so cool to see this come together. You seem very good at setting up an office."

"Oh, thank you. I have some experience in it. I run a chain of radiology clinics in LA."

"Good business, medical clinics."

"Together with my—" she paused. "My as-soon-as-heavenly-possible-ex-husband."

Gerald laughed. "Why?"

"Caught the asshole turning a blind eye to our son pilfering pills. We're partners in the clinics, so I've been tied to him. But when this happened, I said 'Enough.' And just then, Shelly called. So I dropped everything, packed Robbie on a plane, and dragged him out here. He's down on Allie's farm now with Shelly's father."

I'm talking too much, thought Bev. *But he really does look interested. And it sure is nice to talk to an adult without craning your neck.*

"So I guess we're both here for kind of the same reason."

"What do you mean?" asked Gerald.

"To get away from our exes."

Gerald looked at her.

"I know about the tape and everything," she said.

He blinked. *No one's ever said that to my face before.*

"It must really suck to have shit like that played out in public."

And certainly no one's ever said that.

"I should have learned my lesson after my first marriage," she confided.

"This was my third," Gerald commiserated.

"Never again," vowed Bev.

"Never again," vowed Gerald, and they bumped their little fists. "We're just two miserable runaways."

"Where do you want this?" asked a guy with a water cooler on a hand truck.

"In the break room." She pointed without turning. "Pretty good place to run away to, though, isn't it?"

"Sure is."

Gerald's phone rang. It was the head of the AOL internet division in Metro Cleveland.

When Shelly got to the station, there was a small crowd milling around on the sidewalk. "Just to be nearby," explained a young mother with a stroller. Two guys were hawking We Are Decapede! T-shirts from a van at forty bucks a pop, and people were buying. Shelly was so tickled that she bought one and stuck it in her tote bag.

Bev and Johnny and Brandi all jumped up excitedly when Shelly came in. Gerald was waving his arms up and down, calling her a sorceress and a miracle worker, turning Shelly the shade of a Harbinger peach in May. Finally Shelly got them all settled down and into their seats.

When she told them about finding Mendel, they all gasped at every twist of fate in the tale, and beamed at his final "Yes."

When she told them about Kathleen, Bev lowered her eyes. Gerald bit his lip, and his eyes turned red. Brandi burst out in tears.

When she told them about Justine, they were stunned into silence. Johnny kept shaking his head and mumbling, "Unbelievable. Un-fucking-believable."

Each of them sat processing Shelly's fantabulous tale.

Finally, she put her hands down on the table. "Okay, come on, guys. I'm just as dazed as you. We have a lot to do. Where do we stand here?"

Johnny told her about the commotion at the station following Vaneshi's reincarnation as Mendel. "When I tell the story of Kathleen and Justine?" he said. "Shelly, it's going to be pandemonium."

"How much is the girl going to be a part of this?" asked Gerald Bridges.

"Don't count on her for anything more than a few pictures," said Shelly. "She's young, she's withdrawn. She's been through an awful lot."

Bev told her about the advance orders for the CD and that all the Cleveland TV stations and newspapers had requested a press kit and interviews. Brandi told her that stations in Indianapolis, Detroit, and Pittsburgh were starting to play "Creston Gold."

"I've been following the hits on YouTube," said Mr. Bridges. "Something remarkable is going on there. All last week the numbers were growing at an impressive speed, a few thousand a day. Incrementally. But in the forty-eight hours since Johnny announced Mendel, it's grown by twenty-six thousand. That's already exponential," he said with great gravity. "And we know what that means, right?"

"That they're starting to watch it all over," said Brandi and snapped her gum three times.

"Like a snowball," said Bev.

"Like a brush fire," said Shelly.

"Like a *virus*," said Johnny with relish, and everybody looked at him.

"I like that," said Gerald Bridges, writing it down. "We should use that. 'The clip that's spreading like a virus!' " They all agreed that it was a catchy expression. "So what's next, Ms Sorceress?"

"What's next?" Shelly repeated. She sat thinking.

She pulled the T-shirt from her bag and held it up to show them.

"We Are Decapede!" they all mouthed in astonishment.

"Profiteers outside. Forty bucks a pop."

Johnny and Brandi and Bev and Mr. Gerald Bridges looked at each other. Shelly pursed her lips. Everyone waited. Shelly tapped her pen on the table. Everyone waited. Then she stopped tapping her pen and looked at them.

"Something's happening here," she said. "What it is, I'm not sure. But there's a groundswell going on out there." She slapped the pen down on the table decisively. "This is the way I see it," she said. "We have a critical mass. Three original members of the band, plus Bev, plus Kathleen's daughter. I say we go for it," she said, looking at Gerald Bridges.

"What is 'it'?" he asked.

"A weekend. This weekend. At Gruenhaus. Photos, interviews. Maybe making some music."

"Today's Monday. We'll never get ready that fast," said Bev.

"I'll bankroll it all. Carte blanche. On one condition," said Gerald Bridges. Everyone looked at him. "Johnny films it."

"Like Woodstock," Johnny winked at Gerald. "The producers lost their shirts at the festival."

"And made a bundle on the movie," said Gerald Bridges.

"Johnny, can you do that?" asked Shelly.

"Sure," he said. "Use a steadicam, Maysles style. Follow

them getting together, hanging out, fooling around. It'll be great."

"He went to film school at NYU," Gerald explained proudly, "together with Martin Scorsese."

"Wow," said Bev and Shelly.

"Decapede Reality TV," said Brandi.

"Exactly," said Gerald Bridges. "No problem selling that to the cables." He looked at Shelly and smiled. "Deal?"

Shelly answered with a broad smile. "Deal," she said.

"Well, then, go for it, girl."

As the meeting was breaking up, Gerald pulled Brandi to the side and handed her a wad of cash. "Go downstairs and get me some of those T-shirts, will you?" he whispered to her.

Brandi cracked her gum. "Sure," she said loudly. " 'Sir.' "

Gerald looked around to be sure no one was listening. "See if they have small sizes."

37

Those Eyes

– June 7, 2006 –

Shelly waved with excitement when she saw the girl and a grinning Jamaican man with dreadlocks coming through the Arrivals gate. Justine waved back shyly. She was wearing baggy black pants and T-shirt, and her straggly dark hair hung almost to her shoulders.

Winston had been promoted from housekeeper to chaperone and was decked out for his big trip in a sunburst shirt, turquoise with rich gold and scarlet embroidery, a blue knit cap encompassing his mass of braided locks, and a patient and knowing smile. Shelly tried to estimate his age, to no avail.

Before they even left the airport parking lot, Shelly's phone rang, and she put it on speaker.

"Can you talk?" Bev asked.

"Say hi to Justine and Winston," said Shelly, and everyone exchanged greetings. "Bev's down at Gruenhaus, getting it ready for the weekend," Shelly explained to Justine and Winston. "What's up?"

"How many people will we be?" Bev asked.

"Let's see. Aaron, Gavin, Mendel."

"Your father, Robbie. That's five. Me and you, seven."

"Justine and Winston, nine," added Shelly. "And Johnny, that's ten. Mr. Bridges and Brandi will come down Thursday.

"That's twelve. Matt!" Bev shouted away from the phone. "Can you tell Penka to prepare two more rooms? And can you and Petar get rid of the old refrigerator? The new one's coming any minute." She returned to Shelly. "Sorry. Things are just a little crazy here."

"Who are Petar and Penka?"

"A couple Matt found us to help with the housekeeping. I think he knows everyone in Northeast Ohio. They don't speak much English. I think they're Bulgarian."

"How's Gruenhaus?"

"Oh, Shelly, you'll love it," Bev said excitedly. "There must be close to twenty rooms here. There's tons of linens and dishes and everything, neatly stored, with an inch of dust on everything. It's all this old dark wood, solid, sturdy, you know? Three floors. There's a music room on the first floor and a big common room. I had Matt and Robbie and your father move some more furniture in there so we can use it as a place for people to hang out. Matt brought a couple of his construction buddies to help him with the plumbing, the electricity, replacing a couple of broken windows. And some of his baseball friends and their girlfriends to help with the heavy cleaning. The kitchen's enormous. The dining room can seat about twenty. We're still looking for a cook."

"Hey, shugga? Dis is Winston. I mebbe know how to do something in de kitchen."

"Can you cook for a dozen people?" Bev asked.

"Oh, mebbe I can do dat," he smiled coyly.

"He's a magician," called Justine from the back seat.

"Yeah?" said Bev.

"Jamaican, Indonesian, Thai," said Justine proudly. "Even American."

"Bev, you heard?" asked Shelly.

"Got it," said Bev. "Winston, as soon as you get here, we'll make a list of supplies, and I'll send Matt on a run to Akron."

"Okay, shugga," smiled Winston, his dark skin framing his very white teeth.

Shelly hung up, and they continued south on I-71.

"Shelly?" asked Justine.

"Yeah, hon?"

"Will we have time to go see Lake Hope?" asked the girl guardedly.

"Of course we will, tomorrow. I promised, didn't I? And then on Thursday, Aaron, Gavin, and Mendel will be coming in. Over the weekend there will be some press. Bev is organizing interviews—radio, TV. And a photo shoot."

"What am I supposed to do?" asked the girl guardedly.

"You'll do whatever you want, and you won't do whatever you don't want." She looked at Justine in the rearview mirror. "Okay?"

Justine nodded.

"That's what I promised your aunt."

"Das right, Boo," said Winston. "You doan do nuttin' you doan want, yeah?"

"Okay," she said quietly, looking out at the flat, green fields. After a while, she asked, "Who's Robbie?"

"Bev's son. He's just finishing high school. They're from California. You're a junior, right?"

"What's he doing here?"

"Just hanging out, helping. He and Johnny Walker are driving down to the lake with us tomorrow."

"Oh." She stared out at the flat fields. "Bev, she knew my mother too?"

"Do you know what she told me?" said Shelly, looking at the girl in the rearview mirror. "She told me your mom was the coolest person she ever met."

Justine continued to stare out the window.

They parked the car next to the annex but found it empty, so they walked around to the front of Gruenhaus. The long front porch had been swept and cleaned, and now held a dozen chairs with a view of acres and acres of lush farmland. There were four or five little children playing tag on the front lawn, weaving around and laughing. Shelly led Winston and Justine up the steps and into the tall entrance hall, where people were darting from place to place, carrying and cleaning and moving, shouting and banging and dragging.

"Anybody home?" Shelly called.

"Watch out," called Colonel Griffin as he and Robbie pushed past them, struggling to lug a heavy old sofa in the direction of the music room. Winston jumped to help Robbie on his side. Shelly attempted to do the same on her father's side, but he brushed her away.

Bev came out of the kitchen through the dining room, wiping her hands on a towel. "Hey, Shelly, good to see you."

They gave each other a quick hug.

"Whose kids are those?" Shelly asked.

"Oh, they belong to Petar and Penka. Most of them, anyway. They're actu—"

And then she saw Justine and froze. Bev stood staring at her, her mouth agape.

"What?" said Justine.

"Jesusfuckingchrist," said Bev.

"What?" asked Shelly.

"You don't see it?" whispered Bev.

"See what?" Shelly repeated.

"Those eyes? The cheeks, the lips? It's Kathleen incarnate." Justine looked away.

"Come here, you," said Bev, and she hugged the girl so tightly Shelly imagined she heard a bone pop. Justine smiled in embarrassment.

"Hey, Shel," said the Colonel.

"Hi Dad. I see Allie's got you working."

"Oh, he's making himself useful," Allie joshed, and the Colonel smiled at her. Shelly blinked twice, and he was still smiling.

"Hi, you Missus Allie?"

"Yes, Winston?" Gruenhaus had never before seen a dark-skinned man with an overwhelmingly bright blue and red-and-gold embroidered shirt, dreadlocks, and a knit headcovering.

"Das me. Justine here, she take care of me," he said with a giant smile exposing many very white Jamaican teeth, rubbing his hands together. "Somebody tell me you got a kitchen here in dis Gruenhaus."

"Well, I believe there is," Allie said with a smile, taking his arm and leading him off.

"Robbie, this is Justine," said Shelly.

"Hi," he grunted.

Justine lifted her eyes enough to peek at him. "Hi," she said, barely audible.

"Robbie, why don't you show Justine the house?"

"Okay," he mumbled.

"Justine," said Shelly, "is that okay?"

The girl shrugged. "Okay," she said indifferently.

And they trudged off, the two teenagers, both of them dragging their feet.

That night Shelly and Bev sat on the front porch swing, sipping Winston's coffee and resting up from a hard day's work.

"I thought that we'll use this porch for the interviews if the weather's good," said Decapede Weekend Director-General Dr. Beverly Pettiford. "We'll put Aaron and Gavin and Mendel out here and bring in the media people one at a time, give them each half an hour. So far there's six teams. I figure two each afternoon, Friday-Saturday-Sunday. That sound okay?" she asked Shelly.

"Great. How are things at the office?"

"Brandi's terrific."

"I love that girl."

"She's running it like a ringmaster. Everyone's terrified of her."

"That vampire look of hers?" smiled Shelly.

"I wouldn't mind if she wore a little bit more clothes," said Bev.

"I thought you saw stuff like that all the time in California."

"It doesn't bother me. But it sure keeps the guys sniffing around her. Anyway, she's driving down on Thursday with Gerry. To be here when the band arrives."

"Gerry?" said Shelly, teasing.

"Gerald. Mr. Bridges."

"*Gerry?*" said Shelly.

"Shut up."

"He's coming down for the whole weekend?"

"That's what he told me."

"What for exactly?" asked Shelly.

"You'd have to ask him," answered Bev.

"You don't think he'll be in the way?"

"Oh, Shelly, he's not like that at all. He's helping Brandi run the office. He's been coming in early, staying late."

"No kidding? Doing what exactly?"

"Bullying suppliers, signing checks, going out for dough-nuts. He's having a ball."

"Mr. Gerald Bridges is doing the coffee run for the office?"

"And loving every minute of it," said Bev. "Gives him something to think about other than that tape, poor guy."

"It sounds to me like you've been talking to him a lot more than I have."

"Well, someone has to work while you're off gallivanting."

"Bev?"

"What? No. I told you. Never again. It's a work relation-ship."

Shelly looked at her.

"A convivial work relationship."

The two women sat looking out at the stars and the moon

and the night sky, rocking gently.

"You never did tell me what happened in Mason City, Iowa," said Bev.

"That's because nothing happened in Mason City, Iowa," said Shelly.

"Really?" said Bev.

"Really," said Shelly. "Buddy Holly died there."

Shelly could hear faint music from inside, Robbie on the newly-tuned Steinway baby grand, Justine on her guitar. All of a sudden she jerked upright in the rocking chair.

"Instruments!" she said to Bev, panicked.

"What instruments?" asked Bev, alarmed.

"Drums, guitars, amplifiers, and stuff. The guys might want to play—"

"Coming in by truck tomorrow from Akron."

"You knew what to order?" Shelly asked.

"Robbie talked to them."

"Oh," said Shelly, exhaling and sitting back in her chair. "Okay, then."

And so, they sat there on the porch, looking out over Medina County in the moonlight, staring out at the stars and beyond, these two women, free-flying through this fantastical dream, pondering what had passed, what was passing, and what was yet to come.

38

Road Trip

– June 8, 2006 –

Bev set eight o'clock as their departure time for the drive down to Lake Hope. Robbie whined about getting up so early, but the smell of Winston's blueberry pancakes enticed him out of bed. Shelly noted with great satisfaction that Allie sat next to her father and engaged him in easy conversation, a feat that had eluded Shelly for her entire forty-three years.

Johnny, in the passenger seat, was behaving like a kid on a school trip, filming everything and chatting and jabbering far too much and too loudly for the early hour.

"Mr. Walker," Robbie said, "can I ask you something?"

"Mr. Walker?" said Johnny, looking around the car. "Who's that?"

"What should I call you?" Robbie asked.

"Anything you want. I promise you I've been called worse than anything you can think of."

Robbie didn't know how to respond to that.

"Johnny. Call me Johnny."

"Is it true that George Harrison gave you his own Fender Stratocaster?"

"Well, ah, yes, that's true."

"Really?" asked Shelly, impressed.

"Yup," said Johnny. "My big claim to fame."

Justine watched from her corner of the back seat.

"How?" asked Robbie, leaning forward.

"George was touring the US in 1974. I was working for this booking agent as a gofer. And he's bringing George fucking Harrison to Cleveland. Whoops," he said, looking at Shelly. "I guess I'm not supposed to use language like that around kids."

"It's okay, Johnny," said Shelly, patting his hand, "I think they can handle it."

"Anyway, big excitement. Middle of the winter. And there's this mother of a snowstorm. They sent me out to the airport to pick him up because I had my brother's four-wheel-drive pickup that could plow through an iceberg. And my girlfriend, who's now my wife, said there was no way she wasn't coming with me to meet George fucking Harrison. So, we get to the airport, get him and Olivia—"

"Who's that?" asked Justine.

"At the time, she was a secretary at his record company in LA. He was still married to Patti, but that was almost over. He had just met Olivia, and they were really, really into each other. Lovely, lovely woman, Olivia. So we're at the Cleveland airport, the four of us, and they announce that the show's been canceled because the whole city is snowed in, so all of a sudden, he has three days free. And he asks me how far it is to Mammoth Cave, there's a crystal cave there that he wants to see. George fucking Harrison. But it's snowing like nobody's business. So I check the weather, and I see that if we get moving southwards right away, we can outrun the worst of the storm. That's what we did. We hung out down there at Mammoth Cave for three days, the four of us. We had a pretty good time, some of the details of which I might share with you kids when you get much, much older."

The boy and the girl exchanged short glances.

"And the guitar?" Robbie asked.

"When I drove them back to the airport, George wanted to give me something. All he had with him was the guitar. So he just handed it to me. Said he had another one with the tour equipment."

"Wow," said Robbie.

"You know, you could have a go on it, too, if you like."

"Oh, man, I think I just died and went to heaven," said Robbie, falling back in his seat.

Shelly peeked in the rearview. Justine was huddled in the corner of the back seat, but her eyes were following the conversation.

"Where'd you hear about the guitar?" asked Johnny.

"The Johnny Walker Show."

"You've been following it?"

"Back home."

"We don't broadcast in California."

"People record the show. I downloaded it from Napster."

"What is that exactly?"

"It's the peer-to-peer thing people are using these days. It's pretty new," he added.

"What people?" asked Johnny.

"Anyone who's interested in a certain subject. They upload something interesting for them. Like the first show when you talked about the brewery and the song and the band. That one's really popular. Then people anywhere in the world can download it and listen."

"No shit?" said Johnny. "Brave new world, this interweb stuff."

"No shit," said Robbie. "It's called file-sharing. Since Decapede started, people have been downloading your shows."

"Is that legal?" Johnny asked.

"No," answered Shelly, "but anything you play on your show, people can download. That's why we're in such a hurry to get the music licensed and out there commercially. So that the DecaInc can start—"

"What's that?" Robbie asked.

"Decapede, Incorporated. That's my nickname for the company."

"What does it do?" asked Justine.

"It's the legal framework for this whole thing. To protect everyone's interests. So that the band should get money from people listening to their music. Including you, young lady. To pay my salary and Bev's. Doesn't that sound fair?"

"Could I get a job, too?" asked Robbie. "I mean, like, a real paying job? I mean, I'm happy to help any way I can, like I already put broadband internet into Allie's office and into the workroom I set up for my mom, and I could help out with sound at Gruenhaus, I was even looking at the music room, thinking how we could improve the acoustics, to get it ready for some—"

"You're hired," said Shelly.

"For what?" he asked.

"All of the above and more of same and more of other. Okay?"

"Okay!"

"Maybe he could teach me some of that technical stuff, and with the phone and everything?" Johnny asked Shelly, half in jest.

"Oh, you don't need to pay me for that," said the boy.

"I'll talk to your mom," said Shelly. "We'll work out an equitable deal, okay?"

"Okay!" he said, elated.

In the rearview mirror, Shelly caught Justine looking at him and almost smiling.

"Justine?"

"Mm-hmm?"

"You know, Robbie is the one who started all this," said Shelly.

"Really?" she said, looking at him.

Johnny turned in his seat. "That was you who put that clip of 'Creston Gold' on the YouTube?"

Robbie grinned proudly.

"Tell me," said Johnny, pointing the camera at him.

"I used to digitize stuff for people, make some pocket money, you know, usually audio and video cassettes. But someone asked me if I could do reel-to-reel. So I was digging around in my mom's closet and found the Decapede box. And—boom," he grinned to the camera like a peacock in full-feathered display. He glanced at Justine.

"When does the CD come out?" she asked.

"Tomorrow," said Johnny. "I'm going to do a special, listen to it on the air for the first time, live."

"Oh, damn," said Shelly, fishing in her purse, "you reminded me, Brandi put this on my desk this morning. I have no idea what it is." She pulled out a square white envelope with a cellophane window and, inside, an unmarked CD. She slipped it into the player.

"Ready?" said a voice, and then another counted, "One, two, one two three —" and a thumping piano and clear, agile tenor began to sing, "*If you see me walking down the street ...*"

"It's them!" shouted Johnny.

"Omigod!" said Shelly, slowing down the car and turning up the music.

Robbie and Justine both sat forward. The four of them listened, looking at each other in amazement and grinning like fools.

"Oh, what a show I'm going to do with this!" said Johnny.

Shelly pushed Pause. "But you said you were going to listen for the first time on the air."

"Well, I just need to check it, to make sure there isn't any foul language or anything, don't I?" said Johnny.

"Prudent," said Shelly, "very prudent," and she pushed Play.

They heard some scuffling and muffled noises. Then, someone asked, "How was that?" and someone else answered, "Thas about the whitest music ever get made in this room. Awright, y'all ready? 'Peggy Sue,' Take One."

And then a muscular, hoarse voice ripped into a driving

"Peggy Sue," more commanding and soulful than any of them could have imagined, "*If you knew Peggy Sue,*" riveting in its intensity. Every time he said *Mah-hah Peggy Sue-ha-hu,* Shelly pictured Kathleen. The song ended, and Johnny pressed Pause.

"Wow," said Shelly.

"Wow," repeated Robbie, shaking his head.

Johnny shook his head in amazement.

"What did you think, Justine?" Shelly asked.

"Yeah, wow," she said almost inaudibly. "He was pretty incredible."

"I guess that's what they mean when they say Sam was the heart and soul of the band," said Johnny.

"Boy, if you could find him ..." said Robbie.

Shelly shrugged. "It doesn't look like that's going to happen."

"What do you know exactly?" asked Justine.

"As far as I can piece it together, Sam Miller and your mom drove down to Lake Hope to find a guitarist for the band, Mendel, who was called Vaneshi back then. You'll meet him tomorrow. He's very, very nice. They came in your mom's car, Robbie, a maroon 1968 Mustang convertible."

"Cool," said Robbie.

"Cool," said Johnny.

Justine smiled.

"They visited Vaneshi-Mendel in the trailer where he was living. Apparently it was a very special day for both of them, because 'Creston Gold' came out of it." She paused. "That's it. That's the whole story."

"The snow globe," said Justine, still staring out at the flat fields.

"Right. Justine's mom kept a souvenir from that day, a snow globe. From Nick's Gas Station."

Justine pulled the snow globe out of her purse and showed it to the men. "See, 'Lake Hope State Park.' "

"If we can find that trailer, it'll make some great footage," said Johnny.

"You sound excited," said Robbie.

"I love getting back behind the camera," said Johnny. "Haven't done it in years. I could teach you some of the basics, if you're interested."

"Hell yeah," said Robbie, beaming.

"First rule: Turn the damned thing on. You never know when something memorable is going to happen. Now can we hear some more music?" He pressed Play.

Someone cleared his throat and played a chord on the guitar. There were several seconds of silence, and then that raspy, sensual baritone began, naked and vulnerable and oozing hunger, "*Just—you—know—why*," and the band came in with a gentle swing. Johnny and Robbie and Justine and Shelly listened, enrapt.

"Whoo," said Robbie.

"He's really good," said Justine.

"I've heard a lot of singers in my time," said Johnny. "He's really something."

Shelly turned up the air conditioning.

The band started playing a thumping gospel riff punctuated by Aaron's low, funky piano chords. And then, again, Sam's wonder of a voice. "*If you ever change your mind about leaving, leaving me behind ...*" He sang it soulfully, at the top of his register, straining and shouting with utter abandon.

At the end of the song, after a couple of seconds of silence, the band broke into whoops and shouts of exhilaration. Shelly pressed Pause.

"My God," exuded Johnny. "People are going to go crazy."

"It's an oldie?" Robbie asked.

"Sam Cooke. Everybody covered it—John, Paul, Van, Burdon. None of them come close to this. Oh, what a show I'm going to ..." He pressed Play.

And then the next song came on, with a loping, tinkling piano leading a familiar folk-rock intro. Several bars in, the band stopped.

"Can you give me a little more piano in my headphones?"

"Aaron," said Shelly.

"Ah give you piano up the wazoo, man."

Johnny asked Shelly who that was, but she shrugged.

"Can we just play the fucking thing?" growled another voice.

"Sam," she mouthed.

"Did anyone see my water?" asked a female voice.

Shelly looked at Justine in the mirror. The girl was staring out the window, her legs folded up against her, chewing her knuckle.

"It's right behind you."

"Gavin," said Shelly.

A pause, with some fiddling on the guitar, drums.

"One! Two! Three!" Aaron said crisply, leaving the "four" empty, and again came the familiar tinkling piano intro.

"*You and I travel to the beat of a different drum ...*"

"Stop the car, please," said Justine suddenly.

"What?" said Shelly.

"Could you please stop the car?" Justine repeated, her voice catching.

Shelly pulled the car sharply off the two-lane highway onto the shoulder. Justine jumped out of the car, slamming the door behind her, and stomped off, almost running, stumbling through the high weeds.

Shelly, Johnny, and Robbie looked at each other.

"Aren't you going to go after her?" Johnny asked Shelly, his voice shaky.

"I will," she said. "Give her a minute."

The song continued to play. The singer laid back on the beat and punched out, "*Oh, you cry-y*" in a syncopated funk.

Shelly got out of the car and pushed through the brush to where Justine was sitting on a rock, her head cradled in her arms. Shelly sat next to her wordlessly. After a minute, she put her arm around the girl.

"She used to sing that song to me," Justine said, her voice muffled and choked with tears. Shelly slipped her a tissue, holding her as she blew her nose.

They sat in silence as Justine's breathing grew steady.

"She used to sing that song to me," Justine repeated.

"I know, sweetie," Shelly said quietly. "Shh. It's okay."

They walked back to the car, hand in hand. Shelly pulled back onto the road. They rode in silence.

"Can you play it again, please?" Justine asked in a small voice.

As the last chord faded, the girl singer tittered with joy, and they all smiled broadly. Shelly pressed the Pause button.

"What a beautiful voice," Johnny said respectfully.

They rode in silence.

"Should we play the next one?" Shelly asked after a minute. In the rearview mirror, Shelly saw Justine wipe her nose and nod.

Aaron's piano hit a sassy, confident chord progression that everyone recognized immediately, and then Vaneshi's guitar came on top in a raucous jangle to build a wall of glorious, butt-moving music, and they all joined in together, "*Well, he walked up to me, and he asked me if I wanted to dance!*"

By the second line, Justine was singing along, too, and by the second verse, she was letting go in full-throttle rock 'n' roll. Johnny ramped up the volume, unbuckled his seat belt and began bouncing and waving his hands all over the car, laughing. He pulled Justine into his squashed-up, middle-aged dance, "*and then he kissed me!*"

The song ended with Gavin's flashy drum roll, and Shelly pressed Pause. The disgruntled brat, the aging hippie, the brokenhearted orphan, and their intrepid leader, all shrieking whoops of joy at the astonishing, exhilarating music that had never been heard since the day it was made.

39

Lake Hope Renewed

– June 8, 2006 –

The red-white-and-blue plastic sign in front of the little old red-brick building said Exxon with the price per gallon, but above the door was an old, weather-worn sign.

NICK'S GAS
BAIT TACKLE & SOUVENIRS

Behind the counter stood an old man wearing a frayed, formerly white shirt buttoned all the way up to his neck, looking like he had modeled for American Gothic.

"Hi," said Shelly brightly.

"Hello," he responded gravely.

"Have you been working here for long?"

"Yup."

"Did you ever carry these?" She fished Justine's snow globe out of her purse.

He looked at the inscription **LAKE HOPE STATE PARK** and turned the globe upside down. The tag read **Nick's 79¢**.

He glanced at it. "Yup."

"Do you remember how long ago?"

"Yup."

"How long ago?"

"Till about 1981."

"Right. Maybe you can help me with this. I'm looking for a trailer up by the lake. Used to be painted in crazy colors. Do you know the place I'm talking about?"

Nick stared through his rimless glasses at Johnny and his nehru shirt and ponytail. "Dunno."

"Do you know anyone around here who might know?"

"Gardner, mebbe."

"Where would I find him?"

Robbie and Justine laid down their booty of junk food.

"Tell me, sir," Johnny asked him straight-faced, "have you ever heard of Decapede?"

"Decapede? There ain't no such thing," he scorned and began to ring up the pile of sugar.

"Tootsie Rolls?" asked Shelly. "Kids still eat that stuff?"

"My mom used to have them around the house," said Justine.

"Yes, so, this Gardner?" Shelly asked Mr. Gothic.

"'Bout a mile and a half up 278, you got your turn-off to Lake Hope State Park? So you go another couple hunrit yards, you got a little road off to the right. You take that and follow it for half a mile."

"Okay! Thanks very much."

"Then there's a wooden gate, but it's gonna be locked."

"Are you guys following this?"

They all nodded.

"So you climb over it, and walk up this dirt road about another two hunrit yards."

"Okay! Thank you."

"Then there's a little path going up through the trees to the right."

She waited.

"You follow that, and up at the top, that's his place. Right on the lake."

"Okay, great, thanks so much."

"Used to be there, anyways. I ain't been up there in years."

"Great, thanks."

"You watch how you go. He don't cotton much to strangers."

They tried to follow Gothic Nick's directions but disagreed as to whether they had found the correct gate. Shelly ordered Johnny to stop filming while she climbed the fence. As Shelly walked along the dirt road, she watched Johnny zooming in on two squirrels arguing hysterically over an acorn while Robbie and Justine walked up ahead.

Robbie had metamorphosed from a sullen, hooded punk into a frisky colt, stretching and kicking and checking out his newfound muscles and bones. He was flinging sticks and stones as far as he could, balancing himself on a log, smiling and shouting something at Justine, but she walked ahead with her head down. She was still in baggy black pants and a T-shirt, her hair drooping aimlessly. Shelly tried to imagine what was going on inside this poor sixteen-year-old's mind and heart, alone in the world, hearing her vibrant young voice singing out from the past, retracing her dead mother's footsteps. Shelly remembered her own feelings of abandonment and fear when her mother died, and she had been in her twenties. To be left alone in the world at twelve, with no anchor, no real home, no sense of belonging anywhere in this cold world? That was a crueler fate than Shelly could fathom.

"How you doing?" asked Johnny as they walked.

"It's nice to have a day to catch my breath," she said.

"You've been running around a lot."

"And now I get all my emails on my BlackBerry, so there's no rest," she said.

"See, there are advantages to being a Luddite," he laughed.

"Tell me, how long have you known Mr. Bridges?"

"Forever. He was the little kid next door, a few years

younger than me. And I suppose he looked up to me."

"Of course he did," teased Shelly.

"I guess you could say he wasn't the most popular kid on the block, what with his size and—" Johnny hesitated. "Between us, yeah?"

"And?" Shelly grinned.

"Well, let's just call it his 'deficient' social skills."

"Tactfully put," smiled Shelly. "Abrasive, maybe?"

"Obnoxious. Anyway, one Thanksgiving vacation, I must have been in college, and my parents were away, so I threw a bit of a bash. And this whiny little momma's boy from next door was always hanging around. I felt sorry for him, so I told him he could come. He must have been about fifteen, I guess."

"And very short," said Shelly.

"And very short," laughed Johnny. "Anyway, apparently little Gerald Bridges had a couple of bottles of Creston Gold, and some hippie girl who must have been severely intoxicated or benevolent or whatever decided to bestow upon him a lesson in Life Science—"

Shelly was laughing so hard she had to stop walking,

"And he's never forgotten it." Johnny looked around, as if the squirrels might be eavesdropping. "And then, you know, he went on to make all that money. But he always kept in touch with me."

"Do you see him?"

"Every time he comes to Cleveland to visit his mother, I take him to see whoever's in town, take him backstage, make him feel cool."

"His mother?" Shelly laughed.

"She must be about a hundred and six years old. One foot in the grave for fifty years now." Johnny gave Shelly his hand as they climbed over a fallen tree trunk. "And then, when he was trying to impress that tennis player, I got him backstage passes to a Stones show."

Just then a mangy, knee-high, gray-brown dog came

bursting out of the woods, barking furiously at the intruders. Justine crouched down on one knee and extended her hands to the side, cooing at it softly. The dog hesitated, startled, then renewed its hysterical barking. The girl kept low, calm, and still, answering its howling with her reassuring, soothing "Good boy, good boy." The dog tried to maintain its fury, but the girl continued stroking him with her voice, undeterred. "Come here, boy," she said gently. "Good boy." The dog came a step closer to her, barking but with pauses, listening to the girl. She extended her open hand toward the dog. It approached cautiously till it was close enough to smell her hand, or to bite it.

"That's a good boy," she said, leaning forward to touch the dog's muzzle. It jumped back, but she edged toward it, still on one knee, and the dog let her touch its head, then pat it, then scratch it behind its ear. The dog's yowling had become a pitiable, insecure whine, and finally it surrendered onto its back so that she could stroke its belly.

They turned onto the path through the woods, the dog trotting next to Justine, till they saw the back of a small sun-blanched trailer surrounded by an odd assortment of tools, a disembodied car seat, and a tidy vegetable garden, half-a-minute's walk from the lake. The woods were silent except for the chattering of the squirrels and the lapping of the lake on the pebbly shore.

"Could this be the place?" asked Robbie.

"I told you we turned too soon," said Johnny.

Shelly knocked on the trailer door, but there was no answer. On the door she could just make out the traces of a faded amoeba-shaped design. She opened the door a crack. It looked like a human abode but smelled like the den of some denizen of the forest. There was a little old refrigerator with a six-inch gash in the door, an unmade cot, a single table with tools for making some sort of flies for fishing, a few books, and a disused radio-cassette player on a shelf. A battered acoustic guitar was propped against the wall.

She closed the door behind her and took a deep breath of the fresh lake air.

Robbie and Justine plopped down on the car seat with their plastic bags of goodies, the dog wagging its tail and trying to smell Justine's crotch and whining for attention at her feet. Shelly walked down to the edge of the lake, with Johnny following her, filming.

"Sure is beautiful here," she said. "I can understand why they named it Lake Hope."

That was when Shelly saw the man approaching along the rocky lakefront, carrying a fishing pole and wearing a stained Wellington Academy Lacrosse Team sweatshirt despite the warm mid-May sun.

"What are you doing here?" asked the man gruffly.

"Hi," said Shelly sunnily, "Mr. Gardner?"

The man stood in front of her, his eyes darting nervously. He had shaggy, self-butchered sandy hair and a grizzled stubble of a beard. He smelled like the forest.

"Wadda you want?"

"I'm Shelly Griffin," she said, extending her hand, trying unsuccessfully to make eye contact. The man backed away a step, and Shelly lowered her hand.

"We're looking for a crazy-colored trailer that used to be somewhere around here a long time ago," she smiled charmingly.

The man shot a wary look at her, uncharmed.

The dog came running around the corner of the trailer, barking again furiously at Shelly and Johnny, showing the man how well it was protecting their home.

"The clerk at Nick's said you might know—" Shelly tried, but the barking was too loud for her to hear herself talk.

"Shut up, dog," the man barked, but the dog persisted, abashed at having allowed the interlopers in. "I said *shut up!*" he said, kicking dirt at it, but the dog ignored him, knowing it could get away with the barking as long as it didn't bite.

"Have you lived here for long?" Shelly asked.

"What's it to you?" growled the man, sneaking a furtive, suspicious glance at her.

"I'm just trying to find that trailer—"

"Hey!" the man shouted sharply, turning to see Johnny filming him.

"It's nothing, we're making a documentary—" Johnny attempted.

"Get the fuck out of here," he snarled, breathing hard.

"Oh, sorry, I didn't mean—" said Johnny, backing away.

"Get rid of that thing," he barked, moving jerkily towards to Johnny. The man slapped the camera out of Johnny's hand, knocking it to the ground. The dog howled with frenzy.

"Hey, what are you—" blurted Johnny, startled and angry. The man gave Johnny a stinging, ringing, open-handed slap across the face.

"What the fuck?" Johnny cried, holding his cheek.

"Hey, mister, back off!" said Shelly, insinuating herself in front of him, shoving him back fearlessly with her body.

"Ge— Get the fuck—" stammered the man, stumbling a step back. His nostrils were flared, and his eyes were wild and careening.

The dog continued its deafening hysteria.

Robbie came running down from the trailer, with Justine following behind.

"Hey, leave her alone!" Robbie shouted at the man. Shelly stood her ground.

But the man had stopped motionless, frozen, staring with wide eyes over Shelly's shoulder at the girl. She looked back at him with her large gray eyes, undaunted. The dog continued its ear-piercing protest.

"Who're you?" he asked.

"Justine."

He walked around Shelly and stood panting in the girl's

face, but she didn't shy away. Even when he bent forward to sniff her, she didn't flinch.

"Shut the fuck up!" he barked at the dog, but the dog ignored him and continued yowling.

"We're not going to hurt you, mister," said Justine calmly, staring him right in the eyes. "We're just looking for this old trailer."

"Nng," he said, and tried to look away, but she wouldn't let go of his eyes.

"Do you know of a crazy-colored trailer somewhere around here, right near the lake?"

The man was stealing glances at the girl, looking at her, looking away, looking back, his breath gradually slowing.

"Do you?"

"Wadda you want it for?" he said finally.

"There's this band that they're talking about a lot on the radio, Decapede. Have you heard of them?" asked Justine gently.

He stared at her for a long moment.

"There's a guy from that band who lived in a funny-colored trailer somewhere around here once upon a time." She spoke softly, almost touching him. "His name was Vaneshi. We just wanted to see where he lived."

"What for?" he asked, his raspy voice lowering to meet hers. His eyes tried to sneak away, but she pulled them back.

"Because this band has become crazy popular. Maybe you've heard the song on the radio, 'Creston Gold'? *'Storm clouds are gathering way out there'*?" she sang softly.

He stared at her as though she had three eyes and was speaking Martian.

"This is Shelly Griffin," the girl continued in a soothing voice, "from WFOR, the radio station in Cleveland. She's running the whole thing. This is Johnny Walker, the DJ that's promoting the project."

"Who're you?" he asked.

"Justine. My mother was in the band."

"Where is she?"

"She's dead."

The man's hands moved slowly to embrace himself. He lowered his head and stared at the ground, rocking slowly.

"Mister?" said the girl.

"We're the ones who are getting the band back together," said Shelly, moving closer.

"What for?" he asked, squinting at Justine.

"It's become this craze," explained Justine patiently. "The whole country is dying to learn more about this band."

"It's all over the internet," added Robbie.

"Who're you?" asked the man.

"Robbie. My mother used to work with the band."

"Yeah?" he grumbled, scratching his grizzled cheek.

"Yeah," answered Robbie bravely, trying to show he wasn't afraid.

The man continued to steal glances at the girl, his jaw muscles flexing underneath the stubble.

"You want some candy?" she asked, holding up the plastic bag.

"What is this, Halloween?" he snarled.

"Trick or treat?" Justine baited him, holding his eye.

The man glared back.

"You want, yes or no?"

Where did this slip of a girl get the courage to face down this cantankerous hermit? Shelly wondered.

"Depends what you got," he answered.

She rifled through the plastic bag, reading off names. "Pringles, Cheetos, Jolly Ranchers, Twinkies, Corn Nuts, Slim Jims, Almond Joy, Suzie Qs. You want a Mars Bar?"

"Nah, they don't have any chew to them. What's that?" he said, spying the Tootsie Roll.

"That's mine," she said.

He grunted. "So give me half."

Justine shrugged and tore the bar in half. He stuck his

half in his pocket and sat on the car seat to pore through the bag. Robbie pulled over a wooden crate and a backless folding chair. A couple of squirrels edged close to the man to beg for food, but he ignored them, and when the others tried to feed them, they skittered away in terror.

"So, Mr. Gardner," asked Shelly, "do you know of a painted trailer like that somewhere around here?"

"Maybe. Let me think about it." He stood, pocketed a handful of the plunder, and turned to Justine. "I got a fishing line I have to check. You, come."

Justine stood up.

"Justine—" said Shelly.

"We're just walking down to the shore," said the man. "You can see us from here."

Shelly hesitated.

"Do I look like a child molester?" he asked, spreading his arms to display his derelict mien, and guffawed with abandon at his own joke.

"It's okay, Shelly," said Justine.

"You people keep out of my garden," he called over his shoulder as he walked away. Justine followed, unquestioning.

They walked side-by-side in silence, the girl picking her way over the rocky shore as lightly and hesitantly as a week-old doe.

"What's your dog's name?" she asked.

"Just 'dog'," he answered.

"Not much of a name," she responded.

"Not much of a dog," he said. "So where do you live?"

"In Florida, with my aunt. Since my mom died."

"Nng. How long ago's that?"

"Four years."

"Father?"

"Test tube."

"No shit?"

"No shit."

"Fuckin' far out," he said. They walked in silence. "How old are you, then, twelve or something?"

"Sixteen."

"Ah." And then, after a moment, he added, "I didn't mean that you don't look your age or anything. I'm just not too good at that kind of stuff."

"That's okay," she said, looking up at him, smiling. And then the man sort of smiled, too.

As they walked, the man began to pick up flat stones and skip them across the water.

"How about you?" she asked.

"What about me?"

"How'd you wind up here?"

"Once upon a time—I got hurt. I needed a place to mend. This place here was empty, so I stayed for a while. That turned into a summer. Which turned into a winter. Et cetera." He slung a stone masterfully, skipping almost a dozen times, and chuckled. "I got used to the quiet."

"You live here all by yourself?"

"Yup." They stopped, and the man skipped rocks as she watched. "I do some gardening up at the lodge."

"Doesn't it get lonesome?"

"Nah," he said. "I don't like people too much."

"Not even me?" she teased.

"You're a kid. That's different." He looked up at the trailer. Shelly was watching them, shouting distance away.

"Why not?" the girl asked after a while.

"Why not what?"

"Why don't you like people?"

"Can't trust 'em."

Justine picked up a stone and tried skipping it, but it plopped straight to the bottom.

"No, put your foot back. Hold it from the edge, like this."

She tried, but the stone disappeared.

"No, like this!" he said impatiently. "See?"

"I see!" answered the sixteen-year-old.

"So you wind up like this, and then as you step forward, you gotta whip your wrist. That's where you get your action on the rock."

She tried, but it plopped.

"You just gotta figure out when to flick your wrist and when to let go of the stone. You practice. You want to do something right, you gotta practice."

"Okay," she smiled, sensing that he was trying to be nice in his awkward way.

"So what's the deal with this band?" he asked.

"They're playing that song 'Creston Gold' all over the radio and everything. It's a hit."

"A hit, huh?"

She nodded. "Everyone wants to know about the band. Shelly's been trying to dig them up. That's how she found me."

"What's in it for her?"

"She's not like that at all. She's about the nicest person I've ever met in my life."

"You came all the way up here from Florida?" he asked.

She nodded. "Yesterday. The guys she found are coming to this big old farmhouse for the weekend. The drummer, the guitarist, and the guy who played piano. So I wanted to be there, too. Because of my mom, you know."

The man said nothing.

"And I wanted to see Lake Hope."

He looked at her.

"It was special for my mom."

"Yeah? Why's that?"

"There was this guy from the band—Sam. The one Shelly can't find. He and my mom spent the day here. I think he wrote the song about that day. '*Lake Hope lapping at the shore / This must be the place I've been searching for,*'" she sang softly, looking out at the lake lapping at the shore.

The man skipped another stone.

"She said it was the most beautiful day of her life," added Justine pulling out the largemouth bass snow globe from her bag. "See?" she said, showing him the **LAKE HOPE STATE PARK** inscription on the base. "She kept it on her dresser."

A gnarled sound came from the man's throat.

"Are you okay?"

"Yeah." He wiped his nose on the sleeve of his battered sweatshirt. He patted his pocket and pulled out the stub of the Tootsie Roll.

"We should go back," said the girl.

As they approached the trailer, they saw Robbie playing on the man's guitar.

"Please don't get angry," the girl said to the man quietly, touching his arm. The man jerked, but said nothing.

Robbie stopped in mid-phrase, watching the man warily.

"Listen," said the man in Johnny's direction, but avoiding his eyes, "I'm sorry about that. I— I don't see many strangers around here."

"Yeah. I guess we surprised you," said Johnny, rising and extending his hand. "Peace?"

"Peace," mumbled the man, touching Johnny's hand.

Robbie was still holding the guitar, embarrassed and not a little afraid. "I'm sorry, Mr. Gardner, I hope it's okay. The case was just sitting here."

"Nah, it's okay. Not bad."

"Thanks. You play?"

"Here and there. What about you, girl?"

Justine shrugged.

"What kind of answer is that?" he asked gruffly. "I asked if you play guitar."

"Here and there!" she shot back at him, mimicking his gruff baritone.

"So play something for me," he said.

"No," she said.

The man took the guitar and pushed it into her arms.

Justine strummed a few chords. *"You and I travel to the beat of a different drum ..."*

That was when Sam Miller lowered his head and began to cry.

40

Loudmouth
Bass Deboned

– June 8, 2006 –

Shelly quietly slipped him a packet of tissues from her bag. Sam blew his nose several times and wiped his eyes before he lifted his head.

"Your turn," Justine said to him, holding out the guitar.

"Nah," he said, squirming.

She continued holding the guitar towards him.

He waved his hand in dismissal.

"What kind of answer is that?" she said in a mock gruff baritone.

He shot a look at her, took the guitar, held it close to his body for a long time, then positioned it and began to play the familiar introduction. He closed his eyes and began to sing.

"*Storm clouds are gathering way out there / Soon it's gonna rain— but I don't really care,*" he sang, his voice tight and struggling. But when Justine began to sing her mother's harmony, he broke and let the guitar slide gently to the ground.

After they had all dried their eyes, Shelly told him about Allie. "And then I just happened to find a clip of 'Creston Gold' on YouTube."

"That's part of the internet," explained Johnny.

"So then we got Johnny to talk about it on his show—" said Shelly.

"Who's 'we'?" Sam asked.

"Me."

"So, say 'me.' "

"And it just caught on. People started calling the station, asking to hear it. Again and again."

"Hmph," said Sam, scratching his scraggly beard.

"Do you know how many people have seen the clip, Sam?" Shelly asked.

"How would I know that?"

"It was a rhetorical question. I asked it for dramatic effect."

The grizzled man shot a glance at her.

"Over eighty thousand people. In the last two weeks. It's a hit."

Sam looked at the others to see if she was riding him, but no one was laughing.

"My song?"

"They're playing it all over. Not just on WFOR. Chicago, Philadelphia, the West Coast even," said Robbie.

"It's spreading like a virus," said Johnny, winking at Shelly. "And the CD won't be released till tomorrow."

"All we knew about the band was the name and this picture," said Shelly, pulling the *Plain Dealer* magazine from her bag. On the cover was a blurry, faded color picture of Decapede standing on the sidewalk in front of Pedro's, with the banner caption "Decapede Guitarist Found!" above, and underneath "Exclusive — Previously Unpublished Color Photos." He leafed through the magazine, looking at the pictures.

The dog sat with its head on Justine's knee so she could continue scratching him behind the ear. Shelly looked at the girl and tried to imagine what she was feeling.

"That's Vaneshi?" asked Sam, pointing at then-and-now pictures of the guitarist.

"His name is Mendel now."

"Far fucking out."

"That's Gavin."

"Gavin. Jeez. Who's that?"

"Dr. Beverly Hunt Pettiford. Bev Hunt. Bev."

"That half-pint girl who jabbered all the time? Beaver?"

"You might say," said Shelly, enjoying watching him step in shit.

"Fuck me."

"She's my mom," said Robbie.

Sam looked at the boy, and back at the picture. "Double fuck me," he said, shaking his head.

"And that's Aaron," she said.

"Fucking Aaron," he said, peering closely. "Still the pretty boy."

"And tomorrow, they're all coming!" said Robbie.

"To Gruenhaus," added Johnny.

Shelly had wanted to broach the subject at her own speed, but now it was out.

"What's that?" Sam asked.

"Allie's place," said Shelly. "Up near Creston. Everybody's coming there tomorrow afternoon for the weekend."

"Up near Akron?"

"Right," she continued quickly, trying to steer the conversation. "There's a big farmhouse. Everyone's meeting there tomorrow. And of course we want you there, too."

"You do, huh?" he said, biting off a chunk of the Tootsie Roll.

"For the reunion of the band!" said Robbie. "It's a really cool house, and everyone's going to be there. Radio and TV and reporters and interviews and—"

Shelly tried to catch Robbie's eye to shut him up, but it was too late.

"You can forget that real fast," said Sam testily, tossing the newspaper to the ground, rising.

"Sam, listen—"

"Forget it," he said, beginning to pace agitatedly. "Go, get back in your car—"

"Would you please just listen to me for a minute?" Shelly pleaded, trying to get him to look her in the eye, but he kept zig-zagging nervously to get away from her.

"Go, go away!"

"Would you just listen for a minute?" she asked, touching his arm.

"Get out of here," he shouted, brushing past her, "you and your stupid-ass band!"

"Don't say that!" cried Justine, her mouth agape, her eyes tearing up.

"You're coming for a walk with me," Shelly ordered in a tone that brooked no room for appeal.

"I don't want to take a walk," he glared.

"Now!" she barked. She turned and stomped down to the lakeside.

He growled, but followed.

As soon as they were out of earshot, she turned to him and pointed her trigger finger at his nose, angry enough to poke out his eye.

"If you *ever* make that girl cry again, I will grind your testicles into powder and feed it to the loudmouth bass in this lake. Don't you *ever* hurt her like that," she hissed, almost crying herself, jabbing him in the chest and stalking away down the rocky shore.

"It's the truth," he called, chasing after her. "It was a shitty little band that nobody gave a fuck about. Are you going to tell me that's not true?"

He heard her muttering as she walked away. He couldn't hear the words, but they didn't sound very complimentary. Shelly continued to pick her way over the rocks, stumbling in her low heels, till she reached the same rock he had been sitting on with Justine and sat down angrily. The rock was warm from the summer sun.

"I'm sorry, okay?" he said.

"You ought to be," she hissed again, livid.

Up at the trailer, they could see Johnny and Robbie talking to Justine, consoling her. The dog lay at her feet, watching.

"I didn't mean anything," Sam mumbled.

"My God, Sam, she's only sixteen!" she said, cooling only slightly. "She has no one in the world. She lost her mother when she was twelve. She has *no one*. Can you even begin to imagine that?"

"Yeah, I can," he muttered.

"You can? Did she show you the snow globe?"

He nodded.

"She carries it around with her."

"Okay, I get it!"

"That's what she has left from her mother," said Shelly, her voice rising again, the image of Justine's tears welling up within her. "A snow globe and a second-hand dream. And then she meets you, the real Sam Miller, and all you can do is growl and slap Johnny and shit all over the most precious memory the poor girl has left."

"I'm sorry, okay?" he snapped, angry and embarrassed.

But Shelly had no intention of letting him off the hook.

"How dumb can you be? Don't you remember how fucked up and confused you were at sixteen?"

"How do you know what I was like?"

"I'm taking a wild guess."

"You don't know squat about me."

"I've learned enough to put one and one together. I know that something very special happened between you and Kathleen here that day. There's a very beautiful song testifying to that. And I know that something happened to mess it up, and that you've been hiding from the world ever since."

"You know that, do you?"

"Am I wrong?"

"Yeah, you're wrong. Maybe I just got sick of the world

out there, all the lies, the deceit. Maybe I figured out that I'd rather live out here with the trees and the sky and the lake and the squirrels and the fish. They don't lie, you know? The birds sing for a reason. They're not just mouthing the words. They mean it. The sun rises right there, on the horizon, every single morning. No bullshit. No, no—*duplicity*."

"You're really an asshole, you know?" she said, ignoring his bluster. "Don't you understand anything? In real life, humans interact. They meet, and they talk to each other, and if they're really lucky, they get involved and fall in love, and sometimes they have their hearts broken. And then they pick themselves up and pull themselves together and start all over again. That's how life works."

"Maybe yours. I'm happy right where I am," he said, looking out at the lake.

"Oh, you're a real bundle of joy, hiding out here in the woods, attacking anyone who happens by. You've really got the world by the balls, Miller."

"I ain't complaining."

"Neither are your loudmouth bass."

"Largemouth."

"Sam, this is no life. You fucked yourself up once. People don't get second chances like this."

"You can't turn the clock back."

"And you can't make it stand still."

"Fuck you, you know?" he said, disconcerted and confused. "You come barging in on me here. I didn't invite you. I don't want you here. I don't need you. Go away!"

But Shelly didn't budge.

"What the fuck do you want out of my life?"

"What do *you* want? Your birds and your squirrels?"

"Not your damned circus, that for sure," he said. He picked up a small flat rock and slung it angrily at the surface of the lake. It skipped over the surface eight or nine times before giving in and sinking to the bottom of Lake Hope.

"Wow, that's very impressive," said Shelly.

He looked at her.

"And here I thought you could keep it bouncing over the surface forever."

"Oh, fuck off," he said, without conviction.

"They all say that you were the spirit behind the band. Even Aaron. I've heard stories."

"Boy, what I don't need is you coming in and dredging up all that crap. Go get in your car and—"

"Sam, you had brilliance. They all say so."

"That was a million years ago. It doesn't mean diddly squat."

"Yeah? Well, there's tens of thousands of people out there who would disagree with you. But, you know, the whole world's wrong. Sam Miller's right."

"Fuck you," he said.

But now Shelly smelled blood.

"Humans need contact with other humans," she said, right in his face.

"Not this human."

"What do you do if you break your leg?"

"What are you, my mother?"

"No, but I'll bet you this isn't what she had in mind when she was raising you."

"You should leave."

"Really?" she scoffed, as if he'd suggested that she sprout wings and fly. "And I think you ought to go pack your guitar, because you're coming with me to Creston to meet the band."

"And what makes you think that I'll do that?"

"Well, one," she said, pummeling him with reality, "if you don't, by this time tomorrow, you'll have twenty news crews here tramping through your vegetable patch looking for the infamous Sam Miller, and you can just go and slap them all to your sweet heart's content. Two, I'm guessing that if you're living out here in the Tahiti Hilton, you don't have a fortune in gold doubloons buried. If you cooperate, you'll be making a shitload of money. *If.* And three," she said gently, "I'm going to give you the opportunity to make music and have a lot of fun. Together with a bunch of good people."

He kicked loose some rocks with his toe and began to fling them as far as he could.

"Without you, there's no band. With you, we have Decapede."

"The others? They're on board?"

"All three. Aaron was the first to agree."

He had a strong arm, and she watched the stones arch and plop into the lake farther and farther from shore.

"What would I have to do?"

She paused a moment, then gave voice to the fantasy she had been nursing since the first time she heard "Creston Gold."

"Play with the band. Record. Perform."

"Oh, bullshit," he said, flinging a stone in a low, whipping sidearm with a long, looping arc, a good ten feet further than any of his previous throws. It plopped into the lake with barely a ripple, like a hooked fish in its last throes of resistance.

"Wait till you see Gruenhaus. It's a great place. It'll be like summer camp."

"Archery lessons and all?"

"The house is gigantic. There's lots of room. There'll be a small crew of really nice people taking care of everything. I'll set you up a recording studio. There's a whole farm. There's even a lake."

"Woodshedding," he mumbled.

"What's that?"

"That's what the old blues guys used to call it," he said. "They'd go out to the woodshed to play, where there wasn't anybody around to bother them."

"Exactly," she said. "I guess you're kind of a record holder in that field," she smirked.

He scowled at her.

"Don't you get it, Sam? I'm making all this up as I go? I'm

just as scared as you are."

"Bullshit," he said.

He stood looking out at his lake.

"Come here, sit next to me," she said.

"I don't want to," he said.

"I know you don't. But I'm asking you to, anyway," she said softly.

He scowled at her. She smiled at him. He sat down, pouting.

"I'll make it really nice, you'll see. Very laid back. I'll do everything I can to make you comfortable. You'll have fun." He was listening. "Money is no object. Don't you get it? There's nobody telling us what to do. We can do whatever we want. How often does that happen in life?"

"I can do whatever I want right here," he said.

"You know, there are things you can't do alone."

"Nothing that interests me."

"You're not that old," she needled him.

He looked at her sideways.

"To make some great music with a great band? Do you know what we were listening to in the car coming down here, for the very first time? Decapede's tape."

"I don't even remember that we made a recording."

"Like hell you don't."

He flung another stone into the lake, but from his sitting position it didn't go far.

"That's all we need to do? Make music?"

"There'll be some promotional stuff. Interviews, photo shoots. Johnny's filming a documentary."

"Do we get matching monkey suits?" he grouched.

"Sam, I want everybody to enjoy this," she said, formulating the thought as she spoke. "To have a good time. I'm not going to drive you crazy."

"My ass."

"Well," she added, " 'crazy' by the world's standards, not by yours."

"Funny," he said.

"But I'll tell you this, Sam Miller. I'm going to sign you on a contract that obligates you to behave like a normal adult, as absurd as that might sound to you. And if you fuck with me— are you listening to me?" she asked threateningly.

"Yes," he hissed, kicking at the stones.

"If you fuck with me, if you screw up this project, I will make you wish you were one of your loudmouth bass deboned, breaded, and deep-fried."

He leaned towards her, close enough for her to smell his breath. It smelled like he had been living alone in the woods for thirty-some years. "You know you're a bully?"

"I'll take that as a compliment."

"You should be a debt collector."

"Maybe I am. Time will tell," she said, smiling sweetly.

Sam reached into the pocket of his stained work pants and pulled out the last chunk of the Tootsie Roll. He brushed off some of the lint and dregs and stuck it in his mouth.

"We're going to have fun. I promise," said Shelly.

"You promise?"

She weighed her words. "Yeah, I promise."

"How can you promise something like that?"

"You'll just have to trust me."

He snorted.

"Sometimes you need to trust someone."

"No I don't."

"Yes, you do."

They looked out at the lake in silence.

"Sam, I know you didn't ask for this. But, like it or not, you're a star. You can't hide anymore."

He said nothing.

"So you might as well try to enjoy it. Tell me what will make it good for you, and I'll do my best to make it happen."

He chewed on the wad of chocolate.

"Can I bring the dog?" he asked.

"Sure," said Shelly.

"Aw, fuck it," he said. "Call the girl."

"She has a name," answered Shelly.

"You think you're tough, don't you?"

"You don't want to find out, buster."

Sam continued chawing. "Please call Justine down here," he said in his grumpiest voice.

"Call her yourself."

"She won't come."

"Try."

He spit the brown glob into the water. "Justine!" he bellowed.

Together Sam and Shelly turned to watch the girl slumping down from the trailer, dragging her feet and looking at the ground.

They stood together, the three of them, the water lapping at the shore.

"I'm sorry, okay?" said Sam. "Sometimes I say crap."

Justine nodded without raising her eyes.

Sam shifted his weight in discomfort, staring out across the water.

"You know how much you look like your mother?"

She nodded again.

"So, Shelly here wants me to come up to Creston, to join this circus she's putting on up there." He paused. "You think I should?"

Justine raised her eyes and nodded, bruised but hopeful.

"I got a condition," he said to both of them.

"You don't have squat," said Shelly.

"Maybe not. But without me, you don't have a band, do you?"

Shelly didn't answer him. Justine stood watching.

"The girl sings in the band."

Shelly and Justine looked at each other. Sam squinted out at Lake Hope.

"I think I can go along with that," Shelly said, suppressing a smile. She turned to Justine.

"I don't—" said the girl, and blinked several times. "I've never sung in front of people."

"It's no big deal," said Sam. "You just close your eyes."

The girl hesitated, then nodded assent.

"All right then," said Sam. "And one more thing."

"What now?" asked Shelly.

He looked at the girl. "That snow globe? It's mine."

Justine looked him right in the eye. "No, it's not," she said. "It's mine. It was my mother's."

"She bought it for me," he said.

"Tough," said the girl, toe to toe with him. "Now it's mine,"

"No, it's mine," said Sam.

The girl folded her arms and stuck out a hip. Shelly sensed she was smiling inside.

"I could take it from you, you know?" said Sam, straight-faced.

"Oh, yeah?" she answered, stretching up till her eyes met his chin. "Let's see you try."

"You don't look too tough."

"Tough enough to fight you, mister."

"Oh, yeah?"

"Yeah."

"I'll tell you what. You give it to me, I'll tell you some stories about me and your mom right here."

"I don't want to hear any of your dirty old stories."

"Geez, these kids today," said Sam, fighting a smile, "the way they talk."

41

FUUUUUUUCK!

– June 8, 2006 –

Shelly sent Sam to pack up for the trip and walked back down to the lake's edge, pacing, her mind hurtling through the universe. *Focus*, she thought, *focus*. She focused. After a long moment, she dialed and prayed for reception.

"Oh, jeez, Shelly, am I glad you called! It's a madhouse here. Listen," Bev began to rattle off in rapid-fire, "Matt will pick the guys up at the airport tomorrow. They should be at the house by about four o'clock—Could you guys stop banging for just a minute?—and I set up a series of half-hour interviews starting Friday morning at eleven with WFOR and WWHY TV—"

"Bev—"

"Gerald made a very nice exclusive deal with them—"

"Bev!"

"Then the *Plain Dealer*, the *News-Herald*, and a photo session with—"

"Bev, would you shut up for a minute?!"

"Yeah, okay, sorry. Is everything okay? We really need you back here. Where are you?"

"Bev, go outside."

"Okay, wait a minute. Hey, be careful with that, will you?"

Shelly waited.

"There, okay, can you hear me okay now?"

"Yes. Can you hear me?"

"Loud and clear. Where the heck are you? I really need—"

"Bev, stop talking and sit down."

Bev stopped talking.

"Are you sitting?"

"Wait a sec. Yes, Ms Griffin, I'm sitting. Is everything okay?" she asked, worried. "Is everything okay with Robbie?"

"Everything's fine. Will you just shut up for a minute?"

"I shut up."

"Are you ready?" she asked, pausing, smiling, relishing the moment.

"Yes, Ms Griffin, I'm ready." Shelly imagined Bev smiling as well.

"I FOUND SAM!" she shouted so loudly that the birds stopped chirping and flew up into the sky above Lake Hope.

"You *what?*"

"I found Sam!"

The line went silent.

"Bev?"

"I don't think I heard you right. Could you repeat that?"

"You heard right. Bev, are you there?"

"I'm here. I think."

"We're still down at Lake Hope. I'm getting him packed into the car right now. We'll be back—" She looked at her watch. "By about six. Bev? Are you with me?"

"Yeah? Huh? What?"

"Listen up, we don't have time. He's a real case. High-maintenance. It wasn't easy convincing him to come. He's kind of—feral. So we need to handle all this really carefully."

"He's coming here? Now?"

"As soon as we get him packed. Oh, Bev, you have no idea. I don't know if he owns a toothbrush," Shelly laughed, speaking in a rush. "Oh, yeah, I almost forgot. Want to hear what his one condition was? Didn't ask about the money, didn't ask for how long. One little condition."

"What?" squealed Bev.

"Are you still sitting? He wants Justine to join the band!" said Shelly. "And she agreed! Justine's going to sing with Decapede!"

"FUUUUUUUUUUUUUUUUUUUUUCK!!!!!!!!!!!!!!!!!!!"

"Exactly. Now listen. Are you listening?"

"I'm listening. Oh, shit, Shelly."

"Are you crying?"

"What if I am?"

"We don't have time for that."

"How did you do it?"

"No time. I want to get him on the road before he changes his mind. Bev, are you with me?"

"Yeah." She blew her nose into the phone. "Yes. Okay. Go ahead."

"It's a whole new ballgame now."

"What are you going to do?"

"I have no idea. Bev, this just happened. Ten minutes ago." The line went quiet.

"FUUUUUUUUUCK!!!!!!!!!!!"

"I know. Me, too." Shelly paused, thinking. "Listen Bev, Sam's really fragile. I don't want anything to spook him. Protective bubble. Do you understand?"

"I understand. Shelly?"

"What?"

"You found Decapede," said Bev.

"I guess I did," said Shelly, and took a deep breath. "Okay, listen, you have your clipboard? Write this down. Tell everyone who needs to know. Tell them—this changes everything. Cancel the interviews. We need to give them time to get acquainted. Call the guys and Justine's aunt, tell them to pack some extra clothes."

"They'll all agree?"

"Gavin and Aaron will be thrilled. Justine knows." Shelly

paused, pushing at a stone with the toe of her shoe. "Have Gerald talk to Mendel."

"What should he tell him?"

"Tell him to make him an offer he can't refuse," she said, laughing at herself. "And, listen, Bev, I want the house sterile. Just the core staff and the band, as few people as possible. I want a really calm, relaxed atmosphere."

"Got it. But you're on your way with him? It's for sure?"

Shelly thought for a moment, pinching herself mentally. "Yeah. I guess it is."

"Did you talk to Sam about Aaron?"

"I just glossed over it. I told him that Aaron's on board, that's all."

"How did he react?"

"I didn't give him time to dwell on it. He was pretty overwhelmed by the whole business."

Neither Shelly nor Bev spoke, both of them thinking the same thoughts.

"Shelly ..." said Bev.

"I know. We'll just have to jump off that bridge when we come to it," said Shelly.

"I guess."

"I want them making music as soon as they get there. I figure that's the safest way to break the ice."

"That's good," said Bev. Neither of them spoke for a moment. "Shelly, do you realize what this means financially?"

"Oh, yeah."

"The media is going to go ballistic. DecaInc shares are going to go through the roof."

"I know." Shelly paused for a moment, thinking. "Johnny needs a mobile broadcast unit. Can you set that up?"

"On it. Anything else?"

"Anything else? Gee, maybe one or two other details, do you think?" said Shelly, laughing giddily. "Listen, if you want me back there, I have to get going. We have a drive ahead of us.

Can Winston have something ready for us to eat?"

"Of course."

They blew each other kisses, and Shelly hung up.

"Robbie, come down here," Shelly called.

The boy came running down to the lakeside and screeched to a halt in the pebbles in front of her.

"We need to set up a studio in the music room."

"Cool!" he said, grinning like a seventeen-year-old.

"How long will it take?"

"I don't know exactly. It depends on what you want to do. Who's going to do it?"

"You are."

"Me?" His smile faded. "I've never done anything like that. I have Pro Tools at home, but for something like that, you'd need to soundproof the room, put in paneling and stuff. You'd need an expert."

"Where could you find an expert?"

The boy thought for a minute. "There's probably a store in Akron."

"Find someone. Hire him."

He looked at her agape. "Shelly, I'm just a kid."

"You wanted a job? You got a job. Do you have something to write with?"

He patted his pockets. From her bag, Shelly dug out a pen and a printout of the picture of Decapede and handed them to him. "Write on this. Get yourself a notepad or whatever."

Robbie stared at her.

"Write!" she said.

"Get notepad," he wrote.

"Hire an expert," she dictated. "Money is no issue. Time is."

"Hire expert," he scribbled.

"What do we need to get them playing?" Shelly asked.

Robbie's eyes opened wide, his mind racing. "Uh— uh— well, we have instruments."

"Everything they'll need?" she asked.

"I ordered drums and amps and a bass guitar. Sam has his guitar. We have the piano," he said, doing the inventory in his head. "There's some tambourines and percussion stuff. Some kind of old zither thing with a keyboard. A double bass. It needs new strings."

Shelly pointed at the piece of paper.

"Get bass strings," wrote Robbie. "Are Mendel and Aaron bringing anything?" he asked.

"Call them, ask them what they need."

"Me?"

"You. Introduce yourself and ask them what they need. What they *want*," she corrected herself. "I want them to be able to start playing tomorrow. Are you listening?"

He nodded vigorously as he wrote.

"If you run into any obstacles, solve them. If you get stuck, straight to me or your mother. Absolutely top priority. I want them making music as soon as they arrive."

"Okay, okay."

"And I want them recording. Absolutely as soon as possible. Okay?"

He nodded, writing.

"Questions?"

He shook his head, writing.

Shelly watched him and smiled. *This is going to be fun*, she thought to herself. "Get on it as soon as we get back. Nothing in the car. I don't want to spook Sam."

He nodded, writing.

"Go."

He walked back up towards the trailer, still writing.

"Do you have any decent clothes?" Shelly asked Sam as they walked to the car. Johnny was walking ahead of them backwards, filming. The dog was trotting up ahead alongside Justine and Robbie.

"This is my nice shirt."

"One?"

"It ain't Broadway here, case you didn't notice."

Shelly fished in her tote bag and pulled out the We Are Decapede! T-shirt she had bought from the scalpers.

Sam looked at the print on the shirt and then at Shelly. He tossed it in the trunk, together with his guitar case, fishing pole, and two shopping bags. One held a pair of battered work boots. Several carrots spilled out of the other.

"They have carrots in Creston," said Shelly.

"You sure?"

"I'm pretty sure."

"Well, just in case I get hungry on the way." He stuck a couple in his pocket and slammed the trunk shut.

Sam climbed into the back seat and whistled for the dog, but it shied away from the big metal thing. "Come here, dog!" he commanded, but the animal shrunk away. Sam climbed out of the car and tried to grab the dog. Sam was wiry, quick for a man of his age, but the dog was quicker.

"Fuck it," said Sam, panting, "leave him here."

Justine crouched down and approached the animal slowly. "Dog. Hey, Dog. Come here, boy. That's a good Dog," she said, stroking it, lifting it into her thin arms. "That's his name," she explained to them, " 'Dog.' " The dog licked her face, slobbering. "Yes, good Dog," she said, cuddling it and carrying it protectively into the middle seat. Robbie scooted in next to her. Johnny sat next to Shelly, filming. As the car began to move, the dog jerked free of Justine and began to jump around the back seat frantically. Justine struggled unsuccessfully to calm the anxious animal.

"My dog likes to put his head out of the window," said Johnny as they turned onto the highway. Justine lowered her window a crack, and the dog clambered over Robbie, crushing his nuts, and onto his lap, then stuck its snout out into the wind. The open air playing across its face calmed it, and after a few minutes, the dog relaxed. By the time they hit Route 33, Dog seemed to be smiling.

"We gotta stop at the lodge," said Sam

"Where's that?" asked Shelly.

"Not far. I'll show you."

They drove for ten minutes through the lush, thick forest till they saw a sign reading **LAKE HOPE STATE PARK.** They pulled into a large parking lot next to the lodge. Sam opened the door while the car was still moving and jumped out.

"Hey Patti!" he said excitedly to a woman in a T-shirt and overalls lugging two industrial-sized bags of toilet paper. She stopped and mopped her brow. She was a plain woman in her forties, with broad shoulders and her hair pulled back.

"Hi, Sam," she said guardedly. "Who're your friends?"

"This is Shelly."

"Hi, Patti," said Shelly, getting out of the car and extending her hand.

"And that's Johnny. Johnny Walker, from the radio. I haven't yet figured out why a radio announcer is taking movies. I'm hoping someone will explain that to me."

"Ah-hah?" said Patti cautiously.

"And that's Justine and—what's your name again, kid?" he asked through the open window.

"Robbie."

"Right," said Sam. "Justine and Robbie. I used to know their mothers."

"How nice," she said.

"Listen, Patti, I'm going away for a while."

"Away?" she asked, alarmed.

"Yeah," he said, "Sam the Adventurer!" He guffawed, spreading his arms like an eagle in flight. "Amazing, huh? I'm going up to Creston. Up near Akron."

"Up past Wooster? What're you gonna do up there?"

"I'm gonna play in a band and make a shitload of money, that's what I'm gonna do!" He laughed so hard he bent over coughing.

Patti looked at Shelly.

"Who are you exactly?"

"We're from Radio Station WFOR. You've heard about Decapede?"

"What is that, some bug Sam found in his trailer?"

Shelly chuckled. "No, that's the name of a band that disappeared thirty-six years ago. And now they have a hit record. Written and sung by Mr. Sam Miller here."

Patti looked at Shelly and her gang, unconvinced and mistrustful. Shelly extracted a Decapede business card from her bag and handed it to the lady.

"It's all over the news, radio, TV, internet, everything. Maybe you've seen something?"

"I don't use the computer." Shelly looked at her askance. "Morgan has one in the office he uses for work. But we don't want our girls growing up looking at screens." She pointed at the lake and the forest surrounding it and the clear blue sky.

"I get that," said Shelly. "We're going to have a kind of closed camp for a while. Up in Creston. To play some music and have some fun and make Sam here some money."

"Really?" asked Patti, beginning to believe.

"Sure," said Sam. "My garden can get along on its own for a while. As long as we get some rain. Are the girls here?"

"Down by the dock," she said.

"Tell them to keep an eye on the trailer, will ya?"

"Go tell them yourself. Can you drop these off at Housekeeping on the way?"

"Okay," he said, hoisting the bags. "I'll be back in a couple of minutes."

"And tell Morgan you're leaving," Patti called.

The women watched him trudge off.

"How old are your daughters?" Shelly asked.

"Bunkie's nine, Teal's six. We homeschool them," she added.

"Oh?" said Shelly.

"Right now, Morgan's teaching them to build a canoe. From scratch."

"Wow," said Shelly. "That's very cool. What's the connection with Sam?"

"They hang out at his trailer. He teaches them about the bugs and the birds around here. Sometimes they bribe him with candy to make up songs for them," Patti added.

"That's really sweet," said Shelly, sensing Patti was deliberating on what to share.

"If they're bothering him, he just tells them to leave. They have an understanding," she smiled.

"It sounds like you're fond of him."

"Well, I worry about him. Listen, Shelly, I don't know you, I don't know what your intentions are. But I really don't want to see Sam get hurt. Or hurt anyone."

"What do you mean?"

Pattie sighed. "Look, there's a reason why he's living out here all by himself." Shelly saw she was searching for the right words.

"Patti, listen, crazily enough, Sam's song is becoming a hit. I've been running all over the country, digging up this band. Decapede is turning into some sort of crazy phenomenon. Sam is the missing piece. In a day or two, his picture is going to be all over the news, radio, TV, internet, everything."

"Does he know that?"

"More or less. Hell, even I don't know what's going to happen, and I'm supposedly in charge of the whole thing. But I'm guessing it's going to be quite a carnival. Sam was the heart of the band. He's the key. And a lot of people are going to be counting on him."

Patti weighed that. "Listen, day to day, he's fine, around me, Morgan, the girls, with his gardening. But he—" She led Shelly away from the car, out of earshot from Johnny and the kids. "If he feels threatened or pressured, he can just fly off the handle."

"I saw. He attacked Johnny."

Patti nodded. "He really doesn't like people coming near

his trailer. Or trespassing in his own little world. You take him to a strange place, with God knows what kinds of pressure and demands—heaven knows how he'll react."

"How does he live?"

"Mostly he minds his own business. He does the gardening for us and some odd jobs. Almost never leaves the park. When he needs supplies, we bring them in for him. But he doesn't need hardly anything. He fishes, grows his own vegetables. Sometimes he'll let me give him some leftovers from the kitchen here, but for the most part he just keeps to himself."

"That's pretty sad, isn't it?"

"When Morgan and I moved here, we had him come up to the lodge on winter evenings to play for the guests. He plays really well. But I guess you know that?"

Shelly nodded.

"I thought it was a great arrangement. The guests loved it. And Morgan would pass the hat for him, so he made a few bucks. But there would always be some problem. Some guy would get drunk and insist he play 'Stairway to Heaven' or something. More than once, it got ugly."

"Your daughters?"

"He gets along great with kids. I never worried about that. It's adults that he can't handle. Especially when he feels someone is getting too close. Then he can just—well, you witnessed it yourself."

They saw Sam returning, two curly-haired girls in tow.

"Pattie, listen, I really have to run," said Shelly. "First of all, could I have your phone number? Just in case. You have mine on the card."

"Thanks," said Patti, and gave her the number of the lodge. "You watch out for him, will you?"

"I will," said Shelly gravely. "I promise."

"Good luck to you, Sam," Patti said.

"I'll see you," he said, smiling nervously.

"Can I have a hug?"

"What are you going to do with it?" he winked.

"Come here, you ape," she said, hugging him self-consciously and even giving him a peck on the cheek.

"Bye, Sam," waved Bunkie.

"Bye, Sam," echoed little Teal.

As she drove, Shelly's mind was in a tumult, imagining nightmare scenarios of Sam and Aaron meeting, fretting about whether the kitchen in Gruenhaus had enough cutlery for Winston to feed everyone, wondering if Robbie would remember to order strings for the bass. She looked in the rearview mirror. Robbie and Dog were looking out one open window, Sam out of the other. She caught Justine's eye in the mirror. They looked at each other for a long moment. Shelly smiled, and Justine smiled back. Johnny reached over and squeezed Shelly's hand.

"How does it feel?" he asked softly, just between them.

"Numbing," she smiled.

"What happens now?" he asked.

"Johnny, I have no idea whatsoever. I guess this is what they mean when they say to be careful what you wish for," she said, looking in the rearview at Sam with the wind blowing in his face. "I don't know how to do this. I don't even know what 'this' is!"

"Shelly," said Johnny warmly, "do you know what I see when I look at you?"

She shook her head.

"I see the flustered, frustrated young woman who lied her way into my office a few weeks ago, who has gone on to conjure up this whole damned magic carpet ride. I am utterly in awe at what you've done. Madame," he said, bowing in his seat. "And I have utter confidence that you know exactly what you're going to do. And that it will be wonderful."

"Would you please *stop?*" she said, laughing and coloring.

Near Mansfield, Johnny pushed Play on the CD and turned around to film Sam Miller hearing himself sing "Creston Gold."

Sam closed his window to listen.

Robbie and Justine and Johnny and Shelly watched Sam as they sped north on I-71, all of them struggling to grasp that this ragged recluse was actually the legendary Sam Miller, in the car with them, listening for the first time to himself singing in a recording tens of thousands of people already knew by heart.

"Oh, man!" said Robbie, rolling his eyes, "this is so cool!"

"Turn it up, will you?" said Sam, leaning forward next to Shelly's shoulder.

"*The world out there don't look so kind, but I don't care, 'cause love is blind,*" sang the guy on the CD.

Shelly looked at him in the rearview mirror. *Is this really the Sam Miller who sang that tender, loving song? "Carnal," Gavin called him. Bev said he had all the girls squirming. He reeks of the forest.* His face was grizzled with a colorless stubble, his features craggy. His hair was a dusky mess. His body was wiry, taut and wary, an animal ready to bolt. Or attack.

His eyes were locked on the CD player, trying to figure out if it was predator or prey.

I'm driving a loose bottle of nitroglycerin over a country road full of potholes. Shelly watched him staring at the music.

Sam caught her looking at him in the mirror and smiled, revealing a missing back tooth.

Or a volcano, waiting to erupt.

On the other side, Robbie was looking at Justine. She lowered her head and smiled demurely. Dog saw that the humans were happy, and began whacking his tail hard into Robbie's face. But he kept his snout out in the early evening wind as the sun began to set and the day gradually cooled down.

42

Meanwhile, Back on the Farm

– June 8, 2006 –

"There it is," Justine elbowed Sam excitedly, pointing through the fading light at the sprawling green farmhouse in the distance, looming on a hillock over the narrow country road.

"It's got a music room and a lake and a zillion rooms," said Robbie. "And I'm going to make you a recording studio."

"Uh-huh," said Sam, soaking it in.

"I think Dog will be happy here," said Justine to him judiciously.

But choking the entrance to the long driveway leading up to Gruenhaus were one police cruiser, half a dozen vans, the WFOR mobile van, and a small swarm of reporters, photographers, and cameramen. Shelly slowed the car to a halt.

"I thought the location was a secret," said Johnny.

"I thought so, too," said Shelly.

A policeman walked out of the cluster of newsmen and began to swagger his way up the road towards them.

"Oh, fuck!" growled Sam, fumbling for the door handle. He began banging his shoulder at the door.

Shelly tried to twist around to see the commotion.

The dog saw the strange human with big black eyes

344

approaching and began throwing himself madly at the window, pinning Sam against the door, futilely trying to leap at the interloper's jugular vein.

Shelly lowered the window. "Hello, Sheriff," she said. "How can I help you?"

He peered into the car and identified an aging hippie, a derelict and two teenagers. "Is one of you Sam Miller?" he called over the dog's hysterical yowling.

Johnny pointed at Sam.

"Would you please step out of the car, sir?" requested the officer of the law through Sam's window.

Sam tried futilely to push the dog off him with one hand while he fumbled with the door handle. Justine wrapped one arm decisively around Dog's neck and with the other reached over to open Sam's door. He tumbled out and righted himself before the law.

"You're Sam Miller?" asked the voice. His aviator sunglasses were as large and black and threatening as The Fly. His right hand was on his billy club.

"Yeah?" said Sam, backing against the car, his hands moving to protect his ribs and his balls.

The Fly extended his hand to Sam. "Sir, on behalf of the Medina County Sheriff's Office, I'd like to welcome you here to Creston, and anything we can do to make your stay more pleasant, please feel free to contact us," he recited and handed Sam a card.

Sam looked at it warily. "Get Out of Jail Free?"

"Sheriff, is everything all right?" asked Shelly. Somehow, Justine had quieted down Dog.

"Oh, yes, ma'am," said the young officer, removing his glasses. "I'm Sheriff Aubrey Krupnik."

He turned back to Sam.

"I'd just like to tell you how proud I am to meet you, sir," he grinned, displaying a broad gap-toothed smile. "Would you mind signing an autograph for my mother-in-law?" he asked, holding out the pad and pen.

"Oh, fuck me," muttered Sam.

"He'd be glad to," said Shelly to the officer.

"Her name's Aubrey, too," said the officer.

"Write that," she said to Sam, taking the pad and pen and handing them to Sam.

"She's from over in Beaver Falls. Heard Decapede back then. Said you were the greatest."

"Am I supposed to write that, too?" asked Sam. He stared at the police officer's glaring shield against the intimidating blue uniform and tie and that big fucking gun on his hip and the billy club on the other hip and the very dark, very unsettling glasses.

"Sam," said Shelly, "write."

Sam wrote.

"You're Shelly Griffin, aren't you?" said Sheriff Krupnik.

"Pleased to meet you," she said, extending her hand.

"I've been assigned by Medina County to take care of security around Gruenhaus here."

"I'm not sure we'll need much security," said Shelly.

"Ah, these reporters can get pretty rambunctious," he said, watching Sam write. "I just want you to know that the Medina County Sheriff's Office will be happy to do whatever we can to help you all out."

"I appreciate that very much," said Shelly.

"So if there's anything you need, you just call me any time," he said.

Sam handed him back the pad.

"To Aubrey 2—Sincerely, Sam Miller" read Sheriff Krupnik, smiling sunnily. "Oh, this is going to make her very happy." He pumped Sam's hand with a smile of awe. This was a moment he would recount to his grandchildren. "Any time, sir, anything you need."

"Oh, fuck me," said Sam.

Shelly elbowed him.

"Yes, sir, Officer," said Sam politely. "And thank you for your service."

They looked down at the people and vehicles clustered around the entrance to the driveway.

"Do you want to say hello to them? Let them take your picture? Answer some questions?" asked Sheriff Krupnik.

"You're asking me?" said Sam, looking at the cop and then at Shelly. They both nodded.

"Hell, no," he said, proud of his newfound sway.

"Would you like me to secure your route?"

"Nah," said Sam with a sly grin that Shelly didn't trust.

Sam walked a few steps down towards the newspeople and waved. "Hey!" he shouted, waving his arms high in the air. "It's me! Sam Miller." Johnny was standing next to the car, filming with delight. Sam pointed at himself, shouting at the top of his voice. "Sam Miller, Sam Miller." The swarm began to buzz up the road towards them, the cameramen and sound-men struggling with their equipment and their cables, the women presenters hobbling on their heels. He kept waving his arms and pointing at himself, but in a low voice that only Shelly and Sheriff Krupnik could hear, he muttered, "Come on, you bloodsuckers." When the swarm got to about fifty yards from them, Sam shouted, "In the car!" They all jumped in and slammed their doors.

"Go!" Sam shouted to Shelly. She hit the gas and sped past the pack, up into the driveway and up behind the annex, out of sight from the road, where Bev, Allie, and Mr. Griffin were waiting for them.

Johnny continued to film while Robbie and Justine scampered off, with Dog bounding after them.

"Sam," said Shelly, "this is Allie Bauer, the owner of Bauer's Brewery, manufacturer of Creston Gold, and hostess for this whole happening."

Allie smiled warmly and held out her hand. "It's a pleasure to meet you, Sam. We're all so glad that you're here."

"Thank you, ma'am," he said, shaking her hand. "I've been a fan of your beer for a long time."

Johnny filmed everyone smiling.

"And this is Colonel Charles Griffin," said Shelly. "He's legal counsel for the, ah, events here. And, well, my father," she added awkwardly.

"Colonel?" said Sam, extending his hand skeptically.

"Mr. Miller," said the lawyer, shaking his hand even a bit more strongly than usual, disdainful of this vagabond that everyone was making such a commotion over. But Sam had quite a strong grip himself.

"And this," said Shelly, turning to Bev, who had been hanging back, staring at Sam and biting her knuckle, "this is Dr. Beverly Pettiford. Bev."

"Beaver. Fuck me," he said with genuine warmth. Bev bounded up to him and wrapped her arms around him, her cheek against his heart. When she stepped back, they all saw she was blubbering.

"I said I wasn't going to do this," she said, laughing through her tears, wringing her hands in frustration, over-whelmed. "Damn it!" she said, sniffling and laughing together with everyone.

"How you doing?" Sam asked, flustered but smiling.

"I'm *okay*," said Bev with emotion. "I'll tell you this—it really is nice to see you, Sam."

Sam nodded and smiled. Bev gave him another hug, and this time he hugged her back.

Just then, a rich, vibrant bell began to peal. It reverberated through the summer eve, carrying down past the frustrated newspeople below.

"What's that?" asked Sam.

"That's dinner," said Allie. "We all waited for you."

"You waited for me?" Sam asked.

"Shelly said you'd be hungry."

"Hell yeah."

"I would like to ask, though," Allie said gently, "that you refrain from profanity here at Gruenhaus."

Sam caught a waft of meat cooking. "Oh, yes, ma'am, I'm very sorry."

Allie led them up the steps to the kitchen porch, where Winston was waiting.

"And this," said Allie, "is Winston, Justine's chaperone and chief chef of Gruenhaus."

"Hey, man," said Sam, waving at Winston, with his dazzling multicolored tunic and dreadlocks.

"Oh, so this be our guest of honor! Welcome, Mr. Sam," he grinned, displaying his entire whiter-than-white smile.

Justine and Robbie and Dog came running up, laughing at some private joke.

"Here she be," said Winston, jumping down off the porch to greet Justine. "How do my Boo? You have a good day?"

"Oh, it was great!" she said, giving him a hug, happier than he had seen her in months. "This is Dog. Dog, say hello to Winston."

"Well, hello, Mr. Dog," said Winston. "You hungry, too?"

Dog barked hungrily.

"You let me feed these human people first, then Winston fix you something special, okay, Dog? You like bones mebbe?"

"Arf," answered Dog.

Allie led them into the kitchen. Justine called for Dog to follow, but he refused to enter, barking nervously at the doorway.

"Leave him," said Sam. "He'll be fine."

"Come on, Dog," Justine coaxed, but the animal stood its ground, yapping.

"Doan you worry, Boo," said Winston. "I make him a doggy bag."

They walked through the spacious kitchen. Shelly figured the counters and shelves and closets and linoleum floor were almost a hundred years old, but there was a massive stainless steel refrigerator with the tags still on it. In the dining room, a long table was set for seven. The cutlery and utensils and glasses and delicate dishes were Old World, laid out on embroidered placemats. At each setting was a cold bottle of Creston Gold. In the center was a vase with freshly cut flowers.

"There's a place to wash up through there," said Allie. "You've had a ride."

"Come on," said Johnny to Sam, "I'll show you."

As soon as they were gone, Shelly and Bev and Allie made a quick huddle.

"Do we need another table?" Shelly asked.

"I'll have one brought up from the basement," said Allie.

"There's a whole truckload of kitchen equipment coming tomorrow morning," said Bev. "Don't worry, Shelly, we've got it under control."

"Okay. Figure fifteen, twenty people altogether."

"Won't there be visitors?" said Allie.

"Dad, could you please join us? No visitors," replied Shelly emphatically. "I really want to keep it as calm and homey as possible. Listen," she said to the four of them, "tread carefully. He's—volatile."

Bev nodded.

"He seems fine so far," said Allie.

"I think it's really important for him to get settled physically. You know, his room and all."

"I gave him a very nice one," said Bev. "On the second floor, all the way at the end, in the corner."

"Let's just keep our fingers crossed," said Shelly. She took a deep breath. "And if there's any problems with him, anything at all, come straight to me. Okay?"

They all nodded.

"He looks pretty—shabby," said Colonel Griffin.

"I know," said Shelly. "I'm going to have Brandi take care of that."

The women nodded as Johnny and Sam returned.

"Miss Allie tell me you like Mexican food, so I make chili

con carne. Iss good?" asked Winston.

"My man!" said Sam. "Where do I sit?"

"The place cards won't be ready till tomorrow," said Shelly nervously.

Sam looked at her.

"I'm kidding. Sit wherever you want."

He sat and took a long swig from the bottle. He looked at Allie. "Heavens to Murgatroyd, that's *good*."

Winston placed a deep bowl of steaming chili before him. Sam inhaled and looked up at Winston. "I think we're gonna get along just fine," he said, and Winston grinned.

"Is there anything else you need?" Shelly asked, sitting opposite Sam, but she had lost him to the chili.

Bev sat next to him, saying little but gazing at him with adoration. Next to her, Justine and Robbie were absorbed in their teenage conversation. Johnny was circling the table, filming every moment. Colonel Griffin and Allie sat next to each other at the far end near the kitchen. When Shelly saw her father get up, unsolicited, to help Allie and Winston serve, she choked on her chili.

Sam caught Shelly and Bev staring at the way he was wolfing down the chili. He sat up straight, held his tablespoon properly, slowed his pace, and continued slurping up the spicy stew. "God*damn*, that's good," he said.

"Sam," said Allie.

Sam stopped, his spoon poised just before his mouth. "Oh, ma'am, I'm really sorry. This chili is just so good it kind of went to my head."

Allie bowed her head with a gracious smile. Sam blew on the steaming, heaping tablespoon and shoveled it in, chewing with relish. Allie and Winston exchanged looks of satisfaction.

Winston leaned in to fill his glass with Creston Gold.

"Aw, you don't have to do that, man," said Sam.

"Juss today," grinned the Jamaican. "You be de guess of honor today."

Sam drained half of the glass in one rapturous swig, leaned back in his seat and belched with gusto. He smiled guiltily, and everyone laughed.

"You like some more?" asked Winston.

"Can I?" asked Sam.

"Anyting you likes," grinned Winston. "And another beer?"

"If you insist, man."

Bev had hardly said a word. Shelly nudged her.

"Shh," said Bev, "don't wake me. I'm in the middle of this incredible dream."

Shelly squeezed her hand.

"*Thank you,*" Bev mouthed silently, and Shelly blushed.

"Allie, that was spectacular," said Johnny, wiping his mouth with the cloth napkin.

"Thank Winston. He's got the hands of gold."

"Iss Miss Allie's recipe. I just make what she say."

"Golly bejingles, that was good!" said Sam, his hands resting on his stomach, sated. " 'Golly bejingles,' that's okay, right?"

"Yes, Sam," said Allie, "that's just fine."

Sam turned to Shelly. "We gonna eat like this every day?"

She turned to Allie and Winston. They looked at each other and back at Sam and nodded.

"Winston aim to please," said the chef in the spectacular tunic, grinning.

"I sure appreciate that," said Sam, he said, patting his bloated belly

"Well, there is one thing," said Shelly.

"What now?" Sam sat up straight.

"Do you know why we're all here?" she asked him. Everyone went quiet, even the kids.

"Well, yeah, the band and everything."

"Who started it?" she asked, suppressing a smile.

"You did, with all your meddling with the past," he said.

"No, actually you did. With a certain song." Shelly waited

for him to figure out what she was driving at.

"Oh. Oh. I get it." He scratched his jowl. "Yeah. Sure, okay."

Robbie leapt up and brought in Sam's guitar case as if it were the Crown Jewels.

Sam gave the battered old guitar a quick tuning and began to play.

"*Storm clouds are gathering way out there / Soon it's gonna rain— but I don't really care ...*" he sang in his rich, warm baritone, the voice they already knew so well, singing a song of youthful optimism wizened by decades of bitterness. On the chorus, Justine hesitantly sang her mother's harmony. They all sat enrapt, together, this little gang of eight fans and facilitators. In the last verse, Sam faltered over the words, but Robbie whispered them to him, and Sam finished the song without missing a beat. Everyone sat motionless, transfixed. Finally, he stood up and put away his guitar.

"Allie," said Shelly, breaking the silence, "perhaps you could take Sam up to his room, get him settled?"

Johnny excused himself to go prepare the press release. As the others began to rise and disperse, Shelly went over to Sam quietly and put her hand on his shoulder. He started but didn't jerk away.

"Sam, is that okay with you?" Shelly asked. "I've got a lot I need to do down here."

"Sure," he said.

"You okay?" She led him into the entrance hall.

"Yeah, I'm fine," he said, examining the tall, stately foyer. "I'm tired, that's all."

"Allie'll get you set up in your room. If you need anything, come find me. Okay?"

"Okay. Shelly?"

"Yes, Sam?"

"Do you think we could have that chili again tomorrow?"

"I think maybe we can arrange that."

Sam nodded.

"So I'll see you later?" she asked, but he was climbing the stairs next to Allie, carrying his guitar and fishing pole in one hand and, in the other, two shopping bags with his carrots and his one good shirt. She watched him shuffling off and breathed a deep sigh of relief.

Passing the Old World mirror in the dining room, Shelly saw a vaguely familiar stranger.

You did it, girl.

Yes, I did. Did what?

43

Shelly Griffin, CEO
– June 8, 2006 –

She turned to see her father and Bev homing in on her from opposite directions.

"Shelly, can we—" said Colonel Griffin

"Shelly, I really need—" said Bev.

"Go ahead," said the Colonel, ever the gentleman.

"No, please," said Bev, respectful and a bit intimidated.

"Dad, what?" said Shelly. She felt an overwhelming fatigue and a deep need for a shower.

"I thought you'd want to know—Mr. Bridges called to tell me that Mendel agreed to a one-month contract."

Shelly felt a jolt of energy. "Really?" she exclaimed, grabbing her father's hands.

"I spoke with Mendel myself about the details, and he sounded very pleased."

"Oh, Daddy, that's great!" she said, giving him a big, embarrassing hug.

"And I'm drawing up letters of agreement for all of them to sign as soon as they get here."

"Justine's aunt?"

"Is flying up over the weekend to sign."

"You're a lifesaver!"

"Just remind me—where do we keep boilerplate contracts?"

"Drive M. Under 'Boilerplates,' " she said.

"I looked there, couldn't find it."

"I'll send it to you by email as soon as I get to my computer, okay?"

"Right," said the Colonel. "I'll be in Allie's office if you need me." And off he marched, a man with a mission.

Shelly and Bev watched him go.

As soon as he was out of earshot, Shelly called after him, "I'm proud of you, too," and made a strangling motion with her hands.

"Aw, isn't that sweet? Daddy's little girl," joshed Bev. "You know, he's been spending quite a lot of time in the annex."

"Meaning?"

"He works in Allie's office."

"Meaning?"

"Working on the brewery, for all I know."

"And?"

"That's all I know."

"You're no help at all. Show me my office? I must have a billion emails waiting."

"Wait a sec," said Bev, stopping her. "How are you doing?"

"Could we start with an easier question?" she chuckled tiredly, leaning her head down onto Bev's shoulder. "How are you?"

"Me?" Bev rolled her eyes rapturously. "I feel like I died and went to heaven. Sam fucking *Miller!*"

"Wait till the guys get here."

"Oh, God, Shelly, don't. My heart can't take it."

"Come," she laughed, "show me."

"Okay, so this is the foyer. People come in here. They can either go right to the dining room or left to the common room. Past the dining room over there are the kitchen and the pantry. Up the stairs here, we've prepared fourteen bedrooms, eight on the second floor, six on the third floor."

"That's a lot of stairs."

"I figured we'll put the younger people on the top floor. Including you, my dear," she laughed.

"I'll take that as a compliment. The bathrooms are okay?"

"Yeah. Matt had a couple of guys in yesterday, fixing up everything."

"He's been a help?"

"Oh, God, Shelly, I couldn't have done this without him. Anything needs doing, he knows someone."

"That's so great."

"The living room here will serve as a common room." The lofty old room with the ten-foot-high bay windows was filled with musty, plush loveseats. "I was thinking of replacing these two-seaters with something more modern, more comfy. What do you think?"

"No, leave them," said Shelly. "I like the look. Just, if you could, ask the guys to arrange them so everyone can have eye contact."

Bev made a note on her clipboard and led her through the long common room to carved wooden double doors at the far end. She flicked on the light. "This is the music room that Robbie's converting into a studio. He said to ask you if he can drive into Akron tomorrow."

"What for?"

"He needs to drop off measurements and photos for an acoustical engineer he found."

"That was fast!"

"You said you wanted it fast," said Bev proudly.

"As long as he's back when the guys get here," said Shelly, looking at the dark wood paneling and the high ceilings.

"Shelly, he's a changed kid. Do you realize in how many ways you're transforming my life?"

"Shut up, will you? Those Germans knew how to put together a beautiful house. Did anyone check the electricity?"

"Matt said they redid it all in the Sixties, 'back when they were still building to last.' It's all triple-phase and solid as the pyramids."

"Matt said that?" joked Shelly.

"Okay, maybe I added the part about the pyramids," said Bev. "Shelly, you're sure about entrusting Robbie with all this? He's just a kid."

"He's smart," Shelly reassured her. "He knows the basics better than anyone else around. He'll learn as he goes. We just have to keep an eye on him. But I think I'd rather have one of our own do it than bring in a stranger. I really want to keep things as calm and familiar as possible. No traffic of people going through here."

"Because of Sam?"

"Absolutely."

"He's that—"

"Bev," said Shelly, shaking her head as she replayed the scene in her mind, "he just lashed out and smacked Johnny."

"You invaded his territory."

"And the way he never makes eye contact?"

"Yeah, I saw," said Bev. "So you want to keep it quiet for him."

"Not just for Sam. For the entire band. For everyone. For you and me. I promised Sam this wouldn't turn into a circus, and I meant it."

"Well, good luck with that," said Bev, leading her through a side door into a long hallway dividing the front of the house from the back.

"So here are three rooms for offices. Robbie hooked up broadband all over the house, even wi-fi. Desks for Gerald, Brandi, and myself, and one room with a computer for the band members. The Colonel's working out of the office in the annex."

"Beautiful. Perfect. Except for the band. No computers, no phones."

"Seriously?"

"Yup. If they need to, they can make calls from here. Internet usage goes through you. And if they ask, tell them it's broken."

"Seriously?" asked Bev.

Shelly smiled. "Use your own judgment. Hey, what about me? Don't I warrant a desk?"

"Wait," Bev said, bubbling with excitement. "My *piece de resistance*. You ready?" At the end of the hallway was a stately oak door with a brass sign: Shelly Griffin, CEO, Decapede.

"Okay, that's really embarrassing," said Shelly, smiling.

Four stairs led down into a warm room with a wall of windows on the far side. Beyond, a long grassy hillside sloped down to the corner of the lake. In the center of the room were two facing rust-and-butterscotch sofas with a coffee table between them, some old stuffed chairs, and tawny rugs strategically scattered about. In the far corner was a desk, Shelly's laptop waiting in its charging port. Bev watched proudly as Shelly admired the long panel of amber curtains reaching from the ceiling to the oak floor.

"Oh, Bev!" said Shelly, genuinely touched. "It's too nice."

"No, it's not. I figure you're going to be spending a lot of time here. Allie says it was the smoking room, where the men would go after dinner to play gin rummy and smoke cigars and make decisions."

"There's not going to be any smoking in here now, I'll tell you that," she said, running her hands and her eyes over the decor. "How did you get it fixed up so quickly?"

"All these guys Matt knows are hungry for work. You pay them a good wage, and they work their very handsome butts off." Bev led her past the screen door leading outside to a half-hidden nook in the back corner. "Ta-da!" It was her own private Eisenhower-era bathroom, lined with peach and aqua Old World tiles, complete with a shower stall.

"Oh, Bev! It's a girl's dream!" she said, gazing around the room, taking it all in. She plopped down on the sofa facing the sloping lawn, kicked off her shoes, lifted her feet onto the coffee table, and laid her head on the warm, cradling cushion, dizzy from the day's drive, from Sam, from the million critical and crucial and urgent missions and tasks and obligations and details racing around her brain, from this whole massive Gruenhaus that was beginning to feel more and more like an ant colony than a farmhouse.

"Wake me up in September," said Shelly, closing her eyes, when her cell phone rang.

"Hi, Johnny," she said wearily. "What's up?" She listened patiently. "I'll be right out," she sighed. She groaned and put on her kitten heels.

"All I want is a shower and a bed," she said to Bev.

"I know. You've had one hell of a day," said Bev as they walked. "Shelly?"

"Yeah?" she answered through the fog in her head.

"You did it," said Bev. "You found Decapede."

"Yeah, I guess I did," she smiled wearily and walked down Gruenhaus's wide porch stairs to the front lawn, where Johnny and the kids were waiting for her. "Hey, what's up?" she asked, feeling like she was running on fumes.

"Hey Shel," said Johnny. "Pretty exciting, huh?"

The evening air braced Shelly, cool and refreshing. The grass in front of Gruenhaus smelled sweet, gathering dew. The night was soft and clear. Down on the road by the WFOR van, a police barricade held back a cluster of journalists and gawkers.

"Listen, I'm about ready to film the press release about Sam and Justine, and I'd really like to let people see her face—"

"But Justine's chicken," teased Robbie.

"I'm not chicken," protested Justine. "I just don't want to go on camera."

"Why not?" asked Shelly.

"Pock-pa-pa-pa-po-ock," Robbie clucked at her.

"Cut it out," Justine protested, swinging a punch at his shoulder, but he bobbed out of reach, laughing.

"You're going to have to sooner or later," said Johnny.

"So, later," said Justine.

"Aw, come on," said Robbie, "to be on television? It'll be so cool."

Johnny looked to Shelly for help.

"Come," Shelly said, taking the girl's hand, "walk with me a little."

Justine fell into step with Shelly, walking along the grassy hillside in the dark, the dog following close behind.

"Stay here, Dog," Justine commanded.

The dog looked up at her.

"Stay here with Robbie," she explained.

Dog followed close on her heels.

"So?" Shelly asked.

"I—I'm just not ready."

"Scary, huh?"

"I guess. And my hair's all a mess."

"Brandi will be here in the morning. She does hair."

"And I didn't bring enough clothes. I was just supposed to be here for the weekend."

"Brandi."

"Who is she?"

"She was a receptionist at the station, but she's become sort of like the office manager. But ever since this Decapede thing started, she's been dressing me. She's great. Just don't be frightened by her appearance."

"Why, what's her 'appearance'?"

"It changes, but usually there's a lot of black, a lot of skin, a lot of jangly metal things around her and in her."

Justine laughed.

"But she's really, really sweet, you'll love her. She'll help you with anything you need."

"Okay, great," said the girl.

"You saw your room? Everything's all right?"

"I'm fine. Why?"

"Just checking. Pretty exciting day."

"Oh, yeah."

Shelly half-expected Justine to be as exhausted and over-whelmed by the day's events, but the girl was animated, apparently high on adrenaline. Or maybe just sixteen.

"You know, it's going to be quite a circus. Are you ready for all this?"

"I guess," she said.

"Justine, you get that from tomorrow on, you're going to be a rock star? Literally."

The girl smiled to herself and nodded.

"It's okay to be nervous. It's natural."

"Are you?"

"Are you kidding? I'm peeing in my pants."

In the moonlight, Shelly saw the girl smile, and she felt a flush of warmth in her heart.

"You'll be great," said Shelly, putting her arm around the girl's shoulder and giving her a squeeze. "You know that I'm here for you. Whatever you need. Anything, anytime. Yeah? You got that?" Shelly gave her an extra-hard squeeze to show she meant it.

The girl nodded.

"How's it going with Robbie?"

"Okay, I guess." Shelly had no idea what a sixteen-year-old meant by that.

"You'll like the guys in the band. They're all really nice. Mendel's great. And Gavin's a peach. And wait till you meet Aaron. They'll all be really nice to you."

"Okay," she said.

"They all liked your mother a lot."

"You talked to them about her?"

"Of course. I was trying to track her down."

"Oh, right," said the girl.

"I guess you haven't had much chance to talk to people who knew your mother from those days."

Justin shook her head. "Shelly, can I ask you something?"

"Of course."

"Do you know why the band broke up? What the fight was about?"

Shelly's heart plummeted. "Ah—"

"Is it true that Sam punched Aaron?"

Shelly hesitated.

"Yes, I think that's what happened."

"They were fighting over my mother, weren't they?"

"I don't know that."

"Sam, he loved my mother very much, didn't he?"

"I think he did, yes."

"And Aaron?"

"I don't know exactly what happened."

"Are they still angry with each other?"

"Justine," said Shelly, wishing her phone would ring, "maybe we should just let that lie."

"Come on, Shelly," insisted the girl. "I'm a member of the band. I need to know what's going to happen."

"Pushy little thing, aren't you?" Shelly smiled and turned to her. "I don't know. I have no idea how they're going to react to each other. My guess is that they don't know either. Aaron's a good guy, he's not going to make any trouble."

"What about Sam?"

Shelly shrugged. "Your guess is as good as mine. Probably better."

The girl nodded.

She seems composed, considering, thought Shelly. *Well, she's been through so much at her age, she must be tough inside. And she sure looks a lot happier than she did in Florida.*

"If anything, you know, happens—between Aaron and Sam—I hope you'll help keep things cool," said Shelly.

"Me?"

"Yeah, you."

"I'm just a kid," Justine said.

"Sam, he—" Shelly groped for the word. "*Relates* to you."

"That's because I remind him of my mother."

"Bev says you're the spitting image of her."

Justine shrugged. "I mean, I know I'm taking her place in the band because I'm her daughter. But I'm not her. I couldn't be her if I wanted to. I mean—I never really even knew her. As a grown-up."

Shelly took her hand as they walked over the cool evening grass. They could hear the croaking of frogs from down at the lake.

"I hope I can do it okay. I've never sung in front of an audience before."

"You've got a great voice. And you look terrific. You'll be great. I'm sure of it."

Justine looked up at Shelly and smiled.

"Why don't you just say 'hi' to the camera for Johnny? No interview or anything. Just a hello and a smile. Can you do that?"

"Okay," said the girl. "I can do that."

"Come here," Shelly said, and drew the girl into a hug. Dog barked nervously. "Don't stay up too late," she said. "You have a big day tomorrow."

"I know. If it's okay, I'm going to go into Akron tomorrow morning with Robbie. He has some errands for the music room."

"The guys are supposed to get here around four. You'll be back?"

"We'll leave first thing. We'll be back for lunch."

"Okay, well, drive carefully."

"We will. Thanks."

"Do you want me to talk to Johnny?" asked Shelly.

"I can do it," said the girl.

"Go," said Shelly, and she gave Justine a little pat on the back. The girl scampered off towards the TV lights.

Johnny waved at Shelly with a thumbs-up. She waved back and trudged up the porch steps to her room, which Brandi had stocked with oodles of delights from Tower City Center. She kicked off her shoes and plopped back onto the deep, swathing bed. Then she took her BlackBerry and dialed Brandi, who answered immediately.

"Oh my God, Shelly, I can't believe it! How are you?"

"I'm good," Shelly said, "just feeling pretty bushed. Thanks so much for getting all my clothes here. And the new stuff looks great."

"Come on, give already! What's he like?"

"Sam? He's—He's a handful. He's been living out in the woods by himself all these years. Living in his own world. Angry. Unpredictable."

"Bad boy?"

"You'll see for yourself tomorrow."

"Oh, fuck me!" she squealed.

"When will you get here?"

"Mr. Bridges and I are driving down in the morning. They've already packed the van with all the stuff we need from the office."

"Great. Listen, I need a couple of things. I hate to ask, at this hour."

"Are you kidding? Who can sleep? What do you need?"

Shelly considered getting up to find her bag with the little green notebook, but she was too exhausted to extract herself from the soft bed.

"First of all, clothes for Justine."

"There's one bag of stuff packed in the van already. I want to meet her before I get any more."

"Great. And your hairdressing equipment? To tell you the truth, she could use some help with the way she looks."

"Packed already."

"One other thing," Shelly paused. "Sam? He's pretty—how can I put this gently?—*scruffy*. Do you think you could maybe spruce him up a little?"

"Shelly, when I get finished with him, he'll look like the Marlboro man."

"And do you by any chance know how to give a shave?"

"With three brothers? I used to do them all every Friday afternoon. He's a medium?"

"Hard to think of him as a medium anything, but I guess so."

"I'm bringing him some clothes. Just in case."

"He said he has 'a nice shirt.' "

" 'A nice shirt'? For the whole summer?"

"Brandi, I'm telling you, this guy is barely housebroken. Anyway, yes to bringing clothes for him. If you can get him into them."

"Well, first we'll have to get him out of what he's wearing," she said, shrieking in laughter at her own innuendo.

"Rein it in, sister," said Shelly, laughing. "See you in the morning."

Shelly hung up and stared at the ceiling, the moonlight coming in through the window. The day had begun as a picnic at Lake Hope and had ended in a different universe. She closed her eyes, hoping the electrons racing around her brain would settle down.

"Huh?" she said, unsure if she'd said it out loud, confused at what was happening. She looked at her watch. Eleven-twenty. Something rapped again.

"Shelly," said a raspy whisper. "Hey. Shelly."

"Wait," she mumbled, pulling herself up. She'd fallen asleep in the day's clothes. She needed a shower badly. "Sam. Hi. What?"

He opened the door and entered halfway. "I can't sleep."

"Why can't you sleep?"

"The bed's too soft."

"I'll have them change it tomorrow."

"There's too much noise here."

Shelly listened. Gruenhaus was asleep.

"I don't hear anything."

"People flushing toilets all the time. Traffic."

"Traffic? What traffic?"

"Every half hour, there's another car driving by."

"Sam, the road's all the way down at the bottom of the hill."

"Listen, you'll hear it."

"I'm not listening to anything other than my own snoring right now."

Sam stood at the foot of the bed, looking miserable in the moonlight.

"And I'm not used to eating so much."

"The chili was good, though, wasn't it?"

"Damn good."

"Do you want to talk to Bev?"

"What for?"

"She's a doctor."

"Beaver's a doctor? A real doctor?"

"Well, a radiologist, but yeah."

"No shit." He seemed to be pondering the option. "Nah," he said finally.

"Where's Dog?" Shelly asked.

"Huh? Oh, I don't know. Ran off with the kids."

"He seems to be having a good time."

"Yeah. Well, you know, they're probably a lot more fun than me."

She looked at him and chuckled. He sort of smiled back. No cars drove by, no toilets flushed.

"Are you nervous about tomorrow?" she asked.

"Me? What is there to be nervous about?" He looked at her and cackled, and she realized he'd been joking.

"It'll be fine," she said.

"You sure of that?" he said.

"No," she admitted, "I'm not. But we'll try to make it all fine. Okay?"

He nodded.

"It's up to us, you know."

"You think?"

"I hope. Who really knows?"

"Looks to me like you do," he said.

"There's this girl, Brandi, she works as a receptionist at the radio station. Pretty lively girl. She's going to clean you up a little tomorrow. Give you a haircut and a shave, if that's okay with you."

"I like a good shave. Is she bringing me a clown's suit too?"

"No, just a haircut and a shave. Maybe a clean shirt. On the outside chance that you might need a second one. Is that okay?"

"Yeah, what do I care what I wear?"

"Great."

"Yeah."

"Sam?"

"Yeah?"

"I need to go to sleep now."

"Oh. Okay," he said. He turned and walked out without closing the door behind him.

"See you in the morning," said Shelly to herself.

44

Rock Star Sam

– June 9, 2006, Early Morning –

Sam rose with the birds, but Gruenhaus was still sound asleep except for Winston, humming along with Decapede's "Bring It on Home to Me" on the radio as he assaulted large piles of eggplant, tomato, carrots, potatoes, onions, squash, and pumpkin with a sinister-looking twelve-inch knife, chopping more quickly than Sam's eye could follow. An intoxicating bouquet wafted through the large old kitchen.

"Damn, that smells good," said Sam, fishing pole in hand. "You making that chili again?"

"Hey, mon. Mizz Shelly say, 'Sam want chili,' Sam get chili. You de boss. Big day. How you be doin'?"

"I don't know. Some pretty strange stuff going down here."

"Fresh pot o' coffee der," Winston offered.

"Nah, thanks, I want to get down to the lake before people here wake up," he said, chewing on a carrot. "Sure smells good, though."

"Got good water here. Mebbe I make you up a little sumpin you take wit' you?" he asked, grinning his dazzling Jamaican grin.

"Well, if you twist my arm," said Sam.

"You gon catch me some fish?" Winston asked, indicating Sam's pole.

"I'm sure gonna try."

Sam peered out the kitchen porch door, then snuck down the steps quietly with the matching Hopalong Cassidy lunch pail and thermos in one hand, the fishing pole and gear in the other. At the bottom of the long driveway, a small throng of reporters was waiting by the police cordon and the radio van, even at this early hour. He watched a beat-up red Ford pickup stop and chat with a cop, then continue up the long driveway and pull up sharply next to him. A sandy-haired young man in his mid-twenties jumped out wearing a backward baseball cap, a tight light blue We Are Decapede! T-shirt, and a wide, agreeable smile.

"Hey, mister, going to try your luck down at Lake Traumsee?" he asked.

"Good spot?" asked Sam.

"People in these parts who know their fishing come up here. Biggest bass and bluegill in Medina County."

"Yeah?" Sam brightened.

"They say there's something in the water down there. That's where they take the water for Creston Gold. Did you know that?"

"No shit?" said Sam.

"Anyway, there's a nice little boathouse down there on the far side, with a wood dock in front. You set up there, you'll do good."

"Okay, I'll see you around then," said Sam, moving to leave.

"Matt Hinton," said Matt, extending his hand.

"Gardner," said Sam, shaking his hand.

"Seen Miss Shelly this morning?"

"Everyone's asleep 'cept Winston."

"Maybe I came a little early. They called and said Miss Shelly wants to talk to me, but I'm a little nervous because I don't know what it's about. It's got something to do with a property my Great-Uncle Lonny left me, where Decapede first played, but I didn't even know Uncle Lonny 'cause he lived all the way over in Wooster and he died when I was just a—"

"You talking about Pedro's?" asked the Gardner.

"You heard Johnny Walker's radio show about it?"

"Oh, yeah. Fucking Pedro's," he said to himself, shaking his head.

"I've been helping out here at Gruenhaus. Doing some odd jobs for Dr. Bev and Miss Allie and the Colonel. But now Miss Shelly herself wants to talk to me, so—"

"Right, see you, man," said Sam, itching to go.

"Is it true what they're saying on the radio?"

"What's that?"

"That Shelly found Sam Miller and brought him here?"

"They said that on the fucking radio?"

"Did you see him?" asked the lad, his eyes wide.

"Mighta caught a glimpse," said Sam.

"What does he look like?" asked the boy, his eyes widening even more.

"Oh, he's one handsome devil."

But just then a shiny black WFOR van stopped at the police cordon, and when the shaded window rolled down to reveal the bald-domed driver with a ring of hair over his ears and neck, the snarl of journalists began to push and photograph and jump and shout and film in a frenzy. Sheriff Aubrey removed his very dark sunglasses and smiled widely at the cameras, then waved the van up.

Mr. Gerald Bridges, the Barracuda of Buyouts, jumped down out of the van. He was wearing an oversized We Are Decapede! T-shirt and plaid Bermuda shorts. Brandi came running from the other side, jangling as her heels sank into the gravel, her tiny black skirt riding even higher, shrieking, "I gotta pee! I gotta pee!"

Together, Matt and Sam and Gerald watched her rattle up the kitchen porch stairs. Gerald Bridges took off his clip-on sunglasses, squinted into the sun, and put them back on.

"Gerald Bridges," said Gerald Bridges to Matt and Sam,

pulling himself up to his full sixty-one inches, sticking out his hand and bracing himself to be recognized as the most notorious cuckold in the Western world.

"Matt Hinton, pleased to meet you." Matt smiled as he enclosed Gerald's hand like a pop fly in his shortstop's mitt.

Gerald Bridges turned to the shabby fisherman.

"Gerald Bridges," he said, holding out his hand, bracing himself.

"Gardner," said Sam, edging away in the direction of the lake.

"So," said Gerald, breathing a sigh of relief at not being recognized, mixed with a dash of disappointment. "Big day, huh?"

"Cool shirt!" said Matt, pointing at Gerald's emerald green We Are Decapede! T-shirt.

"Cool shirt," Gerald responded proudly, pointing at Matt's light blue We Are Decapede! T-shirt. "You work here?"

"Yeah, I've been helping out, fixing up some stuff around Gruenhaus. Gardner here," confided Matt, "he *saw* Sam Miller!"

"Seriously?" asked Gerald. "What's he like?"

"I'll tell you this," drawled Sam in his rank Wellington Academy Lacrosse Team sweatshirt, "from what I hear, he's one ornery son of a bitch."

"No!" said Matt and Gerald to each other.

"But I'll bet deep down he's really nice," said Matt.

"Nah," growled Sam, "from what I hear, he's a real asshole through and through."

"Still," said Matt. "I promised my Meemaw that I'd try to get his autograph. If I actually get to meet him."

"Know what I have in the van there?" preened Gerald. "The CD."

"But they said on the radio it doesn't come out till nine-thirty," said Matt in disbelief.

"Want to see one?"

"Could I?" asked Matt.

Sam hesitated. He sure wanted to have a go at the biggest bass and bluegill in Medina County, but the new Decapede CD sounded pretty interesting, too.

Gerald was struggling with the sliding door of the van, so Matt reached in to pull it open, revealing a ton of cartons and amps and mic stands and a small mountain of toilet paper and boxes labeled Decapede T-shirts and Decapede Mugs and Decapede Tchotchkes, and on the top, Decapede CDs. Matt reached up to dislodge it.

"Careful," said Gerald, "they're heavy as hell."

Matt shifted the top carton till he could grasp its girth, his shoulder muscles bulging under the load, and set it down gingerly on the gravel. Gerald and Sam peered over Matt's shoulder as he slit open the carton with his pocket knife and drew out a pristine CD wrapped in skin-tight cellophane: "*Decapede—The Sheek Sessions*" over the iconic, faded photo of the band now in color, digitally enhanced.

"Wow," said Matt reverently.

"Wow," said Gerald reverently.

"I'm going fishing," said Sam, and turned to head down to the lake.

"Hey!" a voice called out, as sharp as Winston's chef knife.

Sam turned to see Shelly glaring down at him from the kitchen porch.

"Where do you think you're going?" she asked in a voice strikingly like her father's.

Sam held up his fishing rod and tackle. "Bowling," he said.

"Get over here right now," Shelly commanded.

For a fleeting moment, Sam considered running.

"You don't want to make me chase you, Miller—" she warned him, fire in her eyes.

"You're—" gasped Gerald

"Y— y— y—" stammered Matt.

Gerald looked up at Shelly and back at Sam.

Shelly bustled down the porch stairs and up to them. She

wrapped her hand firmly around Sam's sinewy arm. "Sam," she said, giving him a painful pinch, "I'd like you to meet Gerald Bridges."

"Oww," said Sam.

"Be nice to him," hissed Shelly.

"Already had the pleasure." Sam glowered at Shelly, but he shifted his fishing pole to his left hand and stuck out his right towards Gerald Bridges.

Matt's mouth was open, but no sound came out.

Allie and Colonel Griffin and Winston and Brandi and Bev had gathered on the kitchen porch while Johnny walked carefully down the stairs, his hand on the railing, his eye in the viewfinder of the camera.

"That's him?" Brandi grabbed Bev's arm. "That's Sam Miller?"

Bev nodded.

"Hello, sir," said Gerald Bridges, pumping Sam's hand with both of his own, "Gerald Bridges. I'm very pleased to meet you."

"You might want to reserve judgment on that till you get to know me better," responded Sam.

"What a joker you are, sir!" gushed Gerald, still pumping Sam's hand.

"And stop calling me 'sir,' " said Sam, toeing the gravel.

"I'll try. If you call me Gerald."

"Well, I'll tell you what—if I call you, I'll call you Gerald. How about that?"

Dog was sitting in the shade of the porch, his tongue hanging out of the side of his mouth, panting, taking in the scene with equanimity, while Johnny moved in a little closer but very cautiously.

Matt gaped at Sam. "You're really—"

"You got a wasp up your ass, boy?" Sam peered at him sideways. He could feel the Hopalong Cassidy thermos hot against his leg, filled with fresh, steaming coffee, and he thought about the biggest bass and bluegill in all of Medina County.

"Oh, sir, you should know, the people of Northeast Ohio are *so* proud of you!" panted Matt, the floodgates open. "You're—you're our hero, my friends and me. All the people around here. We think your song 'Creston Gold' is the most beautiful thing we've ever heard, and we can't wait to buy the CD! And our friends all over the country, they keep writing and calling and asking us if we actually know Steubenville and Lake Hope and Creston and asking if we know if Decapede is going to record together, or even perform, because for us, you guys are like something out of a movie, and now, actually meeting you, face-to-face, oh my gosh, I don't know how I'm—oh. Sorry, sir. I don't mean to—"

"Pshee!" said Sam, looking for a hole to hide in.

Shelly smiled.

Bev, Brandi, and Allie stood at the porch railing, watching the seedy legend, the diminutive tycoon and the strapping infielder in the tight turquoise Decapede T-shirt with the line of sweat down the back.

"You grow them healthy out here in Ohio, don't you?" said Bev.

"Hardy young man, isn't he?" said Allie.

They looked at Brandi.

"Nyeh," said Brandi, "not my type."

"Seriously?" said Bev.

"I knew a million of those guys back in Canton. Country bumpkins."

But her gum was popping like a pot of popcorn.

"Could I have your autograph, sir?" Matt asked.

"No, you can't have my fucking autograph! Sorry, Allie. And would people stop calling me 'sir'?"

"It's not for me, sir, it's for my Meemaw. She saw Decapede back in '70. Talks about them all the time. People treat her like she came over on the Mayflower. She has your picture up on her refrigerator!"

"What picture?" growled Sam in consternation.

Matt reached into the cab of his pickup and extracted a newspaper. "SAM MILLER FOUND!" proclaimed the banner headline. Underneath it was a picture of Sam waving at the press from the top of the hill. The picture was greatly enlarged, with Sam as pixelated as Bigfoot. Johnny zoomed in on him studying the paper.

"Please, sir," said Matt, holding out a pen to Sam. "Could you sign that? It would mean an awful lot to her."

Sam glared at Matt.

"Her name's Sue. Sue Hinton."

Shelly took the pen from Matt and handed it to Sam. "Write 'Best Wishes, Sam Miller,' " she instructed him.

Sam looked at her, squinching his eyes. "You got my dancing bear outfit there in the van?" he rasped.

"Sign the picture," she commanded him in a whisper she'd learned from the Colonel.

Sam grumbled something, but wrote.

"Gerald," said Shelly, nudging him towards the house, "we really do have a lot to talk about."

"But—" protested Gerald.

"You'll have plenty of time to get to know Sam, I promise. Here, Gerald, this is Allie Bauer, our hostess."

"It's a pleasure to meet you, Mrs. Bauer," said Gerald, turning on his grown-up charm.

"Allie, please," she said. "Welcome to Gruenhaus."

"I suppose this is quite an intrusion," said Gerald, wondering if she'd seen his ex's home movie.

"Oh, it's a pleasure to see Gruenhaus come to life like this," beamed Allie.

"And the Colonel, you've met," Shelly continued.

"We have this Decapede thing under control, don't we, Charlie?" joshed Mr. Bridges, whacking the Colonel on the shoulder.

The Colonel maintained his military dignity with a grimace camouflaged as a smile.

"And this," said Shelly to Gerald, leading him on, "is Winston, our chef."

"Nice to meet you, man," grinned Gerald as he shook his hand vigorously, then turned to whisper to Johnny, "This is better than being backstage with the Stones! This is the thing actually happening! In real time!"

Johnny clapped him on the shoulder.

"Hey you," said Gerald, smiling at Bev.

"Hey you," said Bev, smiling at Gerald.

Shelly nudged her.

"All right, everyone, listen up," said Bev in her best camp-counselor voice, reading from her clipboard. "Gerald, Colonel Griffin, Shelly, to Shelly's office. Brandi, you take Sam to get a shave and haircut."

"Later," said Sam, leaning toward the lake.

"Sam!" Shelly lassoed him with her voice. He turned to look at her, then at Bev, then back at Shelly.

"You heard her," said Shelly.

Sam gave her a dirty look, grumbled something unintelligible, and leaned his fishing pole against the side of the house. "Keep an eye on that," he said to Dog, who looked at him with no comment other than to pant contentedly with his doggy tongue hanging out.

"Everybody reports back to me as soon as you finish," Bev called. "Matt, you stay with me, I'll show you where to put all those boxes."

Robbie and Justine were listening to the WFOR Decapede special celebrating the release of the CD as they drove into Akron. From seven in the morning, the station had been playing all eight tracks in a loop, punctuated by Johnny's commentary from the WFOR mobile van "somewhere in Northeast Ohio."

"We're in the Twilight Zone here, right?" asked Robbie.

"Way beyond that," said Justine.

"Can you believe—" he began, but had no idea how to finish the sentence.

They agreed that Aaron's "Walk on By" was intoxicatingly beautiful, that Sam's "Peggy Sue" was as powerful as a fist to the gut, and that Kathleen's "And Then He Kissed Me" made them want to stop the car right there on I-76, get out and start dancing.

"I can't wait to hear you do it," said Robbie.

"Omigod," she said, "don't even say that."

"Why not? It's going to be your song."

"I don't want to think about it."

"Why not?" he asked.

"Are you kidding? How am I going to match that? She's so good."

They grew serious and attentive when "Cuyahoga Rising" played, trying to figure out the intricate harmonies as they drove.

"Sam wrote that?" Justine asked him. "It's so beautiful."

"My mom said she was at the rehearsal when he sang it for the first time."

"I need to learn the words," she said, chewing on her lip.

When "Different Drum" came on, Robbie saw Justine grow somber, and said nothing.

"How old were you when your mom died?" he asked after the song was over.

"Twelve," said Justine.

"Jeez," said Robbie. "It's hard for me to imagine."

"Yeah," she said. "Me too."

They drove in silence, listening to Sam singing "Creston Gold."

"How can a guy that crazy write something so sweet and beautiful?" Robbie wondered.

"He isn't crazy," she replied quietly.

"You saw how he attacked Johnny."

"He was just scared."

Robbie mulled that over.

Gerald and Bev found a quiet corner in the kitchen near the pantry.

"Hey you," said Gerald.

"Hey you," said Bev.

"Seems like ages."

"It's only been two days."

"Two very busy days," smiled Gerald.

"Pardon me," said Winston, slipping between them into the pantry.

"Two *very* busy days," smiled Bev. "Welcome to Gruenhaus."

"Good to be here." *It sure is nice talking to someone at eye level,* he thought.

"I got you a good room, right in the row with the guys in the band," said Bev.

"Pardon me again," said Winston, cutting between them, lugging two large sacks of potatoes.

"I want to hear how Shelly found Sam."

"I only heard bits and pieces. Later."

"Please?" said Gerald.

"Later!" said Bev. "Shelly's waiting for you."

"Duty calls," he sighed dramatically, and Bev smiled at him.

"Excuse me, ma'am, did you see Dr. Bev anywh—"

Brandi turned to face Matt.

Matt stared at her black tatters and white skin and metal trim.

Brandi looked at him with scorn.

Matt stared back at her and smiled.

"What?" she snarled at him threateningly.

Matt stared at her and smiled and wiped the palm of his

right hand on the calf of his jeans.

"Matt, there you are," said Bev. "Come help me unload the truck."

"And how in the world did it happen that Justine joined the band?" asked Gerald.

"It was Sam's idea," said Shelly.

Gerald's jaw dropped.

"Seriously?" asked the Colonel.

"More than that. It was a 'precondition,' " she laughed.

"And Justine agreed?" asked Gerald, leaning forward on the edge of the rust-and-butterscotch sofa. "Just like that?"

"Just like that. She and Sam were communicating on some kind of paranormal wavelength, I don't know. But, yeah, he made it a condition, and she agreed."

"She's sixteen?" asked the Colonel. "And fragile, you say. Do you really think she's up to this?"

Shelly nodded slowly, considering the question. "She will be," she said gravely, and then shifted gears abruptly. "Shall we get started?" she asked, looking at Gerald.

"I'm ready," he said.

"Well, I thought perhaps you would want to take the lead here," said Shelly hesitantly. "I mean, with your experience ..."

"Oh, no, ma'am. No chance. This is your baby. You've worked miracles up till now. I have no intention of getting in your way."

Shelly looked at the Colonel. Not a flicker, she thought, as her ghost-self reached for his throat.

"I'm here to sign checks and answer phones and maybe kibbitz a little. But this is your baby. Go for it, girl," said Gerald, sinking back into the rust-and-butterscotch sofa with his BlackBerry.

#

"Sit!" commanded Brandi, indicating the chair backed up against the bathroom sink, but Sam hung back.

"Maybe later," he said.

"Shelly said now."

But still he refused to move.

"You wouldn't be afraid of me, would you?" she asked.

"No, why?" he asked from the doorway, his eyes fixated on the tattered remains of the white T-shirt covering very little of her black bra.

"The way you're staring at me," she smiled, fully aware of what he was staring at, and why.

"I was just thinking about how 'underwear' got its name."

"You don't like the way I look?" she asked.

"No, it's fine," he said, shifting his feet uncomfortably. "Just a little different from what I'm used to."

"And what is it that you're used to?" she asked, putting her arm around his shoulder, leading him to the chair, her breast rubbing against his arm.

"Huh?" he asked, allowing himself to be led. She seated him, draped the sheet around his neck and pulled it so tightly it choked him before insinuating the point of the safety pin through the compliant cotton and clipping it shut with a snap.

"Are you comfortable?" asked Brandi, adjusting the collar. He could feel her hot breath on his ear. The lacework of her bra was an intricate filigree of soft twists and weaves, more delicate than anything Sam had seen in a very long time.

"Hey, that's tight!" he said.

"Here, let me loosen it," she said, leaning forward and reaching behind his neck to tighten the collar, the very soft skin of her very soft breasts almost touching his nose.

"I wouldn't want to get any hairs on your shirt," she said, snapping her gum right in his ear so loudly he jerked.

"It's seen worse. You know what you're doing here?" he asked.

"I could give a better haircut than this blindfolded and

with one hand tied behind my back."

"I did it myself," he protested.

"I'll bet you did," she said, looking right into his eyes so close he could feel her breath on his face. "But I can do it so much better."

"Heh."

She leaned his head back into the sink, letting the hot water run through the chaos on top of his head. She squirted a spurt of shampoo into his wet hair and began to knead the suds, lathering him firmly and deeply, her fingers stroking and plying through the thickets and tangles of his scalp.

"How's that?" she asked.

"Oh, fine," he said, his voice cracking.

"You're so tense!" she said.

"It's been a while."

"Try to relax," she said, her fingers probing and working the slick lather, the suds rising and bubbling as she stroked him.

"Heh."

"Don't worry, I don't bite." She snapped her gum. "Unless you want me to."

"Heh," he said, an octave higher.

She rinsed the shampoo out of his squeaky clean hair and stood behind him, brusquely toweling him dry.

"Hey, be gentle," he said.

"Oh, I can do 'gentle,' " she said. She began to run the comb through his hair, the teeth tugging at the jungle of his follicles, gently prying loose each tangle and knot, combing and smoothing with her fingers, comb and smooth.

She took the long pointed scissors in her hand, sliced the air with two menacing slashes too near to his nose, and began to snip, lift and snip, lift and nip.

"I've never done a rock star before," she snipped.

"I ain't no rock star."

"Fuck you aren't," she said, looking him right in the eye. "And I'm going to make you look like one."

45

Rock Star Justine
– June 9, 2006, Mid-Morning –

"Can I ask you something?" Justine asked hesitantly.

"Sure," said Robbie.

"Do you know what happened, why the band broke up?"

He looked at her. "Not really," he said. "I thought you'd know."

"Me? How would I know? Nobody tells me anything. I thought maybe your mom said something—"

"Nah, she doesn't talk to me about that kind of stuff."

"She never talked to you about the fight?"

"Not really," he said unconvincingly.

"What?" Justine insisted.

"I've overheard some stuff."

"Like what?"

He looked at her.

"Go on," she told him.

"That they had a big gig somewhere. And right on stage, Aaron and Sam had a fight. And Sam just walked away. They never even played."

"And afterwards?"

He shook his head. "They never saw him again."

"My mother loved him so much. He must have loved her. What could have made him do that?" she wondered half aloud.

"You could ask him."

Justine shrugged.

"Why not?" he asked.

"That's too weird for me. Romantic triangles, my mother, these strangers—"

"Sam acts like he's known you forever."

"Maybe, but I don't know him."

"I don't know. He acts different with you."

Justine pondered that as she gazed out the window at the used car lots and gas stations.

"Hey, Justine?" said Robbie finally.

"What?" she asked.

"I'm scared, too, you know," said Robbie.

Brandi continued to work on Sam deftly, lift and snip, lift and nip, her arm brushing accidentally against his arm.

"Can I ask you something?"

"You can ask me anything you like," she said.

"What's that thing in your tongue?"

"You mean this?" she asked, wagging the silver piercing up close to his nose. "It's called a stud."

"What's it for?"

"I'll let you use your imagination," she said, her eyes twinkling.

Sam pondered that for a moment. "Oh," he said, swallowing hard.

"Never seen one before?"

"Not that I recall."

"You can touch it if you like," she said, her breath warm on his face.

"Some other time," he said, squirming.

"Oh, don't be a baby," she admonished him, taking his index finger, enveloping it in her mouth, and demonstrating to him just how a tongue stud works.

He withdrew his finger. "Heh," he said.

"They're called piercings. People put them all over. In their eyebrows, in their cheeks, in between their eyes."

"No shit?"

"Yeah. Even some more intimate places that I'm too bashful to mention."

"Oh, yeah?"

"But mine are very conservative."

"You got more?"

"I have a couple more." She lifted the tatter of her T-shirt to allow him to examine her navel.

Sam gazed at it closely. "Oh," he said.

"And one more somewhere where the sun never shines," said Brandi, looking Sam right in the eye.

"Oh," he said, but it came out in falsetto.

Comb and lift and snip, comb and lift and snip.

"Could you sit still? You're all fidgety," she said.

"This chair's getting hard," he said.

Comb and lift and snip, comb and lift and nip. Comb and smooth and comb.

"Let's see," she said, assaying her work. "Fucking Marlboro man!"

She ran the comb through his hair on the right, then on the left, and then on the top. Then, the comb slipped from her hand right into the middle of his lap.

"Whoops! I'm so clumsy," she said as she fished for it among the folds of the sheet.

"Hey, well, gee," he said, clambering to his feet. "It's, ah, I gotta, ah, go do that—"

Brandi watched, grinning, as he ran out of the door, her gum popping like automatic fire from an AK-47.

"But why cancel all the interviews?" said Shelly's father, an accusation wrapped in a question.

"The way *I* see it," she said, eyeballing her father, "we're talking about a whole new ballgame now. Before, we were talking about a weekend with some old guys reminiscing. Now, we got ourselves a band. I think I'll say that again. We got ourselves the whole cotton-picking old-new Decapede. That's a big deal," said Shelly.

"That is indeed a big deal," said Gerald.

"How long do you think this fad is going to last?" asked the Colonel respectfully. The cover story of last month's Forbes was "Gerald Bridges—Fortune Teller."

"One month," said Shelly.

"How do you know that?" asked the Colonel.

"Aaron is having a hip replacement right after the Fourth of July weekend, and Mendel has two daughters giving birth then. We have them for a month."

"How much can you accomplish in one month?" asked the Colonel skeptically.

They looked at Shelly.

She walked over to the tall glass windows to gaze down the long slope to Lake Traumsee. "One month," she said to herself.

The Col. (Ret.) Judge Advocate General and the Barracuda of Buyouts watched Shelly think.

"Do you really believe Decapede has commercial viability?" the Colonel asked Mr. Gerald Bridges.

"Charlie, the clip on YouTube? Thirty-six K in the last *twelve hours*. There's never been anything like that. Ever. It looks like Decapede might drive digital sales past physical sales for the first time in history!" said Gerald, glowing. "The reunion of the band is above the fold in all the media all over Northeast Ohio. We got feelers from all three networks and CNN, and Warner Reality Channel is about to make us an offer for exclusive rights. It's all people are talking about, Decapede reuniting thirty-six years after an acrimonious breakup, complete with mad recluse and orphan girl—all live on camera! Johnny said,

'It's like watching a dinosaur egg hatch in the middle of a soap opera.' If you ask me, the sky's the limit." Gerald leaned back and crossed his arms, his chest all puffed out.

"But how do we do that if we only have a month?" asked the Colonel.

Gerald shrugged with a grin. "Ask your daughter."

Shelly turned to them from the window.

"This is what we're going to do," she said.

Justine looked at Robbie. "What do you have to be scared about?"

"Shelly's expecting me to set up a studio."

"But you had one in California."

"In my room. For me and some friends to fool around on. But this is big-time shit."

Justine looked over and gave him a little smile as the final chords of "Creston Gold" played on the radio.

Hi there, what's your name?

Freddy McNeil.

What brings you here today, Freddy?

I'm from over in Chagrin Falls, I'm a driver for Goodyear. It's my littlest one's birthday today. She's gonna be fifteen, and she's all excited about this Decapede CD. She really wanted to buy it herself this morning, but she's in school. So I figured I'd surprise her, pick it up for her.

It looks like you're going to be in line here for a while. You don't mind?

Aw, for my little Cathy? I know how happy it'll make her.

Some people are saying that Decapede is the biggest thing to hit Northeast Ohio since LeBron James.

Ah, man, don't even mention them in the same breath. Lebron's great and all. But you know, bottom line, it's all about him. Him and his giant ego and his giant salary. Decapede—that's us!

Thanks, Freddie, and congratulations to Cathy McNeil on her fifteenth birthday. This is Art Murray broadcasting from Bent Crayon Records for WFOR.

"I guess we're all a little scared," said Justine.

"You think?" he said, smiling.

"Well, maybe everyone except Shelly," said Justine. They stopped for a red light. "Can you pull over for a minute at that CVS?"

"Shelly said not to hang around."

"I need a couple of things. It'll just take a minute."

"Okay," he said, "you're the rock star."

"Oh, shut up," she said, smiling.

"This is what we're going to do," said Shelly. "One show."

The men stared at her.

"We have them for a month? We take away their cell phones, no internet. Rehearse their asses off. Record right here. And then at the end, one big show. Rehearse. Record. Perform. One show."

The men looked at each other, then back at Shelly.

"Will they be up to that, musically?" asked the Colonel.

Shelly looked her father right in his skeptical eye. "Of course they will," she said, her heart thumping.

"With Johnny as fly on the wall, we completely own the media flow," said Gerald. "It's brilliant."

"Where?" asked the Colonel.

"I don't know. Somewhere big."

"When?" asked Gerald.

"On the Fourth of July," said Shelly. She listened to the sound of that. "Yeah," she said, "on the Fourth of July."

"Hey, here's some nice floor wax," said Robbie.

"Would you please go away?" said Justine, hiding her smile.

"You don't need any floor wax? How about some instant glue? Oh, here's a real nice electric pencil sharpener. You never know when you'll need—"

"Robbie, would you shut up already and let me concentrate?" she said, repressing a giggle.

He mugged zipping his lips.

"What do you think," she asked, mulling over the sunscreen, "forty or fifty?"

"Oh, fifty, definitely. Go wild. How does this look on me?" He was wearing a wide-brimmed red sunhat with large white polka dots.

"Perfect. Matches your eyes. Would you please let me concentrate?"

"Hey, did you see little notebooks anywhere?"

"Right behind you."

"This is all they have," he said, holding up a pocket-sized pink Little Kitty pad.

"Suits you," she said, and he tossed it into the basket she was carrying.

"What do you need more shampoo for?"

"I don't like what they have at Gruenhaus."

"Shelly said we can have that girl order in whatever we need."

"Brandi."

"She said no alcohol."

"Oh, you're so funny!" she said, yawning a giant yawn.

"How about some furniture polish? That always comes in handy—"

"Robbie!"

"What?" he said innocently. "Oh! Wait a minute!" He ran to the end of the aisle and returned with a dog collar and a box of Greenie doggy treats.

Justine smiled sweetly at him.

Robbie's heart gave a little flip.

"Robbie, now go away!" she stage-whispered, suppressing her laugh. "Go look at car magazines or something."

"Ooh, do you think they have comic books in Ohio?"

The moment his back was turned, Justine made a beeline

for the Feminine Care aisle. Checking that he wasn't looking, she shoved a box of tampons into her basket and covered it with a red T-shirt with Cleveland and 23 printed in garish yellow letters. She went straight to the checkout counter, hoping to avoid Robbie, but there was a young mother in front of her buying a mountain of baby supplies.

Justine pulled a pack of chewing gum from the candy rack next to the register, then spied the Tootsie Rolls on the bottom shelf. She took one, thought a moment, then bent down and picked up an entire unopened box.

Robbie tossed two cans of Coke and a copy of *The Irredeemable Ant-Man* on top of the Cleveland T-shirt.

"You read this stuff?" Justine asked.

"Ant-Man? He's great."

"Would you go please start the car?"

"We need to make a quick getaway?" He was looking at the tabloids.

"Would you please just—"

"Justine, did you see this?"

He pulled a copy of *US Enquirer* from the display and held it up for her to see.

"Oh, no!" Justine cried loudly enough for the young mother and the cashier to turn to look at her.

On the cover of the rag was a picture of Justine's eighth-grade swimming team with the banner headline "MYSTERY DECAPEDE SINGER REVEALED" and underneath "Exclusive Color Photos!"

"I'm going to die!" she moaned to him. "The whole world is going to see that picture?" The girls were all wearing ugly one-piece uniform suits over their curveless bodies.

"Wow, some bod there!" he snickered.

"Stop," she said, punching him in the shoulder. "That's so embarrassing. Where did they dig that up?"

"Anything else, ma'am?" said the girl at the register, ringing up the comic book and the tabloid.

Justine saw Robbie averting his eyes from the O.B. box.

"No, that's all," said Justine, handing her the credit card Shelly had given her and moving quickly to pack up her personal purchases in a separate bag.

"Did you hear," the cashier asked them as she handed Justine the change, "that Decapede band is staying right over here in Creston?"

"Decapede?" said Robbie, "what's that?"

"Very funny," said the cashier.

Bev knocked and stuck her head in. "Are you ready for Matt?"

"Sure," said Shelly.

"Give us a minute first, please," said the Colonel. "Shelly, you're just looking for trouble."

Shelly looked at Gerald, but he was reading an email on his BlackBerry.

"Pedro paid for those recordings, Dad. You can't ignore that," she retorted. "He bequeathed his estate to Matt. That makes Matt the prima facie owner."

"There's no evidence of ownership in the first place," argued Attorney-at-Law Griffin. "Some hearsay rumors, thirty-six years later," he said, fixing his eyes right on hers without wavering, a sort of eye wrestling he used to get his way.

Shelly fixed her eyes right back at him, folded her arms, sat back and crossed her legs. "It's the right thing to do," she said. "I want to do right by him."

"And I say you're stirring up a hornet's nest."

"Have you met Matt Hinton, Dad? I would not call him a hornet."

"You haven't seen what I have, Shel. When a lot of money is involved, opportunists start crawling out of the woodwork."

Gerald's phone rang. "Charlie, that Matt, he's a good kid. Give him some stock. Sorry, I have to take this. It's Warner," he said. "Simon, how are you? Actually, I'm with her right now.

Shelly, Simon says to tell you he's a giant fan of Decapede. Simon, I think we're going to get along just fine," he said from the doorway, winking at Shelly and his new buddy.

Shelly and her father watched the door close behind him.

"*That*," asked the Colonel, "is the sixth-richest man in the world?"

"His social skills are a little out of whack, I'll admit," said Shelly. They both stared at the door.

"According to the trade papers, he's a cutthroat," said the Colonel. "People are terrified of him. *Countries* are terrified of him. What in God's name is he doing here?"

"He's a fan of the band. He just wants to be on the inside." She looked at her father and whacked him on the shoulder. "Charlie."

"What do you listen to music with?" Robbie asked as he browsed at the aisles of Computerland.

"An old iPod," said Justine, "but I left it in Florida."

He tossed a couple of iPod 5s into his cart.

"Why two?" she asked.

"In case someone else wants."

Robbie laid it all on the counter, the Pro Tools work station and all the assorted nerd goodies he had grabbed.

"That will be $1,425.67," said the pimpled cashier, not much older than Robbie and Justine.

Robbie handed him the Bridges Media credit card.

"Can I see some ID, please?" he asked.

Robbie handed him his driver's license.

The boy handed it back. "This is from California."

"Yeah, so?"

"I'll need a local ID."

"Sorry, I live in LA," said Robbie. "But this card is good."

"Regulations. It has to be a local license."

The nineteen-year-old cashier called over the twenty-year-old store manager with a complexion even worse than the cashier's, but wearing a clip-on tie as a mantle of authority.

"I'm sorry, sir, but we'll need some local identification. How about you, ma'am?"

"I'm from Florida," she shrugged.

"Sorry, we need a local license," said the acned young man. "Those are the regulations."

Robbie looked at Justine and then at the two young salesmen. "Did you watch Johnny Walker's broadcast last night?"

They looked at each other and nodded.

Robbie looked at Justine. The two young salesmen looked at Justine, then back at each other. Then back at Justine and then back again at each other.

"You're—"

Robbie and Justine looked at each other.

The young manager hurriedly processed the purchase as the younger salesman bagged their purchases.

"Could you please sign here, sir?" he asked Robbie. Then, handing Justine a piece of Computerland stationary, he added hesitantly, "And would you sign this for me?"

Justine smiled shyly, but signed, embarrassed.

On their way out, Robbie stopped to gaze at a rack of the New Super Mario Brothers video games. "Look what they have in Hicksville," said Robbie.

"Great," she said. "Come on, we need to get back."

"Just a minute," he said, reading the back of the box. Justine saw the manager whispering to a huddle of young salesmen and the cashier talking to someone on his phone. Everyone's eyes were fixed on her.

46

Legal Air

– June 9, 2006, Late Morning –

"Just don't frighten him," said Shelly.

"Me?" asked the Colonel.

"He doesn't think too well on his feet."

"Hmpf," said the Colonel.

Matt knocked.

"Mr. Hinton," said the Colonel, extending his hand, "come in, please."

Matt wiped his right palm vigorously on the leg of his jeans before extending his own hand. "Excuse me, sir, I'm a little nervous," he said, smiling broadly, terror in his eyes.

"Come, sit next to me," said Shelly sweetly.

"I understand that you're the owner of a commercial property at 1660 Market Street in Steubenville, most recently leased to Dee's Hair & Beauty Supplies, currently vacant, is that correct?" asked the Colonel curtly.

"Yes, sir."

"Could you explain exactly how you assumed ownership of the property?"

"Me?" asked Matt. "Oh, I didn't assume it. My Meemaw gave it to me."

"Meemaw is?" prompted Col. (Ret.) Judge Advocate General Charles Griffin.

"My grandma. She's buried over in Massillon," Matt smiled, about to disintegrate. When the Colonel continued to glare, he added, "That's where she lived. When she was alive."

"Mr. Hinton, do you consider yourself to be Lonny Hinton's legal heir?"

"What exactly is legal air?" he asked.

Shelly put her hand on her father's forearm. His iron jaw continued to clench.

"Okay, so Lonny Hinton?" Shelly nudged Matt back into the groove.

"I hardly knew him," babbled Matt. "Maybe I met him once or twice at family weddings, but I really don't remember him. Just that he had this big wart right under his nose—"

"Lonny was Meemaw's brother?"

Matt nodded enthusiastically, greatly relieved to be asked a question to which he knew the answer. "Right, and he didn't have any kids, so Meemaw got all his stuff when he passed. Not that there was much to get. A rusty old eighteen-foot outboard, twelve hundred bucks in the bank, and some worthless old properties he owned around this area." He began to innumerate on his fingers. "In Steubenville, there's the one what was Dee's over on Market, and another empty one on 4th Street."

"By Dickenson's Hardware?" asked Shelly.

"Right," said Matt casually, assuming that Shelly knew everything about everything. "And two over in Massillon. One's a tattoo parlor, the other's empty. One in Dover. Used to be a sporting goods store, but they closed down last year. Four," said Matt. "Anyways, they're mostly empty. They're not worth much to speak of, but I gotta keep paying taxes on them every year. So I'm just stuck with them. I keep trying to rent them out, but everything's dead in this part of the state."

"So how do you make a living?" asked Shelly.

"Odd jobs, repairs and stuff. Construction work during the off-season. Me and my friends play semi-pro over in Cuyahoga Falls. The Cuyahoga Rapids, that's us," said Matt. "I play shortstop."

"Mr. Hinton," said the Colonel magisterially, "it has come to our attention that your great-uncle Lonny Hinton was involved in facilitating the original Decapede recording session. As a gesture of goodwill, Decapede Incorporated is proposing to offer you a one-time disbursement of three thousand shares of corporate stock in antecessum of any future—"

Matt stared at the Colonel, smiling and wiping his palms on the leg of his jeans.

"Matt," said Shelly, "do you know what 'stocks' are?"

"Robbie, come on, pl—" Justine urged him.

"Excuse me," said a girl with braces and pimples, not much older than Justine, clutching the arm of her boyfriend, "are you really Justine Brinker?"

Justine looked around the store. There were about twenty customers and six or eight employees. They were all staring at her. A couple of them had cell phones with a camera and were snapping Justine.

"Uh, yeah," she said.

"Oh my God," squealed the girl, bouncing from excitement, jerking her boyfriend's arm as she clung to him, "I can't believe this. Can we do a selfie?"

Without waiting for an answer, she pulled a little camera from her bag, handed it to her boyfriend, draped her arm around Justine's shoulder and grinned maniacally. "Come on, Goose, just click the button."

"Okay!" he said, flustered. "One more. Now me," he said, switching place with the girl. Justine meanwhile noticed that everyone in the store had begun to cluster around them. Goose smelled like soggy feathers.

"This is SO exciting!" said the girl. "I can't believe I'm actually meeting you in person! We lo-o-ove Decapede! Are you guys going to perform soon?"

People were pointing and moving in closer.

"Is it true that Decapede is holed up over near Creston?"

"What's Sam Miller like?"

"Is it true that he was living like a hermit?"

"What's it like being an orphan?"

"Do you hear there are lines of people in all the stores waiting to buy your CD?"

"Is Aaron still that handsome?"

"When do we get to see Decapede?"

"Will Decapede be on the Johnny Walker Show soon?"

"Hey, man," said Robbie as the crowd began to press in on them, jostling them roughly as the cacophony grew. "Hey, watch it!"

"Can I take a picture with you?"

"Justine, will you sign this?"

"Will you be singing your mother's songs?"

One of the salesmen grabbed a camera out of a display case and climbed onto the counter to get a better angle.

"Is Decapede going to record a new album?"

"Were you there when the band first met up again?"

"Hey, back off," said Robbie, struggling to keep his balance.

The store's front window was lined with people peering in.

A simian linebacker shoved his way forward, knocking people backward. "Justine, will you marry me?" he guffawed and grabbed her in a forceful embrace, landing with all the force of his two hundred and ten pounds on her little foot.

"Robbie!" she cried.

"Matt?" Shelly prompted him.

"I'm sorry, ma'am. Could you repeat the question?"

"Do you know what stocks are?"

"It's a thing where rich people gamble, I think."

"Exactly. Listen, Matt, I'll explain what Colonel Griffin said to you when things quiet down, I promise. But for right now, I want to explain to you about your great-uncle Lonny and Decapede."

Matt smiled at Shelly with no clue as to why he was smiling.

"Lonny paid for Decapede to do the recordings."

"That's nice," said Matt, smiling.

"So I think you should get some of the money that comes from selling the CD."

"Oh, that was way before I was even born. You don't have to pay me anything, ma'am." Matt's eyes and smile were frozen, but his palms were perspiring like sprinklers.

"And I believe it will be a nice amount, Matt," said Shelly.

But just then the door opened and Johnny came through, eye in the camera, Brandi guiding him down the four steps into Shelly's office.

"Don't look at the camera, just keep doing what you're doing," he said, slowly circling the group.

Shelly tapped her pen on her notebook.

"You know what, Matt? You've been a tremendous help to us here—"

"Oh, that's my pleasure, ma'am."

"—bringing in guys to get Gruenhaus ready—"

"Oh, they were happy to do it, ma'am."

"—and helping us find hands for the brewery—"

"Oh, ma'am, you have no idea how happy my friends are to have that work."

"—that I'd like to hire you. To work with Decapede as—Community Liason."

"I'm not sure what that means, ma'am," said Matt, smiling.

"Just keep doing what you're doing. We'll pay you a nice salary for the next month's work. When things calm down, I'll explain to you about your stocks and gambling," she smiled.

"Oh, thank you, ma'am, you don't need to pay me. My buddies and me, we're just so proud to be helping out Decapede."

Johnny meanwhile was zooming in and out at Matt, at Shelly, at the Colonel to his utter consternation, at one point climbing on a chair to shoot from a high angle. The chair wobbled, and Matt leaped to grab Johnny's arm and help him down.

"Whoa, thanks," said Johnny. "Why are you proud? Talk to the camera," he said to Matt and continued circling the powwow.

"Decapede—" said the shortstop, looking at the camera, "it's the first time people have ever felt cool about being from around here. The whole country's looking at us on the internet, talking about Steubenville and Creston and Warren and Youngstown and Akron and stuff. And, I mean, we all feel like it's *us*. It's not just happening here. It's *part* of here. I mean, this is Decapede Country, man. And Decapede is like the coolest thing in the whole world. So, you know, it kind of makes us cool. And proud just to be from around here."

"Nice haircut, handsome," said Bev, blocking the kitchen doorway with her entire little frame. "Where do you think you're going?"

"I went with that Brandi girl like you said, barely got out alive, and now I'm aiming to check out the fishing down at Allie's lake."

"Sorry," she said, consulting her clipboard, "I have you down here for kitchen duty."

"Show me?" he said.

Bev showed him her clipboard. Sam squinted to read it. The top page was titled "May 9—Morning" in large bold letters. Underneath it was a densely detailed table with Personnel listed across the top row, Shelly's name first, followed by each of the other members of the staff in alphabetical order. The left column listed time blocks of thirty minutes each. Under Sam Miller 9:30-11:00 was written Kitchen Duty. He looked down at Bev, took the pencil from behind her ear, crossed out Kitchen Duty with two emphatic strokes and wrote in its place Fishing. He handed the clipboard back to her.

"Winston here's got it all under control. Don't you, Winston?" said Sam, looking down at Bev.

"Morning, Miss Bev. Get you a cup of coffee?" he offered, far too wise to get between them.

But Bev stood her ground, glaring right back up at Sam. "Kitchen Duty."

Sam began to sing scoffingly in her face, "*I'm a-goin' fishin', you can come a-fishin', I'm a-goin' fishin' too.*" He turned and began to walk out to the back porch.

But Bev snatched the pole from his hand and took off running so fast through the kitchen into the dining room down the hall towards Shelly's office that when Sam lit off after her she already had a good head start on him. He chased her down the hall, Bev squealing with glee. Gerald went running after them to catch all the action.

Winston watched them go and resumed his chopping, humming along with "Peggy Sue" from the radio.

"You're crushing my foot," cried Justine, trying to move the Neanderthal, but he was holding her with his ape arm, mugging for the camera.

Robbie put his foot behind the heel of the behemoth and shoved with all his might. The goon fell backward, clearing space around them. Robbie grabbed Justine's hand and yanked her towards the door. Through a blur of shouts and clicks and groping hands, they ran through the crowd and out to the car, threw the packages in the back seat, jumped in and drove away as quickly as they could.

Justine was sobbing. Robbie asked if she was all right, but she continued choking on her tears. Robbie reached into the back seat, his hand trembling, grabbed a can of Coke and handed it to her. Justine took it from him and fumbled to open it, but it erupted in a fizzy shower all over her and the seat and the dashboard and her face and her window and the windshield and Robbie.

"F-U-U-U-U-C-K!" she wailed in frustration and began

sobbing even harder. Robbie pulled into the first parking lot and stopped the car. Justine clambered out and stood with her hand on her chest, gasping for air.

"Are you—"

Justine threw her arms around Robbie's neck and sobbed into the crook of his neck. Robbie stood there, confused, and finally put his arms around her to try to comfort her, but the girl continued to blubber inconsolably. His heart was thumping, even as his breathing became regular. He felt the heat of her breath and the wetness of her tears against his neck and began to get hard. Justine was holding him so close that he was sure she could feel it as well, the boner of an aroused seventeen-year old stoked with adrenaline. Confused and embarrassed, he moved back, but somehow their eyes locked and became a fumbled attempt at a kiss. Justine shoved him away, rattled and distraught.

They drove in embarrassed silence.

"Justine, I'm—"

"Don't say anything."

"I didn't mean—"

"Just shut up!"

Bev bounded down the four steps into Shelly's office, shrieking and laughing, carrying a fishing pole taller than herself, Sam hot on her heels. Shelly and the Colonel and Matt and Brandi and Johnny and Johnny's camera all turned to stare.

"Give me back my pole, you little—" shouted Sam.

"Hey, we're working here!" said the Colonel.

"Cut!" ordered Shelly.

Everyone stopped talking.

"What's going on?" she asked Bev calmly.

"There's a ton of stuff that needs to be done," Bev panted, "so I put Sam down to help out—"

"I finished what you said—" he attempted.

"Hup!" Shelly silenced him. "Bev's—"

Then she turned to look at Sam, but it wasn't Sam. It was a younger, cleaner, domesticated Sam Miller. Shaved and shorn. With a naked face. With strong, weather-worn creases. That could be used for smiling. A very comely face.

"—talking!"

"Winston's got a ton of work for tonight, so I asked Sam to help out in the kitchen, but he says he's going fishing." Then she added in a whisper, "You said to come right to you."

Shelly turned to Sam.

"I did what you told me," he said, trying to sound surly. "I got my hair cut. I can't take all this commotion, all this—"

"Outside," snapped Shelly.

Sam followed her through the screen door out to the lawn.

Bev and Brandi and Gerald and Matt and Johnny and even the Colonel ran to the windows to watch.

"Maybe you shouldn't film this," said the Colonel.

"Are you kidding?" said Johnny, his eye in the viewfinder.

"Look," Sam huffed, "I've been cooperating with this whole circus of yours. You tell me come up, make some music. Fine. You tell me to get my hair cut, fine, even though I barely got out of there alive. You want to put me in new clothes, I don't care. But, man, I just want to go down to the lake now and relax a little. I didn't sign up here to wash dishes."

A different person. The fucking Marlboro man. "You done, Miller?" she hissed.

"Yeah, I'm done," he said, with waning confidence.

"Now you listen carefully to me. Are you listening?" she said, knives in her voice.

He grunted.

"What you signed up for is to come live in society. This is how society works. You cooperate with other people. They do things for you, you do things for them. Are you following me?"

Sam was gazing down the long sloping hill at the lovely, placid Lake Traumsee.

"Are you following me?" Shelly snarled. Without all that messy stubble, she could see him stifle a smile.

"Could you go over that one more time, just a little slower?"

"You're not a hermit here, Sam. You're living with other people. Get it?"

"I just wanted to settle down a little. To calm myself."

"I ain't buying it, Miller. Aaron and Gavin and Mendel will be here in a couple of hours. There's a ton of stuff to do. A whole house to get ready, mouths to feed. And you want to go *fishing*?"

Still, the lake beckoned him, more placid and more distant by the moment.

Bev and Brandi and Gerald and Matt and Johnny and the Colonel stared through the tall windows at their blond boss berating the legendary Sam Miller.

"Why is she yelling at him like that?" Matt asked Johnny.

"It's just pretend," said Johnny. "I think."

"You don't want to help?" Shelly continued. "No problem. I'll bring you in a servant. I'll bring in an army of servants. You're rich, Sam, do you get that? You're a millionaire."

"I'm a millionaire?" he scoffed.

"Yes, Sam. Seven figures. From royalties on 'Creston Gold' alone."

He scratched his newly-shaven jaw and gazed longingly down at the lake. Shelly grabbed him by the shoulder and turned him to face her.

"Look me in the eye, you shiftless son of a bitch! If you want, I'll bring you in your very own personal chef and your personal butler and your personal valet and a personal fucking shoeshiner," she said into his face, jabbing him rhythmically in the chest. "You just tell me how many servants you want following you around all summer. Five? And then five for each of the other members of the band, and five for me. About fifty more people here in Gruenhaus, that should cover it, don't you think? And if you think that's not enough, we can—"

"Okay!" Sam cut her off. "I get it."

Bev and Brandi stood together, watching Shelly pummel Sam Miller mercilessly in mime.

Bev looked at Brandi. "They're not—?"

"Nah," answered Brandi, after a pause.

They continued watching.

"Are they?" Brandi asked Bev.

"But if you don't want that, then you'd better get it through that thick skull of yours that you're going to be living according to the rulebook of The Real World. And drop the 'Sam Miller, Irascible Recluse' act."

Sam turned his gaze from the lake to Shelly, the lines in his well-formed face smiling.

"What?" she steamed.

"You're funny when you're mad," said this new person.

Shelly felt herself turning red, so she turned and stomped back across the lawn to her office.

"Nice view you got here," he called after her.

"Winston's waiting for you," she called back without turning.

Bev figured she could go out the front door and sneak up on Sam in the kitchen from outside. Down on the road, two policemen were moving news vans and reporters and cars and spectators, clearing the entrance to the driveway.

Dog was lying in the shade of a tree by the annex near the parking area, waiting for Justine to return. Bev bent to scratch him behind his ear. Dog complied warily, never having been scratched behind the ear by anyone other than Justine. He seemed to find it pleasant, and even whacked his tail on the ground halfheartedly a couple of times. Bev heard voices from the kitchen and tiptoed carefully up the wooden stairs of the back porch, aching to catch Sam in an act of indolence. She stood next to the open door, out of sight, and listened.

She could hear water running, some utensils moving, and the chop-chop of a vegetable knife.

Then she heard Sam's voice say, "Okay, you ready?" and a whispered "One, two, one two three—"

And then Sam and Winston were singing—shouting more than singing, at the top of their voices—"*If you wanna be happy for the rest of your life, never make a pretty woman your wife,*" repeating it over and over until she walked in. They saw her, and both convulsed in unbridled adolescent hilarity.

"All right, you guys," said Dr. Pettiford, drawing herself up to her full miniature height.

"*Awright?*" Sam shouted at Winston, ignoring her.

"*Awright!*" Winston shouted back.

"*One more time?*" shouted Sam.

"*Two more times!*" answered Winston even more loudly.

"All right! All right!" proclaimed little Bev.

Sam tossed his potato peeler onto the large pile of freshly peeled potatoes, grabbed her by the hands and dragged her into a circle dance with him and Winston, singing it over and over, Bev singing and laughing with them.

"*If you wanna be happy for the rest of your life, never make a pretty woman your wife—*"

They finally wound down, laughing and panting for breath. Bev put her hands on her knees and inhaled deeply. She straightened up, her brow furrowed and her eyes sharp as a hawk's.

"What's that smell?" she demanded.

"What smell?" asked Sam, choking a laugh.

"Wa smell?" repeated Winston, poker-faced.

"Have you two been smoking?" she asked.

"No, Miss Bev," said Winston, wide-eyed and innocent, "thas my secret seasoning for de chili."

Bev planted herself in front of him, fists on her hips, and attempted to look imposing.

"What seasoning would that be?" she demanded.

"Oh, das a secret!" said Winston, setting Sam and himself off on a peal of laughter.

"What's the commotion?" asked Shelly, poking her head through the door, Allie right behind her.

Bev turned to her sharply. "Do you know what these two—"

But Sam was too quick for her, grabbing Shelly and Allie by their hands, Winston following his lead and pulling in Bev, with Sam leading them all into a reprise of the circle dance in the middle of the kitchen, singing at the top of their lungs, Sam and Winston and Shelly and even demure Allie, with Johnny now filming from inside the circle, drowning out Bev's protestations. "*If you wanna be happy for the rest of your life, never make a pretty woman your wife—*"

They heard a car pull up outside and Dog barking excitedly.

"The kids are back," said Bev, and ran down to greet them. Through the driver's window she saw on Robbie's face a helpless, vulnerable look she hadn't seen on him in years. Justine threw open her door and jumped out before the car had fully stopped, almost tripping over Dog. She stumbled gawkily towards the porch, limping badly, Dog leaping and yelping in a frenzy. The girl threw her arms around Sam, burying her head against his chest and sobbing hysterically. Sam stood frozen, his arms outstretched, baffled and bewildered, looking over little Justine's quivering shoulder at Shelly for a clue about how to comfort a sobbing sixteen-year-old girl.

Hesitantly, he tried patting Justine's back while Allie stroked her wet, tangled hair, cooing to her soothingly. Still, to his utter consternation, Justine clutched Sam's chest, hiding her tears, sobbing.

"Oh, sweetie," said Allie, brushing the girl's matted hair back to see her eyes, "what happened, honey? Are you all right?"

The girl shook her head against Sam's chest, convulsing in starts, clutching him even tighter.

"Come," said Allie, extricating her from flummoxed Sam,

who watched as the women led the girl away, not knowing whether he was supposed to follow. Dog was barking furiously at the door through which Justine had disappeared, but refused to enter the house. Sam looked at Winston, who shrugged. The door to the annex was open, so Sam followed them in.

Allie's annex was full of photos and pictures and knick-knacks, and Sam immediately whiffed something freshly baked. Allie and Shelly seated Justine on a chair at the wooden table in the homespun little country kitchen. They crouched in front of the girl, vigilant and consoling and protective, ministering to her with love and a glass of water.

"What happened, sweetie?" asked Shelly gently when the girl's sobbing had subsided, "Tell us."

"They—they attacked me," she whimpered, sniffling.

"Who did?" snapped Sam, ready to leap into battle to defend her. But there was no one to defend her against, and the women were all ignoring him.

"Who attacked you?" asked Shelly gently.

"In the store," she said.

Allie handed her a tissue from the box on the kitchen table, and Justine blew her nose three times forcefully.

"They recognized me in the computer store. From television, last night."

"Oh, no," said Shelly softly, stroking Justine's hand.

Next to the box of tissues, Sam sniffed a plate full of buns. They were still warm.

"They went *crazy*," said the girl, looking at Shelly and then at Allie. "Taking pictures, and shouting, and *grabbing* me." She tried to contain her crying. "And this ape grabbed me and smashed my foot—" She began to sob again.

Shelly hugged the girl to her and stroked her back.

"Are you all right?" asked Allie. "Did they hurt you?"

She buried her face in Shelly's breast. "Robbie got me out. Barely."

"Do you want Bev to come take a look at your foot?"
Justine shook her head.

"It must have been very frightening," said Shelly.

The girl nodded emphatically and wiped her nose.

"Would you like to lie down for a little bit?" asked Allie softly.

Justine nodded.

Sam watched as the women led the girl into Allie's bedroom.

Allie peeled back the covers and sat Justine on the edge of the widow's bed.

"Are you sure this is okay?" asked Justine.

Sam counted seven buns on the plate.

"You just lie down and close your eyes," said Allie. "No one's going to hurt you here."

Shelly bent down to remove Justine's tennis shoes. Underneath the bed was a strikingly familiar pair of men's slippers.

Allie laid Justine onto the bed and covered her with a down quilt, tucking her in. Through the door, Sam saw Shelly close the blinds to darken the room. He rearranged the six buns on the plate.

"You just close your eyes and relax, honey," said Allie, motioning to Shelly that she could take over. "I'm here. Okay?"

Justine nodded into the pillow.

Outside, Sam snarled at Shelly. "See what you started?" Dog was still barking furiously.

"What do you mean?" asked Shelly.

"All your rock star shit. See what it did?"

"You want to blame me for this?" she said, bristling, the color rising in her face and chest.

"Hell yes," he said. "Who else?"

"The girl had a shock. She'll be okay," said Shelly, her ears burning like a thief's.

"Yeah? How do you know that?"

In truth, Shelly wasn't sure at all that Justine was going

to be all right. Or any of them, for that matter. But someone had to hold this whole stampede together, and everyone was looking to her for answers. So she invented one.

"Because she's been living in a little cocoon, and she's in a crazy new situation, and she's going to be hitting some bumps along the way."

"The girl gets attacked, and you call it a bump?"

"She'll survive it!" said Shelly, convincing herself as she spoke. "It's part of growing up."

"You should just leave people alone," he said.

"So she can waste away her whole life like you in a dumpy trailer in the middle of the woods? Welcome to the real world, Miller," barked Shelly and stomped off through the dining room.

"You call this 'real'?" he shouted after her, but Shelly was gone, and Sam wasn't sure if she had heard him.

47

Hi Guys

– June 9, 2006, Afternoon –

Shelly and Bev stood on the front porch, staring anxiously at the bend in the road on the crest of the hill on the country road leading to Gruenhaus, waiting for sight of the band members.

Sam watched through the tall, stately windows of the common room to avoid the prying zoom lenses of the cameras down on the road. His eyes wandered over the high-ceilinged room, with its gloomy *fin de siècle* German immigrant décor. But one of those women had already splashed around some orange and yellow pillows and whatnots, which looked actually kind of nice, he thought to himself, and continued staring out the window.

Justine came to stand next to him at the window. They stood in tense silence, watching the road. In addition to the news crews, police officers and cars, the crowd below had swelled to several hundred spectators. There were even two mounted policemen. People were milling with tangible excitement behind the wooden barriers the police had placed around the entrance to the driveway. Somewhere a tinny loudspeaker was playing "Creston Gold." Several posters were held high reading "Creston ♥ Decapede" and "We Are Decapede!" Justine slipped her slender arm through Sam's and lay her head on his shoulder.

"How's your foot?" he asked.

"It's okay now," she said.

They continued waiting in silence. Police cars were stationed every hundred yards along the road leading to the Gruenhaus driveway. Finally, a shiny black van with tinted windows came around the bend at the crest of the road and slowed to a stop. The throng of spectators was vibrating in excitement.

The van made its way slowly down the hill through the gauntlet the police were struggling to maintain and turned into the driveway when Sheriff Aubrey signaled it to stop. Matt got out and stood talking to him. The din from the throng was swelling, and the air began to pulsate. Matt waved at the restless horde with a grin and was answered with a raucous cheer. Shelly and Bev walked quickly down the driveway to see why the van had stopped. Sam watched them discussing something with Sheriff Aubrey, gesticulating animatedly. The crowd was shifting and undulating, the shouting becoming more boisterous.

"You want to go down and see what's happening?" asked Sam.

"Oh, no," said Justine, gazing at the clamor down on the road, holding his arm tightly. After a long moment, she spoke. "Would you stay with me?"

"You scared?" Sam gave her a little shove with his shoulder.

"And you aren't, hotshot?" she answered back, and gave him a bump with her hip.

"You ever been to a circus?"

The girl shook her head.

"C'mon," he said, taking her hand and leading her briskly down the front steps and down the long sloping lawn to where the van had stopped. Dog was trotting beside them, his tail wagging suspiciously. But when he scented the crowd—more humans than he had ever seen in all his dog years—hopelessly outnumbered, he shied away and slunk back towards the house. Shelly and Bev were still talking to the sheriff and Matt, who seemed to be mediating. Meanwhile, the hum of the crowd was becoming a buzz. People were pressed against the railings, jumping and shouting. The TV crews, pinned behind the police line with the common folk, were shouting towards the van, straining to catch a glimpse of even an elbow of the mystery men inside. Johnny was standing apart on a rise in the lawn, filming the pandemonium.

Shelly spied Sam and Justine walking down towards them. She tried shouting at them to go back, but the tumult from the crowd drowned her out, and then the mob spotted them. Shouts began to rise of "There's Sam Miller!" "Justine, over here!" The crush at the barriers began to swell and fall, breathing and heaving.

"Don't look at them," said Sam, his arm around the girl's waist, hurrying her towards the van, half lifting her off the ground.

Somehow, one barrier was knocked over, then the next, one after another, like a row of Southeast Asian dictatorships, and the crowd began to flood through the breach. Sam pulled Justine towards the side door of the van, where Matt was blocking the onslaught. Sam slid in behind him, flung open the sliding door and heaved Justine in.

"Come on!" Sam shouted, trying to grab Shelly, but she was pulled away in the sea of commotion and swirling bodies and cameras. Matt lifted Sam up, flailing, tossed him inside and slammed the door after him. "Lock it!" Matt shouted above the din.

And there they were.

Outside was a cacophony of shouts and banging, the van trembling, rocking. The noise became a chant. "De-ca-pede! De-ca-pede!"

Sam and Justine and Aaron and Mendel and Gavin looked

at each other, crouching away from the storm outside. No one spoke. Each pair of eyes examined the other four faces, one at a time.

It was Mendel who finally moved. He squeezed his bulky frame up the narrow aisle to Sam and enveloped him in a bear hug, whacking him loudly on his back and laughing.

"Justine!" said Gavin, grinning so widely he looked like he was about to pop. "I'd recognize you anywhere. You really do look so much like your mother!"

"Hi," she said, and gave him an awkward little wave, then they both rose as high as the roof of the van would allow and embraced each other in a get-acquainted hug. The van became a bucket of slippery musicians, worming around each other between and over the seats, greeting one another with bewildered smiles and hugs and kisses on the cheek.

But somehow, everyone was watching when Sam and Aaron came face to face, Gary Cooper and John Wayne eyeballing each other, ready to draw.

Aaron smiled his beguiling smile and stuck out his hand. "Hey, Sam. Good to see you."

After a second's pause that lasted for an eternity, Sam held out his own hand and shook Aaron's.

"Aaron," he said with a stiff smile.

There was an insistent banging on the front window. Mendel leaned over and unlocked the door for Shelly, who jumped into the driver's seat, turned on the ignition, rammed the van into gear, pressed down hard on the horn and didn't let up until the sleek black van had extricated itself from the mob.

She pulled up on the gravel by the kitchen porch in back, out of sight from the road, and turned around in her seat. She looked at Gavin, then at Mendel, then at Aaron, then at Sam, and finally at Justine. They all looked at her.

"Hi, guys," she grinned. "Welcome to Creston."

They spilled out of the car, Aaron and Gavin and Mendel

stretching their middle-aged bones from the trip, blinking at the bright country sunshine, gazing at the back of the large green house, the lawns surrounding it, and the pastures and hills beyond. Gavin was wearing coffee-brown slacks with an elegant, tailored lime shirt. Aaron was in a white cotton tennis shirt, tan slacks, and his now-famous smile. Mendel's imposing bulk was almost all black—black pants, black shoes, peppered black prophet-length beard, black skullcap, and an unseasonably heavy dark black frock coat down to his knees, half covering the white but yellowing fringed garment on top of a white shirt open at the collar. Justine, shy as a fawn in her baggy black T-shirt, hung back by newly-shorn Sam. Allie and Colonel Griffin and Winston and Robbie and Mr. Gerald Bridges himself and Brandi and Matt all stood around them, watching in hushed awe, the sole witnesses to the convocation that people from Alaska to Zimbabwe were dreaming of at that very moment.

Bev came chugging up the driveway with Johnny behind her, filming as he walked. Bev jumped up on Gavin and hung on his neck, hugging and rocking and squealing. She turned to hug Mendel, but he backed away.

"I'm sorry, Bev," he said with embarrassment. "I don't touch women. But it sure is nice to see you."

"Couldn't I call you 'Vaneshi' and hug you just once?"

"Just this once," he laughed, giving her a light, formal embrace. "But from now on, it's Mendel." Everyone laughed.

"Hey, what about me?" asked Aaron. "I don't rate a hug?"

Bev looked at him for a long moment, then catapulted into his arms so violently he rocked backward. He hugged her long and tight, swaying her back and forth, her feet a full foot off the ground.

"Wow, isn't this cool!" said Matt to Brandi. She turned to pop a jumbo bubble right into his face. Then she turned back to watch the gathering of demigods. No one noticed that Allie surreptitiously squeezed the Colonel's hand.

"Hey, where's Shelly?" asked Johnny, but she was nowhere to be seen. Mendel opened the driver's door of the van and Shelly climbed out, all bustling and businesslike. Her eyes and nostrils were red, and she was clutching a wadded-up tissue.

"Oka—" she tried to speak, but her vocal cords wouldn't obey her. "Ok—" she attempted again, but her voice failed her. Winston came bounding down the porch stairs and handed her a bottle of water. She gulped the water greedily while everyone watched, choked with emotion. Johnny panned the pensive faces of the congregation.

Shelly cleared her throat and spoke, clutching business like a life preserver. "Okay, this is what you're going to do, the five of you. You're going to walk around to the front of the house together and wave to the crowd from the porch. Let them take some pictures."

"Here we go," growled Sam.

Shelly turned to him icily. "In a few hours, people all over the world are going to be looking at pictures of Decapede on the front page of everything. Do you want them to see Justine in her eighth grade swimsuit, a mob attacking a van, or five smiling faces waving from the porch?"

Sam glared in her general direction.

"That was a rhetorical question," she snarled back at him. "Justine!"

The girl snapped to attention.

"You lead."

"Me?"

"Yes, you. You know the way," said Shelly. "We'll meet you in the foyer."

"What about you?" asked Gavin.

"You should be with us," said Aaron.

"Just the band," decreed Shelly.

No one was about to argue with her.

Shelly looked at Justine. "Go!" she barked, and nudged the girl with a pat on the back.

Justine took grumbling Sam's hand and led him around the corner of Gruenhaus, out into public view. Aaron and Mendel and Gavin followed in a row, waving and smiling as they walked. Behind the front porch railing, they turned to face the crowd below. The police had managed to move the crowd back behind the wooden barriers. From the porch, the band could hear the crowd chanting "De-ca-pede!" and see them holding the posters high in the air and waving frantically.

Justine and Sam and Mendel and Aaron and Gavin waved back graciously, if somewhat bewildered, the royal family of Medina County and the universe.

"Fucking circus," muttered Sam through his grimace of a smile. Justine kicked him in the shin.

"Ow," he said.

"Shut up and smile," she said, waving, smiling at the crowd.

Shelly and Bev watched through the common room window as Decapede waved regally at their subjects below.

Bev's mind drifted back to Steuben College and the faded memory of the magical days with the band. Afterwards came med school, then a lousy marriage, then starting a business, then as the business got better, the marriage got worse—but it was all a detour. This was her dream destiny. Right here, right now, in the common room of Gruenhaus in Creston, Ohio. She took Shelly's hand, and Shelly squeezed it too tightly.

"Ow!" said Bev, and they continued staring at the band's backs. "Are you okay?" Bev asked. "You're like emanating this aura of vibrations or something."

"I don't think I can do it," Shelly said almost in a whisper, without moving her eyes from the band.

"Shelly, you're hurting me. Do what?"

Shelly released her grip, but didn't move her eyes.

"Do you want a pill?" asked Bev, getting concerned.

"What?" She turned to look at Bev. "No, no. I'm fine. I'm just a little whzzzzzzzzz" she said, making a spinning motion around her head.

"Nervous?"

"Nervous. Excited. Overwhelmed. I keep expecting to wake up. And I keep having to pee every five minutes."

"I know you'll do great."

"I'm glad you know it. Wish I did."

Shelly went over to the next window, where the Colonel was watching the band waving at the raucous crowd below. She stood right up close to him, facing him, her father, the Colonel, stern and stiff, but concerned. She put her arms around him and lay her head on his chest, Daddy's little girl.

"What, Shel?"

She looked up at him. "I'm not sure I can do it," she said into his suit jacket.

"You sure put a lot on your plate. Stop chewing your fingernail," he told her softly, with a hint of a smile.

Shelly stopped chewing her fingernail.

"Scared?"

Shelly looked up at him and nodded.

"What do we do when we're scared?"

It was the mantra he had taught her during those awful two years when they nursed her mother together. Shelly had always imagined it was taken directly from the US Army's "Manual of Disciplined Behavior under Stressful Conditions."

"Focus on the mission," she said.

"That's right," said the Colonel, squeezing her shoulder in encouragement.

"You know what?" she said, drawing herself up, tugging at her blouse, and touching her hair.

"What?" he asked.

"You'll excuse me," she said, "I have some work to do." And she marched off to meet the band.

Master Sgt. Bev gathered them in a circle in the foyer, clutching her clipboard to her breast, even though she knew her precious schedule by heart. The guys were grinning at each other, overwhelmed, struggling to concentrate.

"Okay, everyone, listen up," she said.

Everyone listened up.

"First of all, for all you men with a fifty-five-year-old bladder, there's a bathroom right back there. Your bedrooms are on the first floor to the left. There are signs on the doors, and a shared bathroom at the end of the hallway. You can go dump your stuff there. There are light refreshments here in the dining room. Sam, Aaron, you go with Shelly now."

"What about the refreshments?" groused Sam.

Johnny was circling the cluster, intent on filming every word. His eyes were on the camera, and he tripped over Gavin's suitcase, but Mendel caught his arm to prevent him from falling.

"Sorry," said Johnny, "just ignore me."

"She's something, isn't she?" said Aaron to Sam as they followed Shelly down the hallway, testing the ice.

"Don't run into her in a dark alley," said Sam, and Aaron forced a nervous laugh.

They walked through the door at the end of the hall and down the four steps. "Nice office," said Aaron, surveying the room.

"It's Bev's doing," said Shelly, all business, seating them next to each other on the sofa opposite her.

"You've come a long way since El Charro's," said Aaron, still scanning the room.

"That's where Aaron and I first met," explained Shelly to Sam in the most factual tone she could muster. "I went out to Chicago to meet him."

"Then, we flew to Iowa to dig up Gavin," smiled Aaron. "In a private two-seater."

"Sounds like you had a real good time," said Sam.

"Okay, listen you two," said Shelly sternly, focusing on her mission, "I'm going to say this once and once only. A lot of people have spent a lot of time and energy and money to get you here. And I don't need to tell you, the whole world is watching and waiting to meet Decapede. In a little while, I'm going to go out there and say a lot of inspiring stuff and raise a lot of expectations for a lot of people. But before I say anything, I need to know that I'm not going to make a fool of myself."

She was staring accusingly at each of them in turn, but all three of them knew which one she was addressing. Aaron was sharp enough to act like he was also being grilled.

"I want to know that the two of you came here to work. To do a job. To make music." Here she turned directly to Sam. "To jump through some hoops, to do whatever needs to be done."

Sam snorted. Aaron looked at him and bit his tongue and smiled.

"But before I say a single word to the rest of the band, to the crew here, to the whole damned world, I want to hear it from the two of you—are you in this, *together*, or not? No bullshit. Yes or no?"

Aaron looked at Sam.

"Sure," said Aaron. "That's why we're here."

Sam scratched his smooth jowl, missing his stubble.

"As far as I'm concerned," Aaron continued, "the past is past. No baggage. I look forward to making music together."

"Sam?" said Shelly.

"Su-ure," he grimaced. Shelly couldn't tell if he was being sincere or bitterly ironic or simply that his smiling muscles were stiff from disuse.

"Sam?" she demanded.

"What do you want?" he growled. "Find me a hatchet and I'll bury it." He looked around at the office. "Or maybe I'll just use it to chop my own head off right now and save myself all this headache."

"Sounds like a good line for a country song," said Aaron.

Sam considered that for a moment. "What rhymes with 'chop'?" he asked with a hint of a smile.

Shelly pressed a button on her desk phone. Bev answered immediately.

"Send 'em in," she said.

48

We Are Decapede!
– June 9, 2006, Afternoon –

Justine plopped down on the soft sofa between Aaron and Sam. Mendel brought over a chair, and Gavin sat next to Shelly. Dog was sitting outside the screen door, his tongue hanging out, staring in at Justine.

Bev stood on the steps and looked at Shelly. "I—I don't know—if I—" she hesitated, embarrassed.

It was a question Shelly hadn't anticipated. There was an awkward silence.

"Isn't she our manager or something?" said Sam, and the room breathed a sigh of relief.

"Absolutely," said Gavin.

"As much Decapede as we are," said Mendel.

"Manage us," Aaron proposed, holding his arms out, smiling that smile, and everyone quickly agreed.

Bev looked at them for a long moment, then scribbled something on her legal pad.

"What are you writing?" asked Shelly.

"A reminder to myself to have your father draw me up a contract."

Then she laid down her pad and ran to hug each of the guys, except for Mendel ("Sorry, we made a deal, one time only, but I really am glad that you're here"). At the end, she gave a somewhat overwrought squeeze to Justine. The girl made wheezing noises, and everyone laughed.

Shelly's eyes moistened, but she dug her Brandied nails into the balls of her thumbs. *Focus on the mission.* She closed her eyes and tried to convince the stars spinning through her mind to slow down.

Bev pulled over a chair, grinning widely. "Okay, come on, guys," she declared, clipboard on her lap, "let's get to work."

Everyone turned to look at Shelly. The room was wobbling, and Shelly clung to the agenda in her green notebook. Outside, Dog dozed in the afternoon sun.

"Well!" she said, smiling confidently. "You've all read and signed the basic contract, right?"

"The three of us have gone over it all together," said Aaron.

"Aaron's lawyer helped explain it to Mendel and me," said Gavin.

"It seems very equitable to us," said Mendel.

"Very generous," said Gavin.

Sam twisted his neck to try to look out Shelly's windows, down the hill, all the way to the lake.

"More than fair," said Aaron. "Whose work was it?"

"The Colonel's," answered Shelly. "Colonel Griffin. My father. We believe in nepotism here," she smiled. "He's been acting as Decapede's de facto legal advisor until we get things in place."

"Shelly told him what to write," said Bev.

"Bev!" said Shelly.

"What?" she said. "They should know that it was you."

"Mr. Bridges also helped," added Shelly.

"Gerald Bridges himself is actually here?" asked Gavin.

"That little bald guy?" Sam asked Justine. "He's famous?"

"Sam's had the pleasure of getting to know Mr. Bridges a little," said Shelly.

"What's he like?" asked Gavin.

"Like a mosquito in your ear when you're trying to sleep," said Sam.

"He's involved in the details?" asked Aaron.

"Fully-fledged member of the team," said Shelly.

"Making you money and washing dishes," Bev added.

Aaron, Mendel, and Gavin looked at each other and shrugged.

"He'll be here at Gruenhaus with us for the duration," said Shelly.

"How did you get someone like him involved?" asked Gavin.

"Johnny's next-door neighbor growing up," explained Shelly.

"He's your biggest fan," gushed Bev. "He worships you guys."

"Sam, tell them," said Shelly.

"That Gerald guy? He's okay," said Sam. "Just rich."

"And he thinks Shelly walks on water," Bev added.

"Come on, guys, the contract," said Shelly, bringing them back to base. "Justine, your Aunt Diane explained everything to you?"

Justine nodded. "She said she'll try to get up here over the weekend to sign."

"Sam?"

"My lawyers are all off surfing in Australia. Not answering their phones."

Shelly glared at him.

"Yeah, your father explained it to me. I signed. Okay? Are we going to be talking about contracts all day?"

"Questions?" she asked the others, ignoring him.

"Yes, well, one," said Aaron. "The percentages and the terms, as I said, they seem very generous to us." Mendel and Gavin nodded in agreement.

"I'm glad," said Shelly.

"But do you think you could kind of, you know, fill in

the blanks? We really don't know how much, uh, *income* we're talking about here. For us, I mean."

"We'll know a lot more in a few days," Shelly answered.

Everyone was staring at her intently.

"Well, Mr. Bridges gave me some numbers this morning," she said, flipping open her laptop. She scrolled down to the bottom line.

"I think it's safe to say that by the time we finish with you, you'll be—whew—comfortable for life."

They continued staring.

"Seven figures." She paused. "Maybe eight." The room was deafeningly silent. "Those are Mr. Bridges' predictions. But— giant 'but' here, folks—they're all based on the following proposal." Shelly turned the page in her notebook.

Everyone's eyes were fixed on her except Sam, who was looking out the window.

"For the next month, you will all live here in Gruenhaus and do nothing but work your butts off on your music. Full-time. No distractions whatsoever. A closed camp. During that month, you will: one, rerecord the Decapede CD; two, record a new CD; and three, give a single performance in a major venue on the Fourth of July."

"That's one month," said Gavin.

They all took a moment to digest the magnitude of the task, then burst out jabbering about what a short time it was and how it would be impossible to—

"And!" Shelly barked so sharply that they all sat up straight. "And this will all be documented in living color, in real-time, by Mr. Johnny Walker, aka 'The Sixth Decapede,' the face of this group until today and unto whom you five and all the rest of us should be eternally grateful because without him we wouldn't be here—" She paused. "And who will be living with us and filming everything that goes on here, and, with a bit of tasteful editing, will present a weekly ninety-minute show in the US and, so far, sixteen other countries, on the Warner Reality Channel."

They all took a moment to absorb what Shelly had just said, and again burst out babbling and gabbling about privacy and glass houses and—

"I'm not finished!" Shelly said sharply, and they all stopped mid-sentence. She eyed the band. "Do you remember all those zeroes you got so excited about a minute ago?"

They all understood that Shelly didn't really expect an answer to that question.

"Well, Warner is one of them."

"I don't understand," said Justine.

Aaron turned to her and explained, "If we don't want to live in an aquarium, we can knock off one zero from that number Shelly mentioned before."

"Oh," said Justine.

"Oh," said Gavin.

"Oh, indeed," said Mendel.

Aaron smiled, pleased with the idea.

Sam yawned loudly without covering his mouth.

Shelly smiled sweetly and plowed forward. "You'll be able to record without leaving the house. Bev's son, Robbie, is preparing the music room for recording right here."

"He's okay, that Robbie," said Sam. "Knows computers and stuff. Like a genius, just without glasses."

"We had the piano tuned for you," Bev said to Aaron. "And there's a stand-up bass."

"They got a little dolceola you hold on your lap," Sam said to Aaron.

"Seriously?" asked Aaron.

"You might like it a little," said Sam, the corners of his eyes wrinkling.

That could be the first civil sentence I've heard from him, Shelly noted.

"It's a shame Shelly couldn't track down the, ah, 'recording engineer' at that 'studio' where we made the tape," said Aaron.

"The guy in the booth!" recalled Mendel, guffawing in his deep belly laugh. "What was his name?"

"I think Bev would remember, no?" mugged Aaron.

"You shut up right now!" Bev punched him in the shoulder, and they all rolled with laughter.

"J— Ju— Junior!" whooped Gavin, clutching his stomach in laughter.

"Sheek Records!" added Aaron, rocking so far back in his chair that he almost fell over.

"Right!" shouted Bev and Gavin and Mendel together, convulsing with the memory. Even Sam was laughing, despite himself.

Shelly and Justine looked at each other and shrugged. "Okay, come on, guys, you'll have plenty of time for reminiscing," Shelly said, and waited till they quieted down. "So. What do you say? Come on. Can you do it?" They all turned to Aaron.

Aaron looked at Sam. "Do you still play?"

"'Nuff," Sam grunted.

"Don't forget, you're going to be working on this full-time," said Shelly. "Sam called it 'woodshedding.' "

The guys nodded, soaking that in.

"Of course we can," said Aaron. He turned to his band. "Have you heard how good that CD sounds? Forget about all this Decapede craziness. That's some frigging fine music we were making, guys. Us, the five of us." Justine coughed. "Well, more or less. And here we are, under ideal conditions. Why shouldn't we be able to do it again?"

Shelly watched Aaron turning the charm on them, cheering them, focusing them, leading them, and she smiled. Then she looked at Sam, with his handsome new face, gazing longingly down at the lake. But he seemed to be listening, and Shelly felt as though something had shifted in the room.

"Practice the old stuff, record it," Aaron continued to exhort them. "Put some new songs together. Do a show. Why not?"

"Mendel?" asked Shelly.

"You're the miracle maker. We're just mortals. But we can try."

"Gavin?"

"Don't ask me," said Gavin. "I'm just the drummer." Everyone laughed.

"Sam?"

"Making music's the easy part," he said, crooking an eyebrow at her.

"Justine?"

The girl started at being addressed. "What? Oh. Yeah. I guess," she said, looking at the four men.

"Okay, then," said Shelly, proud and relieved, "we have a plan."

"You mentioned a 'closed camp,' " said Aaron. "What exactly did you mean by that?"

"It's crazy out there," said Bev. "Shelly wants you to have things relaxed here."

"Relaxed is good," said Sam.

"No distractions," said Shelly. "And I don't want strangers walking around here, cleaning the bathrooms or washing the floors or working in the kitchen or talking to you. It's just us, the core team. There's a couple who'll come in to do the basic housekeeping, but they speak no language known to mankind. Other than that, everyone needs to pitch in. Everyone will get their house duty assignments from Bev. And you'll do them, no arguments. Clear?"

Everyone except Sam nodded.

"How should we dress?" asked Aaron.

"Good question," said Shelly. "Be comfortable, of course. But don't forget, Johnny's going to be filming the whole time, so you want to be presentable."

"What sort of style?" asked Gavin. "I'm not sure what I brought is suitable. Casual? Elegant casual? Sporty? Sharp?"

"Chop off my head now, please," said Sam to the ceiling.

"You can wear whatever you want," she said, smiling. "You can *be* whoever you want. Nobody knows you guys. You can wear a Prussian general's dress uniform or his wife's dress, I don't care. Look at it as a chance to redefine yourselves."

"I think I'm set," said Mendel, and everyone laughed.

"I only brought clothes for the weekend," said Justine.

"There's a young woman on the team, Brandi. I've been on the run ever since this started, so she's been dressing me. She's fantastic."

"And she does hair really well, too," said Bev. "You should have seen Sam 'before.' "

Sam tried to protest, but the words got caught, and he began to cough loudly.

"Anything you need, we'll bring you," said Shelly. "But you're sequestered. No one in, no one out. No cell phones, no visitors. This summer is literally a once-in-a-lifetime opportunity. For the next month, nothing but music."

"And washing dishes," grumbled Sam.

"You didn't seem to be having such a terrible time with Winston this morning," said Bev.

He grumbled something but didn't disagree.

"Well?" Shelly asked.

Everyone grouched about being separated from their phones, including Sam, who had never even touched one. But the men were all musicians, and the idea of immersing themselves in their craft had great appeal.

"You have Friday nights and Saturdays off thanks to Rabbi Mendel here. It's his day of rest."

"Yeah?" Sam asked Mendel.

"Yeah," smiled Mendel.

"Hmm," said Sam, mulling that over. "I just might be Jewish all week long."

"Well, come on, guys," said Shelly, clapping her hands together and rising, "the team is waiting to meet you in the dining room."

As everyone filed out into the hallway, Aaron pulled Shelly aside, their first moment alone since Chicago. The terry-cloth robes flashed through her mind. *Tell them and they'll listen,* he'd said to her at the airport, ten days and a million years ago. *Well, you did,* she told herself. *And they did.*

"Hey, how you doing?" he asked gently.

"You know, a bit overwhelmed," she said, squeezing his hand. "Okay. I guess. How're you?"

"What could be bad?" He laughed. "I'm a rock star. Tell me the truth, how are you?"

"Okay, just, you know, lots of details."

"Everything you've done here? It's incredible. The guys love it."

"That's very sweet," she said. "Thank you."

"The band's behind you, Shelly. You lead, we'll follow."

"Even Sam?"

"Especially Sam. Shelly, believe me, I know. Even Kathleen couldn't handle him like you do."

"Really?"

"Really. Shelly, he's terrified of you."

"Well, I'll tell you, it's mutual. I've seen how he can act when he feels cornered."

"So have I," he said with that Colgate smile. "Remember?"

She nodded. "But I can't help but worry. He's the reason I came up with this whole woodshedding idea. To keep the world away from him."

"It's exactly the right thing, Shelly, not just for Sam. For all of us. For Decapede, the whole event."

"There's an awful lot at stake here."

"I promise you we'll do our best. We want this more than anyone else."

"You're always optimistic, aren't you?" she jibed.

"You betcha."

"You going to make us some great music?"

"I'm sure going to try. And Shelly?"

"Hmm?"

"We're cool?"

"About what?" she said.

"You know. About—"

"Oh, that? Of course," she said with a dismissive wave of her hand, flushing despite herself.

And they gave each other a hug and a peck on the cheek the way warm friends do.

"I'm glad," he said.

"But you know," she said as an afterthought, "maybe it would be better to not mention it to Sam. You never know how he's going to take things."

"Right. Gotcha."

As the band walked down the hall to meet the team, Sam stopped Aaron.

"Look at this," he said and flicked on the light to the music room.

Aaron looked at the Steinway baby grand, the drum kit, the guitars, the mic stands, all waiting for them.

"Bev's kid did all this?" asked Aaron.

"Sam, Aaron, come on," called Bev from the end of the hallway, where Shelly and the band were waiting.

"Yeah. Sweet, ain't it?" said Sam.

"Aaron!" called Bev.

"A whole lot better than we had back then," said Aaron.

"Sam!" called Shelly.

Sam and Aaron stood together in the doorway, gazing at the cornucopia of instruments and equipment, trying to get their minds around what they were expected to do.

"Sam, Aaron, would you get over here already?" called Shelly. "The team is waiting."

Sam shot Aaron a fuck-it grin. Aaron grinned back.

"Yeah?" asked Sam.

"Oh, what the hell," said Aaron. "That's why we're here."

Aaron went to the freshly-tuned Steinway Baby Grand and tinkled a few notes.

"Nice," he said.

Sam picked up an acoustic guitar, plugged it in and flicked on the amp. He played a couple of soft chords and a quick run all the way up the neck. Aaron sat down on the old piano bench and played a familiar lick. Sam looked at him and began strumming and picking the introduction.

"Sam!" hissed Bev, sticking her head in the door, "everyone's waiting for—" But Sam was running the chord sequence of the introduction to "Creston Gold" as Aaron was exploring, block chords with his left hand, melodic lines with his right.

"Do you remember it?" asked Sam.

"I might have gone over it once or twice in the last couple of weeks," Aaron smiled at the keyboard.

Bev stood transfixed. Then Shelly was behind her, and then Gavin, who slipped past them, gave a quick look around the room, and grabbed the bongos from behind the drum kit. Then Mendel was strapping on his guitar, supplying a few filler licks as he found his footing, then taking over the melodic lead.

"You're speeding up," Aaron called to Sam, who nodded and reined in the tempo.

Justine was staring at them from the doorway in front of Shelly. Shelly put her hand on the small of the girl's back and gave her a gentle shove into the room. The guys were still exploring the introduction to the song, repeating the same chord sequence over and over.

Then the door opened from the common room, and the whole team was there, gaping at this ghost band incarnate. The guys kept looping the introduction, Mendel leading them through a soft and winding waft of a memory of the time when everyone was young and had their whole lives in front of them. Finally, when they began to feel comfortable in the groove, they shifted into the first verse. Sam flicked on the mic and sang, "*Storm clouds are gathering way out there,*" but no sound came out. Mendel led them back into the pattern of the intro while Robbie scrambled to the mixer and began fiddling frantically with faders and switches. He went to Aaron's mic and tapped on it to check that it was working. Then he grabbed a mic from a stand, turned it on and handed it to Justine. But it was heavier than it looked, and it slipped from her hand, hitting the floor with a painful bang. Robbie picked it up for her. She snatched it from him, her hand trembling. Johnny was crouched on one knee right in front of them, zooming in on each face in turn, then back out to try to get all of them in the frame. The girl waited for her entrance, her back to the camera. Sam reached the chorus again and began to sing in his storied baritone, "*Storm clouds are gathering way out there / Soon it's gonna rain—but I don't really care.*"

Shelly closed her eyes and smiled. Bev took her hand and squeezed it. When Sam reached "*Lying with you on the ground,*" Justine came in on the backing "*ooh,*" but the sound was far too loud, crackling and distorted. Robbie quickly turned down the mic from the console. Heart thumping and tears in her eyes, Justine tried to sway a bit to the music, which made her feel even more self-conscious and foolish. "*Grass and sunlight all around / Nothing's gonna bring me down.*"

On the refrain of "*Have another Creston Gold,*" Justine came in on the lilting harmony line Vaneshi had composed for Kathleen Brinker a lifetime ago, but what came out of the speakers was an earsplitting bleat. She slammed the mic down on an amp with a loud bang and tried singing as loud as she could, but no one could hear her. Robbie wondered in a sweat if he should try to find her another cable and mic while the song was going on, but Johnny was filming, and he didn't want to get in the way again. Justine continued singing, unamplified and unheard.

The performance was hesitant, slow and cautious, without revelations or epiphanies, but without calamity. They started together and ended together, and they remembered the chord changes and almost all the words. The guys stood looking at each other, relieved and pleased with themselves that the resurrected Decapede had managed to get through their first song intact. They were, they smiled with satisfaction, still a band. Justine stood to the side, wishing she could disappear.

Those graced to witness that first song clapped softly in hushed appreciation—Matt, Winston, Robbie, Gerald, Brandi, Shelly, Bev, the Colonel, Allie, Gruenhaus, and all the ghosts of the Bauer family, with Johnny Walker documenting for posterity every moment of the rebirth—an audience smaller than the one at Pedro's Cantina that very first night thirty-six years earlier, when Sam Miller walked in and saw Aaron Woodwright and the New Waitress on stage.

Robbie went over to Justine as unobtrusively as he could. "I'm sorry about the mic—" he tried.

"Oh, just go away!" she snapped sharply, so he did.

49

Johnny's Woodstock

– June 9, 2006, Evening –

As everyone was finishing their dessert of fresh watermelon and chocolate flan, Bev stood to her full 4'11" and tapped on an empty Creston Gold bottle with a knife, but the room was so full of excited chattering that no one heard her. She rapped again, harder, but the clamor was too great.

No one noticed when Robbie stood up and went over to his mother. But when he bent over to whisper to her, hiding a little black box tied with a red ribbon behind his back, the room suddenly fell silent, everyone staring. Robbie looked around and cleared his throat and stood up straight, a head and a half taller than his mother.

"Excuse me, everyone. I just— Mom, I'd just like to thank you for bringing me here to meet all your old friends. I never knew until now what a cool mother I have," he smiled sweetly, and everyone in the room smiled as well.

"Remember what he looked like when he first came to Gruenhaus?" Allie whispered to the Colonel.

"You mean that sullen face of his just begging to be slapped?" whispered back the Colonel with what for him was a smile. Allie gave him a playful nudge with her elbow.

"And I have something here that I thought might help you with your job." continued Robbie, and handed her the box.

He peeked at Justine, who had been watching closely, but she turned away and took another swig of beer.

Bev opened it and extracted a blue-and-red lanyard with a whistle on a hook.

"Is this—?" asked Bev, staring down at the plastic chain.

"Uh-huh," said Robbie.

Bev pressed it to her lips reverently, then to her breast. She kept her head down, but everyone could see she was crying.

"What is it?" asked Shelly.

Her head still bowed, Bev held it up for a moment for everyone to see, then clutched it to her chest again.

"That's the whistle she would use to call us to order," said Gavin, and paused. "I remember when Kathleen gave it to her." His voice choked a bit, and he turned to Aaron and Mendel, then to Sam. "Remember?"

The three men all nodded.

"She never took it off," said Aaron.

"Where did you find it?" Bev sniffled.

"In your closet with the Decapede tapes," said Robbie proudly.

Bev slipped the lanyard over her head and reached up to give him a long, emotional hug, to his great embarrassment. She gave the whistle a piercing toot. "Still works," she grinned.

Everyone was smiling and surreptitiously wiping the corners of their eyes. Dog was barking hysterically outside the kitchen door. Justine jumped up to see what was bothering him, and when she opened the door, he scurried past her into the dining room, barking furiously at the room, at so many humans. Justine ran to him, crouched, and enveloped him in her arms, stroking him and soothing him, her cheek resting on the dog's neck. "Shh, shh, Dog, good Dog, shh," until the dog quieted down.

"Allie," said Justine, "I think he wants to stay here with me."

"Sure, honey," smiled Allie, "but if he makes any mess, you're cleaning it up."

Justine led the dog back to her chair. Dog curled up and rested his snout on Justine's foot.

Johnny stood up. "With your permission," he addressed Bev and Shelly, "I'd like to make a toast." Everyone smiled and nodded. Johnny put his reading glasses on the end of his nose and checked a small piece of paper with a few handwritten notes. He folded up the glasses and put them in the pocket of his collarless white linen shirt.

"Hey there," he said, and smiled warmly at the room in his familiar, soothing voice. "It's quite a relief to see you all here. Up until now, I've been, to a great degree, the face of Decapede, but that was just while you guys were busy being rumors and legends. But now that Shelly's found you, it's your turn to get up there and strut your stuff."

The band looked at each other, and everyone tried to imagine what was going through their minds.

"Sam, Aaron, Gavin, Mendel, Justine, you guys are the reason we're here. You're the band. But we here all know who the real sorceress is, the one who created a life-changing phenomenon out of thin air. Ladies and gentlemen, the incredible *Shelly Griffin!*"

Everyone stood and applauded Shelly. Sam thumped his beer bottle on the table a couple of times, and Dog whacked his tail on the wooden floor.

"I threw a snowball," she said to Johnny, her heart thumping, her head spinning. "You turned it into an avalanche."

"Yeah, yeah," said Johnny, and everyone laughed. He looked around the room. "Every one of us here could tell a story about how Shelly and Decapede have changed his or her life. With your permission, I'd like to say a few personal words, about how Shelly has changed *my* life. When Shelly Griffin first came into my office—you know what, we're all family here, let's call a spade a spade—when Shelly Griffin first *lied* her way into my office after she'd stalked me at home—as I was trying to get Brandi to throw her out of my office, she stopped me in my tracks. She told me the whole story of Bauer's Brewery, and right there in my office, she broke my heart. And then she had me listen to 'Creston Gold,' and I heard this amazingly beautiful song."

Sam snorted. Johnny looked over at him.

"Like it or not, Sam, I'm officially an expert. I'm a permanent member of the selection committee at the Rock and Roll Hall of Fame. And I say it's a *great* song."

Sam saw Shelly grinning at him, her cheeks flushed. He fought off a smile, but his eyes crinkled a little. Gavin and Aaron and Mendel were beaming. Justine was peeling the label off her beer bottle.

"Anyway," said Johnny to the congregation, "right there, on the spot, I was hooked."

"Me, too," said Brandi with a proud pop of her gum.

"So I played it on the air, and it changed all of our lives. Not just ours. Metro Cleveland, Northeast Ohio. You know what? It looks like it's going to affect the whole darned world. Over the past three weeks, we've played the song hundreds of times on WFOR. This morning, on the YouTube, it got its millionth point."

His audience drew a breath and murmured. Brandi whispered something in Johnny's ear.

"Its millionth hit. And now the CD has hit the stores. I'm told that today alone it might sell a hundred thousand copies, no one knows. No one can even imagine. Except for Shelly, of course."

He held his notes at arm's length and squinted.

"Now, during my life in music, I've seen it all—Elvis and The Beatles and Disco and Punk and Dance and Madonna and Michael Jackson and Rap—and I've never seen anything like this. In my entire professional life, I've never had so much fun. And I've never been so proud."

He paused.

"Decapede has reminded me who I am. I'm a child of the

Sixties, a passport-holding citizen of the Woodstock Nation, and I'm damned proud of it! Because we were special. Our generation wanted to make the world a better place. Our parents, what did they want? A nice house in the suburbs and a new car. Our kids? All they want is no friction. And now their kids, the ones growing up in this new century? They're the saddest ones of all. They don't want anything at all."

He looked at the band, and the guys nodded their heads.

"There's something about 'The Sixties' that grabs people's imagination. I'm always being asked by young people about Hendrix and Joplin and The Doors and Led Zeppelin and Hair, not to mention Dylan and The Beatles. You talk about disco, they're not interested. You want to listen to music from the Eighties, the Nineties? Go to the Oldies But Goodies corner. But 'The Sixties'? That's not just music, it's an ideal."

"*Imagine all the people ...*" sang Aaron.

"Exactly. Do you know how many requests I still get for that song from kids? Even today, 'The Sixties' represents a time of innocence. A time when people believed in a tribal togetherness. Loving one another, helping one another. That's what Woodstock was all about. Living in *peace*. No one trying to rip off the next guy, no fights. Half a million horny kids, drunk and stoned and half naked, rolling around in the mud, with no food and no facilities. It was a utopia, just without toilets."

"Were you actually there?" asked Robbie.

"Hell yes I was there," he answered. "Sorry, Allie. Still am in many ways. This all may sound a bit anachronistic in this cold, computerized world. I know that today, kids just sit in front of their screens. Heck, they even 'talk' to each other over the internet in little notes and call it 'communication.' Soon, kids will be dating on this AOL thing. I guess at the end of the evening, they'll kiss the screen goodnight."

There was a smattering of appreciative applause.

"But you know what these kids will be watching on their

computers, with that blue light from the screens sucking the blood out of them like vampires of the soul? Do you know what they'll be watching? Jimi Hendrix playing the national anthem. Janis Joplin tearing out another little piece of her heart. Innocent, loving young people rolling in the mud for three days. And now—Decapede. *'Storm clouds are gathering way out there / Soon it's gonna rain—but I don't really care.'* Because everyone longs for innocence and trust, especially in this cynical world today. Teenagers, and clubbers, and nerds in their twenties, and couples in their thirties with mortgages and families to raise, and people in their forties struggling and sweating nine to five for their measly paycheck at the end of the month, and people in their fifties wondering where their life has gone, and people in their sixties trying to remember what it felt like to be eighteen and optimistic—Decapede speaks to all of them. Decapede takes them back to the innocence and the goodness that they long for in their own lives."

"He's good," Aaron whispered to Shelly. She squeezed his hand.

"So, in my office that day, Shelly Griffin reminded me that we all have an obligation to try to make the world a better place, a happier place. That's what I've been trying to do on the air, and that's what 'Creston Gold' has been doing for people all over the world. You've become a symbol of hope for a better world. I'm thrilled that I've had the opportunity to help a little bit, and I'm very proud to be here with you."

Everyone sat still for a long moment.

Finally, Bev stood up. "All right now, listen up. I'll post the schedule for the coming days on the whiteboard in the entrance hallway. That's where all the updates and last-minute changes will be announced, so make sure you check it every time you're nearby. I don't want to go chasing around to find you! Sam, you got that?"

"Yes, ma'am," he said, still chewing, but no one believed that he heard her.

"In twenty minutes, I want the band and Johnny on the front porch. Everyone else is free except for the people on KP. Just keep within shouting distance in case we need you."

"What's KP?" asked Justine.

"Kitchen Patrol," said the Colonel.

"Everyone pitches in," said Shelly, "including the band."

"And no bitching about assignments," added Bev. "Just don't stay up late. Rehearsal tomorrow starts at nine o'clock sharp."

"Seriously?" said Gavin, looking at Shelly.

"That is a little early," said Aaron.

Shelly looked at the band. "Nine-thirty?" she suggested to Bev.

Bev made a face. "Nine-fifteen. Breakfast from eight-thirty."

Everyone looked at her. She looked back at the whole team. "Come on, let's go!" she commanded, and then gave a painful toot on the whistle.

As everyone was filing out of the dining room, Shelly pulled Justine to the side.

"You okay?" she asked.

"Yeah, I'm fine, why?" The girl was holding an almost-empty beer bottle.

"Well, take it easy."

"Are you kidding?" said Justine, looking at the floor. "With everyone staring at me?"

"Everybody's staring at everybody."

"Not like at me. What happened in the music room? It's just a big joke that I'm here."

"That's not true at all!"

"It's worse than a joke," she said, her eyes welling. "It's just a giant mistake. I shouldn't have agreed to be in the band."

Shelly bent over, trying to make eye contact. "Do you think I'm not nervous? I was peeing in my pants in there!"

"No, you weren't. You're always on top of everything."

"I just hide it. Believe me, I'm a puddle of melted putty inside."

Justine made a half-hearted effort to smile. Shelly lifted the girl's chin and made her look at her. "Relax. Everyone's rooting for you."

The girl just shrugged and lowered her eyes.

"Justine, listen to me. None of us knows how to deal with this. Not you, not me, not Aaron, not even Mr. Bridges. And certainly not Sam. How does he seem to you?"

"How should I know?"

"Because you just do."

The girl looked up at her. "I don't know. You saw, he's hardly talking. He's all tense and fidgety."

"Yeah, I saw. Listen, try to keep him calm, will you?"

"Me?"

"Well, he seems to listen to you."

"I don't know how to talk to him."

"You're doing just fine."

"He scares me."

"Yeah, me too," said Shelly.

"Shelly? I don't think I can do this," whimpered the girl.

"Of course you can! Just—focus on the mission."

"Shelly," called Bev, "can you come over here for a second?"

"You'll be fine," said Shelly. "I promise." She gave the girl a quick hug and went to take care of some urgent business.

Robbie had been lurking, waiting for Justine to finish, and he edged over to her cautiously.

"Justine?"

"What?" she said curtly, facing away.

"I just wanted to say how sorry I am about what happened with your mic." He waited for a response, but she just stood with her cold shoulder to him. "And I really hope you're all right, your foot and everything—"

"I'm fine!" she cut him off without turning.

"And that I really hope you don't think that I was trying to take advantage of you in Akron. I was just trying to—"

"Oh, God, you're such a dickhead!" she hissed and stomped off.

50

Shattered and Splattered

– June 9, 2006 –

Gruenhaus was perched on the highest hillock around, the front porch commanding a soft panorama of miles of rolling hills. Shelly and Bev and the band sat in a circle around a low wicker table, with neatly arranged trays of guacamole with tortilla chips, a large crystal pitcher of freshly squeezed lemonade with sprigs of mint, and a dozen bottles of Creston Gold. They all sat watching the sun set slowly as the frenetic day faded into a quiet early summer's eve, sipping their drinks and relaxing on the padded old straw chairs. Justine was curled up on the porch swing next to Sam, with Dog curled up on the floor directly below her. In the background, bullfrogs from down at Lake Traumsee croaked their low, steady drone.

"Listen, guys," said Johnny apologetically from outside the circle, his camera on his shoulder, "I know it's going to be a pain in the neck having me around all the time. I'll try to stay out of your hair as much as I can."

"We don't have all that much hair left," said Mendel.

"Don't worry," said Shelly. "Everyone's on board, right guys?"

Almost everyone agreed.

"Sam?" said schoolmarm Shelly.

"Hey, 'Cooperative' is my middle name." He raised his beer bottle to the camera in a salute.

"Johnny," said Aaron in his group leader's voice, "we appreciated everything you said before. I think you did a great job expressing the way we all feel."

"Well, thanks," said Johnny, "I meant every word of it," and he leaned over to give Aaron a warm buddy hug.

"Okay," said Johnny to the band, "now here's how we're going to work this. I know some of you haven't even had time to say hello to each other. So we're going to go around the circle to catch up, one person at a time."

"Forty years in forty words," snorted Sam. Justine poked him in the rib. "Ow," he said, almost smiling.

"And what Decapede means to you," added Johnny, "where it caught you in your life."

"And what you've been doing musically," added Aaron. "We don't even know who's still playing, that's how crazy this is," he mugged an aside at the camera, pretending to be bewildered.

"Great," said Johnny. "I may toss in a question here and there. But just talk among yourselves. Ignore the camera as much as you can. I'd like to do it in the order in which Shelly found you, so—Aaron?"

"Nothing very romantic or remarkable," he said. "I settled in Chicago. I have my own wholesale hardware company."

"Family?" asked Mendel.

"A couple of marriages, neither lasted too long," said Aaron. "I've always enjoyed my, ah, freedom," he said with his most charming smile. "And the business pretty much takes care of itself. So, yeah, this actually comes at a very good time for me. I'm completely geared up to do my part in making this incredible adventure a success."

"You must have been pretty shocked when Shelly approached you," prompted Johnny from behind the camera.

"Yeah, of course. But don't forget, I was the first one. When she showed me the article from the Steubenville paper, there was no Decapede hysteria. It was just this crazy blast from my distant past dredged up by this funny blonde bulldozer."

Sam leaned forward to take another bottle. Justine nudged him to pass one to her. He hesitated for a moment, but then shrugged and passed her another Creston Gold.

"To tell you the truth," Aaron continued, "I hadn't thought about Decapede in years. But she came in like a whirlwind, and we flew out to Iowa on the spur of the moment. It all struck me as kind of a lark."

Right, said Shelly to herself.

"I was definitely up for something out of the ordinary. A bit of an adventure. But I never imagined anything of this magnitude." Aaron said.

"Have you been playing at all?" asked Gavin.

"Believe it or not, I still play Thursday nights in a bar. Just for fun."

"Fun of the female persuasion?" asked Bev.

"Me?" said Aaron. "Nah." And everyone laughed. "Now that I think of it, it's pretty much the same gig I had at Pedro's." He paused to think. "Except no Sam, no New Waitress." He looked at Sam, and Johnny panned the camera to catch Sam looking back at Aaron, still guarded but less jumpy.

"New Waitress?" asked Justine, sipping her beer.

"That's what I used to call your mother," said Aaron.

Everyone saw Justine nod, taking that in, and they all wondered together what thoughts could be going through the girl's mind.

"In fact, I still sing some of the same songs from back then. It's a 'mature' crowd."

" 'Walk on By'?" asked Gavin.

"You betcha," he answered and looked at Sam. " 'True Love Ways.' But not as well as you."

Again Johnny panned for a reaction shot, and Sam raised his bottle in salute.

"And, ah, 'Different Drum,' " added Aaron.

"Really?" asked Mendel.

"It works for a guy singer, too. Just differently."

"My mom used to sing that around the house," said Justine.

"It was her song," said Sam.

"What do you mean?" Justine asked, but Sam didn't answer.

"That was her 'featured' song," Aaron offered. "Usually a band will try to give each member at least one song that features him. Or her."

"That song was always one of the high points of the show," Bev explained to Justine. "The guys—oh, geez, the guys in the audience used to call for it."

"Really?" asked Justine. Dog raised his head for a moment but fell back asleep quickly, exhausted from all the strange events of the day.

"And *bam bam-bambam*," sang Mendel.

" 'Then He Kissed Me,' " said Aaron.

"Oh, what she did with that song," sighed Gavin.

"She would have the whole audience jumping up and down, singing with her," said Aaron.

"The girls, at least," said Bev.

"There were plenty of boys jumping up and down, too," said Gavin.

Johnny came back to Aaron.

"So I'm really looking forward to seeing what we can do musically. And also personally, how we'll meet the challenge to work together, to band together. Because that's what people are coming to hear. A band." He looked at Johnny and the camera.

"Did I do okay?" Aaron asked Johnny, ever the pleaser.

Boy, he loves a camera, thought Shelly.

"Oh, yeah, great," Johnny answered. "Gavin?"

"Well, Aaron and Shelly just caught me with one foot out

the door on my way to Colorado for a skiing vacation. I left my partner, Dale, out in Aspen to come here."

"Have you been playing?" asked Aaron.

"Actually, after college I played with a pretty good band on weekends back in Washington. Rhythm and blues, soul. I got into that kind of music thanks to Decapede, by the way. But then Dale got this incredible job offer, and we moved to, ahem, Mason City, Iowa, itself. The things you do for love. He promised it would only be for two years, but it's been almost thirteen. I've been teaching farm boys trigonometry at an engineering college. I never dreamed it would be that—*flat*. And they're not particularly amenable out there to alternative lifestyles, you know. I was about to dive head-first off a cornstalk when Shelly appeared. And now this!" he said with a glow.

Winston came in with a bowl of watermelon cubes and set it down on the low table. He started to pick up the empty bottles, but Sam stopped him. "Hey, man, we'll clean up, you don't have to do that."

"Iss okay," said Winston, grinning. "I jus' gonna wait on you tonight because tonight special. Mebbe tomorrow night, too. Then, you all on you own. Somebody need somting here?"

"No," said Gavin, "I think we're just fine. We can't thank you enough for that delicious meal."

Winston beamed. "Mr. Sam's request."

At which point, Sam let out a loud belch for emphasis. Justine made a face, but the guys all laughed.

Sam the joker, thought Shelly. *Will wonders never cease?* Still, he kept a wary distance from everyone, and everyone gave him space. The little he did say always seemed to have an edge to it. *Will I ever get past worrying that he might explode at any moment?*

"It's all just scrumptious," said Gavin. "Really, thank you so much." Winston grinned and took his leave. "Where was I?"

"Provincial Iowa," Johnny cued him.

"Right. And I wasn't teaching over the summer, so there

was really nothing holding me back from coming here. Dale wasn't too pleased that I bailed on him in the middle of a vacation. But between you and me? I would have been happy for any excuse to get out of there. And sure, the money is—what can I say? Very nice." He smiled shyly. "But to be truthful, the real draw for me is the excitement. I mean—who would have thought?"

Everyone smiled. Gavin was as sweet and gentle and guileless as he had been back then.

"Mendel?" prompted Johnny.

"Yes. Well, with me, it's quite different."

"That's pretty apparent," said Aaron. "You used to be a different person."

And they all chuckled at the obvious.

"After college, I moved back to Brooklyn. I got a gig playing guitar in a Hasidic wedding band, just to pay the rent. I already had the beard. The only thing I needed was shoes," he smiled warmly through his thick, graying beard.

"And clothes," added Aaron.

"Well, yes, that too."

"I'm sorry, I don't know what that is," said Justine, "a Hasidic."

"Hasids are a kind of very religious Jew," explained Mendel. "We usually live in our own neighborhoods, keep to ourselves. Wear special clothes. Don't do anything on Saturday except pray and eat."

"Didn't you see 'The Big Lebowski'?" asked Aaron.

"I guess," said Justine.

"And make babies," added Shelly. "I was in Mendel's house. They make a lot of babies!"

"Yes, we do," said Mendel proudly.

"How many kids do you have?" asked Bev.

"It's considered bad luck to count them."

"Don't worry, we don't allow any bad luck in here," said Shelly.

"Eight children, thirteen grandchildren, *keinehora*. With a few more on the way." Everyone struggled to grasp that. "So, obviously, the money will come in very handy. Anyway, eventually I started getting involved in the band and this one particular Hasidic group with a wonderful musical tradition. Every single year, the Rebbe composes about a dozen new *niggunim* for Rosh Hashana, the New Year holiday. Great, great, soulful music. So I started learning their music and playing it, and we became very popular. Anim Zmiros, we were called. We were playing almost every night. Weddings are a big deal in these communities. Fathers save their whole lives to put on a big show. I did that for almost twenty years till the hours got to be too hard for me."

"That's very cool," said Aaron. "What kind of music did you play?"

"We were a quintet. But we sounded like more because we kept changing our instruments. One song would be all about electric guitars, the next one horns, the next clarinet and accordion. The guys were great musicians, everyone could play all the instruments, so we just rotated."

"Wow," said Aaron.

"You'd like it, I think. You know klezmer?"

"You mean like 'If I were a rich man, yubba dibby dibby dibby dibby dibby dibby dum,'" Aaron attempted.

Mendel laughed. "Well, kind of. But it's trickier than that. They use some pretty far-out scales and rhythms. I'll show you tomorrow."

"It sounds like you've been playing more than any of us," said Gavin.

"Yeah, well, twenty years, six nights a week."

"And on the seventh, he rested," added Johnny from behind the camera.

"So, yes, I'm really looking forward to getting back to

playing. Oh—I didn't mention—I play mostly violin now."

"Really?" said Aaron, already interested.

"Oh yeah. And even some clarinet, sax. Accordion. And guitar, of course, I still keep up with that. Banjo, if I need to. But mostly violin. That was the lead instrument in most of our repertoire."

"Cool," said Aaron.

"Cool," said Gavin.

"So, you're happy to be here?"

"That's really a tough question. I mean, of course, I am, in a way. It really is great to see you guys. But I have a wife, two kids still living at home, and the grandchildren all around and everything. I know they're going to miss me. I won't deny it, when Shelly first got me to commit to signing the contract, it was mostly for the money. I really don't like leaving home. All this Decapede craziness—sure, it's exciting. And I'm still a kid at heart, like all of us. But when I finish here, God willing, I'll be going back to the life I was living before. Just maybe with a couple more bedrooms."

"And what about you, young lady?" Johnny asked Justine.

"Me?" she said, sitting up straight and putting down her empty beer bottle. "Well, you know, I'm sixteen, and right now, I'm missing my final exam in Trig, so of course I'd rather be here."

Everyone laughed, partly from relief at hearing her crack a joke, partly because she told it well.

"And, yes, I really am a test-tube baby. So it was just me and my mom. We lived in New Jersey, in a little town called Dover, near Morristown. Mom taught Phys Ed at a college nearby. Swimming. And then, one night, when I was twelve, she was coming home from a yoga class and swerved for a deer. Poof—I'm an orphan." She delivered the line as a joke, but this time no one laughed. "The only family I had was my

Aunt Diane, down in Florida, so I went to live with her. But she's a Florida state senator, works up in Tallahassee most of the week, so she's not around too much. She tries, but she's not a mother. Winston's a great cook, and he's a really sweet guy. But basically, I've been on my own."

Sam, in the corner of Johnny's frame, reached down for another beer. Dog was lying on his side, snoring lightly.

Alone in the world at twelve, thought Shelly to herself, and her heart winced.

"How did it happen that you joined the band?" asked Aaron.

"It was Sam's crazy idea," said the girl. "You can't blame me."

"You got a problem with that?" Sam asked Aaron, piling watermelon cubes on a plate.

"No," said Aaron with a smile, "I think it's great."

"It's perfect," said Gavin.

"Smart guy," said Mendel.

"Always was," said Aaron. "Johnny said on his show that you sing, play guitar?"

"Not like you guys. Just a little, to accompany myself," she answered self-consciously. She picked up Sam's half-finished beer and took a gulp.

"She sings okay. Guitar, not so much," said Sam, taking a large watermelon cube in his fingers and ingesting it in a single bite.

"I'm no expert," said Shelly, shooting Sam a look of reproof, but he was focused on the watermelon, "but what I heard sounded great."

"I've never even sung in front of people," said the girl.

"Funny," said Aaron.

"What?" she asked.

"That's exactly what your mother said," said Aaron.

"What do you mean?" asked Justine, looking up at him.

The crickets had joined the bullfrogs.

"I remember the first time I invited her to sing. At Pedro's, that very first night."

"I remember that," said Bev. "You had to practically drag her up onto the stage."

"Some stage," recalled Gavin. "There wasn't even room for my drum kit. I had to set up on the floor."

"But she got into it really fast," said Aaron.

"Yeah, well, I'm not her," Justine muttered to herself.

"She was a natural," agreed Bev. "Do you remember the first song she sang with you?"

Aaron thought for a minute and shook his head. "Nope. Do you?"

" 'Different Drum,'" said Bev. "Just before I went on. I remember everything about that night."

"Boy, she used to kill that song," said Mendel.

"You had to pull her up on stage," Bev continued to remind Aaron, "but when she got there, she acted like it was as easy as serving a plate of tamales."

"By the time I joined," said Gavin, "she was already like an old hand. Full of confidence. And that was just, what, a week or two later?"

Justine belched too loudly with no attempt to disguise it, chasing it with another big swig from the bottle.

"Something like that," said Bev. "Remember?" she asked Sam.

He looked at her with half a smile. "Yeah," he said, "I remember."

"She had such gumption," said Gavin. "She just grabbed that mic like she was born to sing. Looked the audience straight in the eye."

"With that peasant blouse down over her shoulders?" recalled Aaron. "Oh, she was one very good-looking waitress. She—" he began, but caught Shelly's look and stopped.

"What?" asked Justine sharply, taking a swig of Creston Gold.

"No, nothing," he said, embarrassed.

"I want to hear," said Justine with an edge.

"Really, nothing," said Aaron, backpedaling.

"Justine, maybe take it easy?" said Shelly in a low voice, but everyone was listening.

"Hey, I'm a rock star, remember?" she said to Shelly with reckless bravado. "I can have a couple of beers." She turned to Aaron contentiously. "So, tell me about this Kathleen lady."

"Justine," Bev attempted, "we were college students. It was 1970, Flower Power."

"Yeah, I know," she sneered, "sex, drugs, and rock and roll."

"I'm not sure any child should hear everything about his parents," said Mendel. "There are certain things that we don't want to remind ourselves about, let alone tell our children."

"Technically, I'm not a child, you know. I don't have any parents."

"Still—" said Bev.

"Maybe it's time we all went to bed," said Shelly, rising.

"Stop treating me like a kid!" Justine bleated, reeling. "You guys knew my mom—" She faltered, her brain trying to catch up with her tongue.

"Justine, not tonight," Shelly tried to soothe her, but the words kept spilling from the girl.

"Why do you think I flew up here?" she said, her voice rising. She took another wobbly slug. "To hear what a natural she was, how fast she learned, how sexy she was—"

Shelly touched Justine's arm, but the girl jerked away, careening down a steep and dangerous hill, her brakes overwhelmed by beer, terror, and fury.

"It's not my fault you got stuck with such a lousy replacement," the girl bawled, wild-eyed and frantic. "How do you expect me to take her place if you won't even tell me who she was?"

Gavin and Bev and Aaron and Mendel looked at each other uncomfortably.

"Johnny," said Shelly, "I think it's time to call it a night—"

"I need to know!" she demanded.

"She was very attractive," said Aaron, trying to extricate himself. "The guys all went wild over her. That's all I was trying to say."

"No it's not," insisted Justine. "Tell me what happened."

"Justine, please, for everyone's sake, just drop it," Aaron implored.

"No," said Justine, her voice rising to a pitch they hadn't heard before. "Stop tiptoeing around it."

"Justine—" Shelly attempted.

"Don't *Justine* me!" shouted the girl.

Dog jumped up out of his deep sleep and began to bark.

"Why?" she demanded from Aaron. "Why did you fight?"

"Ask him," said Aaron, crossing his legs and turning his head. "I don't go around punching people."

Justine turned to face Sam. "What was the fight about?"

No one moved. Dog's barking sounded like the soundtrack of a disaster movie.

"It's none of your business," Sam said to the floor. "Why don't you just sit down and shut up?"

"Don't you tell me to shut up!" she wailed at him. "You got me into all this. Answer me!"

"I— I—" he stammered, his hands gripping his knees. "Shut up, dog!" he shouted, clambering clumsily to his feet, and threw a piece of watermelon at it, but Dog ignored it and continued its strident barking.

"You hit him, right? Right?" the girl insisted. "Answer me!"

"Yeah, I hit him!"

"Johnny, please stop—" Shelly tried.

"Why?" Justine hit Sam on the chest with her fist. "Why did you do that?"

"He— He—" said Sam, glaring at Aaron. He gasped several times, struggling to speak. His eyes widened like a trapped animal, darting between the faces staring at him and at Justine.

"Why did you have to ruin everything?" she sobbed, pounding on his chest.

"Ask him!" Sam snarled, warding her off.

"You're going to try to pin this on me?" said Aaron, his temperature rising.

"You had nothing to do with it?"

"I don't go around punching people."

"All smiling and agreeing with everyone and making everyone love you. Mr. Perfect. Everyone loves Aaron. Everyone except— except— Kathleen."

"Yeah?" said Aaron, his lip curling unattractively.

Sam glared at him, seething, his chest heaving. "You smug prick."

"As if I'm the problem," said Aaron with contempt.

"Why? Why did you have to go and ruin everything?" Justine bawled in Sam's face.

"Get off of me!" he shouted at her, shoving her aside roughly. "Go on, you chickenshit," he growled at Aaron. "Tell her what you said."

She turned to Aaron.

"I don't even remember," said Aaron, crossing his arms and legs and looking off to the side.

"Stop bullshitting me!" she yowled, swaying on her feet.

Shelly and the others looked on helplessly.

"Tell her, you chicken-shit prick," said Sam, his eyes wild, his nostrils flaring. "You had a big enough mouth back then."

"Tell her yourself, asshole!" shouted Aaron, unfolding his legs. Mendel put his hand on Aaron's arm.

Dog's barking was grating, deafening.

"He said—" Sam panted, "he said—"

Johnny zoomed in for a close-up.

"He said that he screwed her!" Sam croaked in anguish, kicking the low table into the air, beer bottles and tortilla chips and guacamole flying. The crystal pitcher of lemonade crashed, shattered and splattered, and Sam stalked off down the porch stairs to disappear into the night.

51

Aftermath

– June 9, 2006, Night –

Everyone sat stunned, staring at his exit. Shelly blanched. Gavin uprighted a few dripping bottles and made a feeble stab at wiping up the mess.

Justine rose groggily to her feet, stumbled to the porch railing, leaned over and heaved, gagging and spewing the beer and dinner down into the rose bushes below. Shelly wrapped one arm around the girl's thin shoulders and steadied her head with the other.

"It's okay," said Shelly soothingly, bracing her. "Let it go. Let it go. Let it all out."

The girl's back convulsed as she made horrible retching sounds. Dog was howling hysterically. Shelly shot Bev a look.

"Okay," said Bev to the guys, "enough excitement for one day. We're all exhausted. Go get your sleep. We'll see each other in the morning."

"I hope I didn't—" attempted Gavin.

"It's no one's fault," said Mendel.

"We'll work it—" Bev tried but stopped, unconvinced herself.

Aaron looked at them, shaking his head in angry despair. "Déjà vu. Thirty-six years, and he's still the same self-centered asshole," he muttered, and walked back into the house.

"Go," said Shelly to the rest of them, still holding Justine through the final throes of her retching.

Gavin, Mendel, and Johnny filed out despondently.

"Can I—" asked Bev.

"Just go," said Shelly, holding onto the girl as she gagged.

Finally the girl's gut calmed down, and Shelly led her back to the porch swing where the girl slumped down, lifeless, except for the occasional afterbelch. Splotches of dinner clung to her matted hair. Shelly sat with her hand resting on Justine's back, feeling her breath growing regular. She looked up at Shelly.

"I really screwed things up, didn't I?" she sniveled.

Shelly reached down onto the table and handed Justine a napkin dripping lemonade or beer. Justine wiped her nose and her mouth, then buried her head on Shelly's chest, whimpering.

"Shh," said Shelly, stroking her back and her hair, oblivious to the smell and the stains on the lovely peach tunic Brandi had brought her. They sat on the porch swing for long minutes, Justine lying in silence with her head in Shelly's lap.

Dog was already back asleep, exhausted from having defended the girl.

"I was twenty-two when my mom got sick, twenty-four when she died," said Shelly quietly. The only sounds were the creaking of the porch swing and the toads and the crickets in the night. "That might sound to you like I was already grown. Compared to you, I guess I was." She spoke softly and slowly, almost in a whisper, stroking the girl's hair. "But I remember what a giant hole she left in my life. I felt like—I don't know, this giant nothingness. Nothing mattered. I didn't have the strength to get out of bed in the morning."

The girl sniffled into Shelly's lap.

"When I look at you, I try to imagine what it would have

been to lose her when I was twelve. But I just can't grasp it, not having a chance to really get to know your own mother. I just—I just can't imagine how empty the world must seem to you sometimes." And she continued to stroke the girl's hair in silence.

Finally, Justine spoke.

"Why did I have to open up my mouth like that?" she sniveled.

"Shh," said Shelly.

"What made me think I have the right to talk to Sam like—"

"Cut it out," Shelly said gently. "You weren't wrong. It's only natural that you want to know what happened. And I suppose you even have a right."

Shelly stroked the girl's matted hair in silence.

"It was bound to come up sooner or later," Shelly said quietly. "Maybe it's better that it happened now."

"You're just saying that to make me feel better."

No, I'm saying that to make both of us feel better. "Well, maybe this wasn't the right time to confront him."

"I'm such an idiot."

"You're not an idiot. You're a kid who made a mistake." Shelly was quiet for a long moment. "It's probably not the last one you'll ever make in your life. Or even this month. There's an awful lot of heavy baggage floating around here, and a lot of awfully heavy responsibility on your shoulders. But we've got a big job ahead of us. So you're going to have to figure out a way to deal with these things better. Okay?"

The girl nodded into Shelly's lap.

"And now, young lady, we're going to go inside and get you into bed. Tomorrow's your first rehearsal."

"I can't go in there!" She sat up, panicked. "Everyone will be staring at me."

"You'd better get used to it. You're a rock star now, remember?"

Shelly half-carried Justine into the foyer. No one made a

pretense of not staring.

Robbie moved towards Justine tentatively, but when she saw him, she buried her face deep in Shelly's shoulder and wailed at him to go away.

Shelly got the girl to her room, undressed, and into bed. Justine groggily pulled a beat-up teddy bear from under the pillow and clutched it tightly to her chest. Shelly sat by her bed until the girl's sobbing died down. Then, she got up and walked down the wide staircase, determined to focus on the mission, spinning her wheels to figure out what the mission was. Everyone was perched forward. Shelly pulled Bev to the side and spoke quietly.

"Do you know where Sam is?"

"He was headed down towards the lake. How is she?"

"She'll survive."

"Are you sure?"

"It's not open for question."

"I'll go check on her," said Bev.

"No," said Shelly, and she waved to Brandi, who came clumping over quickly on her platform shoes, clinking and jangling.

"Go keep an eye on her, okay?"

"On it."

"Make sure she gets a night's sleep."

"I'll stay with her."

"She smells pretty bad."

"I've slept with worse," said Brandi. "Anyone got an aspirin?"

"I'll get some from the kitchen," said Allie, jumping up.

"Where are you going?" Bev asked Shelly.

"To find my other singer."

The grassy slope was full of dew, so Shelly took off her low heels and carried them, enjoying the feel of the cold, wet grass. There was little moonlight, and she walked in the direction of the lake until she almost tripped over him. He was sitting balled up on the wet grass. *Well, here go these nice slacks*, she thought as she sat down on the slick grass next to him. He didn't even turn to look at her.

She gave him a couple of minutes to get used to her presence, but when she finally touched his arm, he jerked away sharply.

"Sam?" she said quietly.

He didn't answer.

"Sam, it'll be all right."

"How can you say that?" he bleated, turning to her, his face twisted in anguish. "I ruined everything."

"You didn't—" she attempted, laying her hand again on his shoulder, but he knocked it away and accidentally swatted her in the nose.

"Ow!" she cried.

Shelly saw his shock, and rubbed her nose more than necessary, but he just shook his head in self-contempt. "Why?" he mumbled to himself, rocking back and forth, his head buried in his arms.

"Shh," she whispered and laid her hand gently on his back. He tried to shrug it off, but she kept it there. He was trembling. "Shh."

"I've ruined everything, haven't I?" he asked, wiping his nose on his shirt.

"You sure haven't made things easier."

Finally, he worked up his courage to ask. "Is she okay?"

"She'll be okay. She's stronger than you think," she said, praying it was true. "She drank too much."

"Why did I have to open my mouth?" he mewled through clenched teeth. "Why? Why? Why?!?" he cried, banging his clenched fists against his head.

"Sshhh, come on," she said, holding his arm.

Shelly just sat quietly, feeling his heartbeat settle down gradually.

"I never meant to hurt her," he choked.

"I know. Ssh." She took his hand in both of hers.

"She must hate me so much," he choked. "I—" But he couldn't continue.

"Don't be dense. She loves you."

"She'll never come near me again in her life."

"You really are an idiot, you know?" Shelly whispered.

"Wha—"

"She wants so much to love you," she said gently. "More than anything in the world."

"After what I said to her?"

"She'll get over it."

"You don't just forget about a thing like that!"

"No, you don't forget it. But you deal with it. You don't just go running away to hide in the woods. Hearts can mend, Sam. If you let them."

He looked at her, wretched and despondent.

"What am I supposed to do now?"

"Talk to her."

"What, like heart-to-heart and stuff?"

"Do you know what heals a heart, Sam? Exercise. Living. Interacting with other humans. Loving them, hating them. Having feelings. It strengthens your heart muscle."

And this poor mongrel, she thought to herself, *he hasn't used his heart in so long that it's atrophied. All of a sudden, all these things are happening, and it's just too much for him. He's having an emotional heart attack.*

"I wouldn't know what to say. One minute she's like a little kid, the next she's like an adult."

"Yeah, Sam. It's called 'sixteen.' Weren't you ever sixteen?"

"Not like that."

"You both loved Kathleen. You both miss her. Couldn't that be a good place to start?"

He mulled that over.

"How do you know she'll talk to me?"

"I know."

"How do you know?"

"I promise."

"How do I know you'll keep your promise?"

"I don't lie."

"Would you help me? Talk to her?"

Shelly felt a tingle in her breast.

"Of course I will," she said. "In the morning. Come on." She stood up, muddying the knee of her pants, and reached out her hand. "Come on."

"I can't go in there," he said.

"Yes, you can," she said. "Come on."

"I am such a worthless piece of shit," he said.

"Yes, you are," she said.

He looked up at her.

"I thought you were going to encourage me."

"I told you, I don't lie."

"Great," he said wretchedly.

"Come on," she said, holding out her hand to him, "I need the bathroom."

"I can't face them all," he said.

"We'll go in through my office. Come on. Let's get you cleaned up and into bed."

He trudged obediently up the hill behind her towards her screen door. "Wait," he said, turning and unzipping himself. "I gotta pee."

"We have indoor plumbing here, Sam," she said sternly.

"Fuck," he grumbled, zipping himself.

"The bathroom's in there," she said.

"I thought you said you had to pee?" he asked.

"I lied," she said. "And while you're in there, take a shower."

"What for?"

"Because you smell," she snapped.

"Now, is that the truth, or is that a lie?" he crinkled.

"If you have to ask, you'll never understand the answer,"

she smiled back at him.

He shuffled in and closed the door behind him. The stream of his pee sounded like a fire hose. She wasn't pleased that this ripe denizen of the woods was soiling her pristine privy, but reconciled herself to the sacrifice.

"Do you have any clean clothes with you?"

"That Brandi girl put a bag of something in my room," he called over the sound of the shower. "You know, that girl is dangerous."

"You want her on your side in a bar fight," she called in. "A bag of clothes?"

"I don't know, I didn't open it."

When she heard the shower running, she huffed up the back stairs to the men's rooms on the second floor. The room with "Sam Miller" on the door already smelled like the woods. She almost tripped over his fishing pole. In the corner she found the bag of clothes Brandi had brought for him. She found him some plaid boxers, baggy safari shorts, rubber sandals, and a pink Spice Girls T-shirt. Shelly smiled and trudged up to the third floor to check on Justine. Dog had camped himself directly in front of her door. Shelly had no idea whether he had delusions of protecting her or he simply wanted to be as close to the girl as he could, but when she leaned over him to peek inside, he lifted up his eyes without raising his chin. Justine was underneath the covers, Brandi lying on top of them next to her, on her stomach in her black underwear, her arm over the girl, both of them sleeping the sleep of the just.

Shelly closed the door quietly and lumbered back down to her office. From the stairway she heard what sounded like the fitful spurts of a buzz saw. Sam Miller was lying face down, buck naked on her brand-new rust-and-butterscotch sofa, dreaming his way ferociously through an entire winter's supply of kindling. Even asleep, he was restive, jerking and snorting. She looked down at him in the moonlight. His back was lean and wiry, his skin rough and ruddy from living with the elements. Shelly leaned forward. Shaved and shorn, he had strong, rugged features. Showered, he wafted an earthy musk. He must have smelled her in his dream, because he flipped over sharply in his sleep. His body was taut and tight, his prick languid. Shelly stared at it for a moment, sighed, and covered him with a beautiful handmade patchwork quilt, leaving the clean clothes on a chair next to him. The peach-and-aqua bathroom looked like it had suffered its own private tsunami.

She closed the door in exhaustion and looked at her watch, having completely lost track of time. It was only a quarter after ten, but she felt fatigue washing over her. *Well, Shelly,* she thought to herself, *I guess this is what they mean when they say, "Be careful what you wish for."* She sighed and began to drag herself toward the common room to assess the storm damage.

Robbie and Matt were in the music room, arranging sound equipment, while Gerald, Johnny, and the Colonel were gloomily discussing business in the common room, and Allie and Winston were sweeping the dining room. They all turned to stare as Shelly walked in.

"Where's the band?" she asked.

"We're out here, cleaning up," called Gavin from the porch.

She stood in the entrance hall and spoke aloud. "Can everyone hear me?" She felt woozy and had no idea what she needed to say. "Okay, listen up. Everyone's under a lot of pressure here. It's going to be a long month, and we're going to have all kinds of ups and downs. We'll work through this. Everything's going to be fine." Everyone was still looking at her. "I suggest we all turn in. It's been a big day, and tomorrow isn't going to be any easier. Bev? Could we please make rehearsal a bit later?"

"Is there going to be a rehearsal?" she asked.

"Of course there is," she said. The room wobbled.

"Shelly, are you okay? Your pants are all full of mud."

"I'm just a little—" She put her hand on the back of a chair to steady herself.

"Come," said Dr. Bev, supporting her. "Jeez, Shelly, you stink!"

"I—" she put her arm on Bev's shoulder to steady herself and let Bev lead her out to the porch, where Mendel and Aaron and Gavin were waiting. Bev put her in a chair and lifted her feet onto the low table.

"Sorry for the mess," said Shelly, letting her body go, feeling like she was falling. "You guys cleaned up nicely."

"What's going on?" Mendel asked.

"I really don't know." They were all leaning forward. The room was still tilting. "Justine's asleep. Brandi's with her."

"And Sam?" asked Bev.

Shelly sighed. "He's asleep, too. I talked to both of them."

"Do we still have a band?" asked Mendel.

She looked at them. "To tell you the truth, I don't know. I'll get them together in the morning and try to work things out."

"Shelly," said Aaron, "I feel so bad for what happened. I keep going over it in my mind, wondering what I could have done differently—"

"Oh, Aaron, don't take this on yourself," she said. "It's not your fault. It was bound to come out at some point. Let's just hope we get past it." He didn't look convinced. "Come on," she said, reaching over and shaking his shoulder in encouragement. "I need you."

He looked up at her and nodded.

"What did they say?" asked Gavin.

"Nothing that made much sense. The two of them, they're both overwhelmed. Think of how you guys are feeling, and you're mature adults."

They all smiled ruefully.

"Look, try not to talk too much about Kathleen."

"But she keeps asking us," said Gavin.

"Talk about her personality. Tell stories. But try not to make comparisons about her singing."

"Nobody expects her to sing like Kathleen," said Mendel.

"But she doesn't know that. You need to tell her. Make her feel it."

The three men nodded.

"She's very, very self-conscious."

"What's with Sam?" asked Aaron.

Shelly shrugged. "I'll talk to both of them in the morning. Cross your fingers."

"Are you okay?" Mendel asked her.

"I'm just bushed." She looked at Mendel. "Pray for me?"

"You got it," he said and winked.

"Aaron," said Gavin, "you should tell her."

Aaron hesitated.

"Tell me what?" she asked.

"He's right," said Mendel. "It can't make things any worse."

"What?" she insisted. Aaron hesitated. "Tell me. What happened?"

"It was one time," said Aaron somberly. "With Kathleen. Just one time. Before she even knew Sam. I mean, it was just, you know, a lark. We were kids. But she knew he wouldn't be able to handle it. So she made me swear I wouldn't tell him." He paused. "But then, in Columbus, it was all so—so *intense*. And Sam, he was just riding me and being a real pain in the ass, and—" He sat for a long moment looking at the floor. "She was so damned cool, that Kathleen. And I—I was jealous." He looked up at them.

Shelly, Bev, Gavin, and Mendel sat looking at Aaron, feeling his embarrassment with him.

"I never meant to hurt anyone."

It was Mendel who finally spoke. "Aaron, I don't pretend to understand everything that went on between you two. You three. But we were right there watching. Nobody blames you."

Bev and Gavin nodded their agreement.

"Just that one time?" asked Shelly.

Aaron nodded.

"Before he even knew her?" she asked.

"Of course," said Aaron. "After they were together, they

were inseparable. You couldn't help but be jealous. I've never seen two people so glued to each other."

Gavin and Bev and Mendel and Shelly and Aaron sat looking at each other glumly.

"Next time, I'm gonna find me a band that isn't so fucked up," Shelly said, and they all smiled.

Plodding back to her room, Shelly pictured the quaint communal shower upstairs. And her private, personal, Shelly-only, brand-new, virgin, never-been-used-by-anyone-else-before, private, peach-and-aqua toilette. And the mud and guck and God only knows what other droppings were left in the aftermath of Hurricane Sam. And that naked man on her butterscotch-and-rust couch with his lax prick and his cowboy jawline. *I just hope he didn't mark the couch*, she laughed to herself.

After her shower, she sat down on the lush, white-sheeted, old bed. She poured herself a glass of wine and read Brandi's instruction sheet: *Friday—sleeveless green top with big white flowers, jeans (white plastic hanger), light denim jacket if you need it.* She hadn't even had time to get a good look at the oodles of goodies Brandi had stocked her closet with. She took tomorrow's outfit from its hanger—Brandi had removed all the pins and hung them to uncrease—and laid them on the chair. She set her alarm for seven o'clock and turned out the light. The room was dark and quiet except for the flashes of Justine screaming uncontrollably at Sam, and Sam's demons ripping and tearing at his soul right before everyone's eyes.

Coddle her? Reason with her? Scold her? How much can I push him before he bites me? Are they going to even let me open my mouth?

She sat up, reset her alarm for six thirty, and fell back into the soft bedding.

Part 3

We Are Decapede!

52

The Morning After

– June 10, 2006 –

Shelly was standing on the patio just outside the screen door of her office in a long red-and-gold striped Moroccan lounging robe, looking at the thousands of people gathered all the way down the hillside to the lake. In front were Sam and Justine and Bev, behind them Shelly's mother and father, Kathleen, Sheriff Aubrey, the Hasidic Santa Claus, creepy Marvin George from the hardware store basement, George Harrison, and thousands of others, their faces fading in the distance, all looking up at her, waiting for her to speak, waiting for the gospel, but she had nothing, she could only stare at them in frozen, speechless terror, as the very earth beneath them split the grassy hillside, the people spilling into the dark like a Bosch painting when the alarm rang.

It was ten of eight.

Shelly opened her eyes, staring at the old bedside lamp, exhaled hard to expel the smog from her brain, and sat up resolutely.

She dressed and washed up quickly. She paused to look in the mirror. *You will not let it fall apart now! You will think of something to say. Or you can just twist their goddamn necks into submission.*

She crossed the hallway to Justine's room and leaned over Dog to open the door a crack and peek in. Brandi and Dog raised their heads to see who was intruding, but the girl was still deep asleep. Shelly put her finger to her lips and closed the door. Then she went down the back steps and put her ear to her office door. She could hear the woodsman still sawing logs to stockpile for the winter.

Bev was huffing down the hallway towards her.

"Did you change my alarm?"

"I'm your doctor."

"No, I've got so much to do!"

"You can't function without a clear head."

"Where is everyone?"

"Puttering around, waiting for breakfast. No one knows what to do. Nice outfit."

Shelly nodded.

Johnny was ambling down the hallway, camera in hand.

"And heeere's Johnny," whispered Shelly so that only Bev could hear. "Hi, Johnny. Please please please, not now."

"A little late for keeping secrets from me now, cutie," he said, giving her a warm hug with his non-camera hand. "Don't you look lovely this morning?"

"But you're not getting near the room when I talk to them," she warned him.

"Clear," he agreed.

Shelly's voice dropped to a serious, low tone. "And nothing at all of Justine, okay?"

"Duh," he said, this old ponytailed teddy bear.

She turned to Bev. "And?"

"The Colonel is in Gerald's office. They say they need you immediately, that you need to talk to them the very first thing—"

Shelly touched Bev's arm. "Let me just think for a minute."

Shelly thought. Then she looked at her watch. Then she turned to Bev.

"You stand guard here. If Sam stops snoring, call me immediately. Okay?"

Bev nodded.

"And you don't move from here, no matter what, okay?"

"All right, all right! Where are you going?"

"I want to grab both of them before they have a chance to collect their thoughts," Shelly said over her shoulder.

"What are you going to say to them?"

"I have no idea. Got any suggestions?"

Bev shrugged.

"I'll be right back," said Shelly, but the Colonel was lying in wait for her as she tried to get past the office.

"Where have you been?" he asked, peeved.

"I'm sorry, Dad, I can't talk right now—"

"Shelly, we need to talk about—"

"I'm sorry," she said, walking away from him backward, "I have to—"

"Shelly, would you please stand still while I'm talking to you?" said her father.

Shelly wrapped her hands around his neck and squeezed until—

"Dad, I don't know if we have a band at all. I'm trying to put Humpty Dumpty back together again, okay? So, please! Not right now."

And she set off, undeterred, a woman with a mission.

The kitchen was a beehive. Matt was beating the pancake batter with a fury, Gerald was cutting a variety of fruits into symmetrical little squares, Winston was cracking eggs into a large bowl with one hand, flipping pancakes with the other while instructing Gavin in the fine art of frying sausages, the four of them chatting like contented housewives.

"Winston, everything under control?"

"Sure ting, Miss Shelly. Brekfass ready half hour. How my Boo?"

"Oh, she'll be fine," said Shelly, realizing she'd begun to

fib without blushing. "Listen, I need a pot of coffee taken up to Justine's room as soon as possible. Have someone wake her and Brandi as soon as it's ready."

"I'll do it!" volunteered Matt cheerily, wiping his short-stop's hands on his apron.

"Make it strong," said Shelly. "Immediately, the minute it's ready."

"Okay, no problem," Winston smiled.

"And in half an hour, I'll need a nice big breakfast tray for three in my office. I'll let you know exactly when."

"I make it special," he twinkled.

"And go heavy on the sausages."

Someone was rapping emphatically on the door. Brandi jerked awake and sat up with a start. "Who is it?" she asked woozily.

"Hi," boomed a voice as bright as the sunny summer morning. "It's Matt."

"What?" slurred Brandi as she struggled to clear the jungle of cobwebs.

"Winston sent me," he hollered through the door. "Can I come in?"

Justine groaned and turned over onto her stomach. "Wha isfm dgrufng?" she mumbled.

Matt opened the door and stuck in his grinning face. At his knee, Dog stuck in his snout. "Go-ood morning," he said cheerily, carrying a tray with a pot of steaming coffee. Dog padded over to Justine's side of the bed and began to whimper up at her for attention.

"What do *you* want?" Brandi growled uninvitingly, clutching her pillow in front of her very black underwear and her very white skin.

Justine slid her hand out from under the covers and scratched Dog behind his ear.

"Dr. Bev said to tell you that Shelly wants Justine in her

office in half an hour," he smiled broadly.

Dog panted contentedly.

"What time is it?" Brandi asked, looking around the room for her clothes.

"Eight fifteen."

"Fuck," she said.

Matt stood entranced, staring at Brandi with his impossibly optimistic grin, his sandy hair and dimples, and his tight, beige We Are Decapede! T-shirt.

"What are you staring at?" she hissed.

"Me? What?"

"Put it on the table there," she snapped, indicating the tray.

He put the tray on the table.

"What are you waiting for, a tip?" she snapped.

"Huh?" he asked, staring transfixed at Brandi's bare shoulders.

Justine opened one bloodshot eye to peer at him from underneath the covers.

"Get out of here!" Brandi barked.

"What? Oh. Okay," he said, backing out of the room sheepishly, gaping and smiling, and closed the door behind him with a bang.

"Ow!" said Justine, sitting up.

"Good morning, Sunshine!" said Brandi.

Justine surveyed the room with her one open eye, trying to figure out where she was and what she was doing there. Then she remembered, and flopped down with a groan to hide her face in her pillow.

"Sorry, girl," said Brandi, yanking the covers off her, "boss's orders."

"No!" she protested, grabbing for the blanket, but it was gone.

Brandi pulled her out of bed, force-fed her two aspirin, and stripped her of the last remnants of the night's excesses.

The girl was too fuzzy to present any serious resistance. Dog watched as Brandi wrapped her in a sheet and led her across the hallway to the shower. She shoved the girl into the stall, squawking and yawping. Eventually, the girl's protestations subsided as the steaming water purged the sludge from her brain, layer by layer. Then, Brandi toweled the girl roughly and led her back to her room, where she wrapped her in a fresh sheet, sat her on a chair, and handed her the Winnie the Pooh mug of steaming coffee.

"I don't drink coffee," said Justine, brushing her hand away.

"This is definitely the time to start."

"Winston remembered my mug!"

"Great. Drink," Brandi ordered.

Justine sipped at it. "It's bitter!" she said.

"Yeah, life's a bitch, ain't it? Drink."

Brandi tried to comb Justine's jungle of tangles as the girl sipped the coffee.

"Don't you ever touch your hair?" Brandi asked. "Wait here." Brandi ran out of the room and ran back in with her hairdressing kit in one hand and the duffel bag of clothes she'd bought in the other. The girl hadn't moved except to sip the hot coffee. Brandi began to comb and brush and lift and snip, lift and nip.

"Whar you doin'?" asked the girl.

"Making you presentable," answered Brandi. "You have a big day today."

"A giant mess, you mean." Holding the cup with both hands, the girl slurped her coffee.

"That's true." Brush and comb and lift and snip, lift and nip. "So you gotta look really good. 'Fuck 'em,' you know?"

"Did you hear?"

"I hear everything."

"Everyone?"

"Yeah, pretty much so."

"I'm never going out there again."

"Yeah, yeah. I remember the first time I got drunk. You're what, sixteen?"

"Almost seventeen."

"Well, it's about time."

"Why, how old were you?"

"Fifteen? Probably not, even. Scott Page took me out to the stock car races one Friday night in his Galaxie convertible, got me tanked. Figured he'd take advantage of me."

"Did he?" the girl asked.

"Well, I'm not sure who was taking advantage of who."

The girl mulled over that.

"Among some other things, I puked all over his shiny black upholstery." Snip and lift and nip. "Damn, that car had one roomy back seat."

"What's everyone saying?"

"That you drank too much."

"Other than that?"

"That Sam's an asshole. But we all knew that already."

"Come on, seriously."

"What?"

"About—what we were shouting about," the girl whined.

"What is there to say? Once upon a time, some guy stuck his wee-wee into some girl's woo-woo. Big fucking deal," said Brandi and cracked her gum in her ear.

"Ow!" said Justine.

"Sorry," said Brandi.

Justine took another big slurp of hot coffee.

"How's your head?" Brandi asked as she snipped and nipped.

"Feels like a train ran over it."

"It'll pass. Next time take aspirin before you pass out."

"Next time?" said the girl. "Never again."

Brandi snickered. Snip and lift and nip.

Shelly figured she had time for a quick survey of the troops before the court martial. In the music room, Mendel and Aaron were fiddling with a computer and a bunch of black boxes of various sizes.

"Hey, how's it going?" asked Shelly.

"Okay, you know," said Aaron. "Just waiting to hear. Robbie's been showing us around this Pro Tools program. It's amazing what you can do by yourself today."

"Any news?" asked Mendel.

"They're still asleep. I'm going to wake them up soon."

"What do you think?" asked Mendel.

"Do we have a band?" asked Aaron.

Shelly looked at them long and seriously. "I have no idea," she said. "You'll be the first ones to know."

They glumly wished her good luck. As she walked away, Aaron began to play Chopin's "Funeral March."

"That's not funny," said Shelly over her shoulder.

"Yes, it is," said Mendel.

Matt met her at the door. "Shelly, you're wanted on the phone."

"I don't have time for—"

"By the police."

"Yesterday was supposed to be—magic," whined the girl. "And everything went wrong. Everything!"

"I'm going to shorten it a little here and layer it here, okay?"

The girl shrugged. Brandi snipped.

"I heard you got trampled in Akron."

Justine told her how she was recognized, how she was mobbed, and how Robbie extricated her. By the time she got to the Coke spraying all over the car, they were both laughing so hard that Brandi had to stop cutting her hair and sat down on the bed.

"So he stopped the car, and I got out, and I started crying and everything, and I was kind of, you know, hanging on him, crying. And he tried—he tried—"

Justine was trying to make the story sound tragic, but Brandi kept laughing harder and harder, flopping back on the bed and whooping till Justine had no choice but to laugh herself.

"Wait, wait, wait!" Brandi shrieked, convulsing with laughter.

"What?" said Justine, laughing but not getting the joke.

"He rescued you from a mob, and then right after that, you were crying on him and hugging him?"

Justine nodded.

"How, like with your head on his chest?"

"I don't remember," said Justine.

"Bullshit," said Brandi.

"No," admitted Justine, "like this."

"Crying right into the crook of his neck?"

"I guess so."

"You guess so. Oh, man, give me a break!"

"What?" Justine asked.

"Seriously? You go all helpless and gushy, and pressing up against him and crying *hot, wet tears* right into the crook of his neck?"

"What?"

" 'What?' " Brandi mocked her. "Jeez, I didn't figure out that one till I was nineteen."

"I don't understand!" said Justine, frustrated and embarrassed and laughing.

"The hell you don't. Hot tears in the soft part there? Little head kicks in, big head conks out. Remember that, girl, you'll thank me someday. Hopefully, many days."

"You're crazy."

"Do you like him?"

"I—I don't know—"

"He's got a nice little bod on him."

"Brandi!"

"Well, when you think about him, do you think dirty thoughts?"

"Stop!"

"What?"

"I'm not going to tell you my thoughts!"

"That's a relief. I was starting to worry."

Snip and lift and nip. Snip and lift and nip.

"Can I ask you something?" said the girl.

"As long as it's inappropriate." Snip lift nip.

"That guy, Matt?"

"Who?" said Brandi, cracking her gum twice.

"Ow. Matt, the guy who brought the coffee."

"Oh, him."

"Cut it out. Everyone thinks he's such a hunk."

"I didn't notice."

"Aw, come on. The guy looks at you and his eyes go all glassy and stuff."

"So what?"

"Why are you so nasty to him?"

"Not my type," she said curtly.

"What is your type?" Justine asked.

"Generally I believe in equal opportunity."

"So what's wrong with him?"

Brandi stopped clipping.

"I grew up with guys like that. Born in Hicksville, raised in Hicksville, happy as a turtle to spend his whole life there. That's not me. I'm going somewhere."

"Where?" asked the girl, fascinated.

"I don't know, but somewhere far from here. Look," said Brandi, handing her a mirror.

Johnny squeezed into the office ahead of Shelly so he could catch her coming in.

The Colonel was sitting at a computer, his hand over the mouthpiece of the phone. "It's the sheriff. He wants to talk to you," he whispered.

"Tell them you can't find me," Shelly whispered back.

"I'm not going to lie to the *police*," whispered back the Colonel.

"Well, I don't have time to talk to them right now," whispered Shelly.

The Colonel sat up straight and cleared his throat. "I'm so sorry, Sheriff, we can't find her right now. But I'm sure she's somewhere on the grounds, and I promise we'll get back to you as soon as we can. I'm sorry?" he said gravely. "I really can't comment on that at this point in time. Well, thank you very much, sir. I'll pass that on to the band," and hung up. "The sheriff sends his—"

"What did he want?" asked Shelly.

"Traffic jams," said the Colonel. "Apparently, Creston has become quite an attraction. He said the traffic is snarled from Hulbert Road on the east and all the way to I-71 in the west. It's just piling up, and cars keep coming."

"What in heaven's name does he expect me to do?" Shelly demanded. "He's the police!"

The Colonel shrugged. "And Shelly—he asked about the ruckus on the porch last night."

"How does he know about that?" she demanded angrily.

"No idea," said the Colonel.

Big help, thought Shelly.

"What do you think?"

Justine examined herself.

"It's nice," she admitted.

"Try it for a couple of days. If you don't like it, we'll do something else."

"Thank you," said Justine.

"Oh, you're so polite!" joked Brandi. "Okay, now we got to get you out of that baggy shit you've been wearing."

"But that's what I like!" she protested.

"Forget it," said Brandi, studying her. "You look like an old Spanish widow. When you go out, what do you wear?"

Justine shrugged. "I don't really go out much."

"What TV shows do you watch?"

"I don't really watch much TV. I don't know. 'The Simpsons'?"

"Oh, jeez. Teenage shows?"

"Nah, they're all so silly."

"Great. Singers. Who do you listen to?"

"I don't know, all kinds. Ella. Sinatra. My mother's old stuff from the Sixties."

"No one, like, alive?"

The girl shrugged.

"Do you have any posters on your wall?"

"Picasso. That blue guitar player."

"God, you really are a mess."

"What do you mean?"

"Girl, this is where you decide. You're going downstairs in a minute, and you gotta wear something. And it ain't gonna be that black widow shit. Now, who are you? Time to decide. Who do you want to be?"

"Me."

"Yeah. Who are you? Come on, Shelly's waiting."

"How should I know? I'm only sixteen. I haven't done anything."

Brandi scrutinized her head to toe and fiddled with her lip ring.

"Perky," she said finally.

"What?" asked the girl.

Brandi bent down and began plowing through the duffel bag. She held up a pair of baggy jeans.

"Those aren't bad," said the girl.

"Hun-uh, sister. You're done hiding it." She tossed them on the floor and continued digging.

"What do you mean?"

"Here, put these on," she said, holding up a pair of cut-off denim shorts.

"I don't think—"

"Put them on," Brandi ordered.

Justine put them on. "They're kind of skimpy, aren't they?"

"They're health shorts," said Brandi.

"What?"

"They let the skin breathe all over your leg."

Brandi held up against her a cute little yellow-and-orange striped top with a deep scoop neck.

"Uh, it's a little—*little*."

"Try it on."

She pulled it over her head and wriggled into it with a little dance.

"Oh, it's way too tight."

"Perfect."

Justine looked warily in the mirror at the three inches of skin showing above the tiny teeny shorts and frowned.

"Oh, loosen up, will you?" Brandi scolded and continued digging. "You're sixteen, a fucking rock star, you have a terrific little figure, and you're going to stop hiding it."

"But everybody will be looking at me!"

"I know. Some girls have all the luck. Here, try this."

Brandi placed a floppy brown buckskin hat on Justine's head.

The girl looked in the mirror and adjusted the hat to give it a slightly jauntier angle.

"I like it," Justine smiled.

Brandi gave the girl a final once-over and nodded with satisfaction.

"It's a start. Come on, Shelly's waiting for you."

53

Humpty Dumpty
– June 10, 2006, Morning –

Shelly pushed open the door and peeked in. Sam was still lying on her couch, his bare butt facing her. She slammed the door as loudly as she could.

"Wha?" He sat up, startled, looking around, covering his privates with the beautiful hand-made quilt. "Where are my clothes?" he mumbled.

"There, on the chair," Shelly said.

"Those aren't mine," he said.

"Yes they are. Put them on."

He covered himself with them as he rose. "I gotta pee."

"Aim well and don't come out till you've cleaned up the mess you made last night," she barked, as he stumbled towards her private bathroom.

Shelly folded the blanket and straightened up the sofa, trying not to hear the fire hose emptying into her aqua toilet. She sniffed the cushions he'd slept on.

"Did you clean up after yourself in there?"

"Yes!" he responded sullenly.

She went to the bathroom to check. "Pick up the rug," she instructed him.

He scowled, but did as she ordered him.

"Now wet the towel with hot water and go over the sink

482

and the toilet bowl. Not that towel!"

"Which one?" he grumped.

"The one that used to be white," she barked back. She watched over him till she was satisfied.

"Okay?" he asked finally.

Someone knocked. "Who is it?" called Shelly, fire in her voice.

Justine opened the office door a crack and peeked in. At her knee, Dog was whining and trying to squeeze in.

"Keep him out!" ordered Shelly.

"Stay!" Justine ordered Dog as she pushed out his snout and closed the door behind her like she was going to meet a firing squad.

Justine and Sam stared at each other from opposite sides of the room.

"What are you staring at?" she growled at him.

"You look different," he said.

She looked again at the grizzled man of the woods, saw his Spice Girls T-shirt, and let loose a whoop, but stopped abruptly and touched her forehead.

"Oh, shut up!" growled the old man.

"You shut up!" retorted the girl.

"Cut it, the both of you!" snapped Shelly in a voice that brooked no objection. "No talking! Sit, both of you." She pointed to the sofa opposite her. The girl sat as far from Sam as possible. They avoided each other's eyes, both of them with their arms folded.

There was a knock at the door.

"Come in," called Shelly without looking.

Allie came in carrying an elegant black lacquered serving tray laden with white porcelain dishes, pancakes, sausages, scrambled eggs, freshly baked rolls, butter, a selection of preserves, and a large silver pot of steaming coffee.

"Oh, Justine, don't you look lovely! So—lively!" said Allie. "Very nice!"

"Thank you," said Justine, averting her bloodshot eyes.

"Sam!" prodded Shelly.

"What?" he said.

Shelly rolled her eyes.

"Take the tray from her, you jerk," whispered Justine.

"What? Oh." He jumped up and took the tray from Allie. "Sorry. Thanks. It looks, ah, very delicious."

"My pleasure," she smiled, glancing around Shelly's office. "Bev sure fixed up this room."

"Nice bathroom, too," said Sam, thinking that perhaps was a sociable thing to say.

Allie took her leave, and Sam placed the tray right in front of himself on the low table. He picked up a fork and speared a sizzling sausage, but before he could get it to his mouth, Shelly spoke.

"Put it down!" she commanded.

"Why?" he asked.

"Because I said so!" said Shelly.

He hesitated.

"Now!" Shelly snapped.

Sam slowly returned the hot, savory sausage to the plate.

"What?" he groused. "I washed my hands and everything."

Shelly pulled the tray away from him. "You eat when I'm finished talking."

Sam looked at the coffee pot.

Shelly pulled the tray to her and methodically poured herself a cup.

"Hey!" said Sam.

"Hey what?" asked Shelly, stirring in a teaspoon of sugar.

"How come you get to?"

"Because I didn't act like an asshole last night!"

"Hah!" sneered Justine.

"I'd watch my mouth if I were you, young lady," warned Shelly.

Justine crossed her arms and sat back with a pout. Sam whiffed the fresh brew and grumbled something inaudible.

"Justine," said Shelly, pointing her knees at the girl, "you behaved like a spoiled brat. You're sixteen—"

"Almost seventeen."

"Sixteen, and you've never drunk anything before, but you're smart enough to know what could happen, and you let it happen, and you made a fool of yourself and everyone around you."

"I wanted to get it right. And then the microphone didn't work—"

"That's what set you off?" said Sam. "A mic that didn't work? Big fucking deal!"

"Oh, shut up," said Justine. "You wouldn't understand."

"You've got to understand that no one here is trying to judge you," said Shelly. "Nobody gets things perfect the first time."

"Apparently *she* did."

"Don't you use that tone about your mother, young lady!" said Shelly.

The girl began to sniffle.

"Hey, stop picking on her," said Sam. "It wasn't all her fault."

Dog was scratching at the screen door, having figured out how to run around the house to Shelly's side entrance.

"It's too much!" the girl whimpered.

"You haven't even started, and you're giving up?" asked Shelly.

Justine burst out in tears.

"Look what you've done!" said Sam, rising in distress. "You made her cry!"

"So what?" said Shelly.

Sam looked from Justine to Shelly and back, confused. "But—but—"

"Oh, sit down!" said Justine through her tears, grabbing a

tissue from the coffee table.

Sam gaped, utterly at a loss.

"Sixteen-year-old girls cry, you know?" said Shelly.

"Just like that?" asked Sam, bewildered.

"Yeah, just like that!" Justine snapped and blew her nose.

Dog was still watching them through the screen door, whining and scratching.

"Shaddup!" barked Sam, but the dog ignored him.

Justine went to the door, opened it, stroked Dog's head and whispered something to it. The dog quieted down. Justine closed the door, and they all sat back down.

"Listen," said Shelly, softening her voice and speaking slowly, "this whole business—it's a crazy thing for anyone to deal with. Right, Sam?"

Sam sniffed the sausages and nodded.

"Did you really think it was all going to be smooth?"

The girl shook her head and wiped her nose.

"Justine, everyone is here for you. I'm here for you. Bev is here for you. And Allie. And Brandi. And the guys. Even Sam."

The girl blew her nose. "It doesn't feel that way."

"Right, Sam?" prodded Shelly.

"What? Oh, yeah. Sure. So, like, if you ever want to talk about, you know, your feelings and stuff. You can try. Talking. To me."

"To you?" scoffed Justine, sniffling.

"Well, you know. Yeah. I guess. I might be a little out of practice. But if you want to, you can, you know, try."

"Like you could understand."

"You know, I—" Sam began and stopped.

Shelly and Justine looked at him.

He spoke in a low, gravelly whisper. "I grew up without a mother, too."

Shelly and Justine looked at each other.

"I never knew her," he said. "I went through the system. Foster homes and stuff."

They waited.

"At your age, I was out on my own. Trying to figure out a place to sleep and how to fill my stomach. And a lot of other stuff I try not to remember." He stopped. "So, yeah, I maybe know something about—you know—"

The girl reached over and touched Sam's hand.

Sam blinked a couple of times.

Justine sat up, sniffling and smiling, and reached for the coffee.

"Oh, no," said Shelly, "I'm not finished with either of you."

They sat back unhappily.

"I am so sick and tired of your ghosts. You know how you get rid of ghosts?"

Justine shook her head.

"Garlic?" offered Sam.

"You turn on the lights!" she said, glaring at him, then at Justine. "You wanted 'the truth'? All right, then, let's lay it out on the table. No more secrets, no more lies."

They both looked back at her with apprehension.

"You met Kathleen. You fell in love with her, and you loved her like you've never loved anyone before or since. Right?" Shelly said and glared at Sam, waiting for an answer.

He glared back.

"I asked you something!" she barked.

"Yeah, that's right."

"And for some unfathomable reason, she loved you, right?"

"I guess so."

Shelly rolled her eyes. "But before she knew you, she had a meaningless, one-time fling with Aaron. Right? Answer me!"

He nodded reluctantly.

"Say it," she said.

"Say what?" he growled.

" 'She had a meaningless one-time fling with Aaron before she knew me'!"

"I heard you."

"Say it!"

"I don't want to."

Shelly raised the plate of steaming, savory sausages to her nose and inhaled deeply. "Mmmmmmm!" she said.

He glared at her, but she wasn't budging.

"She had a one-time thing with Aaron," said Sam finally.

"She had a *meaningless* one-time *fling* with Aaron *before she knew me*," Shelly dictated.

"Okay, what you said."

"Say it!"

"She had a meaningless one-time fling with Aaron before she knew me!" he shouted at her.

"And she didn't tell you about it because she *didn't want to hurt you*," Shelly said gently. "Because she loved you. Do you under*stand* that?"

"You don't know that."

"Yes, I do. She knew how much it would hurt you. She knew you better than anyone."

"It sounds different when you say it like that."

"And just as you went up on stage in Columbus, everyone was nervous, and you were driving Aaron crazy."

"What, you were there spying on me?"

"True or false, you pushed him to it?"

Sam refused to answer. Shelly waited. Still, he refused.

Shelly smelled the sausages. "Mmmm."

"Maybe I egged him on a little, but everyone knows that Aaron can be such a—"

"We are not here to discuss Aaron!" she quelched him. "Don't you understand what you did? You ruined people's lives. For nothing!"

"It was a stupid college band—"

"I'm not talking about the band, you imbecile!" She wanted to punch him. "You could have stayed and let Kathleen love you the way she wanted to. You—you could have been—*normal!*" She banged her fist on the coffee table so hard that coffee spilled from her cup onto the china saucer.

"You think you're so smart?" he said, laying down his trump card. "She saw it. She was standing right there when I hit him. Do you know what she said to me?" He paused dramatically. " '*I never want to see you again.*' "

"And you just walked away?" asked Justine.

"Yeah. I walked away."

"My God, you really are dense," said Justine. "She used to say that kind of stuff to me every time we had a fight. 'I'm going to sell you to the gypsies.' 'The sperm donor must have been Darth Vader.' "

The women stared at him.

"You see, now," he attempted, "I didn't have that information at that time—"

"Well, you do now!" cried Shelly. "You screwed up people's lives back then, and now you have the opportunity to make it right, to *build* something. So I'm begging you, Sam. Grow a pair. Get out there and face the world. Do this thing. With your heart."

Sam and Justine were both quiet.

"So, decide now, the two of you. You can go back to your stinky little trailer, and you can go back to hide in your aunt's house, and you can both spend the rest of your lives kicking yourselves for ruining everything for everyone. Or you can do what the whole damned world is hoping you'll do, which is to make some music and make a lot of people happy."

Shelly sat back and folded her arms. "I'm waiting," she said.

Justine and Sam looked at each other.

The girl spoke first, looking at Sam. "I'm very sorry for what I did out on the porch. I didn't mean to make a mess. I just—I—I'm sorry. " She looked at Shelly. "I know this is going to be the biggest thing in my life. I promise I won't let you down."

Shelly and Justine looked at Sam.

"I get it, Shelly," he said finally. "I get it. I might be crazy, but I'm not dumb. I know I'm—well, you know. This whole circus of yours—it's, you know—okay. Look, I'm not used to being around people. But I can try, you know, to, like, *communicate* with *people*." He said it as if he were swallowing a tablespoon of castor oil.

"And you're going to behave yourself?" asked Shelly.

Sam considered that. "Yeah, you know. In principle. But I can't make any promises if some drunk teenager comes puking all over me again."

Justine smiled at him, and Sam sort of smiled back.

Shelly smiled to herself.

The girl scootched across the sofa, wrapped her arms around him, and lay her head on his chest.

Sam just sat there and let her hug him for a long moment. "Okay, come on, let go already. I'm not your boyfriend."

She sat up, and they both looked at Shelly.

"Can I leave the two of you here without getting into trouble?" she said, rising.

"I ain't going anywhere," he said, grabbing a plate and fork.

Justine curled her legs underneath her and cuddled her Pooh mug.

Justine watched Sam as he ravaged a heap of scrambled eggs and sausages, tamped with a fresh roll, and then gulped down the syrup-sodden mound of pancakes.

"What?" he asked.

"Nothing," she said.

"What, am I supposed to, like, make small talk while we dine?"

"Are you really that much of a jerk?"

"What do you mean?"

"Or is it just this grouchy old fart role you like to play?

"Hey, watch your language," he said through the mouthful of pancake.

"Is it?"

"What?"

"An act?"

He looked at her. "Think I'm gonna tell you all my secrets?" Justine didn't answer, but he continued to look at her as he ushered another forkful of pancakes into his mouth, chewing like a voracious cement truck.

"What?" she asked.

"What what?" he answered.

"Why are you looking at me like that?"

"Your eyes," he said and swallowed. "You got her eyes."

"That doesn't mean I'm like her."

"I know," said Sam, slurping the coffee as he reached for another roll. "She was nicer."

"Oh, yeah? You didn't know her like I did," said Justine.

"You didn't know her like I did," said Sam.

Justine watched him chew on the roll and took a sip of the hot, bitter coffee in her Pooh mug. "I think I was nicer before—she died. It's hard to remember."

Sam chewed some more.

"I like your T-shirt," she said, straight-faced.

"Fuck you," he said, pouring maple syrup on another mound of pancakes, quartering it, and spearing a forkful. "You look—you know, nice."

"Fuck you," she said, smiling.

But then in stomped Shelly, fire in her eyes.

Sam and Justine quickly lost their smiles.

She set her laptop on the table facing them and glared at them as they read.

"**Decapede Breakup?**" read the leading headline of *Yahoo! News*, and under that, "**Orphan and Recluse in Dramatic**

Screaming Match—Exclusive Yahoo! Video."

Shelly clicked on the arrow in the middle of the black rectangle, and after an eternity, an eighteen-second clip appeared. A distant ghostly green Justine and Sam were gesturing at each other angrily. Then Sam stumbled down the porch steps, waving his arms wildly and on out of the frame. Then Justine was puking over the porch railing. The soundtrack was a lot of background noise and muffled shouting. The clip had been posted just after midnight and had already garnered over 17,000 views.

Shelly looked at their stunned faces.

"Apparently, they used a telescopic night-vision lens. The police are doing their best to keep them back, but the reporters are all over."

Justine and Sam looked at each other and at Shelly.

"Oh, but wait," smiled Shelly, a smile that did not reassure them. She clicked on Comments.

Sam turned away.

"Scared to look?" asked Shelly.

"That thing hurts my eyes," he said.

The girl scrolled and began to read.

Justine, are you alright? My daughters saw this and went to bed crying. Please send some sign that your ok.

Is it true she got trampled in a store in Akron? Does anyone know if she's allright?

Today I was released from hospital after a recent suicide attempt. As I waited to be discharged, I was listening to the new Decapede album on my iPod. For the first time in a long time I felt a sense of hope and faith and like things would maybe get better. I have a long road ahead, I got to sober up—but the song Creston Gold in particuler—

"He spelled it wrong," the girl noted.

—gives me strength. So inspireing. I'm so glad I'm alive now. Justine, if your reading this, listen to me: Lfe is worth living!

"People really write creepy stuff like that?" Sam asked.

"Welcome to the twenty-first century," said Shelly.

"I'm not sure I'm staying," said Sam.

All my friends slept over last night. We stayed up all night listening to the Decapede CD and praying for Justine!

Justine u are so hot I want to tear off your— She mouthed a few more words in silence. "Yech!" she squealed in disgust and closed the screen.

"Anyone can see that?" asked Sam.

"The whole world," nodded Shelly. "And they're going to keep watching until we feed them something else."

"Fucking twenty-first century," said Sam.

"What are you going to do?" whined the girl.

"I have no idea!" snapped Shelly. She turned on Sam. "Do you, Rock Star Genius Sam Miller?"

"They still out there? The reporters?" asked Sam.

"Sharks never sleep," said Shelly. "Why?"

"With cameras and stuff?"

"Why?"

"What?" asked Justine.

"Come on," he said, pulling the girl after him and heading for the screen door.

"What are you doing?" called Shelly, scrambling to her feet. "Sam!"

But he was walking purposefully, pulling Justine by the hand down the hill, with Dog loping behind them jumping and barking happily and Shelly trying to keep up with them, but her kitten heels kept sinking into the ground. When Sam neared the hubbub of news crews and fans, Justine tried to pull back, but he put his arm around her waist and half-dragged her alongside him to face them.

"Hey, y'all, how you all doing?" Sam called out to the crunch of gapers and gawkers and news crews, while a handful of policemen struggled to keep them behind the cordon. Everyone was filming and shouting and pushing to get close to him. Sam put his fingers to his mouth and gave an ear-piercing whistle. Justine touched her forehead in pain, and the little mob went silent.

"Is Decapede breaking up?" called out one reporter.

The swarm began to buzz and clamor, but Sam raised his hands, and they stopped to listen. Justine clung to his arm. The flashbulbs continued to pop furiously at her new hairstyle and cutoff shorts and midriff tank top.

"What's your name?"

"Tim Nilsson, *Cincinnati Enquirer*."

"Well, Don, I'm glad you asked that. No, of course we're not breaking up. So far, we're just catching up on old times, but we came here to make music, and that's what we're going to do."

"What was the argument about last night?" shouted another.

Shelly had caught up with them and was poised to leap into the fray.

"What argument?" Sam responded innocently.

"The video of you and Justine from last night," someone called.

"Haven't seen it," he said. "We were playing tag as an ice-breaking activity, maybe that's what you saw." He looked to Justine.

"Must have been," she confirmed.

"Sam, are you a big Spice Girls fan?" shouted one of the reporters.

"Oh, absolutely," he answered with great sincerity. "They've always been an inspiration to me, musically and personally."

"Justine, love your new look," called a short woman with a pointed nose. "What's it like to try to take your mother's place in Decapede?"

Justine took a breath. "We haven't even had our first rehearsal yet, so you'll have to ask me later. In the meantime, the guys are being really nice to me." She smiled sweetly.

"Sam, is it true that you wrote 'Creston Gold' for Justine's mother?"

"No, I wrote that one for Rocky Colavito."

"How does it feel to have the fastest-selling single since Eminem?"

"Melts in your mouth, not in your hand."

"Sam, what's the secret of Decapede's success?"

"Ah—" he paused, scratching his clean-shaven cheek. "I'll tell you." He leaned forward to speak right into the microphone. "The secret is that Shelly Griffin lady over there. Wave to the nice reporters, Shelly," he grinned at her.

Do I strangle him or shoot him? Shelly wondered as she waved back and smiled, showing her gritted teeth.

"But, listen," Sam said, addressing the throng with casual aplomb, "I got a favor to ask of everyone. We just got here, and all this is happening real fast. We appreciate all the support and attention. But we need to focus on getting our act together, you know? And I don't imagine the police here enjoy playing cops-and-robbers with all the fans and reporters and stuff. So it would be great if everyone could, you know, just back off from Gruenhaus here and give us a little breathing space for a while."

Justine squeezed his hand.

The reporters all began to shout questions.

Shelly felt that Sam had already pressed his luck too far and stepped in. "You'll have to excuse us," she said affably to the throng, "but these two have to get back to the house for the band's first rehearsal."

Sam and Justine waved goodbye to all their newfound friends and trudged back up the hill.

"That should give them something to write about, no?" grinned Sam, all pleased with his performance.

"I told the band that you're not to talk to reporters except through me!" hissed Shelly. "Keep walking! They can still see us. Weren't you listening?"

"I heard you. I just ignored you. By the way, you're red as a pimp's ride."

54

The First Rehearsal
– June 10, 2006, Mid-Morning –

When the band finally stood in front of their instruments for inspection, Bev looked at her clipboard and then at her watch. "You were supposed to be here half an hour ago," she addressed them sternly. The silence was deafening.

"We were waiting for you to toot," Sam drawled finally. Gavin tried to stifle it but burst out laughing, then Mendel and Aaron, and Justine and Shelly, and Robbie, and finally even Bev herself. Johnny bit his lip to avoid shaking the camera. Dog barked a doggy laugh.

"Okay, okay, listen up," said Shelly briskly, clapping her hands, "you all saw what happened on TV?"

"Sam Miller on Channel Eleven!" said Gavin, clutching his stomach.

"Hogging all the publicity," whooped Aaron.

Shelly waited till they all calmed down. "Can't happen," she shook her head, smiling but serious. "You can't just do what you want like that. Miracles happen, and Sam pulled off a successful imitation of a rational person. But we can't risk a train wreck twice a day! Take some responsibility, people! I'm not your fourth-grade teacher," she said in a voice quite like a fourth-grade teacher's. "Now, when I walk out of here, I want

496

to hear you making music. No more dramas! Do you understand me?"

They all nodded.

"Do you guys need a babysitter?" she asked, indicating Bev.

"Why is she always looking at me?" Sam asked Gavin in a stage whisper.

"And when I say 'you guys,' I'm most definitely including you," said Shelly, eyeballing Justine.

Justine hugged her Pooh mug and smiled innocently.

"Oh, she's one of the guys, all right," said Aaron.

"Bev and I will be right across the hall. Taking care of all kinds of important grown-up business things so you don't have to worry your pretty little heads." They all hooted good-naturedly. "All you have to do is play together nicely." Shelly stood up. "And I expect everyone to cooperate with Johnny."

"Yes, Ms Griffin," said Sam.

"Yes, Ms Griffin," said Gavin, stifling a whoop.

"Yes, Ms Griffin," said Mendel, grinning through his bushy beard.

"Yes, Ms Griffin," said Aaron, flashing his Aaron smile.

"No promises," said Justine.

They all looked at her.

"Kidding, okay? I was kidding!"

Sam let out a long, cascading guffaw.

"Am I supposed to stay here?" Robbie asked his mother quietly.

"Of course," said Mendel, slapping the boy on the shoulder warmly. "We can't play without you."

Robbie lit up as if God had just switched on the sun. He caught Justine smiling, and he lit up even brighter.

"I need him for just one minute," Shelly said to the band, pulling Robbie into the hallway.

Aaron turned to the band.

"So," he said, and smiled charmingly. "A journey of a thousand miles starts with a single step, right? We're good to go?" He looked at the band.

"Before you start," said Justine, looking at him and Gavin and Mendel, "I'd like to say something."

"Sure," said Aaron.

"I just wanted to say that I'm really sorry for what happened last night. And I promise you it won't happen again."

The guys reassured her and told her not to worry. Then they looked at Sam.

He looked at each of them—at Mendel, at Gavin, at Aaron.

"Yeah, what she said," Sam grumbled. "The part about being sorry, anyway. The part about it not happening again—well, you all know what an asshole I can be, so I won't go making any promises about that. But I'm, you know"—he looked at Aaron—"I'll try to behave myself better."

"Listen, Robbie," whispered Shelly, "I'm going to be right here across the hall from you. You are my eyes and ears in there. Anything starts to go sideways, anything at all—you get your buns over to me faster than a speeding bullet. You got that?"

Robbie wasn't sure if her threatening tone was really a joke, but he nodded vigorously.

Aaron began passing out a list of all the songs they ever played. "The ones from the CD are starred," he said. "Let's start with them."

"I'm sorry," said Justine. "I—I don't know most of these. I've only heard the CD a couple of times." She glanced at Robbie.

"Which ones do you know?" asked Aaron.

"Uh, from the CD, just 'Creston Gold' and, uh, 'Different Drum,' uh, and, uh—oh, 'Then He Kissed Me,' kind of. But I'll need the words."

Robbie wrote "Justine iPod whole list" in his Little Kitty notepad.

"Us old guys might not remember all the words either," said Mendel.

"I printed out lyric sheets," said Aaron. "Okay? We're going to start with—"

"I'm sorry, can I ..." said Robbie.

"Yes?" said Aaron. The men and Justine all looked at him.

"Yesterday, Justine had some trouble hearing the other voices," he said hesitantly. "So I thought maybe these would help." He handed her a headphone set.

"I've never used these," she said.

"Just put it over one ear," said Aaron, winking at Robbie. "You'll hear Sam and Aaron's vocals better like that, and you'll follow the band acoustically through your other ear. Try it," he encouraged her.

The girl wasn't completely sure what he meant, but she donned the headphones.

"Can everybody check their mics, please?" asked Robbie. *Me*, he thought, *me telling Decapede what to do. Crazy.*

"Who's taking notes?" asked Shelly.

"My spelling is embarrassing," said Gerald.

"I'm a doctor," said Bev. "Illegible."

"Where's that Brandi girl?" asked the Colonel.

"She said she had to do something," said Shelly.

" 'Had to do something,' " muttered the Colonel as he took the legal pad.

"So, let's start with our big hit," said Aaron with a smile. "Justine, you and I come in on the second verse, yeah?"

The girl nodded.

The first time around was methodical, Sam forgetting to sing into the mic, Mendel needing more bass in his monitor, and Robbie adjusting faders on the console and tweaking settings in Pro Tools.

"Could you hear okay?" Robbie asked Justine.

She nodded. "Thanks."

"Sam, give Mendel eight bars on his solo," said Aaron. "You came in after four."

Sam nodded in agreement.

Johnny opened the door from the hallway and peered in. "Is it okay now?" he asked.

"Sure," said Aaron, as positively as he could.

"Ignore me," he said, as he put down his equipment in the corner, dragged a chair over next to the wall and clambered up onto the deep window sill for a good cover shot of the whole band.

Sam sang it again, drily, watching Johnny move around the room for different angles. But after they got through it without stumbling, Sam closed his eyes and relaxed inside the song, his voice filling it with warmth and love and innocent longing. Johnny zoomed in for a close-up on him, then panned to catch Justine staring enrapt. She saw the camera and turned her back.

"Guys," said Johnny when the song ended, "I promise to shut up, but I have to tell you—that sounded really great. Just great."

Everyone was genuinely pleased and bubbling.

"What's next?" asked Mendel.

"Let's make some noise," said Sam.

Shelly listened politely to Sheriff Aubrey's detailed traffic report.

"Sheriff, I'm sure—"

Shelly listened a while longer.

"Well, Sheriff, I'm afraid I'm not going to be able to solve that one for you. But right now, I'm sitting with the entire management team, and as soon as you let me off the phone, we'll—"

Just then the screech of an electric guitar shook the room.

"Bev," said Shelly, covering the receiver, "go!"

"Hey, guys, we're on the phone with the police," Bev hollered at them. "Could you keep it down?"

"No!" answered Sam and Aaron together.

Bev looked at Aaron, who shrugged and smiled an Aaron smile. "You gotta play rock and roll *loud*."

"That's why we're here," said Mendel.

Gavin gave a drum roll with a rim shot.

They all stared at her.

Bev backed out of the door.

"Okay," said Aaron with a boyish grin, "take it from the top. Gavin?"

Allie came out of the pantry with a mason jar. Winston stopped whipping the batter for her to pour in a few splashes of the amber liquid.

"Wha dat, Miss Allie?" asked Winston.

"My Uncle Herman used to make his own schnapps. Aunt Berta said it gave the fried chicken a little tang," she tittered. "But don't tell anyone!"

"You secret safe wid me," he tittered back.

Aaron ran the rehearsal efficiently, calling the songs one after another—"Peggy Sue," "True Love Ways," "Bring It On Home to Me," "Walk On By"—fielding questions and working out kinks. Sam waited patiently while Robbie fixed a technical glitch or Aaron coached Justine on her harmony parts, which the girl handled reasonably well, except for avoiding Johnny's camera and finding excuses to put off her solos. Aaron got them through most of the songs from the CD in two or three tries, all of them pleasantly surprised at how quickly it all came back—"Like riding a bicycle," said Mendel.

Even Sam didn't look unhappy.

"I got this cousin over in Youngstown. Dennis. Well, he's not a real cousin, his sister is married to—"

"Matt," said Shelly, "take a breath."

Matt took a breath. "He has a roofing and paneling company. Over in Youngstown. He's done a lot of soundproofing."

"The sooner, the better," grouched the Colonel to Shelly.

"We need to find out how long it'll take," she said to Matt.

"A crew of four could do it in two days," said Matt.

"How do you know that?" Bev asked.

"I called Dennis yesterday."

Shelly and the Colonel and Bev and Gerald looked at each other.

"I was helping Robbie measure the room. I figured you'd probably need someone to do the work," said Matt.

"Could a crew of eight do it in a day?" asked Shelly.

He paused to do the math. "Sure," he said.

"Tomorrow?" asked the Colonel, but it wasn't a question.

"On a Saturday, it'd be time and a half," said Matt.

They could feel the floor trembling from the bass guitar.

"Just get it done fast," said the Colonel, plugging his ears.

"Ten guys, double time, six hours," said Shelly.

Gerald raised his eyes from his BlackBerry and winked at her. Shelly smiled back.

Aaron looked at the list of songs. "All right, next, 'Different Drum'! You know the words, right?" he asked Justine.

Justine walked over to him. "Could we maybe do that after lunch?" she asked quietly.

Aaron forced himself to smile. "Sure. Okay then," he said,

shuffling through his folder, 'Cuyahoga Rising.' "

"Gosh, I haven't thought of that song in—well, thirty-six years," said Gavin.

"It's a beautiful one, though," said Mendel.

"Remember it?" Aaron asked.

"Sure," said Gavin, "just a tambourine at the beginning, then I come in with some brushes on the third verse."

"I'm going to try it on violin, if that's okay," said Mendel. "For that meeting-house sound, you know?"

"Great," said Aaron. "Sam?"

Sam was studying his very comfortable new rubber sandals.

"Sam?" said bandleader Aaron. " 'Cuyahoga Rising'?"

"Remind me how it goes?" he said.

Aaron played through a verse, then a chorus, stopping just a couple of times to check a chord or a voicing. Sam tried to follow.

"You wrote it, didn't you?" asked Robbie. Johnny panned the camera to catch the boy hiding something behind his back.

"They say I did," said Sam, and the guys hooted at him. "Sure don't remember the words, though," he said.

"Because I just happen to have this," smiled Robbie, handing out some handwritten sheets of paper, some crumpled, some stained. In bold letters on top was written in a girlish hand, **Cuyahoga Rising**, and underneath that, **Music and Lyrics—Sam Miller**, followed by the lyrics, the I's dotted with little hearts. To the right of the first verse was written "Sam;" next to the second, "Aaron;" to the right of the third, "Kathleen."

They all stared at the sheet.

"That's your mom's handwriting," said Aaron to Robbie.

"They were in the box with the reel-to-reel tapes," he grinned widely.

"I don't know this one at all," sniffled Justine.

"No problem," said Aaron, "I'll sing it today, and you can

learn it from the CD, okay?"

The girl nodded. "Thanks," she said, keeping her back to Johnny.

Brandi entered the office in a clatter of jewelry and platform heels on the sturdy old wooden floors. Matt and Gerald and Charles stared.

"Allie was showing me around the basement," she said. "There's boxes and closets full of clothes going all the way back to the 1930s. In perfect condition!"

"Wow," said Bev and Shelly.

The Colonel made a face and handed her the legal pad with his scribbles. "Well, I wish you would stay here to take minutes next time."

"Oh, and you're going to dress the band for their photo shoot?" said Brandi.

Matt stifled a laugh.

Bev and Gerald exchanged a look and bit their tongues.

I love that girl, thought Shelly.

"*Cuyahoga wash your sins away*," Aaron sang, and played a big final chord. The verses had gone well, with Aaron singing Justine's verse for her and leading the arrangement with his piano, but they couldn't work on the harmonies of the chorus until Justine learned her part. Aaron looked at his list. All that was left were Justine's songs.

"Okay, guys, great," said Aaron, "let's just run them one last time—"

"Enough already," said Sam.

"While they're still fresh," said Aaron. "We need to, you know, *practice* them."

Sam looked at him. "Anybody know when lunch is?"

"Not for another half hour," said Gavin. "But it's only sandwiches."

"Sandwiches?" said Sam, turning to look at him.

"They're preparing something special for tonight," he confided.

"So we have time to run them again," said Aaron.

"Nah, I'm done," said Sam, pulling the guitar strap over his head.

"I think we should run the songs one more time," said Aaron. Johnny framed the two of them facing each other. "That's what we're here to do."

"I'm hungry," Sam said, setting down the guitar.

"We need to get them out of the house tomorrow for four-five hours at least," said Shelly. "And the roads are impossible. Any ideas?"

"We could have a picnic down by the lake," said Allie brightly. "The Bauers used to do that on Saturday afternoons in the summer, back when I was a little girl, have a lovely big picnic for the entire family. We'd grill down there, and everyone would go swimming, and then the men would play baseball and the women would lie in the grass and gossip, and the kids would play. Oh, it brings back such memories!"

"How far is it?" asked Shelly.

"An easy ten-minute walk there, a little longer coming back."

"Can you and Winston handle it?" Shelly asked.

"Oh, sure!" said Allie. "It'll be so much fun. Won't it, Charles?"

"What? Oh, yes," said the Colonel, "absolutely."

"I'll be happy to help," chimed in Gerald.

"Shelly," panted Robbie as he burst through the door, "you'd better get in there."

The room went silent as she entered with a scowl inherited from her father.

"Sit," she said to the band.

"It's okay," said Aaron, "everything's under control."

"Sit," she repeated.

They sat.

"In a circle," she said.

They moved their chairs into a circle.

Robbie hid behind his console.

Shelly sat at the head of the circle.

"Maybe Johnny doesn't need to film this part?" suggested Gavin.

"Johnny stays," she snapped. She leveled her eyes at Sam. "Remember the part where we talked about 'no more dramas'?"

"I remember that breakfast," he winked at Justine.

"Watch it," Shelly warned him.

Sam didn't answer that.

Shelly crossed her legs and folded her arms. "So?" she asked.

"Nothing, really," lied Aaron. "Everything's fine."

She looked at Sam.

"We were just having a dis-*cuss*-ion," said Sam.

Shelly rolled her eyes and looked at Mendel. Johnny continued moving around the circle.

"What Aaron said," said Mendel from behind his beard.

She glared accusingly at Gavin, who smiled back angelically.

And last but not least, she looked at Justine, who scooched her chair right next to Gavin and slipped her hand through his arm.

The bell for lunch pealed through the halls of Gruenhaus.

"All right, then," said Shelly, smiling at her fourth-graders. "We have a lot of business issues to discuss with you," said Shelly, "but we'll do that over lunch."

"Sandwiches?" groused Sam.

Shelly shot him a murderous look, and everyone laughed.

#

"Thanks," Justine said, handing Robbie her headset as he rolled up a long black cable. "It really helped."

"You're welcome," he said without looking up.

"Robbie?" she attempted, but he kept his eyes on the cable, resolved to do nothing further ever again in his life to impinge on her very precious private space.

"I'm sorry for what I said to you last night."

He wrapped the end of the cable around the coil and began to roll up another.

"Robbie," she told him, "don't make this hard on me."

He rolled that coil tighter and tighter, and with it, his resolve to never—

"Robbie, please," she pleaded, touching his shoulder, her voice quavering in distress. He dropped the cable and his resolve and faced her.

"Here," she said, her eyes brimming, and handed him the headphones. "Thank you. They really helped."

"You're welcome," he said as begrudgingly as he could.

"And I'm really sorry for what I said last night," she sniffled.

"It's—you know," he mumbled as the tears melted his anger. "It's okay."

They stood looking at each other awkwardly.

Finally, Justine spoke. "Are you coming in for lunch?" she sniffled.

"I have to straighten up the equipment first."

"Can I help you?" she asked.

"You don't know how to roll cables," he said.

"You're joking, right?" she said, smiling.

"Are you kidding?" he responded, almost smiling. "It's a whole science." And he began showing her how to roll and coil and wind and loop and twist and entwine and wreathe all the errant cables.

"I thought you sang really well," he said.

"No, I didn't," she snapped.

They lined up the rolled cables in an orderly row.

"Thank you," she said. "I'm sorry, I don't mean to snap like that, I'm just—"

"I saw."

"What?" she asked.

"How you were avoiding the camera."

"I wasn't avoiding any camera!" she snapped again.

She re-straightened the row of rolled cables.

She stamped her foot. "I thought I hid it!" she pouted, and began to laugh at herself.

"What's the big deal?"

"I look so stupid."

"You don't look stupid at all."

She looked at him.

"Justine, I—you—you looked—fine," he said. "I mean—you know, *good*," he said, stealing glances at her cutoff shorts and midriff tank top. And he added, after an embarrassing pause, "And you sounded great."

"Bull," she said. "I hardly sang at all."

"You have a terrific voice."

"How would you know?"

"When you sang 'Different Drum' down at Sam's trailer? I'll never forget that. That was just so—so—really, wow."

"Thanks," she said with a small smile.

"If the camera bothers you so much, why don't you just tell Shelly?"

"No!" she snapped. "I swore to her that I'm going to be a good little girl. She said Johnny stays."

"I bet she'd understand."

"No! I don't want to ask her. And don't you go getting any ideas, either, okay?"

"Okay," he said.

"Promise?" she demanded.

"Promise," he agreed reluctantly.

"Pinky swear?" she smiled.

"Pinky swear," he agreed.

And they did.

"Thanks," she said, looking him in the eye.

"That's okay," he glowed. He had no idea what she was referring to, but he didn't care.

"I guess we should go eat," she said.

"Yeah," he said.

Justine grunted, lifting the tray piled with plates and dirty coffee cups.

"I got it," he said, taking the tray from her and walking next to her into the dining room. Dog padded along behind them.

55

Saucy Little Flick
– June 10, 2006, Afternoon –

In the dining room, the guys were clustered around one table with Bev and Shelly, deep in conversation.

"Justine, come, we're waiting for you," said Aaron, indicating the place he'd saved for her at the table. Everyone greeted her with smiles. She slipped into the chair between Aaron and Gavin, leaving Robbie holding the tray with the dirty dishes. He carried it into the kitchen.

"Oh, tanks," said Winston, taking it from him. "You go eat, I take care of it."

Robbie helped himself to a tuna sandwich, potato salad, and an apple from the buffet sideboard. Johnny was sitting alone at the other table.

"Can I sit with you?" asked Robbie, trying to look cheerful.

"Of course," said Johnny. "What, your girlfriend's busy with the band?"

"She's not my girlfriend," said Robbie.

"Well, it's a long summer yet," said Johnny. "Hey, you did a really good job on the board, kid."

"Thanks," said Robbie. Justine was laughing at someone's joke, hanging onto Gavin's arm.

"Seriously, I've been around bands a lot. You were really on top of things."

"Thanks," said Robbie, chewing listlessly. "What did you think of how they played?"

The band members were all listening to Shelly and talking animatedly among themselves.

"I thought they were great. I was really surprised, they fell right into the groove. What did you think?"

"Me? Oh, I don't know. I was sweating, trying to get some kind of acoustic balance. You know."

"Oh, I do. Great job," Johnny said, chewing. "Hey, we got a lot of response to my broadcast on how you found the tapes in your mom's closet and put the song up on the YouTube."

"Johnny," said Robbie, putting down his sandwich, "can I ask you something, just between us?"

"Sure," he said, chewing cheerfully.

"But you have to promise not to say anything to anyone. Promise."

"Between us," Johnny said. "Man to man."

"Maybe you noticed that Justine is a little camera-shy?"

"Hey, kid, I'm not blind." He bit into a pickle.

"I was thinking—they're going to do her songs next. Maybe you could, you know—"

"Get lost?"

"Well, give her a chance to get used to singing without worrying about—"

"You got it, kid."

"*Really?*"

"No problem. I should have thought of it myself. Give the girl some breathing space."

"Are you sure?"

"No big deal."

"But Shelly said—"

"Don't you worry about Shelly. I'll just tell her I have editing to do down in the van."

"Really, you'd do that?"

"Just call me if anything interesting happens, okay?" he

said, stifling a burp, and clapped Robbie on the shoulder. "And don't forget, you promised to teach me how to read emails on this Blueberry thing."

"BlackBerry," said Robbie.

Johnny stood up, and Shelly called him over to the band's table. Robbie sat chewing on his tuna sandwich, which was pretty good, though he wasn't a fan of potato salad, and he sure would have preferred a cola to iced tea. He looked across the room at Justine, sitting and laughing with the band. *Idiot*, he said to himself. *She's a rock star. Did you really think she's going to be interested in you?* Dog bumped up against his leg. Robbie tore a corner off his sandwich and dropped it on the floor. Dog gobbled it down and whacked his tail against Robbie's leg in gratitude. The boy strained to hear.

"Next," Shelly read from her notepad, "Bev and I want to come and listen for a little while, if that's okay with everyone."

"Oh, goodie," said Justine.

"Fine with me," said Aaron, and the band all agreed.

"Next. We're vacating the house tomorrow for some quick construction work on the music room. So we're going to have a picnic. If anyone needs a bathing suit or anything, talk to Brandi."

"Don't forget," said Bev, "photoshoot Sunday. Everyone has to show Brandi what you're planning on wearing."

Sam reached across Shelly to grab the last tuna sandwich.

"Slow down," Shelly whispered to him, "they'll make more."

"Nrgf," he said.

"Next," said Shelly aloud. "Filming. Johnny told me that you were good boys and girl this morning. I want to keep hearing that."

"Yes, Msgz. Grffn," said Sam through the tuna sandwich.

"Shut up, Miller," she said.

"Gimme me that coleslaw over there, will ya?"

"Next," she read from her notebook and smiled slyly. "We got our venue," Shelly said, smiling broadly. "Decapede," she said, aping Johnny's rich bass, "will be giving its one-and-one-time-only show on the Fourth of July at—*Cuyahoga Hollow!*"

"The amphi in the park?" asked Gavin.

Aaron and Mendel looked at each other, impressed.

"I saw Iron Maiden there," grinned Matt, laying down a fresh tray of tuna sandwiches. Sam hooked one before the tray hit the table.

"What is it?" asked Justine.

"It's a music venue, over in Cuyahoga River State Park, just half an hour from here," explained Johnny. "Very classy. Big stage, great acoustics."

"How did we get a place like that at such short notice?" asked Aaron.

"Gerald," said Shelly. "He just got off the phone with the governor. Turns out he's a big fan."

Sam reached across Shelly for the potato salad, but she snatched it first, and passed it to him slowly, and with a courteous smile.

"Grnf," he said.

Justine heard the platform shoes before she saw her. Brandi clomped in, surveyed the band's table, and went to sit with Robbie.

"Last item," said Shelly, "recording. How's it going with that—what did you call it, Pro Tools?"

Justine watched as Brandi leaned across the table, talking to Robbie a mile a minute, looking over at her and the band, asking him questions, clearly trying to pump him for information about the band. Which he seemed to be providing her, because she was hanging on his every word as she leaned way forward, even putting her hand on his arm for emphasis.

"And we can double-track vocals right on the spot," enthused Aaron.

"It's amazing how easy it makes everything," agreed Mendel.

Justine watched Brandi take the big Red Delicious apple from Robbie's plate, delicately remove the gum from her mouth, impale it on her blood-red pinkie fingernail, and take a big, juicy, crunchy bite of the apple. She chewed hungrily as she listened to Robbie's stories from inside the rehearsal room, Justine guessed, because Robbie seemed to be referring to the band members and Brandi kept glancing over at them. Dog nudged Brandi's foot with his paw, and she leaned over to scratch him behind the ear. The dog rolled over on his back in hopes that she would scratch his tummy. She took a last big bite of the apple, handed it to Robbie, and got down on her knees to play with Dog.

"Ordinarily," explained Aaron, "we'd have to send the tracks out for mastering."

"Good dog," said Brandi, rassling roughly with Dog. Justine had only ever petted him or cuddled him gently. But there was Brandi, pulling his jowls and jerking his paws, and he seemed to be having a ball, snarling and sparring. Justine looked at Robbie watching Brandi bent over, with a front-row view of her feminine charms.

"So you can do this remixing yourselves, right here? Justine, are you listening?"

"Where's Johnny?" Shelly asked Robbie as the band plugged in.

"Oh, he told me he had some work to do in the van," said Robbie. He saw Justine looking at him.

"Robbie," called Aaron, "did you finish mic-ing the piano?"

Justine was looking at Robbie in a way that made him more than a little jittery. She reached out and took the headphones he was holding.

"Robbie?" Aaron repeated.

"Yeah, you shouldn't have to bang so hard now."

"Oh, great, thanks. 'Different Drum,' in F, yeah? Everybody ready?" called bandleader Aaron.

Justine looked at Shelly and Bev, and Shelly gave her a wink. Justine tried to concentrate on her breathing, a lesson she'd learned in the pool from her mother.

Gavin waited for quiet. He looked at Justine, who licked her lips and nodded. He smiled back encouragingly, called out "One-two-three-four!" and Decapede began the song, with Sam providing the punch with his rhythm guitar and Aaron supplying the Baroque trills and frills on the piano with his right hand.

Justine swayed right and left through the eight-bar intro, holding the mic and gazing out at the back wall of the stately old music room, then entered perfectly with a warm, confident contralto, "*You and I travel to the beat of a different drum ...*"

She smiled at her audience of Bev and Shelly, and they both smiled back, proud as mother hens.

She laid back on the beat and punched out, "*Oh, you cry-y,*" in a syncopated funk that made Aaron smile broadly at the keyboard. Then, she looped a giant slur down over, "*... and a-a-all you can say,*" and Sam and Mendel grinned at each other. She sang the second verse with even more confidence and control.

"A natural," Bev whispered to Shelly, squeezing her hand.

But then Justine spun to face Robbie and locked her eyes on his.

He stared back slackjawed as she sashayed back and forth saucily, singing to him, with smiling glances at the band.

"*So, goodbye ...*" She turned her back on him abruptly with a saucy little flick of her derriere.

"Where did *that* come from?" Bev whispered to Shelly in wonderment.

"It's called 'hormones,' Dr. Pettiford," Shelly whispered back.

The song ended in a flourish and exuberant applause from

everyone in the room. Justine took a deep, exaggerated bow, clearly pleased with herself.

"Wow," said Mendel.

"I heard worse," said Sam.

"It's easier when I actually know the song," she said, flush with excitement.

"What a shame Johnny wasn't here," fluttered Gavin.

Shelly said nothing, glowing and squeezing Bev's hand.

Robbie swallowed hard, trying to decipher what had just happened.

"Again?" said Aaron.

"Yeah," said Sam.

They ran the song several more times till they all felt they had it locked down.

Shelly and Bev showered Justine with hugs and kisses and praise and excitement and took their leave to get back to business.

Justine was grinning like a Disney princess.

"Okay, the last one!" said Aaron, " 'And Then He Kissed Me.' Kathleen, are you ready?"

"Justine," Gavin corrected him.

"Shit, sorry," said Aaron.

Justine was studying the lyric sheet, so Aaron suggested that they run through it instrumentally first, which they did a few times till it rocked to everyone's great satisfaction.

"What a great song!" said Mendel.

"Justine, want to try it with maracas?" asked Gavin.

"Next time," she said.

"Ready?" Aaron asked.

"Sure," she said hesitantly.

She began to sing mechanically, reading from the lyric sheet.

"Closer to the mic!" called Aaron.

She moved closer, but then the mic kept getting between her and the sheet, and when she wasn't losing her place, her singing was hesitant and thin.

"Kick it up, girl!" Sam told her.

She shot him a dirty look and tried to raise her voice, but it was unsteady and shallow.

"And then he kissed me."

Sam stopped playing, and the song ground to a halt.

"Jesus, you sound like a little girl," Sam growled. "Give it some huevos."

"I'm giving all the huevos I have!" she snapped back.

"Well, you sound like a little girl. Look at the words."

"I am looking at the words."

"Well, sing them like you mean them."

"I am!"

"Well, it sounds like you're singing to a teddy bear!"

"Sam—" said Mendel.

"I don't play with teddy bears," she tried to answer, her eyes watering.

"Hey, Sam, cool it," said Aaron.

"I mean, Jesus, girl, haven't you ever been kissed?" he growled.

Justine's jaw dropped open.

"Sam!" said Gavin in his clipped Quebecois accent. "That really was tactless."

The room fell silent.

And then the hallway door swung open, and in walked Winston, carrying a tray of two bottles of champagne and two rows of elegant champagne glasses, followed by Shelly and Bev and Gerald and the Colonel and Allie and Brandi and Matt and Dog and Johnny with his camera rolling.

Shelly looked at her band and held up a piece of paper with a grin. "This just came in by fax," she said. " 'Creston Gold' entered the charts at Number One."

Everyone looked at each other in stunned silence, then they all began cheering and shaking hands, slapping backs and hugging and jumping on each other.

56

Elmer Fudd

– June 10, 2006, Evening –

During the scrumptious Old German Ohio farm dinner of pan-fried chicken, mashed potatoes, corn on the cob, and fresh greens, everyone chattered excitedly about having a #1 Hit and the music they were beginning to make. Afterward, they filed back out to the front porch, as dictated by Bev's whiteboard.

"Justine, can I talk to you for just a minute?" attempted Robbie, holding a CVS bag.

"Sorry," she said without stopping, "I have to go sit with the band. I'll catch up with you la—" and she was gone.

Idiot, he thought to himself. *Idiot!*

"We're back here?" wondered Mendel aloud, looking at the low wicker table Sam had attacked the night before.

"Getting right back in the saddle?" suggested Johnny.

"Revisiting the scene of the crime?" offered Aaron.

Sam headed for the watermelon cubes, and Justine demonstratively zipped her mouth shut, but was smiling a lot, bouncing and buoyant.

"Allie's idea," said Shelly. "She said it's too pretty out here to let it go to waste."

They all agreed that the evening was very peaceful indeed, with the dusky shadows slowly blanketing the low, sloping green hills of Medina County, the sweet breeze on the stately hundred-year-old porch, and the chirping of the crickets and the burping of the bullfrogs that heightened the quiet all around them.

When they had all poured themselves iced tea or Creston Gold—with Sam sworn to a limit of two and Justine to one, but she declined even that—everyone turned to Shelly.

"Well, guys, how was your day at the office?"

Bandleader Aaron smiled his now world-famous smile and informed her proudly that they'd gotten through all the songs from the CD, that most of them had gone surprisingly smoothly but still needed ironing out. And learning the words by heart, he added, without looking at Justine.

Johnny and his camera followed from a judicious distance outside the inner circle.

Bev explained that in honor of Mendel and the Sabbath, there would be no formal rehearsals for the next twenty-four hours, and that everyone would be spending tomorrow at the lake so that Matt's construction friends could soundproof the music room.

They were all very happy with the idea of a free day for settling in, stretching out, and trying to wrap their minds around their unfathomable new situation.

"So, how does it feel to have a Number One record?" Shelly asked.

They all smiled and agreed that it was pretty amazing.

"Apparently, the CD sold out in all the major outlets within hours," said Shelly. "They're already making a second pressing."

"At a plant down in Dayton," said Bev. "Gerald wanted to have it done in Mexico, but Shelly insisted we do all the manufacturing locally."

"This may cost you guys some money in the long run," said Shelly, "but I got the feeling that you like it this way."

Aaron, Mendel, and Gavin agreed while Justine's foot

stealthily crept across the swing to tickle Sam under the ribs, causing him to swat at her and spill iced tea on his Spice Girls T-shirt.

"He got this plant to agree to work three shifts over the weekend to have another half-million pieces ready for Monday," bragged Bev.

"There's a lot of talk about how Decapede is single-handedly creating a local economic boom," said Johnny from behind the camera.

"Which makes everyone just love Decapede even more," added Shelly.

The guys looked at each other.

"I love it," said Aaron, sincerely impressed.

"We all love it," said Mendel with a broad, bushy smile.

"We all love you," said Gavin with a shy, cherubic smile. "We don't know how to thank you."

Even Sam looked at her and nodded approval.

"Look at her blush!" burst out Justine, pointing, and everyone laughed, including Shelly.

The laughter finally died down to a relaxed quiet.

They sat together, listening to the frogs and the crickets and the creak of the porch swing.

" 'We are Decapede,' " said Aaron softly, astounded.

"We're a movement," said Gavin, shaking his head in bewilderment.

"I'm thinking about running for office," growled Sam, straight-faced.

The laughter cascaded so raucously that Robbie and Dog could hear it, sitting by themselves down on the grass in the dark.

Johnny cleared his throat.

"So," said Shelly, "Johnny needs us to pick up from where we were so rudely interrupted." She turned to Sam with a smile on her lips and daggers in her eyes. He took his very comfortable new rubber sandals off the wicker table and sat up straight in the swing.

"What am I supposed to say?" he grumbled suspiciously.

"What have you been doing for the past thirty-six years?" prompted Johnny.

"Doing?" said Sam.

"I heard you've been taking care of my trailer," said Mendel.

Sam ingested a large piece of watermelon in a single mouthful and ruminated as everyone waited. "It could use a new water heater. Guess I can treat myself to one now."

"You going back there when all this is over?" asked Justine.

"That's a stupid question," he said to her.

"Why is that a stupid question?" she answered right back.

"How the fuck should I know where I'm gonna go?"

"Well, I just asked. You don't have to shout at me."

"Well, it was a stupid question."

Shelly caught Bev's eye and smiled.

"Sam, try not to swear when I'm filming, will you?" said Johnny.

"Oh, sorry," he mumbled.

"So, how's Lake Hope?" Mendel asked.

"The lake? Oh, it's fine, it's fine," said Sam.

"Pretty quiet?" asked Aaron.

"Be surprised," said Sam.

"Like what?" asked Gavin.

"Well, trespassers, for one," he said, eyeing Shelly and Justine and Johnny. "Come crashing in with cameras and Tootsie Rolls and stuff and disturbing the peace of the, uh, residents."

Everyone laughed.

Sam Miller, raconteur, thought Shelly. She looked at him, newly shorn and smiling.

"Summers, there's whole troops of assholes staying at the lodge, making all kinds of noise and mess and racing their boats around like a bunch of—*people*." He spit the word like a curse. "There was this one kid," he continued in a flat voice, "about Robbie's age. I was standing on the shore, watching him and his friends fooling around on an outboard, drunk, throwing beer cans into the lake, swerving and twisting and stuff, faster than they should have been going, and this kid, he just flipped off the back and sank. Never came up."

"You didn't try to save him?" asked Justine.

"He was too far out," said Sam. Then after a pause, he added, "I never learned how to swim."

"You live next to a lake, and you don't swim?" said Bev. "Don't you see the irony in that?"

Sam looked at her sideways. "Never thought about it before."

"So what do you do to keep yourself busy?" asked Aaron.

"Oh, there's always plenty to do. Sometimes I help out with odd jobs at the lodge. And I fish. And I got this garden. Carrots and cucumbers and stuff. That takes some looking after because of the damned rabbits. I gotta watch over that garden like, like old what's his name? From the Bugs Bunny cartoon?"

"Elmer Fudd," said Gavin.

"Right," said Sam, "Elmer Fudd! That's me!" And he started rolling with laughter at the image of himself guarding his carrots with a shotgun and a lisp, while the others looked at each other and wondered why this lunatic recluse was finding it so funny. "Ahh," he said, drying his eyes on the sleeve of his Spice Girls T-shirt.

"Do you get to play any music?" asked Mendel.

"I had this cassette player thing, but it broke."

"He meant if you still play guitar," said Justine, poking him with her foot.

"I know what he meant," said Sam, swatting at her foot and missing. "It ran on batteries, and I used to take it out with me, listen to some music while I was fishing. Turned out the fish liked the music."

"Come on," said Shelly.

"Especially those walleyes."

Aaron caught Shelly's eye. Shelly looked back at him and shrugged.

"But then," Sam explained, "the cassette thing broke, and they stopped biting."

No one knew how to respond, but no one questioned him.

"So what did you do?" prodded Shelly.

"I started taking my guitar out with me. Playing for those damn fish, so they'd come back. I figured if I kept at it long enough, maybe they'd get distracted, take a little nibble of something they shouldn't of oughta." He winked at the camera. "They bit."

Everyone looked at each other.

"So, yeah, I do play some," Sam said to the camera and then turned to Justine. "See? I was coming to the point."

"What sort of songs?" asked Aaron.

"Well, not really songs. Just kind of—"

Justine reached behind Aaron's chair and handed Sam the guitar.

"Nah," he refrained.

"You going to chicken out like a little girl?" she asked in Sam's gruff baritone.

Sam grunted with a half-smile and took the guitar.

He began to play, strumming and picking sweet, melodic lines. The music was tranquil, swaying. He began to hum softly in unison with the melody line, then in wordless syllables in harmony with the melody on the guitar, but it was mostly his fingers caressing the strings with a lover's touch. Here and there, he added *oohs* and *yo-de-wah-ahs*, and a couple of times, "*Moon dancing over the water, fish dancing under the sea.*" It went on for several minutes, and not even his bandmates could figure out if it was a set piece or something he was making up on the spot.

When the music ended, everyone sat in silent acknowledgment. He looked at Shelly with a mischievous glint in his eyes. "That one's a big hit with the walleye."

"Wow," said Aaron. "Where the heck did that come from?"

"Made it up," he shrugged.

They all looked at each other in wonder.

"What?" he asked.

"Open tuning?" asked Mendel.

"Un-huh," said Sam, noodling a lick. "It gives it that nice round sound."

"Maybe we could do something like that with the band," suggested Aaron.

"Why, you planning on taking up fishing?"

Sam Miller, life of the party, thought Shelly.

When the laughter had died down, Mendel turned to her. "Listen, Shelly, it's getting towards sunset. If we're through here, I need to go pray."

Shelly looked at her notepad and then at Bev. "Sure," she said, "go ahead. We're finished."

Mendel excused himself and went off to the far corner of the porch. He took a small black book from his pocket, and began to rock back and forth, mumbling and humming softly.

"I'm going to get myself a cup of coffee," said Gavin. "Anyone want anything from the kitchen?"

"I'll take a cup," said Shelly. "Thanks."

"If you're finished up here," said Johnny, excusing himself, "I have a lot of editing to do," and everyone wished him a good evening.

57

Pairing

– June 10, 2006, Evening –

They sat peacefully, Shelly and Bev and Sam and Aaron and Justine, watching the evening shadows grow over the hills. They listened to Mendel singing softly, "*Bye-de-bye-bye bye*," a mournful, poignant, wordless prayer.

"That's beautiful," said Aaron.

Sam began to hum along softly with Mendel's prayer. Justine smiled at him, curled her legs under her and joined in, the two of them humming the melody together in unison. Then Aaron added a poignant harmony on top.

"Excuse me," apologized Gerald, who emerged holding his hand in the air with a red-spotted napkin wrapped around it. "I seem to have had an accident."

"What happened?" asked Dr. Bev, jumping up to examine the wound.

"I was washing dishes. I guess there was a knife I didn't see—" he winced.

"That looks pretty ugly," she said. "We'd better go dress it. My bag is up in my room."

"Do you think I'll need stitches?" he asked as they walked into the house.

"I'm not sure it was medical attention he was looking for," said Aaron, and Shelly laughed.

They sat without talking, enjoying the lovely evening air.

Sam began to hum Mendel's twisting, tearful melody again, and Aaron began to follow along in harmony. They looked at each other.

"Wanna go inside?" suggested Aaron.

"I gotta pee anyway," grunted Sam as he stood up.

"Hey," Shelly called after him, "you stay out of my office! Use the one by the dining room."

He waved acknowledgment without turning, whether to confirm or to brush her off, she wasn't sure.

"You must be exhausted," said Shelly.

"No, I'm all right," said Justine cheerfully.

"Are you?" asked Shelly.

"Oh, yeah," she said with genuine enthusiasm. "You heard 'Different Drum.' "

"It was great," said Shelly.

"And once I know all the songs better, it'll be fine."

"You feel comfortable? Everything's okay?"

"Oh, the guys are great. They're making me feel like one of the gang. Aaron's really on top of things. Mendel doesn't talk much, but he's really understanding. And Gavin, you just want to hug him, you know?" she said.

Shelly nodded, smiling. "Hey, didn't he say he's bringing coffee?"

"He likes hanging out in the kitchen, I think," said Justine.

"How's Sam doing?" asked Shelly, changing channels.

"I think he's good," said the girl. "He seems to be kind of having fun, you know?"

"Hmm," said Shelly.

"Why 'hmm'?" asked Justine.

"No, I'm just, you know, cautious."

"Don't worry so much. He's okay."

"For now," said Shelly.

"For now," Justine conceded.

"And how's the sound engineer?"

"Who, Robbie? He's doing a really good job, I guess. I mean, I don't know, I'm new at all this. But the guys seem to really like what he's doing. And they're working on Pro Tools, him and Aaron and Mendel, so that they can, I don't know, mix the channels—"

"I mean, how is it going—with the two of you?"

"What do you mean, 'the two of us'?" she asked sharply, sitting up straight. "I haven't even talked to him—"

"Just—okay, that's your business. You're a big girl now. You're a rock star. Just know that I'm here if you need me, okay?"

Justine nodded.

But Shelly couldn't help herself. "Can I say just one thing without you getting all adolescent on me?"

Justine grinned. "Try me."

"Don't ignore him."

Justine stuck out her tongue at Shelly and sat there thinking. Then she got up, gave Shelly a hug, and scampered off down the steps toward the long, sloping lawn.

"That chicken was just scrumptious," said Gavin.

"Thas Miss Allie recipe," responded Winston. "You try my food? Hoo-hoo!"

"Ooh, that sounds exciting."

"What you like?" Winston asked.

"Oh, I don't know. All sorts of exotic things. Indonesian. Indian. Sushi."

"You like cooking?"

"I adore it, but ..."

"Wha but?"

"But my partner, Dale, he has a stomach condition. And allergies. So I don't have much opportunity to, you know, try new things."

"You want, I show you some stuffs."

"Really?"

"Sure, mon. Dats my ting. But you busy all de time wit' de band."

"Oh, I'm just the drummer. I have plenty of spare time."

"You wan help get tings ready to grill tomorrow?"

"I'd love to. If I won't be in the way."

"You can chop vegetable, clean corn—how you say dat?"

"To husk it?"

"Yeah, dat," smiled Winston.

"I think I can handle that," smiled Gavin.

"You do dat good, I show you how you got to seasing de meat."

"Ooh!" Gavin cooed. "Where do I start?"

"First, you putting on a apron. Doan want you get tha pretty shirt dirty."

"Finished praying?" asked Shelly.

"No, I'm just getting started," answered Mendel. "But I think I'll go upstairs. This has been one heck of a day."

"I guess we're all happy to have your Sabbath right now."

"Hey, I wanted to thank you for that. I know it makes your impossible job just that much harder—"

"A promise is a promise," she shushed him.

"Well, thanks, anyway. For everything," Mendel smiled from within his bushy graying beard.

"It was okay, the rehearsal?"

"It'll be fine. Don't worry. We're four solid musicians, we can still communicate musically, no problem there. Aaron runs the rehearsals well. It'll be fine, God willing."

"Amen to that," she said. "Justine?"

"She's very camera shy. But she's—" His eyes crinkled. "Special."

Shelly felt a warm flush.

"Sam? Tell me the truth."

Mendel thought about that for a moment. "You know how you're never quite sure just how much is real and how much is a mask?"

"Exactly!" Shelly agreed. "Bev was just saying the same thing."

"That thing of playing to the fish?"

They shrugged together, and Mendel went off, leaving Shelly alone on the porch, looking out at the last glimmer of this fantastical day.

Sam hummed the melody line. "Play just that, no left hand," said Sam.

Aaron fingered the melody on the piano.

"Make it go up at the end, do it a second time," said Sam, and Aaron did.

"Again," said Sam. He vocalized the wordless melody in a husky, plaintive voice that sounded as if it had been singing this mournful melody for a thousand years. Then Aaron played the verse a second time, adding a harmony a minor third above Sam's lead. "Again," Sam urged him, and sang a counterpoint line intertwining with the melody, and then Aaron added a harmony line to that.

"Something like that?" smiled Sam slyly.

"Wow," said Aaron. "Let me work on that."

Over the raucous belching of the bullfrogs, Robbie and Dog heard Justine calling from the direction of the house.

"Dog? Hey, Dog!"

Neither of them answered. She called again, and Dog finally answered with an unenthusiastic woof.

Justine made out their shapes on the grass and came bouncing down towards them.

"Excuse me, is this seat taken?" she asked.

Robbie shrugged and Dog said nothing, so she plopped herself down cheerily on the night grass next to Dog and gave him a big hug, but he squealed and pulled away towards Robbie.

"Could you hear what we were singing up on the porch? It was so-o-o cool," she jabbered, high on adrenaline. "Mendel was praying and singing this really beautiful melody without words, and then Sam started singing it really softly—"

Dog got up from between them and moved off a decent distance to pee.

"And then Aaron and I joined in, and it sounded *so* good—"

"Great," he said.

"Is something the matter?" She asked.

"You have the Number one record in America—what could be wrong?"

"Well, you sound like something is wrong."

Dog returned and lay down on Robbie's other side.

"No, it's nothing," he said. He wasn't going to open up again. He was done.

"What?" she said, reaching over the space that Dog had left to lay her hand on his forearm. "What is it?"

"I—don't know what it is you want," he burst out. "One minute I'm the most important person in your life, the next minute you don't even know that I'm alive. I know, you're a rock star, and you're on the cover of *16½ Magazine,* and I'm just this—this *dick* you got thrown into this crazy situation with, but you know, I have feelings too, and when you—"

Justine rose towards him on one elbow, put her hand behind his head, pulled his astounded eyes towards hers, and gave him a forceful, determined, closed-mouth kiss on the lips.

Dog watched, panting lazily, his tongue hanging out of the side of his mouth.

Then she plopped back down on the grass. "Hah!" she said.

"Huh?" said Robbie.

"Screw Sam Miller."

The whirlpool inside Robbie's head screeched to a halt.

"What?" said Robbie, realizing that he'd just been used.

"That's the last time he'll tease me about never being kissed!"

"Oh," said Robbie, and realized that he really didn't mind being used like that.

"So, whatcha got in the bag?" she asked.

"Hi," said Aaron, "am I disturbing you? I need that guitar."

Shelly was sitting by herself, staring out at the darkening sky. "Sit with me for a minute?"

"I really want to get back to Sam. We're working on something. Everything okay?"

"Yeah, great. Perfect. You?"

"Are you kidding?"

"How is it going in there?"

Aaron stopped for a moment. "Shelly, I'm a good musician. You know, competent. Predictable. Sam, he's crazy. But, man, his mind operates on a whole different level."

Shelly smiled and nodded. She could see that he wanted to get back to his music.

"Go," she said.

"I'll catch you later," he said as he headed back to the music room.

Shelly moved to the porch swing, kicked off her shoes and put her feet up on the wicker table. She stared out into the darkening sky and tried spotting each star as it emerged.

"Whew," she said.

"Ow!" said Gerald, as Bev swabbed his finger.

"Oh, don't be such a baby," she said.

Johnny heard snatches of a piano and a guitar and peeked

in. Aaron Woodright was playing a sinuous, mournful melody on the piano while Sam Miller picked a flowing figure underneath on the guitar and hummed an intertwining counterpoint line. Johnny raised the camera to his eye, but Aaron looked up and shook his finger.

Johnny closed the door quietly and tiptoed down the hall and around through the common room. One of the doors to the music room was open a crack. Johnny peeked in and saw their backs.

Johnny nudged open the door with his foot and began filming them from a distance, as quietly and unobtrusively as a long-legged fly on the surface of Lake Traumsee.

He filmed for a minute, then slipped out the door as quietly as he'd entered.

The Colonel was pecking with two fingers at the computer in the annex office when Allie walked in.

"Charles?" she said. "I was looking all over for you."

"Oh, hi. I'm getting the contracts ready for Justine's aunt to sign."

"Can't that wait till morning?" she asked. "It's such a pretty night."

"It's taking me a long time," he said. "Shelly always used to do these things."

"Come on," she said, taking him by the hand and pulling him from the desk. "Take a walk with me."

"Hey, Shel?" said Johnny. "No one wants to talk to you?"

"I'm so enjoying the quiet. It's been a while since I've had a minute when the world wasn't spinning around me."

"When you weren't spinning the world," he said.

"Oh, cut it out," she smiled.

Allie and the Colonel ambled down the lawn in the dim moonlight.

"Looks like everyone's pairing up," Johnny said.

"Just you and me left," winked Shelly.

"Hey, are you hitting on me?" joked Johnny.

They both chuckled.

"How's the filming going?" she asked.

"We made a seven-minute trailer. I got this incredible shot of people attacking the van when they were coming in, and then the band waving from the porch down at the journalists—your brilliant idea. Anyway, apparently the network really loved it. They put it on the YouTube. In eight hours, guess how many points?"

"Hits," she said. "How many?"

"Guess!" he said as eagerly as a kid.

"Five thousand," she said.

"31,534! In eight hours! Can you believe that?"

"No," said Shelly thoughtfully, "to tell you the truth, I can't."

They both smiled at the craziness they'd engendered, and Johnny took his leave to go do a final editing session down at the van before bed.

"There you go," said Bev, snapping her black doctor's bag shut. "That should do it."

"You're very good at that, Dr. Pettiford," said Gerald.

"Most of my nursing skills come from mothering."

"And a very good one you are. I'm still waiting to hear the story you promised me about the trip the band took to Columbus."

Bev hesitated.

"But I guess you should be getting back to the band."

She hesitated for one moment. "Not if I have a better offer," she smiled.

"I just happen to know where Winston hides the good

wine. And I hear the stars are out tonight."

"Oh, really?" she said.

Sam found Shelly sitting alone.

"Pretty nice out here, isn't it?" she asked.

"Yes it is," admitted Sam.

"Come, sit with me."

He sat on one of the old wicker chairs opposite her.

"Here," she said, patting the swing seat next to her.

"I'm afraid of you," he said.

"Well, I'm afraid of you, too. Come, sit."

He came and sat.

Winston was standing next to Gavin over a large bowl of prime chopped beef, instructing him in the nuances of seasoning for the grill.

"So you putting some salt, like dis. Den, some garlic powder, like dis. Den, some teriyaki, like dis. An' den, de chop onions. Yeah, das good," he said, smiling his pearly smile right at Gavin. "Now, de barbeque sauce. Juss a little, now. Thas good. And now, de eggs."

Gavin poured the bowl, and the half dozen eggs plopped onto the meat, one after another.

"Now, stick in your hands."

Gavin hesitated modestly.

"Go on, mon. Is good," he encouraged him.

Gavin sank his fingers into moist, red meat and smiled back at Winston.

"Squeeze it," said Winston. "Doan you 'fraid."

Gavin dug his hands into the raw meat up to his wrists.

"Thas right. Now mix it up."

Gavin began to work the meat with his fingers.

"No, man," scolded Winston, "wit' love, mon! Like you

giving you lover a massage. You can do dat?"

"Sure," said Gavin shyly and began to knead the oozing mélange with his dexterous drummer's fingers.

"How's that?" asked Gavin, looking right at Winston, who was standing very close to him, making sure he worked the beef with the proper love.

"So?" asked Shelly.

"What?" said Sam.

"How was it playing with them after all these years?"

"Harder to hit the high notes."

"Very funny. Seriously, how do you like being in a band?"

"They're pretty good."

"That isn't what I asked you."

"What did you ask me?"

"Isn't it better playing with them than you and your damned fish?"

"Fish don't talk so much," said Sam. He took a big cube of watermelon from the bowl with his fingers and shoved it in his mouth whole.

"There are forks there," she said.

"I'm off the clock," he said, sitting back, chewing with a smile.

"How was it with Aaron?"

"He's a pain in the ass," he said, "but he runs stuff pretty good."

Shelly smiled to herself.

"What were you doing in there with him now?"

"Fiddling around with something new." He turned to look at her. "His playing hasn't changed much. Always knows the right thing to do."

"So why do you get in his face about everything?"

"Who wants someone being right all the time?" he snorted with a smile.

This new Sam Miller, sitting on the swing here. With me. Chatting. And smiling. At me.

Aaron was alone at the piano, crafting Sam's noodlings of Mendel's mournful *"Bye-de-bye-bye bye"* into a thirty-two bar theme, working out harmonies.

"Here?" asked Gerald, pointing at a spot in the middle of a wide grassy slope. He was carrying a blanket in one arm and a bottle of wine with two glasses in the other.

"A little further down," suggested Bev, pointing to a place further down the hill, where the lights from Gruenhaus didn't reach.

"How did Justine do?" asked Shelly.

" 'Different Drum' she did fine," said Sam. "All the other stuff, she didn't sing for shit."

"Why not?"

"She wouldn't sing in front of the camera."

"Did you say something to Johnny?"

"None of my business."

"And what's this I heard about you teasing her that she's never been kissed? In front of everyone? Did you really do that, Sam?"

"It's not like it sounds."

"So how is it?"

"She's gotta get toughened up."

"Take it easy on her, Sam, she's just a kid."

"That'll pass," he said.

"Sam, you have to look out for her."

"Me?" he snorted.

"It was your idea to bring her into the band."

Sam pondered that. "Moment of weakness."

"She's a good kid, isn't she?" smiled Shelly.

"Yeah," he said, almost smiling, "she's okay."

He looks softer in the moonlight, Shelly decided.

Allie and the Colonel strolled down the grassy hill in the night. Her arm was wrapped through his, and she gave him a little squeeze.

"You chilly?" he asked.

"No, I'm just fine," she said. "You?"

"Oh, I'm fine. Fine."

"That thing about fair prices for all the merchandise and stuff?" Sam said.

"Yeah?" Shelly answered.

"That's good."

"Well, I'm glad you like it."

They sat in easy silence.

"Thanks," he said finally.

"Damn!" said Shelly and gave the arm of the swing a little whack with her fist.

"What?" asked Sam, looking at her sideways.

"Bev and I bet on how long it would take before you said 'thank you' for anything. I said it would take at least a week. It's only been three days. There went twenty bucks."

"I can float you a loan, if you need. Seems I'm rich."

They both chuckled.

"You know you really should talk to a financial consultant about—"

"Oh, shut up," said Sam.

"Don't you tell me to shut up."

"Then don't talk business on such a sweet night."

Sam Miller the romantic. "So what do you want to talk about?"

"Who said I want to talk?"

"You did."

"No, I said I don't want to talk business. That's not the same as saying I want to spoil the evening by chattering."

Shelly smiled in the dark, and they sat next to each other, swinging gently, watching the stars come out, one by one.

"Hey, guys," said Matt cheerfully. "How's it going?"

"Iss good, iss good," smiled Winston. "What you need?"

"Just wanted to get myself a bottle of beer," said Matt.

"In de frigerator. Hey, Matt, you mebbe help Gavin wit' a li'l problem he got?"

"Shoot," said Matt.

"Gavin, he need to buy some clothes. Mebbe you know a place he find sumpin 'round here, you know, wit' style?"

"So whatcha got in the bag?" asked Justine.

"The stuff we bought in Akron," said Robbie.

"God, that was a hundred years ago," she said. They were lying on their backs on the grassy hillside, their hands cupped behind their heads, their elbows almost touching. "I have no idea what we bought."

Somehow the spinning of the earth nudged them so that their elbows actually did brush.

"Come on," she gave him a playful kick. "Let's see!"

He propped himself up on an elbow and dropped the bag between them. He reached his hand in and felt around. "Oh, what have we here?" he said dramatically, and pulled out, with a wave of his hand, a plastic bottle of sunscreen, and she giggled.

He tossed it back in, fished around, and pulled out a closed box of Tootsie Rolls.

"God, a thousand years ago!" she said, propping herself up on one elbow.

His fingers felt her pack of chewing gum, but instead he pulled out the *US Enquirer* with the picture of her from her eighth-grade swimming team.

"Give me that!" she said, grabbing for it, but he held it away from her, and she leaned over his chest, pressing down on him. She grabbed the newspaper and flung it over her head off into the night air. It made a flapping noise as it landed a few feet away in the dark.

Dog barked vigilantly.

Then Robbie reached in and handed her the bag of doggy treats.

"Oh, that's so sweet," she sighed. She could see Robbie grinning in the dim moonlight.

"And this," he said proudly, handing her a dog collar.

"Aww!" she said smiling at him. "Dog, come here." But Dog was on the other side of Robbie and did not budge.

"Move!" she said to Robbie, giving him a playful shove.

"I'm comfortable," he smiled, not budging.

She gave him a little tickle under his arm, and he sat up straight. She leaned against him, her breast pushing against his leg as she reached over him to put the collar around Dog's neck. But Dog resisted, whining and pulling away from her.

Robbie tore open the bag of Greenies, pulled one out and offered it to Dog on his open palm. The dog sniffed it and lapped it in with one swift swoop of his warm, slobbery tongue, chewed loudly, gulped it down, and barked for more.

Robbie and Justine laughed, their shoulders touching. Robbie offered him one more, but kept it inside his closed fist so Justine could collar him. Dog was whimpering and licking and nibbling to get at the Greenie. Robbie studied the dark little hairs on the back of Justine's neck as she leaned forward in her yellow-and-orange-striped tank top to hook the collar around Dog's neck, her breast again pushing up against his leg.

Then Robbie took a handful of the treats, waved them under the nose of the sweet-crazed Dog, and flung them out into the night. "Go get 'em, Dog!" he shouted, and Dog ran off into the night to do just that.

They were sitting close enough to see each other's faces in the near dark. They paused, hesitating.

She swallowed audibly. "What else you got in that bag?" she asked.

Shelly and Sam watched the stars emerging together. Finally, she asked, "How are you doing, Sam?"

"Me? What do you care? You got your dancing bear."

"Now that was just nasty, and I'm going to choose to ignore it."

"I'm sorry," he said after a while.

"There went another twenty," she said, and he chuckled.

They sat listening to the bullfrogs.

"I do care, you know?" said Shelly.

"Do I get a say in the matter?"

"Doesn't look like it, does it? I asked you a question. How are you?"

"What, you mean like my feelings and stuff?"

"Yeah, like your feelings and stuff."

"Yo, Ziggy, Matt here. Oh, man, yeah, crazy. Listen, are you still at the store? Any chance of you opening it back up for one special customer? Oh, just a certain *Gavin Grover*."

He grinned at Gavin and Winston and held up the phone in their direction to hear Ziggy shouting and whooping and jumping up and down. Matt put the phone back to his ear.

"They'll be there in twenty minutes," he smiled and hung up.

"But Shelly said we're not allowed to leave," protested Gavin.

"Go on," said Matt. "It's late, no one's gonna notice."

"It's not an inconvenience for him, this Ziggy?"

"Outfitting Decapede's drummer? Do you know what that'll do for his business?"

Gavin looked at Winston.

"Here, take my truck. The store's over on Market Street this side of Akron. I'll write you out the directions."

Still Gavin hesitated. "The kitchen's a mess."

"I clean up when we come back," said Winston.

"Oh, I don't mind," said Matt, handing Winston the keys and donning an apron. "I'll cover for you. Go!"

Gavin and Winston looked at each other and snuck off into the night.

Sam didn't answer.

Shelly studied him in the moonlight. Brandi had done wonders. His light brown, peppered hair hung nicely just over his ears. And without the stubble on his face, she could imagine him at twenty, singing with all that pent-up passion. *Carnal*, Gavin had called him.

"All these people," said Sam.

Shelly said nothing, hoping he'd continue.

"I'm not used to all the noise," he explained.

"You were pretty loud in there."

"That's not noise. That's music."

"I get that, Sam. I think you're doing a really good job."

"Yeah? Really?"

"Yeah, really. Considering all that's going on here?"

"Even with the thing with Justine last night and everything?"

"Yeah, Sam," she said. She put her hand on his and gave it an encouraging squeeze. "You're doing great."

He looked at her hand and nodded slightly. "I'd say 'thanks,' but I don't want to cost you another twenty."

"You know you can talk to me if you ever need to."

"Yeah," he said. "I know."

"So what are you going to do with all your money?" she asked, taking her hand back.

"Ask me that last week, I would have known what to answer you."

"What's that?"

"A new water heater for the trailer," he said.

"And now?"

"*Nothing's gonna bring me down / Have another Creston Gold,*" he sang softly in his raspy, intimate baritone.

"No, seriously."

"Seriously—you come turning my life upside down, you expect me to know what it all means?"

"No," she admitted, "I guess not."

"What do *you* want?" he asked, looking out into the night at the faint shapes of the hills of Medina County.

"It's funny," she said, "when this whole Decapede thing started, someone asked me what my dream was. I didn't have to think twice: To put Decapede back up on the stage. Guess I'll just have to find me another dream," she chuckled.

"What was it before Decapede?" he asked.

"Why, Mr. Miller, are you actually making conversation?"

"You better watch out," he said. "Pretty soon I'm going to sign up for Emily Post."

"I'd pay a lot to see that," she laughed easily, and he grinned, too.

They sat in silence for a long moment.

"So what was it?" asked Sam.

"What?"

"Your dream. Before the band."

She shrugged. "Like any other girl from Warren, Ohio, I guess. A house with a white picket fence. A loving husband to greet me at the door in his apron at five thirty, kiss me on the cheek, and say 'How was your day at the office, honey?' And before I could answer, he'd call upstairs, 'Dave, Ricky, your mom's home, dinner's served.' "

#

Brandi walked into the kitchen to get one of those delicious Red Delicious apples she had tasted at lunch.

Matt was standing with his back to her, wearing earbuds, singing, "*Peggy Sue, Peggy Sue*," horribly out of key. She moved to the side to watch him plunging his hands into the hot, sudsy dishwater, soaping a round white plate over and over, around and around, the suds gushing through his muscular fingers as he massaged the foaming disc, his shoulder blades undulating under the skin-tight We Are Decapede! T-shirt.

Brandi turned and walked out of the kitchen without her apple.

"I don't think anyone's going to notice," said the Colonel to Allie as they strolled serenely over the grass in the balmy night, her arm through his.

"It's hard to keep any secrets around here," she said.

"We can be discreet," he protested.

"No," she said. "It doesn't look right."

"It's the twenty-first century," he said.

"It's Creston, Ohio," she retorted.

"We're not doing anything wrong."

"I'm not having any public shenanigans going on in my house."

He looked up at the stars and pondered that.

"Well, how would you feel about making it official?" asked the Colonel.

Allie looked at him.

"Charles, if you have something to say, come out and say it."

The Colonel took a deep breath.

"How would you feel about ..."

"What?" she asked.

"About us, ah, getting married."

She removed her hand from his arm.

"Say it properly," she said, smiling in the dark.

He grumbled, embarrassed. They stopped walking.

"Allie Bauer," he said ceremoniously, "will you marry me?"

She looked at him.

"I'll think about it," she said.

"What?"

"Thought you'd never ask," she said, slipping her hand back through his arm, and they walked back up towards the house, arm in arm, serene and silent, through the balmy evening.

Shelly and Sam gazed out into the dark sky, at the pinpoints of stars flickering in the warm night.

"Did you hear that?" asked Sam.

"No, what?"

"Bev's whistle."

"Nope, didn't hear anything."

They listened, but the only sounds were the crickets and the bullfrogs from all the way down at the lake.

Shelly curled her legs under her and leaned her head against the cloth padding on the swing. It smelled of the fifties, a warm, lived-in smell.

"What are you so happy about?" grouched Sam.

"Nothing," she smiled.

Aaron was singing a rough version of the new song quietly to himself when a woman's husky voice behind him said, "Excuse me." He turned and saw a tall, handsome woman in a tailored business suit with large gray eyes.

"Omigod," she gasped, covering her mouth with both hands and taking a step back.

"You—ah, what?" he said, rising and smiling.

She pointed at him with one finger, her other hand still covering her mouth. "You're ..."

"Yes, I am," he said, chuckling at this impressive woman's behavior. "Ah, hi. Hello. Can I—ah, er, help you with something? Would you please say something?"

She gave herself a little shake, recomposed herself, and cleared her throat.

"Hi," she said in a suddenly low, resonant voice, stepping forward and taking his hand in a very self-assured grip, "I'm Diane Hobgood."

"Aaron Woodwright," he responded, smiling his world-famous smile, for she was a fine-looking woman. *If this is what stardom is going to be like,* he thought—

"I'm Justine's aunt," she said, smiling back at him. "Kathleen's little sister."

"Whew," he said. "Justine, Kathleen, you. Of course. The congresswoman."

"Cross your fingers. And tell all your fans in Florida to vote for me."

"I have fans in Florida?" he asked.

"And don't think my campaign manager isn't pressuring me to play it up, being Justine's aunt," she said, smiling.

"Sorry, it's going to take me a minute to process this."

"I guess you've been having a lot of those moments recently."

"Wow," he said sincerely, "you have no idea."

They smiled at each other.

"So, ah, can you tell me where I can find my niece?"

"What else you got in that bag?" asked Justine.

"Oh-ho!" he said and proudly drew from the crinkly bag the brand-new iPod 5 he'd so carefully prepared for her, with all the songs from the Decapede CD organized in folders, including out-takes from the original tapes and all the cover versions he could find on Napster of Aaron's list of other songs that the band used to play.

"How does it work?" she asked him, leaning forward to look closely, her bare arm against his.

"See, like this." He pressed a few buttons and showed her the lyrics on the little screen. "You can listen and see the words at the same time. I figured that it would be a good way to practice—"

"It's perfect!" she said, smiling sweetly at him. He could feel her breath on his face, and smiled a broad, geeky smile.

"Look," he said. He put one earbud in her ear, the other in his own, and pushed a button.

"*Well, he walked up to me, and he asked me if I wanted to dance,*" the Crystals came on singing, Justine reading and singing along.

Robbie raised himself up towards her, but she leaned back and began to sing along with the second verse, peering to read the words. She pressed the Stop button.

"This is so cool. It'll really make it easy to learn the words and the parts—"

"I know, that was the whole idea."

"That is so sweet!" she said.

He leaned in to kiss her, but she hung back.

"I already proved my point to Sam," she said with a smile.

"Turn the song back on," he said.

"What for?" she asked.

Robbie reached over and pressed Play, moved his hand to Justine's neck, and pulled her slowly towards him when they both heard a faint "Justine!" from the porch, and they sat up quickly. It was Shelly calling out into the dark.

"Justine, come up here."

58

Sans Trousers

– June 11, 2006, Morning –

"Morning, guys," said chipper Shelly.

"You're up early," said Gavin, who was sculpting fresh, raw ground prime beef with his deft drummer hands and stacking patties neatly in a plastic container, a sheet of waxed paper separating each one.

"Miz Shelly hungry arready?" chirped Winston cheerfully, chopping onions with a fury.

Shelly inhaled the powerful potpourri of kitchen aromas and took a step back.

"No, thanks," she said, swallowing hard to quash a small wave of nausea. "I'm looking for the Colonel."

"Haven't seen him," said Gavin in his apron, kneading and pattying with a steady whoop-BOP-splat.

"Is Allie up?" asked Shelly.

"Oh, she de first one up evvy morning," said Winston.

"She's in the annex," said Gavin, indicating the connecting door.

Shelly knocked, opened the door a crack, and saw her father sitting at Allie's kitchen table, raising a cup of coffee to his lips.

In his white boxer shorts.

He looked at Shelly, frozen, his mouth puckered to sip the

coffee. Shelly stared at him, wide-eyed. Shelly quickly closed the door and her eyes.

"*Delete*," she said to herself. "*Delete, delete, delete.*"

Allie opened the door wearing a faded orange seersucker nightrobe. Her father had disappeared.

"Well, don't just stand there," said Allie, irked. "You might as well come in."

Shelly stepped into Allie's kitchen, her face as red as the Ohio state bird. The image of him sitting there sans trousers was indelibly engraved in her mind's eye.

"I—I—I'm so—I knocked, I—" she stammered.

The Colonel entered the kitchen, wearing pants.

"Good morning, Shelly," he said, his lips iron-tight.

"Um, I was just looking for the papers for Justine's aunt to sign, I wanted to go over them before—"

"Oh, sit down," said Allie, pulling out a chair sharply. She walked to the counter, poured Shelly a cup of coffee, and plunked it down hard on the table.

"I didn't mean to—" she said.

"Well, you're here now," said Allie.

They sat in embarrassed silence. Shelly sipped her coffee.

"You see, Shel," said her father and stopped. "I meant to say something. That I, uh, you know, I've been finding it relaxing here. In the office here. The annex office. To work here. I've gotten everything set up, and in the office over there, there's so many—"

"What Charles is trying to say," said Allie impatiently, "is that he's been spending somewhat more than just working hours in the annex here."

"Oh. Oh! OH!"

"And I told him that it doesn't look right, him being in here like this," she said, annoyed, "but these *men* ..."

Colonel Griffin looked like he was about to sink into apoplexy.

"Oh, Allie," said Shelly, scrambling to find her voice, "don't worry about me, I—"

"Charles, would you say something already?" snapped Allie, piqued.

The Colonel cleared his throat. His voice stood at attention.

"Shelly, I have asked Allie to marry me," he said.

Shelly looked at her father, who had known only duty and work his entire life and monastic widowhood for the last fifteen years. She wiped her eyes, walked around the table to her father, and gave him a big, warm hug and a kiss on the cheek. "Aw, Daddy," she said. She hugged him again and then let him retreat to his chair. As she moved back to her seat, she gave Allie a hug on the shoulder and a peck on the top of her head.

The Colonel cleared his throat again and started to stand up again. "The papers are all ready. They're on my desk here, I'll just—"

"Hey, Dad," she cut him off.

"What?" he said in his military voice.

"Smile."

"What? Oh." He tried unsuccessfully to smile.

"Come on, you can do it," she said, relishing his embarrassment.

"Shelly, can we please be serious here?"

"No. Smile first."

He looked at her, frustrated and consternated.

"Aren't you happy? Dad?"

"Yes," he said grimly, "I am happy."

Allie looked at Shelly and rolled her eyes.

Just as Sam was about to enter the upstairs bathroom, a woman came out wrapped in a towel, her hair and body still dripping from the shower.

Sam stared at her large gray eyes. "Fuck," he said.

Justine's aunt stared at her late sister's legendary lost lover, the face on the current issue of *Cosmopolitan*. "Fuck," she said. She clutched the towel with her left hand and held out her right. "Diane, uh, Brinker."

"Sam Miller," he said, twitching and looking over her shoulder at the bathroom door. "I gotta pee."

Aaron set his coffee cup on a coaster on top of the piano. He loved its touch, this Depression-era Steinway baby grand. He played scales for a good quarter of an hour to limber up, as he had been doing every day since the whole thing began.

He was thinking about Justine's very elegant aunt and how embarrassed she was when she saw him, and he began to doodle a spunky, cheeky melody. "*Pah-peh-de-dah, dah,*" he sang, "*start all over again.*"

"Hey," said Sam to Justine, who was sitting on the porch swing with her legs curled up under her. Then he saw she was listening to a little white contraption with earphones and couldn't hear him. She was mouthing the words to a song. When she saw him, she started swinging her shoulders and singing aloud, "*Well, he walked up to me,*" and smiling a big happy smile.

She removed the earphones.

"You get clothes yet for that photo thing?"

"Un-huh," nodded the girl. "Brandi got me some really cool stuff."

"Oh," he said and stood there.

"What?" she asked.

"Nothing," he said, but just continued standing.

"*What?*" she asked.

"I gotta get clothes from her," he said.

"So?"

"They're in the basement."

"I know. There's tons of old clothes down there."

Still he stood there.

"What?" asked Justine, but he couldn't answer. "Jeez, Sam, talk!"

"Would you come down there with me?" he blurted out.

Her first impulse was to laugh, but she caught herself.

"Are you afraid of the dark?" she asked gravely.

"No, I'm afraid of that Brandi," he said.

"Sure," she said, bouncing up from the swing and slipping on her flip-flops. She grabbed Sam by his arm, calling, "Hey, Robbie, c'mere!" as she pulled Sam towards the basement stairs.

"Where are we going?" asked Robbie, running to catch up.

"On an adventure," she said in a spooky voice. "Clothes shopping in the deep, dark basement."

They walked down a long, dark corridor, Justine tugging Sam with Robbie close behind, towards the lighted room at the end, where they found Brandi bending over and into a large cardboard box. Robbie leaned forward to see, but Justine moved to block his view.

"Hey, Justine," said Brandi. She stood up and gave the girl a peck on the lips. "How's it going?"

"Good, all good," answered Justine, not looking at Robbie.

"How do those knit tops fit?"

"The red one is perfect."

"Great. Hey, your aunt was just down here. Nice lady."

"What did she want?"

"A bathing suit. Wait till you see what I found her. Okay, Sam, come with me."

"Where to?"

"My torture chamber," said Brandi, pulling him by the wrist. "You kids feel free to look around, see if there's anything that interests you. Just don't make a mess. Come on, scaredy-cat."

She pulled him towards a small, dark inner chamber, but Sam held back until Brandi had flicked on the light.

"See that box?" she asked, pointing at a large carton at the bottom of a stack. "That one. Bring it out."

"Hey, as far as I'm concerned, you can take all these costumes and—"

"Shelly's orders."

"I'm her boss, you know," he said.

"Right," snickered Brandi.

He toted the boxes and lifted the cartons, grunting and glowering at her as she popped her gum, enjoying herself.

"That stuff around your eyes, it's blacker than usual, isn't it?" he asked.

She blew a bubble. "Open it."

He stooped to open the box and lifted a 1950s baseball glove, fitted it onto his hand, and pounded his fist into it. A cloud of dust billowed around him in the dank light. Then he picked up a ball, snapped it into the pocket of the glove sharply several times, and nodded approvingly.

"Made 'em nice back then," he said.

"Look inside, dummy!"

He picked up a mothballed baseball jersey. On the front was an emblem of the Cleveland Indians. On the back, the number 6.

"This is—" stammered Sam. "How did you—"

"You said in that interview of yours that Rocky Colavito was your hero."

"You saw that?"

"It's all over the news."

Sam fondled the jersey gently, blinking rapidly.

"I looked him up on the internet."

"They got Rocky Colavito on the internet?" he asked in true wonder.

Justine and Robbie wandered through the dark, stuffy racks. Justine draped a mink stole seductively around her neck, and Robbie tried on a tough-guy fedora.

"Ooh," she squealed, "gimme, gimme!" She donned it and posed coquettishly.

They forged a path through a jungle of summer jackets and suits and slacks and skirts and shirts before Justine stopped to examine a sleeveless bright green blouse with bold white polka dots. "What do you think?" she asked him, pushing aside the hanging clothes for him to see.

"Nice!" he said, hoping really hard that was the correct answer.

"Turn around," she said.

"What for?"

"I want to try it on," she said, moving the hanging clothes to block his view. "Will you turn around already?"

He turned, demonstratively unwillingly, bumping the hangers apart as much as he could as he turned.

"Stop peeking!" she said.

"I'm not peeking," he protested.

"Yes you are," she said.

"So what if I am?" he said, peeking.

"Well, don't!" she scolded him with a little smile.

Mendel sat in his wicker chair on the front porch, facing out at the fine morning sun. He was holding a little black book and wearing a long white prayer shawl with heavy black stripes and fringes along the sides and a bunch of strings on each corner. His lips moved quickly and silently, as he rocked back and forth in whispered prayer.

"Excuse me, Allie?" said Justine, knocking on the annex door.

Allie opened it. "Well, someone around here knows how to knock. Yes, dear, what can I help you with?"

"This strap is torn."

"My sewing basket is in the closet over there."

The girl hesitated.

"What's the matter, dear?"

"I—I don't know how to sew too well."

"Really?"

"No one ever taught me."

"Well, you just sit right down here, young lady."

59

Vigilant and Shirtless
– June 11, 2006, Morning –

Shelly and Bev reclined side by side on low striped canvas lawn chairs, perched on the grassy slope overlooking the lake. Shelly was wearing a light tunic with long sleeves against the sun in the shade of a wide umbrella, pecking at her laptop like a hyperactive sparrow. Bev was broiling herself in a stylish Californian tankini, a thick layer of sunscreen, a nose guard, and her whistle on its lanyard.

Down by the picnic tables, in the shade of a towering sycamore, Allie was laying out *le dejeuner sur l'herbe* while Winston and Gavin were grilling and grinning. Out past them, Diane and Justine were sitting under a smaller tree, chattering and laughing, blind to the world. Justine was wearing her teeny cutoff shorts and a We Are Decapede! T-shirt tied up at the midriff. Diane was in the swimsuit Brandi had found in the basement, a bright green WWII-era affair tied at the nape of the neck, which somehow looked elegant and contemporary on her.

"What do you make of Aunt Diane?" asked Bev.

"I guess they're pretty close," said Shelly, her nails clicking on the keyboard.

"It must have been hard for her to take on a teenager all of a sudden," said Bev.

Shelly stopped typing to look at them chitting and chatting, then went back to the daily financials.

In the lake, Brandi was swimming in long, steady strokes out to the raft and back, while Matt watched from the lifeguard tower, vigilant and shirtless.

On a flat field off to their left, the men were playing catch with some old baseball equipment Sam had dragged up from the basement. Robbie fungoed a high pop fly which Johnny circled under, waving everyone else off, but it fell behind him, and Sam and Mendel collapsed on the grass in laughter.

"You had no idea they were, you know, ah, cohabiting?" asked Bev.

Shelly nodded.

"Did you hear what I asked you?" Bev repeated.

She finished typing the sentence and looked up. "I'm sorry, what?" she said.

"I asked how you didn't get that your father and Allie were—"

"Well, I have been kind of busy, you know," she answered.

"It was pretty obvious to everyone else," said Bev, but Shelly's eyes were back on the screen. "Are you listening to me?"

"Yes, I'm listening," said Shelly typing. "It was obvious to everyone else. I don't know. My mind is exploding here from—things."

"So close it."

"I can't. I have eighty-two emails that I need to answer."

Bev propped herself up on her elbow, reached over and pulled the computer from Shelly's lap, snapped it shut, and lay it on the ground where Shelly couldn't reach it.

"Hey!" said Shelly.

"Doctor's orders," said Bev.

"Would you please give it back?"

Bev put on her serious voice. "As your physician, I am ordering you to give your mind a break."

"I have too much—"

"You know what they say about all work and no play?" Bev lay back down in the warm sun, stretched luxuriously, and closed her eyes.

Shelly gazed across the lake, the dock, the picnic tables, the broad hillside, and the field where the men were scampering around after the ball, except for Winston and Gavin, who were bustling and bumping around the picnic tables. Brandi emerged from the lake, dripping and glistening and jiggling. She raised her hands to squeeze the water out of her hair, and the baseball game paused.

"So, are you going to tell me how it was?" asked Shelly.

"How what was?" answered Bev.

"I saw you sneaking off into the night with Gerald."

"I'm a grown woman," Bev smiled smugly.

" 'Never again'?" Shelly chided her.

"I still abide by that principle," laughed Bev, "in principle."

Shelly watched Brandi saunter coolly past Matt's tower in her skimpy little yellow bikini.

"Hey, Brandi, do you need a towel?" he called, but she just sashayed on by without noticing.

"Where did it come from, all this, this—horniness?!" asked Shelly.

"Must be something in the water," said Bev, stretching her whole body contentedly in the sun.

"Oh my," said Allie. "You look so different!"

Brandi was still dripping from the lake. The water had washed away her raccoon eyes. All her chrome trimmings were gone, as well as the few clothes she wore. There was no towel in sight, just the mere suggestion of a bathing suit.

"Different how?" asked Brandi.

"Different nice," smiled Allie. "There's a box of Decapede T-shirts behind the coolers," said Allie.

Brandi donned one, having been raised to respect one's elders.

"How was the water?" asked Allie.

"Really nice. Gosh, the lake is beautiful."

"Thank you. Did you know we take the water for Creston Gold from here?"

"I did not know that," said Brandi.

"Around these parts, they say there's something in the water here, that's what makes Creston Gold so special."

"Really?" asked Brandi.

"Yes, that's why my grandfather chose this spot for Gruenhaus. When I was a girl, the entire family would picnic out here Saturdays. Everyone would go swimming, and the men would play baseball, and the women would lie on the grass and gossip, and the kids would play. Oh, what am I rambling on for? Did you need something, dear?"

"I just wanted something cold to drink."

"There's iced tea and beer in those coolers."

Brandi looked around to check that no one was listening. "Is it, like, official?" she whispered.

"Not yet. But I guess everyone knows?" Allie whispered back.

"Duh," said Brandi, popping a perspiring bottle of Creston Gold. "Oh, Allie, I think that's just so great. Aren't you happy?"

"Of course. It's just a little—fresh."

"My gammy got married again at about your age, after she was a widow for a long time, and she always said it was the best time of her life."

"How nice of you to share that."

"And he wasn't half as cute as the Colonel," Brandi winked, and Allie hugged her arm, laughing like sisters. "Anyway, I really do wish you and the Colonel lots of happiness. You both deserve it."

"Thank you, dear, that's very sweet."

#

Shelly was staring at Sam fucking Miller, ex-recluse, running and shouting and grinning and sweating. He sure is fit for a man his age, she thought. Well, living out in the woods ... She drummed her fingers on the wooden arm of the lawn chair. "Can I have my computer back?"

"No," said Bev, basking in the fine June sun. "Did you see the way Diane was coming on to Aaron at breakfast?"

"It looked pretty mutual to me," said Shelly, adjusting the wooden beach umbrella.

"Well, you know," said Bev. "Aaron."

"Aaron," agreed Shelly, and they both laughed.

Aaron tried to move laterally for a slow grounder, but pulled up limping.

"Did you talk to him about his hip?" asked Shelly.

"He has replacement surgery scheduled for next month. It's a pretty simple procedure today."

The Colonel fielded the ball in the outfield and threw it back to Aaron in a long, precise arc.

"Has he changed a lot?" asked Shelly.

Bev mulled that over. She propped herself up on her elbow and looked down at the men.

"It's weird, you know? Seeing him all grown-up. Don't get me wrong—he's still one very fine-looking man. But when I close my eyes, I see him back then. Oh, God, Shelly, he was so hot. I went mushy every time I talked to him."

Bev lay back down on the wicker lounge chair and closed her eyes.

"Was there ever any—"

"Oh, hell no. I was just this little nonentity tagging around. Don't forget, he was a local celeb even before Sam."

Mendel blocked a slow dribbler at third with his chest, picked it up and tried to throw it to Robbie at home plate, but missed him by fifteen feet.

"Know what Aaron said to me yesterday?" asked Bev, her eyes closed to the sun. "He apologized for the way he treated me back then."

"How did he treat you?"

"Polite. But you know. From up high," said Bev.

"He's been very nice to you up here at Gruenhaus," said Shelly.

"Oh, he's a pleaser. And we've outgrown that stuff, haven't we? Shit, thirty-six years."

"So, what's Aaron like?" Diane asked, long and elegant in her Betty Grable swimsuit.

"Diane!" said Justine, crooking an eyebrow in mock disapproval. "I know that tone."

Justine had been her aunt's confidante for four years now, the sounding board for all the ups and downs and ins and outs of her various suitors and squires.

"What tone?" Diane protested unconvincingly. "C'mon, tell me."

"He's really nice. Serious about the work, responsible."

"Good guy?"

Justine thought about that for a moment. "I guess. But if I were married to him, I'd put him on a very short leash."

"Well, I'm not planning on marrying him," said State Senator Diane Brinker Hobgood, smiling.

Gavin was bent over with laughter, watching Winston flipping burgers higher and higher.

"Hi, Mrs. Bauer," said Matt, smiling his Colgate smile at Brandi.

"Why, hello, Matt," Allie answered. "Have you abandoned your post?"

"Nobody's in the water, so I figured I'd take a little break, go play some ball," he answered her, trying to avoid gaping at Brandi's wet white We Are Decapede! T-shirt, "with the guys."

"Matt, while you're here, could you pull those two picnic tables end-to-end? I want everyone to sit together."

Brandi watched him as he dragged the massive old tables together. Shirtless. He wiped his brow and grinned. She put the tip of the perspiring bottle of Creston Gold to her lips and took a deep swig.

"Well, if there's no one in the water, I guess I'll go join the guys," Matt repeated. "Play some ball."

"Do you want me to write you a note?" asked Brandi.

Matt slapped his abs and went off to play ball.

"Might I ask you something, dear?" said Allie.

"Sure," said Brandi.

"Why are you so snitty with that Matt?"

"What do you mean 'snitty'?" asked Brandi.

"You know perfectly well what I mean," said Allie

Brandi didn't reply.

"He really is a nice young man. Good manners."

"Oh, no question about that, he has very good manners," said Brandi.

"He even asked me if he could come to church tomorrow with Charles and me."

"*Well, whoopity doo-dah for him,*" Brandi thought to herself, but she didn't say it out loud.

"And he certainly is good-looking."

"If you like that type," said Brandi.

"What do you mean by 'that type'?" asked Allie.

"Local yokel," said Brandi.

"Oh, now, you know he's just a little shy," said Allie. "He certainly could keep a woman warm on a cold night."

"Allie!"

"What? I'm old, I'm not blind."

They worked in silence, arranging blue-and-white-checkered

tablecloths on the picnic tables.

Brandi tried to crack her gum, but it came out as a fizzled little pop.

"I'm going to take Shelly some iced tea," she said.

"There are pitchers over by the cooler. It's lovely how you take care of her."

"Someone has to. She worries about everyone else."

"Poor girl," said Allie, "she works like a dog."

Allie looked down at Dog, lying underneath the picnic bench, chewing lazily on a large bone from a side of prime sirloin steak. Dog looked up at her and continued chewing.

Shelly watched Sam circle under a high pop-up. He caught it deftly and slung back a bullet, shouting at Matt to put some muscle into it. "And Sam? How has he changed?"

Bev mulled that over. "Back then we didn't interact much. He didn't interact with anyone much. Except for Kathleen. But there was this one incident, I'll never forget it as long as I live. I was bringing the band some food from Pedro's. I think it was their very first rehearsal, because that's when they chose the name, Decapede. Anyway, I was just a gofer, this pipsqueak trailing around them. It was Sam who invited me to stay. That's what I remember about Sam Miller. He's got a really good heart."

"We're talking about the same Sam Miller?"

Bev smiled, her eyes still closed.

Shelly was warm, even under the umbrella. She stared at Sam as he lunged headlong, like a hungry wolf chasing a rabbit, to snatch a liner just before it hit the ground, skidding on the grass. He jumped up holding the ball, shouting and showing everyone that he had come up with it, proud as a prom queen.

"Hey, Brandi," he shouted across the grassy slope, "I got grass stains on my Rocky Colavito jersey!"

"Don't worry, I got magic hands," she called back saucily with a little twitch of her very visible buttocks as she climbed up the hillside, balancing a tray with three glasses and a pitcher.

"And Sam?" Diane probed her niece.

"He's—*different*." Justine spoke slowly. "Like, sometimes he talks kind of—sideways."

"The way he won't look you in the eye? You know, that's certifiable."

"I know. But then, sometimes—it's like he sees *through* things," said the girl.

"You sound like your mom when you say that," said Diane.

Justine told Diane how they'd found him in the woods, how he stared at her like he knew her. "And then, on the first night the guys were here, he was being a real asshole. But so was I, I guess. We were all really, you know, tense. And then there was this whole big fight."

"You mean that clip they showed all over the news of you and Sam on the porch?"

"Oh, you saw that?"

" 'Oh, you saw that?' " Diane mimicked her in a little singsong voice.

Justine fingered the blades of grass.

"What people don't get is how afraid he is. More than me, even. So we've kind of wound up being afraid together." She looked at her aunt. "You know what I mean?"

Matt fungoed a gentle looper towards Gerald, who was watching Brandi walk up the hill and didn't even see the ball sail right past him.

"Oh, you're an angel," said Shelly.

"That's so sweet," said Bev.

Brandi poured the tea into three glasses, each with a slice of lemon and a paper straw. She pulled off the wet Decapede T-shirt, spread it out to dry, and lay next to Bev on the green grass, her pale skin soaking up the fine summer sun after so many nights in the dens of iniquity of Cleveland's nightclubs.

The three women sipped their iced tea and looked out at the men romping around. Sam was wagging the bat over his shoulder. Matt pitched him a smoker, and Sam whacked a long fly ball far over the heads of the outfielders. He jumped up and down in glee, pounding his chest and roaring.

"Bev?" said Brandi.

"Yeah, yeah," said Bev, "I see."

"See what?" asked Shelly.

Bev and Brandi looked at each other.

"How can she be so smart in some stuff and so clueless in others?" Brandi asked Bev.

"Got me," laughed Bev.

"Did you see this?" Brandi opened Shelly's computer and typed something. She held it up for them to see.

It was the cover of People's 'Sexiest Man Alive!' issue with the banner "**AARON or SAM? 20 Celebs Pick Their Favorite Decapede.**" Aaron was smiling his Aaron smile right at the camera. Sam was half-blurred, caught in mid-turn, flashing a suspicious, guarded scowl.

"Read it!" said Bev, sitting up.

"Give me back my computer!" said Shelly.

Brandi sat cross-legged on the grass facing them. "Jennifer Aniston?"

"Aaron?" said Bev.

"Aaron," said Brandi. "Oprah?"

"Aaron," said Bev.

"Sam," said Brandi.

"Give me back my computer," said Shelly.

"Angelina Jolie?" said Brandi.

"Sam?" said Bev.

"Sam," said Brandi.

"Seriously?" said Shelly.

" 'Sam Miller is the hottest man walking the planet today. Except for Brad, of course,' " read Brandi.

Shelly snorted.

"Paris Hilton?" said Brandi.

"Aaron," said Bev confidently.

"Aaron," said Brandi. "Nicole Kidman?"

"Aaron?" said Bev.

"Sam," said Brandi.

"No way," said Shelly.

"Way," said Brandi. "Beyonce?"

"Sam?" said Bev.

"Sam," said Brandi. "J.K. Rowling?"

"Aaron, for sure," said Bev.

"Sam," said Brandi.

"Seriously?" said Shelly

" 'He can park his slippers underneath my bed anytime he wants,' " read Brandi.

"J.K. Rowling thinks Sam Miller wears slippers?" scoffed Shelly. "Tell her he chews on them."

They watched him whack a liner over Aaron's head down the first-base line.

"He's an animal!" protested Shelly.

"Yeah," smiled Brandi.

"Grrr," said Bev.

"You didn't see the cave he was living in!" said Shelly.

"You could use a little caveman action," said Brandi, and Bev tittered.

"He's crazy!" said Shelly.

"He's *Sam* fucking *Miller*," said Bev.

The three of them sipped their iced tea and gazed at the guys.

Sam took his place on the improvised pitcher's mound to

limber up his arm. Matt took the bat and took some practice swings.

"You swing like a fucking golfer," Sam taunted Matt, "Let's see what you do with a moving target." All the guys gave them both a round of Bronx cheers. Matt took the bat, one hand at each end and flexed it behind his neck. Brandi gazed at the ripples of his bare back and pictured him soaping the dishes in the sudsy sink.

The sun was hot, and she swatted a fly on her thigh so hard it left red fingermarks. She stood up. "I'm going swimming," she said, and strutted purposefully down the hillside.

Gerald and Bev waved at each other.

Sam toed the imaginary rubber. He stretched. He wound up tight as a spring and fired an impressively fast fastball down the middle of the zone. Matt swung and whacked a line drive that flew straight at Gerald, bounced out of the pocket of his Herb Score glove and into the bridge of his nose.

"Oh, no!" shouted Bev. She leapt up and ran towards the scene of the accident. She shoved the men out of the way and knelt down next to him.

"Gerry? Are you okay?" she asked anxiously.

"Those damned old mitts," spoke Gerald Bridges stoically, his head in Bev's lap. "They don't have any webbing."

"Shh!" she said. "Lie back. Robbie, go get an ice pack!"

"Where?" asked the boy, frantic.

"From Allie!" she barked at her son, who stumbled as he turned to run and get it.

"Get lost, all of you," she ordered. "Give him some air!"

60

Sur l'Herbe

– June 11, 2006, Morning –

Shelly lay surveying the pastoral scene as the game dissolved. Mendel went off to sit under a tree. Matt returned to his lifeguard's tower to keep both eyes on Brandi and her long, smooth strokes. Aaron and Sam and the Colonel and Johnny went to sit together on the hillside in comfortable manly silence, nursing bottles of cold Creston Gold on the warm summer day, panting and aching and proud of their prowess on the playing field.

The men watched as Brandi pulled herself up onto the raft in the middle of the lake. She lifted her arms to wipe the hair out of her face. Only a sliver and two blotches of sorely stretched yellow polyester came between her and the sun.

They sipped their beers.

"Charles?" called Allie. "Have you finished your beer? Can you come help me here?"

The guys looked at the Colonel. He looked back at them, shrugged, and smiled. "Coming," he called, grunting as he stood.

"Where does a guy take a leak around here?" said Johnny, standing.

Sam looked at him, not understanding the question.

"Behind the boathouse," suggested Aaron.

568

"Ah, thanks," said Johnny, and he trudged off.

"Well," said Aaron, rising as well, "I think I'll take a swim."

Mendel sat in his wicker chair, leaning back against an oak tree next to the lake. He had shed his long black coat and was wearing only black dress pants and a white shirt, with a white serape over his chest with fringes along the sides and a bunch of strings on each corner. He was holding a very large black book, mouthing softly a debate in a foreign language, in a sing-song of ups and downs, punctuated with his thumb.

"Hi, ladies," said Aaron, smiling his Aaronest smile. "Can I disturb you?"

"I doubt you could do that," smiled Diane.

"Sit," grinned Justine, patting the grass.

"Ay! My hip," he explained, sitting. "Nice suit!"

"You like the Betty Grable look?"

"Love it. Even though I'm a Lana Turner guy," he said.

"It was all Brandi could find for me in Allie's basement."

"Yeah, she really likes dressing people," said Aaron.

"And undressing them," said Justine, laughing.

"Juss!" said Diane.

"Rumor has it you swim," said Aaron.

"And who might be the source of that rumor?" asked Diane coyly.

"Oh, a gentleman never tells those things. Do you think you could make it all the way out to the raft?" he asked.

"Hmm," she said.

"She'll kick your ass," said Justine.

"That's the way you talk now?" said Diane.

"It's okay," said Aaron, "she was officially voted in as one of the guys."

"What the heck?" said Diane.

"Come with?" said Aaron to Justine.

The girl shook her head.

"Aw, come on," said Aaron sincerely, but Diane gave him a look, and he shut up.

"Ay!" he said, standing.

"It's his hip," explained Justine. "He's an old man."

"Brat," said Aaron.

"Can you swim with that?" asked Diane, indicating his hip.

"Try me," he said, holding out his hand chivalrously to help her up.

No one was looking, so Shelly opened the laptop, scrolled down and began to read. Kate Beckinsale—Sam. Jennifer Lopez—Sam. Natalie Portman—Sam. Dr. Ruth: "Sam Miller is the ultimate sex symbol for modern women. He feeds their danger fantasy with his animalistic impulsiveness. Think of Lady Chatterley's John Thomas ..."

Shelly pictured Sam languishing naked on her rust-and-butterscotch couch and snapped the laptop shut. She watched Aaron and Diane wading together into the water.

Justine moved out of the shade of the tree, peeled off her We Are Decapede! T-shirt, plugged herself into her new iPod and lay back in the grass to sun herself and listen to the best-selling CD in the entire United States.

"I hope I'm not keeping you away from Justine," Aaron apologized as they waded into the water. "You came up here to see her."

"We were up late talking, don't worry."

They picked their way gingerly over the stones on the lake bottom, some sharp, some smooth.

"Kathleen was a swimmer," Diane explained. "She was training Justine. It was a thing they shared."

Aaron waited, sensing there was more.

"Since she died, Justine doesn't swim."

"Poor kid," said Aaron.

They looked back at her on the shore, lolling on the grass, listening to music.

"Ow," said Gerald, his head cradled in Bev's lap.

"Lie still," she said, applying the cold compress lovingly but firmly.

"With my own mitt, I would have had it," he said.

"Shh," she said, stroking his bald pate. "You know, Gerald, you don't have to damage yourself to get my attention."

"I wish you had told me that earlier," he said, smiling valiantly through the pain.

"Hey, Miller!" Shelly called from under her umbrella to Sam down by the picnic tables, "Bring me a beer!"

He cupped his ear. She called louder, but again he cupped his hand to his ear.

"Pass me another Creston Gold!" she shouted at the top of her lungs, and all over the hillside, the entourage turned their heads to look.

Sam Miller, the most infamous malcontent recluse in the world, just pulled a playful prank on me, Shelly thought and chuckled to herself.

"Queen of Lake Traumsee up here," he said, panting.

"Take a load off," she said, indicating the other recliner.

He dragged it out of the way, pulled the vintage Cleveland Indians jersey over his head, bundled it up for a pillow and stretched out on the grass next to her in the sun.

"You'll get your shirt all wrinkled," she said.

"I got a grass stain on it," he said, "but that Brandi girl can get it clean."

"I can take care of it for you," said Shelly.

"You know how to do that stuff?"

"Yes, Sam, I know how to do 'that stuff.' "

Shelly looked down at him, his tight, sinewy chest shiny from running around in the sun. All those years living out in the woods, eating rabbits and carrots or whatever had sure toughened him up.

She sipped her beer.

Angela Jolie? Seriously?

Okay, there's something appealing about him. Something earthy.

Like walking in mud barefoot.

He was smiling to himself, lying back in the sun, his eyes closed, his brow relaxed, his hands behind his head resting on his bunched-up baseball jersey.

Sam fucking Miller.

Shelly shooed away a fly. "Want my beer? I hardly touched it?"

Sam sat up, took it, and drank down half the bottle. Then he pulled a brand-new Tootsie Roll out of his shorts pocket and began to peel it.

Beer and a Tootsie Roll? Shelly squinched her brain at the thought.

"Where'd you get that?" she asked.

"The girl gave me," he said, peeling.

"Nice of her," said Shelly, smiling.

Sam bit off a chunk with relish.

"She has a name, you know."

"I know."

"You looked like you were enjoying yourself out there."

"What, the baseball?" He considered that. "Yeah. Yeah, that wasn't bad."

"I told you so."

"What?"

"There are things you can't do alone."

He bit a chunk off of his Tootsie Roll and ruminated on that.

All the baseball games that Derek used to drag her to flashed through her mind for a nanosecond and vaporized.

"How would you like a real game? Nine on a side, fastball, with a diamond and everything?"

"Yeah, sure," he said, chewing on the gooey glob.

"I could arrange that."

He stared at her as though she'd just levitated.

"We could mark you out a diamond over there on that field. It's pretty flat. Get Matt to round up some of his friends. I have a sneaking suspicion he could do that."

"You'd do all that for me?" asked Sam.

"Sure," said Shelly, flushing. "Why are you so surprised?"

Sam looked at Shelly and chewed on his Tootsie Roll. He washed it down with the rest of her beer. He leaned back against the foot of Shelly's recliner, looked out at the panorama of the grassy hillside and the lake and the woods beyond, and made a little burp.

Shelly resisted the impulse to scratch him behind his ear.

"Whoo!" said Diane, as she collapsed on the raft.

"Damn, you're fast!" said Aaron, who'd been beaten by two lengths.

"Actually, you're the one with the reputation," she teased.

"Where'd you hear that?" he panted, lying on the raft next to her.

"Johnny did a whole program on you."

"You listen to him?"

"Every word, are you kidding? Haven't you been following?"

"Shelly has us in strict quarantine. No screens, no radio. Just us making music," he said with pride.

"You're kidding!"

"No distractions."

"You do everything she tells you?"

"She's our momma!" he said in undisguised admiration.

"So, ah, what did they say about me?"

Diane chuckled a low little laugh.

"Sam the Man, looking good out there!" said Gavin as he chopped vegetables on the picnic table with a very big knife.

"Yeah, thanks," said Sam. "It's been a while. Hey, careful there." He snitched a sliced carrot. "We don't want no nine-fingered drummers 'round here!"

"You're in a good mood," said Gavin.

"Shelly said she's gonna rustle me up a real baseball game."

"Well, you watch your fingers. They're worth millions."

Winston flipped a burger for a double gainer.

"Something sure smells good around here!" sniffed Sam.

"You put yo teeth back in yo mouth, Samiller," said Winston, shooing him away from the grilling meat with a long, pronged fork.

Sam pulled him over and whispered something to him. Winston nodded and asked Gavin, Allie, and Charles to watch the fort for a few minutes.

Robbie stood staring at Justine lying on her back on the grass, sunning herself, her ears plugged into the iPod he had so fastidiously loaded for her. Her hair was dark and shiny against the green of the summer grass. Her eyes were closed, but her mouth was moving in a whisper.

She was wearing her little cutoff jeans shorts, a less-than-convincing gesture to her dwindling bashfulness, and the top of her little blue two-piece.

He stared long and hard at her bikini top, his eyes running reverently over the curves and shadows—the hillocks of the nubbly blue material, swelling and rising with each mesmerizing breath, the unfathomable, enthralling white skin of the top of her breasts, open to the warmth of the sun and the caress of his eyes. His throat went dry.

He inched forward a step to examine the tiny cracks and shiny planes of her pink lips mouthing the words to the song. *"Lying with you on the ground / Grass and sunlight all around / Nothing's gonna bring me down / Have another Creston Gold."* Her tongue flicked over her lips, moistening them such that they glimmered in the sun. Her flat, delicate stomach rose and fell in a gentle rhythm. Robbie's groin stirred.

"What are you looking at?" she said, sitting up.

"I—I—didn't want to disturb you," he said.

"I was just practicing," she smiled, shading her eyes with her hand to look up at him. "The iPod is great."

If she was flustered by his staring, she was hiding it. She was sitting at an angle that relaxed the pressure of the bikini top, opening to his eyes the entire mound of her breast—even, trying not to stare too hard, the dark crest. He felt himself growing hard. He made himself look out at the lake, but she didn't seem to be noticing, so he stared again, shifting slightly to the left to see past her shoulder and down into the magical shadows. For a short, miraculous moment, the planets suspended their movement in the skies.

She smiled, squinting into the sun, and brushed her hair back out of her eye.

His shorts bulged flagrantly.

"Come, you can practice with me," she said, patting the grass next to her.

Robbie lay down quickly on his stomach.

Matt was watching eagle-eyed over the lake. He leaned forward as Brandi stepped out of the water, the three undulating yellow splotches highlighted against her wet white skin. He surveyed the view from his perch, a wooden tower with a crow's nest, from which he could see the entire lake, the picnic area, the hillside, the woods, and the hills beyond.

All of a sudden, Brandi's head appeared at his feet. Dripping and glistening, she ascended the ladder like a siren emerging from the depths.

"Oh! Ah—" he stuttered, sitting up straight. "Hi," he grinned.

She stood on the ladder, her waist at floor level, her hair dripping on his toes. He crossed his legs.

"You—do you—I have—would you like ..."

She climbed onto his little wooden perch, plucked the towel from his lap and began to dry herself.

Matt watched as she patted and smoothed her very white skin. He took a long gulp from his beer and crossed his legs to the other side.

"I needed some good rays," she explained. "The higher the hotter, right?"

"What? Huh? Right. Closer to the sun. Sure."

"Could you close that umbrella?"

Matt leapt up and climbed up on his chair to fiddle with the mechanism. He saw her watching and turned his back to her to hide the swelling bulge.

"This is the highest spot in the whole county. See, in that direction is Chippewa Lake, about eight miles over, past those hills. And then over there is Ashland. See that little shade on the horizon? And just a ways past that is Mansfield ..."

He babbled on as Brandi spread the towel on the floor of the wooden tower and lay face down. Her back was stupefyingly smooth and white except for the little green tattoo on her shoulder of Animal, the Muppet's drummer. She popped the catch restraining the string of her top, and Matt's breath caught in his throat.

"You got any sunscreen?" she asked, her voice muffled by the towel.

"Uh, sunscreen, yeah, here, I have this one, it only a thirty, but I guess it—"

"Would you please shut up?" she said.

Matt shut up and stared at the contours of her spine, from the neck all the way down to her coccyx, where his eyes rested.

"Well?" she said impatiently in her muffled voice.

"What? Oh. Me? You want me to—" Matt figured maybe he should stop talking. He unscrewed the top of the bronze plastic bottle and squeezed. A line of creamy, thick white lotion spurted out onto his hand.

"How much of this secret sauce does Winston want us to add to the hamburgers?" asked Allie.

"I'm not sure," answered Gavin, turning over the steaks gingerly, one by one. "He'll be back soon. Colonel, do you see the celery salt over there?"

"It's in that box under the table, Charles," said Allie.

"Here you are," said the Colonel.

Gavin decided against making a joke about his Betty Crocker apron.

"You seem to know your way around a piece of meat," said Allie.

"I do love a good steak," beamed Gavin. "To tell the truth, I've missed it. For quite a long time, I was a vegetarian. Well, my partner was. Is. Was/is," he said, shrugging his shoulders.

"No longer a vegetarian?" asked Allie.

"No longer my partner," said Gavin. "We were on vacation out in Colorado when I got the call to come here. There was this ski instructor that Dale seemed to be more interested in than me. We haven't spoken since I got here."

Gavin chose his words carefully, sensing that Allie and the Colonel were less than comfortable talking to someone of his color and flavor.

"Well, you've been pretty busy here," said Allie sympathetically.

"And a lot happier than I have been in a long time," said Gavin. "Winston's been teaching me so much."

"He's a wonder," Allie agreed. "The hands of a master chef."

"Oh, I couldn't agree more," said Gavin.

"Is there anything I can do to help?" asked the Colonel.

"You can put those salad bowls on the table," said Allie. "And, Charles, make sure they all have serving spoons."

Johnny ambled up with his camera slung over his back, sniffing the fleshy fragrance.

"I heard this is where a guy can get a cold beer on a hot day."

"In the cooler," said Gavin. "Not filming?"

"Ah, even Scorsese gets an hour off here and there. Sure smells good," he said, leaning over to inhale the sizzling prime sirloin steak.

"You hold your horses there," said Allie, shooing him away. "Lunch will be ready in just a little while."

"Hey," said Johnny with a big grin, "I understand congratulations are in order."

"Shh!" whispered Allie, checking that the Colonel hadn't heard. "Thank you, but it's supposed to be a surprise."

"Gotcha," he whispered back. "Anyone seen Sam?"

"He went thataway," said Gavin.

"Call of the wild?" asked Johnny.

"I think he wanted to do something he didn't want anyone to smell," Gavin whispered.

"Oh yeah?" said Johnny, and he ambled off in the direction of the boathouse in his shorts, white legs, and gray ponytail, with a Creston Gold in hand and his camera slung over his back.

"If you see Winston, tell him we need him," called Gavin.

Johnny gave him a thumbs-up.

Gavin turned shyly to Allie and the Colonel. "Could I ask you something? I know both of you have business experience. Tell me if this sounds crazy."

"What is it, dear?" asked Allie

"I'm apparently going to have all this money now. And some name recognition, I suppose. And I really don't want to go back to Iowa. I was thinking of opening a restaurant. Here in Cleveland. With Winston as chef."

"Really?" asked Allie.

"To let him go wild with his ideas. Everyone here loves his cooking, I don't see why other people wouldn't as well. A boutique restaurant. Small, for people who appreciate fine cuisine."

"What do you think, Charles?" asked Allie.

"It sounds to me like a sound investment," said the Colonel, greatly relieved to be back on familiar ground. "Have a business as a basis for your financial structure—not a bad idea at all. You need a business plan—I can recommend some people if you decide to pursue that."

Allie looked at her retired-military fiancée, then turned to Gavin.

"I'll tell you, dear, I've seen a lot in my life. And if there's one thing I have learned, it's that you only live once," she said, slipping her arm through the Colonel's, and smiling at Gavin warmly. "You're blessed with health and financial security? Go follow your heart!"

"Oh, thank you," said Gavin. "Thank you so much." He opened his arms and gave Allie a big hug. Then he turned to the Colonel, hesitated, and stuck out his hand to receive the Colonel's bone-crushing grip.

Behind the boathouse, Johnny peeked around the corner, where he found Winston and Sam sharing a Tootsie Roll-sized joint.

He approached, sniffing and grinning.

Winston hid his hand behind his back.

"He was at Woodstock," said Sam.

"Hey, what are you two hoodlums up to back here?" grinned Johnny.

"Oh, just breathing in some nature," said Sam.

"I'm a big fan of nature," said Johnny.

Winston grinned and held out the joint to him.

"That's one big piece of nature," said Johnny in admiration, and took a short, sharp hit, holding it in, rolling his eyes.

"Das how we do in Jamaica," said Winston.

A couple of tokes later, Johnny remembered to tell Winston that he was needed at the grill.

"How you doing?" asked Johnny, holding his breath.

"You know, another day, another hit record," said Sam, and Johnny laughed, coughing and choking on the smoke.

"Pretty cushy setup here," said Johnny, passing Sam the joint.

"Better than a sharp stick in the eye," said Sam, holding his breath.

"What's in here?" asked Johnny, opening the back door of the boathouse a crack.

"Are you sure we're allowed?" asked Sam.

"Man," said Johnny hazily, "you have the number one record in the United States. You can do whatever the fuck you want. Oh, and Japan."

Sam tried to scratch his stubble, but it was gone.

Johnny pushed the door, and it swung open. A dank smell wafted out, but it was too dark to see anything. He fumbled on the wall and found a light switch. He flicked it, and a large naked bulb actually flickered on, revealing a tableau of wonderful things.

Johnny looked at the line of oars hung neatly on the back wall. He ran his finger over one, drawing a line through a thick layer of dust. "Fuck," he said.

Sam looked at the six rowboats perched on racks with pulleys and rollers. He gave a lever a creaky turn, and the pulley began to lower the rack towards the water. "Fuck," he said.

Johnny brushed the cobwebs off a case of Creston Gold. He pulled out a bottle and wiped the dust off the label. It was the original red-and-gold label, the one he had known as a college student. "Fuck," he said.

Sam opened the wooden door of a tall cabinet to find a cornucopia of fishing tackle—elegant old rods standing at attention in orderly rows and tackle boxes full of floats, lures and nets, hooks, lines, and sinkers. "Fuck!" he said.

Johnny blew the dust off an old *Look* magazine with a cover photo of Frank Sinatra and Ava Gardner, then brushed a cobweb off a wooden radio set. "Fuck," he said.

Sam picked up a half-full pack of unfiltered Old Golds and gave a nudge to a dusty wicker rocking chair. "Fuck," he said.

On the lakeside wall was a wide double door. They each pulled back a lever, swung the two doors open, and stepped out onto the wooden dock facing the lake. On the far side, the Decapede team was scattered around, swimming, cooking, and reclining on the hillside. Up the hill in the distance, they could see the screen door of Shelly's office at the side of the house. They gazed at the sweep of the land in front of them, the vivid greens of the grass and the trees, the deep blue of the lapping water, and the placid turquoise sky.

"Know what you could do here?" said Johnny.

"Yeah," said Sam.

And then they heard the squawk of Bev's whistle and people calling "Lunch!"

Robbie and Justine were lying on their sides facing each other in a dip in the grass, secluded behind the maple tree, each with one earbud, singing the Decapede lyrics over and over and smiling, a mere earbud wire apart.

He looked at her lips moving, inches away, and at her eyes looking at him.

"You're looking at me looking at you looking at me looking at you ..."

"Hah," said Justine, moving a millimeter closer to him.

And that's when his mother blew her goddamn whistle for lunch.

61

Le Dejeuner
– June 11, 2006, Lunch –

"Some spread, huh?" said Aaron, spearing a steaming hamburger patty.

"Wow," said Robbie, forking two of them onto his plate.

"Hey, Miller, c'mere, I saved you a seat," called Shelly.

Sam came trotting up, panting and grinning.

"I thought you got lost," she chided him.

"Johnny and I snuck into the boathouse," he said, squeezing in next to her, hips bumping. "They got this whole wall full of old fishing gear, wooden rods, stuff you never see anymore—"

They were squinched together so closely that she could smell him, all warm and outdoorsy. Shelly felt herself blushing, and there was nothing she could do to stop it.

Sam's nose twitched, and his eyes widened at the cornucopia of grilled sirloin steaks and hamburgers and frankfurters, potato salad, baked beans, coleslaw, fresh grilled corn, and sliced tomatoes with onions. He stretched across the table to grab the platter of steaks, and Shelly knew she had lost him.

He kept bumping up against her as he shoveled his plate full, keen and hungry. He saw her smiling at him, grinned back, then bit into the succulent prime sirloin, hot and dripping.

The Colonel tapped with his fork on a bottle of Creston Gold for attention.

Johnny turned on his camera.

The Colonel cleared his throat. "Before we begin, I have an—"

Allie tugged on his sleeve and whispered to him to take off the Betty Crocker apron.

"Before we begin this beautiful meal, I have an announcement I'd like to share with you," he spoke with gravity, at which point Brandi stood up, raised her hands in the pose of a conductor and began to lead everyone in a loud and raucous *"Going to the chapel and we're gonna get ma-a-a-ried!"* Even Dog barked along, and they all clapped and laughed.

"Well, it seems it's impossible to keep a secret around here," said Allie, and everyone laughed again.

"When's the wedding?" asked Diane.

"We'd like to do it as soon as possible," said the Colonel properly.

"Should I bring my shotgun?" said Sam through the steak, and everyone burst out in laughter, even Allie. Shelly turned as red as the Creston Gold label, tears running down her cheeks.

Justine jumped up and ran to give Allie a big hug. Then she planted her feet stiffly right in front of the Colonel, snapped her heels together, and saluted him sharply so that even he broke into a wide smile. Everyone went over to the couple, hugging Allie warmly and giving the Colonel a firm handshake.

When everyone had sat back down, Allie turned to Mendel. "Would you do the honors?"

Mendel smiled through his thick, peppered beard, held up his kosher hot dog bun, and recited a blessing over the food in a foreign language. Everyone said "Amen" happily and began to partake.

Allie smiled at Charles and squeezed his hand under the table. He squeezed back and smiled.

"The food's delicious," he said.

"Well, I'm glad you like it," said Allie. "It's all Winston's work."

"Well, it's delicious."

"Just don't go expecting me to cook like this for you," she cautioned him.

Sam was attacking the mound of meat on his plate, slicing off large chunks of the succulent steak with his knife, spearing it with his fork, and tearing off large bites with his teeth.

"Hey," said Shelly, nudging his shoulder with hers, "slow down. Nobody's going to take it away from you."

"Ynevrno," said Sam, grinning as he chomped.

"I'm so sorry about your nose, sir," said Matt to Mr. Bridges, "I didn't mean to—"

"I'm fine," said Gerald bravely. "The webbing on those old mitts just isn't—"

"Don't worry," Bev reassured Matt, "he's going to be very proud of his shiner." Gerald smiled at her and squeezed her hand under the table.

"It looks like you have some very satisfied customers here," Gavin smiled at Winston, looking down the length of the table.

"Das why I'm here," Winston grinned back.

Brandi sat opposite Matt, watching him eat with athletic gusto. She accidentally bumped his shin with her toe, and he looked up at her. She was holding a frankfurter in a bun loaded with sauerkraut and mustard and ketchup. She looked him right in the eye, lifted the frank to her mouth, opened wide, and took a big, juicy bite. Then, she took a blue paper napkin that matched the checkered tablecloth and daintily dabbed a smudge of mustard from the corner of her mouth.

Matt emitted a little peep.

"Hey, Matt," called Shelly.

"Yes, ma'am," he jerked and turned to face her.

"Hey, watch your mouth, kid!" she chided him.

"Sorry, mm—Shelly."

"This guy Sam here, who just happens to have *the* number one record in the entire US of A—"

"And Japan," added Gerald.

"—expressed an interest in participating in a regulation baseball game, nine on a side, hardball. Now, as far as I remember, you are the community liaison here."

"That's right, ma'am," he said, sitting up straight, "yes, I am."

"Do you think you could possibly prevail upon some of your take-me-out-to-the-ballgame hoodlum friends around here to participate in such an endeavor?"

Matt grinned at her with his limpid blue eyes and his dimples. "You're going to make me the most popular unemployed handyman in Northeast Ohio."

"Maybe we can play against the cops, kick their be-hinds?" said Sam.

"Shelly, do you know how good that would look?" said Johnny. "Team Decapede against the Medina County Police Department?"

"Neat!" said Robbie.

"Oh, cool!" said Gerald.

"I believe the doctor placed you on the disabled list," said Bev.

"Right, of course," said Gerald.

"Million Dollar Hands," Gavin excused himself, wiggling his fingers in the air and grinning angelically.

"Doctor, my hip!" said Aaron.

"Oh, my guys from the Cuyahoga Rapids, they'll be honored to wear the Decapede uniform." Matt turned to Sam. "The cops will never know what hit them." And they gave each other a big grinning high five.

"It's a shame you can't stay over," said Aaron.

"I promised my campaign manager," said Diane.

Aaron stuck out his lower lip.

"You know I'd love to stay," she said, laying a hand on his

arm, "but a woman's got to do what a woman's got to do."

"Everything good?" Winston asked Mendel, who was working on the mound of kosher meat grilled specially for him.

"*Baruch Hashem*," said Mendel, grinning like a big furry bear.

"How's the hamburger?" asked Justine, smiling.

"Delicious," answered Robbie, smiling back.

"I hope you didn't put any onion in it," she said casually.

Robbie continued chewing slowly, processing what she'd said, then gulped and began coughing so loudly that Aaron had to whack him on the back.

"You okay, kid?" asked Aaron.

Robbie nodded, still trying to clear the traffic jam in his esophagus.

"Any idea how it's going up at the house?"

"There's like two dozen guys working really hard, really fast," said Robbie excitedly. "Oh, man, it's gonna be *so* cool."

"We got ourselves a studio?" grinned Aaron, raising his hand to give the boy a fist bump.

"We got ourselves a studio," grinned Robbie, bumping back.

"Hey, Sam," said Johnny, "tell Shelly about the boathouse."

"We fn a ho bnchf fshng—" said Sam through a mouthful of steak and beans and coleslaw and pickle.

"Finish chewing first," said Shelly.

He began to chomp faster to get it down.

"Sam, you'll choke yourself," she said, laying a hand on his arm. "Slow down."

He masticated methodically and looked at Shelly.

"Che-e-e-w," she crooned. "Savor it."

He slowed down and savored it. Shelly was right.

She was wearing a wide, white sunhat over her light, long-sleeved-against-the-sun tunic, her cheeks a cheery red from the food and the bonhomie and the warmth of the sun. She felt a glow at the sight of him eating good food, chewing it well. *When did I become my mother?* She smiled to herself.

"See?" she asked, smiling at him goofily. "Tastes better like that, doesn't it?"

He nodded and swallowed.

"Now say what you wanted to say," she instructed him.

"That old fishing gear down there in the boathouse," he said. "Do you think it'd be okay if I used it?"

"Sam," deadpanned Shelly, "I'll check with Allie. But if you're careful with it, I'm sure there won't be any problem."

She shifted her weight on the hard wooden picnic bench and tucked her leg under her, bumping up against his arm.

"What are you grinning about?" he crinkled.

"Do you think you can get drunk on happiness?" she asked him giddily.

"Look who you're asking," he chuckled. He turned to look at her. "Damn, your cheeks are red!" he said, and returned his attention to the next forkful.

Dog was deep asleep under the table, dreaming about the half-pound of sirloin he had just gorged upon, his doggy tummy stuffed close to bursting.

62

Something in the Water

– June 11, 2006, After Lunch –

After pecan pie and watermelon, Allie shooed everyone away so that she, Winston, Gavin, and the Colonel could clean up without people getting in their way.

"Hey, wanna go fishing?" Sam nudged the dog with his foot, but Dog showed no intention of awakening in the foreseeable future.

Justine and Robbie ran off in the direction of their private corner.

"You just ate!" Bev called after them, and they both waved acknowledgment unconvincingly.

"No! He doesn't need me in his hair!" protested Diane as Shelly dragged her by the arm.

"He doesn't have any hair," said Shelly, pulling and pushing her towards the wide oak tree where Gerald and Bev were sitting together in the shade, holding hands, digesting their picnic feast.

"Gerald, Diane Hobgood," said Shelly. "Diane, Gerald Bridges."

Gerald stood up to shake her hand.

Diane stood a full head taller than him.

"Please, join us," he said.

"I don't want to disturb you," said Diane, shooting a look at Shelly to show him whose idea it was.

Bev gave Gerald a look.

"Don't be silly," he said, "sit."

"How's your nose?" asked Shelly.

"Oh, it's nothing," he said courageously. "People should just stop making a fuss."

"I'd like to say that it's a real honor to meet you, Mr. Bridges," said Diane.

"Gerald, please," he said modestly.

"If I may say so, I think the way you've been pushing back at China—I think that shows real foresight. In another year or two, everyone's going to be kicking themselves that they didn't listen to you sooner."

"I don't know whether to hope you're right or wrong," he said, and Diane laughed at his wit. "I'm going to keep up the pressure until the White House wakes up."

Bev caught herself fingering the whistle hanging around her throat. She smiled when she remembered Gerald tooting it on the lawn under the stars the night before.

Robbie was lying in the grass right next to Justine. "Want to take a swim?" he suggested.

Justine didn't answer, but her smile faded.

"Bigshot swimmer, afraid to get her toesies wet," he goaded her.

"I can beat you," she answered.

"Race you to the raft."

The girl said nothing.

"Or are you afraid that a lowly soundman is gonna kick the ass of the big hot-shit star?" he said, nudging her leg with his foot.

"Cut it out," she said, slapping his foot away.

"Chicken?" he said, tickling her under her ribs.

Justine sat up.

"Chicken?" she sniffed. "*Chicken?*"

She jumped up lithely, popped off her little cutoff shorts, and ran down into the water, squealing at the chill, then called over her shoulder, "Beat me to the raft and you might get a prize." She gave a little bounce and disappeared under the water.

"So," said Gerald, "what's going on with your race down there?"

"Tell me what you've heard," Diane smiled, sipping her iced tea and crossing her Betty Grable legs.

"I know that you were working as an attorney for an NGO helping illegal islanders, that you got elected four years ago to the state legislature, that you have the reputation of being an idealistic, loudmouth, take-no-shit, pain-in-the-ass reformer."

"I'll take that as a compliment," she smiled.

"It was meant as one," he smiled back. "And that you're running for Congress as an independent in the twenty-third district against a Republican who believes the world is flat and a Democrat who has white powder on his nose. And that no one gives you a snowball's chance in hell."

"You have good intelligence, Gerald."

"That's my business," he said with the pride of a five-foot-one tycoon. "And that you're running a campaign on the issues?"

"Yes," she smiled.

"No attacking the opponents, no spice, nothing but *issues?*"

"Yes," she repeated.

"How old school. Skeletons?" he asked sympathetically, a man of the world.

"No!" said Diane emphatically. "I just want to keep Justine out of it as long as possible."

"The press hasn't made the connection yet?"

"Maybe they won't."

"Don't bet on that. She's going to be on the cover of *16½ Magazine* next month. They'll dig up everything."

"How do you know that?" asked Diane.

"I own the magazine," said Gerald. "You really need to control the spin."

"I don't know. I don't want to exploit her."

"That's very admirable, but you've made yourself a public figure. Like it or not, so has Justine. I'm just saying you should tell the story the way you see it. Don't leave it in the hands of others."

Diane pondered that. "But she's so shy," she said.

They looked out at Justine and Robbie, rollicking around in the lake like teenage dolphins on a school trip.

"Shelly, what do you think?" asked Gerald.

Shelly cupped her hands around her mouth. "Justine! C'mere a sec," she hollered. The girl dove smoothly off the raft and swam to the shore in sleek, strong strokes. She came bounding up to them in her little blue bikini, all smiling and glowing. Diane tossed her the towel from around her shoulders.

"Yeah, what's up?" she panted, patting herself dry.

"Nice strokes," said Gerald chummily.

"Nice shiner," twinkled Justine, holding up her fist for a bump

"You should see the other guy," he joshed, bumping her back.

"Justine," asked Shelly, "how would you feel about helping Diane out with some campaign publicity?"

Justine took Diane's iced tea from her hand. "Sure," she said, gulping down the entire glass. "What do you need?"

"Just let Johnny do an interview with the two of you," said Gerald.

"Sure, no prob," she said, the summer sun shining on her wet body.

Gerald looked at Diane. "Ted Turner's been pestering me to get him some exclusive visuals," he swagged. "He'll be happy to run it. Especially in Florida."

Diane smiled and crossed her legs. "That's so generous of you, sir. Gerald," she said.

He pshawed her magnanimously. "Hey, Johnny!" he called.

Johnny ambled over, Creston Gold in his right hand, camera in his left. He stumbled over the root of a tree, and Justine grabbed his arm.

"Steady there," she said. "All good?"

"All mellow," said Johnny with a serene smile.

Gerald pulled Johnny aside. "Listen, we need to get Diane's face on the map in that congressional race down in Florida. Do you think you could whip up a segment tonight? You know, a nice little interview with aunt and niece. Something personal, heartwarming?"

"Groovy," said Johnny. "They're crying for personal stuff about Justine."

"And mention, you know, by the way, that Diane's running for congress?"

"Gotcha."

"Tasteful," Gerald explained. "Wholesome."

"Cool," said Johnny.

"And make sure you get in the angle on the power woman sacrificing her career to take care of her orphan niece."

"Right on," said Johnny.

"Gerald?" called Bev.

"Just a minute," he called back. "And try to get Justine to talk about her tragically deceased mother, working with her old band, her old lover. You know—"

"I gotcha," Johnny smiled serenely. "Tasteful, but meaty."

"Tasteful, but meaty," smiled Gerald Bridges, clapping Johnny on the shoulder. "I love the way you put things."

"Gerald," Bev called more insistently, her lanyard around her neck, "people are going out in rowboats."

#

"I hope I'm not disturbing you," said Aaron.

Sam was leaning back in a rocking chair with a Cleveland Indians baseball cap over his eyes, his feet up on a dock post, and his fishing line lying flaccid in the lake.

"You ain't disturbing diddley shit here," said Sam out of the corner of his mouth. "Damn fish went on vacation."

"Brought you something," said Aaron.

Sam peeked out from under the baseball cap and saw that Aaron was carrying the little antique keyboard and a guitar. He jumped up, the rocker rocking.

"Gimme that," he said, grabbing the guitar from Aaron, sitting back and tuning it deftly. He strummed a few chords and began to pick a sweet, lulling arpeggio.

"I thought maybe you'd want to—"

"Shhh!"

Aaron waited, but Sam just kept picking the same translucent chords over and over. Finally, Aaron shrugged and dragged a dusty old chair out of the boathouse.

"SSHHH!" hissed Sam. Aaron lifted up the chair and set it down opposite Sam, who was still playing the same misty phrase over and over.

"You gotta keep it simple in the beginning, draw 'em in," whispered Sam. "They ain't too sophisticated, musically."

Aaron looked at him.

"They're suckers for hooks," said Sam.

Aaron processed that. "Did you just—"

But Sam just chuckled.

Aaron joined in as stealthily as he could, comping a couple of soft chords here and there. After a few verses, he began to take a sporadic melody line with his right hand, but Sam shushed him.

"You'll confuse 'em," he whispered. Thirty-two bars later, the line jerked erect. Sam thrust the guitar at Aaron and grabbed the fishing rod with both hands to begin a tug of war. Finally, he reeled up the catch and netted it. He set down the pole, reached in, and pulled the hook out of the mouth of a flapping four-pound walleye and then held it up proudly right in Aaron's face.

"Beautiful," lied Aaron.

Sam tossed it in the tin pail next to him, where the poor walleye flapped out the final throes of its fishy little life, lured astray by a song.

"That didn't really just happen, did it?" said Aaron.

"They're back," grinned Sam as he rebaited and recast and settled back into the rocker. "You can play a little fancier now. Just nothing too, you know, scratchy."

Sam wiped his hands on his grass-stained shorts, picked up the guitar, and began to pick the same tranquil, fish-alluring tune he'd played for them on the porch the night before. Again, Aaron comped with chords, and Sam listened closely, working around them, opening his pattern to make room for Aaron's melody, growing and taking shape verse after verse. Sam began to add his *oohs* and *yo-de-wah-ahs*, and then that haunting "*Moon dancing over the water, fish dancing under the sea.*"

Aaron began strengthening the chords in his left hand and gradually increasing the intensity of the right, pushing Sam to begin pounding chords more and more insistently till he burst into a flying line of wordless phrases.

"Again," shouted Aaron, and they moved back through the chords, over and over, working it, kneading it, forging it into a progression, defining the melody, the jumble of music gradually taking shape as a fully formed, wondrous song.

"Not bad," said Sam.

"Not bad at all," said Aaron. "What do we call it?"

"Walleye," said Sam. "From the top."

When the fishing line yanked taut, Sam ignored it and continued his scatting above the music. "He's hooked," sang

Sam, and repeated it over and over, going deeper and higher into the music.

"I'll edit it tonight," said Johnny to Diane. "Gerald said he'll have it on the news in Florida tomorrow."

"That's so sweet of him," said Diane.

"He was showing off for Bev." Johnny winked, and Diane laughed.

"Oh, look," she said, pointing across the lake at the boathouse, where Aaron and Sam were playing. "Can we go listen?"

"You want to leave them alone right now," said Johnny.

"Why?" asked Diane.

"That's where the magic happens."

Allie saw the Colonel looking at Gavin and Winston with discomfort as they rowed by, sitting next to each other to row in tandem, laughing.

"Oh, Charles," she chided him, "it's a new world."

"So it seems," he grimaced.

"Finally," said Shelly, pulling up a lawn chair next to Diane in the shade of the big oak tree right by the edge of the lake.

"Finally," said Diane, "face-to-face, alone, with my niece's kidnapper."

"Speaking of which, did the Colonel sit with you—"

"He barely let me finish my breakfast. Yes, every last signature. By the way, I loved the way you structured everything with Justine's trust. Very generous, very sensitive."

"Thanks," said Shelly. "We try to be fair."

"Justine told me, even about the price of T-shirts."

"Yeah. Well, we don't see any reason to rake people over the coals. That's not what we're about."

"She also told me who that 'we' is."

"Not true. I've been getting a lot of help. Mr. Bridges, the Colonel, Bev, Brandi. Everyone's been really stepping up."

"Speaking of which, congrats on your father and Allie!"

"Oh, thanks."

"Justine told me that you introduced them?"

"Yeah, I did, actually," Shelly remembered, smiling. A hundred years ago. "He was alone for a long time."

"How long have you worked for him?"

"Oh, fourteen years now."

"Except now he's working for you," said Diane with admiration. "How's that going?"

"You know, when you're trying to hold onto a bucking bronco, you don't have too much time to think," she said. Then she added, "He doesn't really understand all this, but he's handling it pretty well. The Army prepares you for that."

"Dat Sam Miller, he changin'," said Winston, looking over at Aaron and Sam playing on the dock.

"He's a different person," said Gavin.

"More happier?"

"I've never seen him so relaxed."

"Dey play good togetter when dey not fightin'?" asked Winston.

"Oh, you have no idea," said Gavin wistfully.

"He one good-lookin' guy when he smilin'," said Winston.

"You should have seen him back then. We were all so young and good-looking."

"You still young an' good-lookin'," said Winston with his sparkling teeth.

"Looks like Gavin's getting along with my Winston," said Diane.

"Oh, he's in seventh heaven," said Shelly.

"Drumming and cooking," observed Diane.

"Drumming and cooking," Shelly repeated, laughing hard. "What do you mean *your* Winston?"

"Don't think you're keeping him here when after all this is over."

"Shh!"

"What?" said Diane.

"That phrase—"after all this is over"—not allowed to use that around here."

Diane laughed. "What's Mendel like?"

"A giant teddy bear," said Shelly, and Diane laughed. "Aaron and Sam kind of rein it in around him, if you know what I mean."

"Hey, Mendel, how's it going?" asked Johnny, sitting next to him.

"Great," said Mendel, closing his big black book. "Take a load off."

Johnny sat next to him on the grass. "You having a good time?"

"Oh, yeah, it's great," he said.

"But?"

Mendel looked at him from within all his bushiness. "Shabbos. I miss my family."

"Yeah, I miss my wife, too," admitted Johnny.

"Well," said Mendel, "it's only for a month."

They looked across the lake at Aaron and Sam playing on the dock in front of the boathouse.

"Woodwright and Miller," said Johnny.

"Yes," said Mendel. "Déjà vu all over again."

"Bring back memories?" asked Johnny.

Mendel watched them.

"Nitrogen and glycerin. Mix them carefully, you get alchemy.

Shake it? Boom." He made the shape of a mushroom cloud with his hands.

"It was always like that?"

Mendel thought about it. "Yeah," he said finally.

"You think you guys are going to make some good music?" asked Johnny, leaning back on the grass.

"Once Justine gets her feet on the ground, I think we'll be fine."

"Do you think she will?"

They both looked at her cavorting on the raft with Robbie. "She'll be fine."

"Remind you of her mother?"

Mendel smiled and reflected on that. "She's got those same eyes."

Johnny nodded. "Other than that?"

"Well, she's still a kid. Kathleen was very—womanly."

Johnny waited patiently. He knew when to give an interviewee room.

"But the way Justine gets to Sam?" said Mendel after a long moment. "That reminds me of Kathleen."

They sat watching the rowboats—Gerald and Bev, Winston and Gavin, the Colonel and Allie.

"Sure is a lot of coupling going on here," observed Johnny.

"Sun, lake, food," suggested Mendel. "Not to mention music, media attention."

"They say there's something in the water here," said Johnny.

"Could be," said Mendel.

63

Start All Over Again
– June 11, 2006, Afternoon –

"It's nice here," said Woodwright, sitting on the dock next to Miller, looking out at the lake and the long hill sloping up to Gruenhaus.

Sam looked at the whole wide panorama. "Nice place for the band to play."

Aaron surveyed the hillside. "Yeah, I can see that," he said. "Know what's been running around my head? That thing of Mendel's."

Sam sang a snatch of the haunting *"bye-de-bye-bye bye,"* then Aaron played the entire melody on the little keyboard with his right hand, precisely, up at the end the first time around, down the second.

"Again," said Sam.

Aaron began to play, but then stopped to listen to Sam sing the mournful Hassidic melody, born of generations of pogroms and poverty and piety. He sang it with his eyes closed, his voice naked.

He finished, and they sat without speaking, listening to the water of Lake Creston lapping at the piers of the dock beneath their feet. Sam got out of his rocker to check the bait on his line, cast again, and sat back down.

#

"I thought you were very nice to Diane," said Bev.

"Glad to help her a little," preened Gerald as he heaved on the oars, but the current or the breeze kept pushing them backward. Bev lay basking in the sun in the bow of the little rowboat.

"My turn?" she asked.

"Your turn," he agreed.

"Mmm—" she deliberated, her finger on her chin, "what was it like being married to that model?"

"Please, not her, anything else."

"You said anything," smiled Bev, running her big toe up his calf.

"Grr," he pouted and caressed her ankle with his hand. "It happened in a moment of weakness. One which cost me an awful lot of money in the end."

"Is she as dumb as they say?"

Gerald pondered that. "Five feet eleven, a body to die for, and dumb as a clam," he admitted. "A clam with a very smart lawyer."

"Shelly, is that my Justine out there?" asked Diane as the girl shoved Robbie off the raft into the lake.

Shelly smiled, sipping her iced tea in the shade of the sycamore.

"Or do you have a la-*bor*-atory in the basement where you transplant victims' brains?"

"Shit, I've been outed."

"I don't recognize her."

"Yeah, a lot has happened," mused Shelly.

"She's told me everything."

"How much everything?"

"She told me how she got stupid drunk on the band's first

night here and acted like a total twat and almost broke up the band before they got started."

"True," laughed Shelly, "but it wasn't all her fault."

"And she told me what happened with Sam and how you held it all together."

"They really need each other. I just, you know, helped them get acquainted."

"How you've been steering her through this whole adventure."

"Steering her? Do you think I know where I'm going?"

"Stop deflecting, Shelly, I'm trying to be serious," insisted Diane. "I remember you sitting in my Florida room—"

"Crying like a baby in front of a total stranger—"

"*One week ago.* Do you get that?"

"No," laughed Shelly.

"Dreaming this crazy, impossible dream, and poof—doing it. Shelly, you have performed a miracle."

"A lot of stuff fell into place."

"Shelly, every day I go toe to toe with those old white men in the State Legislature who think they're entitled to run the world however they see fit. And I hold my own with them because I'm one tough motherfucker. But you? You're ... Superwoman."

"Okay, let's take it down a notch," said Shelly, blushing.

"I'm in a chat room on AOL with other women politicians in the South. Do you know what they say about you?"

"*Me?*"

"You're becoming a symbol."

"Weren't we talking about Justine?"

"She told me how you protect her when she needs it and how you give her a kick in the butt when she needs it."

"I've just been trying to watch out for her."

"Shelly, would you shut up for a minute and listen to me? Do you know what Justine thinks of you?"

"What? We get along okay."

"Do you know what she says about you?"

"That she rues the day I walked in your door?"

"That you're the *strongest* person she's ever met, the *sweetest* person she's ever met, and the *smartest* person she's ever met," said Diane.

"Well, she doesn't get out much."

"Shelly!"

"Justine said that?"

"Her words."

"About me?"

"No one else."

"She's at an impressionable age. Okay, I admit it. I really love that girl."

Diane lay her hand on Shelly's arm. "And she loves you."

"That's what I'm afraid of."

"Of what?"

"She's gone through so much in her life. Before this crazy blonde hurricaned in on her."

"And?"

"I feel responsible! I'm afraid of—I don't know what I'm afraid of. That's exactly the point. I dragged her into this, and I have no idea what's going to happen. I don't want to see her get hurt."

"Shelly, you can't control the future. Not with Decapede, not with Justine. I'm really glad Justine has you."

"Thank you," said Shelly. "That's very sweet."

Diane reached over and squeezed Shelly's hand.

And I'm glad I have Justine, thought Shelly.

"Tell me about the first night Sam showed up at Pedro's," said Gerald, wrestling with the oars.

"Gerald," said Bev, "I told you the whole story last night."

"I know," he said. And then he added sheepishly, "Could you tell it again?"

#

"Can I play you something I've been working on?" asked Aaron.

"Let's hear," said Sam.

"It's nothing deep," said Aaron apologetically, fiddling at the keyboard.

"Let's hear," said Sam.

"Just a rocker. Fun," said Aaron.

"Damn, you talk a lot," said Sam.

"Something like this," said Aaron.

Aaron played if for Sam, a driving, move-your-butt feel-good rocker, mumbling some of the words, playing a bouncy stride left hand, "*Na-na-na-na-na-na, Start all over, Na-na-na-na-na-na, (boom-chuck!) Start all over again.*"

Aaron stopped and looked at Sam. "Well?" he asked.

Sam scratched his jowl and picked up his guitar. "You got a middle part for it?"

"No," said Aaron, smiling like a Cub Scout achieving his first merit badge, "it's brand new."

"Do it in B flat," said Sam, and Aaron showed him the chord progression. "Play the verse again," said Sam.

When he got to the end of the verse, Sam motioned for him to stop and plucked a few notes, then a minor chord, then another, then a third, and then repeated the three of them several times, trying out different tempos.

"Now, tell me about Aaron," said Diane.

"Looks like you don't need any help from me," smiled Shelly.

"He's, ah, married?"

"Quite to the contrary."

"So, he's like—"

"Oh, yeah, completely. Go for it."

"You're not—?"

"Me? Oh, no."

"He sure is pretty."

"Oh, that he is," Shelly agreed.

"You don't have any—"

"Me? Nah. Who has time for that stuff?"

"You'll come with me to church tomorrow?" said Allie.

"Church?" said the Colonel.

"Yes," said Allie, "church. I want to introduce my new fiancé to everyone."

The Colonel said nothing, pulling on the oars in strong, purposeful strokes.

"What's Robbie like?" Diane asked. "Good kid?"

"He was trying to act like a real little punk when Bev brought him here," said Shelly. "Sullen. The kind of face you look at and want to slap?"

"You'd never know."

"He got challenged, he stepped up."

"What's that saying? 'Some are born great, some achieve greatness, and some have Shelly thrust upon them.' "

Justine reached the raft a full length ahead of Robbie. She was holding onto it, panting and laughing, when he caught up.

"You had a head start!" he complained, laughing, giving her a little shove on the shoulder.

"Oh, the poor little boy has an ex-*cuse*!" she shoved him back.

Their hands were holding onto the raft just a few inches apart. Their knees, treading water, kept bumping into each other. Her face was glowing, and the water was dripping down over her smiling cheeks. She brushed the hair out of her eyes. Again, their knees bumped.

"You okay?" he asked.

"Yeah!" she answered, still panting. "You?"

Robbie smiled a big, wide smile, took a deep breath, pushed himself up as high as he could go with one hand on the raft, put both of his hands on top of her head, and pushed her down under the water as far as he could, then scrambled to hide on the back side of the raft, where no one on land could see.

She emerged, splashing and sputtering and laughing and kicking at him.

"Bastard!" she said. She swam to him and tried to grab onto his shoulders to dunk him back, but he held fast to the raft with one hand, and she only managed to get his head underwater for a second.

He came up laughing, shaking the water from his hair and grinning. Their hands were touching on the raft. Their knees were touching under the water. Her breasts brushed against his chest, and then her hips against his hips. And then his hips against her hips. He could feel her breath on his face, still panting from the race. She could feel his breath as well.

And then, somehow, Robbie's desire overcame his apprehensions, and their lips were touching. She tipped her head to the side, and he kissed her deep and long. She began to slip down into the water, and he put his free hand under her behind to boost her up.

"Hey, watch it, buster," she said but made no attempt to move away.

He put his arm on the warm skin of her back to hold her close to him, and kissed her again. He nudged her lips with his tongue, and she hesitantly opened them to receive him. She looped her hand around his neck for support, drawing their loins so close that they both felt his hard-on growing and pushing up against her.

They broke for air, and Justine hoisted herself up onto the raft. Robbie watched her bottom as it rose right past his nose in a splash. She looked at him, leaned back on her hands, and shook herself in the sun like a dog.

"Whoo," she said.

"Did you really like Gavin's idea of opening a restaurant?" asked Allie

"Absolutely," said the Colonel. "He's going to have a lot of money coming in, he needs some good investments."

"Restaurants are notoriously risky."

"I know, but he's got a name. I'm sure downtown Cleveland could do with an upscale restaurant."

"Where you could take your fiancée out to a nice meal sometime," said Allie.

"Of course," said the Colonel, forcing a smile.

Johnny thought he could get a nice panoramic shot of the lake from the lifeguard's tower, so he slung the camera over his back and began to climb the wooden ladder. He poked his head up through the floor and saw Matt and Brandi.

"Whoops," he said, and climbed back down as quietly as he could.

"Where are you?" called Justine as she broke into the air, but Robbie grabbed her ankle and pulled her underwater. She squirmed away from him, and they emerged together, gasping for air and grasping the raft.

"You bastard!" she shouted, laughing, the water splattering off her lips and onto his nose and his eyes, and he tried to kiss her again, but she slithered away, giggling and panting.

"They can see us," she protested.

Jeff Meshel

"No, they can't," said Robbie, trying to grab her underwater.

"Cut it out," she said, struggling without going anywhere, and smiling at him.

Robbie hesitated, confused.

And then she kissed him.

Aaron sang through "Start All Over Again," including Sam's middle section, in his clear, confident tenor. He made up nonsense words for the phrase where they hadn't finished the lyrics—*Ooby cha-cha one more time, oh, my scrambled eggs.*

"Yeah, but then at the end, it should be, you know, grittier," said Sam.

"That's the grittiest I can do without ripping my vocal cords apart," said Aaron. "You try it."

"Nah, it's your song."

"Let's hear."

Just to be cooperative, Sam sang one verse of the lyrics they'd just written while Aaron accompanied him on the dolceola.

"When I sing, it sounds pretty," said Aaron. "When you sing it, it sounds real. That rasp."

"Nah, it's your song, man."

"No, come on, you sing it. I want to try a harmony for Justine," said Aaron, and he began playing the introduction to the song.

"Everly style?" said Sam.

"Exactly," said Aaron.

"It's so bizarre, you know," said Diane.

"What?" said Shelly.

"All these interconnections. Aaron and Sam. Kathleen and Sam. Kathleen and Aaron. Kathleen and me. Kathleen and Justine. Justine and me. Justine and you. Aaron and you."

608

The Greatest Band that Never Was

"There is no Aaron and me," Shelly interjected quickly.

"Sam and you."

"And there certainly is no Sam and me!"

"C'mon, Shelly, seriously?" Diane scoffed. "The way he looks at you?"

"I'm his ... trainer."

"Bullshit. Half the women in the world would give anything to be in your place."

"Hey, Justine!" Aaron called out to the raft where she and Robbie were playing King of the Mountain.

"Aw, leave her alone," said Sam.

"What?" she yelled back.

Aaron mimed playing guitar.

"Aw, crap, I have to go work," she said petulantly and turned to Robbie. She stuck out her lower lip, pantomimed collecting a tear with her fingertips, and moved towards him slowly, deliberately, with the lovelight in her eyes, then shoved him with all her might backward into the lake. She dove off the raft, slick as a seal, and swam right up to the dock. Sam reached down to help pull her up, with her dripping and grinning, and Aaron handed her the towel that was hanging around his neck.

"What's up?" she asked, drying herself.

"Listen to this," said Sam.

Aaron handed her a piece of paper on which he had scribbled the lyrics. "Are your hands dry? That's the only copy."

They played through "Start All Over Again," with Sam singing the melody and Aaron demonstrating Justine's harmony to her. She nodded as she followed, her still-wet brow furrowed in concentration.

"Again," she said, standing behind Aaron to read the lyrics, and sang it through with him.

"Again," she said, looking Woodwright and Miller right

609

in the eye, both her hands holding the towel that was draped around her neck as she sang her part with confidence, barely glancing at the lyrics, with even a touch of bravado.

"So, I was singing my song," said Bev, "and this bunch of frat boys were being pretty rude."

"To you?" asked Gerald, hanging on every word as he struggled with the oars.

"Yeah."

"Like how?"

"Like heckling and stuff. You know."

"If they were here now, I'd break their necks. Okay, go on."

"And he just appeared out of the dark," said Bev, wearily retelling him the legendary incident yet again, "like Zorro or something, and whacked this wrestler with big ears with his guitar case, and a whole brawl started up, like in the old Westerns—"

"Sam fucking Miller!" said Gerald, his eyes glazed with adulation.

"—but then, somehow, Kathleen got it calmed down."

"And then?"

"And then Aaron brought him up on stage."

"Do you remember how he introduced him?"

"Jesus, Gerald, this was thirty-six years ago!"

"Okay, okay." He pulled with all his might on the oars. His muscles were beginning to cramp. "Do you remember the first song he played?"

"Gerald, enough! Could we talk about something else?"

"Just that, please?"

"I don't remember, it was probably 'Peggy Sue.' He used to start with that."

"You're not sure?"

"Look!" she said, pointing behind him at the dock, where

the picnickers were beginning to gather around Woodwright and Miller.

Gerald struggled to turn the rowboat.

"... but de secret is—an' lissen, you can tell no one about dis because iss my family receta secreta, you tell someone, I got must kill you," Winston threatened Gavin, and they laughed so hard that they rocked the boat.

"Oh, look," said Gavin, pointing at Sam and Aaron. "They're starting to play."

"I've been practicing, too," said Justine.

"The breaststroke?" said Sam.

"Very funny!" said Justine, and she kicked him in the shin, sending him into mock shrieks of pain.

"No," she said, "the words to the songs. I know the whole CD."

"My ass, you do," teased Sam.

"Try me," she said saucily, and Aaron began the introduction to "Cuyahoga Rising," and she nailed every single syllable in her solo verse without hesitation.

"Not bad for a first time," said Aaron.

And she stuck her tongue out at him and grinned proudly.

"Oh, look," said Shelly to Diane under the tree, "they're singing."

"Give her something hard," said Sam, jumping into the thumping rhythm on his guitar, pumping fat chords up and down, while Aaron played the famous bum-be-dah-da figure on top with the tinkly dolceola.

"*Well, he walked up to me, and he asked me if I wanted to dance,*" she sang, her eyes looking right at Miller and Woodwright, one hand on her hip, the other beckoning to Robbie, who was watching from the raft. As soon as he saw Justine crooking her finger at him, he dove into the water and began swimming towards the dock, churning the water with all his horny might. Shelly and Diane hurried down the path around the lake towards the dock, right behind Johnny, who was walking as fast as his rubbery legs would take him, camera on his shoulder, already filming.

Justine watched Robbie frothing water furiously as she sang about how the boy in the song looked kind of nice while she twirled the towel around her neck like an ostrich feather.

Winston and Gavin rowed hard towards her, each on one oar.

"Oh, look, Charles," said Allie, "everyone's going over to the boathouse."

The Colonel forced a smile and began to row them towards the dock with precise, efficient strokes of the oars, commander-in-chief of his own little vessel.

Awakened by the hubbub, Dog scrambled to his four feet to chase after Shelly and Diane, who were scurrying along the trail and up the wooden steps to the dock.

The girl sang to the world about how closely they danced, all smiling and proud of herself.

Johnny stood right in front of them filming, Aaron and Sam whooping it up, Justine dancing and bopping and strutting her stuff for the camera like a sixteen-year-old with the world in the palm of her hand and her new paramour paddling through the water towards her like a dolphin calf in heat. She smiled at Winston and Gavin as they pulled up, her hand open on her flat little tummy, and even gave them a wink and a sexy little bump with her hip.

"Isn't she adorable?" said Gavin, and Winston grinned back.

"Oh, come on, Charles, put a little back into it," chided Allie.

"Used up all my energy last night," he countered racily.

"Stop making excuses and row," smiled Allie.

Brandi and Matt peeked over the little wall around the lifeguard's perch to see what the commotion was, but no one noticed them, and their heads disappeared.

"Do you want me to help?" Bev asked Gerald.

"No!" he snapped, straining to straighten the craft.

Shelly slipped her arm through Diane's and laid her head on her shoulder.

As Justine sang the line about the boy walking the girl home, Robbie clambered up onto the wooden dock, dripping and panting and smiling.

Gerald was still in the middle of the lake, struggling desperately to turn the boat around.

Justine tossed the end of the towel to Robbie, who tried to dry his face, but she tugged on it, reeling him towards her as she sang about the starlight. Johnny pushed past everyone for an extreme close-up, right in Justine's face. Aaron and Sam brought the music to an abrupt halt, leaving everyone hanging. Justine kept the beat going with her foot, surveying her audience in silence with a sly smile.

"And then he kissed me!"

Justine puckered up right into the eye of the camera, grabbed wide-eyed Robbie behind the neck and gave him a smack right on the lips.

And that was the picture that appeared the next morning on the front page of the Sunday edition of every major newspaper in the land.

64

Decaheads
– June 11, 2006 –

The sun was sinking, and people were climbing slowly up the hill back to Gruenhaus. Sam was still fishing over by the boathouse. Shelly knew she had all those emails waiting for her in her office, but she walked over to the dock anyway.

"Hey, you," she called over the bullfrogs.

Dog whacked his tail on the wooden dock.

"Hey, you," Sam smiled at her.

Shelly smiled back at him and plopped down in the wicker chair next to him. Dog pawed her leg for attention, so she reached down to scratch him behind the ear.

"How you doing, Dog?"

Dog whacked his tail on the deck and panted.

"How you doing, Sam?"

"Cleaning these up for Winston," he grinned as he inserted the fillet knife into the nether end of the fish, opened a smooth slit up to between its gills, spread the belly open, scooped out the innards with his bare hand, and flicked them into the lake.

"Oh," said Shelly.

"Wanna do one?" he grinned at her, holding the disemboweled walleye up to her nose.

"Very funny." She squinched her nose and shoved his hand away.

"Don't you like walleye?" he laughed, pushing the fish back towards her face.

"On a plate, you—fish-gutter, you! Stop it!"

They settled down and sat side by side, gazing at Justine and Robbie out on the raft, enjoying their last cavort in the fading light. Dog pawed Shelly's foot again.

"Ow," said Shelly, and then she resumed scratching him.

"He's just waiting for the kids to come out," said Sam.

"Hey," Shelly called out to them, "we're packing up."

"Okay!" called Robbie, waving.

"I don't want you kids in the water anymore!"

"Yes, Mommy," called Justine as she shoved Robbie, squawking, into the water and dove in after him.

"Where do they get all that energy?" Shelly asked Sam.

"They'll get over it," said Sam, swigging his beer.

"How're you doing?"

"Enjoying the quiet."

"Quiet?" she shouted over the bullfrogs.

"That's not noise, that's nature," he explained.

They watched Robbie and Justine horsing on the raft and jumping into the lake while all the grownups trudged up the long hill.

"She did good today," said Shelly.

"She did real good," said Sam.

Shelly looked at him. *Half the world's women are fantasizing about him,* she thought, *and they have no fucking idea.* She was about to reach over and touch his arm when he grabbed another listless walleye from the bucket, plunged the knife deep into its belly, and sliced—

Shelly turned her head and stood. "Justine, Robbie, out of the water now!" she barked.

The sun was beginning to set, the bullfrogs were serenading the cowfrogs in full-throated ease, and Sam was cleaning the fishing gear carefully, returning everything to its place. He even made sure the old all-steel rod he'd used was standing in a straight line with the others. He looked at his day's catch with satisfaction, several nice bass, half a dozen walleyes, and a bluegill that must have weighed well over six pounds. *Hoo, what Winston's gonna do with that!* he mused to himself.

"Hey, dog, you wanna go take a dump with me?"

Dog barked enthusiastically, and together they walked off behind the boathouse, along the trail around the lake, and up into the woods. He found a clearing to do his business, and was proud of himself that he had thought to bring a wad of that soft toilet paper from the house, which was a whole lot better than the newspaper he was accustomed to. As he stepped over a log, careful not to scuff his new rubber sandals, he saw a two-foot black rat snake slither off into the undergrowth, but he knew they weren't dangerous. It was calming, the sounds and smells of the woods, but he kept thinking about Shelly and the ballgame and that lunch and the music with Aaron and Justine gleaming as she sang, and the whole Gruenhaus family glowing right back, himself included.

He walked on through the woods and out to a clearing rising up to a knobby hill. He thought of climbing up to take a look, but he wanted to get back for the huevos rancheros Winston had promised him for supper. Just as he was about to turn back, he saw someone across the field. The man waved to him, and Sam waved back. He was in his thirties, with a straggly beard and hair. Dog ran ahead to him, wagging his tail, and nuzzled the man's groin vigorously in greeting.

"Hey, bro!" said the man, smiling, scratching Dog behind the ear. "You too?" They were wearing the same We Are Decapede! T-shirt.

"Me? Oh, yeah," said Sam.

"You seen a little cocker bitch running around here? Light brown, answers to the name Lady? When she answers."

"Nah, just this mutt. Ran off on you?"

"Yeah, I think all this fresh air out here is making her horny," the man said, and they both laughed.

"City dog?" asked Sam.

"Toledo. You?"

"Down past Zanesville. What brings you out here?"

"Me and my girlfriend and another couple figured we'd come hang out up here, just to, you know, be close by. Maybe even catch a glimpse of the band. And then we ran into a bunch of others doing the same thing. One family from down near Columbus. Some people from somewhere outside Pittsburgh, I think. So, we all just pitched our tents together, about a mile north of here."

Sam scratched his newly shaven jowl.

"We've been grilling and just sitting around, playing guitar, singing Decapede songs. You?"

"Pretty much the same," said Sam.

"Yeah?" said the stranger. "You all should come over and join us. We're hardcore," he said. Then he added proudly, "We call ourselves Decaheads."

"Decaheads, huh?" said Sam.

"*Grass and sunlight all around / Nothing's gonna bring me down / Have another Creston Gold*," sang the man, grinning.

"Hey, where'd my dog go?" said Sam.

The man and Sam looked around, but Dog had disappeared.

"Hey, dog!" called Sam, but there was no answer, just the frenzied croaking of horny bullfrogs serenading the end of a warm summer day.

Robbie and Justine were lying in the last faint light in their private dip in the grass by the lake, oblivious to the amphibian choir croaking and ribbiting to their froggy hearts' delight.

Justine lay next to Robbie, his arm under her neck, her head on his shoulder, her eyes closed, her knee on top of his knee. Robbie looked at her and smiled, and Justine looked back at him and smiled, too. Then he closed his eyes as he pulled her lips to his and kissed her deeply, with his tongue. She accepted, hesitating, then shyly began to explore in return. Robbie shifted under her and slowly moved his hand up from her thigh, to her hip, over her ribs, to the blue terry-cloth edge of the bikini bra, and then back down over her ribs to her hip across the string of her nubbled bikini bottom and to her thigh and back up slowly across the now charted but still intoxicating bodyscape up to her breast, which he cupped hesitantly and gently. Justine felt the warmth grow inside her as Robbie probed her mouth with his tongue, and her tongue fluttered back against his, and he slipped his fingers inside the cup of her bra when Sam clomped down on Robbie's out-stretched leg with all his weight.

"OW!" shouted Robbie, grabbing his ankle with both hands and sitting up sharply, almost fracturing his boner. "OWW!"

"What the fuck?" cried Sam.

"What are you doing?" shrieked Justine, leaping up with her arms crossed in front of her. "Go away!" she screamed, stamping her foot. "What are you doing here? Go away!"

Sam backed off, wide-eyed, and tripped backward over a tree branch.

"If you say one word of this to anyone, I'll kill you, Sam Miller, I swear I will!" she hollered after him as he scrambled up the hill towards the house. "Do you hear me? One word!"

Shelly was at her desk, writing an email to the governor himself explaining why he wasn't going to be invited for a photo shoot with the band, when she saw something moving out on the lawn in the last light. She went to the window. It was a person pacing back and forth. She opened the screen door and stepped outside.

"Sam?" she called, but he didn't respond. She walked a few steps in his direction and called again over the bullfrogs. "Sam, don't make me walk all the way down there. Sam?"

She sat down next to him on the grass. "What's going on?" she asked.

"Something bad happened," he said, looking at the ground between his legs, shaking his head. "Really bad."

"What is it?" she asked, laying a hand on his shoulder.

He jerked, but didn't shake her off. Shelly could hear his breath coming in sharp, accented starts and stops.

"Sam. Hey, Sam, come back!" She touched his knee, growing concerned, but he just shook his head back and forth. "Come, help me up," she grunted, holding up her hand.

He stood up without looking at her and pulled her up.

"Come on," she said, linking her arm into his, leading him up the hill. "Let's talk about it inside." As they walked, she tried not to think about her breast rubbing up against his arm.

She sat him on her sofa and sat next to him. "You want to tell me what's going on?"

"I can't," he mumbled.

"Why not?"

"Can't tell you that either."

"Did you do something wrong?" she asked gently.

"No," he said, straightening up. "No no. No."

"Did someone do something wrong to you?"

"No, nothing like that."

"Is it connected to Justine?"

"How did you know that?" he jerked.

"What is it, Sam?"

"Let's say," he tried, "just for example, that I knew something about Justine. Something I shouldn't know. Something I don't want to know. And she made me promise not to say anything. But, like—this is all just an example, yeah?"

"Right," Shelly reassured him, suppressing her smile, "just an example."

"But let's say I think maybe I should say something. To someone. About something."

"Why do you think you should say something to someone about something?"

"Because—I don't want her to get into trouble."

"What kind of trouble are you afraid she might get into? In this hypothetical example?"

"You know, like—you know."

"No, Sam, I don't know. Not unless you tell me what you saw," she teased.

"But she made me promise not to tell!" Sam implored, and Shelly realized he wasn't joking.

"Well, then, you're just going to have to decide. What's more important, your promise to her or trying to keep her out of trouble?"

"I don't know!" Sam floundered. "I *promised*. I promised her, and I promised you and everyone that I'll keep my promises and do everything right, and smile at the cameras and be nice to people and everything. And I'm trying. Jeez, Shelly, I swear, I'm really trying. But I just don't understand this stuff!"

Shelly looked at him, a boy lost in a world of grown-up emotions. She felt something inside her soften.

Shelly took his hand in both of hers. Sam looked at her and said something, but her brain shorted out.

"What did you say?" she asked him.

"I said you gotta *help* me."

They looked at each other. Her hands were holding his, resting on her knee. They could feel each other breathing. Shelly touched his cheek with her fingertips.

And somehow, as naturally and inexorably as the waxing of the tide, they drew closer, till their lips were touching, a twelve-year-old's first kiss—hesitant, confused, brain function frozen, lips pressing on lips for a brief, confusing moment. Then they both backed off, staring at each other. Sam slid his hand slowly from Shelly's hands. Then he stood up and turned and walked out of the room.

Shelly felt her cheeks burning.

Exactly what you need right now.

Justine and Robbie were talking on the swing, knee to knee. Robbie jumped up when Sam approached them.

Sam stood there, staring at the porch railing, his jaw grinding.

"I'm going to the kitchen," said Robbie. "To get one of those—you know, those waddayacallits ..." But they weren't listening, and he scurried off as quickly as he could.

"What?" she snarked.

"Listen—" he said, and stopped. "You should—I mean, you shouldn't—you know—"

"God, Sam, I'm almost seventeen," said the girl.

Sam stared at the porch railing.

"Don't worry, we haven't done anything yet."

Sam peered at her.

"And I'm not going to lose my head or go crazy or anything."

Sam scratched his jaw.

"And when I do decide to have sex, it'll be with a condom."

Sam swallowed hard and looked back down at the porch railing.

"And I'm sorry for the way I screamed at you down there," said Justine. "You scared me."

Sam looked at her.

Justine bounced up and came to him, pecked him on the cheek, and skipped into the house to find Robbie.

Sam stood watching the porch swing rock back and forth.

The dinner bell rang, so he turned and walked back into the house.

65

Yawns
– June 11, 2006, Evening –

The entire team was lolling around in the common room, half-asleep, worn out from the sun and the fresh air and the water and the food. Sam was picking his jazzy figures on the guitar, Aaron filling in around him on dolceola. Shelly was chatting with Diane and listening to them. Mendel and Johnny were each stretched out, snoozing. Brandi was asleep on one love-seat with her head in Matt's lap. Bev was curled up against Gerald on another, his hand resting several inches above decent on her thigh. The Colonel and Allie sat on straight-backed chairs, listening politely. Justine was next to Robbie, whispering animatedly, too shy to touch in front of the adults. Gavin and Winston hunched together on the floor, playing backgammon on an elegant old board with polished wood and inlaid ivory.

Aaron caught Sam's eye and played the opening notes of Mendel's Hassidic melody.

Sam nodded, laid down his guitar, and stood. Everyone went quiet. He closed his eyes, took a breath, and began to sing the soft, mournful *"bye-de-bye-bye bye."*

Mendel opened one eye, and Johnny picked up his camera.

Sam sang it through once softly, the entire room hanging on his grainy, mournful voice. The second time, Aaron stood next to him and joined in harmony, just the two voices of Woodwright and Miller filling the spacious, gently lit common room with the high windows and old oaken paneling.

For the third verse, Justine rose and stood between Aaron and Sam, looped her arms through theirs, and completed the mournful chord from above. Everyone was staring now, riveted by the three naked voices singing the aching melody, surrounded by the silent shadows of the room.

Mendel shook his head in wonder, slipped out through the newly soundproofed double doors of the music room, and returned with his violin.

He nodded to them to continue and joined on top of them, beside them, darting in and out of their chords, adding colors, filigrees, the scent of a long-gone Polish village, the wordless endless story of a vagabond troubadour fleeing the Cossacks, an odyssey as long as the Diaspora. No one thought to count the number of verses, but according to the counter on Johnny's camera, the journey lasted over twenty minutes.

"I could die right now," whispered Gerald to Bev.

Diane's eyes were on Aaron.

Matt stared and smiled, while Brandi slept soundly, her head in his lap.

"Bug Juice," said Gavin.

Bev sat up sharply. "Yes!" she said.

"What? What?" asked Gerald.

"Vaneshi's big solo," said Aaron.

"Who's Vaneshi?" said Mendel, and the old bandmates laughed with him.

"At the Kiwanis, this hall we used to play in," explained Aaron to the others, "we had to do a forty-five-minute set."

"And we only had about half an hour of songs," recalled Mendel. "So one night Sam and Aaron and I, we were just fooling around, improvising. Remember?" he asked Sam.

"Yeah, I remember," Sam answered with a small smile.

"It was just a bunch of spaced-out chords," said Aaron.

"And Mendel started playing this long guitar solo—" fluttered Gavin.

"This endless *trippy* guitar solo" said Mendel, and Gavin and Bev and Aaron and Sam and Mendel all laughed together while the others watched, fascinated. Johnny was tracking them frantically, capturing every word.

"—that the audience went crazy over," said Bev. "They'd clap and yell and chant 'Va-ne-shi, Va-ne-shi!' "

"It would go on for half an hour sometimes," said Gavin.

"The solo," laughed burly Mendel in his deep bass, "not the applause."

"Even more," said Bev.

"And it became part of our set," said Aaron.

"The *high* point of the set," said Gavin, and the old-timers laughed at the memory.

"Yeah," said Sam, "that was pretty good."

"It was incredible," said Bev.

"What were the other ones that we used to pad out the set with?" asked Mendel.

" 'Shout!' " shouted Bev.

"Right!" said Mendel and Gavin together.

" 'Rock Around the Clock,' " said Aaron.

"Oh, Kathleen used to kill that," sighed Gavin.

"I know all the words!" piped Justine. "Mom used to sing it all the time! '*Put your glad rags on,*'" she began, but the guys looked at each other, reluctant to dispel the magic that was still floating around the room.

"Oh, please!" said Justine.

"I'm pretty bushed," said Mendel.

"Tomorrow," said Aaron.

"Promise?" asked Gerald.

Aaron, Mendel, and Gavin promised, and Sam didn't object.

"Rehearsal, eleven o'clock," Bev reminded them, "breakfast at nine." She didn't toot her whistle, but everyone groaned anyway.

"I think I'm going to turn in," said Mendel.

"Yeah, it's been a long day," said Shelly.

"But it was great," he said, and everyone waved goodnight to him as he climbed the big staircase.

"Yes, I think I'll say goodnight, also," said Allie, rising.

The Colonel stood up.

Allie looked at him.

"I think your fiancé is tired, too," said Johnny.

The Colonel stood looking hopefully at Allie.

"Oh, come on," she said. The Colonel gave Johnny a grim nod, and everyone stifled their smiles as they headed back to the annex.

"And I have a midnight flight," said Diane, standing. "It was incredible meeting you all. I hope to see you again soon."

Everyone wished her a good night. Aaron followed her from the room and caught her in the hallway.

"Couldn't you stay over?" he asked, holding her arm.

"I wish," she said. "It's been quite an experience, Mr. Aaron Woodwright."

Aaron looked around, and then at her, and she looked back at him, and he pulled her to him for a long, deep kiss.

"Wow," she said. "Where did that come from?"

"I've been a rock star for—what is it, almost a week now? I figure it's about time I start reaping the benefits."

"Oh, I'm just another one of your groupies?" she smiled.

"If you want to be," he smiled back, rubbing against her.

"Mick Jagger incarnate," she chided him, rubbing back.

"Stay," he urged, kissing her again.

"I have a budget committee meeting in the morning."

"Skip it."

"I'm the chair."

"And I'm the table," he said, nuzzling her.

"No," she said, her hand on his chest. "I really do have to catch that plane."

He nuzzled her neck again, and she breathed in deeply.

"But if you don't mind watching me pack, we can have a chat about how convenient this midnight flight is."

Aaron followed her up the stairs.

Gerald whispered something right into Bev's ear, and she tittered like a teenager.

"Don't we have some stuff left to do in the kitchen?" Gavin said to Winston, standing and stretching.

"Yeah," said Winston, "sure do."

"Stuff?" said Sam with a cocked eyebrow, and they laughed and took their leave.

"Hey," said Justine suddenly, "where's Dog?"

"He ran off on me, down by the lake," said Sam. "He'll be back when he gets hungry."

"Oh, no!" said Justine, standing. "I'm going to go look for him."

"I'll come with you," Robbie offered politely, leaping up from the sofa and following her out.

"Robbie, don't stay up too late," called Bev.

"Mom, please!" he protested.

"You, too," called Shelly to Justine.

She called back something from the porch.

"Breakfast is at nine o'clock," Bev called after them, but they were gone. She looked at Shelly. Shelly looked back at her and shrugged. Shelly looked at Sam, who was busy scratching his jaw.

Gerald stretched widely and gave out a yawn so loud that Brandi stirred and sat up, her eyes three-quarters closed.

"Wt strngvsh?" she mumbled.

"Good morning," said Shelly.

Brandi squinted at the room. "Where is everyone?" she mumbled.

"People are going to bed," Matt informed her.

Brandi looked at him, stood up, and began shuffling towards the stairs in her bunny rabbit slippers. She stopped and turned back to him grouchily. "What do you want, a written invitation?"

"Am I—" said Matt, rising. "I mean—Yeah. Okay. Goodnight, folks," he said politely and followed her up the stairs.

"I guess all the excitement's over," laughed Johnny, closing up his camera. "I'll say g'nite, you all," he said, and headed upstairs.

Bev stood to her full little height and stretched. "Wow, what a day," she said.

"What a day," agreed Shelly.

Bev turned to Gerald.

"Oh, come on, you," she said. Gerald jumped up, winked at Shelly and Sam with his black-and-blue eye, and followed her upstairs.

Alone in the vast, shadowy common room, Sam and Shelly looked at each other. He was still standing where he'd sung Mendel's tune. Shelly was sitting on one of the loveseats, pink from the sun. The room was silent but for the distant croaking of the bullfrogs.

"Listen, Sam, about what happened before—" she began.

"Yeah, I mean, I'm sorry," he stammered. "I didn't mean to—"

"Because we can't—" Shelly felt her cheeks burning.

"No, no," he agreed, shaking his head.

"I mean, you understand, right? Because—"

"Oh, yeah. I—sure, right."

Sam stood looking at Shelly.

"But you can sit down, if you like," she said.

Sam sat. They sat together in silence.

Finally, Shelly spoke. "So, how did your talk go with Justine?"

"Oh, that? Fine," he said. "It was fine. We talked it over. It was fine."

"Ah," she said.

Again, they sat in silence.

"The way she sang 'And Then He Kissed Me'?" said Shelly.

"Yeah," he agreed.

"Wow. She—she blossomed."

"Kid's got game."

"She's a natural performer."

"Just like her mom," Sam said.

He took his guitar and began to play those open, jazzy chords. Shelly lay her head back and closed her eyes. Her mind wandered over the whole splay of the land at the lake, the hillside, the grass, the water lapping on the shore, Sam and Aaron making music together, Justine showing off for the camera, the couples coupling. *And here I am, being serenaded by Sam fucking Miller. Sam fucking caveman Miller.*

"That's very beautiful," she said.

"Mm," he said, and continued picking.

She nudged his leg with her bare toe.

"Hmm?" he said.

"You're supposed to say, 'Thank you.' "

"Mm."

She nudged him again.

"Thank you." He continued picking, his eyes on his fingers.

"How you feeling?"

"Me?"

"Yeah, dummy."

He stole a glance at her, and smiled a sly little smile. "There you go again, spoiling a nice evening with all your jabbering."

She smiled and shut up.

"That lake's a good place for music," he said, plucking a lolling figure on the strings.

"Why's that?" she asked,

"The bullfrogs."

"What do they have to do with anything?" she smiled, curling her leg under her on the loveseat, her knee almost touching his.

"They fill the air with that nice low B flat." He sang a low, humming drone that made her tingle. "It's a good vibration."

Shelly watched his fingers plucking the strings.

"Good for fish."

Tell me he's pulling my leg. Please tell me.

"Good for music," he said.

As she listened to him play, Shelly pictured the band on the dock. *It would be a great backdrop for Johnny. The boathouse has electricity.*

"Want to set up down there tomorrow?"

Sam stopped playing and looked at Shelly. "Just like that?" he smiled at her.

"Yup," she smiled back, hooking her hands around her knee and leaning back.

Sam shook his head and went back to playing those beautiful, jazzy figures.

I can do that, she smiled to herself. *Apparently, I can do anything. I can even make this crazy guy smile.*

Shelly gazed at him as he played, his face soft and gentle in the dim light.

"Okay," she said, standing briskly. "I'm bushed."

Sam looked up at her, the guitar in his lap.

"Good night," she said, looking at him.

"Good night," he said, looking back at her.

The bullfrogs continued their endless croaking.

"You want to give me a hug?" she said.

"A hug?" he said.

"Yeah. A hug," she answered. "We humans do that sometimes. As a gesture of affection."

"Oh. A hug," he said, and half-rose as she bent down for an awkward, politely warm, little embrace.

Shelly looked at him and started to say something, then changed her mind, turned, and climbed the stairs up to her bedroom.

Sam waited until she disappeared. The house was quiet except for the squeaks and creaks and grunts that an old Ohio farmhouse makes at night when everyone is asleep. He sneaked quietly down the hallway to Shelly's office. He closed the door behind him without turning on a light. There was enough moonlight in the room for him to fumble his way to the bathroom, where he peed into Shelly's vintage toilet. Then he washed his hands and went to lie down on Shelly's rust-and-butterscotch sofa. He sniffed the cushion, pulled the patchwork quilt over himself snugly, and slept the sleep of the just.

66

Hickey

– June 12, 2006, Early Morning –

Sam was used to rising with the sun, but since coming to Gruenhaus, he'd been staying up long after dark. So, when he heard some kind of noise outside, he jerked up from Shelly's couch, startled.

It was Justine, alone on the early morning lawn with the little white things in her ears and a little white box hooked to her little jeans shorts, bouncing back and forth to the music, shooting her hands in the air and singing too loudly, "*Na-na-na-na-na-na, Start all over, Na-na-na-na-na-na, (boom-chuck!) Start all over again!*"

Sam pulled on his We Are Decapede! T-shirt and his khaki shorts and the rubber sandals Brandi had gotten him that were without a doubt the most comfortable footwear he had ever owned, and walked out to Justine on the grass.

"You're up early," he said.

"You're up late," she answered.

"Watcha doin'?"

"Practicing the lyrics."

"You look all happy," he said, his grouchy side still asleep.

Justine shrugged with a smile.

"Know all the words?" he asked.

"Uh-huh," she said.

"*Na-na-na-na-na-na, Start all over,*" she sang, and Sam joined in, "*Na-na-na-na-na-na, (boom-chuck!) Start all over again.*" They made it through together with only a couple of small glitches.

"Again," said Sam, and they sang it again, almost perfectly.

"Again," said Justine, and they nailed it.

They sat side by side on the grass, looking down the hill at the lake.

Sam looked at her. "Ready to be a rock star?"

"I already am."

"You are, huh?"

"I thought I sang pretty well yesterday."

"You ain't done diddly till you sing in front of people."

"No big deal," she said with bravado.

"Chicken?"

"Don't you chicken me, you old rooster."

"We're gonna set up down by the lake."

"Cool," she said.

He turned to go back into the house, but stopped and turned to her. "You ought to go look in a mirror."

"Why?" she said, alarmed.

"You got one hell of a hickey there," he said, and turned with a smirk and walked into the house through Shelly's door. He took the back stairs two at a time up to the room marked Aaron. He knocked three times, waited two seconds, then three times more, but louder, calling, "Hey Aaron, you up?" When he heard a muffled voice, he opened the door and walked in. "Come on, get up."

"What the fuck?" said Aaron, sitting up and rubbing his eyes.

"We're setting up down on the dock."

"When?"

"Now," said Sam.

"Now?" said Aaron, looking at his watch on the night-stand. "It's not even eight o'clock yet!"

"Wha—" slurred Diane, sitting up, holding the sheet to her.

"Come on, let's make some noise."

Aaron and Diane looked at each other.

"Get out of here," said Aaron to Sam with a sigh and a smile. "Let a guy get dressed."

Sam stuck his head into the common room. Mendel was standing in a corner, rocking back and forth, little black boxes on his forehead and arm, and a big white prayer shawl with black stripes wrapped around him.

"Hey, Mendel, we're setting up down at the lake."

Mendel flashed him a thumbs up and rocked a little harder in his prayers.

"Where is everybody?" Sam asked the kitchen crew.

"Still sleeping," said Gavin as he deftly peeled a cucumber.

"Allie and de Colonel dey went to church," said Winston.

"Hey-hey, good-lookin', whatcha got a-cookin'?" sang Sam, inhaling the frying blueberry pancakes.

"Breakfast a' nine o'clock, Samiller," said Winston, swatting at the pilferer's fingers before he could swipe a sausage off the skillet.

"Aw, c'mon," said Sam. "Just one?"

"Juss one," said Winston, "'cos you a rock star an' you payin' all our celery," and he burst out laughing at his own joke.

"Hey, Gavin, we're gonna set up down at the lake."

"Cool," said Gavin, guillotining the tip of the poor vegetable with relish.

The office was empty. Sam picked up the receiver of a complicated phone and pushed on buttons till he heard a dial tone. He fished a crumpled wad of paper out of his shorts pocket and dialed.

"Hey Pattie, it's Sam," he called into the receiver. "Hey, how you doin'? You saw *me* on the internet? Sonofagun! No, they're treating me fine. Good fishing. Hey, listen, you know, this band I'm in up here? They got a nice little lake here, and we're playin' down there today. Any chance you bring Bunkie and Teal up here to Creston, give a listen?" Sam looked out the window. "They give you any trouble at the roadblock, ask for Sheriff Aubrey."

The only sound on a quiet Sunday morning other than the birds chirping was Sam Miller walking down the long front lawn to the road, whistling "Start All Over Again." "Yo, Aubrey," said Sam, knocking on the window and waking the sheriff with a start.

"Oh. Mr. Miller. Good morning."

"Listen, I got some friends coming up in a little while. Woman and a couple of girls. Drive a brown pickup with Lake Hope State Park on it. Can you show them the back road down to the lake?"

"Sure. What's going on at the lake?"

"The band's setting up down there. Gonna play a little."

"Really?" said Sheriff Aubrey, wide awake now.

"Yeah, play for the fish, iron out some of the kinks," said Sam.

"Boy, would I love to hear that," said The Law, removing his sunglasses and looking up at Sam.

"You would, huh?" said Sam. "Well, I guess you could come on over."

"Really?"

"Yeah. Give us a little audience."

"Would it be okay if I brought my mother-in-law? I mean, I don't mean to impose, sir, but she's your biggest fan in the world, saw you live back then, in Steubenville."

"Fuck," Sam smirked. "Bring whoever you want."

They plugged in and tuned up, and Aaron ran them through the songs from the CD, starting with the easy ones, so that each of the singers had a chance to warm up—"Peggy Sue," "Walk on By," "Different Drum." Then they ran "Cuyahoga Rising," and everyone was very satisfied.

"The harmonies sounded really good, guys," said Aaron.

"It helps when you know the words," Sam said to Justine, and she made a face at him.

"Just make sure you always stay the same distance from the mic, otherwise Robbie can't keep up with you," Aaron cautioned her.

"Oh, he can never keep up with me," she said saucily.

"In your dreams," called Robbie from the console, grinning.

They got through "True Love Ways" and "Bring It On Home" hesitantly, so Aaron had the band run them till they felt comfortable.

"By George, I think we've got it!" said Aaron, beaming.

"About time," growled Sam, but everyone could see that he was pleased as well.

"Only took thirty-six years," said Mendel.

"I guess you just needed my help," said Justine, and everyone laughed.

"Who are they?" Diane asked Matt, indicating a couple sitting down along the dock, speaking in a foreign tongue. Near them was an array of children running around on the grass.

"Oh, that's Petar and Penka," answered Matt. "My cousin J.D. found them. They help out around Gruenhaus with the housekeeping."

"Where are they from?"

"I'm not really sure, ma'am," said Matt. "They don't speak any English."

"Okay," said Aaron, consulting his set sheet, " 'And Then He Kissed Me.' Gavin, count us in?"

"No, don't you remember?" said Gavin. "Kathleen used to call it."

"Right!" said Mendel.

Aaron and Sam looked at each other.

"How?" asked Justine.

"Ah-one, ah-two, ah-one two three *four!*" demonstrated Gavin.

Justine grinned and looked at her band with the mic in her hand. "Ready?"

"But keep it clean this time," said Sam, indicating Robbie over at the control panel.

Justine stuck out her tongue at him, raised the mic to her mouth, and shouted it out. "Ah-one, ah-two, ah-one two three *four!*"

"She's enjoying herself," said Bev.

"Yes, she is," agreed Shelly.

"She's a natural," said Brandi.

"Just like her mom," said Bev.

"Just like her mom," agreed Diane.

"This is so cool," Gerald grinned.

The girl sang it facing the band, and they ran through it without a hitch.

"Once more?" asked Johnny.

"It was fine," said Sam.

"For the camera," explained Johnny.

Sam made a face.

"Sam!" said Bev.

"We need publicity shots," called Shelly sternly. "Do what Johnny says."

"Once more," said Sam with an exaggerated smile, "for the camera."

"The band looks great," said Diane.

"Brandi," explained Shelly.

Brandi had attired them all in black We Are Decapede! T-shirts. Aaron was wearing a dapper gray blazer over his and sporting the most buoyant forelock anyone had ever seen on a fifty-six-year-old. Sam was wearing his vintage Cleveland Indians jersey, open to display the Decapede motto. Gavin's T-shirt was tucked into his tan pants, partially covered by a pear-green vest. Mendel had removed his long black coat and was wearing the T-shirt that Allie had prepared especially for him with long white fringes at the corners. Justine was in her tiny denim shorts, the T-shirt tied at her midriff to display her taut little tummy. She was wearing the fedora from the basement and a red cowboy bandana around her neck.

They played it again, Justine looking right into Johnny's camera, all five Decapedes smiling as brightly as the mid-June sun on a sunny Sunday morning on the dock of Lake Traumsee.

"Okay," said Aaron, "all we have left is, ahem, the Number One song in the country. Mr. Miller?"

"Nah, we know it good enough. Let's do that new thing of yours," said Sam. "Aaron's got this new thing, 'Start All Over Again,' " he explained.

"I'd rather finish—" Aaron attempted, but Justine began to sing into the mic, showing off that she already knew the song, "*Na-na-na-na-na-na, Start all over, Na-na-na-na-na-na, (boom-chuck!) Start all over again.*"

"What is *that*?" asked Gavin, his eyes widening.

Aaron smiled and played a snatch of the song on the keyboard.

"Whenever did that happen?" asked Mendel in admiration.

"Somebody's gotta work while you guys are fooling around," said Sam.

"Yesterday, on the dock," said Aaron, "in between the bass and the walleyes."

"He kept pestering me while I was trying to fish," deadpanned Sam.

"That's nice!" said Gavin.

"That's *very* nice," said Mendel.

Sam began playing the chunk-chunk opening chords, and Aaron joined in, smiling widely but focused on his fingers.

"Play the introduction again?" said Mendel, fiddling on his guitar.

Aaron played the chord progression in his left hand, the melody in his right, and Mendel laid a playful new figure on top of the chords in a counterpoint to the lead, giving it an uplifting bounce.

"Again," said Aaron, and they continued smoothing it out through the verse, Sam strumming along his rhythm chords.

"I'm good. Go ahead," said Mendel.

Gavin slid back behind the drum kit and Aaron counted them in. They began to walk through the song methodically, gingerly, the four of them dancing carefully in tandem, feeling out each other's moves. Aaron was grinning as he played, and Mendel was looking up into the blue sky and weaving a joyful tapestry, while Gavin insinuated a warm, funky groove. Sam kept a straight rhythm, his brow furrowed in concentration, his eyes staring at his fingerings. They played through the verse once, then again. Aaron played Gavin and Mendel the B part, and as soon as they understood the mechanics, Aaron took it from the top.

"So, AAB, break on A, BA," said Aaron, and everyone nodded. "Once without vocals."

They ran it through once and then again. Justine was sitting next to Robbie behind the console, gabbing in a whisper, their heads together.

"Robbie, can you give me some more bass in the monitor?" asked Mendel, reminding the boy that he was working.

After several runs, Aaron was satisfied. "Okay, now with the vocals. Justine, care to join us?"

Justine jumped up and moved her mic stand right next to Sam so she could try to look him in the eye for their tight harmony. They stumbled over the entrance to the B part, but Aaron pushed them through it. Mendel picked notes sparingly in his guitar break, feeling his way. By the last verse, Sam and Justine were locked together in major thirds with just a touch of twang. When they'd finished it safely, the whole band began chattering excitedly about how good it sounded, but Aaron shushed them and called to run it again from the top. They played it a second time, and a third, and a fourth, smoothing and polishing their new song.

Mendel saw that Justine was beginning to droop. "Could we take a break?" he suggested.

"Yes," said Gavin. "I could use a breather."

"Okay," said Aaron, beginning to relax. He looked over at Diane and smiled. "Take ten."

"Wow!" said Shelly to Justine as the grinning girl plopped down in the chair next to her on the dock. "When did that happen?"

"Yesterday, at the picnic," said Justine proudly. "It's so cool that Aaron wrote a song like that."

"What do you mean?" asked Shelly.

"Well, it's like Sam's always the writer. And the singer. And Aaron gets, you know—"

"Insecure?"

"Yeah!" agreed Justine.

"Men," said Shelly. "Look and learn."

"Boy, I'm bushed."

"Hard work being a rock star?"

"It's a tough job, but someone's got to do it," the girl grinned at her.

Aaron and Diane were off by themselves, talking softly and smiling. Sam pulled his chair over to the edge of the dock, dug a handful of breadcrumbs from his baggy pocket, and tossed them into the water just below his feet. A mob of fish attacked their surprise snack in a floppy frenzy, and Sam began to play his fishy guitar theme.

"Hey, Robbie, crank me up a little, will ya?" he called to the boy.

"No fishing pole?" Robbie asked.

"Nah, today I'm just gonna soften them up," answered Sam.

Shelly and Justine looked at each other and laughed.

The guitar theme was magical, enchanting. Everyone stopped their chatter. Aaron, holding Diane's hand discreetly and whispering in her ear, turned to listen. After a moment, he got up and went back to his keyboard. Justine lay her head on Shelly's knee.

Sam sang his siren refrain, wordless but for the single, haunting "*Moon dancing over the water, fish dancing under the sea,*" his eyes closed. The lilting music wafted through the quiet Sunday morning and over the lake.

Shelly watched Sam's hands fingering the gossamer refrain, his lips warbling wordless curves and swoops, the elusive rhythm of unexpected pulses and surprise stresses.

"You're all red," said Justine.

"It's the sun," said Shelly, adjusting her hat.

But suddenly the music stopped, and Sam went running off the dock, sprinting like a goofy rabbit, to greet a woman coming down the hill, waving at him, two little girls running down behind her.

"Shelly?" called Bev from behind a big oak tree where she was tête-à-têtting with Gerald.

Shelly squinted into the sun. "Oh, gosh, it's Sam's neighbor from down at Lake Hope."

"Hey, Shelly," said Sam excitedly, "remember Bunkie and Teal?"

"Sure," said Shelly, holding out her hand to the older one. "Hi, remember me? I'm Sam's friend, Shelly."

Bunkie shook Shelly's hand solemnly while Teal hung back behind her.

"And this is Kathleen," said Sam.

"Justine," Justine corrected him.

"Shit," said Sam.

"Quarter," said Bunkie, holding out her hand.

"I don't have it on me. But I'm good for it. I'm rich now."

"You don't look rich," said little Teal.

"Well, you don't look like a bullfrog," said Sam. "So there!"

Teal giggled at silly old Sam.

"How old are you two?" asked Shelly.

"I'm eight," said Bunkie. "Teal's only five."

"Almost five and a half," said Teal from behind her older sister.

"Hi, Pattie," said Shelly. "What brings you here?"

"Hey, Shelly. Sam called this morning, asked us to come up. I hope that's okay?"

"Sure, I'm just a little surprised."

"I want Bunkie and Teal to hear the band," said Sam. "Between them, they got five good ears."

"Just four, actually," Bunkie explained to Shelly.

"I saw you on the computer," said little Teal.

"You did?" exclaimed Sam. "How many ears did I have?"

Teal held up two fingers.

"He makes jokes like that sometimes," Bunkie explained to Shelly and Justine. "He thinks they're funny."

"I know," said Justine, nodding her head in sympathy, and Bunkie smiled at her.

"I leave, and you let them use the computer?" Sam teased Pattie.

"Well, they caught Morgan watching your band, and they started driving him crazy to watch it over and over," said Pattie with a laugh and a shrug.

Bunkie put her fists on her hips to demonstrate her impatience. "We came to hear you play," she said sternly.

"Well, then, what do you want to hear?"

"The one that's on the radio all the time," said Bunkie. " 'Creston Gold.' "

"How does that go again?" he asked her.

Justine rolled her eyes at Bunkie, and Bunkie rolled her eyes back.

"Come on, guys, we got a very important audience here," Sam called, and they assumed their positions.

"Who are they?" Gavin asked Justine.

"Sam's friends," she answered. "He says they're the best judges of music he knows."

Gavin looked at Justine skeptically.

"Don't look at me," said Justine, "that's what he said."

The girls sat next to each other, right in front of the band, cross-legged on the dock.

"I've been following you on the news," said Pattie, sitting next to Shelly. "I had no idea."

Shelly smiled. "What do you think of your Sam Miller?"

"You mean that guy up there? Lousy impersonation."

Sam Miller's band played the Number One hit song in the US for the little audience of two.

"Well, wadja think?" he asked them.

Bunkie looked at Teal. Teal looked back at her, then at Sam. "It was very loud," she said.

"That's so a whole lot of people will be able to hear us when we get famous," he explained, and he turned to Bunkie. "Well?"

"It's too fast," said Bunkie.

"Yeah?" said Sam.

Bunkie just shrugged.

Sam looked at Aaron.

"We could try it a drop slower," said Aaron. "Gavin?"

"Maybe she's right," admitted the drummer.

"What else do you want to hear?" Sam asked the girls.

"Play 'Rogarown'!" said Teal.

"I don't know no 'Rogarown,' " said Sam.

"You shouldn't tease her," said eight-year-old Bunkie. "She's too young."

"Oh, '*Rogarown*'!" said Sam. He adjusted his mic stand and played a chord.

The housekeepers' kids joined Bunkie and Teal, sitting right in front of the band and whispering excitedly in their other language.

"What are we doing?" asked Aaron.

Sam just smiled. "In D." Sam played the chord again and leaned into the mic, looking directly at little Teal. "*One, two, three o'clock, four o'clock rock ...*"

67

The Congregation
– June 12, 2006, Late Morning –

The band jumped in behind him.

At the end of the first verse, Aaron called out, "Take it, Mendel!" and Mendel did. Johnny was weaving in and out among the cables and kids and monitors and mic stands, ecstatic with the footage.

Sam looked down at the kids gazing up at him. "Come on, get up off your *be*-hinds!" he commanded them, and they began to jump around on the dock in front of the band, flapping their arms and flailing their legs.

Winston jumped up in his wildly colored shirt and grabbed his boss, Diane, by the hand, laughing and game. He began to whirl her back and forth, slick and swinging.

Matt grinned so widely his dimples almost popped as he rose and pulled Brandi up to join the revelry. She rolled her eyes, but followed him onto the little improvised dance floor on the dock right in front of the band. Johnny wove and dove between the couples, catching their smiles and their bodies bouncing and bopping.

Aaron shouted out the lyrics, shaking his famous Aaron Woodwright shock of hair. Justine let out a teeny-bopper's scream of adulation, and her guys all broke out laughing without missing a beat.

"Come on," said Bev, holding out her hand to Gerald.

"I'm not much of a dancer," he shouted into her ear above the music.

Bev pointed at Brandi and Matt. She was making honky-tonk zombie moves, while he jumped around her in a circle, waving an imaginary lasso over his head.

Gerald shrugged and took Bev's hand, and they began to jump around with abandon, laughing and having perhaps the best time of their lives.

Winston saw Allie whisper to the Colonel, who shook his head emphatically, so he danced over to them and drew Allie into the ruckus, tittering and following his toned-down gamboling. Diane leaned over to the Colonel, took both of his hands, and without asking, led him into a mature back-and-forth swing.

Johnny was in the middle of it all, bouncing and circling and filming all the grinning faces and bobbing heads.

Then, all of a sudden, the housekeepers Petar and Penka were in the middle of the little dance floor, spinning and bouncing. He was wearing a shiny black shirt and flared white pants, she a tight white blouse and a wide skirt full of puffy, bouncy crinoline, with her hair pulled back in a flittering ponytail. Penka slid under Petar's legs and flipped over his back. They went careening back and forth with him like paired balls in a pinball machine.

"Where did they learn that?" Shelly asked one of their kids in amazement, a mustached boy of eleven.

"They jitterbug champion in Shqipëri," he said proudly.

"What's that?" asked Shelly above the music.

"No Tirana, all Shqipëri champion," he explained.

"Oh," said Shelly, as everyone formed a circle and watched them swirl and circumvolute, Mendel egging them on with yet another verse of his jubilant solo.

"Sam!" shouted Aaron, motioning to him to take over the lead. Aaron rose from his piano, cut in on the Colonel, and began a very nimble jitterbug with the congressional candidate from Florida. He swung her in and out, out and in, and then when she came back in—just as Johnny turned to catch them in his frame—wrapped his arm around her waist, bent her all the way back, and planted a deep, pulsating kiss on the lips.

Sam sang with a wide grin, ragged and raucous, with Justine sharing his mic right up next to him. Then, she danced over to Robbie and pulled him out from behind the sound console. They began bouncing with the entire little crowd, the pier groaning under the weight. Johnny moved in close to catch them together. Justine watched Aaron and Diane's steps and tried to emulate them, but Robbie turned out to be quicker with his fingers than his feet. Johnny shoved the camera into the boy's hands and grabbed Justine by the hand. "Keep it rolling," he shouted to Robbie, and began leading the girl in an authentic Dick Clark jitterbug with startling pizzazz.

"Johnny?" said Shelly in amazement to the chair next to her, but it was empty.

"Yo, Aaron," called Sam into the mic, and Aaron bopped back to his keyboard.

Aaron pounded the keyboard and shouted out the lyrics, with Sam and Mendel and Gavin grinning and rocking and rolling.

Sam laid down his guitar and undulated along the pier to where Shelly was sitting.

"*We're gonna rock around the clock tonight,*" he serenaded her, taking both of her hands and coaxing her up.

"I don't dance," she shouted over the music, coloring.

"I don't negotiate," he grinned, pulling her firmly to her feet, placing his right hand on her hip and taking her right hand in his left.

He began to sway her back and forth, their bodies moving together in a gentle swing, so close she could breathe him in, grinning right at her, and she smiled back at him, flustered and buoyant.

"You're getting all red," he said into her ear with a smile.

"Shut up and dance," she answered back.

On the beat, he pushed her sharply away, then snapped her back tight up against him, and again, and again, harder and harder, with a cocksure smirk, then swung her left, then swung her right, rolling her and rocking her till she forgot all about gravity. He twirled her under his arm and then wrapped her tightly up against him. Then, he wheeled her around backward, knocking down little Teal, but before she had a chance to realize she was hurt, Sam scooped her up into his arms and began spinning her, singing, "*We're gonna rock, gonna rock, around the clock tonight!*" He spun her so hard that Teal had to wrap her arms around his neck tightly, squealing in delight.

Bunkie and Shelly watched them clowning around.

"He's funny, isn't he?" said Shelly, gazing at him, her heart still pumping as she caught her breath.

Bunkie nodded. "Are you his girlfriend?"

"No!" answered Shelly.

"Wow," said the little girl, "your face gets red really fast."

And then, as if on cue, just as the last jubilant chord was echoing across the lake and up the hill, suddenly Dog came bounding out of the woods, his tongue flapping in the wind and his paws barely touching the ground, flying up the steps and along the pier, dodging the chairs, weaving through the crowd of couples in front of the band till he found Justine, where he began barking raucously, jumping up and down.

"Dog!" she shouted, "Dog, Dog!" She got down on her knees and wrestled her arms around his neck as he jumped and jerked and licked her face and finally tore himself free, only to resume his hysterical herky-jerky dance around her.

Sam lunged at him, but Dog easily eluded him and ran a complete breakneck circle around the band, braking hard at the drum set.

"He's peeing on my high hat!" protested Gavin.

"He's excited," explained Justine.

Dog ran away back out to the end of the pier, where they were all startled to see a blonde cocker spaniel waiting impatiently for him. She didn't even bother to bark, but Dog came running up to her. They smelled each other's crotches and trotted off together back into the woods, the blonde leading the way.

"What was that?" asked Shelly, flushed and panting.

Justine stuck out her lower lip. "Did you see how he just ran off like that?"

"Let that be a lesson to you in life, young lady," said Sam, "they'll break your heart every time."

"What the hell?" said Shelly, gaping at the woods behind the boathouse. Sam and Justine and the whole little party turned to stare as figures began to emerge from within the trees, in twos and threes and fours, old and young, tall and short, bedraggled and smiling beatifically, all wearing We Are Decapede! T-shirts.

Shelly saw Sam greet a lanky young man with disheveled black hair down to his shoulders, a headband, and a chest covered with wampum beads. Next to the man was a short woman with two long black braids, whose We Are Decapede! T-shirt was sorely stretched by an eight-month watermelon in her stomach, on top of a skirt that looked like it had been handmade from animal hides, with a baby swaddled in a Decapede T-shirt on her back.

"Brother," said the young man, eyes glazed.

"Yo," said Sam. "You found your dog."

"And you found yours. You're Sam Miller."

"I am."

"Who the heck are you?" puffed Shelly, catching up

"Ronnie. Ronnie Bayer."

"But everyone calls him Running Bear," smiled the squat woman.

"I mean, who are all of you?" asked Shelly, flustered at the incursion. Dozens of them had now appeared, all gaping at the band.

"We are Decaheads," spoke Running Bear as Johnny circled them, then panned the entire tribe hanging back timidly at the edge of the woods. "We heard the music—"

"Hey, we can use an audience," said Sam. "Come on in."

"How many of you are there?" Shelly asked Running Bear nervously, but it was too late. They materialized from the woods, lines of them, families and couples and small groups of all sizes and ages and shapes, dozens of them, all gazing wide-eyed at the hillside and the lake and the pier and the mythic Decapede itself.

"Sam!" Shelly called to his back, but he was already looping his guitar strap over his shoulder.

"What are you doing?" asked Aaron.

"We're gonna give 'em a show," said Sam, adjusting his mic.

"No!" said Justine. "I'm not ready."

"Hell you're not," he grinned, and without even telling them what song he was playing, Sam counted off four beats and began to sing. "*If you knew Peggy Sue ...*"

The band jumped in behind him, Aaron and Justine and Gavin and Mendel, eyes fixed on each other, all beaming. They finished the song with Gavin's drum roll flourish, and the clusters of Decaheads all stood, cheering and applauding and pinching themselves.

"Hey there," said Aaron into the microphone, "can you hear me okay?" and the tribe cheered and applauded even louder. "Welcome to Lake Traumsee." Aaron's voice echoed off the lake and the hill and the woods, and all the Decaheads clapped and shouted and whistled. "We Are Decapede!" called the scraggly man from the sloping lawn, as Dog and Lady scampered around him in circles, and the entire little congregation on the hillside cheered and applauded.

"What the heck is that?" asked Gavin, pointing his drumstick at the crest of the hill above the Decaheads as a line of round-brimmed uniform hats poked their peaks over the horizon. Gradually, a dozen men in dark blue uniforms with guns and badges appeared on the ridge.

"Oh, shit," said Sam, "it's the fuzz."

"It's the Seventh Cavalry," hooted Johnny, and Aaron played the bugle charge on his piano.

But the fuzz was carrying picnic baskets and blankets, with their chunky wives and tow-headed kids in tow, dozens of Medina County's finest and their families flowing down the hillside, intermingling with the Decahead tribe.

"Yo! Mr. Miller!" called the cop in the lead. It was Sheriff Aubrey, coming down the hill towards them, followed by three chubby rug rats, an inflated wife with flabby white legs, and her even larger old mother.

"Miller?" shot Shelly at Sam, poisoned arrows in her eyes.

"Me?" he protested innocently.

"Hi, Ms Griffin," said Sheriff Aubrey. "Mr. Miller? This is my mother-in-law, Aubrey, too."

"Omigosh, Sam Miller!" tittered the blubbery lady. "I can't believe it! Sam Miller!" She was panting from the walk and the celebrity and looked as though she were about to swoon, but she held out her arms and ingested him in an embrace from which Sam was afraid he might not return. She planted a big blubbery kiss on his cheek, and Sam grimaced with a pained smile.

"And this is Aaron Woodwright," said Shelly, steering her to the piano man.

"Oh!" squealed the woman. "As I live!" she said, clutching her hands to her copious bosom.

"I'm pleased to meet you," said Aaron, donning his Aaron smile.

"I saw you perform at the Kiwanis in Steubenville!" she fluttered, all two hundred pounds of her.

"Well, you must have been just a baby," said Aaron.

"I swear, you haven't aged a bit," she ga-gaed. "You're just as cute as you were back then."

"Mom, they need to play," said Mrs. Sheriff Aubrey.

"Can I make a request?" asked Mother Aubrey.

"Sure," said Shelly, glaring at Miller.

"Could you play 'Creston Gold'?"

"Of course," said Aaron as Shelly steered them all away from her band.

"Aaron and his groupies," Sam grinned.

"You're just jealous," Aaron answered and then called out, "Creston Gold," to the band. They began the lilting introduction, and every single person at Lake Traumsee felt a shiver—the Decaheads, the Medina County Sheriff's Department and their fleshy families, the DecaInc team, Justine and Gavin and Aaron and Mendel and Sam themselves—witnessing the most popular song in the world performed live, in front of an audience for the very first time, after thirty-six years in a shoebox.

Shelly looked out onto the hillside, where the crazy hodgepodge of an audience was now swaying as one to the music on this fine Sunday, singing along with Sam Miller, *"Grass and sunlight all around / Nothing's gonna bring me down / Have another Creston Gold."*

Shelly looked at Sam singing his heart out, his eyes closed, his lips touching the microphone, his grainy voice filling the heart of every person there.

"She holds me close and takes me in / To a place I've never been / Never want to leave again / Have another Creston Gold."

What was he thinking about? she wondered. *The audience? Kathleen? His own crazy self?*

"And when she holds my hand / I know she understands, understands ..."

And then Sam opened his eyes and looked right at her. Shelly smiled and lowered her eyes.

Decapede finished the song, and the motley congregation

at Lake Traumsee, over a hundred strong, those on the hill-side and those on the dock, started jumping and hollering and whistling and clapping and shouting till their arms were aching and their voices were hoarse.

Sam and Aaron and Justine and Mendel and Gavin looked at each other, overwhelmed and speechless.

Justine looked at Sam, her heart thumping, and he winked back at her. Then she looked at Robbie and saw him smiling at her so widely that she thought her heart might burst right there and then.

Bev looked at Robbie looking at Justine. The boy looked dizzy from happiness. Gerald groped for Bev's hand, squeezed it painfully, and then went back to applauding madly with everyone else.

Allie squeezed the Colonel's hand, and they smiled at each other. "Very nice," he said.

State Senator Diane Hobgood's eyes were fixed on Aaron.

"I've seen a lot in my time," said Johnny, his eye in the viewfinder, "but *this* is *history*."

Shelly and Sam were looking at each other. She could still feel the touch of his hand on her hip.

"Thank you, th—" said Aaron, but he stopped, overcome by the applause and his emotions. After an endless ovation, Aaron spoke, interrupted by occasional screams and shouts. "Thank you so much. We—we—" He looked around at his bandmates. "We are Decapede!" and the hillside exploded in screams and shouts. "We are so happy to be here," he continued finally. "It's been a long, strange trip." And everyone laughed appreciatively. "And we really do want to thank you," he said, looking at the crowd. "We're here because of you, and we're here for you!"

And again, the grassy slope went wild. Families continued to stream down the hillside, picnic basket in one hand, kids in the other.

"But truth be told," Aaron continued, "all these shenanigans going on here are going on because of this one lady sitting over here." He looked her in the eye and pointed at her. "Let's give it up for *Shelly Griffin!*"

And everyone stood on their feet, turned to Shelly, and applauded her.

Bev nudged her, and she stood up. She was as red as a ripe Ohio watermelon.

Aaron and Gavin and Mendel and Justine and Sam came forward to the edge of the dock and stood clapping their hands with sober faces. Justine wiped her eyes. Torn between filming and joining the chorus of appreciation that was going on and on, Johnny opted for duty.

Shelly looked at Sam. He looked at her and smiled as he applauded her.

"Play something, dammit!" she called.

Aaron lit into a joyous, ebullient "Walk on By," and a gaggle of teenyboppers squeezed onto the trail at the lake's edge, as close to the band as they could get, screaming and yelping and pulling their hair.

Johnny wove between the band members, catching extreme close-ups of them grinning at each other, sweating and dazed.

"And now—thank you," said Aaron, waiting for the applause to die down. "And now—Now—Thank you. Thank you."

Finally, they let him talk.

"Our next song features our youngest Decapede. I suppose you know that the lady you heard singing this song on the CD couldn't be with us. But we've got her daughter, and we think she's pretty darned terrific, ladies and gentlemen, Miss Justine Bri—" but he was drowned out by the shouts and cheers.

Gerald was standing on his chair, cheering so loudly that the chair began to wobble, and Bev had to grab his hand to steady him.

"Get down from there before you break your neck," she told Gerald, and he did.

The crowd had swollen to several hundred people now, a real audience, clapping for Justine, loud and long and raucous.

Sam saw her turn her back to avoid Johnny's close-up and stepped up to the mic. "Just a minute," he said, his rugged baritone resonating over the lake, and held up his hand. The entire hillside fell silent in anticipation. "Now, you all might notice that our little Justine here is wearing a bandana around her neck, and you might be wondering why." He looked at her with a sly smile.

"Sam Miller, you shut up," the girl warned him.

"Now you might think it's a fashion statement—"

"Sam Miller, I will cut your throat right here—"

"But actually—"

Justine grabbed her mic and shouted out at the top of her lungs, "*Ah-one, ah-two, ah-one two three FOUR!*" and the band began to play. Justine looked out at the crowd from underneath the brim of her fedora. Then she cocked her little hip and began to sing.

"*Well, he walked up to me, and he asked me if I wanted to dance.*"

The girl put her forefinger on her chin and began to walk provocatively towards Robbie at the soundboard, but then she pivoted sharply and came up behind the drum set to give Gavin an audible smooch on the crown of his head.

"*And then I kissed her,*" bellowed out in unison half a dozen of Medina County's finest, locked arm in arm, their billy clubs clacking against each other's gear, Creston Gold in hand, singing along with their favorite song in the whole wide world.

Gavin beamed without missing a beat.

The crowd continued to swell, filling the hillside, from where no one knew or even bothered to wonder, in twos and threes, families, teenagers, an entire Little League baseball team in uniform, together with their coach, his wife, and a double stroller bouncing over the grassy slope. And everyone was on their feet and dancing, grandmothers with punks, police with decadent Decaheads, strangers with even-stranger strangers.

As she sang, Justine sauntered up to Aaron Woodwright, pulled his cheek to her puckered lips, and gave him a *big* smack on the cheek. The screams of the girls in front were piercing, even over the band. She stood next to Mendel and mimed him rocking back and forth in prayer, and he grinned an angelic grin from beneath his bushy beard. She slipped her arm through Sam's, laid her cheek against his shoulder, and gazed up at him lovingly with her famous gray eyes, fluttering her sixteen-year-old eyelashes at him. Then she broke from him and blew a giant kiss to the screaming crowd.

"*And then he kissed me!*" Justine turned and motioned to the band to keep it going.

"*And then he kissed me!*" the band repeated.

"*And then he kissed me!*" she sang, motioning to the hillside to clap along with her.

"*And then he kissed me!*"

"Sing it with me!" she commanded the audience, and they did, a giant chorus shouting in unison on a sunny Sunday.

"*And then he kissed me!*"

Gerald climbed back up on his chair.

"*And then he kissed me!*"

The crowd's voice swelled and grew.

"*And then he kissed me!*"

"*And then he kissed me!*"

"Find somebody to kiss!" she ordered, prancing back and forth along the pier. "Go on, don't be shy."

"*And then he kissed me!*"

Gerald jumped down off his chair and gave Bev a big kiss, right in public.

Colonel Griffin looked at Allie, and she looked back at him, and they both smiled.

"*And then he kissed me!*"

Johnny panned the swelling crowd. "*If I don't fuck it up,*" he thought to himself, "*this is going to win me an Oscar.*"

Several songs later, Aaron smiled into his microphone. "I hope you all are having as much fun as we are." The crowd roared that they were. "That was the last song from our CD—" The hillside let out a groan of protest. "But we have a new song we could play if you—" he started, and the crowd drowned him out with their shouting and cheering and whistling and clamoring and ruckusing. The gaggle of teenyboppers at the edge of the lake had become a multigenerational bevy of besotted femmes careening towards collective apoplexy.

"I'll take that as a 'yes,'" said Aaron to the hillside, and the crowd cheered wildly.

"Aaron here wrote this song just yesterday," said Sam, and the crowd yelled even louder.

"Sam helped out, too," shouted Aaron. "It's called 'Start All Over Again,'" and Gavin counted them into their brand-new song.

"Look at them," Bev nudged Gerald, showing him that the entire hillside was on its feet, dancing and clapping.

"That should be their next single," said Gerald.

Justine was grittily holding her own in the middle of the makeshift stage, right between Sam and Aaron. But to Shelly, she appeared spent, so while the throng was still applauding the new song, Shelly pulled Aaron aside.

"Maybe that's enough? You've been playing for almost four hours."

"Oh, I could go on all day," he said, grinning widely, panting, and wiping the perspiration from his matted bushy forelock.

"Justine looks bushed," she said.

"You think so?" Aaron said, disappointed. "Yeah, I guess. Okay, one more!" Aaron gathered the band for a quick huddle.

"We're going to play our last song now," Aaron said into the mic, panting and glowing. The hillside responded with a collective groan. "I know," he smiled charmingly, "but we haven't done this for a while, and—*we've got blisters on our fingers!*" The hillside laughed. "It's been really wonderful playing for you. Quite a trip," he said, shaking his head with tangible emotion. "Back in the old days, in Steuben, we used to end our shows with a kind of a jam, and we'd like to bring back that tradition. So here's another new song, featuring our incredible multi-instrumentalist Mendel 'Vaneshi' Shochenstein. It's called: 'Shabbos.' " The crowd applauded politely.

Robbie arranged three mic stands right at the front of the improvised little stage. Sam laid down his guitar and took his place at the center mic.

"Sam, I love you!" screamed a girl's voice from the hillside. He squinted out over the water at the tribal gathering. "You might feel different if you got to know me a little better," he cracked, and the hillside rocked with laughter and cheers.

Aaron played a B-flat chord. Sam closed his eyes and began to sing the mournful, haunting melody, "*Bye-de-bye-bye bye,*" his lips touching the mic. He sang slowly, passionately, and hundreds of people listened in rapt silence. At the end of the first verse, Aaron joined in harmony, the silence between phrases broken only by the lapping of the lake and the occasional shrieks of adulation. Then, to a smattering of fervid shouts, Justine took her place between them and joined in on the top voice. As the intensity of the song swelled, Justine slipped her hand into Sam's. Aaron rested his hand on Sam's shoulder, and Johnny lay on his back in front of them to shoot them from below, three demigods against the endless turquoise sky.

Then, Mendel stepped up next to them with his violin and began to add his magical, mystical adornment, weaving and looping through the voices. They did one verse, then another, till finally the entire lakeside was singing along with them, their voices rising in a communal benediction.

"Oh, Charles," whispered Allie to the Colonel, "isn't this wonderful?"

The refrain went on and on. Camera on his shoulder, Johnny walked off the dock and up the hillside, capturing hundreds of faces, a crazy salad of shapes and sizes, joining in a single voice, spellbound by the rapture of the music. Finally, the song ended. For several seconds, there was only the lapping of the lake. Then, the hillside exploded in an uproar of chanting, "Mendel! Mendel!"

"Thank you," said Mendel, moved, smiling shyly, "thank you."

"Thank you," said Aaron, back at his keyboard. "Thank you. Thank you very much." Still, the audience applauded.

Sam waved at the crowd, and the cheering swelled. Aaron brought the five of them to the center of the dock, where they stood in a row waving at the crowd. Finally, as they were filing off the dock, Sam saw Patti and the girls waving at him. "Hey, come on up to the house afterwards!" he called, not bothering to check if Robbie had turned off the mics.

68

After-Party

– June 12, 2006, Afternoon –

The common room, the foyer, and the dining room were packed with uniformed policemen, their portly families, scraggly Decaheads, and a wide assortment of interlopers, all buzzing and animated, peering around at the legendary Gruenhaus itself, snapping pictures and touching things and gossiping. On the front porch, a dozen men were standing patiently in line at a keg of Creston Gold. Johnny was filming interviews one after another, with Robbie pressed into service as soundman. Allie and Diane and Gerald and Winston and Gavin and the Colonel and Brandi and Matt were running around the kitchen trying to lay out some sort of improvised refreshments.

Each one of the band members was surrounded by a cluster of gawkers. Mendel was posing graciously for photo after photo, decked out in his exotic black regalia, careful to avoid touching any women. Justine was in a crush of young girls and men of all ages, with Robbie keeping vigil that no one came too close. Aaron was sitting on a sofa, Creston Gold in his hand, with Bev next to him, spinning yarns from back in the day for an adoring group of women. Sam was trapped in a corner, pinned in by Mrs. Sheriff Aubrey and her mother, indistinguishable but for thirty years and thirty pounds.

"So me and my girlfriend Barbara Sue, we was just fifteen, we couldn't drive or nothing, so we got Bobby's brother Lewis to drive us over to Steubenville for this concert we heard was going on. We never heard of no Decapede or anything, but there was all these college kids and hippies and stuff we never saw around Beaver Falls, so we wanted to go see."

"Excuse me," said Shelly, pulling him out of the corner and leading him towards the hallway, "I need to speak with Mr. Miller about a certain pressing matter ..."

She pushed him through the door into the quiet hallway and snapped the door shut behind them.

"Well, Miller, you having fun?" asked Shelly, smiling at him up close and glowing.

"Who invited all these damn people?" he said, trying unsuccessfully to suppress a smile.

"I wonder," grinned Shelly, "who could it have been?"

"There he is!" said Patti, and the girls came running down the hallway to Sam.

"Well, how'd you like it?" asked Sam eagerly, crouching down to meet them at eye level.

"It was pretty good for a first show," said Bunkie.

"We saw you on the computer," said Teal shyly.

"So how'd we sound?" asked Sam.

"It was nice," said Teal.

"You need more slow songs," said Bunkie.

Sam looked at Shelly.

"I liked that one where all three of you sang and then the man with the beard played violin."

"Yeah, I like that one, too. He's a really good guy," said Sam. "Come on, girls, I want to show you something."

"They miss him," Patti said as they watched him lead the girls down the hallway with their little hands in his.

Shelly watched and nodded.

The house was milling with fans and friends and strangers, the noise was oppressive, and Shelly was feeling stuffy. As soon as she was introduced to Pastor Tim and his wife, Eleanor, to Mr. and Mrs. McAlister from the next farm over, as well as to Roger Fadinka, the pharmacist who also served as Creston's mayor, Shelly slipped into the kitchen for a moment's quiet. The kitchen team was still working frantically.

"Das all we got left," said Winston, indicating a tray piled with peanut butter sandwiches. "I can mebbe get you sumting?"

"No, I'm fine, thanks. Great, what you guys are doing here."

"Cut them in fours," Diane instructed Gerald.

"Gavin, you should get out there and circulate," she said.

"I'd really rather help out in here, if it's okay," he said.

"Sure," winked Shelly. "Hey—good job down there."

"Yes," said Gavin, glowing like a choir boy, "wasn't it lovely?"

"So, how did you like the show?" she asked her father.

"Nice, Shelly, very nice," he said. "You know, if you like that kind of music."

She eyed the carving knife on the counter.

"But it was very thoughtful the way Sam mentioned you," he added with a smile, and squeezed her arm.

The dining room was full of strangers drinking beer from plastic cups and munching on peanut butter and boysenberry jam sandwich wedges, celery sticks, and pretzels. The foyer was full of policemen standing around, joking and having the time of their lives. The common room was full of more strangers.

Sheriff Aubrey's mother-in-law was busy telling Penka, the Balkan housekeeper, long stories in English about the Decapede of old. In all the hubbub, Shelly spied Pattie chatting with Mendel.

"Have either of you seen Sam?" she asked.

Mendel shook his beard.

"No," said Pattie. "I think he went off somewhere with my girls."

As she neared the door of her office, Shelly could hear singing. The door was open a crack. "*Rain on the roof goes pitty-patty, pitty-patty when you're riding in my car-car.*"

She peeked in. Sam was sitting on the floor with his guitar, leaning back against her rust-and-butterscotch couch. Bunkie and Teal and Petar and Penka's kids and a passel of other unidentified juniors were sitting around him in a circle, entranced.

"Take me for a ride in your car-car, take me for a ride in your car ..."

Caveman Miller, she teased herself, and felt a warm flush. Sam saw her and motioned with his head for her to come in.

"Sam is sitting in Sam's seat, Aaron's sitting in Aaron's seat, Shelly's sitting in the driver's seat when you're riding in my car-car."

He smiled a crinkled smile at her. Shelly felt herself flush.

"Boom-chukka boom-a chukka boom-boom," he sang, and Shelly went to sit next to him.

He finished the song, and all the tykes smiled at each other and clapped their little hands.

"Sing puffa maja," said Teal.

"I don't know that one," said Sam with a twinkle.

"You know that one!" insisted Teal.

"Oh, 'puffa maja'! Why didn't you say so?" he grinned, and began strumming. *"Puff, the magic dragon lived by the sea,"* he sang, his husky voice gentler and softer than Shelly had ever heard it.

She sat next to him on the sofa, looking down at him sitting on the floor, the kids of all sizes and shapes and colors scattered over the facing sofa, the chairs, everywhere, all listening to Sam Miller, transfixed. She laid her hand on his shoulder as he played and let it rest there. Then she leaned her head back onto the soft cushion.

When Shelly awoke, the room was dark. She was lying on her sofa, covered by the quilt. Sam and the kids, she remembered. She sat up sluggishly. The house was quiet but for a distant, deep humming.

She stumbled foggily into the hallway, where Brandi was

running an industrial-sized vacuum cleaner that sounded like a jet engine, while Matt was dragging out two super-jumbo black plastic garbage bags. She groped her way into the common room, where her team was collapsed in post-bacchanalian exhaustion. Johnny was lying stretched out on one loveseat, snoring happily. Bev and Gerald were spread out on another, publicly displaying their affection. Diane was curled up with her head on Aaron's knee while he was chatting animatedly with Sam, who moved his leg for Shelly to drop down next to him.

"How long was I asleep?" she asked groggily.

"Since Sunday," said Sam.

Brandi finally turned off the sweeper. The silence was thundering.

"Finally, some quiet around here," said Sam.

"Whose idea was this?" asked Diane.

"Ask the singer," yawned Shelly.

"Why is she always blaming me?" asked Sam innocently.

"Because it's always your fault," said Mendel, and everyone laughed, Sam loudest of all.

"Allie," said Shelly, "I'm so sorry. I hope they didn't make too much mess."

"Oh, don't be silly," said Allie. "It was the most excitement we've seen at Gruenhaus in years."

"She's the only one around here got any game," said Sam.

"I'm not sure what that means," said Allie, "but thank you."

Gavin and Winston came in, each carrying a silver serving tray with tall crystal champagne glasses.

"Ho, ho," said Johnny, sitting up and taking his camera in hand.

"Whose idea was this?" asked Shelly.

Gerald pointed proudly at Bev.

"I thought a little celebration was called for," Bev said, and everyone nodded.

"Where's Justine?" asked Shelly.

"I think she had some technical issues to discuss with the soundman," said Sam, and everyone laughed.

"We used to call that snipe hunting," smiled the Colonel.

"Dad?" said Shelly, feigning shock.

"Cover your ears," said Bev to everyone, and gave a long, piercing tweet on her whistle. Shelly cringed, still half asleep. A minute later, Robbie and Justine came in, as serious and proper as if they'd just come from their Civics homework, their clothes in perfect order. Justine's bandana was still in place, but her fedora was gone.

"Everything all right?" mugged Sam.

"Yeah, fine," croaked Robbie innocently.

"Fine," agreed Justine.

"Where you hat, boo?" teased Winston.

Justine put her hand on her head to find it gone, and everyone laughed.

"Oh, leave them alone," said Diane.

Shelly failed to suppress a wide, loud yawn. "I'm sorry," she said, "I just conked out."

"You deserve it," said Bev. "You've been working like a dog."

"Hey," said Matt, "where's Dog?"

"He was chasing after that spaniel bitch," said Sam.

"Men," said Shelly and Justine together, shaking their heads in disdain. Justine took a glass of champagne.

"One glass," said Shelly.

"Hey, I'm a rock star," protested Justine.

"A sixteen-year-old rock star," said Shelly. Justine stuck her tongue out at her, and Diane laughed.

Everyone took their champagne in hand and looked at Shelly. She started to pull herself to her feet, but was feeling heavy and not yet awake. "Johnny," she said, "would you care to do the honors?"

Johnny smiled, handed the camera to Robbie, and raised

his glass for a toast. Everyone grew serious.

"I'd like to congratulate Decapede on an incredible show, their first after a thirty-six-year hiatus. It's been too long. You are," said Johnny, looking at the band and then at Shelly, "literally a dream come true."

"Tell that Shelly lady she ought to be more careful what she dreams," said Sam.

"But today, I saw that you aren't just a legend come back to haunt us," continued Johnny. "You guys really are one kick-ass rock band."

Everyone smiled at each other.

"Ladies and gentlemen and Sam," said Johnny, raising his glass, "to Decapede!"

The team raised their glasses and drank.

"One more thing," said Johnny. "Sam, when you started playing 'Creston Gold'? Well, it got me thinking. About the old days, and about you guys. And, well—"

He reached behind the loveseat and held up an elegant auburn guitar.

"Is that the George Harrison guitar?" asked Robbie in awe from behind the camera, then remembered to move in for a close-up.

Gerald sat up. "For real?"

"Sam, I'd like you to have this," said Johnny, handing it to him. "I think the original owner would have approved."

"Jeez," said Aaron.

Mendel stared, speechless. Gavin shook his head. Bev touched Gerald's hand, and he closed his mouth. Sam ran his fingers over its elegant brown body.

"That's the guitar you told us about?" asked Shelly, and Johnny nodded.

Aaron and Mendel and Gerald clustered around Sam. Robbie ran to get a little amp.

"It's very pretty," said Matt.

"It belonged to George fucking Harrison, you idiot," said

Brandi, snuggling deeper into his arm.

"It's a Fender Rosewood Stratocaster," said Mendel.

Gerald reached in his finger to touch it.

Sam plugged it in, strummed a chord and played a lick, dumbstruck.

"Say something," Shelly prompted him.

Sam looked at her, then at Johnny.

"Oh. Oh, man," he managed to say. "I—Yeah, this is really ..." He stood up and gave Johnny a hug and a couple of manly smacks on the back. "Thank you." He scratched his jaw. "Shit, man."

"Play something," said Shelly, and the team all sat back to listen. Johnny took back his camera from Robbie.

"Play something, huh?" said Sam as he adjusted the tuning. His fingers fiddled around while he tried to think what to play.

"I can't believe this," said Gerald, squeezing Bev's hand in excitement.

"Ow," said Bev, and squeezed him back.

"Maybe this song got played on this guitar before," Sam said and began to pick a familiar, reflective line. He closed his eyes and sang softly in his gravelly voice. *"There are places I'll remember ..."*

At one point, his fingers stopped playing for a long moment, frozen in extreme close-up in Johnny's lens. Gavin and Winston looked at each other. Mendel's hands were behind his head, his eyes closed. Diane was lying with her head on Aaron's knee, his hand on her shoulder, their eyes riveted on Sam. Bev was nestled under Gerald's arm. They both held their breath. Allie and the Colonel sat on hardback chairs, poised. Brandi snuggled up against Matt, and he smiled happily. Justine and Robbie sat close, watching and waiting, but not touching.

Shelly's head was nodding.

Sam continued playing. Shelly jolted alert.

The last *ting* of the guitar hung in the air. Finally Johnny broke the silence. "Got any more bubbly there, Winston?"

When people finally began to stir and move and talk in subdued voices, Sam turned to Shelly. They looked at each other, and she squeezed his hand.

"Shelly," said Bev, "don't you want to, you know, say something?"

"What?" she said, stifling a yawn. "I'm sorry?"

"Don't you want to, like, summarize the day for everyone?"

"Yeah, sure. Yes. Of course."

Bev tapped on her empty glass and refilled it. Everyone turned to listen to Shelly.

Shelly pulled herself up again, tugged her tunic into place, and raised her champagne glass. Her brain was a fog.

"Well, well, well," she said, and everyone beamed together with pride and happiness and excitement. "First of all, thank you to Mr. Miller here, who, in his infinite irresponsibility, provided us with a most entertaining day's activities."

Everyone laughed and looked at Sam, who took a deep bow.

"Something happened today. Something—big. In so many ways." She paused, hoping her brain would give her mouth something to say. "For Northeast Ohio. For Allie Bauer and Bauer Brewery. For all the people pressing the CDs and sewing the T-shirts and answering the phones in the Cleveland office and the DJs playing 'Creston Gold' on the radio." She looked at the band. "For your music. For your fans around here, for the fans all over the world who'll hear and see what happened here today. For the future of Decapede, for yourselves." She looked around the room. "For every member of this team, and for Aaron and for Gavin and for Sam and for Mendel and for Justine—" Again, she paused. "And for me." She smiled. "If I start trying to describe all the things I'm thinking and feeling—I wouldn't know where to start, so I'm not going to."

Everyone smiled at each other.

"Know what today was?" she asked, scouring the faces the faces of her troops. "Today was your first show. Four weeks from tomorrow, July fourth, you're appearing at the Cuyahoga Hollow."

"I saw Iron Maiden there," said Matt.

"The whole world is watching you. You have four weeks to make your mark. Let's give them something to remember, yeah?" Everyone nodded and agreed. "So," Shelly continued, "congratulations. And let's get to work! " she said, raising her glass.

Everyone clinked glasses and drank a champagne toast and chattered excitedly.

"You're not celebrating?" asked Sam, indicating Shelly's untouched glass.

"No," she said, stifling a yawn. "Oh, I'm sorry. I mean, yes. I'm celebrating. I'm just feeling so bushed all of a sudden."

Sam guzzled down her champagne, and Shelly gave in to a giant yawn.

69

The Summer

– June 2006 –

The weather that June, everyone agreed, was perfect.

By the end of the first week at Gruenhaus, the band had finished recording all eight songs from the Sheek CD. Hour by hour, Aaron had forged them into a band, and even Sam had been patient as they ran through take after take. Justine and Robbie kept up with the adults in the studio, though outside of rehearsal, they tended to go off by themselves. The single of "Bring It On Home to Me" was released and entered the charts at #2, behind "Creston Gold."

Bev worked out a schedule to suit the band's needs: Breakfast at nine, studio work ten to six with a forty-five-minute break for lunch. But sometimes, Sam would get up early and go down to the boathouse with his tackle, his prodigal dog and his guitar, coming back only when Winston sounded the dinner bell. "Leave him," Aaron told Shelly, "that's where the magic happens." The band had plenty to do without him—Gavin in the kitchen, Aaron and Mendel and Robbie mixing the recordings, Justine practicing the bass.

One day, a crew came to do a photo shoot of Justine for *16½ Magazine*. Shelly wouldn't let them in the house, so they shot her out on the porch swing, on the lawn, and perched on the branch of a tree in the backyard.

In the evenings, the gang would sit around chatting in the common room, playing guitars and singing old songs they all loved, just for fun. Johnny caught every minute of it.

On Sunday, the band set up again down at the lake. Although no one announced anything, word got around, and a stream of neighbors, locals, couples, packs of teens, families with toddlers and grannies, Decaheads, and picnickers carrying their picnic baskets and blankets all gathered on the hillside, twice as many as the week before. Decapede played their entire repertoire, including "Rock Around the Clock," a twenty-three minute "Shabbos," and, acceding happily to the chants of the crowd, "Creston Gold" and the brand-new "Start All Over Again" three times each. Johnny caught every minute of that as well.

During the second week, bootleg recordings began to circulate on Kazaa, as well as a short, jerky clip of Justine's raucous "And Then He Kissed Me." At first, Colonel Griffin was outraged over copyright infringements, but when he saw the sales figures, he begrudgingly reconciled himself to the phenomenon.

On the days when Sam went fishing, he would sometimes send Dog to call Aaron down to the lake to help him polish something he was working on. At the end of the day, Sam never failed to bring home a bucket brimming with fresh bass and bluegill, to Winston's delight.

While he was waiting, hoping for new material from Sam, Aaron began working on some new covers, each member choosing one song. Gavin chose Buddy Holly's "I'm Gonna Love You Too" "because it all started in Mason City." Sam and Justine sang the airtight harmony in tandem, with the girl playing bass for the first time. Justine chose a song by Laura Nyro "because she was Mom's favorite." "Bi-i-i-ill! I love you so!" she sang in a rousing overflow of joy. Mendel taught them a rollicking Hassidic melody. On a bet they lost to Justine at pool, Sam and Aaron chose each other's song. Sam came up with "Ruby Baby" for Aaron, which he sang with a swag and brag destined to syncopate many a female heart. And in return, Aaron picked for Sam Bo Diddley's raunchy hoot blues "I'm a Man," which Sam sang in a low, gravelly growl, with his eyes closed and his lips touching the microphone, caught by Johnny in an extreme close-up.

Johnny explained on his show that due to overwhelming demand, tickets for the Cuyahoga Hollow show would only be available via lottery, $20 a shot, and that there would be a maximum of twelve thousand tickets available. The governor, his secretary, and her two teenage daughters were all comped with backstage passes.

If she wasn't too tired from the endless phone calls and emails and distractions and decisions, at the end of the evening, Shelly liked to turn off her BlackBerry and take a walk to clear her head. Sam and Dog would tag along, and they'd talk about the day's events—Justine's progress on the bass, Allie's rhubarb pie. Shelly had no idea if Sam even remembered the halting kiss that night in her office. For her part, she was careful to avoid the subject.

On the second Saturday afternoon, the Medina County's police force was defeated 13-2 by the Decapede team (Sam and a bunch of Matt's friends from the AA Cuyahoga Rapids). Sam went two for four—a single and a double, as well as one snazzy catch in left field. He was so exultant at the end that he picked Shelly up and spun her around in the air, ignoring her squeals of protest.

On the following Sunday, people started showing up early to grab a spot for their picnic blankets. Cars came from as far away as Chillicothe, Altoona, and even Kalamazoo, and traffic backed up for miles along little East Mill Road.

Shelly had Matt draft his endless supply of friends to bring in porta-potties for those too delicate to use the woods. They came with food trucks, concession stands for T-shirts and CDs and mugs, balloons and cotton candy, and even a pony ride.

One stand sold nothing but fedoras ("Justine hats," the kids called them).

The band played for a full three and a half hours, the crowd of over a thousand calling for the old songs and the new songs again and again. As soon as they got back to Gruenhaus, the whole team collapsed from exhaustion and exhilaration. The logjam of cars going home lasted for hours.

During the third week, the band spent long hours in the studio, racing against time to generate enough new material for their comeback CD. By the end of the week, they were polishing two new originals—"You Never Know," an introspective ballad, and "Allie's Rhubarb Pie," an upbeat rocker, both of which were written almost entirely by Sam but credited at his insistence to Woodwright-Miller. "Your name's fancier," he said.

The "Creston Gold" single went platinum. "Bring It On Home" and "Start All Over Again" were declared million-sellers. The Sheek CD was #6 and climbing.

Johnny's "Inside Decapede" was expanded to two nights a week, with unprecedented viewership for a "reality" show. The revenues from advertising and syndication were, in Gerald's word, "significant."

The Colonel was spending more and more time at the brewery, where they had reactivated the two retired production lines and leased eight new trucks. He used every ploy he could think of to get Shelly to drive down with him, but she adamantly stood her ground, insisting he take "that Brandi girl" instead.

For the first time, independent candidate Diane Hobgood drew statistically even with her opponents in the Florida 38th District congressional polls, spurred to no small degree by the photo of her and Aaron Woodwright kissing in the middle of the dance party on the dock.

Each evening at nine o'clock, Sam and Dog would appear at the screen door to Shelly's office to pull her away from her computer. They would walk all the way down to the lake and back, Dog walking happily between them. Shelly explained to Sam why so many people were watching Johnny's videos of Decapede eating breakfast or playing Frisbee on the lawn. He explained to her the difference between the swaggering mating call of a horned bullfrog and the coy response of the hornless cowfrog.

On the third Saturday, several hundred people watched and cheered and drank a lot of Creston Gold as the Decapede team walloped the Medina County Police by 21–6. Sam went three for six (two singles, a double, two RBIs, and a stolen base) and pitched a scoreless seventh inning in relief.

Early Sunday morning, Sheriff Aubrey closed off East Mill Road from both ends, but several thousand Decapede fans made their way by foot, undeterred. The band played for hours, and clips were shown on the evening news in fifty states and sixty-two countries.

By the fourth week, four new songs were in the can, and Aaron, Mendel, and Robbie were working evenings to finish mixing the rest. The days were spent polishing the performance for the big show. Sam bitched when Aaron explained that they were limited by union regulations to playing for no more than two and a half hours, but he more or less behaved himself as Aaron ran them through their paces over and over till he was satisfied.

"Start All Over Again" was released as their new single with Justine's "Wedding Bell Blues" as the B-side, and it entered the Billboard charts at #1, above "Bring It On Home" and "Creston Gold," giving Decapede the top three songs on the Hot 100, the first act to do so since The Beatles. The Harlem Gospel Choir's version of "Cuyahoga Rising" charted at #17.

Sales of lottery tickets for the Fourth of July show at Cuyahoga Hollow passed the three-hundred-thousand-mark, filling DecaInc's coffers beyond Gerald's most optimistic forecasts.

Decapede appeared on the cover of Newsweek, including a full-page "DecaMomma" spread on "the legendary" Shelly Griffin, "the vibrant new icon of women's empowerment."

All day long, Shelly was on the phone and Skype meetings and answering emails, dealing with publicity and finances and logistics and backscratching. Often she would make a mental note to tell Sam about some work dilemma on their evening walk. She would pare the matter down to his very limited span of attention for "business shit." But when she could get him to listen, she found he always had a straight way of thinking that, well, cut through the bullshit and saw the heart of things.

And then, finally, the Fourth of July weekend arrived.

Diane flew up on Friday to join everyone for the last Friday night dinner. Johnny's camera caught Aaron and her holding hands on the white tablecloth as Mendel was singing the blessing over the wine.

Shelly wouldn't allow Sam to play ball on Saturday, for fear of a broken finger, but Sam allowed Justine to give him a swimming lesson. He got as far as walking in up to his chest, holding her hand. Shelly and Dog sat on the dock and watched.

Sunday was spent at Cuyahoga Hollow, long and tedious, and Sam Miller was grouchier than ever because Shelly and Aaron had canceled the last Decafest at Lake Traumsee for a "chickenshit sound check."

70

Sausages and Wind
– July 4, 2006, Early Morning –

Outside, the early morning Fourth of July sun was shining gloriously to greet The Big Day, only an occasional rambunctious gust of wind stirring the trees around Gruenhaus.

Inside, Shelly's face was glowing in the light of her computer screen. First she checked the weather update: **Turbulent front over Lake Erie headed towards Canada, will avoid Metro Cleveland.** She felt her body relax. Then she read the very flattering Daily Financial Report from the Cleveland office. She closed the file with a smile and clicked on the *Plain Dealer* site. **OUR DECAPEDE!** ran the banner headline over a giant photo of the band.

She clicked through Yahoo!, CNN, MSNBC, even BBC— every home page featured links to articles about the Decapede show, about the Decahead cult, about the Decapede corporate culture, about the revenues generated, about the record-breaking reality show's viewership, but mostly gossip about the band.

A number of the articles quoted Johnny's epithet, "Like watching a dinosaur egg hatch in the middle of a soap opera." She peeked at profiles of Sam, of Justine, of Aaron, of the "celeb groupies" Diane and Gerald, and of someone named Shelly Griffin, **Mother of the Decapede Miracle**, even though she had resolved not to read any of them until after the show.

The *New York Times* led with **Not Just Music: The Decapede Revolution**, crediting the band's unprecedented success to the growing availability of broadband internet, citing Decapede's groundbreaking popularity in emerging social media, such as Myspace ("the magic ingredient in the Decapede potion"), Facebook ("hundreds of thousands of friends and strangers chatting together about Decapede"), and YouTube ("the first musical video clip with over a million views, a viral-like phenomenon").

She clicked through: **Decapede—Sole Performance Today Near Cleveland,** and under it was a photo of Sam singing in front of the boathouse. Shelly clicked, even though she had seen it a dozen times, the jiggly audience video of Sam singing the song that first Sunday down at the lake. She read the description as she waited for it to load—**"Creston Gold" by Decapede (Sam Miller)—First public performance ever, thirty-six years after ill-fated Decapede breakup**—but the video file was taking too long to load, so Shelly closed it and opened her private email, shellyg63@yahoo.com.

There was a rap at the door and in came Winston with a breakfast tray, all bustling and cheerful.

"Just the coffee, thanks," Shelly smiled.

He was wearing his brightest turquoise scarlet-and-gold-rainbow shirt, freshly ironed for the big day. He handed Shelly her We Are Decapede! mug.

"Nice hot brefess," he said, laying the tray on the corner of her desk, "Hard-workin' boo like you need to eat good."

"Is everyone up?" she smiled.

"Yah, peoples done breakfast, take it easy, like you say."

Shelly knew she should go out to say hi to everyone, but she felt so good that she decided to give herself another few minutes. She sipped her coffee as she skimmed through her old emails, all of them trivialities from a previous lifetime,

till one caught her eye, Congrats and Invitation from
bwalters@abc.com. She opened it and glanced at the signature.
Shelly's heart broke into a sprint.

```
Dear Shelly,
    I hope you don't mind me writing to your
private account. Gerald Bridges gave me your
address, so you can blame him.
```

That tray that Winston left. Those sausages. The room
tilted slightly.

```
    I just want to tell you what a big fan
I am of Decapede and of you professionally
and personally. It would be my pleasure to
host you on The View at your earliest possi-
ble convenience. I look forward to speaking
to you as soon as you've caught your breath.
```

Oh, God, those sausages.

```
    In the meantime, very best of luck to
Decapede and to you on your big day. I'm
sure the show will be great. I'll be cheer-
ing from afar,
    Barbara
```

Shelly turned away from the screen, her stomach yawing.
She drew a deep breath and looked out at the treetops horsing
around like unruly schoolboys.

Girl, she told herself, *get a handle. You've made it this far.
Focus on the mission.* Her stomach shifted position. She tried
to fill her nostrils with Winston's coffee, but the sausages
slipped through, churning her insides. *Just the weather, then
I'm going.*

Morning—Sunny and clear, with a high near 78. South wind around 11 mph. Chance of precipitation 0%.

Yes!

Afternoon—Sunny and clear, with a high near 82 with occasional breezes 13 to 16 mph. Chance of precipitation 0%.

Barbara Walters, she smiled to herself, light-headed.

Evening—the show would be over by then—*Partly cloudy, with a high near 61. Occasional gusts of wind 14-24 mph. Chance of precipitation 8%*

But those greasy, spicey sau—

She waited for the radar map to load, holding her breath. A drunken amoeba crawled jerkily across her screen. Her stomach queased.

The quickly developing cold front moving northeastwards, she skimmed, holding her nose closed with her fingers, *will remain over Lake Erie unless wind direction—*

Shelly gasped for air, but with it got a deep draft of Winston's hot, greasy bratwurst. Her stomach lurched. She stood up, shoving her elegant executive chair back against the wall, and slid as quickly as she could out from behind her desk to flee the smell, in between the two rust-and-butterscotch sofas, up the four steps, and out the door to the hallway where Brandi was headed towards her.

"I thought you were gonna sleep through your big day," grinned Brandi. She had shed her raccoon eyes and her zombie garb for a tight ponytail, a pair of very tight jeans, and an extremely tight white We Are Decapede! T-shirt.

"Just checking my mail," said Shelly. "Everything okay?"

"Everything's under control. Just a couple of questions." Brandi flipped through the pages of her legal pad. "The mayor of Cuyahoga Rapids asked for two comps."

"Brandi, we can't go giving away tickets to every hick town mayor—" said Shelly, trying to expunge the smell of Winston's bratwurst.

"The State Park is part of his town. He's like the host."

"Good catch. Do it. Next?" Shelly kept walking.

"The guys at the brewery made me promise to thank you for thinking of them." Shelly had instructed her father to give every employee of Bauer's Brewery, past and present, a pair of tickets.

"My pleasure," said Shelly. "Next?"

"The governor's office. They need six more seats in the VIP section."

"You couldn't find me. Next."

"Some guy named Derek Turnbull, says he's a close personal friend. Asked for a pair of comps."

Shelly snorted. "Tell him to go fuck himself," she snapped.

"Who is he?" asked Brandi, grinding at her gum.

"That asshole football coach I used to date."

"Him? Screw him!" said Brandi, crossing a thick line through his name.

"Wait, you know what?" said Shelly, smiling smugly. "Send him two."

Brandi gazed at Shelly. "Can I be you when I grow up?"

The sausages were still in her nostrils. *Keep moving*, she said—new air, new smells. She stuck her head into the little office where Gerald was talking into the microphone of a headset, his Bermuda-shorted legs propped up on a chair, paring an orange into one long curly peel with a long, sharp knife, with a toothpick in his mouth and a glint in his eye.

"Jack, I don't have time to negotiate. Three and a half million per thirty-second spot, take it or leave it." He offered Shelly a slice of the orange as he listened, but she quickly declined. "I can give you three in the first hour, three in the second, one in the third for"—he did the calculation in his head—"twenty-two million. No, you decide now. I got a line of people begging for slots." He smiled and winked at Shelly. "I'm sending you the papers."

He hung up and looked up at Shelly. "Nike," he said. "Do you know what Coca-Cola offered to sponsor the entire show?"

Shelly shook her head, holding her breath.

"I'll give you a hint. It was very close to nine figures."

"That's a lot of figures. What did you say?"

"Not for sale. The show will be sponsored by 'Bauer's, brewer of Creston Gold since 1872.'"

"There you go," she grinned. *Keep moving*, she thought.

"There you go," he grinned back as his phone rang again. "What time do we leave?"

Shelly looked at her watch. "We have a couple of hours yet," she said.

The front door was open, and she gulped the fresh air.

Sam was sitting on the front porch swing, picking on his George Harrison guitar. Aaron and Bev were at the other end of the porch, chatting and laughing. Shelly knew that Sam was still irritated over the Sunday bash at the lake being canceled for the sound check. The trees swayed in the breeze. Shelly took a deep breath of the sunny Independence Day morning and turned to Sam.

"Hey, watcha doin' out here, Mr. Rock Star?" she smiled through the churn in her gut.

"Just watching the weather," said Sam.

"It's going to be a beautiful day," said Shelly chipperly. *I wish those damned trees would stop swaying.*

Sam just continued plucking.

"What?" demanded Shelly.

Sam shrugged.

"What? Say it!" Shelly covered his strings with her hand.

Sam looked up at her. "It's gonna rain," he said, and resumed his annoying picking.

"Well, the National Weather Service says it's going to be a beautiful day," she snorted.

Sam just shrugged and continued playing.

"God, you can ruin anything, can't you?" she said and

went to the other end of the porch to be with friendly people.

"Look at this day, will you?" said Shelly, inhaling deeply.

"It's going to be a beautiful day," said Aaron.

"A beautiful day," agreed Shelly. The grass was swishing like waves.

"A beautiful day, and a big day," said Bev.

Sam plucked a little louder.

"We've come a long way since Alejandro's," said Aaron.

"The restaurant where Aaron and I first met," Shelly explained to Bev. Shelly breathed deeply through her nose and steadied herself against the porch railing.

"Here you are," said the Colonel, as if he'd caught her shirking.

"Dad, you're dressed already?" said Shelly, all smiles. "We still have—"

The Colonel was wearing his freshly pressed business suit, his cell phone in his hand, and a worried look on his face.

"I just got off the phone with Sheriff Aubrey. State Police say traffic is already starting to back up on the interstate, and that if we want to get to Cuyahoga Rapids on time, we'd better get a move on."

"Dad, are you serious?" asked Shelly, blanching.

"Silly question," said the Colonel. "Shall I tell the sheriff to have the police escort here in half an hour?"

Shelly looked at Bev.

"I need to organize the band," Bev read from the checklist on her clipboard, "organize all the equipment, and make sure everything gets loaded onto the bus."

"I can take care of the band, if that'll help," offered Aaron.

"You're an angel," said Shelly. "Dad, police escort in thirty minutes, yes, go."

The Colonel went to make his call, and Shelly began to spurt bursts of orders.

"Aaron, go find the band, make sure they're packed, outfits for the show in garment bags, no excuses!" A gust of wind brushed her hair into her eyes. "Have them put all their personal things here in the foyer. Brandi has the lists. Have them in my office in—" She looked at her watch. "Twenty minutes. Go," said Shelly, and Aaron was off on his mission. The trees began to bump shoulders like corner boys looking for trouble. Her stomach roiled, and she gripped the railing.

"Are you okay?" asked Bev, touching Shelly's shoulder.

"I'm fine," she inhaled deeply. "Tell Robbie to collect all the stuff he needs from the music room, and have—have Matt pack the bus. If they need more hands, get Gerald and my father. I don't want any of the band carrying things today." Shelly was leaning on the railing, trying to hold her head up. "I'll go tell the rest of the team."

"Are you sure you're okay?"

"Yes, yes!" insisted Shelly. "Go!"

And Bev was off on her Energizer-Bunny legs.

Shelly turned sharply to Sam. "Didn't you hear?" she scowled.

"*Cuyahoga rising,*" he sang, "*river gonna overflow.*"

"Oh, go back to your cave!" she hissed at him and stomped into the hallway, her stomach flailing.

"Shelly!" wailed Justine right into her face, "I can't find my hat!"

Shelly skirted her, quickening her steps.

"I know that I left it on my bed with the rest of my clothes for the show—" cried the girl, almost in tears.

Her gut was pitching and heaving as she hurried past Diane and her ironing board.

"—but now it's gone ..."

Around the corner and down the hallway, the girl on her heels—

"... everybody expects me to wear ..."

Past Gerald's office—

"... can't leave till I ..."

Shelly closed her throat and tried to breathe through her nose.

"... you listening? I *have* to find it!" the girl rattled hysterically.

But Shelly was running now, with the girl chasing after her, down the hallway and through her door and down the four steps and between the two rust-and-butterscotch sofas and past her executive desk and the screen door and around the corner and into her pristine Old World bathroom where she flung open the toilet seat and threw up her very guts.

Justine stood in the doorway, staring at Shelly on her knees with her head in the bowl, retching.

The screen door banged in the wind.

Shelly retched again, longer and harder.

The screen kept banging.

"B-Bev!" said Justine and bolted out of the room.

Shelly stumbled out of the bathroom, wiping her mouth with a tissue. Justine came running back in, panting and spooked. Shelly pointed at the offending breakfast tray. "Get that out of here!" she shouted at Justine. The girl opened the screen door and threw the food out onto the grass for Dog.

Shelly sat on her sofa, sipping water from a bottle and staring glassy-eyed out the window down the hill towards the lake. The wind was shoving the trees around, huffing at them, looking for trouble.

Justine sat down next to her and put her hand on Shelly's.

Bev came bustling in, lugging her black doctor's valise. She pulled a chair up next to Shelly and took her wrist. "What's going on?" she asked in her doctor's voice as she measured her pulse.

"What?" answered Shelly, annoyed. "Nothing's going on. I'm nervous. A person isn't allowed to be nervous on a day like today?"

Bev fished her stethoscope out of her bag and looked at Justine. "Goodbye," she said.

The girl stuck out her lower lip and scootched closer to Shelly.

Bev stuck a thermometer into Shelly's mouth and listened to her chest and back.

"Grinf lsermw—" she protested.

"Shh!" ordered Dr. Pettiford. She checked the thermometer. "When did this start?"

"When I got up this morning," answered Shelly impatiently. "Yesterday, I was fine,"

"Eat anything special?"

"I've been too busy to eat. A little attack of nerves, I'm fine now!" she said, rising.

"Sit!" said Bev.

"The bus is—"

"Sit!" said Bev. "I'm ordering you."

"I'm your boss," said Shelly. "You don't have the authority."

"And nonetheless, I am ordering you." said Bev. "Sit, please."

Shelly sat.

"Have you ever thrown up from nervousness in the past?"

"I've never had a whole fucking phenomenon on my head before!" Shelly barked. "Can we please—"

"Have you ever thrown up from nervousness in the past?" repeated Dr. Pettiford.

"No," answered Shelly.

"Have you been feeling nauseous recently?"

"No," said Shelly.

"Are you sure?"

"Maybe once or twice."

"Have your breasts been sensitive?"

"No!" answered Shelly.

"Are you feeling bloated?"

"Thanks, kick me when I'm down. Now, could we please—"

"When did you have your last period?"

"I don't know!" she shouted. "I have a giant fucking extravaganza to put up, and you're asking me—"

"When?" demanded Bev.

"Bev, not now," Shelly pleaded.

"When?" asked Dr. Pettiford.

Shelly tried to remember. "I—" she flushed. "I'm not sure. I was spotting a little the last few days. I couldn't—I mean, I didn't really pay attention."

"Are you usually regular?"

"I used to be. Before all this."

"When did you last have sex?"

"Maybe I should wait outside," said Justine.

Shelly looked at Justine, blinked, and grabbed her hand.

"When?" asked Dr. Pettiford.

Shelly swallowed and colored. "A couple of months ago, I guess."

The wind and the trees were butting heads. A plastic bucket tumbled recklessly across the grass.

"Do you pee a lot?"

"Define a lot," said Shelly.

"Now," said Bev, and she pulled a white stick and a plastic cup from her black bag.

"I don't have time for that," said Shelly, rising. Bev and Justine blocked her way.

"Now," said Bev, all business.

Shelly went into her bathroom.

Bev and Justine looked at each other.

"Who?" mouthed Justine.

"I have no idea!" mouthed Bev.

"Ask her!" mouthed Justine.

"You ask her!" mouthed Bev.

The wind began to yowl.

Shelly put the cup down on the table, and Bev stuck in a white strip of paper. They sat staring at it. Shelly took Justine's hand.

"Ow," said Justine, and Shelly loosened her grip. "What's supposed to happen?"

"One line is going to appear there," said Shelly.

They kept staring at the stick. Shelly's hand was grimy from sweat, but Justine held on tightly.

Slowly, two dark, parallel lines emerged.

71

Two Lines

– July 4, 2006, Morning –

Justine clapped her hands to her mouth. "Omigod!"

There was a frantic knock at the door, and Matt stuck his head in, "I just got a phone call that—"

"Get out!" they shouted in unison, and he did.

Bev looked at Shelly. She was still staring at the plastic stick.

"Okay, then," said Shelly, standing, "we'll have something to talk about after the—"

But Bev leaped up to block her way. "How much spotting?"

"Spotting, I don't know," said Shelly. Bev glared at her. "Some red specks. For a couple of days. Maybe a week."

"Shelly, you need an ultrasound and an OBGYN right now."

The wind whistled through the rafters of Gruenhaus.

"Well, that ain't gonna happen, is it? So let's get this show on the road—"

"Shelly!" demanded Bev, taking her by the shoulders. "Are you listening to me? Do you not realize how serious this could be?"

Focus, Shelly said to herself. Shelly tried to focus, but all she could see were those two lines.

"What do you mean?" asked Justine.

"It's impossible to know anything without an ultrasound. But you're bleeding, and that shouldn't be happening. At your age—"

"Now you're flattering me?"

"—this is a high-risk pregnancy. You shouldn't be on your feet till you see an OBGYN."

"Oh, right," said Shelly, looking at her watch. She turned to Justine. "Come on, we need to—"

"Shelly, do you understand what I'm saying? You could harm the pregnancy! You could harm yourself!"

"Are you saying that as a doctor or as a friend?"

"As a doctor, absolutely."

"And as a friend?"

Bev hesitated.

"And as my right hand in this whole circus, with the bus waiting?"

"Please don't ask me that!" said Bev.

The door to Shelly's office burst open and the guys tumbled in, bubbling with energy. "We're all packed," announced Aaron, followed by Mendel and Gavin. Sam shuffled in behind them.

Shelly stared into space for a moment, then jerked. "Sure," she smiled brightly, "let's do this!" and invited them to sit.

Justine and Bev looked at each other. They sat. An angry gust unlatched the screen.

"Can someone take care of that?" asked Shelly, and while everyone was watching Gavin open the door and secure the banging screen, she scooped the little plastic cup into her hand. Her stomach gurgled.

"Right," smiled Shelly, surveying her troops. "So, listen, guys, we don't have time for a pep talk, and anyway you don't need it. You guys are the greatest. I've always known it. Now the whole country knows it. The show will be great, I'm sure of that."

Shelly's stomach began to brawl. She looked at Sam and

Jeff Meshel

Aaron. She closed her eyes. Kathleen was standing between them, about to go on stage in Columbus. She opened her eyes.

"What I want you to remember," she said, looking directly at Sam, "is that there are going to be a lot of people and commotion, watching every move every one of you makes, every minute, on-stage and off. So be on your best behavior." Shelly paused to breathe. "We've all worked long and hard for this, so let's get out there and give them a show they'll re—" She halted, squelching her breath. "A show that they'll remmm—" Her eyes widened. Frantically, she hauled herself up from the sofa, spilling the cup of pee onto the coffee table, splattering Gavin's beige slacks. Shelly lurched towards the bathroom, her hand covering her mouth, slammed the door behind her and upchucked viciously.

Gavin, Mendel, and Aaron stared at the soggy yellow strip of paper with the two black lines lying in a puddle in the middle of the coffee table in front of them. Aaron blanched. Justine and Bev looked at each other. Sam stared at the closed bathroom door.

The sun disappeared behind a cloud, and the screen door was slamming again. They could hear Shelly heaving. Sam took a step towards the bathroom.

"Leave it," snarled Bev, blocking his way, a full head shorter.

"What—what's—" Sam stammered, breathing heavily.

They could hear the water running. Then Shelly came out, wiping her mouth daintily and smiling brightly. "Sorry," she said, taking her garment bag from the coat rack by the door. "Everybody ready?"

But everyone was staring at her.

"Come on," Shelly ordered everyone, "we have a show to do." No one moved. "Let's go," she insisted. "Move it!" Hesitantly, they began to move towards the door.

"Shelly!" protested Justine.

"On the bus," Shelly ordered her.

The girl turned to Bev. "Say something!" she insisted.

"I'm her doctor," refused Bev.

"Well, I'm not," said Justine. She turned to the guys. "Shelly's pregnant, and Bev said she shouldn't move!" she pronounced.

"Justine!" shouted Shelly, but the words hung in the air as the wind shrieked outside.

Shelly and Aaron looked at each other.

Shelly looked at her band. They were all staring at her. "Well, I feel absolutely fine," she said sunnily, "and now we're all going to get on that bus—"

"Mazal tov!" said Mendel. "Who's the proud father?"

Everyone watched Shelly's face turn from pale peach to blushing tomato.

"A—an old boyfriend," said Shelly. Everyone continued staring. "Not in the picture." Her face achieved chili pepper red.

Sam turned to Bev. "That true?"

"What?" squirmed Bev.

"What Justine said," said Sam. "About her not moving."

"Sam, it's none of your busi—" Shelly attempted.

Sam looked down at Bev. "Did you say that?"

"Any pregnancy in her age group and with her symptoms is by definition high risk," said Bev. "I said that it's advisable for her to stay off her feet till she's examined, but that doesn't mean—"

"'Advisable'?" said Aaron.

Sam turned to Shelly. She was still holding her garment bag.

"Sit," said Sam.

"What?" said Shelly.

"Siddown."

"I'm not sitting down."

"Bev said you need to sit."

"Look, Sam," said Aaron, "if Shelly says—"

Sam whirled to face him. Aaron stopped talking. Sam turned back to Shelly.

"Forget it, mister," she said, standing her ground. "I've put too much into this. We've come this far—"

"So what?"

"What do you mean, 'so what?' The whole world's out there waiting to see you perform, and I'm going to see that it—"

"You don't sit down, I ain't getting on that bus."

"Don't be an idiot, you know that—"

Sam sat on the couch.

"You're being an asshole."

"Lady, I'm an expert on assholery. So, I know when I'm looking at one."

"Oh, fuck you, Miller!" she shouted, staring him in the eye.

And he stared her right back in the eye, just like a normal person.

"Sam," she pleaded, "we've worked so hard for this!"

Sam folded his arms and crossed his legs.

No one moved.

Outside, the wind was losing its temper.

There was a knock and Matt stuck his head in. "Sheriff Aubrey says that if we don't leave now—"

Everyone turned to glare at him. Matt closed the door.

Sam crossed his legs to the other side.

No one in the room breathed.

"God-*damn* you, Miller!" Shelly shouted into his unflinching face. "I should have left you out there in the woods!"

Sam snorted.

Shelly sat down hard, seething, and crossed her arms.

"All right," Bev hesitated, "chop-chop, everyone on the bus."

No one moved.

"GO!" Shelly shouted at them.

Sam rose first, and then they began edging towards the door. Justine came and hugged Shelly and rocked her.

"Don't sniffle in my hair," sniffled Shelly, and they all shuffled out.

Sam hung back.

"Go on, get out of here," she snarled. "Before you get caught up in the traffic."

Sam took a step toward her, and she stood up, her heart slamming like the screen door. She looked at the floor. "Would you go already, please?"

He took another step and stood in front of her. "Sam, it was a shock to me, too," she quaked. She could feel his breath on her face. "We'll talk about it after—" Shelly faced him speechless, her insides collapsing.

Sam raised his hands to her shoulders and enveloped her in a warm, cradling hug. They stood, not moving.

"You don't move off that couch, you hear?" he said softly into her ear.

Shelly nodded.

"Promise?"

"I promise," said Shelly.

Sam stepped back from her and pointed to her seat on the rust-and-butterscotch sofa.

Shelly sat.

"Okay, then," he muttered and stood there looking at her. "Yeah," he added finally and turned to leave.

"Hey, Miller," she called. Sam turned. "What if I need the bathroom?"

He rubbed his jaw and smiled at her.

"Use the grass," he said and was gone.

72

Storm Clouds
– July 4, 2006, Afternoon –

The sky was losing its holiday sheen. Shelly watched the wind flatten the grass and bend the trees. Old Gruenhaus groaned. "My God!" she said aloud, and went to her desk to look at the weather site, but service was down.

Next to the keyboard was her notebook. "Rhubarb→Set List!" She dialed Bev frantically, but the line was busy.

Shelly stared out the window. The wind was howling like a choir of cats in heat. *Goddamn that weather station*, she thought. *Goddam Sam! 'It's gonna rain.' Goddamn medicine man.*

She dialed Brandi, but her line was busy, too.

Shelly saw the mess on the coffee table. The treacherous white strip was lying face down in a puddle of pee, soggy and bloated, but the two lines were still there. She got a towel from the bathroom. The wind was relentless.

What if they run into traffic? she asked herself with a jolt.

They have a police escort, she answered. *They'll use the siren.*

Right, she thought, and she relaxed.

Then she wiped up the table. Then she picked up the dirty tissues and other mess and straightened the pillows. Then she sat. Just like she had promised. The sky had turned a dull, steely blue. The wind was whipping the trees. Gruenhaus creaked and groaned.

Shelly dialed the switchboard at Cuyahoga Hollow. The on-hold music was the familiar sound of those two guitars, with the bongos. And Sam Miller singing. It felt like weeks since she had last listened to the song. She leaned her head back and closed her eyes.

Storm clouds are gathering way out there
Soon it's gonna rain—but I don't really care
Lying with you on the ground
Grass and sunlight all around
Nothing's gonna bring me down
Have another Creston Gold.

Fucking Miller, she sniffled.

Lake Hope lapping at the shore
This must be the place I've been searching for
She holds me close and takes me in
To a place I've never been
Never want to leave again
Have another Creston Gold
Have another Creston Gold.

He hugged me.

And when she holds my hand
I know she understands
Understands ...

When he sang those words down at the dock, he opened his eyes and looked at me.

Sometime tomorrow we'll be far away
All we have for sure is what we have today
The world out there don't look so kind

But I don't care, 'cause love is blind
You're the one thing on—

An up-and-down bleep blared into Shelly's ear, and she hung up.

The wind was brawling with everything it had. There was still no internet. Shelly tried calling Bev again, but all she got was a busy tone.

Shelly closed her eyes. *Maybe when I open them, the whole team will be there in party hats with noise makers and balloons, laughing and shouting, "Just kidding!"*

Except they weren't. She watched the surly wind out looking for trouble.

She pictured them riding in the bus, Johnny filming everyone chattering in excitement. *If there are any big problems, Bev will know what to do. And Brandi will keep the band in line. Sam will be sitting by himself, looking out the window, confused and tense. Maybe Justine will be sitting with him? No, she'll be teenagering with Robbie. What can you expect of a girl? "Shelly's pregnant!" she'd blurted out, right in front of everyone. Grew a pair, didn't you, honey? Ah, I don't blame you. You did what you thought was best. I've probably scarred you for life with everything I've dragged you through. I didn't even wish you good luck!*

Shelly held her head in her hands. *Oh, please, let the show go well,* she begged. *For Justine's sake. For the guys, for the team. For the fans. For me.*

Let Sam get through it unscathed. And unscathing. She pictured him again, sitting there alone, looking out the window of the bus, not saying a word, watching the traffic and scratching his jowl. *He must be so scared.* She took another tissue. *"Go back to your cave."* She hit her forehead with the heel of her hand.

The wind was moaning like a banshee on fire, and clouds were beginning to gang up. Shelly felt a shift in the air. The old barometer on the wall read 28.5. Shelly didn't know what that meant, but she was guessing it wasn't good.

There was a scratching at the screen door. Since it was halfway between the couch and her bathroom, Shelly figured she was within the boundaries of her promise to Sam. She opened the door a crack, and Dog slithered in between her legs. She pushed the door closed against the wind. Dog was yelping excitedly. He ran twice in a circle around Shelly in an outburst of canine gratitude for being brought in from the storm. He tried to jump on her, but she pushed him away and sat back down on her sofa while Dog went to sniff out the room.

The sky had turned a grave pewter. Well, so much for the National Weather Service forecast.

The phone rang, and she grabbed it.

"Shelly?" said a woman's voice. The line snapped and crackled. "It's Kimberly, the manager at Cuyahoga Hollow."

"I tried calling you. The band left already," said Shelly. "The police told us that—"

"Shelly, can you raise your voice? The line is terrible."

"THE BAND IS ON ITS WAY!" she shouted over the popping in the background.

"I CAN'T HEAR YOU!" shouted Kimberly. "LISTEN, SHELLY, WE HAVE A BIG PROBLEM HERE. THE WIND IS GOING CRAZY. IT KNOCKED DOWN A BIG TREE RIGHT AT THE ENTRANCE TO THE PARK, AND THERE'S A TRAFFIC SNAG TRYING TO GET TO—"

And the line went dead. Completely dead, no matter how many times Shelly tried.

Shelly stared at the maelstrom brewing outside. The sky was losing control. Shelly shivered and covered her legs with Allie's quilt.

Dog came up to Shelly on the couch, wagging his tail, not a care in the world. He stuck his nose into her crotch and nuzzled her ardently. Shelly pushed him away, but Dog whined and tried to climb up on the rust-and-butterscotch sofa with her. "You're all dirty," she explained, but Dog whined more pathetically and pawed the sofa. Shelly sighed. He squirmed and protested while she toweled off his paws, and then he jumped onto the sofa and snuggled up next to her like it was his rightful place. His fur was damp and funky.

"You stink," said Shelly.

Dog grinned at her, panting, his tongue hanging out of the side of his mouth.

"Happy Fourth of July," said Shelly.

The Fourth of July. She tried to remember the last time she was with Derek. Before she discovered him humping his ex-wife.

It had been snowing. March, latest.

Oh, shit.

The Hampton Inn in Mason City. Aaron and his smile and the adrenaline. May sixth.

Dog sniffed her crotch. "Ah," he yawned.

"What do you mean, 'ah'?" said Shelly.

"You've been mounted," said Dog.

"Go to hell," said Shelly.

Dog snorted. "Pretty old for that, aren't you? Even in human years."

"You want to go back outside?" threatened Shelly.

Dog knew when to shut up.

"Yes," Shelly answered finally.

Dog looked at her.

"Yes, I'm old to be knocked up. Even in human years." Shelly blew her nose. "It's not that I'm not—It's just—you know? I figured it wasn't going to happen, so I pushed it out of my mind." Dog listened sympathetically. "And then Decapede. And now this."

"And Sam," said Dog.

"What does Sam have to do with anything?" snapped Shelly.

Dog nuzzled Shelly's crotch. "Get out of there, you smelly mutt!" she said, pushing his snout away. Dog play-chewed on her finger. "Ow!" She pushed him back, and he play-snarled and pretended to bite her till it turned into a wrestling match, the two of them pushing and laughing and biting and growling and hugging until Shelly collapsed on the couch, sobbing. Dog squeezed free from underneath her and began licking her cheeks and eyes anxiously, until Shelly pushed him away and sat up, laughing through her tears. She blew her nose.

They must be getting to Cuyahoga around now. Walking from the bus into The Hollow, a crowd of fans and journalists straining to get a glimpse of the reincarnated Decapede ghosts. Gavin and Mendel waving and smiling. Aaron and Diane, media's darling couple of the year, holding hands and glowing. Justine, trying to hide behind Robbie, giggling and waving shyly. Who's with Sam? He can't manage a gauntlet like that on his own.

Relax. Bev's there, Justine's there.

And then there they were, the band standing in the wings while Johnny made a long-winded introduction, and the crowd buzzed in anticipation.

"... my privilege and my pleasure to hang out with these guys ..."

Bev was in front with Gavin and Mendel, waiting for the signal to send them out on stage. Justine was standing behind them, between Sam and Aaron.

"... like watching a dinosaur egg hatch ..."

And the crowd begins the rhythmic chant, DE-CA-PEDE! (clap), DE-CA-PEDE! (clap).

And Sam is twitching and fidgeting, and he looks over at Aaron, who has his arm around Kathleen. Sam knocks his hand away, and Aaron smiles back tauntingly. "Yeah? Well, I fucked her first."

And then there was a sound louder than an explosion, as if the entire universe was imploding, shaking poor old Gruenhaus to its foundation. The shadowy room lit up like a strobe, sharp and vicious. Then a second bone-jarring blast, then a third. Then the lights all went out. Dog howled at the heavens, to no avail. Shelly pulled him to her. He strained to assail the invisible intruder, but Shelly held him firmly, and stroked him and cooed to him till he believed her that everything would be all right.

She sat in the dark, staring out at the slate gray sky, Dog's chin on her lap.

"Cuyahoga's probably on a different electric grid, right?"

Dog didn't disagree.

"To tell you the truth," said Shelly, "I don't know. I don't know that. I don't know what electric grid Cuyahoga is on. And I don't know what's going on out there, and I don't know what's going on in here. I don't know anything anymore, Dog."

Then there was another flash of light, and Shelly hugged Dog tightly through the thunder. He tensed up but allowed her to hold him.

"Aaron wouldn't say anything, would he?" she asked.

Dog looked up at her.

"Of course he wouldn't," said Shelly.

Dog wagged his tail and licked her on the mouth.

She wiped her lips with her sleeve. "He did once. Oh, God, please, no."

Dog yawned. His breath stank.

"Aaron wouldn't let anything ruin his big day."

Dog didn't look convinced.

"Déjà vu all over again," said Shelly. "It's not enough for one past to haunt me? I need *two*?"

Dog had no answer for that.

The barrage of thunder was almost constant, the lightning flickering, lighting up the dark house. The air was growing thick.

Dog looked up at her.

"Yes, I did. I told him to go back to his cave. Pretty cool, huh? That's how I send Sam out in front of twenty thousand people?"

Dog had no words of consolation.

What a mean, miserable, knocked-up piece of shit you are, Shelly

Griffin. She blew her nose. Dog really did smell rank, but she scratched him behind the ear anyway.

"So, when he asks me whose it is, what am I supposed to say, huh?"

"I wouldn't know. Dogs don't care much about that stuff," Dog said.

"Well, humans do. Some, anyway."

He hugged me. The first time he's ever touched me like that.

"What about the time you kissed?" asked Dog.

"Get out of my head!" Shelly snapped, and pushed the dog down off her rust-and-butterscotch sofa.

The wind was roaring.

This must be what the end of the world sounds like.

73

Words and Stuff
– July 4, 2006, Late Afternoon –

Sitting on the couch in the dark, Shelly and Dog heard it at the same time, a slamming door and a voice.

"Who's there?" called Shelly, and Dog was already across the room and up the four stairs and into the house. "Who's there?" she called again anxiously.

Dog came running back in, jumping and barking happily, followed by Justine and Sam, panting and windblown. They did not look like they were bearing good news.

"Why are you here?" cried Shelly.

"How are you?" asked Justine.

"What's going on?" demanded Shelly.

"Are you okay?" demanded Sam.

"Of course I'm okay! Why aren't you on stage?"

She looked at both of them. They looked at each other.

"Well?!"

"I gotta pee," said Sam, and ran into Shelly's bathroom.

Shelly stared at Justine.

"Can I sit?" asked the girl. "We've been walking for miles."

"Why are you not on stage?" Shelly repeated.

Over the wind, Shelly could hear the stream of Sam peeing, but she didn't care.

"This storm," the girl panted, "it's going crazy! As soon

as the bus left, they said there's way more traffic than anyone expected, so all the roads to Cuyahoga got clogged. And then this tree fell at the park, so the traffic got all backed up, and the bus got caught, too. We were stuck there for a really long time."

"Gridlock," said Sam, zipping his fly.

"And then Sheriff Aubrey got on the bus and said part of the roof at The Hollow blew away, and the concert was canceled."

They both watched Shelly.

Dreams don't come true, she said to herself. *You should know that. You should have known that all along. You shouldn't even be surprised.*

Sam sat next to Shelly and looked at his feet.

"Shel—" Sam mumbled, and stopped. "I'm sorry."

"Sorry?" she said. "You didn't do anything."

"No, I'm sorry for you." He peered at her. "It was—you know—a big deal. For you."

Look at him, all sweaty in his baseball jersey and his tough-guy jaw and his jerky eyes and worried about me. I could burst out in hysterical tears. Or I could save that for later. Focus on the mission.

What the hell is the mission?

"So, there we are," continued the girl, "stuck in this giant traffic jam, with the wind going crazy. Miles and miles of cars. Sheriff Aubrey said we'd be sitting there for hours till it gets untangled."

"And so this one"—Sam pointed his thumb at Justine—"decides you shouldn't be left alone with the electricity down in the whole county. Says she's walking back to Gruenhaus."

"You did *what*?" shrieked Shelly.

"I was worried," the girl smiled impishly.

"How far was it?"

"Sam said it was only a few miles as the crow flies," said Justine.

"Do you see any crows flying around in this weather?"

701

shouted Shelly. "The two of you! One is crazier than the next!"

"She'd'a gone by the highway, she be out there till tomorrow," said Sam defensively. He sniffed the air. "It's getting bad out there."

"And you let her go?"

"He tried to stop me, but he couldn't," Justine boasted.

"She's as stubborn as her mother," said Sam, scratching his jowl, with a hint of a smile.

"So we walked across these fields—" the girl prattled on, high on adrenaline.

"In this weather?" protested Shelly, but they could tell she was calming down.

"There was this one time," she panted, her cheeks shining, "when I was climbing over that big stone fence, and the wind *literally* knocked me *over*, and Sam actually caught me in his arms, like in the movies!"

And Shelly found herself laughing with them while Dog was nuzzling the girl and whacking his tail on the floor.

The room flashed ghostly white, and a blast of thunder rattled the house. Justine tried to soothe Dog.

"There must be some candles in the kitchen," said Sam. "You be all right for a few minutes?"

"Yeah, I'll be all right for a few minutes," she answered, wiping her eye in the shadows.

The girl came to Shelly and hugged her. "I'm really sorry about the show," she said. "You worked so hard for it."

Shelly dabbed her nose with a tissue. "How are you?"

"I'm fine. Really."

"You're shivering. Go take a hot shower."

Justine hesitated, not wanting to leave Shelly alone.

"Now. Go on, get out of here," Shelly ordered her, and the girl obeyed, with Dog right behind her.

Outside was a dull, gray morass. Heavy drops of rain began to splat on the tall windows. Shelly sat alone in the murky shadows. She looked around the room. *Where exactly does one hide an elephant? I should have asked Dog.*

She tried to think about something else. *Thank goodness I put a force majeure clause in the insurance for the event. And everyone is safe. And there goes Barbara Walters. But the way Justine glowed when she told her story, looking at Sam with such love and trust ...*

Sam came back carrying a tray with a thermos, two mugs with teabags, a little plate of butter cookies, and a single candlestick. His face flickered in the candlelight. He set the tray down on the coffee table and sat next to her.

"Thank you," said Shelly.

"It was Justine's idea," said Sam.

"Well, thanks anyway."

"She went to shower."

"Okay."

"You okay?"

"Yes, Sam, I'm fine. I'm not *sick*."

"Nng," he said. "You been sitting here this whole time?"

"I didn't move. A promise is a promise." She clung to that one truth like a lifebuoy.

"So, how did the guys take it?" Shelly asked.

"You can see it. Johnny filmed it all."

"Tell me!"

"I don't know, I guess they were, you know, disappointed."

" 'I guess they were, you know, disappointed,' " she mimicked. "Maybe you'd like to expand on that?"

"Yeah, it's a big deal for them. Especially Aaron, he took it hard." Sam looked at Shelly for a moment. "But Justine's aunt was taking care of him, you know."

Shelly knew.

"Gavin and Mendel? Bev?" she prompted him.

"Yeah, they were all bummed out. That Gerald guy, he wasn't handling himself too well," said Sam, shaking his head. "Even your father got his panties in a twist. That Brandi?

Crying her eyes out like a baby."

"So everybody's just stuck sitting in the bus in a traffic jam? In this weather?"

"Blowing in the wind. Winston brought a case of champagne for after the show, so everyone was getting a little smashed."

"Justine? How did she take it?" asked Shelly.

"She's a good kid. Got her head screwed on right."

"I was afraid she'd be—devastated."

"She was just worried about you, sitting alone here."

"And how about you?"

"Me? You know."

"No, Sam, I don't know. You have to use, like, *words* and stuff."

"Oh. I was sorry that place got blown away. Sorry for you."

"For me?"

"Yeah. You—you worked really hard for it."

"Yeah, I did," said Shelly.

"How are you—you know, *feeling*?" He approached the word carefully, as if it might bite.

"Why, Sam Miller, did I just hear you correctly?"

"Cut it out. How you doing?"

Shelly shrugged. "Ask me a year from now."

Shelly sipped on her tea. Their faces flickered in the candlelight as they listened to the wind. The rain was rattatatting steadily.

"What happens now?" Sam asked.

Somewhere in the shadows of the dark room, the elephant stirred.

"That's it, it's over," she said. "Tomorrow, everyone goes home."

Sam cleared his throat. "Who's this old boyfriend?" he mumbled.

The elephant waved its trunk nervously.

"It's in the past. Not important."

"What's his name?"

"Derek," said Shelly. "Not in the picture. Non-factor. Nothing."

She could feel her face turning scarlet.

The elephant pawed the ground nervously.

"How did he take it?"

"I—I haven't spoken to him yet. I just found out. Forget about him."

Rain began to lash at the windows, wave after wave.

"But you're gonna tell him, right?"

"I don't know," she said. "I haven't had a chance to think about it." *Please, Earth, swallow me.*

"It's his kid."

"Sam, he's a guy I used to date. Way before Decapede started. I mean, not way before. But before. I'm not even in touch with him anymore. He's not—"

"But it's his *kid*," Sam persisted.

Shelly turned away from the candlelight, deeper into the shadows, hiding her shame. "Sam, he's not interested!"

"How do you know if you haven't even talked to him?"

"I just know!" she said, biting her knuckle. "Could we please talk about something else?"

The elephant raised its trunk towards the sky, trumpeted angrily, and the heavens cracked open. The rain unleashed its crazed assault, thick, wind-driven, rapid-fire drops cracking against the windows.

"So who's gonna take care of you?"

"Who says I need taking care of?"

"Bev. And she's a doctor."

"Nobody knows what's going to happen."

"You're going to have a baby."

"There's many a slip twixt the cup and the—cradle."

"You're gonna be fine," he smiled.

"Sam, I'm too old for this!"

"Says who?"

"Bev! And she's a doctor."

"Well, she don't know diddly." He took her hand. "You'll do great."

Shelly pulled her hand away. Sam looked at her, perplexed. Shelly sat watching the storm. "How long can this go on?"

"Oh, it ain't done yet," he said.

The lightning was as bright as Independence Day fireworks, the thunder coming closer and closer. Gruenhaus trembled.

"Want some more tea?"

She handed him her mug.

"You're *sure* this Derek's not going to be around?" he asked again.

"Yes, I'm sure," she said, but she saw he wasn't convinced. "I promise."

"Because you're going to need somebody—"

"Would you please just shut up?"

"And I don't have any specific plans—"

"Now!" Shelly turned her face away from the quivering candle.

Sam shut up, baffled.

Shelly felt like she was going to explode. *I can't. I can't.*

Sam looked at her, perplexed.

The elephant stomped its foot impatiently.

Shelly rose from the sofa and pulled a chair to sit facing Sam.

Do it.

Don't do it.

She wanted the world to disappear, but there he was, looking at her with trusting puppy eyes. For the last time.

"Look at me," she said. "It happened one time, the first night we met. Way before I met you. It didn't mean anything then, it doesn't mean anything now—"

Sam looked at her and stood up. Shelly lowered her head and covered her face with her hands. "Oh, Sam, I'm so sorry."

When she looked up, he was gone. The door was open, and the screen door was banging in the wind and the rain.

"Justine!" Shelly shouted towards the hallway. "Justine!" she yelled at the top of her lungs, but her voice was drowned out by the rain battering Gruenhaus. She sat, her mind a jumble, till she realized she could go look for the girl herself. Or she could go look for Sam. Or she could stay sitting. Like she promised Sam. Like he insisted.

The girl came running in, Dog on her heels.

"What?" said Justine, smelling trouble. "Where's Sam?"

"He—" she tried and stopped.

Rain was coming in the open door, and the screen door was banging. Justine closed it and sat next to Shelly.

This is crazy. You're supposed to be taking care of her.

"I had a one-time thing with Aaron," Shelly said, "right when all this started. The very first day I met him. We were both very drunk on the idea of Decapede. It didn't mean anything. Except—" Her voice trailed off.

"Okay," said Justine calmly.

She's heard more shocking news in her short life.

"What did he say?"

"Nothing," said Shelly, looking at the door.

"He can't have gone far," said Justine.

The squall was furious, thunder and lightning, lightning and thunder.

"You can't go out in a storm like this, it's dangerous!" said Shelly.

A thunderbolt lit the room and shook the sky.

Justine stood in the doorway looking out at the maelstrom, while Dog barked at it. "Dog, go!" the girl commanded. "Find Sam!" The dog barked. "Dog, find Sam!" she commanded again, but Dog stood yowling, showing no intention of leaving warm Gruenhaus. "Stupid animal!" said Justine. She sucked in her breath and dove out into the deluge.

"Justine!" Shelly shouted into the rain from the doorway, but the girl was gone.

The rain was coming down with the force of mallets rapping at Justine's back and head and face, but on her bare legs, it felt like ice-cold BB pellets. The lawn was a swamp of mud so deep that her bare feet made a sucking sound with each step. She trudged her way down the slope through the tumult, barely able to open her eyes. A foot slipped out from under her, and she fell hard on her behind. She tried to bounce right up before she had solid footing, slipped and tumbled over sideways, flopping face down into the black ooze. She scrambled up, cursing and sliding till she could see the faint outline of the lifeguard tower. The trail around the lake was just a dark quagmire, lit only by the lightning that seemed to be getting closer and fiercer.

Finally, she made out the shape of the boathouse. She trudged through the mud, stinging and aching from the rain beating on her, till she found the wooden steps leading up onto the dock and then the handrail that she followed till she reached the boathouse.

"What the hell are you doing here?" said Sam's voice.

"Where are you?"

"Go away."

She stood close to the wide wooden door, but the rain seemed to be coming from all directions.

She huddled close, facing him. "You can't stay here," she shouted over the clamor of the rain on the lake.

He slumped back against the wooden door and slid down till he was sitting on the dock, defenseless, surrendering to the punishing rain. A flash of lightning lit up his face for a moment, wracked with anguish.

"Please?!" she shouted over the clatter. Sam buried his face in his arms.

Justine crouched next to him, gripping his arm with one hand and turning his rain-drenched face to her, forcing him to look right into her large, pleading gray eyes.

"Please!" she hollered.

Sam opened his mouth to speak, but the heavens short-circuited. The sky lit up brighter than day, shuddered, and Lake Traumsee exploded, knocking them both off their feet. Sam pushed Justine down onto the dock and piled on top of her.

"Wha—" she squirmed under him.

"Lay still!" he shouted, and she obeyed. The air was trembling.

Another explosion shook the dock, but Sam remained on top of her. One more flash lit the lake, and again the ground quaked.

After a long moment, he rolled off her, stood up, and helped her stand. She was holding her hands to her ears.

"Return strokes," he shouted. "They come in bunches."

Across the lake, not a hundred yards away, was the remainder of Matt's lifeguard tower, the torrents of rain fighting to quench the stubborn fire.

They stood gaping, the rain pouring down without mercy.

"My God," she said.

"Jeez," he said.

Justine took Sam's hand and led him off the dock, arm in arm to steady each other, through the mire of mud and rain, up the hill towards Shelly's office.

Dog heard them before Shelly. Sam stood in the doorway, his head hanging down, drooping and sodden. Justine stood next to him, shivering and chattering.

"Hot shower," Shelly commanded and shoved Sam into the bathroom. He went meekly. Shelly closed the door behind him. She leaned on the door, waiting to hear the shower start to run. Her emotions were exhausted, all she had left was efficiency. "You, too!" she said to the girl sternly. "Go."

"He'll be all right," Justine reassured her.

"Of course he will," said Shelly. She squeezed her hand. "Go."

Shelly sat on the sofa watching the storm, and thought about the ark bobbing on the waves. The animals went in two by two, Hoorah! Hoorah! Forty days and forty nights. *Where was I forty nights ago?* She counted backward. *Meeting the wrestler with the big ears who first identified the band. The day I started chasing her dream. Forty days and a hundred years ago.*

Sam came out with a towel wrapped around his waist.

"Aren't you cold?" she asked.

"My clothes are all wet," he said.

She handed him Allie's homemade quilt, and he wrapped himself in it. They stood looking at each other. The floor beneath her was about to collapse and swallow her whole. "There's probably another cup of hot water in the thermos," she managed to say.

Please.

He looked at her, beaten and broken.

Please?

"Well, I'm not going to stand here waiting for you to make up your mind. I'm supposed to stay off my feet," she said, fighting tears, and sat.

Sam wrapped the quilt around himself more closely, and sat opposite Shelly, looking at the floor. The thunder and lightning were taking short breaths between salvos. She poured the hot water over the used tea bag and slid the mug to him across the coffee table.

He took the mug and sipped at it.

"Still hot?"

He grunted.

"Could you ..." she said, averting her eyes.

"What?"

"Cross your legs or something."

He yanked the quilt over his knees. They listened to the rain and the wind.

"I'm sorry," she said.

"You don't have anything to be sorry for. It was before—" he addressed the floor coldly. "Before."

Please, let me just disappear. "Sam, I'm sorry!"

"You're right," he muttered. "I should have just stayed in my cave."

"Oh, Sam, please, you know I didn't mean that—"

Sam snorted. "Doesn't matter," he choked in his gravelly voice. "Everything I go near goes south."

"It's not your fault!"

"I'm a walking fuck-up magnet."

The rain continued to pound the house, wave after wave.

"Stop feeling sorry for yourself! You didn't do anything wrong."

"It doesn't matter anymore," he said to the floor.

"It's me who fucked up. And I'm sorry. I'm very, very, very sorry!" she bawled.

"You should be happy," he corrected her. "You're having a baby."

Goddamn him. She bit her knuckle.

"Sam, I don't want to hurt you," she cried. "That's the last thing in the world I want to do, don't you understand that? Sam? Would you look at me?"

He snorted again.

"Don't you understand why I had to tell you? It's b-be-cause I—" she sobbed, "be*cause* I care about you."

Sam looked at the floor.

"Sam, I care about you too much to lie to you."

He looked out at the rain.

She looked at him through her flooded eyes. "Do you believe me?"

He looked her in the eye. "No," he said.

"We're back," said Bev from the doorway.

74

Ask Me Proper

– July 4, 2006, Evening –

They sat circled around a single kerosene lamp Matt had somehow scrounged up, listening despondently to the unforgiving assault of the rain on Gruenhaus. They were sitting in their customary pairs, except that Bev sent Gerald to sit with Matt so she could talk seriously with Brandi.

"What do we know about this Derek?" whispered Bev.

Brandi looked around to make sure no one could hear.

"Come on, spill!"

"Football coach. Divorced. She caught him screwing his ex-wife," whispered Brandi, squinching her brow to recall details from the night Shelly slept over. "She tells the story really funny."

"I guess it's not so funny now," said Bev.

"I guess not," said Brandi.

"When was that exactly?"

"Wait a minute, I'm counting!" Brandi thought some more. "She slept over at my apartment at the end of May, right when Decapede was just starting, even before she met Aaron."

"Six weeks," said Bev.

"At least," said Brandi.

They sat listening to the rain and thinking the same thoughts.

"But I got the impression she hadn't been seeing much of him before that."

The two women did the same calculation, looked at each other, and shrugged.

"Aaron?" asked Bev.

"She said she didn't," said Brandi.

They looked at each other, unconvinced.

"Sam?" said Bev.

They looked over at Sam and Shelly sitting on opposite sides of the couch, not talking.

"Nah," said Brandi.

"Disappointed?" Mendel asked Gavin.

"Sure. I was really looking forward to playing in that place, with that crowd, with all the lights and the glamor and everything. You?"

"I feel for Aaron," said Mendel. "He's really down. This was a big deal for him."

"For all of us," said Gavin.

"Yes, but for some more than for others. Most of all, for Aaron."

"That's true," said Gavin. "Justine's taking it like a trooper. The way she spoke up about Shelly?"

"She's turned into quite the young lady," agreed Mendel.

"Reminds me of her mother," said Gavin.

Mendel looked over at her and nodded his beard. "Me too."

"And Shelly," said Gavin.

"Poor Shelly," said Mendel. "She worked so hard for this."

"Do you know anything about this old boyfriend of hers?"

"Just that he's not in the picture."

Gavin looked over at Shelly and Sam, sitting on opposite sides of their sofa. "What's with them?"

Mendel shrugged. "Go figure out what's going on inside Sam Miller's head."

"That's true," agreed Gavin.

They sat listening to the rain.

"It's pretty spooky, don't you think?" asked Gavin.

"What?" asked Mendel.

"Well, you know, this whole déjà vu thing."

"This is different. That was Sam's fault. You can't blame him for the rain."

"Still, both times, getting canceled at the last minute?"

"That's true," conceded Mendel.

"Do you believe in coincidences?" asked Gavin.

"No, I'm religious. You?"

"No, I'm a mathematician."

"We have a word for it in Yiddish," said Mendel, "*beshert*."

"What does that mean, cursed?"

"No, more like 'preordained.' "

"Do you think?" said Gavin. "I think we're just jinxed."

"I guess it just wasn't meant to be," sighed Mendel.

"Still, it's kind of spooky, isn't it?" said Gavin.

"Yes, it is," agreed Mendel.

Diane nudged Aaron's knee gently. "How you doing?"

"Okay, I guess," he shrugged listlessly.

She cuddled up next to him and pulled his arm around her.

"It's a shame," she said, looking at the lantern-lit faces, "your last evening together?"

"I feel like I'm in a Greek play, you know?" said Aaron. "It doesn't matter what I think or say or do, Fate's going to flick its fickle finger at me."

"Hey," she nudged him again, "you're a rock star."

"Washed out and washed up," he said glumly.

"A sex symbol," she poked him in the ribs.

The corner of his mouth curved a little.

"Rich as all hell."

The other corner curved as well.

"You have a Number One record."

"And Number Two," he said, smiling a little.

"And a new girlfriend."

"Are you starting up with me?"

She squeezed his knee. "All in all, I'd say you had a pretty good run, wouldn't you?"

"Yeah," he admitted.

"So, what do you know about this Derek guy?" she asked.

"Nothing," gulped Aaron.

"Do you think Dog needs to go out?" suggested Robbie.

"Mmm?" Justine murmured.

"Do you think we need to take Dog out?" asked Robbie.

"No, he'll tell me if he needs to," she said quietly, cuddled up next to him.

They sat listening to the rain.

Robbie had expected her to be all emotional, but she seemed okay, just a little withdrawn. He took a deep whiff of her hair and considered suggesting to her that they sneak off into the blacked-out house, but he figured it probably wasn't appropriate.

"I'm really sorry you didn't get to—"

"Shh." She slipped her arm through his and rested her head on his shoulder at an angle that she could watch Shelly and Sam not talking.

Robbie crossed his legs.

Underneath them, Dog stirred in his sleep.

"Poor Shelly," said Allie. "She worked so hard for the concert."

"Yes, she did," said the Colonel. "What a way to end it all, eh?"

"At least now it'll be easier for her to take care of herself, without all that pressure on her."

"I suppose you're right," said the Colonel and smiled. "You

always find the right thing to say."

"So, you're going to be a grandfather?" said Allie.

"That's what they tell me," said the Colonel.

"Do you know this Derek fellow?"

"Never met him. Don't particularly want to."

"Why not?"

"Shelly never said anything, but I got the feeling he wasn't very nice to her."

They sat listening to the rain.

"Allie," said the Colonel, "would you please reconsider about tomorrow?"

"No sirree, bob-booey, not till we're properly married."

"Allie, it's a new world. Nobody is going to even raise an eyebrow if—"

"I'm not going to have my neighbors talking."

"But we've been—"

"What you got away with when all this commotion was going on is all good and fine. You're more than welcome to move back in. After the wedding."

"Well, when can we do it?" asked the Colonel.

"I'll have to talk to Pastor Tim. The church is booked up in advance. It may take a while."

The Colonel crossed his arms in consternation.

"You do understand, don't you, Charles?" smiled Allie, putting her hand on his arm. "It wouldn't look right."

"Of course," he scowled.

"The old 'Creston Gold' or the new one?" Gerald quizzed Matt.

"The new one, you can hear it better," said Matt, smiling hopefully. "The old one sounds like it's coming from the next room. The new one sounds like it's right up close."

"Well, they have much better equipment today. But there's something so special about that sound, don't you think? And when you remember what was going on in the room. Bev told me that they—"

"I like it more when you can hear it better," said Matt, his smile drooping.

Sam and Shelly sat with their arms folded, listening to the rain. Finally, Shelly broke the silence.

"Are you just going to sit there not talking all night?"

Sam didn't answer.

"Everyone's down enough, you don't have to make it worse."

"Don't worry," he said, "I'll be out of your hair tomorrow."

Shelly's heart wrenched.

Turn off that lantern, maybe all of this will go away.

I don't want it to go away.

For a long while, no one spoke at all. The room was silent but for the rain pounding mercilessly on old Gruenhaus.

Johnny was just setting up his camera, and no one noticed who, but someone began humming. And then someone else, and then everyone was humming it together, and then everyone was singing it together, in a melancholy whisper, barely audible over the rain.

Cuyahoga rising, there's a price you have to pay
Cuyahoga rising, there's a price you have to pay
Ain't no place to hide
Cuyahoga wash your sins away.

They all sat listening to the rain.

"I'm about ready to start," said Johnny.

"Okay," said Shelly.

He waited for her to say something more. "Shelly, are you okay?" he asked.

"I'll be fine, thanks," she said.

"Don't you want to say something to the team before we start?"

"No, that's okay," she shrugged. "Go ahead and do your thing."

"Winston," said Johnny, "could you sit down, please? I want to start."

"Somebody mebbe wan' sumpin'?" he asked.

"Sit!" said Allie. "You've been running around like crazy."

Winston sat next to Gavin and immediately bounced back up. "Boo!" he called, holding up a smashed fedora. "Lookee what I find."

Everyone watched as Justine uncurled herself, walked over to him, took the hat, and dejectedly tried to straighten it out.

"Maybe that was the jinx?" Gavin whispered to Mendel.

"Good evening, brothers and sisters," Johnny spoke somberly to the camera in his resonant, radiophonic bass. "Decapede is sitting here in the dark. Quite an apt metaphor, that. There's a power outage here at Gruenhaus, all the lines are down, so we have no idea what's going on in the outside world. Which may be just as well."

"He's supposed to be cheering us up?" Diane whispered to Aaron.

"But, of course, spirits here are pretty dark as well after the cancellation of today's show. This evening was supposed to be a celebration of the big event at Cuyahoga Hollow, Decapede's reunion, debut, and swan song all rolled into one gala performance. But, in an eerie echo of the band's first incarnation, the big show didn't take place."

"It sounds like a concession speech," Diane whispered.

"But Decapede has left a legacy, nonetheless. They've renewed their great old music, recorded some great new music. And they've given us a lot of good times, for me personally and, I hope, for the audience at home."

"This is so depressing!" whispered Diane.

"Welcome to reality TV," whispered Aaron.

"So," Johnny addressed the camera somberly, "this will be our last show, and as promised, each Decapede is going to share his future plans with the others for the very first time. Aaron, did the band really keep the promise?"

"Oh, absolutely!" said Aaron to the camera. "We loved the idea."

"You mean to tell me you really don't know what Mendel and Justine and Gavin and Sam are doing tomorrow?"

"Nope," said Aaron, smiling charmingly. "You know, when we got here to Gruenhaus, Shelly confiscated our phones. She said she has us for a month, we're all hers. So we really got into that 'woodshedding' mindset. To answer your question, I think everyone here was really happy not to discuss the future so that we could concentrate on the here and now, making music. Right, guys?"

The guys all agreed.

"All right then," said Johnny, "who goes first?"

"Mendel asked to get it over with first," said Aaron. Everyone smiled to themselves in the dark because they all knew Mendel hated talking to the camera.

"My plans?" he smiled at Johnny underneath his long beard. In the light of the lantern, he looked like a time warp. "I'll tell you, Johnny, it's been a wonderful adventure here, but truthfully, I can't wait to get back to my 'natural habitat'—my wife, my family, my home. I have one new grandchild I haven't seen, and two more about to arrive any day, God willing. As for the future—I'm very happy in my life, I'm not going to change a thing. I did quit my salesman's job, that's true. My wife and I will be buying a new house in the same neighborhood where we live now. And I hope to be able to help my kids out, God willing, so they can live nearby," he concluded.

"Lovely!" said Johnny and hugged Mendel while everyone clapped softly with warmth for such a sincere, modest guy.

"I'm not good at goodbyes," said Gavin, wiping his eyes. "This has been the most wonderful month of my life in so many ways. Not just for what has been, but also what's going to be," he smiled slyly. "I'll be flying back to Iowa tomorrow morning"—he paused coyly— "to pick up my things and have them shipped back to Cleveland, where Winston and I are going to open a restaurant." Everyone applauded, surprised and delighted. Gavin smiled broadly and held out his hand to invite Winston to come into the light with him.

"I'll be back in a few days, and we'll start looking for a location. The Colonel has been *soo* helpful—"

"Ah," Johnny wagged his finger at the Colonel, "so you knew his plans?"

"Strictly on a need-to-know basis," answered the Colonel with military bonhomie.

"An' I be here to help Miss Allie clean up from de mess you peoples making," grinned Winston.

"But I'll be back real soon," said Gavin, and they squeezed hands and smiled at each other very happily, their faces aglow in the yellow light of the kerosene lantern. Everyone else was smiling in the dark, even Shelly. Even Sam, she saw.

Johnny turned the camera to Aaron.

"Goodbye? We just said hello yesterday," said Aaron to the camera. "But it feels like a hundred years ago."

"It was," said Bev, and everyone chuckled.

"Johnny said we're not supposed to say thank you's tonight," Aaron spoke directly to the camera, completely composed. "So I'll just say that it's not easy to say goodbye to this whole great team, and especially, of course, to my band-mates, Mendel, Gavin, Justine, and Sam." He looked directly at Sam and spoke distinctly for the camera. "It's been a privilege to play with you."

"Beautiful," said Johnny. "Your plans?"

"I'm flying back to Chicago in the morning. I have things to take care of there," he said, slapping his hip. "Winters in Chicago are getting pretty harsh for me," he motioned to someone to join him in front of the camera, "so I thought about trying Florida." He smiled at Diana as she sat down next to him. "Work on my golf game."

"And squire me to some campaign events," said Diane, crossing her long legs.

"Do you have plans to continue making music?" asked Johnny.

"I was toying with some ideas. But I'll just have to wait to see how the dust settles."

"What about a Decapede reunion sometime in the future?"

"Third time's a charm?" He looked at the bandmates, then at Johnny. "If I've learned one thing this summer, it's to never predict what a Decapede is going to do."

"Lovely," said Johnny, and turned the camera to Sam.

Sam looked off somewhere into the darkness.

"Your plans?"

"I—I'll be leaving after the rain lets up."

"Where will you be going?" prompted Johnny.

Sam shifted uncomfortably in his chair. "Somewhere else," he said.

There was an awkward silence in the room.

"Any parting words you'd like to add?" asked Johnny.

Sam thought for a moment. "Thanks to Miss Allie for the hospitality, and ah, good luck to everyone."

"That's it?" said Johnny.

"Yeah, I guess," Sam mumbled.

Shelly bit her knuckle.

Please, let the ground open up and swallow me. Swallow all of us. No.

"This last month has meant more to me than I have words for," said Justine, looking around the circle. She sat in front of the camera, wearing her fedora and biting her lip to fight back the tears. "You all are the most important people in my life, and I'm not going to say goodbye because wherever you go, you're going to be right here in my heart with me."

Everyone sighed and smiled in the dark.

"And I have some pretty big news," she smiled as she wiped her eye with the back of her hand. She looked around the room coyly, toying with her audience, dragging out the dramatic pause.

"Come on," said Brandi, "we're dying here."

"Give me the letter," Justine said to Robbie, and she kneeled next to the kerosene lamp to read. "This was totally Shelly's idea," Justine smiled excitedly at everyone.

" 'Dear Ms Brinker, In recognition of your unique contribution to the reputation and prestige of Steuben College, our admissions board is proud to extend to you an Exceptional Legacy Invitation (through your late mother, Kathleen Brinker, Steuben College Class of 1972) to register as a freshman for the coming fall semester. We will waive the prerequisite high school diploma,' blah blah, 'full scholarship,' blah blah."

The whole team oohed and ahhed.

"That's really wonderful," said Bev.

"Wait," said Justine, "you haven't heard the best part." She turned to Robbie and motioned to him to join her in front of the camera.

"They asked me to sing at the orientation session, and I told them I couldn't do it without my soundman," she poked him in the ribs and took his hand. He lowered his eyes shyly. She continued reading.

" 'Regarding your query pertaining to Mr. Robert Pettiford, son of Dr. Beverly Hunt Pettiford (Steuben College Class of 1970) and member of the Decapede team, the admissions board has decided to extend a similar Exceptional Legacy Invitation to him. Enclosed, please find an additional application form for him to submit by August 1, 2006. We look forward,' blah blah blah."

Everyone applauded and congratulated them.

"And Allie said we can stay here for the rest of the summer," said Justine, "and come here from school for weekends."

"Or maybe even commute," said Robbie. "It's not that long a drive."

"So Robbie was in on it?" Johnny asked Justine, who shrugged sheepishly. "This is how you people keep a secret?" Johnny admonished the whole room, and everyone laughed.

"Bev," said Johnny, "did you know about this?"

"I didn't know about them getting accepted. Shelly might have mentioned the idea before suggesting it to Justine," she confessed. Bev glanced at Shelly, but she was looking off into the dark.

"So you played by the rules?"

"Oh, absolutely. I'm a good girl," she said, and everyone snickered and laughed, Gerald the loudest.

"And, Dr. Pettiford, as the sixth Decapede, what are your—"

"Wait, wait a minute. What did you call me?" said Bev.

"The sixth Decapede," said Johnny.

"No way, Jose, that's you. Everyone knows that," said Bev, and everyone agreed.

"You're the manager," said Johnny, and everyone agreed.

"You're the face," said Bev, and everyone agreed.

"Shelly's the mother," said Gavin, and everyone agreed.

"It's me," said Justine.

"What?" said Johnny.

"I'm the sixth Decapede," said Justine.

No one quite knew whether to laugh or cry, so they sat quietly for a moment, listening to the rain.

"So then, Bev," said Johnny, "we still haven't heard. What are your plans?"

"I'm going to be sticking around here in Ohio. Keep an eye on the kids. Robbie's not eighteen yet."

"Mom!" he protested.

"We're going to be setting up the DecaInc office in Cleveland," said Bev.

Everyone murmured approval.

"We?" asked Johnny.

Bev waved to Gerald to come join her.

"We'll be staying with my mother in the meantime," said

Gerald, taking her hand in his. "She's not doing too well," he added gravely.

"Your *mother*?" asked the Colonel.

"I've known Fidelia Bridges since I was a boy," Johnny told everyone, struggling to hold back his laughter. "She must be, what, a hundred?"

"Ninety-eight," nodded Gerald solemnly.

"She still lives in the same old house in Chagrin Falls," Johnny was choking to stifle the laughter, "and she's been doing poorly for the last fifty years." He burst out laughing loudly, and everyone joined in except for Gerald. Even Sam smiled. Shelly wasn't listening.

"Brandi, your turn," said Johnny.

"Me?" she said. "I thought this was just for the band."

"As far as we're concerned," said Aaron, "you're a Decapede."

Brandi nervously took her place in front of the camera, wearing her new look, a tight white Decapede! T-shirt with her hair tied back in a severe ponytail.

"Boy, you've changed down here at Creston," said Johnny.

"You have, too," said Brandi and turned to the audience. "He learned how to use a BlackBerry." Everyone chuckled at that.

"So, plans?"

"You know that in between my duties for Decapede, I've been spending some time down at the brewery."

"I understand you've taken over the place," said Johnny.

"Well, they didn't have enough workers to handle all these new orders, so I've been getting Matt's baseball pals to come in and help out between games."

"The Cuyahoga Rapids," said Matt, edging into the frame.

"Don't push," said Brandi, and made room for him to sit next to her. "I got all four production lines working three shifts, nine trucks running day and night, four more coming in this week."

"She's doing a wonderful job down there," said Allie.

"Very impressive," admitted the Colonel.

"Tell Johnny the news, dear," said Allie, beaming.

"Allie's asked me to take over the brewery," said Brandi. "As manager."

Everyone sighed and smiled.

"And she invited me to stay here in Gruenhaus for a while to learn the books."

"I'm so proud of you," said Johnny, glowing.

"It's cool," glowed Brandi. "I get to boss all those hunky guys around."

"Doesn't Matt mind?" asked Johnny.

"Of course he does," she smiled, cracking her gum. "That's the best part."

Matt smiled, too.

"Mrs. Allie Bauer," said Johnny, "I suppose you'll be happy to have your quiet back."

"Well, you'd suppose wrong," said Allie. "This is the most fun I've had in about fifty years. Maybe ever. And I'll be sorry to see it end."

"Well, it won't be completely quiet. I understand the Colonel will be here to keep you company."

"After the wedding," groused the Colonel.

"When's that going to be?" asked Johnny.

"It might take a while," said the Colonel.

"It sounds like you're getting cold feet," teased Johnny.

Shelly turned her gaze from the dark of the room to her father in the lantern light.

"Negative, sir. It's Allie who's dragging her feet," he said, looking at Allie, while everyone hooted and hollered at his ardor.

Allie looked at him. "Me? Don't you try to pin that on me, mister. You just say the word, I'm ready right here and now."

"What about all your neighbors and friends?" said the Colonel.

"Ach," she said dismissively, "this here is more family than I ever dreamed I'd live to see. You get Pastor Tim here, I'll marry you right here and now." Everyone hooted and hollered even louder.

Everyone except Mr. Gerald Bridges, the Barracuda of Buyouts, the sixth-richest man in the world, who began jumping up and down right in front of Johnny, shouting, "Confidential! Confidential!"

Everyone stared at him. Bev tried to put her arm around him.

"Confidential!" he squawked at Johnny. "Confidential!"

Everyone looked at each other, figuring Gerald's cork had finally popped.

"Gerald!" said Bev, "calm down!"

"Johnny!" he hyperventilated, struggling for speech. "*Confidential* magazine, don't you remember?"

Everyone looked at each other.

"The Good Reverend John W. Walker?" Gerald wheezed.

"Oh, my gosh," said Johnny.

"What in heaven's name are you two babbling about?" laughed Allie.

"Johnny is a minister of the peace!" said Gerald.

Everyone looked at each other, then at Johnny.

"Gerald's right," recalled Johnny. "Gee, I haven't thought of that in fifty years. When we were kids, I bought a certificate of ordination from an ad in the back of *Confidential* magazine."

"For $4.99!" squeaked Gerald.

"The Eternal Church of Universal Hope," recollected Johnny.

"The Universal Church of Eternal Hope," Gerald corrected him.

"Right," laughed Johnny.

"So you're really an ordained minister?" asked the Colonel.

"In the eyes of God, the State of Ohio, and *Confidential* magazine, I am Reverend John W. Walker, licensed to perform marriages, funerals—and maybe bar mitzvas, I'd need to check about that."

"Seriously, you're licensed to perform a wedding?" asked Bev, smiling.

"I am, indeed," said Johnny, smiling.

Allie and the Colonel looked at each other.

Everyone held their breath.

"I'm game if you are," said the Colonel.

"I'm game if you are," said Allie.

"Right now?" said the Colonel.

"Let's do it while everyone's here," said Allie.

Justine let out a shriek and jumped up to hug Allie. The women all clustered around Allie with squeals of glee. The men surrounded the Colonel with heartfelt handshakes of congratulations.

Everyone except Shelly and Sam.

Shelly turned to face him. "Come with me."

"No thanks," he said without looking up.

"Would you please come with me?"

Sam gathered himself up and followed Shelly sullenly out the side door and into the pitch-dark hallway. She shoved him back up against the wall and stuck her nose in his face.

"I'm going to say this to you one time and one time only, do you hear me?"

Sam snorted dismissively.

"Are you listening?" she said threateningly.

"Make it fast," he said coldly.

"So listen fast. This is your chance, Miller. You made a big mistake once, and you screwed up your life."

"Get to the point."

"And now you're getting a second chance," she glowered.

"It's over," he said.

"It's not over."

"Your show was washed out."

"Shut up and listen." She looked at him. "Are you listening?"

He kicked at the carpet.

"I need to go out there and tell Johnny what my plans are," she said into his face.

"You're good at figuring that stuff out."

"Well, this concerns you."

"I'll be gone as soon as the rain stops."

They stood in the dark, listening together to the silence. The rain had stopped.

"You can go back to your doghouse—"

"I thought it was a cave."

"—to eat carrots for the rest of your life, or—"

Shelly stopped. Sam looked at her. She could feel her cheeks burning.

"Or I can tell Johnny that you're staying here."

"Here?" said Sam.

"Here," said Shelly.

"At Allie's?"

"At Allie's." Shelly swallowed. Her face was hot. "With me."

"With you?"

"With me."

Sam looked at the floor for a long time.

Shelly couldn't see what he was thinking.

A cheer went up in the common room when someone noticed that the rain was gone.

"I want you to marry me," she said.

Sam crooked an eyebrow. "What did you say?"

"Marry me."

"Are you fucking with me?" He began to twitch.

"My legs are getting tired," she demanded.

"Why would you want to marry me?" he asked.

Shelly squinched his Decapede! T-shirt in her fists.

"Because I want to be around you. Because I feel good when I'm around you, and I don't feel good when I'm not."

Sam listened in the dark.

"You make me feel alive. And happy. And safe. Would you say something?"

"You sure you're talking to the right person?"

"I want to be with you. I want to wash your stupid Rocky Covalito jersey—"

"Colavito."

"Rocky Coladon't give a fuck what his name is. I just want to be around you. And I want you to be around me and—and just be you."

He could barely make out her face in the darkness.

"That's what I want," she said. "That's all I want."

"What about Aaron?"

"He'll be thrilled for us."

"What about the—"

"I don't know, Sam. I'm forty-three years old, if you've noticed."

"You're still in good shape."

"Fucking Shakespeare. Why don't you go write me a song, you moron?"

They looked at each other in the dark.

"I don't want to get my hopes up," she said softly.

"It's gonna be fine," he said.

"What, you're going back into your medicine man routine now?"

Sam smiled at her.

"But, if it does work out"—Shelly leaned her cheek on his chest— "somebody's going to need to teach him to fish."

"You'd really have a wretch like me?"

"Yeah," she said, looking up at him, "I'd really have a wretch like you."

Sam looked at her. "Are you sure?"

Shelly nodded.

"You don't want to take a little more time to think this over?"

"I want to do it now. Together with Allie and my father."

Sam looked at her. "You're crazier than me," he said.

"Well?"

"Well what?"

"I asked you a question."

"What was the question?"

Shelly kicked him.

"Ow," he said and rubbed his shin.

They stood toe-to-toe, looking at each other for a long moment.

"Ask me proper," he said with a twinkle.

"What?" she asked.

"You know," he said.

"Grr," said Shelly.

"You shouldn't be on your feet," he said.

"Oh, all right," she said, standing up straight, taking his hand and looking him in the eye. "Sam Miller, will you marry me?"

Sam blinked twice and twitched his nose. "Yeah, what the heck," he said.

75

Surprise Ending
– July 4, 2006, Night –

Shelly took her seat in front of Johnny's camera.

"Shelly Griffin," said Johnny resonantly. "What a long, strange trip it's been."

Shelly breathed in deeply and smiled. Johnny waited.

"Parting words?" he prompted her.

"Parting words," she repeated to herself. "The first time I heard 'Creston Gold,' I fell in love with a dream. That dream became a reality. A sticky, gooey, complicated reality. But I'm still in love. In sticky, gooey, complicated real love. Ladies and gentlemen, I'd like to introduce you to my fiancé."

Shelly held out her hand, and Sam stepped into the halo of the kerosene lamp with her.

There was stunned silence in the cavernous common room.

"Really?" Johnny managed to say.

"And if you don't mind us jumping on the bandwagon, we'd like to make it a double ceremony," said Shelly.

No one spoke.

"Right here."

No one spoke.

"Right now."

No one spoke.

"I know she's just after my money, but she don't know I know," Sam deadpanned to the stunned audience. He turned to Shelly, looked her in the eye, and they smiled at each other.

Brandi and Bev screamed in tandem. Justine leaped onto Sam, her arms and legs wrapping around him, sending him staggering backward.

The women all flocked around Shelly, the men all huddled around Sam, and Gruenhaus filled with excited chatter. Dog wagged his tail, happy for them in their human happiness.

"Okay, listen up," Shelly called out, clapping her hands for attention. She tried to stand, but Sam put his hand on her shoulder. She brushed his hand away but remained sitting. She peered at her watch in the dim light. "It's six thirty. The, ahem, *nuptial ceremonies—*"

Everyone tittered and chortled.

"—will take place in this room at exactly nine o'clock."

"Thatsnotenoughtime!" screeched Brandi. "I want to make you a bash!"

"You have two and a half hours to bash to your heart's content. Bev, give me your clipboard, will you? And your pen."

"Just not the whistle," said Sam.

"Allie, Winston, Gavin, go bake a cake or something. Gerald, you help them out."

Winston rubbed his hands together and grinned.

"Colonel, you're in charge of—"

She stopped and held out her hands. He came over to her, and she pulled him down to give him a hug and a kiss on the cheek.

"You're in charge of arranging the room. Make sure Johnny has space to work."

"Can I be on the refreshments committee?" asked Sam.

"I saw a wedding dress down in the basement," cried Brandi, stamping her foot in frustration, "but there's no light!"

"I got a flashlight in my truck," smiled Matt.

"Why didn't you say so before?" Brandi accused him.

"Because you'da used it up for something, and then we would'na had it for an emergency," he explained.

Brandi looked at him and cracked her gum.

Matt smiled at her with puppy eyes and dimples.

Aaron approached Sam in the half-light and extended his hand. Sam took it like a gentleman and returned a firm, emphatic handshake. Aaron clapped Sam on the shoulder. "I'm really happy for you, man, I mean it," he said warmly. "Really, really happy."

"Yeah, uh, thanks," grunted Sam.

"You got yourself a wonderful woman there," Aaron smiled.

"Hrmf," said Sam, but he didn't look displeased.

Aaron finally released the handshake.

"And, uh, Aaron?" mumbled Sam.

Aaron looked at him.

"I—I'm sorry."

"For what?" asked Aaron.

"For last time," said Sam.

"What last time?"

"Back then," said Sam. "In Columbus."

Aaron pulled Sam to him in a brief man hug and clapped him on the back.

"Hey, Aaron," mumbled Sam.

"Yes?"

"You got a ring I can borrow?"

"I'll find you one. Don't worry, I'm on it. But, hey."

"What?"

"That makes me your best man."

"It does, huh?" Sam peered at Aaron. "Well, okay," he chortled. He knew that would please Shelly.

#

Everyone formed a circle around Johnny and the couples. Gavin was holding the one lantern in the middle so they could see who was marrying whom. Robbie held the camera while Matt stood on a chair and projected the flashlight down on the actors like a spotlight. Dr. Bev had given Shelly permission to stand for the duration of the ceremony as long as Johnny kept it brief.

Aaron was standing with Sam, holding the heirloom gold band Allie had happily given him. Justine was standing with Shelly, who was holding a small bouquet of flowers from Allie's garden. Bev was standing with Allie, who held an identical bouquet. Gerald was standing with the Colonel, ready to pass on his own former wedding ring.

Allie was wearing a mauve Mamie Eisenhower evening dress. The Colonel was in his crisp business suit. Shelly was wearing a satin WWII-era wedding dress with a high neck and a flowing white train. Sam was wearing his Rocky Colavito jersey, freshly pressed for the occasion.

Johnny cleared his throat, and everyone was quiet. "I wrote it down." He held up an index card to show them, and everyone laughed.

"We are gathered here in Creston, Ohio, on the fourth day of the month of July, in the year two thousand and six, to bind in holy matrimony these two couples—Allie Bauer with Charles Griffin, and Shelly Griffin with Sam Miller."

Johnny bumped the side of his head with the heel of his hand in mock disbelief, and everyone smiled.

"Before we begin," said Johnny, "it's customary to declare banns. So, if anyone present knows of any reason why these unions should not take place, let him speak now—" Johnny peered out over his reading glasses. "Or forever hold his peace. That pertains to women as well." Everyone was smiling in the dim light. Everyone held their breath. No one said a word.

"Do you, Alice Cecily Bauer, take Colonel Charles Lawford Griffin to be your lawfully wedded husband, to have and to hold from this day forward, for better or for worse, for richer or for poorer, in sickness and in health, to love and to cherish, till death do you part?"

"I do," said Allie, and she smiled at the Colonel.

"Do you, Colonel Charles Lawford Griffin, take Alice Cecily Bauer to be your lawfully wedded wife, to have and to hold from this day forward, for better or for worse, for richer or for poorer, in sickness and in health, to love and to cherish, till death do you part?"

"Affirmative," said the Colonel, and he smiled at Allie.

"Colonel, please take the ring and place it on Allie's finger." Gerald handed him the ring, and the Colonel slipped it onto Allie's finger.

"By the authority vested in me by the Eternal Church of Universal Hope and the great State of Ohio," said Johnny, "I now—"

"The Universal Church of Eternal Hope," Gerald corrected him.

"By whatever and the Great State of Ohio, I now pronounce you man and wife."

Everyone smiled and wiped their eyes.

"Do you, Shelly Anne Griffin," Johnny read from his cue card with visible emotion, "take Samuel Aloysius Miller—"

Justine let out a whoop of hilarity, then covered her mouth with both hands.

"—to be your lawfully wedded husband, to have and to hold from this day forward, for better or for worse, for richer or for poorer, in sickness and in health, to love and to cherish, till death—"

"Hey, wait a minute!" said Sam.

"What?" asked Johnny, his heart thumping. Even Dog held his breath.

"I thought it was to love and to *obey*," graveled Sam.

"It used to be," said Johnny. " 'Obey' doesn't fly anymore."

"Ah," said Sam and winked at Shelly. "Okay. You can go ahead."

"To love and to *cherish*, till death do you part?"

"I do," she said, and smiled demurely.

"Do you, Samuel Aloysius Miller, take Shelly Anne Griffin to be your lawfully wedded wife, to have and to hold from this day forward, for better or for worse, for richer or for poorer, in sickness and in health, to love and to cherish, till death do you part?"

Sam looked around the room, then at Shelly.

"Hell, yes," he grinned.

Mendel broke out in a spirited klezmer wedding tune on his violin, while Aaron improvised a deft accompaniment on the dolceola. People danced a bit, but kept crashing into each other in the dark.

Winston brought out a cauldron of steaming punch and trays of guacamole and tortilla chips.

"What's that?" sniffed Sam.

"It was supposed to be our victory punch," said Gavin.

"Whoa, wha'd you put in there, some of Allie's moonshine?" graveled Sam.

"It's a toddy," Allie said proudly, "an old family recipe."

"I'll have you know that's Kentucky's finest single-barrel rye whisky there," said the Colonel.

Sam raised his glass to the Colonel and grinned sideways. "To you. Dad."

Winston discreetly came over to Shelly with a glass of milk.

"I guess there aren't any secrets around here," she frowned.

"Doan you worry none about that, Boo. You just take care youself," he smiled.

"Could you get me some more of that guacamole?" Shelly asked. "They won't let me get up." She watched Winston load her plate. "A little more," she said.

Shelly sat surrounded by Brandi and Bev and Justine while the rest of the party caroused and chattered and drank punch. Brandi and Bev were on their third cup each, swapping wedding stories less than appropriate for a sixteen-year-old. Justine, nursing her single allotted cup, was hanging on every word. Shelly covered her mouth to stifle a yawn.

"You've had quite a day," said Bev.

"I should—I should—" Shelly attempted, but broke into a gaping yawn. "Oh, I'm sorry. Have you seen Sam?"

"I think he's hiding from you," brayed Brandi, and she and Bev and Justine whooped in laughter.

Shelly found Sam snoring on the other sofa. In the moonlight, she could see his erection peeking out from under Allie's quilt. He snorted and shifted. Shelly blushed and covered him.

Shelly took another blanket and lay down on the other couch. She closed her eyes. His snorting and snoring annoyed her at first, but ...

76

Encore

– July 5, 2006, Morning –

The electricity had returned during the night, but the morning sky was still heavy and gray, with the earth glutted from the deluge. Everyone was standing on the front porch to say goodbye to Gavin and Mendel and Aaron. Winston was comforting Justine, who was crying on him like a sixteen-year-old.

"Well," said Shelly.

"Well," said Gavin.

"Well, well," said Aaron.

Mendel nodded his long beard.

"We'll see you ..." said Shelly.

"When we see you," said Aaron.

"All packed and ready," called Matt from the van.

Johnny was filming everyone standing around uncomfortably, not knowing what to say, not wanting to take the first step down from the porch. Aaron walked over to Sam and stuck out his hand. Johnny moved in for a close-up. Sam took his hand manfully.

"See you around," said Aaron.

"Not if I see you first," said Sam with a twinkle, still pumping hands.

Aaron leaned forward and whispered to Sam, too softly for Johnny or anyone to hear. "Good luck, man, seriously. I really wish you the best."

"Grnf," said Sam graciously. "You too."

"And maybe, someday, if it's cool with you, I'll come visit? You know, see you and Shelly and—"

"Yeah," said Sam. "You ought to do that. Make some music, too."

"Any time, any place," beamed Aaron.

Sam peered at the gray sky over Aaron's shoulder. "How about right now?"

"Sam, they have to go," said Shelly.

"I ain't asking you," he answered her, and everyone whooped at his bravado. "Well?"

The guys looked at each other.

"They have planes to catch," said Bev.

"There's always more planes," said Sam. He looked at Aaron and Gavin and Mendel. "Come on, one last time?"

"It looks like it's going to rain some more," said Mendel.

Sam sniffed the air. "Nah, it's over."

"It's all mud," squeamed Gavin.

"Ah, come on, you sissies!" he challenged them. "A little mud never hurt no one!"

They looked at each other reluctantly.

"You can take a hot shower when it's over. Allie got plenty of hot water here. Come on, whaddaya say?"

"Ohpleaseohpleaseohplease," Justine begged her band-mates.

Everyone could see them weakening.

"For Shelly," said Sam.

"For Shelly and Sam," Shelly corrected him.

"And for Allie and me," said the Colonel, cracking up the foyer.

Sam peeked into Shelly's office with his guitar case and a grin.

"I'm sitting, okay?" she said.

He sat down right next to her. "How you doing?"

"I'm okay," she smiled. "How you doing?"

"I'm all right," he smiled.

"Well, all right then," she smiled. "What's going on out there?"

"Matt's running people and equipment down to the lake. Allie said she's not getting on any old land buggy to go slogging through the mud, but your father sure looked like he's having a good time."

Shelly smiled at him. "You're sure the rain's stopped?"

Sam rose and went to the window. "Yeah, I think we had about enough," he said, although the sky still looked pretty dark to Shelly.

The lifeguard's tower was gone, clearing a view from Shelly's window all the way down to the dock.

Sam looked around the room, picked up the coffee table, and placed it behind Shelly's desk.

"What are you doing?" she scolded, laughing.

He rotated Shelly's rust-and-butterscotch sofa.

"You're feng shui-ing me *now*?"

He pulled the other rust-and-butterscotch sofa next to it to make a double bed and piled a stack of pillows at the end facing the windows. He turned and smiled at her proudly. "You prop yourself up here, you'll be able to watch us lying down. If you don't have anything else to do."

Shelly smiled at him.

Outside on the lawn, Matt came slopping through the muck on the land buggy to pick up Sam.

They stood by the screen door for Shelly to give her new husband a proper send-off.

"Isn't that the George Harrison guitar?" she asked.

"Yeah," he said. "I been saving it."

"Saving it for what?"

Sam shrugged. "For this, I guess."

She couldn't resist asking one last time. "You're not worried it's going to get wet?"

Sam looked at the sky. "Nope," he said.

"Well, good luck, then."

"You be okay?" he smiled with a twinkle.

"I be okay," she smiled back. "Go, play good. Sing one for me."

Reclining at the head of the makeshift bed, Shelly could indeed see the teeny little Decapedes setting up down on the dock. She remembered them playing down there that very first Sunday, and wiped away a tear.

"We slogged all the way down here to serenade the mud?" asked Aaron, mimicking Sam's sour puss and gravelly baritone, and everyone laughed.

"We got the mud, we got the birds and the fish," said Sam. "We got some sleepy bullfrogs we gotta wake up. Best audience in the world."

"You just about ready?" Mendel asked Robbie at the soundboard.

"Just a minute," said the boy. Justine was helping him unroll cables while he was plugging in plugs and adjusting settings. A shriek of feedback bounced across the hillside. Sam plugged in his guitar. He picked a few chords and made some quick tuning adjustments.

"Are we sure about this?" asked Gavin, looking warily at the heavy gray sky.

Sam looked up at the clouds over Medina County, walked up to his mic and began to play a familiar, entrancing arpeggio. Then he closed his eyes and began to sing in that rough, time-worn baritone of his, *"Little darlin', it's been a long, cold, lonely winter."*

Aaron stopped what he was doing to watch.

Everyone stopped what they were doing to watch.

"Here comes the sun," he beseeched, his eyes closed.

A patch of blue peeked through the gray sky.

Sam opened his eyes to squint up at the clouds, and the blue began to grow, melting back the gray.

"*Here comes the sun,*" he entreated.

A cluster of brilliant yellow rays burst through the dark clouds, lighting the lake and the hillside around it.

Everyone was amazed, but not particularly surprised.

Nor were they really surprised when the mud-caked Decaheads began to trickle out of the woods, tramping through the muddy mire in solemn reverence, listening to Sam's fervent invocation, gaping at the sky as it opened.

Sam finished the song. The only sound was the lapping of the lake.

The band strapped on their gear and looked at Aaron. He surveyed them, and they all nodded. "Start All Over Again," he said, playing a chord. They all smiled and nodded. Gavin counted them in, and the band let loose with a burst of joy.

Shelly sat on her sofa bed with a serene smile, listening to the music coming up from the lake.

During "Peggy Sue," the muddy locals began to appear on the horizon and slog their way down the hillside in twos and threes and families. They bopped and bounced to the music and slipped and flopped in the sea of mud, then scrambled back onto their feet and bopped and bounced and slithered and floundered some more. Decapede played their old songs, they played their new songs, and Shelly lay with her hands on her stomach, trying to imagine what was going on inside her. *Not even a little worm yet,* she mused. *Well, that's the way things start.*

Sam was in the middle of "Allie's Rhubarb Pie" when he suddenly motioned to the band to stop playing and pointed up to the sky. The entire hillside, muddy townies and muddier Decaheads, turned to look beyond the horizon at a sharp, glorious rainbow. Everyone stared together in stunned silence. Aaron played two notes on his dolceola, an ascending octave. Justine smiled and began to sing in a lithe sixteen-year-old voice full of hope and dreams, "*Somewhere over the rainbow ...*"

All the muddy voices on the hillside joined in. Aaron and the band stopped playing and sang, and Johnny filmed that iconic shot that would one day adorn the "Live at the Lake" DVD, shooting over Justine's shoulder, out at the crowd, everyone singing in unison, their naked voices exalting the miracle of a rainbow. "*Some*—WHERE," they sang with fervor, and everyone applauded Justine and themselves.

"You know," Justine addressed the muddy congregation, "you *can*. You *can* fly over the rainbow. I'm flying over the rainbow right now"—she paused while they cheered her—"thanks to this band—" She waited while they cheered Decapede, cheering and whistling and clapping and stomping their feet in the muck. "And thanks to all of you!" she flattered the audience like a seasoned performer and waited while they cheered themselves. "And special thanks to Shelly Griffin"—she waved up in the direction of the house— "and the whole Decapede team!" And everybody cheered everybody. Even the sun shone brightly on Medina County.

"We're going to play one last song now," said Justine over the protests of the crowd.

Behind her, Gavin was adjusting his stool and holding the bongos between his knees.

"You may have heard this one," she said over the cries and protests and cheering.

Sam and Mendel took their acoustic guitars.

"If you know the words, you're welcome to sing along." Aaron strapped on his bass and counted them in softly.

And that famous opening, the two lilting guitars, the bass, the bongos:

"*Storm clouds are gathering way out there,*" sang Sam Miller, echoed by the entire hillside. "*Soon it's gonna rain—but I don't really care. / Lying with you on the ground / Grass and sunlight all around / Nothing's gonna bring me down.*" The crowd broke out in raucous applause. "*Have another Creston Gold.*"

Shelly could hear the congregation singing. She closed her eyes.

"The lake is lapping at the shore / This must be the place I've been searching for / Holds me close and takes me in / To a place I've never been / Never want to leave again / Have another Creston Gold. / And when she holds my hand / I know she understands, understands ..."

The audience burst out in a spontaneous ovation. Shelly jerked awake.

"Sometime tomorrow some of you people will be *far away / All we have for sure is what we have today / The world out there don't look so kind / But I don't care, 'cause love is blind / You're the one thing on my mind / Have another Creston Gold."*

The hillside erupted in a splattering ooze of adoration. Mendel and Aaron and Justine and Sam and Gavin grinned at each other. The crowd hollered and slopped and hooted. Justine stepped up to her mic, looked right into the eye of Johnny's camera, and winked. "Thank you," she said, "and I hope we passed the audition!"

"One more song!" the audience chanted. "One more song!"

"Come on," Aaron grinned at the band, "one more?"

Sam handed his Stratocaster to Robbie. "Keep an eye on this for me, will you?"

"Sure," glowed Robbie.

The crowd roared even louder when Sam went up to the mic. He looked out at them and held up his hands. The crowd went quiet.

"Listen up," he said, shuffling his feet. "This has been a lot of fun and all, but, ah—" He shuffled his feet some more. "I got me a brand-new bride waiting for me up at the house, so, ah—" He looked at Aaron and winked.

Aaron began that irresistible jingle-jangle introduction. Justine cocked her fedora over her eye, stepped up to the mic, and sang for everyone to hear:

"Well, he walked up to me, and he asked me if I wanted to dance—"

Sam jumped down from the dock and began trotting along the muddy trail around the lake, tripping and regaining his footing, past the cheering mud-sodden locals, past the cheering mud-sodden Decaheads, around the lake, past Justine and

Robbie's secret little hideaway, slipping and sliding, scrambling up the long mucky slope, and through the screen door.

"You're a mess!" Shelly shouted. "Go get cleaned up!"

But he plopped down onto the sofa bed next to her. "Did you see us?" he asked, panting and excited. "Could you hear okay?"

"It was a dream," she smiled, brushing the hair out of his eye.

Sam put his arm around her.

"You're all muddy," she squeamed.

"Yeah," he grinned, and he snuggled up to her.

They talked about this and about that.

And then he kissed her.

Acknowledgments

Thanks to all my Alpha and Beta readers for your comments, support, and encouragement. Thanks to David Schloss, my mentor in writing and much more; your support for Decapede has been invaluable. Thanks to Sally Schloss, my talented editor and most rabid fan. Thanks to Becca Kristovsky ז"ל, the first reader for the first part of the book; you are missed. Thanks to Netta Druckman for shepherding the publication of the book. Thanks to Mike Berlin for being a great sounding board over the years. Thanks to Ian Boyle for your tireless investment and perceptive comments. Immeasurable thanks to Shari Giddens for all the support, literary and other.

Thanks to all seventeen characters in the Decapede saga. It's been a pleasure to hang with you.

Thanks to my family for making it all worthwhile.

About Atmosphere Press

Founded in 2015, Atmosphere Press was built on the principles of Honesty, Transparency, Professionalism, Kindness, and Making Your Book Awesome. As an ethical and author-friendly hybrid press, we stay true to that founding mission today.

If you're a reader, enter our giveaway for a free book here:

SCAN TO ENTER
BOOK GIVEAWAY

If you're a writer, submit your manuscript for consideration here:

SCAN TO SUBMIT
MANUSCRIPT

And always feel free to visit Atmosphere Press and our authors online at atmospherepress.com. See you there soon!

About the Author

JEFF MESHEL has been writing about music since high school. He's been a playwright- director, librettist, lyricist, journalist, music producer, and blogger. He is married, father of two and grandfather of eight. Jeff was raised in Ohio and has lived in Israel since forever.

Visit Jeff at www.jmeshel.com.